The Sociology
of Leisure

The Sociology of Leisure

John R. Kelly
and
Geoffrey Godbey

Venture Publishing, Inc.

Cover Design: Sikorski Design
Production: Bonnie Godbey
Manuscript Editing: Richard Yocum
Printing and Binding: BookCrafters, Chelsea, MI

Library of Congress Catalogue Card Number 91-66393
ISBN 0-910251-51-7

Table of Contents

Section One: Historical Perspectives

Section Two: Issues in The Sociology of Leisure

Section Three: Forms of Leisure

Section Four: The Future

Preface: The sociology of leisure

In the Twentieth Century, leisure has emerged as a critical issue in people's lives. Increased material standards of living, better health, increased levels of education, a declining percentage of life devoted to work, and greater personal freedom have provided, for many, a vastly increased potential for leisure. The use of free time in voluntary and pleasurable ways is an expected, and often realized, part of life in postindustrial societies.

Much of our leisure is experienced through a myriad of social groups, from the family to special interest clubs. Such social experiences shape not only our life satisfaction and self-definition, they also fundamentally affect family relations, friendships, the environment and the economy. While work is still central in society, for many, perhaps the majority, leisure is equally important or even more central to their lives. Thus, leisure deserves to be studied. Since much of leisure is organized by and experienced within social groups, leisure deserves to be studied in a sociological perspective.

Sociology is not a neat discipline. It encompasses at least three major theoretical perspectives with quite different assumptions about the nature of society. Functional theory sees society as an integrated system of institutions that usually change in an evolutionary way. Critical theory focuses on the divisions of a society composed of segments with conflicting interests that clash to create change. Symbolic interaction theory begins with the interpreting social actor and the constructed symbol system that is learned, fragile, and yet continually renewed. This book incorporated all three perspectives.

Nor is leisure a tidy bit of action. It cannot be clearly identified simply by time, space, the form of activity, social context, or even motivation. It is experience and action, opportunity and social space, a matter of meaning and the spirit as well as of material elements. There is no neat list of activities, times, places, or even attitudes that places clear definitional boundaries between leisure and the rest of life. As a consequence, this book ranges widely through human behaviors, cognitions, and emotions to explore leisure.

It may be partly the diversity and variety of leisure that has discouraged many sociologists who take leisure quite seriously in their own lives from giving it a central place in their research and theory. There is, of course, also the goal of any discipline to establish itself as important. Despite the significant place of leisure in most people's lives and resource allocations, the idea of studying it makes scholars uneasy. It is the hope of the authors that those who follow the arguments presented here will develop their own perspectives. To further that aim, research and theory are gathered from both mainstream and marginal sociology as well as from the work of those giving special attention to leisure, recreation, and play. We have at several points branched out from sociology to gain from disciplines such as history, philosophy, psychology, and economics.

There is always the practical problem of weaving central themes together throughout the book and still giving them particular focus in individual chapters. In this book, a number of issues are presented in both ways. Issues of social stratification and disparities in resources and the power of self-determination, of pervasive and pertinent gender distinctions, of the dialectic between individual action and social forces, and of a focus on North America that cannot be separated from the changing and interlinked cultures and economies of the world are woven through the book as well as given designated attention. This results in some summary repetition as well as some artificial segregation of related issues. It's a complex and interrelated world, and leisure is very much a part of that world.

Further, the book is the work of two authors. Our overall perspectives are quite similar, but there are also significant differences in approach to some topics. Rather than attempt to reconcile every difference and produce a bland and homogenized product, we decided to leave some of the differences in the text. It will be possible, therefore, to discern some inconsistencies in detail, vocabulary, and even analysis. If the aim had been to produce the final word on leisure sociology, that would be a problem. Our aim, however, is to introduce issues and to engage the reader in the process of discovery and debate. We see the variations in perspective, then, as complementary and hope that readers will find them more challenge than confusion.

One further limitation is that this is a thoroughly North American book. Both authors have benefitted greatly from years of exchange with colleagues from all around the world, especially through the Research Committee on Leisure of the International Sociological Association and the World Leisure and Recreation Association. The book, however much its concepts reflect what we have learned in Europe, Latin America, and the Pacific Rim, is quite long and complicated enough without taking on the task of continual cross-cultural analysis. Nevertheless, we continue to learn from an incredible variety of colleagues and dedicate this book to them and to the ongoing exploration of leisure in all societies.

John R. Kelly   Geoffrey Godbey
University of Illinois   The Pennsylvania
                                                      State University

CHAPTER 1

Introduction:
The Need for a Sociology of Leisure

There are two questions to begin with. The first is "Why study leisure at all?" The second is "Why do it from a sociological perspective?" Another way of stating the same questions would be "Why is leisure important?" and "What's so special about sociology?"

The quick answer to the first question is simple: *Leisure is important.* It is an important sector of the economy, a significant dimension of the culture, and a major element of the interlocking social institutions of the society. Further, leisure is central to the meaning of life throughout the journey from birth to death.

The second question cannot be answered quite so quickly. It requires looking at life from a somewhat unnatural point-of-view, one that begins with the society rather than the self. A sociological perspective is based on the premise that we are profoundly social beings. All that we know and are, even the language with which we think and communicate, has forms that are learned in a specific society. We are thoroughly ethnic beings with our most fundamental ways of defining ourselves and our world learned in the time and place of where we are in a society that is part of a particular historical culture. The symbols, vocabularies, values, dreams, and definitions of our lives are the product of real institutions of the economy, polity, school, family, religion, and community. There are quite real social forces that are the context in which we work out our lives. To understand any aspect of our lives, we must take into account that social context of cooperation and conflict. The "sociological imagination" (Mills, 1959) is not the only important perspective, but it is an essential one.

Leisure, of course, is peculiar anyway. At first glance, not only we as individuals, but society itself tends to view leisure as secondary to what is really important—work and the economy, survival and the state, or central relationships and the family. Then on second thought we realize that we devote a great deal of our imagination, physical effort, time, and other resources to this allegedly secondary aspect of life. In fact, we may make some leisure commitments and associations quite central to who we are and want to become. We may define that elusive concept, quality of life, very much in terms of the satisfaction we find in doing things we don't have to do to survive. In our own priorities, leisure is not really an afterthought at all.

As an introduction, it will be useful to establish some common ground before going on into the analysis of the incredible variety of the history, forms, contexts, and meanings of leisure. First, we will examine something of the scope of leisure in contemporary society. Second, we will outline the variety of disciplinary perspectives on leisure and the particular value of the sociological. Third, we will introduce an approach to the meaning of leisure in ordinary life. And, fourth, we will offer a brief preview of the remainder of the book.

The Scope of Leisure

To begin, we have to abandon the old definition of leisure as leftover time. Leisure is not what we do when everything important is completed. Of course, everything important is never completed. More central, however, is that what is usually labelled "leisure" is now recognized as taking considerable priority in the economy and other areas of the society. The entire book will illustrate this centrality. In this introduction a few suggestions will suffice (Godbey, 1991; Kelly, 1990).

Leisure is a major segment of the economy. In the United States, total spending on leisure is estimated at about $600 billion a year. The average household spends about 7 percent of its income directly on leisure. These numbers, however, are quite conservative. They do not include the proportion of car expenses, home space and improvements, other travel expenses, clothing, eating out and entertaining. Nor do they include other leisure costs hidden in grocery, energy, financing, media, communications, and other regular bills.

In many countries, leisure-based tourism is the leading source of external investment and spending as well as a major domestic industry. Sports, the arts, and entertainment are big business. Government provision of resources and programs for leisure are important, but in the U.S. 97 percent of the spending on leisure is in the market sector. In terms of investment, leisure-based businesses are viewed as a prime sector of the service sector of the economy that now employs far over half the work force.

Participation in leisure activity is the basis of the myriad industries that provide environments, equipment, access, skill-development, information, financing, organization, promotion, and even the right clothing. If 36 million attended college football and 30 million college basketball, imagine how many went to high school, grade school, little league, softball, and all the other sport events! If 18 million played tennis, 67 million bowled, and over 120 million gardened in 1986, imagine how many walked, talked, ate out, watched videos, and read for pleasure!

Think of all the ways in which leisure opportunities are now provided by the various institutions of each community. Schools have a vast spectrum of classroom and after-school programs in the arts, sports, environmental experiences, and even travel. Institutions of higher education offer concerts, drama and dance, opera, exhibitions in the arts, sport spectacles, festivals, and fairs as well as class opportunities to learn leisure-related skills. In fact, colleges attract many students of all ages who are learning for personal enrichment rather than work preparation.

Churches offer programs of travel, community service, and artistic expression as well as study and worship. Corporations have recreation programs that often go far beyond the traditional company picnic and softball league. Municipalities and counties not only provide facilities and space for a variety of leisure activities, but also develop programs of skill-acquisition and participation for a full spectrum of age groups and different levels of ability and disability. Restaurants offer entertainment. Not-for-profit organizations support the arts, sports, and other expressive activity. Shopping malls and centers have special festivals of entertainment as well as space designed for everyday leisure. Housing developments advertise their recreational attractions and design space, both indoor and outdoor, for a range of activities oriented toward their targeted types of households.

Leisure opportunities and resources are so thoroughly a part of our social fabric that we seldom take note of them. With all the attention given to the economic, educational, and political institutions of the society, the pervasive theme of leisure may go unnoticed. But it is there literally everywhere, taking time, space, money, energy, and attention in the day-to-day round of life.

A Question of Perspectives

Recognizing the scope of leisure is only the beginning. The next issue is that of how to go about studying and understanding it. Is leisure fundamentally an attitude or state-of-mind, a space or environment, a dimension or part of the culture, or a major segment of market and nonmarket production and distribution? Or is it an area of public policy and political action, an important part of the past of any civilization or culture, a subject for philosophical analysis, or a matter of social organization and interaction? Is leisure a phenomenon to be studied by psychologists, geographers, anthropologists, economists, political scientists, historians, philosophers, or sociologists?

The answer would seem to be "all of the above." Leisure is a complex element of individual life, of the social system, and of the culture that may be approached in many ways. Psychologists and philosophers may examine the nature of experiences that are identified with leisure. Geographers and economists may deal with the resources that are involved in leisure activity. Political scientists and historians may place leisure in the context of patterns and shifts in power and protection that both use and impact leisure. Sociologists study the relationship of leisure to social institutions as well as a kind of social action.

All of these approaches have evident value. No one would argue that experience as cognition and emotion are irrelevant to understanding leisure. Nor are space, cultural values and symbols, costs and market goods, state provisions and regulations, the sweep of the past, issues of knowledge and value, or how people act and interact with each other peripheral to the subject. These social and behavioral approaches should not deny the possibility that natural and physical sciences may be employed to address issues related to leisure as well. In fact, if leisure is indeed significant to human life, then no discipline can be arbitrarily excluded.

In Europe and North America, sociology has had a central position in studying leisure. This historical development is based both on the nature of sociology and the nature of leisure. Here, in outline, is an introduction to the connection:

- Sociology focuses on two issues: the structures or organization of people into societies and the common actions of people in relation to those structures.

- Leisure is composed of the actions of people, especially toward and with each other in contexts opened or closed by social structures.

- Sociology has traditionally taken an institutional approach, giving attention to work, family, community, religion, government, and their interrelationships. Yet, these foci omit all that people do that is chosen primarily for the experience rather than the outcomes, all the play and expressive activity that occupies a third or more of waking hours in modern societies. Some sociologists have recognized that this vast area of life cannot be left out of any comprehensive approach to societies and what people do.

- Leisure is always of the culture with forms, symbols, meanings, values, vocabularies, and aims that are learned in a particular social time and place. To understand leisure requires placing it in its social context.

Sociology, of course, is not without its own complexities and varieties. There are at least three major approaches of sociology, each with different premises that direct attention to different issues (Kelly, 1974, 1987; Giddens, 1979). "Systemic" or "structure functional" sociology is based on the premise that the society is a system of interrelated institutions that in a complementary way function to maintain the system. Each institution consists of a set of roles taken by occupants whose actions and interactions tend to maintain the organizational structure (Parsons, 1949; Merton, 1967). Structure-functional theory is based on the work of Emile Durkheim and is addressed to the issue of social solidarity and persistence.

A second theoretical approach focuses on the social actor who acts within a social context that is constructed by the symbolic consensus learned by each actor. This "interpretive" or "symbolic interaction" theory is derived from Max Weber (Giddens, 1979) who focused on the value systems by which actors make sense of life and its social context in a continual process of interpretation. Even the social system itself is fundamentally constructed and reconstructed through the learned symbols that are the conceptual framework through which social action is understood and taken.

The third approach is directed more toward the issue of social change. In contrast to the functional model, the society is seen as divided among two or more segments with different power, access to resources, and interests. In this "conflict" theory, developed from the thought of Karl Marx, the integration of society and its institutions is found to be based on control of fundamental economic power rather than on integrated functions or symbolic consensus. Further, there is always the possibility of a "false consciousness" in which what is ideologically defined as freedom is in fact a form of subjugation and repression that consolidates actual power structures.

There is, then, no one "sociology" that presents a unified view of society or single framework for analysis. Rather, each theoretical approach or "metaphor" (Kelly, 1987) directs attention to particular problems and issues. Systemic theory tends to view leisure as secondary and contributing to the maintenance of the society by providing preparation for and recuperation from work. The view includes a social space for bonding in the family and community, and time for religion, learning in and outside of formal education, cultural development, and the celebration of ideological consensus. Interpretive theory begins with the social actor who in the relative self-determination and openness of leisure expresses and develops the self and reconstructs the symbolic basis of all levels of the society. Conflict theory views leisure as potentially liberating but in reality an instrument of control shaped according to the interests of the power elites of the society.

Without question the systemic and conflict metaphors require quite different perspectives on the nature of the society and on the meanings of social action. They differ on whether social solidarity or integration is a matter of organic complementarity or coercion. In both, however, the primary issue is stability and change in the social system. Both direct attention first toward the society itself rather than the individual. The interpretive approach, however, begins with the actor and the meaning of action within the social context.

These theoretical models may be differentiated in terms of their level of analysis. Do they begin with *structures,* the organization of social institutions and the exercise of power and authority within and among them? Or, do they begin with *agency,* how individuals take meaningful action in a variety of social contexts? A third possibility is that life and leisure are viewed as a *process* in which action and structure are in an ongoing and dialectical relationship (Kelly, 1992; Rojek, 1990). From this perspective, institutional integration, class conflict, and interpretive action are each useful ways of trying to understand a complex process.

It can be argued that the interpretive approach has a special affinity with leisure, a dimension of life that includes expression and action that is focused on the experience itself (Kelly, 1983). However, important issues are raised from each of the theoretical perspectives of contemporary sociology. Therefore, none of the three models will be ruled out in the analysis that follows. Rather, there will be references to the theoretical premises that guide the discussion and even combinations of perspectives if together they seem to illuminate a critical element of leisure in a social perspective.

Leisure and the Common Life

One fundamental premise of all that follows in this book is that leisure is not a separate arena of life cut off from the more central elements of work, family, community, school, religion, and the marketplace. Rather, leisure is woven into the fabric of social action and interaction. It is not unrelated to any major dimension of life; nor is it consistently secondary to and determined by any other. Leisure as expressive activity oriented primarily to the experience is found at just about any time or place. There is off-task behavior in the factory, the office, and the school. Workers may even play with their machines— computers or lathes—as well as with each other in the midst of the work day and workplace.

The resources of leisure may be derived from almost any other relationship or role. So much of leisure is social, communication and interaction with other people, that any way in which we are related to others may become a source of leisure companions. The economic resources for leisure are tied to economic position. The expectations for leisure priorities are often based on family roles that change through the life course. The values that are expressed in leisure decisions may be informed by religious and cultural traditions and background. Access to space is frequently a matter of political decision and policy.

Leisure may take place just about anytime and anywhere. It is a dimension of the common life much more than a special segment of uncommon behavior. This integration with the ongoing round of life may be best illustrated in the framework of the life course. As will be developed more fully in later chapters, leisure may be crucial to the fundamental preoccupations of persons in many periods of life (Rapoport and Rapoport, 1975). For example, much of the developmental learning of children is in play. The exploring of sexual identity among adolescents is mostly in leisure settings. The expression of bonding and affection of parents to their children is at least as much in play as in caregiving. The reevaluation of meaning among later-life adults often focuses on leisure investments and priorities as well as work and significant relationships. The context of social integration critical to satisfying retirement is more often than not some set of leisure engagements.

From this perspective, leisure is more often central than peripheral through the journey of life. It is related to personal development as well as to our bonding with those most important to us. What we do, how well and with whom we do it is connected with everything else that is important. Leisure is a dimension of meaning in which there may be the greatest opportunity to learn and develop through trying out actions that are at least a bit new and different (Csikszentmihalyi, 1981). Leisure, from this perspective, may be both special and ordinary.

Preview of the Text

The "sociology of leisure" is viewed in an inclusive rather than exclusive mode in this book. There is no attempt to draw fine lines and narrow distinctions from any disciplinary or theoretical point-of-view. Rather, the approaches to be incorporated include social history and social psychology in addition to all three of the major theoretical types of sociology: systemic, conflict, and interpretive. Further, useful research and concepts will be picked up from any sources, whether or not the investigators or scholars define themselves as sociologists.

Nevertheless, any book is a construction with some order and coherence, however difficult to discern. A primary objective of the order of this book is to provide a cumulative base for understanding. The order is not random or the selection merely eclectic. The persistent question is "What is required to deal with the issues in focus?" Both authors have backgrounds that direct us toward history as a necessary prelude to the analysis of contemporary issues. Therefore, even though the central direction is toward the present and the future, the first section following the introduction of themes and concepts is historical. Contemporary leisure takes forms and meanings that are based in the radical shift to an industrial economy and urban society. The changes in the location, scale, technologies, and organization of the economy reconstituted every other aspect of life to recreate society. Leisure development in the period of radical change included struggle along with accommodation. Further, change did not stop at any point during or after the Industrial Revolution, but has gone on through the Depression of the 1930s, the mobilization of World War II, and the periods of calm and conflict of the 1950s, 60s, and 70s. Now contemporary themes of "postindustrial" shifts away from the centrality of heavy industry, a world economy, the rise of the service sector, changes in family stability and women's roles and opportunities as well as the emergence of mass leisure provide a new, uneven, and complex context for leisure development. Chapters 3 through 8 will outline this kaleidoscope of historical change.

The chapters of the second major section, 9 through 27, address a wide range of issues from sociological perspectives. Beginning with the symbolic and structural character of social division, the chapters introduce the social basis of issues of the connection between leisure and work, economic organization, culture and ethnicity, religion, the family and immediate communities, second-ary communities and ordinary life, social interaction as leisure, commitment and specialization, motivations and satisfactions, the nature of experience, the life course and human development, sex and sensuality, gender, social roles, time and timetables, leisure in the market economy, and barriers and constraints. All of these chapters have as a general theme the meaning of leisure in its social contexts.

The third major section takes a somewhat different perspective. Leisure as activities has a variety of particular forms, none of which is quite like the others in either personal meaning or social organization. Following an introduction to recreation as organized leisure, tourism, resource-based activity, the arts, mass media, and types of artificially-induced experience are analyzed.

Finally, Chapters 35 through 37 look ahead at the future of leisure in terms of social and value shifts as well as critical and philosophical perspectives.

In every chapter the aim is to provide a basis for the discussion of issues rather than a final word on the topic. A number of explicit and implicit selection criteria have been employed by the authors in the process of developing the overall approach and the emphases of each chapter. The historical and theoreti-cal centrality to the field has usually been balanced with some judgement as to which research and concepts are of greatest value in explaining what is going on today and in identifying the major themes that will lead into the tomorrows of the cross-century period just ahead.

REFERENCES

Csikszentmihalyi, M. (1981). Leisure and socialization. *Social Forces 60*, 332-340.

Giddens, A. (1979). *Central problems in social theory.* Berkeley, CA: University of California Press.

Godbey, G. (1991). *Leisure in your life: An exploration,* Third Edition. State College, PA: Venture Publishing, Inc.

Kelly, J. (1974). Sociological perspectives and leisure research. *Current Sociology, 22,* 127-158.

_____. (1983). *Leisure identities and interactions.* London, England and Boston, MA: Allen & Unwin.

_____. (1987). *Freedom to be: A new sociology of leisure.* New York, NY: Macmillan Publishing Company, Inc.

_____. (1990). *Leisure,* 2nd edition. Englewood Cliffs, NJ: Prentice-Hall.

_____. (1992). Leisure. In E. Borgatta (Ed.), *Encyclopedia of sociology.* New York, NY: Macmillan Publishing Company, Inc. (pp. 1099-1107).

Merton, R. (1967). *On theoretical sociology.* New York, NY: The Free Press.

Mills, C. W. (1959). *The sociological imagination.* New York, NY: Oxford University Press.

Parsons, T. (1949). *The structure of social action.* Glencoe, IL: Free Press.

Rapoport, R., and Rapoport R. N. (1975). *Leisure and the family life cycle.* London, England: Routledge & Kegan Paul, Ltd.

Rojek, C. (1990). Leisure and recreation theory. In E. Jackson and T. Burton (Eds.) *Understanding leisure and recreation: Mapping the past, charting the future.* State College, PA: Venture Publishing, Inc. (pp. 69-88).

CHAPTER 2

Themes and Definitions

L eisure is commonly defined in terms of "freedom" and yet is often constrained by scarcities of time and money as well as by the expectations of other people. It suggests idleness to some and creativity to others. It connotes leftover time and central life commitments, feelings of pleasure and packaged purchases, relaxation and intense involvement. Leisure is not a transparently simple concept.

On the other hand, most people seem to know what they mean by the term. "Leisure is what I choose to do because I enjoy it." Perhaps it is enough to point out the themes of personal choice and a focus on what happens in the experience. There is no virtue in elaborately esoteric or exotic definitions. No special jargon makes a discipline profound because it is inaccessible. One possibility is simply to identify the behaviors that we usually call "leisure" and concentrate on what they mean in the lives of men, women, and children.

There are, however, two problems with such an easy solution to the definitional problem. The first is that a definition has to provide a basis for dealing with critical themes of analysis, with the issues crucial to understanding. The second is that different disciplines will define leisure from their own perspectives and in terms of their presuppositions. A sociology of leisure is required to propose a definitional approach to central terms and concepts that provides a common ground for discussion.

For example, economists tend to define leisure as economic choice conducted in market or quasi-market conditions and measured by economic exchange. Often, leisure is defined as nonwork time which can be assigned a monetary value. Social psychologists tend to approach leisure as an individual state of mind or consciousness displayed in attitudes that lead to activity and choice. Anthropologists approach leisure as expressive activity that is embedded in the value systems and practices of a culture. Sociologists see leisure as activity learned in social contexts and requiring social resources. From their own perspectives, none is wrong, nor do any meet all the requirements of the other disciplines.

Themes of Sociological Analysis

What are the themes that must be addressed by sociological approaches to leisure? The first is that leisure is a social phenomenon. It occurs in social contexts. It is ethnic, of its specific culture. It is historical, the result of sequences of past development in a culture and society. It is learned behavior with particular decision factors, meanings, and associations that have been built up through past experiences. It is social in its relationships with the institutions of its society—school and church, family and community, economy and polity. The opportunities of leisure are found and developed in actual social situations with their combined limits and resources, obligations and expectations. Leisure involves other people, not only as individuals but as they are part of social forces with role-based power to shape and even coerce behavior.

The second theme is that leisure is also existential. Individual actors are not billiard balls on the table of life, bounced about entirely by the impact of external forces. Each person is a social actor, interpreting the possibilities and developing lines of action that fit with her/his developing sense of self in relation to others. Actions have meaning, both to the self and in signifying the self to others. Some meanings may be circumscribed and largely limited to the immediate time and place. Other meanings have long-term dimensions based on what actors would like to become or how they hope to be related to others. The "existential" theme in leisure is composed of elements of decision, however limited, and of becoming. From this perspective, individuals create something of who they are and aim to be through their actions. Social actors are always doing things that have and create meaning.

Leisure, then, is both social and existential. The two themes are not in opposition, but exist in a dialectical relationship. Out of the intersection of social forces and individual act comes something that is always at least a little bit new, an action that both has and communicates meaning. A full sociological definition of leisure—or anything else—cannot disregard either the social or the existential dimensions.

Further, a viable approach to leisure has to incorporate the variety and diversity of the phenomenon in the real world. Leisure is not just disengagement and relaxation; it also includes the most intense and strenuous mental and physical activity. Leisure is not just the solitude of contemplation; it also involves the social interaction of parties and conversation. Leisure is not just the creation of new forms of art; it is also fiddling with a car engine or "hanging out" after school. Leisure is not just the expression of family and friendship bonds; it is also the sale of bodies through prostitution and pornography and preoccupation with drugs. It is relaxed and tense, experimental and conforming, excited and bored, sensual and rational, detached and involved. Leisure is, in fact, so many activities, environments, and meanings that it seems impossible to draw any clear parameters that definitively include and exclude according to universal criteria.

Definitions, Metaphors, and Perspectives

The purpose of definitions is to distinguish whatever is being defined from other concepts or things that are most like it. Definitions, then, would seem to require precise criteria of differentiation. Of course, such precision and clarity are difficult enough in the realm of things and quite rare in the world of ideas. Often "judgement calls" are required at the fuzzy boundaries of definitions. Real-life definitions are more like "as far as we know, most quarks are characterized by a, b, and usually c."

This suggests that definitions may often blend into other possibilities such as metaphors and perspectives. Strictly applied, a definition is "a word or phrase expressing the essential nature of a person or thing, or a class of persons, or things" or "an answer to the question 'What is x?' or 'What is an x?'" (Webster's 3rd International Dictionary). "Essential" to the nature of anything is whatever makes it what it is, its unique characteristics. Therefore, a definition of leisure would refer to whatever gives it its distinct nature.

But what if there are a number of characteristics that are said to make leisure distinctive? Each of these may be a matter of perspective, of the starting point. Is leisure a sociological phenomenon? Or is it psychological, economic, political, anthropological, geographical, physiological, philosophical, or aesthetic? Is it human, found in all human societies, or the product of a particular historical social system? Is it a domain of institutional life like the family or education or a dimension of action that may be found in many domains?

One possibility is that there are many perspectives, each valid according to its own premises. Each of these perspectives is a metaphor that says, "Viewed from this perspective, leisure is essentially like this." This metaphorical approach takes the variety of definitions as complementary rather than competing. Each metaphor focuses on one or more aspects of the complex whole, not denying the others but stressing one. Metaphors of leisure, then, can begin with a stated premise. For example, a psychologist may begin, "Viewed as experience, leisure is . . . " A economist may begin, "Viewed as a market good, leisure is . . . " In the introduction that follows, we will concentrate on metaphors that have a sociological base.

Sociological Definitions and Metaphors

Along with leisure itself, a number of other terms will recur in the chapters of this book and require at least a general definition. They include recreation, play, freedom, work, society, and sociology itself. But first, what do we mean by "leisure?"

Definitions of Leisure

In 1899 Thorstein Veblen defined leisure as the "nonproductive consumption of time." He stressed that leisure is different from work and symbolizes status because it does not produce wealth or income. However, the concept has deeper roots in the culture than any definition presupposing industrialization and capitalism.

Aristotle began by approaching leisure as time free from the necessity of labor (*Politics,* Book I). This time was to be used for contemplation and preparation for the exercise of political power by elite males. Aristotle went on in Book VIII of the *Politics,* however, to draw out how that freedom would be employed in fulfilling activity done for its own sake, as an end in itself. The recurrent themes of later perspectives were all proposed by Aristotle: freedom from necessity and activity that is an end in itself and yet at the same time leads to self-fulfillment and a better society. More recently, Sebastian de Grazia summarized Aristotle as follows:

> Leisure is a state of being in which activity is performed for its own sake
> or as its own end . . . And we call final without reservation that which
> is always desirable in itself and never for the sake of something else.
> Leisure stands in that last class by itself (de Grazia, 1964:13).

Leisure is distinguished from the realm of necessity, of what has to be done to maintain a society, an institution, or ongoing life. Further, its meaning is contained in the act and in the direct results of that action for the actor. In leisure, persons become more of what their nature intends them to be. And, even though leisure is carried on for its own sake, it has social consequences in being the context of the development of the concepts and principles that are the basis of a good and just society.

Such a combination of themes, however, does not satisfy those who want to designate the property that makes leisure different, that is the essence of leisure. For example, Max Kaplan (1975) proposed that there were six kinds of definitions of leisure, each based on a different premise. The humanistic or classic approach is based on a concept of being human that requires freedom of action. The therapeutic perspective assumes that people are less than healthy and require some remediation. The quantitative model presumes that leisure as time can be identified by the form of time usage. The institutional concept views leisure as one element of a social system made up of institutions with complementary functions. The epistemological idea is based on the values embedded within a particular culture. And the sociological approach is based on the view that leisure and everything else is defined in a social context by social actors who are creating their own interpreted universe of meaning. These metaphors are more than a list of alternatives. Rather, each begins with a distinctive view of people and the world.

For years, sociologists seemed to accept the tacit assumption that it was possible to deal with leisure in terms of "activities." Research on what people did and on factors in their participation choices had as their pragmatic basis some list of activities presumed to be leisure. When people read, swam, played golf, went to movies, joined voluntary organizations, and went on picnics, they were engaged in leisure. With a quick bow at ambiguities such as work-related reading and status-determined club memberships, most research designs arbitrarily defined leisure in terms of the particular list of activities included in the study. In general, the activities were conducted outside work time and distinguished from required maintenance of self and household.

Such operational approaches were placed in question by self-evident variations. Almost anything can be done in return for income and as a job. Further, every list was only representative of the hundreds or even thousands of activities that might be leisure. In fact, many lists omitted such common activities as conversation, eating, and family play. More significant questions, however, were presented by two of the pioneering efforts in the field.

In Europe, the sociology of leisure was led by the French scholar, Joffre Dumazedier, who studied the leisure patterns of workers in an industrial town. Finding that the form of the activity did not adequately distinguish leisure, he proposed that leisure must be distinguished from family and socioreligious obligations as well as from remunerative work. However satisfying and central to life, community, family, and religious roles have too significant an element of requirement to qualify as leisure. Leisure, then, is different.

> Leisure is activity—apart from the obligations of work, family, and society—to which the individual turns at will, for either relaxation, diversion, or broadening his knowledge and his spontaneous social participation, the free exercise of his creative capacity (Dumazedier, 1967).

Leisure, from this perspective, is purposive activity, chosen for ends that in some way enhance the self. The differentiation from required activity presumes that life can be clearly divided between necessary institutional activity and activity that is oriented toward expression, diversion, and self-development. Leisure is distinguished by purpose and institutional setting rather than by form.

A second challenge to activity lists was developed in the "Kansas City" studies of Robert Havighurst, Bernice Neugarten, and others from the University of Chicago. This comprehensive study of adults was thoroughly sociological in its inclusion of the meanings of leisure activity, how they articulated with social roles and personal agendas, and how they formed patterns of different life styles (Havighurst, 1957; Havighurst and Feigenbaum, 1959). Although the multi-layered methodology was complex, implications for the study of leisure were clear. Leisure activity is embedded in the entire role complex or set of actors who have some idea of the meaning of their choices and priorities. Leisure is not a segregated set of activities, but a multidimensioned element of the integrated life of the social actor.

Both Dumazedier and the Kansas City consortium found it impossible to deal with leisure apart from the dimensions of meaning or aim and the social context of activity. The dimensions of leisure included not just the form, time, and place of activity, but also some sense of its meaning to interpreting actors for whom life has patterns, connections, and continuities.

Despite these and other multifaceted approaches to identifying leisure, however, two more focused metaphors began to command considerable attention. The first viewed leisure as time and the second as a state-of-consciousness.

Leisure as Time

The most influential employment of a time-based definition of leisure in sociological study was that of the International Time Budget Study (Szalai et al., 1972). This comparative study assumed that leisure could be identified as leftover time. Leisure is tacitly defined as doing things that are not connected with employment or maintaining home and self. This approach is gender-biased in its presumption of the separation of the workplace and the home and the segregation of tasks from expressive relationships. It is assumed that if you know the form, time, and place of the activity, it can be designated as work, maintenance, or leisure.

Leisure can then be quantified as hours and minutes, totals added, means calculated and compared, and trends identified. The question "How much leisure?" can be given an answer that seems self-explanatory. The leisure of different persons or social groups can be compared. By keeping diaries in the "time budget" method, accurate estimates of leisure as time can be assessed. Many dictionaries define leisure as time free from work and necessities. In languages such as German and Spanish, there is no suitable word for leisure, only the phrase "free time." The time definition appears to be both simple and useful.

The complications begin to appear when the emphasis is shifted to the modifier "free." Does free signify time remaining when all obligations are completed and all responsibilities fully met? If so, most people probably never have any. In fact, is any time really free from obligation? We may choose to join a club or play softball, but once the choice is made we are under considerable obligation to get to meetings and do our share. We may delay schoolwork or doing the laundry to take a walk, but even then we are responding to an expectation. Anything we do with other persons involves their expectations and some norms of reciprocity. How "free" is free enough to be leisure?

Several scholars have preferred the term "discretionary time"—time in which the actor chooses the activity. There are at least two problems with this amendment. The first is that all the categorization by form, time, and place is negated. Now it is necessary to know something about the decision process. The second stems from the first. If it is necessary to know how the choice was made and to assess the freedom from constraint or obligation, then leisure is no longer a quantity of time, but its quality. The defining standard is freedom of choice.

These complications, however, should not prevent us from recognizing the value in the time metaphor. First, even though time does not have the same meaning in all cultures, Western linear clock time is employed cross-culturally and provides one means of making comparisons of different times in multiple cultures. Changes in time allocations related to industrialization, urbanization, and economic development for women and men in a variety of economic and family conditions are the basis of important analyses. Second, time is a significant dimension of social organization. Social time signifies dimensions of the economic, political, religious, and social order. Time is structure that shapes the opportunities, the resources, and even the value systems of social actors in any society.

Time, then, is a dimension of leisure. It is a metaphor of significance that reveals both priorities and contexts of decision. It is also a pervasive element of the social world that gives shape to all actions and interactions. It is not, however, a simple concept that in itself defines leisure. Questions about the nature of freedom in "free time" and choice in "discretionary time" lead beyond quantity to issues of quality.

Leisure as Experience

Are there qualities that define leisure? If so, they must be found in the experience that is designated as leisure. Aristotle included the qualities of freedom, being an end rather than a means, and outcomes of self-fulfillment and social benefit. At least the first three might be seen as qualities that define leisure as experience.

Experience is within the consciousness of the actor. Experience is a process that involves the three elements of perception, cognition, and assessment or evaluation (Csikszentmihalyi, 1988). There is the sensual apprehension of what is occurring, its mental reception, and making sense of it. Experience in this sense is always a meaningful process. From this perspective, the qualities of leisure are in the meanings.

From a psychological perspective, those meanings may be the subjective attitudes of the individual. John Neulinger (1974) proposed an attitudinal approach to defining leisure. Perceptions of freedom, intrinsic motivation, and noninstrumentality are said to be the cognitive characteristics that make an experience leisure. It is the attitude of perceived free choice for the sake of the experience itself that defines leisure.

Focusing on the state of consciousness raises the issue of temporality. Since experience is a process with variations in emotional and mental states, when does the defining state of mind occur? Does any moment of the correct attitude define the entire activity? Most research based on this model requires subjects to look back at an experience or even set of experiences and assess or summarize the attitudes. The question becomes "Does concert-going in general have enough of this attitude to make it leisure?"

Shifting the locus of definition to the actor and away from time or the nature of the activity does not resolve all issues. If some feeling of pleasure were identified as central, then leisure could be found anywhere and in any time. If the feeling is a standard for the entire experience, then how much pleasure is enough?

de Grazia (1964:5) argued that anyone can know pleasure, but only a few will know the condition that is leisure. "Leisure refers to a state of being, a condition of man, which few desire and fewer achieve." Josef Pieper also described leisure as a "condition" of the mind and spirit rather than just a feeling. "Leisure, it must be clearly understood, is a mental and spiritual attitude—it is not simply the result of external factors . . . " (1963:40). However rare that condition, leisure becomes more than a passing emotion; it is a fundamental condition of the individual.

From this experiential perspective, leisure is a mental condition that is located in the consciousness of the individual. The content of that condition remains at issue. Is it pleasure, a perception of freedom, a sense of timelessness (Csikszentmihalyi, 1988), or some combination of attitudes? The timing is also at issue. Is the consciousness momentary or some sort of average through an experience, immediate or a summation; a pure feeling or a cognitive evaluation? And, if leisure is individual consciousness, there is the question of what produces the mental state. Is drug-induced euphoria leisure, or is leisure an action condition that produces the attitude? Finally, is a mental state all there is to freedom or self-determination? After all, consciousness may be false. We may feel free when we have been seduced, deceived, or brainwashed. Isn't there more to freedom than feeling free?

Nevertheless, the focus on experience and on the actor is significant. Even if the defining characteristics of the experience remain somewhat fuzzy, the consciousness of the actor is central to distinguishing leisure. Leisure is a matter of meaning. One question is what produces that meaning. It is significant that those who define leisure in terms of experience study it in the context of people doing something.

Leisure as Action

Is leisure a special kind of time or activity? Is it an individual state of mind or consciousness measured in attitudes? Or is leisure the action that produces the consciousness, the lived experience itself? Remember that any definition of leisure must encompass its variety—experiences of disengagement and relaxation as well as intense engagement, imaginative and cognitive activity as well as physical exertion, ordinary activity as well as extraordinary events, casual time-filling as well as committed investment, individual action as well as social interaction.

One possibility is that each approach to leisure presupposes some kind of human action. Whether the focus is on engagement in an activity, making a choice, allocating a resource, or experiencing a kind of consciousness, the individual engages in some sort of action. The action may be physical, intellectual, communicative, imaginative, contemplative, creative, habitual, emotional, or some combination of elements. The action is the context of the experience. Even the most narrow state-of-mind definition presupposes an action context. Something happens in directing attention, processing information, defining meaning, and producing the experience. Prior to all measures and methods is human action, "doing something" in the most inclusive sense.

Human action, leisure or any other kind, always has two dimensions or components. Human action is both existential and social. It involves action with meaning and takes place in a social environment of learned symbols as well as opportunities and constraints. The meanings that actors attribute to actions are learned in social contexts so that the existential and social dimensions of action are related rather than separate.

Leisure as action does not float off into a detached attitude or feeling. It has dimensions of time and place. Its meaning is of its specific culture and historical era. It has form in addition to temporal and spatial reality. At the same time, leisure is experience; it involves the perceptions of the actor going into, during, and coming out of the experience.

If freedom is the essential mark of leisure, then action is implied. Freedom is not the absence of limit or constraint, but involves some critical element of self-determination. In such action, there is some realization of the freedom to be and to become. Leisure is more than an illusion of freedom or a mood of detachment. It is taking action that means something and has outcomes for the actor. The outcomes may be momentary and contained in the experience or be central to some agenda of development. The action may be oriented toward the self or toward social bonding with others. It is action with certain qualities—a central measure of self-determination and a focus on the experience itself.

Leisure, then, is action that both has and creates meaning. It is distinguished from other kinds of action by two crucial dimensions: self-determination and meaning within the experience. The traditional Aristotelian themes of freedom from necessity and noninstrumentality are encompassed in this openness and focus on meaningful experience. Leisure is existential in its self-determination and creation of meaning by action. It is social in the reality of its contexts of both learned form and symbolic meaning. *Leisure is self-determined action with primary meaning contained within the experience.*

All this may seem needlessly complicated and argumentative. It may be enough to say only that leisure is what we do primarily for the experience rather than to meet obligations or to produce predetermined outcomes. Leisure is characterized by relative openness and satisfaction with the action. If this leaves the boundaries fuzzy, then it may be better to be inclusive than too narrow. Yet, in the following chapters focusing on a number of sociological issues, it will be important to begin with a perspective on leisure that retains both its existential and social dimensions.

Recreation as Organized Leisure

Recreation may be defined in much the same way as leisure. The derivation of the term, however, is from the Latin *recreatio* and suggests restoration or recovery. Unlike leisure, which has been defined as a human phenomenon in its own right rather than secondary to work, recreation contains the concept of restoration of wholeness to mind, body, and spirit. It presupposes a primary activity, usually work.

Consistent with its roots, recreation is defined less inclusively than leisure. It is activity with social purposes and organization. Leisure may be constructive or destructive, spontaneous or organized. Recreation is intended to be good for the people of a society in specific ways and is organized and supported to produce such benefits.

There are two elements in this more limited perspective. The first is that of restoration. de Grazia (1964:233) writes from an elitist perspective: "Recreation is activity that rests men from work, often giving them a change (distraction, diversion) and restores them for work." The references to work and to "men" are too narrow. Persons need to be restored for other ends: to be good citizens, to nurture a family, to restore emotional balance, to study more effectively, or just to feel better. Recreation is intended to restore us to health, to wholeness. We do not recreate only to work; we recreate to live. Further, recreation is a part of the balance or rhythm of life. Nevertheless, the element of recovery is the first dimension of recreation.

The second is that of social organization. Recreation is not just for its own sake. Unlike leisure, it is not "anytime, anywhere, or anything" if only it is chosen primarily for the experience itself. Neil Cheek and William Burch made this distinction in their stress on the social organization of recreation. "Broadly conceived, recreation is rationalized leisure; it is the routinization of enjoyment" (1976:224). They analyze the rise of recreation in modern society as an institution of the social system with the purpose of contributing to the maintenance of the system. In a modern industrial society, recreation is provided as an identified part of a complex system because it is believed to offer needed restoration of health and social bonds. Recreation is programmatic; it has organization and purposes. It is a social phenomenon.

Recreation, then, is defined as *voluntary nonwork activity that is organized for the attainment of personal and social benefits including restoration and social cohesion.* It is institutionalized and supported because of its assumed contribution to the social system, especially in recovery for work and in providing a context for the social bonding of the family. It is opportunity provided for the re-creation of the individual and of the social fabric.

Play: The Action of Leisure

Play has also been defined in many and often conflicting ways. Most stress the same themes as common metaphors of leisure: freedom and meaning found primarily within the experience. Often the term "play" is used to refer to the activity of children and leisure to adult engagement. Often, however, we recognize that adults may play and engage in playful action. Children, on the other hand, are seldom said to have leisure. One possibility, then, would be to define leisure and play in essentially the same way—as action chosen primarily for the experience—and continue to use *play* to refer to children and unusually frolicsome adult occasions.

However, the history of definitions and theories of play does not permit such an easy solution. Too often *play* has referred to particular qualities or contexts of action. The term *play* comes from the Anglo-Saxon *plega* referring to a game, sport, or even a fight. The Latin *plaga* means a blow, thrust, or stroke as in a ball game or combat. Since so many games and sports are actually mock combat, the play element came to be used to refer to the nonserious aspect of the action. Now we do or say things "in play" because they do not signify serious intent. We are "playful" in suggesting that the action is all in fun. A play requires a temporary suspension of the distinction between the real and the unreal. Children play house under a tree or even play war.

Play is not totally separated from the "real world," but has meaning that is at the same time representative and nonserious. The meaning of play is temporary, confined to the specific time and place of the action (Huizinga, 1955). Play is doing something for its own sake, for the satisfaction and meaning of the bounded time. The three elements of play, then, are:

1) Play generally refers to the activity of children or to childlike lightness of behavior in adults.

2) Play is expressive with its meaning concentrated on the bounded experience.

3) Play involves a nonserious suspension of consequences, a temporary creation of a world of meaning which is often a shadow of the "real world."

A number of approaches to play suggest particular aspects of the concept that add to the richness of its reference. Csikszentmihalyi (1975) introduced the concept of "flow experience" that suggests the transcendence of some play. *Flow* is the experience of immersion and concentration that may accompany familiarity and mastery in action. Play is one kind of action which may include such a heightened time of doing something entirely for its own sake, for the experience of that moment.

Another psychological approach to play is based on a theory of motivation that is an elaboration of the simple stimulus-response model of behavior. From this perspective, individuals seek an optimal condition of arousal, neither too much nor too little stimulation (Iso-Ahola, 1989). In play, people seek environments that afford a high level of excitement at some times and a lower level providing relaxation at others. Novelty and familiarity, uncertainty and stability, challenge and comfort may all be sought in differing combinations in a variety of times and places. Play from this perspective is action that seeks and develops conditions of optimal arousal that produces an experience of engagement and meaning (Berlyne, 1969).

Play may be any kind of action—communication, directed physical effort, aesthetic production, or a period of social interaction. For example, an episode of social play creates its own temporary symbolic world of communication action. What is special about such play is that its outcomes are not predefined. There is always the possibility of creating something new. Play is the quality of action that is open and that creates its own world. There may be forms and limits. There is at least an inaugural symbol system that permits communication. Yet, in this special bounded world, the action and interaction may create what did not previously exist. Play is open to the novel.

The transcendence of play is developed in the classic book *Homo Ludens* by Johan Huizinga (1955). Huizinga stresses the enjoyment of play made possible because it is "out of the ordinary," a suspension of reality that creates its own world. Due to its temporary nature, play may have its own order and beauty. Within its created order, play may have a heightened meaning beyond its own time and place. Its theatrical or representative character makes possible meaning that is related to more lasting ideas and possibilities. Play is like art in the symbolic potential to be more meaningful than ordinary life just because it may suggest the meanings embedded in ordinary life.

Play may have many forms. Roger Caillois (1961) proposed two kind of play at opposite ends of a continuum. The first is *paidia,* free and spontaneous play. The second is *ludus,* rule-governed activity. Play may incorporate both freedom and order. Particular forms may be more open or regulated. In either case, however, the outcomes are not predetermined. Both freedom and order point to Huizinga's idea that play is connected with the fundamental values, myths, symbols, and stories of the culture. Play, then, is like leisure in being action with its meaning focused on the experience. It also has connotations that stress its special world of order and symbols that make possible action that is open to the creation of the novel and the innovative.

Three Brief Definitions

Leisure and *play* are the fundamental concepts for the chapters that follow. They cannot be defined neatly if we are to engage in the kind of exploration that is the aim of this book. They are themes of action and interaction. As such, they take on slightly different emphases in different contexts and from different perspectives. Along with these metaphors, three other terms should be identified more briefly.

1) "Freedom" is a term that has been used and misused in many ways. It is often more of a slogan than a concept. Philosophers have debated whether or not freedom is real at all. There is no debate on the issue that all action is limited. Freedom from limit or constraint is neither a reality nor a useful idea, except in relative terms. All action is limited in its real world situation in addition to the limitations of the actor. Freedom for action is another issue. Can human action be free in the sense of being consequential? Do decisions and actions make a difference? The alternative is that all actions are so predetermined that they only appear to present alternatives with differing outcomes. The approach here is that, however powerful the forces that shape and influence decisions, there remains the reality of freedom for action. *Freedom is the measure of self-determination in human actions.* Life is bounded and contextual in the actuality of a historical and cultural time and place. Yet, in the sense that what we do does make a difference, there is freedom for action.

2) "Sociology" is, of course, the study of people in society. However, there is considerable disagreement over what is included and excluded (Kelly, 1987). The "systemic" model of sociology includes only organized and institutionalized interaction. The focus is on the "structures" and consistencies that are the shaping context of action. The "conflict" model of sociology also concentrates on structures and forces, but presumes divisions within societies. There is always a dynamic element of conflict-driven change as different interests and bases of power meet. The "interpretive" model takes those structures as a context for action and interaction. The symbol systems of the culture become the basis for the meaningful action of interpreting actors.

All three perspectives will be utilized in this book. The social system is composed of interrelated institutions with their particular functions, purposes, and structures. Despite such a system of organization, there is change that is at least in part based on the different interests of social segments with differential access to power and resources. In the society, there is both cooperation and struggle, stability and change.

The interpretive or "symbolic interaction" model, however, has special relevance to the study of leisure (Kelly, 1983). Insofar as leisure is action with a degree of self-determination and meaning, then understanding must include more than external contexts and forces. Rather, a sociology of leisure requires a dialectical approach that incorporates both meaningful action and the organizational structures of the society. From this dialectical perspective, *sociology is the study of action and interaction in the context of the forces and organizational structures of a society.* It includes meaning and behavior, symbolic communication and institutional structures, change and regularities, and conflict and coordination.

3) "Society" is also more than organizational arrangements. Society is the organization of social actors in identified and bounded institutions that are integrated into common action. Society is culture and history, laws and policies, symbols and contracts, forces of change and arrangements of stability. Society is the learned culture of individual socialization, the intimacy of primary relationships, the laws and rules of the family, the learning of the school, the protection and enforcement of the polity, the production and distribution of the economy, and the celebrated consensus of the church. It is conflict and cooperation, the spiritual and the material, the

results of the past and the aims of the future. It is system and chaos, coercion and consensus, explicit rule of law and implicit world-views and values. Yet, when we refer to a particular national society, we also have some sense of geographical, historical, and organizational definitions that distinguish it from other societies. *Society is the organized life of a people.*

Recurring Issues in the Study of Leisure

The test of any definitions, models, metaphors, or perspectives is how well they provide a basis for dealing with crucial issues. In a sociological approach to leisure, there are a number of such issues that are woven through the analysis of the many forms, environments, orientations, resources, and conflicts of leisure. Among those that will recur over and over in succeeding chapters are these:

1) The relationship of leisure to the social system has a number of dimensions. From one perspective, there is considerable emphasis on the alleged "benefits" of leisure. In a capitalist economic system, does leisure contribute to productivity? Is leisure fundamentally secondary to social bonding, to the development of primary rela-tionships and especially those of the family? From a reverse perspective, is leisure largely determined by more powerful social forces, especially economic and political? Functional sociologists tend to approach leisure as secondary but contributing to more fundamental social institutions such as the economy and the family. Conflict sociologists are more likely to see leisure as a means of social control exercised for their own ends by those that own and control the economy. Interpretive sociologists and anthropologists analyze leisure as a realm of the expression and reinforcement of the central values of the culture. From any perspective, leisure is more than individuals "feeling good" or experiencing pleasure. Leisure is social action tied to the organized forces of the social system.

2) However, leisure is not just a social phenomenon that reflects the institutional structure of the society. It is also a realm of openness in which individuals take action that has consequences for who they are and who they are becoming. There is a developmental dimen-sion to leisure that runs through the entire life course. Children learn and develop in play. In fact, most critical early socialization occurs in play. Throughout the life course, individuals inaugurate and

revise lines of action that are intended to enable them to become the kind of persons they want to be and to have some sort of ongoing community with others with whom they want to share some significant part of their lives. Leisure, then, is closely connected with personal self-definitions and agendas for development. Its meaning is more than momentary, however much it may be focused on the quality of the experience.

3) Leisure is not just individual action and experience. It expresses more than the self in some sort of isolation. Rather, leisure is a significant social space in which actors develop community. Human relationships are not just a matter of organizing and completing necessary tasks. Rather, in social action in which the meaning is on the experience rather than the product, individuals explore, create, diversify, cement, and express relationships with other people. We are, after all, social beings in becoming human and in the fundamental meanings of our lives. Relationships are developed in the contexts of doing things together, of social action. Leisure provides a context for both a concentration and openness in the action that enables community to grow and be enriched.

4) Finally, there is the basic issue of whether leisure is culture-specific or a universal human dimension. There is no question that the forms and symbolic meanings of leisure are specific to the culture and the historical era. Leisure in a centralized industrial society is different from a relatively dispersed agricultural period. Eastern and Western world views based on religious premises give different shape and orientation to leisure. Transcending these specifics, however, there may be a universal theme of life that may be referred to as leisure. At least in any societies in which survival is not a total preoccupation, there are expressive elements. People express the meaning of relationships in nonproductive play. The meanings of life are acted out in games and ceremonies. There is activity that is noninstrumental and yet has some persistent forms and even time frames. It is a premise of the discussion that follows that leisure is indeed a theme of human life that is found in varying degrees and forms in all cultures. Leisure is more than designated activities; it is profoundly human action.

REFERENCES

Berlyne, D. (1969). Laughter, humor, and play. In G. Lindzey and E. Aronson (Eds.), *Handbook of social psychology.* New York, NY: Addison-Wesley Publishing Co., Inc.

Caillois, R. (1961). *Man, play, and games.* London, England: Thames & Hudson, Inc.

Cheek, N., and Burch, W. (1976). *The social organization of leisure in human society.* New York, NY: Harper & Row, Publishers, Inc.

Csikszentmihalyi, M. (1975). *Beyond boredom and anxiety.* San Francisco, CA: Jossey-Bass, Inc., Publishers.

Csikszentmihalyi, M., and Csikszentmihalyi, I. (Eds.). (1988). *Optimal experience.* New York, NY: Cambridge University Press.

de Grazia, S. (1964). *Of time, work, and leisure.* Garden City, NY: Doubleday & Co., Inc.

Dumazedier, J. (1967). *Toward a society of leisure.* New York, NY: The Free Press.

Havighurst, R. (1957). The leisure activities of the middle-aged. *American Journal of Sociology, 63,* 152-162.

Havighurst, R., and Feigenbaum, K. (1959). Leisure and life-style. *American Journal of Sociology, 64,* 4.

Huizinga, J. (1955). *Homo ludens: A study of the play element in culture.* Boston, MA: Beacon Press.

Iso-Ahola, S. (1989). Motivation for leisure. In E. Jackson and T. Burton (Eds.), *Understanding leisure and recreation: Mapping the past, charting the future.* State College, PA: Venture Publishing, Inc., pp. 247-280.

Kaplan, M. (1975). *Leisure: Theory and policy.* New York, NY: John Wiley & Sons, Inc.

Kelly, J. (1983). *Leisure identities and interactions.* London, England: George Allen & Unwin, Ltd.

Kelly, J. (1987). *Freedom to be: A new sociology of leisure.* New York, NY: Macmillan Publishing Co., Inc.

Neulinger, J. (1974). *The psychology of leisure.* Springfield, IL: Charles C. Thomas, Publisher.

Pieper, J. (1963). *Leisure, the basis of culture.* New York, NY: Random House, Inc.

Szalai, A. (Ed.). (1972). *The uses of time: Daily activities of urban and suburban populations in 12 countries.* The Hague, The Netherlands: Mouton.

Veblen, T. (1899) (1953). *The theory of the leisure class,* 2nd edition. New York, NY: New American Library.

Section One:
Historical Perspectives

CHAPTER 3

Preindustrial and Early Industrial Society

P hilosophically, the concept of leisure may be said to have originated in the city-state of Athens a few centuries before the birth of Christ. While this concept is, in many ways, "foreign" to our own culture, in other ways it has served as the basis for much of our thinking. If one generalizes about the concept of leisure within Athens, the following may be said. Leisure was considered to be of a higher order than work and the only real justification for working was to obtain leisure. Leisure, according to Aristotle, was essentially a way of life in which one was free from the necessity of being occupied. Leisure was, therefore, essentially a way of life rather than a brief period of free time. Leisure also meant serious activity undertaken without the pressure of necessity. The Greek word for leisure—"schole"—eventually served as the root for our word "school."

It should also be understood that the Greek ideal for culture and leisure within that culture was based on the assumption that the natural life for humans was in collectives; community was all important. Their ideal involved the perfection of civil and political life. The development of individual citizens would benefit the character of the community. Individual development, therefore, such as might be found in leisure, was not an end in itself. Rather, it was a means to collective social and political development.

For the Athenian philosophers, the purposes of leisure were self-understanding and perfection. Individuals who were freed to pursue such a life, it was assumed, would benefit the state since they would eventually think the great thoughts, write the great poetry and advance understanding. Not everyone was assumed to have the potential to benefit from a life of leisure. In most senses, the Athenian notion of leisure was elite. A slave culture and the semi-slave status of most women was responsible for doing the mundane work of daily life while a fraction of the population led lives of leisure.

A life of leisure, it was believed, had to be prepared for or one would not have the personal resources to confront it. Leisure demanded discipline. It was a life, in most respects, in opposition to materialism. Whatever you owned would in turn own you and distract you from matters of higher importance. Aristotle even advised men not to marry or give up all hope of leisure.

Inherent also in the concept of leisure was a halt to the mundane activity of the world. Contemplation was thought to be the highest form of leisure. Tranquility was much admired. Leisure was not merely a matter of doing—it was primarily a matter of being. It was not merely perceived freedom but actual freedom. To obtain such freedom, one willingly sacrificed many things to obtain that which was best or of most importance. Such contemplation gave the opportunity for the development of philosophical thought " . . . a point of view from which to take in the world" (Pieper, 1952, p. 43). According to Aristotle: "To look for utility everywhere ill becomes free and exalted souls" (In Stocks, 1939, p. 178).

For Aristotle, virtue was linked to pleasure and happiness.

> Virtue is pleasant because it is honorable and good. Virtue is, in itself, the source of pleasure. A good man is one who practices virtue throughout a lifetime. Thus his happiness is continuous . . . A day or a brief period of time does not bring happiness in a true sense. Freedom from the necessity of being occupied meant, for Aristotle, a lifetime, not brief periods away from work or other necessary occupation. We may, he said, use these brief periods for recreative pastimes. These periods are necessary for rest and recuperation so that we can return to work. But amusements and pastimes are not a source of true pleasure or happiness. They are not at all related to leisure (Goodale and Godbey, 1988, p. 23).

The leisure ideal was soon overwhelmed by a complicated sequence of historical forces, but its birth and the notion that a society should and could be based upon leisure rather than work must be attributed to the ancient Greeks of 2400 years ago. It was only in the 19th century that humans began to believe that machines might replace slaves to accomplish the work of society, freeing those in industrialized nations for a life of leisure.

Rome—The Politics of Leisure

While the Romans, like the Greeks, built and planned for leisure, their emphasis on law and custom rather than on learning and exploration gave leisure a different meaning (Kelly, 1990). Leisure became viewed more as consumption than as creation and a political instrument rather than the highest human good.

While leisure, over the centuries, slowly became less a matter of participation and more a matter of observation, this trend was accentuated in Rome, where soldiers who were temporarily idle, slaves who were brought to the city to do the mundane work, and displaced farmers formed a ring of poverty and unemployment around the seat of government. For such individuals, the phrase "bread and circuses" summarized the attitude of government and the ruling class, who sought to blunt dissatisfaction with programs of public welfare and with entertainment spectacles. Just as welfare programs provided some food and shelter for the urban poor, the circus and other spectacles provided distraction. Leisure in the form of mass entertainment served to protect both the political structure and the power of the ruling class by diverting the attention of the masses. "In time, the spectacles became increasingly violent and colorful and the bloodshed and danger intensified to continue the appeal to a population that had lost meaningful direction and no longer participated in the productive life of the society" (Kelly, 1990, p. 108).

For the class of wealthy rulers, who became increasingly distinct from the rest of the population, leisure amenities increased. They had their villas on the edge of the city with gardens, entertainment halls, hunting preserves and, sometimes, a place by the sea for vacations.

Rome demonstrated the potential of leisure to be used as an instrument of social control both for workers and for those who had no place in the economy. In the control of leisure, the ability to subvert attention from social problems and political wrongdoing was evident.

Hunter-Gatherer and Agrarian Societies

It is difficult to say if the concept of leisure applies to societies which hunted and gathered food or grew it. Certainly the line between work and nonwork was less absolute. As Cross (1990) observed, in most preindustrial societies leisure was irregular, often consisting of festivals and holidays which might make up almost one-half of the year. Leisure was limited by daylight hours, was generally sex-segregated, and sometimes served as a period for great emotional release when rigid social rules were temporarily suspended.

While it is certainly true that some preindustrial societies were characterized by long hours of work, many others were not. Additionally, many primitive people tend to approach a great many of their daily activities as if they were play. In their study of Maori culture, for example, Stumpf and Cozens (1947) reported that every aspect of their economic life was characterized by elements of leisure. "Whether engaging in fishing, bird-snaring, cultivation of the fields, or building a house or canoe, the occasion was marked by activities which we would definitely classify as recreational" (Stumpf and Cozens, 1947). These activities—singing, loud talking, laughing—are also features of cooperative work parties which are to be found in many parts of Africa and elsewhere.

Not only was there an element of recreation or leisure in the economic activities of many hunter-gatherer and agricultural societies, but, in some, the amount of time for leisure appears to have been far greater than our own. Anthropologists Allen and Orna Johnson (1978) studied the Machiguenga Indians of Peru for eighteen months and found this to be the case. These Indians survived by growing food in gardens, hunting, fishing, and collecting wild foods.

"They are self-sufficient; almost everything they consume is produced by their own labors using materials that are found close at hand (Johnson and Johnson, 1978). When the Johnsons divided the time of the Machiguenga into production time (using consumer goods for pleasure, eating), and free time (idleness, resting, sleep, chatting) and then compared these expenditures to those in current French society, they discovered that French men and women (both working and housewives) spent more time in production activities than the Machiguenga. The French also spent from three to five times more hours in the consumption of goods than did the Indians. The Machiguenga's free time, however, was found to exceed that of the French by more than four hours per day. The Johnsons argued that while technological progress has provided us with more goods, it has not resulted in more free time for most people living in industrial society. They also observed that the pace of life for the Peruvian Indians was more leisurely; daily activities never seemed hurried or desperate. "Each task was allotted its full measure of time, and free time is not felt to be boring or lost but is accepted as being entirely natural" (Johnson and Johnson, 1978).

These findings agree with those of Sahlins (1972), who found that many hunter-gatherer societies, such as the Australian Aborigines and the Kung San of South Africa, require only three or four hours of work per day to provide the material requirements for their simple way of life. Thus, he pointed out, there are two ways to reach affluence—our own way, which is to produce more, or what Sahlins called the Buddhist way, which is to be satisfied with less.

Free time in such cultures did not necessarily lead to what we in the Western world might think of as "higher" forms of civilization. While it was once believed that by producing large surpluses of food, people would automatically experiment with art, mathematics and written languages, this has frequently not been the case. The Kung San, for example, did not undergo such a revolution even though by working only a few hours per day they consumed a diet which exceeds recommended allowances set by the U.S. Food and Drug Administration (Lewin, 1980).

Perhaps, as Godbey observed, " . . . it is not always correct to say that societies continue to have more and more leisure. Rather, it is more correct to say that the quantity and quality of leisure have varied greatly within different periods of history and within different societies" (Godbey, 1990, p. 25-26).

The Rise of Christianity

While the ancient Greeks and the Romans after them did not place a high value on work, the rise of Christianity began to change that attitude. The notion of original sin made work seem not only necessary but desirable. St. Augustine, who formed the first monastery in the Western world, believed not only in original sin but in predestination. While he argued that man could do nothing to change his predetermined fate in heaven or hell, "Over 1,000 years later, the protest of Martin Luther and John Calvin lead to a different interpretation of the path to salvation, and thus a new ethic, the Protestant (work) ethic" (Goodale and Godbey, 1988, p. 3).

Many monastic orders, such as the Benedictines, organized their lives into perpetual rounds of labor, idleness being considered the enemy of the soul. St. Benedict's pronouncement: "Work, do not despair," became the model for monastic life throughout Europe. Monastic life also became increasingly regulated by sundials and, eventually clocks. Life was ordered into time segments and the tolling of bells signaled to the monks that one activity should end and another begin. Townspeople often heard the ringing of such bells and life began to be divided more precisely into time segments. The basis for modern life, in which human behavior is regulated by time in systematic fashion, may be traced to Christian monasteries.

Science and Economics

While Protestantism challenged Catholicism in Europe, by 1500 so too did scientific explanations of the world and the place of humans in it challenge religion. Not only were there substantial advances in physics and astronomy and other subjects, but also in science as a way of learning and as a philosophy. Knowledge was power, observed Francis Bacon. To truly know anything one must first doubt, according to Descarte. These ideas and other challenged religious notions of fatalism and led the way to the belief that humans, through their own efforts, could improve their lives and their understanding.

For many early scientists, the pursuit of knowledge was, itself, a form of play or recreation. Many were employed elsewhere and science was, literally, their avocation. Gradually, however, science was to become mainly work, done for practical outcomes. This was in keeping with the ideas of 18th century philosopher Immanuel Kant, who thought that knowledge was exclusively the result of mental effort or work. Truth never came effortlessly to the individual (Goodale and Godbey, 1988).

With the Renaissance and the Reformation, the firm grip of tradition and religion was partially broken. Trade and commerce flourished due to exploration and colonization of many lands, including North America. "Individualism, the natural rights of liberty and equality, and a protestant ethic equating success with prosperous employment; all this required some attempt to understand work and the production and distribution of wealth" (Goodale and Godbey, 1988, p. 71). Thus was economics born. These "worldly philosophers" have perhaps shaped the modern world more profoundly than any other scholars. Self-interest was slowly legitimized, as was free enterprise, capitalism and laissez-faire political doctrines. Christianity found ways to not only condone attaining great wealth but to make it an ideal. Attaining wealth was a form of predestination which would actually benefit society at large. Self-interest would lead to the common good. Utility and pragmatism were increasingly common values. Social Darwinism postulated that natural laws were at work with regard to the distribution of wealth about which humans could do little.

The combination of the rise of science and of economics paved the way for the modern world, in which wealth, work and consumption all came to be thought of in unlimited terms.

Asceticism and the Rise of Capitalism

Against Marx, who argued that history was determined, essentially, by economic or materialistic structures and the forces of time, the German sociologist Max Weber proposed that ideas, even religious ideas, could reshape history. Religious ideology, he argued, could have an impact on economic arrangements. Weber saw the rise of capitalism as the most dramatic example of the importance of ideology. While capitalism had existed before Protestantism, he noted that it developed most fully in areas of Europe where Calvinist influence was strongest.

For capitalism to exist, he argued, the primary requirement was the availability of investment capital and the acceptance of the idea that money can make money—investment can be rewarded (Kelly, 1990). There appeared to be a relation between capitalism and the cultural influence of Protestantism, which stressed that life in the secular world was a legitimate arena for faithful activity. Since God was thought to be absolutely sovereign, there was nothing people could do to change the divine decision about their salvation. Their salvation was predetermined and could not be earned by good works. Since no one could know with any certainty if they were predetermined to go to heaven or hell, evidence of the likelihood of their election to heaven might be found in the quality of their life on this earth. "The elect are surely among those who are Godly, righteous, sober, well-disciplined, and faithful and not among those whose lives are characterized by waste, frivolity and dissipation" (Kelly, 1990, p. 116). The elect are often rewarded in this world through the success of their enterprises. "After all, if one works diligently, rationally, and in a disciplined way, then the result is likely to be success" (Kelly, 1990, p. 116).

Industrialization and the Ordering of Modern Life

The process of industrialization, which began over two-hundred years ago and, in many nations, continues today, had a fundamental impact on the ordering of life. The production of material goods was transferred from small shops or spaces within the home or barn to large factories. Technological advances made it possible to combine machines and workers in ways which produced un-dreamed of amounts of consumer "goods." The process of producing such goods was taken out of the hands of individuals or of small guilds of workers and, essentially, transferred into the hands of a small number of individuals who owned the means of production. Work became standardized and hours devoted to work were increased. Since work was done in collectives, it now had to be scheduled much more precisely. Punctuality became critical and workers who were late were often locked out of factories. A large clock hung in many factories and mills; whistles blew or bells rang to signal the beginning or ending of the work day. Since most factory workers had almost no power over the process of work, their attempts at resisting this process were usually unsuccessful. As de Grazia observed, those workers who formed movements to oppose the factory system, such as the Luddite movement, were either deported or hung by management. The Luddites had thought that if they destroyed the machinery in factories they could end the process of industrialization. Their real enemy, according to de Grazia, was the increasingly important organizer of worklife— the clock (de Grazia, 1962).

Industrialization produced cities as workers moved close to the factories and mills, often in wretched quarters. The day was now reordered so that work was scheduled first and everything else became, in some sense, "free time."

REFERENCES

Cross, G. (1990). *A social history of leisure since 1600.* State College, PA: Venture Publishing, Inc.

de Grazia, S. (1962). *Of time, work and leisure.* Glencoe, IL: The Free Press.

Goodale, T., and Godbey, G. (1988). *The evolution of leisure: Historical and philosophical perspectives.* State College, PA: Venture Publishing, Inc.

Godbey, G. (1990). *Leisure In your life: An exploration* (3rd ed.). State College, PA: Venture Publishing, Inc.

Johnson, A., and Johnson, O. (September, 1978). In search of the affluent society. *Human Nature,* pp. 50-59.

Kelly, J. (1990). *Leisure,* 2nd Edition. Englewood Cliffs, NJ: Prentice-Hall.

Lewin, R. (1980). An introduction to affluence. In J. Cherfas and R. Lewin (Eds.), *Not work alone: A cross-cultural view of activities superfluous to survival.* Newbury Park, CA: Sage Publications.

Pieper, J. (1952). *Leisure: The basis of culture.* New York, NY: Mentor Books.

Sahlins, M. (1972). *Stone age economics.* New York, NY: Aldine Atherton.

Stocks (1939). Quoted in T. Goodale and G. Godbey (1988), *The evolution of leisure: Historical and philosophical perspectives.* State College, PA: Venture Publishing, Inc.

Stumpf, F., and Cozens, F. (1947). Some aspects of the role of games, sports and recreational activities in the culture of modern primitive people. *Research Quarterly, 18* (1):104-108.

CHAPTER 4

The Struggle for Leisure

The impact of urbanization and industrialization reorganized life in ways which transformed many aspects of leisure. Daily life was reordered with work at the center. Factories changed the nature, tempo, organization and meaning of work. Gender and class differences became more pronounced in many areas of life.

In this chapter, we will examine some of the ways in which the process of industrialization produced a struggle for leisure in terms of how it should be used and who should shape such use. In later chapters, we will examine the movements which sought more time free of work.

The Impact of Industrialization on Gender Roles

One of the consequences of industrialization was to split "economic" time and "domestic" time. When work was pulled out of the home into factories it represented, literally, the breaking up of households. The family unit which had traditionally labored together was now split up and sent different, often distant, places for their work, education and shopping (Cross, 1990). This split had numerous effects including dividing work and leisure into opposed spheres of life and removing work from the domestic environment, thus making home the haven from a heartless world. "Thus, a cult of 'domestic pleasures' emerged, deliberately privatized in the home and defined over against the world of business and labor" (Lasch, 1977, p. 79). Additionally, the separation of work and leisure tended to separate the generations. Fathers had less control over the vocational training of their children as well as less contact in general.

Perhaps the most subtle effect, according to Cross (1990) was the separation of females from male experiences. Women lost contact with the world of business and labor. While working class females often took jobs, in all but the lowest income households they would retire from these jobs once they married and had children. Since work and family life were no longer conducted in the same place, combining economic and family functions was no longer possible. The necessity of segmenting women's lives into periods of work prior to marriage and the role of housewife after marriage was reinforced by the Victorian ideology that a woman's rightful place was in the home.

Women, then, increasingly had different work and leisure experiences from those of men. Work outside the home was viewed as a temporary situation prior to marriage and family. While the male became time conscious in the emerging strict industrial sense, females in the middle and upper classes often organized their day more as workers in preindustrial eras—tasks were planned for and around such tasks might be opportunities for conversation, decorative arts, or other forms of home-bound leisure.

As industrialism created a "working class," families were increasingly less important as an economic unit. They were replaced by factories, with the result that women workers were increasingly seen as a source of competition by males in the working class. "Thus, the distinction between work and leisure, and between public and private spheres were inflicted with the image of gender difference: work-public-male versus home-private-female worlds" (Clarke and Critcher, 1985, p. 59).

Leisure and Class Struggle

Some sociologists, particularly those who accept conflict theory, contend that leisure did not become a discrete area of human activity in linear fashion simply as a result of industrialization. Leisure, according to such interpretations, like industrial work was "imposed" and "enforced" as a means of social control by those in power. Leisure was controlled, Clarke and Critcher argue, by clergymen, police, magistrates, mill owners and others. Despite religious and moral camouflage, leisure was created, defined and controlled to tame the work force (Clarke and Critcher, 1985, p. 59).

> There may even be in qualitative terms a loss here: leisure becomes demarcated from work as a reaction to, and compensation for it. This antithesis of work and leisure, from which so many contemporary accounts begin, is not a given social fact, but an historical creation. That people may gain in leisure satisfactions they do not derive from work is not a psychological but an historical phenomenon. The form industrialization took in the mid-nineteenth century ensured that what was an artificial imposition would be taken for granted by succeeding generations, including some of the most influential scholars of leisure (Clarke and Critcher, 1985, p. 59).

Certainly those with power have historically shaped the leisure of others. The period of industrialization is no exception. Conversely, there is reason to believe that the peasants who became the "working class" supported many of the changes in structuring work and leisure, if for no other reason that dividing the day into work and leisure gave the potential for work to be contained—for a limit to work, however unreasonable, to be defined. This is not to argue that industrialism was embraced by the working class, at least not until a later period, but only that they often saw fixed hours as the best deal which could be struck.

The process of industrialization did, in many senses, bring about leisure and change what people would voluntarily and pleasurably do. While many of these changes were shaped by the various reform movements, most were not. Leisure, as it emerged in industrializing Europe and later in North America, developed in ways which were appropriate for the needs of capitalism. Its segregated, specialized and institutionalized nature increasingly reflected a market economy, division of labor and the centrality of production. It was segregated not only in time and space but also in that it was made to appear as compensation, retreat or escape from the struggle for material sufficiency. It was also class, gender and age segregated.

Leisure became specialized in the sense that it was a special sphere with component parts which became discrete and differentiated. "Pubs were places for drinking, music halls for being entertained, football grounds for getting excited, parks for walking" (Clarke and Critcher, 1985, p. 70). Later, this specialization began to apply even to people's homes, where middle and upper class families had "rec" rooms.

In another sense leisure became more specialized in that style of participation became more various. Often, people of divergent economic classes did the same things during leisure but style, skill level and meanings of the activity in question became increasingly diverse. In some senses, leisure styles set by the rich and powerful "trickled down" to those in lower classes, who imitated such models of leisure behavior whenever they could. As an illustration, Huizinga (1955) mentioned poor people who wore wigs made of yarn in imitation of the wealthy who could afford wigs made of real human hair.

Finally, leisure became more institutionalized since many leisure pursuits came to require money for specialized areas, facilities, and equipment and such capital could come only from private companies or from government. The major forms of organized leisure, in many senses, were outside of the control of those who used them. Thus, the relation was one of customer and provider. While most of what people did during their free time was still to take place in and around the home, many forms of leisure opportunity outside the home were increasingly "provided" and were ultimately more subject to the control of large, formal institutions.

The Emergence of a Leisure Class

Early industrialization brought with it the emergence of a class of wealthy owners of factories and other means of production. The first leisure class in North America evolved on southern plantations where owners had none of the prohibitions against pleasure that the Puritans to the north imposed, but did have slaves to do the work. It was in the second half of the nineteenth century that "society most flagrantly bent its pleasures to display" (Dulles, 1965). Those who became rich after the Civil War, owners of steel plants, copper mines, textile mills, and cattle ranches sought to establish social leadership through their extravagance in entertainments and amusements. Capitalism and the processes of urbanization and industrialization had brought about increasing divisions within society. One such division was "the Leisure Class."

In 1899, Thorstein Veblen launched an attack on the extravagance of the newly wealthy industrial capitalists. In *The Theory of the Leisure Class,* he argued that all consumption of goods, as well as leisure behavior, was shaped by the desire to impress others and to distinguish oneself from ordinary people (Veblen, 1899). History, Veblen argued, showed a process by which workers, through workmanship, at long last created the material surplus needed for economic security. This surplus, however, permitted a new group of self-centered motives to come into being, and some people "found their pleasure in invidious distinctions at the expense of others" (Riesman, 1953). The primary balance of production and consumption gave way to a world where too much productivity, in countries like Germany and Japan, put a military surplus in the hands of ambitious dictators, while in countries like England and America, too much consumption involved all classes in a meaningless chase to display material goods in an emulative manner.

Leisure, as Veblen described it, was the nonproductive consumption of time, undertaken because of a sense that productive work wasn't worthwhile and also to show that one could afford to be idle. Leisure was thought to be closely related to exploitation, and the achievements of a life of leisure had much in common with the spoils of war or the trophies of economic exploitation. Material goods were such trophies. But, since leisure did not generally result in material goods, those in the leisure class had to provide evidence of nonproductive, immaterial, consumption of time.

> Such immaterial evidences of past leisure are quasi-scholarly or quasi-artistic accomplishments and a knowledge of processes and incidents which do not conduct directly to the furtherance of human life. So, for instance, in our time there is knowledge of the dead languages and the occult sciences; of correct spelling; of syntax and prosody; of various forms of domestic music and other household art; of the latest properties of dress, furniture and equipage; of games, sports and fancy bred

animals such as dogs and race horses. In all of these branches of knowledge the initial motive from which their acquisition proceeded at the onset, and through which they first came into vogue, may have been something quite different from the wish to show that one's time had not been spent in industrial employment; but unless these accomplishments had approved themselves as serviceable evidence of an unproductive expenditure of time, they would not have survived and held their place as conventional accomplishments of the leisure class (Veblen, 1899, p. 178).

The use of leisure by the class of society who had it obviously didn't result in self-perfection or the improvement of culture or the community. Instead, it simply resulted in unproductive uses of time in order to achieve status.

The roots of the leisure class, Veblen argued, could be traced to the ancient traditions of predatory cultures in which productive effort was considered unworthy of the able-bodied male. Thus, a leisure class existed before industrialization. It was the transition to a "pecuniary" culture, however, which brought the leisure class into full bloom. The captain of industry and the tribal chief, therefore, shared some things in common.

This portrait of the emerging leisure class, while containing some truth, is widely thought to be exaggerated. As sociologist David Riesman (1953) pointed out, there came to be lots of variation in motive and behavior of those in the leisure class. Many, particularly women, were in the vanguard of modern movements in the arts and politics. Many became deeply involved in charity, often out of genuine concern. Some of the leisure class also recognized criticisms of them and changed as a result.

Such criticisms work against what is perhaps Veblen's most intriguing idea. This is the idea of economic determinism. If a person gained wealth, they would inevitably use such wealth for purposes of display and conspicuous consumption. While such behavior is perhaps not inevitable, it happened with great regularity during the period of industrialization—as it does today.

Gambling and Drinking—Common Leisure Pursuits

In both Europe and North America, gambling and drinking either accompanied or were the source of most leisure activity of adult males. Historians, according to Cross (1990), identified a tremendous growth in wagering during the late 17th century. While gambling was common to some extent in almost all cultures, the growth of racing and of blood sports, from boxing to cockfights, in both Europe and North America increased greatly.

The practice of card playing for money and gaming in general spread to all sectors of society, involving women as well as men. One explanation for the rise of gambling, according to Cross, was the rise of commercial enterprise and the spirit of capitalism, which took a positive attitude toward risk-taking.

In America, according to historian John Findlay, "From the seventeenth century through the twentieth, both gambling and westering thrived on high expectations, risk taking, opportunism, and movement: and both activities helped to shape a distinctive culture. Like bettors, pioneers have repeatedly grasped the chance to get something for nothing-to claim free land, to pick up nuggets of gold, to speculate on western real estate" (Findlay, 1986, p. 23).

While modern academic accounts of gambling usually center around gambling as an addiction (Kusyzn, 1972), a pathological compulsion (Dickerson, 1987) or as a masochistic desire to punish the guilty self (Halliday and Fuller, 1974), there has been little academic attention to pleasurable aspects of such risk-taking behavior. Much of the gambling which became popular in Britain during industrialization and later in North America certainly had such a pleasurable element. It was a means of displaying wealth and bravery. It also provided, as Goffman (1961) observed, an opportunity for euphoria, a flooding in of the experience of spontaneous yet all-encompassing action. It both channeled the excitement of competition and risk-taking into relatively harmless endeavors and also frequently expressed the value of individuality and the dream of gain (Cross, 1990).

In Britain, government's attempts at controlling gambling were usually restricted to controlling gambling among the poor, while in North America, greater church pressure led to numerous attempts to ban gambling. The Virginia Company sought to outlaw gambling in order to improve work discipline. There was also religious disdain for leaving things to chance, a characteristic of much gambling, as well as for the drinking and rowdiness which often accompanied it. Puritans in New England outlawed card playing and horse racing. While casino gambling didn't prosper in North America as it did in Britain, generally attempts at banning gambling simply failed because people wanted to do it. Additionally, there was the matter of hypocrisy—both the church and state sponsored some forms of gambling, such as lotteries, from colonial times.

The popularity of gambling was such that some sports, such as boxing, horse racing, many forms of card playing, cockfighting, bear or bull baiting and other forms of leisure expression existed primarily to allow for betting. In all such forms of activity, there was eventually considerable attention given to establishing rules which reduced cheating, which was common. Attempts were made to regulate boxing, establish written rules for card games and license the operation of gambling casinos. Cheating, nevertheless, remained an important part of the gambling scene.

The consumption of alcohol was no less popular. Not only were wine, beer and spirits popular because they were an ageless means of conserving fruit and grain in an era before refrigeration, but also because of different attitudes toward drinking. "It 'strengthened' the laborer and got him through a 10 or 12 hour day"

(Cross, 1990, p. 53). Drink played a central role in the taking of meals and in social conversation. Even in Puritan New England, there was much evidence of drinking on the Sabbath. The notion of total abstinence was a nineteenth century phenomenon. "While Puritans and other reformers struggled against its excess, few opposed drink on principle" (Cross, 1990, p. 53). Consumption of alcohol was thought of as much as a food as an intoxicant. "Drink was perhaps even more central to the meal and conversation than it is today" (Cross, 1990, p. 53).

While attitudes toward the consumption of alcohol were different in North America than Europe, drinking was nonetheless common. Alehouses and retail dram shops could be found in every town in the colonies. Rum and other forms of drink were often an integral part of the pay of workers. On the frontier, special occasions such as barn raisings, weddings and corn huskings led to communal drinking of home-made whiskey. Taverns sprang up around water fronts and drinking was an integral part of the life of a seaman.

The Increasing Role of Government in Controlling Leisure

The process of industrialization, in almost every country in which it takes place, brings about the increased role of government in recreation and leisure in two ways: the provision of recreation and leisure facilities, programs and other services as well as the increased regulation of leisure behavior.

In regard to the regulation of leisure activities, government had almost always, within Judeo-Christian cultures, sought to ban certain forms of leisure behavior. What changed under industrialization was the increased extent to which government sought to control such activity and the increased means at its disposal to do so. Clarke and Critcher (1985) discussed the increased role of police in regulating leisure activity, owing to laws passed in the second quarter of the nineteenth century which established organized police forces at the municipal and county level. One of the tasks of such police forces was to clear the streets of nuisances to facilitate travel and commerce. "One of the biggest nuisances was popular culture" (Clarke and Critcher, 1985, p. 65). Street trading, children's games and simply hanging around were now activities which were no longer appropriate for the streets. Police were also increasingly evident at almost any public occasion, including holidays, fairs and wakes. They were also evident inside pubs and music halls.

Licensing was also a way in which the state maintained control over numerous forms of leisure activity. Licensing policies increasingly sought to control and regulate pubs, music halls and the sale of alcohol. These were increasingly regulated and the operation of commercial recreation "rational-ized." Negotiations between proprietors of music halls and local authorities resulted in music halls becoming much tamer and more orderly. "Gone were drink, food and most of the prostitutes. Tables and chairs had been replaced by fixed rows of seats; and semi-professional and amateur performers had been supplanted by full-time professionals tightly controlled by contract, including guarantees that they would not include in their acts any material "offensive" to political figures and institutions" (Clarke and Critcher, 1985, p. 67). The pub, also, was increasingly controlled and lost many of its social functions.

In all these changes, leisure was shaped, increasingly to express the same values which industrialism had brought about rather than to provide an opposition to such values. While the working class often resisted such changes, generally they were only partially successful in keeping some part of leisure free from the emerging ideals of efficiency, rationality and productivity.

The Reform of Leisure

Industrialism, as we have seen, produced changes which made former leisure habits impossible for the peasants who had become the working class. New work patterns, the emergence of capitalism and the urban environment, which was largely an unplanned phenomenon accompanying the factory system, made former ways of life and leisure obsolete. The factory system was a catastrophe for peasant culture. Likewise, peasant culture was a catastrophe for the factory system. Peasants often preferred idleness, drink, working when the mood struck them and the pleasures of the body over the pleasures of the mind. All these situations led to a series of attempts to reform the leisure of the the peasants, who had now become the "working class." Those who were employers as well as upwardly mobile employees believed that to change the leisure habits of the working class was of fundamental importance in determining the success of industrialism. Many, including Charles Dickens (1964), also recognized that leisure time was the only arena for the "re-creation" of the physical and psychological capacity to work. By the 1830s, reformers understood that new work patterns had deprived members of society of the means of expressing their religious, family and self-definitional values. "At the same time, these reformers held that leisure was perhaps the best place to inculcate the personal values essential for a growing commercial economy: self-control, familialism, and respectability" (Cross, 1990, p. 87). As an English reformer Joseph Kay (1977) described the situation, the poor "live precisely like brutes, to gratify . . . the appetites of their uncultivated bodies, and then die, to go they have never thought, cared, or wondered whether . . . they eat, drink, breed, work and die; and . . . the richer and more intelligent classes are obliged to guard them with police." At the heart of much reform of leisure in the early nineteenth century was fear of the urban working poor. Crime increased significantly in the early 1800s. Gang wars, prostitution, pickpockets, even the possibility of insurrection made the cities unsafe.

Certainly urbanization was to blame for much of the crime and pathological behavior which accompanied the transformation of peasants into the urban working class. As American historian Paul Boyer observed:

> The bawdy servant girl was transformed into the painted prostitute solic-iting on the street. The village tavern became the beer cellar in the slum; the neighborly wager on the horserace or a cockfight, the organized gambling of the city. The unruly child and the discontented farm youth quarreling with his father became the multiplied thousands of street arabs and young urban newcomers who seemed to have broken free of all familial control (Boyer, 1978, pp. 68-69).

Much of the effort in the rational recreation and other reform movements was to counter such situations, both from altruistic motivations as well as self-interest. Evangelists on both sides of the Atlantic sought to "Christianize" leisure, through developments such as Sunday School, the Sabbatarian Movement, which sought to ban many forms of leisure expression on Sunday, and the temperance movement,which sought to ban all use of alcohol. In Britain, the temperance movement was not politically very strong but in North America, a combination of clergy and business leaders gained sufficient political power that alcohol use had been restricted in thirteen states and territories by the 1850s (Cross, 1990). Temperance groups were often dominated by women, who saw the saloon culture of men as a threat to both family and community life. The various teetotaler and temperance movements often resulted in fierce disputes; neighbor against neighbor.

There were also movements against prostitution, sometimes called "Social Purity Movements," also often led by women concerned about men who transmitted disease to their wives as well as for "morality." Such groups, in the early eighteenth century, picketed brothels and published the names of patrons. Vigilante mobs occasionally hanged persistent brothel owners.

As British historian Hugh Cunningham (1980) argued, however, the various reform movements wanted not just to suppress, but to transform various leisure behaviors, replacing play which was public, inconclusive and improvised, with play which was more highly ordered and planned. In doing so, the intent was to make the working class more "respectable, more predictable, less dangerous to others, and more amenable to industrial working conditions." Certainly there was also a genuine concern for broadening the intellectual horizons, improving family life and the general health and welfare of those less fortunate.

The means of achieving these ends were as diverse as the promotion of reading, choral societies, structured sport experiences, adult education, and a variety of other nonwork experiences. The nature of many of these efforts were themselves offshoots of the techniques of industrial work. Modern sport, for instance, was born during the nineteenth century during the transformation of work to the industrial system. In Britain, sports such as track and field, swimming, rowing, and soccer became regulated contests with "... techniques drawn from industrial production and from the unfolding world of capitalistic market relationships, modern sports constituted themselves first as a noneconomic sort of competitive behavior" (Rigauer, 1981, p. 56).

While the transformation of work did cause the transformation of leisure, such change was not systematic or complete. Many traditions of preindustrial life remained intact; others were restructured—but some were lost forever.

REFERENCES

Boyer, P. (1978). *Urban masses and moral order in America: 1820-1920.* Cambridge, MA: Yale University Press.

Clarke, J., and Critcher, C. (1985). *The devil makes work: Leisure in capitalist Britain.* Champaign, IL: University of Illinois Press.

Cross, G. (1990). *A social history of leisure since 1600.* State College, PA: Venture Publishing, Inc.

Cunningham, H. (1980). *Leisure and the industrial revolution.* London, England: Croom Helm.

Dickens, C. (1964). *Hard times.* New York, NY: Bantam Books.

Dulles, R. (1965). *A history of recreation: America learns to play.* New York, NY: Appleton-Century-Crofts

Dickerson, M. (1987). Quoted in D. Saunders and D. Turner, Gambling and leisure: The case of racing. *Leisure Studies, 6* (3):281-299.

Findlay, J. (1986). *People of chance: Gambling in American society from Jamestown to Las Vegas.* New York, NY: Simon & Schuster, Inc.

Goffman, E. (1961). *Encounters.* London, England: Penguin.

Halliday, J., and Fuller, P. (Eds.). (1974). *The psychology of gambling.* London, England: Allen Lane.

Huizinga, J. (1955). *Homo ludens: A study of the play element in culture.* Boston, MA: Beacon Press.

Kay, J. (London: 1850). *The social condition and education of the people of England and Europe, Vol. 1,* (pp. 580-581). Cited in R. Storch, "The problem of working-class leisure." Donajgrodzki, A. P. (Ed.). (London, England: 1977). *Social control in nineteenth century Britain,* p. 141.

Kusyzn, A. (1972). The gambling addict versus the gambling professional. *International Journal of Addictions, 7,* 387-393.

Lasch, C. (1977). *Haven in a heartless world.* New York, NY: Simon & Schuster, Inc.

Riesman, D. (1953). *Thornstein Veblen: A critical interpretation.* New York, NY: Charles Scribner's, Sons.

Rigauer, B. (1981). *Sport and work.* New York, NY: Columbia University Press.

Veblen, T. (1899). *The theory of the leisure class.* New York, NY: Macmillan Publishing Company, Inc.

CHAPTER 5

Work:
Centrality, Containment, and Control

The question of what is central in human life is more than philosophical speculation. If life is pushed off center, then there is little possibility of personal development and fulfillment. If significant dimensions are left out, then life will be incomplete. Further, centrality is not only a matter of individual choice. All the forces of a society, the values of a culture, and the reinforcement mechanisms of institutions may combine to define life according to a particular ideology.

Are we primarily existential beings, creating meaning for ourselves in decisive action? Are we essentially social, becoming human and expressing that humanity in our multilayered relationships with others? Are we primarily economic beings with productive engagement central to life? Are we first of all players whose experience-centered expression of free action is most natural to our humanity? Or, is there some balance in life among all those elements of action, relationships, productivity, and expression—perhaps with shifting salience through the life course?

Any social system has one or more sets of values that address the issue of what is central to life. There may be a high degree of integration among the institutions that socialize individuals through life including education, the media, the state, and the church. Or, there may be considerable conflict within a social system, counter-cultures that rebel against the dominant ideologies and even seek to replace them. Further, even in totalitarian societies there is resistance to ruling elites, even when they are backed by the force of a police state.

Ironically, the premise that is either enforced or resisted in both socialist and capitalist societies is that work is central. Productive activity that contributes to the survival and growth of the society, that is recognized as of social worth, is held to be at the center of human activity. Work in this sense is much more than employment, meeting the regulations of the workplace and securing a wage. Work is investment in the productive process, investing the self in the meaningful creation of economic "goods," whether they are ideas, machines, food, shelter, or nurture. Productive work, according to the socialist or the capitalist, yields a sense of meaningful involvement. Alienated work, on the other hand, may become so routinized that there is no meaningful connection with the process, the product, or with other workers. There are two questions, then: "Whether work ought to be central," and "Whether work is central?"

Work Centrality: Ideology and Reality

In the beginning of industrialization in Europe and America, Karl Marx (1939) argued that work ought to be central to being human. In a capitalist system, however, it was alienated into instrumental and controlled activity that served the economic interests of those who owned and controlled the means of production. He also presented a vision of full life in which free and intrinsically-motivated activity would balance productive enterprise. Realized human beings would want to work and to play in community with others. That is what ought to be. In reality, workers were neither free to work nor play, but had become pawns on the capitalist chessboard. All this was said to be an inevitable result of the capitalist system.

Max Weber (1958), writing at about the same time, offered a counter-argument in his analysis of the rise of capitalism. He argued that capitalism developed most rapidly in Protestant rather than Catholic areas because of a different religious value system. Sure that no ritual or ethical acts could secure salvation, Calvinist Protestants concentrated on a this-worldly ethic that demonstrated their election by God to salvation. The ethic stressed sobriety, attention to social responsibility, ascetic restraint in life style, and devotion to work. This ethic contributed to success in business and the accumulation of capital for further development. Labelled the "Protestant work ethic," it supported a this-worldly centrality of work. Weber then explored the extent to which the work ethic actually was dominant in Protestant cultures.

The Marxist thesis, then, was that devotion to work was enforced by those who controlled the social and economic institutions of a capitalist society. A work ethic under such conditions was in the interest of investors, not workers. The Weberian analysis was that a religious ideology reinforced values of productivity that underlay the development of a particular kind of economic system. In both, ideology and practice united to focus the worker on his or her place in the process of production and distribution that rewarded investment capital first and labor only secondarily.

As an ideology, the work ethic clearly was in the interests of some more than others. Those who profited by the industry of others, the owners and managers of businesses, would gain from the work ethic of those who labored for them in the shops, factories, mines, and offices. In the capitalist ideology of Adam Smith (1937), writing at the beginning of the industrial revolution, workers would be rewarded (rented) for money assigned differentially according to their productivity assessed by the owner and his surrogates. Everything has a money value so that wages can be exchanged for whatever is valued ("bread or beer") by the worker. The worker exchanges a commodity, labor, for a medium of exchange by which other commodities can be obtained. In order to gain a profit, however, the owner would always pay wages that were only a portion of the value of the labor. Out of the surplus came the return on investment capital.

Both Adam Smith and Marx agreed that capitalism worked this way. The difference was that Smith saw the process as beneficent, even a natural order, while Marx believed it to be inherently exploitive of the wage worker. Both agreed that someone would profit from a work ethic on the part of wage workers. Smith thought it would be the entire society; Marx held that only the capitalist would benefit.

This issue raised the second question: Is work central to the lives and value systems of workers in actuality? The truth is that evidence is spotty and can be selected to support almost any answer.

In the earliest days of the industrial revolution, working conditions were dangerous beyond belief and wages so low that every able member of a family, children and adults, had to pool their meager wages to support a survival level of existence. Weekly hours of work in the factory or the mine averaged 70 to 80 hours a week. Conditions were hazardous, and there was no provision for health care or continuing income in case of an accident. Marx's associate, Friedrick Engels summarized conditions in Manchester in 1842 with phrases such as:

> Living like rats in wretched little dens . . . in a single room, sometimes without beds . . . women and children in the factories sometimes throwing the fathers out of work . . . arresting the physical development of girls . . . illegitimate motherhood and yet compelling them to come to work when they were pregnant . . . children fed into factories at the age of five or six . . . little care from mothers who were themselves at the factory all day and no education at all . . . would drop exhausted when they were let out of their "prisons" (Wilson, 1972, pp. 159-160).

The slightest complaint or resistance meant dismissal and the loss of the few dollars a week that stood between the family and starvation. Only on Sunday was there a break from the debilitating routine, a brief time to wash, rest, recover, and perhaps to drink. Those who escaped accidents usually died young anyway. What did a "work ethic" mean in such circumstances?

Shopgirls in Chicago earned three to five dollars a week. Children were in the factory six days a week. In the coal mines and steel mills men were destroyed by seven day weeks and twelve hour two-shift days in the 110-degree steel mill heat, poisonous fumes, and machine-paced pressure. Injury or health breakdown meant being reduced to the level of sweeper at 75 cents a day for the "fortunate" who were kept on. In 1842 reformers passed a law in Massachusetts that limited the work time of children under twelve to ten hours a day, but there was little enforcement. In the mines, "breaker boys" descended the shafts at ages as young as six.

It is true that hours gradually shortened, children had more limited hours and eventually were removed from the shop and placed in school, and wages raised above bare survival to allow for basic levels of nutrition, housing, and even a little play. Some of the improvement came as mill owners came to realize that productivity was actually increased in shorter hours by healthier workers. More often, workers with little to lose organized to demand better conditions, shorter hours, and higher wages.

It is no wonder that there was resistance by workers. The Pullman strike in 1883 and the Homestead Steel strike in 1892 were only two of the most bitter and violent of the more than 2000 between 1880 and 1900. The Pullman strike was triggered by five cuts in wages, the last by 30 percent. The Homestead strike was crushed by the force of armed militia with twenty workers killed and 3000 workers fired. With few exceptions until the twentieth century, strikes were crushed by the combined force of industrialists and the government ready to employ troops in the name of preserving order.

A "work ethic" hardly requires such massed force to get men, women, and children to work. Of course, things have changed. Children are in schools, although of quite varying quality. Women moved to the home before returning to the office and the retail shop. Hours shortened so that Sunday, and in time Saturday, became available for home, family, and leisure. The weekday employment schedule was reduced as unions battled for "eight hours for what we will."

What was the meaning of work in such improved conditions? Again, the studies are few and far between. One of the best investigations of the "American dream" in the affluent growth period of the 1950s found that an adequate level of security, sometimes even the ownership of a home, was enhanced by the dream that their children would have better opportunities (Chinoy, 1955). A few years later, Dubin (1963) studied the alleged centrality of work to factory employees. In a study of 1200 workers in three factories, he found that 90 percent preferred that their friendships be off the job and away from the workplace. Only 24 percent of the workers could be defined as even moderately job-oriented. For most, employment was a means to an end. Meaningful human relationships, feelings of worth, and enjoyment were sought off the job.

Why would it be otherwise? The factory is paced to the machine, not the worker. The office is a place of hierarchical relationships, of specified functions and clear levels of subordination. Services involve cleaning up after others, accepting the time-efficient rituals of the fast-food chain, and responding to the whims of strangers—usually at low wages and with limited chance for advancement. Certainly there is work that calls for creativity, innovation, and even communication and sharing. There are jobs in which superior performance can lead to increased rewards of income, prestige, and even autonomy. In such conditions, the possibilities of work centrality and a work ethic are increased, although not universal. For the most part, however, the nature of work is unlikely to produce a sense of meaning and involvement.

First it was Adam Smith (1937) and the manufacture of the pin. He found eighteen specific functions in making the pin that could be divided among ten workers. In such a production-oriented design, at least 48,000 pins a day could be produced. The cost to the workers of losing control of their craft was inconsequential. The aim was efficiency.

The drive for efficiency and productivity has led to jobs being designed around the articulation of tasks and functions rather than to challenge and engage the worker. Maximization of output was the sole criterion of the movement called "Taylorism" by its critics and "scientific management" by its proponents (Andrew, 1981). Its author, Friedrich Taylor, applied the stop watch to design time-and-motion routines that were articulated into a productive process. Higher wages and shorter hours were supported to gains in productivity. All was subordinated to time-motion efficiency. In the Bethlehem Steel Works, Taylor's designs increased steel handling efficiency fourfold. Entire factories were designed to lower the per-unit cost. Even leisure was to be regulated to support work efficiency. Work was not to be fulfilling, challenging in complexity, or designed for the greatest autonomy and self-direction. The worker was defined simply as a complex machine, a cog in the productive process.

At least such workers were paid well above survival levels, although still with the aim of increasing productivity. At the marginal end of the employment scale were the jobs for those who could never claim seniority or security. They worked, and still work, at minimum wages at the weekly discretion of their supervisors. They clean and sweep, dig and polish, often at night when the more secure workers are at home. Most often, they are people who have arrived most recently—from the rural South, lands of Latin culture, or battle-torn Asia. How could their work be other than instrumental, gaining enough income to get through the week and sometimes save a little for an uncertain tomorrow. Families are to be loved; work is to be endured.

The Industrial Society

Industrialization reshaped the world. Nothing remained untouched. The world as we know it is the product of the factory. The city unites a labor force, power, and materials in the factory. The city then becomes a hub for transportation to distribute the products. It becomes a center for finance and communication to direct the process. The metropolis was born, the outcome of industry. Think of some of the changes:

The steam engine powered the factory and the railroad and ship. By 1850, the United States had increased its railways from 21,000 to 170,000 miles. In the office, Remington presented a usable typewriter by 1880 and the office became mechanized. Interchangeable parts and mass production were introduced first into gunmaking and then transposed to all kinds of metal products, motors, and in time that revolutionizing wonder, the automobile. Steel production rose from less than 100,000 tons in 1870 to 25 million tons in 1910. Railroads boosted their freight hauling from 10 billion ton-miles in 1870 to 150 billion forty years later. In the first half of the new century, life expectancy increased from 50 to almost 70 years, the population of the United States doubled, and the number of automobiles went from 13,000 to 44 million. The average workweek declined from 84 hours in 1800 to about 40 by 1950.

Some would argue that the incredible human costs of early industrialization were a price that had to be paid for later advancement. Early death, disease, degradation, conflict, exploitation, greed, and suffering were the price of later comfort. Out of the sweatshop has come the jet airplane; out of the mines the university; and out of the tenement the condominium. Work conditions have improved to the extent that most employees no longer find it necessary (or possible) to be organized. Now there is worker's compensation and insurance for the injured, pensions and social security for the old, a home and mortgage for most families, and some sort of car for almost everyone. There are holidays and vacations, toys for adults as well as children, and hints of a new age of leisure. It may be true that the wealthy are still distant from the majority in resources and life styles. But if the worker is still exploited, conditions are nothing like those that Engels described and Marx decried 150 years ago. In 1850, who could have imagined the blue-collar family piling into their own car and leaving their own home to drive to Disney World for a vacation financed by their own credit cards?

Of course there remain great differentials. In wealth there remain the 5 percent of truly affluent with extravagant life styles (Veblen, 1899) as well as the 15-20 percent who are poor and living on the margins of survival. Moving capital on Wall Street is rewarded highly and moving furniture on a different scale. A "new class" of professionals, technicians, and managers have considerable autonomy in their work while most repeat routines and follow orders. Cynics suggest the new "golden rule," that those with the gold make the rules.

What is work like in this new world? For most, there is a central instrumental dimension. Many work for what is more important, home and family. They work for what is more enjoyable, their relationships and engagements of the evening, the weekend, and the holiday. They work for the future, to gain an economic security that permits facing the future, even old age, without dread. Work remains important. It has its meanings and satisfactions (Kelly and Kelly,

1992). The actual conditions of work vary and do make a difference in meaning and satisfaction (Erikson and Vallas, 1990; Kohn, 1990). Nevertheless, the general lack of autonomy reinforces Mills' observation that "Each day men sell little pieces of themselves in order to buy them back each night and weekend with the coin of fun."

Time at Work

That does not mean that there have been no significant changes since 1850. Work may be instrumental for most, contained in a separate sphere by time, place, and even social relations. Yet, the place has changed: safety and other conditions are improved immeasurably. And the time has changed as well. "Eight hours for what we will" has become a reality for most workers, at least if "what we will" includes all the responsibilities of home, family, and community.

It required a century for the average work week to be halved, from as high as 80 hours in the beginning of the factory era to about 70 in 1850, 65 in 1870, 62 in 1890. 55 in 1910, and 45 in 1930 to about 40 in 1950 (see Chapter 24). Further, the decrease came at a decreasing rate. The factors in the reduction were mixed—increased efficiency with the greater complexity of the mechanized assembly line, union pressures, and even some social reformist elements. In any case, the consequences for family and leisure were profound. People gradually came to have time—time to be with each other, to devote to the home, and to engage in amusements. There was time for pleasure by the hour in the workday as well as on Sunday, half Saturdays, and eventually the vacation (Cross, 1990). There were more holidays, sacred and secular, that were increasingly seen as a "right" of the worker. And in time, business entered the entertainment field with enthusiasm to create a mass industry of economic significance.

Life could be viewed as divided between work in one compartment and the home/family/leisure world on the other. It did not mean that work was just a means to an income. Workers might still identify with their craft, their industry, or their company. They interacted in some ways on the job, however restricted by "Taylorism." Their schedules were still dominated by the factory timetable. Work hours were inflexible as the machines stood waiting for the next shift to set the process into integrated motion. The weekend was now the creation of the factory and office schedule as much as of the church. Yet, as the city grew and the workplace was more and more separated in distance from the residential neighborhood and suburb, work was left behind as one entered the domain of nonwork. Where the worker lived, the fun that could be afforded, and even the educational opportunities of children still depended on the job and its rewards. Economic position was related to everything and yet also a world of its own.

In fact, some of the resistance to the reduction of the work week came because of a fear of leisure (Cross, 1990). The concern was that the worker, released from the constrictions of the workplace, would be unable to cope with all that free time. Rather than engage in re-creative activity that would support work productivity, "he" would dissipate his time and health in the saloon and even in violent games. The family, it was feared, would suffer rather than gain from increases in time. As a consequence, some moralists opposed worktime reductions while others fashioned opportunities for constructive recreation for the worker. "Healthy" sport, festivals, educational institutes, and other programs were fashioned to keep factory hands busy and protected from idleness and the "devil's work" (Clarke and Critcher, 1985).

In the meantime, the forces of capital investment moved into the nonwork arena (Cross, 1990). The movie palaces, amusement parks, professional sports arenas, dance halls, and even vacation destinations became a new set of opportunities. While the economic and social elites had their own exclusive set of venues and opportunities, even status-identified games and sports, the mass markets became recognized as promising investment opportunities. Mass leisure, usually in the form of entertainment, met the increase in nonwork time. Some was oriented toward the home and family, as with radio, games, and even books and music. Some got the family out on the road in the Ford Model T and other cars. Some provided entertainment in theaters, parks, pubs and bars, and private picnic grounds. The trolley and the car opened a new world of entertainment outside the home and neighborhood. The weekend became the symbol of pleasure-seeking activity.

The Depression and the Problem of Leisure

As suggested, moralists feared that leisure would turn into license as work hours were shortened. That was the first "problem of leisure." The second came with the massive unemployment of the Great Depression of the 1930s. Time out of work became identified with unemployment rather than shorter hours. For some, leisure was seen as a solution to the problem; for others it was a danger to be avoided at all costs (Hunnicutt, 1988).

The presumed cause of the depression was overproduction, too many goods chasing inadequate markets. Technology had fostered productivity run amuck. Now, as businesses failed (both those that produced goods and those that distributed them), workers were laid off. Without incomes, they could no longer buy. Demand spiraled downward, more workers were dismissed, and the economy crashed. The investment markets crashed as well, banks failed, once-soaring stocks were worthless, and the crisis permeated the entire society.

The question was what to do. Two solutions, to oversimplify the myriad strategies proposed, were debated. The first, offered by President Franklin Roosevelt as the "New Deal," was a work solution. Government programs would put people back to work. Roads, campgrounds, post offices, and a thousand other projects would employ carpenters, truck drivers, and artists in federal projects. Their wages would recreate demand, production would be stimulated, and the economy would get back on track. This, of course, was the solution adopted—although piecemeal and without widespread results. World War II demand brought the depression to an end.

The second proposed solution was the leisure solution. Rather than expand work, expand leisure. Further shorten work hours and fill in the gaps with the unemployed. Underlying this approach was the technological assumption that productivity could continue to rise as work hours were abbreviated. Wages would become both higher and more widely distributed. Market demand for all kinds of goods would increase. Rather than work its way out of crisis, the economy would play its way out. The objections were predictably sharp. Again, elitists distrusted the ability of ordinary people to deal with more free time. Those who believed in the work ethic predicted social and moral chaos in a world no longer dominated by work. And the fundamental faith in work productivity as basic to the social ideology could not cope with the radical idea of playing rather than working the society through the crisis.

World War II and its control economy transformed the situation. Factories went on 24-hour schedules. African-Americans were transported north to work in the wartime factories, crowding the urban ghettoes of Detroit, Chicago, and other cities. Women were miraculously found capable of heavy and demanding labor for the duration of the war. Unemployment turned into a labor shortage. In the postwar period, pent-up consumer demand fueled economic expansion punctuated by periodic recessions, but never by an overwhelming depression. The development of the world economy has now transformed production and opened new markets for all kinds of goods and services. The next chapter will sketch how such new products and technologies transformed life and leisure.

Marxist critics argued during the depression that the collapse of the capitalist system was inevitable. In *Capital, Volume 1,* Marx analyzed a process in which overproduction would be met by an unwillingness of the capitalists to share the gain beyond cost with workers. Demand would be stifled, unemployment would become rampant, and the system would collapse. What Marx failed to foresee was that despite the priority given to profit, the share of gain from productivity would be shared with the worker at levels high enough to create and support new markets. In fact, some believe that the capitalist age of industrial production is being superseded by an age of consumption with leisure a major segment of the new world economy of consumer goods and services. Investment and production may drive the economy, but the outcome is an expanding demand. Until recent decades, that demand has been concentrated in the developed economies of the West, North American and Western European. Now Japan has led the Pacific Rim into both production and consumption expansion and offered a model for development to Eastern Europe, Latin America, and the rest of the world.

The Containment of Work and Leisure

What is the configuration of this new world? Ecologically, the new metropolis separates production and consumption. Factories line the freeways as they once did the waterways and rail lines. Residential areas become enclaves. Road intersections are blanketed by shopping centers. In space, life is divided into domains of work, family, and leisure. The car transformed more than travel; it also made possible the suburb and the modern city (Cross, 1990).

Work time is less clearly demarcated. The "new class" of technicians, managers, and promoters may no longer be able to confine their production hours to 9-to-5 or to five days a week. Service workers increasingly are on the job on weekends and in the evening with work schedules that offer no fixed set of assignments to work or leisure. Nevertheless, time is a common and convenient index of self-determination. As in the earlier days of labor conflict, there is still the time—eight hours more or less—for "what we will."

Less clear is the extent to which men and women mentally divide their lives into separate domains of work, family and community, and leisure. Dubin (1963) and others may have demonstrated that work is not central for most blue-collar workers, but the configuration of life has not been clearly defined. One study of adults over 40 in a Midwest city (Kelly, 1987) found that two patterns were most common. The first was one of balance in which work, family, and leisure receive significant investment that shifts in salience through the life course. The second pattern was one of primary focus on the family with work and leisure defined as essentially instrumental. A more recent exploratory study found that commitment to family is highest followed by commitment to leisure and work in that order (Kelly and Kelly, 1992). Again, however, for many the relationship was not one of an either/or valuation, but more one of balance.

The other primary finding of the exploratory study was that family and leisure were closely related in meaning. Work, on the other hand, was quite separate in the dimensions of commitment, satisfaction, social relationships, self-determination and involvement, personal development, and sense of productivity. One possibility, then, is that the balance of life for most adults consists of two domains: work and economic roles on the one hand, and family, community, and leisure on the other. And for most, the family/community/leisure set is likely to be central.

This scheme redefines the issues. Formerly, leisure was seen as a "problem" in which assets of time and energy as well as income would be dissipated by workers. Considerable effort was made by reformers and moralists to offer "healthy" recreation to workers who would then be refreshed for productive labor. The possibility that leisure as expressive behavior might have its own legitimacy in the overall balance of life was recognized as an ideal, but not a likelihood except for the educated elite. The further possibility that leisure might be an important context for developing and strengthening familial and other primary relationships was seldom addressed. Leisure was a problem to be solved, not a solution to be valued.

In the current redefinition, leisure becomes at least a partial solution to the problem of work. The routines and frustrations of the workplace, the joyless demands of keypunching and tending robots in the modern office or factory (Braverman, 1974), cannot be waved away by some magical technique (Erikson and Vallas, 1990). Rather, leisure is a sphere of relative openness, separate from work, in which those limited on the job can find some opportunity for challenge, community, personal development, expression, and enjoyment. However partial, there is a leisure solution to work.

Further, such complementary leisure is valued because it may support productivity. Especially leisure that provides opportunity for activity that fosters physical and mental health may be promoted by both public agencies and by the corporation in terms of productivity outcomes. Leisure is valued just because it is separate, different, and compensatory. Leisure engagement is significant because of both its disengagement from work and its reengagement in personal and social investment. It was a problem; it is now an opportunity.

Underlying the redefinition is the persistent value placed on economic productivity. In the first decades of the Industrial Revolution, employers found that long hours and degrading conditions were literally counterproductive. Machines tended by relatively rested, healthy, and fairly rewarded workers produced more than wage-enslaved and exhausted women, men, and especially children. The central value was productivity. Now leisure also is championed as a positive factor in productivity when it leads to attentive, healthy, and obedient modes of work. The old fears are turned upside down. Work and leisure are still separate, but the drudgery of work is the problem and the contrast of leisure part of the solution.

There are at least two elements of this redefinition of leisure in economic perspectives. The first is that leisure is viewed as a healthy contrast that makes the worker more productive as well as providing a context for developing family and community bonds. The second is that leisure is a reward for work performance (see Chapter 25). Compliance in the workplace is ensured, not by direct force or power, but by the threat of withdrawal of income. That income supports home and family, the old dream of the American worker (Chinoy,

1955). Now it does something more; it pays for leisure that can be purchased on the market and promises to insert enjoyment into life's routines and obligations.

Creating Leisure Markets

Leisure still contrasts with work, but as something more than release. Leisure becomes a realm of behavior and meaning. It is a new world of pleasure in which income beyond that assigned to the essentials of housing, food, and transportation can be directed toward legitimized enjoyment. It is now "OK" to have fun, to allocate time and money toward the self. Leisure provides a needed contrast with work that is paid for by compliance with the demands of work. It is reward. Further, leisure is a significant sector of the economy providing a needed outlet for investment capital and jobs for those no longer needed in production.

The major division in the world of leisure is between those with rewarding economic roles and those unemployed or marginally employed who barely make it through the week. Styles and price levels may differ, but everyone in the work force is now expected to have enough discretionary income to buy some fun. That fun may be inexpensive electronic entertainment, eating out at the fast food emporium, and shopping at the discount house. It may be travel by car and lodging on the cheap. It may be mass entertainment and goods imported from the low-wage shops of the developing world. But it is available, affordable, and acceptable. And it may be highlighted with an occasional special family trip to a Disney destination!

In fact, the leisure market has developed a multi-tiered set of provisions graded for a variety of income levels and interests. There is travel on budgets and for up-scale classes. There are destinations in clearly-labelled grades up to secluded wealth. There are mass-produced toys at K-Mart and "quality" selections at the speciality boutiques at Aspen and on Rodeo Drive. The new and sophisticated leisure markets are being prepared to meet almost any level of income and set of tastes. Multi-national conglomerates enter the movie and video business, combine airlines and resort hotels, and buy up the name-brand products to complement their empires.

From the consumer side, the markets present pleasure for sale—packaged experiences and status-conferring possessions. From the producer side, the leisure markets offer a space for expansion when the markets for refrigerators and cars level off, at least in more developed economies. Leisure is a reward to make segmented work acceptable. It is a place for investment capital to seek returns. And, in the process, it may be just enough to dampen criticism over social problems that are not being solved. The history of leisure in the twentieth century is at least in part a history of the expansion of market-distributed entertainment that partly redefines the meaning of work (Cross, 1990).

The Division of Labor and the Division of Society

This expansion of leisure through the market does not imply that opportunities and resources are evenly distributed in any society. The society remains stratified in leisure as in labor (see Chapter 10). At the top are those whose main income is from investment, whose money makes money. Then come the 15 percent or so of professionals, managers, finance operators, and new technical experts who are relatively secure and well-rewarded. The middle mass, up to 60 percent of the population, includes the old working class as well as the new service wage workers with significant variations in income and job security. At the bottom are the 15-20 percent who are marginally employed without any security and the unemployed.

Further, gender makes a difference. Women are less likely to become managers, professionals, or technical experts. In the middle mass, they are paid 60-70 percent as much as men for comparable work. If single parents, they usually have the children, half the time or more without regular support from the fathers. Race makes a difference. At the present, the visible minorities, African and Hispanic Americans are disproportionately at the bottom of every economic ladder. Those caught in the urban ghettoes or rural backwaters are least likely to even get a start in the economy. Low pay jobs without security of any kind are most often assigned to women and minorities when education and other indices of ability are equal. The society is divided: male-female, white and blue collar, salaries and wages, European-African, young-old, and countless other divisions that have no reliable relationship with potential productivity.

Now the majority of the labor force is in services. The fastest growing job categories include health care in nursing homes and hospitals, fast food shops, janitors, clerks, and others in positions where they can be replaced quickly and cheaply. Complex machine processes and even multi-function robots have replaced many workers in heavy production. Computers have reduced the need for office staff. Information may be a growth industry, but there are limits on what can be incorporated into decisions, corporate or individual. New technologies such as the computer replace some workers, but create new jobs as well. The configuration of the work force changes, but there are still jobs. Some workplaces are deskilled while others call for new skills. The fundamental principle of the division of labor continues even though the composition changes.

In this change, leisure is more than a reward for compliant and productive labor. It is also an arena for investment and employment. Recreation business has become a major segment of the economy on every level. It is production as well as consumption, a source of profit as well as of pleasure. And as part of the service sector, the employment is disproportionately at entry level wages rather than high level salaries. The division of labor is maintained even in the world of play.

REFERENCES

Andrew, E. (1981). *Closing the iron cage.* Montreal, Quebec, Canada: Black Rose Books, Ltd.

Braverman, H. (1974). *Labor and monopoly capital.* New York, NY: Monthly Review Press.

Chinoy, E. (1955). *Automobile workers and the American dream.* New York, NY: Doubleday & Company, Inc.

Clarke, J., and Critcher, C. (1985). *The devil makes work: Leisure in capitalist Britain.* Champaign, IL: University of Illinois Press.

Cross, G. (1990). *A social history of leisure since 1600.* State College, PA: Venture Publishing, Inc.

Dubin, R. (1963). Industrial workers' worlds: A study in the "central life interests" of industrial workers. In E. Smigel (Ed.), *Work and leisure.* New Haven, CT: College and University Press.

Erikson, K., and Vallas, S. (Eds.). (1990). *The nature of work.* New Haven, CT: Yale University Press.

Hunnicutt, B. (1988). *Work without end.* Philadelphia, PA: Temple University Press.

Kelly, J. (1987). *Peoria Winter! Styles and resources in later life.* Lexington, MA: Lexington Books.

Kelly, J., and Kelly, J. (1992). *Dimensions of centrality and meaning in the domains of work, family, and leisure.* Submitted for publication.

Kohn, M. (1990). Unresolved Issues in Work/Personality. In K. Erikson and S. Vallas (Eds.), *The nature of work.* New Haven, CT: Yale University Press.

Marx, K. (1939). In R. Pascal (Ed.), *German ideology.* New York, NY: International Publishers Co., Inc.

Smith, A. (1937). In E. Cannan (Ed.), *The wealth of nations.* New York, NY: Modern Library, Inc.

Veblen, T. (1899) (1953). *The theory of the leisure class.* New York, NY: The New American Library, Inc.

Weber, M. (1958). In T. Parsons (Trans.), *The Protestant ethic and the spirit of capitalism.* New York, NY: Charles Scribner's, Sons.

Wilson, E. (1972). *To the Finland station.* New York, NY: Farrar, Straus, & Giroux, Inc.

CHAPTER 6

Suburban Life and Leisure

The suburbanization of America had profound effects on every aspect of life. While living outside the city and commuting into it for work was mainly associated with the rich during the early twentieth century, the mass production of automobiles and mass-produced, low-cost houses paved the way for the development of suburban communities. By the late 1920s, the suburbs were becoming democratized. In Los Angeles, for instance, 3,200 subdivisions were opening up to Midwest immigrants seeking sun and the privacy of a small house with a lot. According to Cross, " . . . suburban domesticity was a creation of an Angelo-Saxon quest for natural surroundings and freedom from the disorder and decadence of the city" (Cross, 1990, p. 189). Such decentralized housing was made possible by both rising affluence and the introduction of low interest, low down-payment mortgages. The Federal Housing Administration of the U.S. Government in 1934 encouraged 30 year mortgages with down payments of only 10 percent. By the end of the 1950s, two out of three American families were homeowners.

Such home ownership and the rise of the suburbs meant that suburban owners retained responsibility for the upkeep of their homes, unlike urban renters. This led to both the do-it-yourself movement and a kind of competition to "keep up with the Jones." The home was a refuge from the ills of the world and its upkeep was critical to success and happiness. In particular, keeping up the house was critical to the identity of the wife. "Each household required its own cook, laundress, and chauffeur for active children. Unlike the husband, whose worth was measured by his salary, the housewife felt her value as a marriage partner depended upon the time she spent at housework" (Cross, 1990, p. 192). It was not surprising, therefore, that housework expanded to fill the time available to do it.

Suburban Leisure

From numerous studies, a portrait of suburban leisure emerged which showed greater mobility, less family orientation, more gender separation, and greater democratization and organization of leisure experience. The removal of the home from the process of economic production, the widespread availability of trains, trolleys and then the automobile; the invention of the radio, television and other technological advances; and increasing economic affluence transformed American life and leisure. Let's examine some of these changes.

Greater Mobility

In regard to mobility, as noted in previous chapters, greater ownership and access to automobiles brought about drive-in restaurants which slowly came to serve as teenage hangouts as did as drive-in movies or "passion pits" as they were sometimes known. Shopping centers, complete with free parking, slowly followed the middle-class to the suburbs. These centers, which served as entertainment as well as shopping areas, further segregated housing from commerce.

As sociologists Robert and Helen Lynd (1937) pointed out, for less affluent automobile owners, every spare cent was put into the automobile. Automobile ownership served to keep the family together. For more affluent automobile owners, however, the opposite was true. Individuals rather than families used cars for leisure and teenagers and their parents often went in different directions.

Automobiles not only pulled many individual family members in different directions, they also changed community life. Sidewalk conversations, social visitation at common gathering places within walking distance and even visiting while traveling on mass transportation such as busses and trolleys declined as people traveled individually or in small groups isolated from the rest of the world.

Gender Separation

Suburban living, as Lundberg, et al. (1934) noted in his study of affluent Westchester County, New York, produced a kind of self-indulgence and conformity. In particular, this life was separated by gender. Middle and upper-class men spent their leisure playing golf at clubs and in many organizations such as the Rotary, the Lions, Elks, or Kiwanis. Women participated in garden clubs and service organizations which planned dances, luncheons and other functions. They also spent comparatively little time in "improvement" activities but almost an hour per day, on average, playing cards. As Lundberg observed, however, such functions were sometimes more work than leisure: "The round of club meetings, visiting, parties, and 'going places' are no longer ends in themselves, but have become part of the obligatory activities of life. They have become instrumental to ulterior practical ends of various sorts and therefore have lost their essential nature as leisure" (Lundberg, et al., 1934). It was, as Kerr (1962) observed, a period which began the decline of pleasure.

Certainly women had been encouraged toward domesticity and the consequent gender separation in earlier times. In the late 19th century, for instance, upper-middle class families had begun to retreat to suburbs in both Britain and North America. "The Victorian home, totally bereft of economic purpose, was transformed into a multipurpose leisure center. This, of course, was only to follow the model of the 'great halls' of the aristocracy, which since the late 17th century had been refurbished to privatize and specialize space" (Cross, 1990, p. 105). While homes had a distinct economic function in farming societies and in the mercantile system, where shops were often in the home, the suburban home became a haven from work done for pay. Women were the keepers of these havens and were encouraged to find self-expression in the upkeep, decoration and management of them. Rooms within the house were often decorated to express male or female traits. The standards of speech of the mother were to be observed in the house. Domestic family activities including board games, reading fiction, piano playing, lawn games such as croquet and parlour games such as charades, were the ideal and the mother was to be the organizer or supervisor for these activities. Women's magazines frequently stressed domestic ideals and reinforced the notion that a woman's place was in the home. Songs romanticized home life as the repository of happiness. "Home Sweet Home" was a motto reflecting the ideals of domestic tranquility and the morally uplifting environment the home was thought to provide. For the male, the home gave refuge; for the female, it gave meaning and responsibility. Thus, the division of both labor and leisure between the genders emerged.

Education prepared the female for these domestic roles, both private lessons for the wealthier and, for all, the home economics courses within public schools. From the Victorian Era on, many girls received lessons in hand-sewing, crocheting and lacework. For the wealthier, private girls' schools stressed skills designed to attract a husband: fashion, singing, coiffure, and piano playing (Cross, 1990).

Suburbs also began an era in which a "fun morality" began to emerge. As Wolfenstein (1958) stated, this was a morality in which:

> Work tends to be permeated with behavior formerly confined to after work hours. Play conversely tends to be measured by standards of achievement previously applicable only to work. One asks oneself not only in personal relations but now also at work: Did they like me? Did

I make a good impression? And at play, no less than at work, one asks: am I doing as well as I should? (p. 93)

A combination of individual influences of competition, conformity, and achievement meant that the area of life which had been for play and passing the time became more serious and increasing judged by standards formerly associated with work. The standards of such judgement however, were different for men and women in suburban communities.

For men, earning money was at the center of life. It was not for women, particularly the wives of businessmen.

> . . . the wives of the business class, gaining nowadays relatively little status from the arts of the housewife, throw themselves into leisure and have become the leisure-innovators of the culture. In this business-class world in which the job itself is so important to status and invites and endless "repaying" expenditure of energy, leisure among men is secondary to work: men work not to get leisure but to get money, to 'get ahead,' to 'get up in the world.' The resulting spectacle—of some of the ablest members of society, the men best educated, best 'off' financially, and conceivably best able to live rich, many-sided lives, spending themselves unremittingly in work, denying themselves leisure and bending fine energies to the endless acquisition of the means of living, a life they so often take insufficient leisure to live—is one factor leading certain contemporary psychiatrists to remark on the masochistic tendencies in our culture. If the leisure of such men tends to get used instrumentally to further their primary business of getting ahead, it also becomes easy under the driving pressure of the 'business game' for the business-class wife to make the leisure of the family contribute to her husband's business activity (Lynd and Lynd, 1937, p. 244).

Greater Organization and Democratization of Leisure Experience

Community-based leisure experience during the 1920s and 30s was becoming " . . . more passive, more formal, more organized, more mechanized and more commercialized" (Lynd and Lynd, 1937, p. 245). Many forms of recreation and leisure were now sponsored by municipal recreation and park departments, by volunteer organizations devoted to special leisure interests, and by an array of commercial leisure service organizations.

Organized Recreation in the Public and Nonprofit Sectors

Both government and nonprofit organizations played a large part in organizing leisure behavior. Federal agencies were formed during the Depression to put people back to work. They developed parks, built swimming pools and recreation centers and otherwise increased the capacity of local government to provide a vast array of recreation activities. Much of the leisure of youth became more organized. In suburban communities, summer camps managed by both local government recreation commissions and by voluntary organizations such as the Boy Scouts, Girl Scouts, the YMCA and the YWCA provided highly structured experiences for youth. Within urban areas, as Cranz (1982) observed, the "reform park" era evolved in which recreation activity for both children and adults became highly organized, since the masses were considered incapable of undertaking their own recreation. Play leaders and directors planned and led a variety of recreation experiences, primarily for children and adult men, which were as structured and specialized as working life. The term " leisure time" began to be used more extensively in society and there was great fear that chaos would result (Cranz, 1982). Organized recreation was divided into categories such as physical, social, and civic. A cafeteria approach to providing recreation services was undertaken, in which residents could choose from many highly structured offerings. While many of these offering were thought of as strengthening the family, they were generally segregated by gender and by age.

Many suburban and urban communities developed public and private, nonprofit recreation facilities during the 1920s and 1930s. Swimming pools became so popular that, in some communities, people had to be admitted hourly. Playgrounds were increasingly common and their design was increasingly similar. In some cases, recreation centers were built on playgrounds, combining the features of playgrounds with those of settlement houses.

The play movement, under the leadership of Joseph Lee, assumed that organized play developed character and that, since children are naturally imitative, play leaders should first and foremost be of sound character. Summer playground programs became typical features of suburban and urban life, providing structure for children who were originally let out of school during warm months to help their parents tend and harvest agricultural crops.

Churches also played an important role in the leisure lives of suburbanites. While churches often viewed recreation and leisure as suspect, organized religion increasingly involved itself with the promotion of various forms of leisure. This was both to increase attendance as well as provide alternatives to commercial recreation and other forms of leisure expression thought to be less desirable. The play and recreation movements of the early twentieth century, which included "character building" as a central idea, found an ally in the church. In the suburbs, where churches were often larger than in rural areas or cities, churches de-emphasized the importance of specific denominations and began serving more as community churches (Lundberg et al., 1934). Protestant churches moved more rapidly toward including recreation in their activities than did Roman Catholic ones. In many Protestant churches, the emphasis was upon seven-day-a-week services and activities, often with a director of youth services or recreation. Social and recreation programs became an expected part of church life. Suburbanites, who often took a less serious approach to religious worship than did their urban counterparts, had to be kept interested, and recreation was a means of doing so. Women's clubs, youth fellowship organizations and many other groups formed within the church and recreational activity was an important component of their undertakings. Many more affluent churches were equipped with kitchens, a library, game rooms, a gymnasium, assembly rooms, a radio room and even tennis courts. Lundberg concluded that " . . . the suburban church has perhaps more interest in leisure than any other suburban institution" (Lundberg, et al., 1934, p. 217).

A large part of the increasing organization of leisure, of course, had to do with fraternal organizations and special interest clubs. Fraternal organizations, such as the Masons, the Odd Fellows, the Knights of Pythias and a host of others, while often providing sickness and death benefits for members, existed primarily for recreation and socialization purposes (Dulles, 1965). Such organization were characterized by secret ceremonies and rituals, colorful uniforms, initiation rites, carnivals, conferences and charitable work combined with social functions. Women often belonged to auxiliaries of these organizations or formed their own clubs. These clubs might be art clubs, book clubs, sewing circles, philanthropic groups or many others. Such clubs, while sometimes extending the intellectual horizons of their members, existed primarily for socialization and for confirming one's identity and status within the community.

Commercialized Leisure

The suburbs did not radically change the increasing tendency for leisure behavior to be shaped by the inventions and products of the commercial sector. Suburbanization and increased access to core cities increased the range of possible leisure pursuits for millions but the bulk of leisure behavior remained passive and shaped by the products and services of the commercial sector. The Lynds described the leisure pursuits brought on by increasing urbanization as follows:

> The characteristic leisure-time pursuits of the city tend to be things done with others rather than by individuals alone; and except for the young, particularly the young males, they are largely passive, i.e., looking at or listening to something or talking or playing cards or riding in an auto; the leisure of virtually all women and most of the men over thirty is

mainly spent sitting down. Its more striking aspects relate to the coming of inventions, the automobile, the movies, the radio, that have swept through the community since 1890, dragging the life of the city in their wake. Yet these newer forms of leisure must be viewed against an underlying groundwork of folk-play and folk-talk that makes up a relatively less changing human tradition (Lynd and Lynd, 1929, p. 226).

From this description it becomes clear that urban and suburban life in the 1920s established patterns of leisure use which are easily recognizable today. That is, most uses of leisure involve other people, are physically passive, and are continuously shaped by technological inventions. Counter to this, however, is the continuation of informal play, socializing, gossiping, loosely organized hobbies that have been with us for centuries. While Americans were to become somewhat more physically active during their leisure in subsequent generations, basic patterns established during the 1920s and 1930s remain.

Many of the manufactured entertainments, for all their drawbacks, represented something that the common person had never before known and often broadened and enriched their lives. Additionally, as Dulles argued, commercial recreation forms never wholly monopolized popular recreation. An almost infinite variety of leisure forms became prevalent with suburbanization and accelerated even further after the Second World War. People might collect stamps or other "collectibles," raise flowers, go camping, play chess, attend a wide variety of concerts and plays, have backyard barbecues, take flute lessons or play on amateur softball teams. Mass production very often meant that a given form of leisure expression came within the financial means of ordinary people. Music instruments, for instance, became both less expensive and more readily available, leading to increased music lessons for school children. Radio brought drama and comedy to millions.

The growth of suburban life was both a consequence of greater democratization in society and, in turn, fostered it. By 1930 the nonworking Saturday half-day had become typical, giving the common person more time for leisure. Books, magazines and newspapers were becoming more widely available, although certainly this did not lead to a revolution in reading habits. Mass forms of leisure such as the movies and radio became increasingly popular and available, and the increased availability of transportation which had made the growth of suburban life possible also meant that there was less restriction to the recreational amenities of both cities and the countryside. Certainly the leisure lives of whites, of males and of the upper classes were more privileged than others. Women's roles were still restricted in many ways. African-Americans still lived in largely segregated neighborhoods and experienced great prejudice in their daily lives. Most forms of public and commercial recreation were still segregated and what was provided for blacks was almost always inferior. Nevertheless, the suburbs produced, for many, comfort, mobility and privacy.

Suburbanites could both garden or travel to the city. They could find entertainment more easily and had greater access to social networks organized around leisure interests. They lived in ways former generations only dreamed of. Leisure did not follow the ideals of the ancient Athenians. However, the suburban ideal increased consumption more than it did learning, socializing more than contemplation. It was the beginnings of lives of ease and abundance for an expanding middle-class.

REFERENCES

Cranz, G. (1982). *The politics of park design: A history of urban parks in America.* Cambridge, MA: The MIT Press.

Cross, G. (1990). *A social history of leisure since 1600.* State College, PA: Venture Publishing, Inc.

Dulles, F. (1965). *A history of recreation: America learns to play.* New York, NY: Appleton-Century-Crofts.

Kerr, W. (1962). *The decline of pleasure.* New York, NY: Simon & Schuster, Inc.

Lynd, R., and Lynd, H. (1929). *Middletown: A study in American culture.* New York, NY: Harcourt, Brace and World.

Lynd, R., and Lynd, H. (1937). *Middletown in transition.* New York, NY: Harcourt, Brace and World.

Lundberg, G., Komarovsky, M., and McInerny, M. A. (1934). *Leisure: A suburban study.* New York, NY: Columbia University Press.

Wolfenstein, M. (1958). In E. Larrabee, and R. Meyersohn (Eds.), *The emergence of fun morality, in mass leisure.* Glencoe, IL: The Free Press, pp. 86-95.

CHAPTER 7

Technology
and Its Impact on Leisure

The age of industrialization was also an age of invention. Mass production replaced craft in the manufacturing process, first in producing guns. The factory replaced the shop and routinization superseded skill in the name of efficiency. But the transformation of the production process was only the beginning. There was also a series of new products, some that transformed ordinary life for the many, not just the few. The technologies preceded their implementation and distribution, but by ever-shorter periods. Invention to product took 56 years for the telephone, but only twelve for television and five for the transistor.

Photography was invented by 1839, the telephone by 1876, radio by 1902, television by 1934, the transistor by 1953, and the integrated circuit by 1961. Note that each technology has had significant leisure as well as industrial applications. Further, there are successions of technology that have transformed patterns of social life. The same kinds of family groups that gathered around the radio for comedic relief from the effects of the depression in the 1930s and for the latest war news in the 1940s turned to television in the 1950s and 1960s. Before long, however, the transistor made radio a portable medium and has led to "narrowcasting" of stations to specialized markets leaving mass appeal to television with its high production costs.

Technologies have transformed particular activities. Fiberglass and epoxies both dominated and expanded the boat markets. Preparing the boat for the water was no longer a strenuous task each Spring. The same material technologies were applied to skiing, permitting revolutions in technique as well as increased safety, and broadened participation. Television not only opened college and professional sport to the masses, but also brought about changes in the rules and presentation of the games themselves. Fiberglass, graphite, and ceramics have permitted the redesign of racquets in tennis and other racquet sports and added power to the games of amateurs.

Far and away most significant for leisure have been the truly *transforming technologies*. These technologies have been so powerful in their impacts and so near-universal in their adoption that no element of common life was untouched by their advent. The two technologies that transformed leisure were, of course, the mass-produced car and television. However, other technologies such as the telephone and jet airplanes have also had profound impacts. Now the electronics revolution promises to continue to change patterns of everyday life as the home becomes a multi-media center. And some would argue that even microwave cooking has had substantial effects on leisure scheduling.

Before dealing with those transforming technologies, they should be placed in the context of the massive shift to an urbanized mass society.

Leisure in the Industrial City

As outlined in the previous chapters, industrialization created the modern centralized city and brought hundreds of thousands of workers out of their rural environments and into close proximity. Everything was changed, including access to more informal recreation events and natural resources. The lack of space and opportunity in the early industrial revolution forced men into saloons, women on to door stoops, and children into the streets. Various attempts were made to "rationalize" and control recreation for working families and individuals by channeling their attention to "constructive" and healthy activity. At the same time, however, neighborhoods, ethnic groups, and work-based associations offered opportunities that were often seen as threats by factory owners and social reformers (Cross, 1990). Silent films in little neighborhood parlors, drinking in unlicensed "shebeens" and bars, self-organized ethnic holidays, dance halls, and worker-instigated picnics were regulated and replaced. Settlement houses, "worker institutes," community celebrations, grand movie "palaces," licensed taverns, and, in time, amusement parks and professional sports expanded the scale of leisure. Simultaneously, informal provisions were repressed and public agencies, private associations, and the business sector stepped in to provide regularized opportunities. In general, the aim was to turn recreation from uncontrolled license to activity that would contribute to economic productivity.

Such provisions had their impacts. Parks and recreation centers offered space along with age and gender-directed programs. Amusement parks at the end of trolley lines were filled on weekends with people of all ages seeking excitement and a change. Public holidays gathered crowds for their parades and celebrations. Libraries, churches, neighborhood settlement houses, and organizations such as the YMCA provided "constructive" alternatives to the proliferation of entertainment. Sports and motion pictures widened their appeal as "stars" became national and international celebrities.

Even in this early period, technologies had significant impacts. The electric trolley and train replaced horse-drawn vehicles and allowed youth and adults to traverse the city in search of entertainment. Coney Island, Riverview, and the other peripheral amusement parks were not called "trolley parks" without reason. Electricity, in fact, was essential to safety and illumination in large halls and theaters. The telephone not only permitted conversation across distances, but facilitated making arrangements for leisure events and gatherings. Movie technology advanced rapidly from nickelodeons to silent films and then to sound, color, and special effects. Photography became a mass activity when Kodak took the unreliable glass plate and in time offered the box camera and the "Brownie."

The beginning of a revolution was the result of another technology, the "wireless" transmission of sound across distances. Eventually radio was transformed from a means of communication to mass entertainment in the home. The home had long been a center of leisure as families ate, celebrated, read, played games and music, and organized family celebrations. The cramped working-class tenement in time expanded into residences with more space inside and out. Most of such residential recreation, however, was produced by action and interaction. Now the radio demanded no more than imaginative listening. Championship prize fights with Dempsey and Louis and the World Series with Babe Ruth were broadcast into homes and bars. Comedic radio series with Jack Benny and George Burns and Gracie Allen shaped the family timetable so everyone could gather before the radio set. For the first time, mass entertainment was introduced into the home, a pattern that paved the way for television. Radio soon began targeting audiences with adventure serials in the after-school hours for children and youth. "Jack Armstrong," "Hop Harrigan," and "Tom Mix" were household heroes. Radio raised critical concern over "passive" leisure, especially for the young. Other media such as "pulp" magazines and comics excited similar adult protests over their escapism and violence.

The Commercialization of Entertainment

Leisure became an industry in the 19th century and developed rapidly (Cross, 1990). The amusement park was designed to intrigue and entertain the masses. The half-holiday opened the possibility of special events such as sports that were still forbidden on Sunday. Real wages increased for industrial workers permitting expenditures on leisure. Railroads made possible travel for pleasure, and entrepreneurs quickly developed the "excursion" taking ordinary people to the seashore, religious festivals, or other events. Recreation businesses tended to be localized, but for the time might involve considerable capital investment. Theaters, trolley parks, and beach resorts required a level of capitalization far beyond the neighborhood enterprise. Then, the motion picture industry combined production studios with chains of theaters. Radio developed national networks that evolved into the television giants of today. As industry, leisure took on an entire new scope. MGM, NBC, and their fellows evolved into conglomerates of vertically integrated production and distribution.

Entertainment and travel pioneers P. T. Barnum and Thomas Cook became legends of the new industries. Romance magazines, touring melodramas, circuses and "wild west" shows, children's weeklies, vaudeville and the music hall, dance halls (as many as 500 in New York alone in 1910), and the saloon were everywhere. The nickelodeon was replaced by neighborhood silent films that could be enjoyed even by immigrants who knew little English, and then by the major feature film. By 1910, movie palaces linked to producers had largely driven the penny theaters out of business. Barnum's "Great Travelling World's Fair," of museums, galleries, and "curiosities" crossed the land with a circus train by 1872. In 1983 Chicago's Columbian Exposition "Midway" was an extravaganza of exhibits alleging to represent the world including the hootchy-kootchy of "Little Egypt," Chinese pagodas, mosques, castles, and South Sea island huts. At the center was the mighty Ferris Wheel towering 264 feet over the exposition.

Travel was at first the exclusive privilege of the wealthy. In time, however, the emerging middle class of Britain's industrial society was lured to the continent by lower-cost travel, lodging, and tours. In the United States, Atlantic City's Boardwalk was rendered accessible by the railroad, first from Philadelphia. By 1872, tourist trains had arrived at Yellowstone Park and the Geyser hotel.

Spectator sport also developed during this period. In Britain football clubs were organized that played before large paying crowds on Saturday afternoons before the turn of the century. Sports that began in elite schools "trickled down" to the working class. In time, sports such as rugby became identified with working-class and even ethnic cultures.

In the United States, baseball became the "national pastime." At first amateur players organized the sport with their National Association of Base Ball Players in 1858. Soon the game was played throughout the nation with even small communities fielding a team for weekend contests. In 1869 the Cincinnati Red Stockings were the first professional team. An association of professional players was formed in 1871. Within five years, club owners formed the National League and wrested control from the players. With financial control and the "reserve clause" of 1879 that bound players to one club, the baseball owners set the pattern for professional sports as business enterprise. Owners maintained control, built urban ball parks, "owned" players, and kept the two major leagues racially segregated for over 80 years.

Football as a spectator sport began in the schools. In 1891, the University of Chicago hired a professional coach, Amos Alonzo Stagg, and gave him a budget to produce a winning team that would enhance the image of the university. Other schools followed suit and football spread across the land and down into public schools. Professional football, however, lagged behind baseball and was given its major impetus only when George Halas moved the "Staleys" from Decatur to Chicago, called them the Bears, and lured the legendary Red Grange into a national tour of exhibitions.

During all this period, the work week for most of those employed was being gradually reduced. More and more household incomes rose above a simple maintenance wage. Weekends began to open up with Saturday time off and Sunday restrictions gradually being relaxed. World Wars mobilized the economy and moved people geographically off the farm and across the country. The leisure expansion and relaxed moral codes in the 1890s and 1920s were interrupted by recessions and the Great Depression of the 1930s. Moralists, educators, clergy, and employers continued to express concern and even horror over all the emphasis on "fun" that seemed to be sweeping the country and eroding traditional Puritan morality. Religious leaders pointed to those of different cultures and churches as dangers to the moral fabric of the nation. Yet, despite objections and reservations, leisure was a wave that could not be stopped.

Amid all this change, there were two technologies that transformed every level and style of leisure. They were the car and television.

Henry Ford and the Expanded Space of Leisure

At first, the automobile was the product of skilled craftsmen, expensive, and reserved for economic elites. Henry Ford, despite his personal conservatism, revolutionized all that. Prior to Ford's introduction of the Model T in 1914, a car cost several times the average worker's yearly income. The Model T was the first mass-produced automobile. Ford had several aims. The first was to widen the market for the product by bringing the cost within reach of the middle class and even factory workers. The second was to standardize the product ("Any color as long as it's black"). The third was to raise worker productivity by standardizing production tasks in linear design. The fourth was to purchase worker loyalty with the unheard-of wage of $5 for a an eight-hour day. Workers would become more reliable and efficient, earn more, lower production costs, and in time become a market for the product.

The results were astounding. From an elite toy, the automobile became a requirement of modern living in most locations. By 1927, 85 percent of the world's cars were built in the United States despite initial development in Europe (Cross, 1990). At the beginning of the Depression one household in five had a car. In the 1920s a Ford, the new Model A, cost about $290. In 1935 a new Plymouth could be purchased for less than $500. Among the outcomes were:

- The new metropolis with its rings of suburbs. Eventually retailing moved out of the city to shopping centers and even manufacturing spread out along superhighways. The city that had been centralized by the factory became decentralized by the car.

- Private transportation came to dominate travel with over 85 percent of trips made by car. The old urban electric trains were bought up by automotive-related industry and closed. The assumption of private transportation shaped the ecology of residential dispersal, business location, and leisure provision.

- An entire complex industry developed around the use of the car for leisure. Weekend and vacation trips were served by resort areas, en route support businesses, and the endless linear "service stations" that tended the less-than-reliable car. The National Park system was revised to accommodate the new tourist arriving in the family car. In time "tourist cabins" were replaced by motels and chains superseded the "mom and pop" accommodations. Even during the Depression, automobile visits to National Parks in the West doubled and then doubled again.

- A variety of recreation businesses responded to the car. Drive-in movies attracted both families with young children and couples seeking privacy in the darkened "passion pits." Drive-in restaurants launched the trend toward fast food and minimal service, in California with "car hops," short skirts, trays that fastened to open windows, and even roller skates. And everything was up-to-date in Kansas City when the first shopping center surrounded by parking was opened in 1923.

The car became more than a means of transportation. The initial standardization was soon replaced by varieties of styles and price levels. The black Buick became the "doctor's car," the long Cadillac announced affluence, and the convertible coupe with a "rumble seat" symbolized a sporty life style. Even in its symbolism, the car was connected with leisure styles and levels of affluence that multiplied in the 1920s and 1930s. The interruption of World War II precipitated a latent demand that led to even more of a "car culture." The "family car" was augmented by sports cars, recreation vehicles, and cars for teenagers seeking excitement and privacy.

The car was the vehicle for family vacations. On a more day-to-day basis, it made possible multiple leisure and work commitments in separated locations. The mother as chauffeur for children became a stereotype. Families anticipated the time when children would become old enough to drive themselves, usually forgetting that the car also offered privacy that facilitated considerable sexual activity.

Ironically, the car produced the suburb with its detached houses, spacious yards, and layers of social organizations including churches, "service" clubs, and special-interest groups. All were part of the overall complex of leisure that had once been associated with the small town. The car, however, not only enabled the spatial character of leisure to be expanded, spread out, and diversified. By making possible the suburb, in time it also led to the loss of the urban neighborhood and the concentration of leisure on the home and family. Private domestic leisure became the suburban ideal (Cross, 1990). Suburban developments, at first for the upper-and-middle classes, were in time developed for blue-collar workers, especially when the factories were also moved to less costly suburban locations where single-level assembly lines could be laid out.

In leisure the car widened opportunity. In combination with the interstate highway system, the car expanded the geography of leisure, especially for city dwellers. Travel times for vacations and weekend trips were cut in half by limited-access highway networks as well as improvements in the car itself. This synergy led to a variety of developments—parks and scenic drives on public land, public beaches and seashores, regional parks for picnics, and other locations that could be reached only by private transportation. At the same time, the market sector responded to and even created new markets by lining highways with services and dotting the landscape with destinations. Even within the community, programs were located and scheduled on the assumption that private transportation was generally available. In short, the car changed almost everything about leisure. As late as the 1960s, one of the most common leisure activities was getting the family in the car for a Sunday afternoon drive.

Television and the Privatization of Leisure

If the car dispersed leisure, the other transforming technology brought it back home. Television was introduced widely in the 1950s, by 1970 was found in 58 percent of American homes, and by 1980 in almost 90 percent. Never has a technology been adopted so quickly and with such impacts on day-to-day living. No study of family or leisure activity done prior to television is of more than historical interest. Even in the 1950s, community studies could ignore television in analyses of patterns of ordinary life. Now any study of how time is used begins with two items, work and television. It is central to activity patterns through the life course and has become the central source of information about the rest of the world (see Chapter 33).

For leisure, television has had several significant impacts:

1) It began to bring leisure home. Now the residence offers a variety of entertainments that are easy, accessible, and inexpensive.

2) It transformed images of play with its depictions of special locales, equipment, dress, associations, and activities that are available primarily through the market for a price.

3) It widened horizons by bringing the arts, sports, and travel possibilities into the home for both children and adults. For those unable to afford such possibilities, however, it may have widened the gap between the poor and those with discretionary income.

4) It reshaped leisure timetables with its "prime time" programming and offering of special events at times once reserved for activities such as family interaction, religion, personal development in skills like music, and even students' study.

And commercial television was only the beginning. As sketched in Chapter 33, the wide adoption of cable transmission with its increasing number and specialization of channels, and the video recorder-player that offers more power of selection at a modest price were only the beginning of an electronics revolution. The home would soon become even more a multimedia entertainment center with a hitherto undreamed-of variety of entertainment possibilities. Fiber-optic technology opened a new range of possibilities that built on the life patterns already set by television.

Other Leisure Technologies

Nothing else approached the transforming power of the car and television. Yet, there are other technologies that had significant impacts on leisure and, for the most part, increased its "democratization."

The most important, although most obscure, were the technologies of contraception. Sexual behavior across all social levels has been radically changed by reducing the likelihood of conception resulting from sexual intercourse. Sexual activity before and outside of marriage increased dramatically. Just as important, the size of families began to decrease so that a smaller proportion of adult life is focused on child care and nurture. Some would also argue that families with fewer children are more adult-dominated and less playful than those with several siblings in a narrow age range. In any case, no element of social life, including leisure, has been untouched by contraceptive technologies and the changes in sexual patterns.

Far less profound in effects were technologies such as the jet airplane. The jet with its greater capacity and speed has opened air travel to the masses. Once largely reserved for business travellers and elites, all sorts of middle mass individuals and families now travel by air, most often for family visits. At the same time, off-price air travel and packages developed between air lines and hotel and resort chains have made the one-week and extended weekend pleasure trip a possibility for hundreds of thousands who previously travelled only by car. The tourism industry with its cruise ships, packaged tours, and other travel-hospitality combinations has been made possible by the jet.

The telephone transformed the shape of business by making immediate communication from office to office easy and inexpensive. No longer did related businesses have to be located in the same building or in the same urban district. Later technologies have extended the dispersal of business, but the telephone made the first dramatic impact on location. Leisure, too, was changed by the telephone. It became a medium of communication in its own right, especially for those housebound by family responsibilities. It also enabled those in different households to make arrangements for leisure events on short notice and without having to meet face-to-face. The old small town pattern of informal dropping in on other families gave way to the phone call and prearrangement. Reservations could be made for meals or tee-off times. In time the telephone, toll-free numbers, and computer systems have made travel reservations a quick and convenient operation.

Another far-reaching technology in the world of finance has been the credit card. Travel has been facilitated so that it is no longer necessary to carry large amounts of cash. Reservations for hotels, air travel, and rental cars are made with the plastic. Meals, equipment, and recreation itself are paid for on credit with the card. Trips for which vacationers have not adequately saved are taken anyway and paid for later through the high-interest borrowing of the credit system. "Play now and pay later" fits the mood of pleasure-seeking that is associated with special events and vacations as well as impulse-buying in the shopping mall and the night out on the town.

All of this became a part of the entire leisure industry that now includes all kinds of opportunities for wide segments of the population. The proliferation of theme parks, theme restaurants, and theme shopping malls blended leisure with other elements of marketing. Spending for pleasure became seen as a right rather than a special privilege. Leisure spending became as much a part of the budget as the house and car payments. More accurately, for many households, leisure that is off-budget is what keeps the credit economy whirring. There are activities such as golf and travel that were once reserved for the wealthy, but now have inclusive clienteles. There are the mass sports such as automobile racing in giant spectacles and local tracks, wrestling in the ring and the mud, and several styles of motorcycle contests. Leisure is all over the place in an incredible variety of styles and price levels. For the most part, the experience that is promoted and sold is entertainment. There seems to be an almost infinite number of ways in which an admission fee can buy a vicarious experience for those whose lives seem to lack excitement or challenge.

The Economic Base of the New Leisure

First, a warning is in order. All this discussion of technology's impact on leisure should not obscure the fact that much of people's use of leisure remained unchanged. There is ample evidence that people still interacted with each other, tried out activities that do more than entertain, and sought some kind of balance in their leisure and in the rest of their lives (see Chapter 15). Nevertheless, technology did reshape leisure. Leisure industries proliferated to offer a vast panoply of entertainments at home and away. Changes in social time, the allocation of time to required activity, have opened up new possibilities for many who had been submerged in work-dominated routines.

All the transforming technologies were not in the leisure sector of the society. As already introduced, the modern factory system reduced hours on the job to increase productivity, especially when there were major investments in the machines. The assembly line and functional specialization did increase manufacturing productivity, whatever might be said about the consequences for the worker. Only now is attention being given to reversing the process and involving the worker more in shaping and directing the production process to restore quality and productivity to the factory.

The aim has always been the same—to design production techniques that maximized the output per unit of investment. Some system of machine and labor interface would be developed to get the most out of both the technology and the worker. In some periods that meant redesigning the nature of the workers' tasks. In others the emphasis has been on new machine tools, assembly integration, or the replacement of human labor by robotics. Over the long term, the goal of maximizing the return on investment capital has changed the nature of work and, until recently, produced dramatic increases in productivity. Those increases have been the basis for raising the material dimensions of the quality of life to ever-new heights. We now take for granted devices and opportunities that have made a difference—not only cars and jet travel but also worker-owned homes, refrigerators, central heating and cooling, hospitals, and electronics. Few would want to return to wood-burning stoves, outhouses, dirt roads, and horse-drawn wagons with their inevitable spreading of deposits.

Over the decades such industrial technologies have had their impacts on life in ways other than the distribution of their products. Entire industries have died. Some have been replaced with expanded opportunities for employment, but others have been less labor-intensive. There has been a gradual shift in employment from manufacturing to the services such as retailing, health, and leisure. Now over 65 percent of the work force is in the stores, restaurants, travel, health, and other services rather than the factory. Some of this work is quite labor-intensive, requiring long hours and high levels of attention. It is, for the most part, quite different from the depths of the mine or the heat of the blast furnace. There remains work that is physically demanding, exposed to the elements, and often dangerous. But the composition of the work force has been transformed by the shift to services and the simple fact that most adult women are now employed outside the home.

What will be the future of work? Will cybernetics linking the computer to the robot replace more and more workers in production? Will consequent structural unemployment cast an economic pall on entire communities and regions? Will labor-intensive production continue to be exported to areas with low wages? Can modern economies support an increase in services, including those providing leisure resources, when they are losing in the worldwide competition to produce hard goods such as cars and television sets? Will new electronic technologies increase productivity to the extent that the production sector of the work force will dwindle as has the agricultural? Will the generalist come into his or her own as specialists are replaced by technology and electronics? Who will put it all together? No economy can grow or even survive on services alone. Mass leisure cannot replace mass production as the engine of an entire economy.

The Limits to Access

Such technology-induced changes in leisure have a dark side (see Chapters 4 and 25). Further, in the United States, a sizable proportion of the population remained so marginal economically that it was left out of new opportunities. Nevertheless, it is evident that leisure became something more than a realm of status demonstration for the wealthy, a tidbit of genteel activity for the middle class, and an occasional overflowing of energy for workers. Leisure seemed to be available for almost everyone. Styles vary widely. Costs, even for the same activity, varied even more. Some resources were relatively open and others quite exclusive. Leisure became a major sector of the economy, a central dimension of the culture, and even a taken-for-granted expectation of rich and poor, women and men, young and old. The evening, weekend, and vacation are integrated into the timetables of life as though they had always been there. In fact, when the work force is increasingly limited by age, gender, and all sorts of credentialing protocols, leisure seemed to be there for almost everyone. Veblen (1899) may have been right that leisure was once elitist, a symbol of superior social position. But times changed. Leisure was now thoroughly lodged in the mass society, in some shape or form available to just about everyone. A question remained, however: What did it all mean?

REFERENCES

Cross, G. (1990). *A social history of leisure since 1600.* State College, PA: Venture Publishing, Inc.

Veblen, T. (1899) (1953). *The theory of the leisure class.* New York, NY: The New American Library, Inc.

CHAPTER 8

Mass Leisure and the Postwar Era

The daily use of leisure has been radically reshaped since the Second World War. Not only has technological change played a major role in this reshaping, so too have changing economic and social conditions as well as our value systems. The mass media, pleasure travel, outdoor recreation, local institutions such as museums, botanical gardens, parks and libraries all became an expected part of the leisure experience of millions of Americans. The post-World War II era was characterized by optimism, materialism, the emergence of a mass society, concern about quality of life and a variety of environmental and social issues, and a heightened belief in science and technology. Leisure opportunity, while still associated with social class, became much more democratic in the years proceeding World War II. Government became heavily involved in the provision of recreation and parks at federal, state, and local levels.

An Era of Affluence

The end of World War II found the United States and Canada in an enviable position compared to much of the rest of the world. While both countries had suffered greatly during the nightmare which was World War II, the war had not been fought on American soil, other than the attack on Pearl Harbor. While much of North America's economic competition in the world, such as Britain, France, Holland and Germany, had been devastated by the war, America had not. Further, both Canada and the United States had built up huge manufacturing capacities to produce materials for the war. As soldiers returned home and started families in record numbers, North American corporations expanded into foreign markets at an unprecedented rate and a material standard of living was established which was the envy of the world. While prior to World War II the United States did not have the highest economic standard of living, after the war the U.S. emerged as the leader. A period of rising incomes and optimism followed during the fifties and sixties. People of the Baby Boom Generation, born between 1946 and 1964, began to marry younger and move out of the cities into suburbs. Houses built in "developments" had lawns and yards and an increasing number of mechanical conveniences such as clothes washers and driers, dishwashers, air-conditioners and vacuum cleaners. Television, by 1950, had transformed American's use of time and had become an important part of our daily lives and character. The era of affluence produced in the aftermath of World War II was such that, by 1960, about 70 percent of the population was in the middle class.

Leisure and the Market

Leisure became big business in the postwar period. In many states and in several countries, for instance, tourism became the second or third largest industry. The viability of rural development was increasingly dependent upon the recreation and leisure resources that were available or developed. In large urban areas, leisure slowly became more important to economic survival until today, when products and services can be produced almost anywhere, it is the leisure infrastructure which allows the city to survive. The theaters, dining and drinking, art galleries, museums and botanical gardens, discretionary shopping, professional sports, urban waterfront redevelopment, conventions, historic restoration, festivals and other forms of leisure expression increasing determined the city's survival.

While economists increasingly sought to measure leisure spending in the postwar era, no one knows the amount of money spent for leisure due to a number of factors. First, there is disagreement about what should be considered a leisure experience. Marijuana, for instance, slowly became the largest cash agricultural crop in the United States. Should it be thought of as a leisure expenditure? Should expenditures such as alcohol be considered a leisure expenditure? Many forms of leisure expenditures are illegal, such as some kinds of gambling, prostitution and drug use. Thus, their measurement is difficult. Additionally, it is difficult to determine what part of government expenditures are for leisure. For example, should rest stops on interstate highways be counted? How much of the budget of the United States Forest Service should be counted?

Finally, there are many individual expenditures which might be considered mixed. That is, some portion of the expenditure is for leisure and some for other purposes. Many of the expenditures made by those attending conferences may be considered a leisure expenditure. Part of the purchase of "athletic" shoes may be for leisure. In spite of this, it seems obvious that the use of leisure increasingly constituted a more important component of the economy than it did prior to the war.

An Expanding Range of Opportunities

The post-World War II Era was one in which leisure opportunity was greatly expanded for millions of people. While poverty and discrimination continued to exist, the majority of the population had a greatly expanded array of leisure opportunities within their grasp. Leisure was becoming more legitimate if earned by work. Leisure, for many, was no longer a short period of catharsis after work but gradually became the quest for pleasure and, eventually, meaning.

Television, which from the beginning was controlled by the commercial sector, showcased a different kind of life and leisure experience for millions of Americans. Television not only rejected the tragic view of life; it also portrayed the notion of the "quick fix." Problems were overcome on televised drama within one-half hour. Things happened quickly on television, since commercial sponsors wanted the widest possible audience, many of whom had short-attention spans and wanted little complexity from the "boob-tube."

The quick fix presented on television often happened as a result of dramatic confrontation, the use of violence and sexuality. It was usually the individual rather than a group who solved problems. Television served to reduce the increasing complexities of life in ways which were easy to accept.

An endless variety of attractive material goods was brought to the attention of the viewer through advertising. Success and happiness, particularly during leisure, were equated with the use of these products. Television also made many viewers observers rather than participants, leading to great concern among educators and youth workers about the detrimental effects of viewing TV. Nevertheless, television viewing became the most time-consuming form of leisure for Americans and remains so.

In many ways, television worked against the traditional middle-class values of deferred gratification and the work ethic. Television commercials and, in many cases, programming, taught Americans that you could have what you wanted now. Television affected the Baby Boom generation in three distinct ways. First, it separated them from traditional social connections, teaching them lessons without the intervention of parents or teachers. Second, it presented a world which was remarkably similar from channel to channel, a "vast waste-land" as Federal Communications Commission Chairman Newton Minow referred to it. Finally, television violence, which was so much more prevalent than the violence which occurred in real life, created a sense of fear about the world (Light, 1988).

If television began to define the world for the Baby Boom generation, the automobile became the accepted way to get to it. Automobiles, which after the war became an increasingly common passion for the middle class, were the machines for personal freedom: freedom to live further away from where one worked, freedom to shop where one wanted, freedom to get away from parental control, freedom to drive just for the pleasure of it. Driving for pleasure, in fact, became the most popular form of outdoor recreation, according to many federal government surveys (ORRRC, 1962). Traditional neighborhoods were dissected with highways to accommodate the automobile. Drive-in restaurants, movies, and even churches attested to the widespread use of the automobile for leisure experience. Drag-racing and customizing cars became popular.

Providing for leisure also became a more important part of public institutions such as secondary schools, local, state and federal government agencies concerned with land management, social welfare, libraries, museums, culture, parks and recreation, transportation, individuals with disabilities, tourism, commerce, rural development, beautification and other missions. New legislation, new mandates and rising expectations of the role recreation and leisure should play in American life grew exponentially. Part of this expansion of services was due to the return of millions of soldiers who had experienced recreation programs and services while in the armed forces and wanted them continued in their own communities. Part was also due to the many programs, such as those sponsored by the Works Progress Administration, which had been created during the Great Depression to put people back to work. These programs were responsible for the creation of many local parks and recreation areas.

At the state and federal level, land management agencies found that more and more people visited their lands and waters for recreation purposes, and the automobile was the way in which they did so. The automobile meant that, in many cases, an area which had never been defined in terms of leisure use by its administrators was suddenly found to be visited for these purposes. The Tennessee Valley Authority, for instance, was concerned with rural electrification; but in creating many large dams, they unwittingly became involved in recreation management since the dams formed large lakes which people drove to for swimming, boating, fishing and camping.

All this meant that leisure choices expanded for most individuals. The middle class grew and an increasingly high percentage of the population went to college, aided by veteran's benefits and other forms of aid. This is not to argue that an expansion of leisure opportunity was universal. In the South, for instance, as well as elsewhere, many public recreation and park facilities, swimming pools, movie theaters and other leisure resources were officially segregated as late as the 1950s. Although the official justification for such segregation was that equal provision was made for both races, in almost no case was "separate but equal" a reality in terms of recreation, park and leisure facilities. As Kraus (1968) documented, African-Americans who were denied access to leisure facilities which were for whites only almost always were left with no recreation facilities or with distinctly inferior ones.

Additionally, provision for individuals with handicaps emerged only slowly in the postwar era. It was not until the 1960s, for instance, that serious attempts were made, during the Kennedy Administration, to provide recreation services for the developmentally disabled. As the rights of individuals with disabilities were increasingly recognized, attempts were made to "mainstream" them into society. With the development of the notion of "normalization," helping such individuals lead a life as much like those without the disability as possible, recreation and leisure became an arena of concern for those who worked with such individuals. Therapeutic recreation became an occupational specialty.

In spite of the incomplete expansion of leisure opportunities, for the majority, leisure opportunity increased exponentially after the war as North America for the first time in its history became the richest nation in the world.

Mass Culture—Mass Leisure

The Baby Boom generation, along with increased belief in technology and science, produced a mass culture which, in turn, participated in mass leisure. The meaning of "mass leisure" is not entirely agreed upon by sociologists, but certainly it was related to the emergence of the mass culture which the Baby Boom generation represented.

While many researchers take pains to point out the diversity of this generation, those of the Baby Boom " . . . grew up in standardized kitchens and houses that came with the building codes of the 1940s, studied the standardized curricula that came with the drive for universal access to education in the 1950s, and lived with the standardized fear that came with the atomic bomb drills and the Vietnam War in the 1960s. They were battered by the nonstop advertising that catered to the material joys of owning rather than the status of keeping up with the Jones, and the nonstop crowding that created a deep need for privacy and individual distinction" (Light, 1988, p. 11).

Mass leisure became a part of the mass culture. In many senses, it is difficult to distinguish between mass culture and mass leisure. In one sense, mass culture may refer only to "cultural elements generally transmitted by the printed press, the electronic media, or by other forms of mass communication, and therefore generally shared in standardized form by very large numbers of persons" (Kando, 1980, p. 42). If culture is used in its broadest sense, however, to mean all the things which exist because humans exist, mass culture refers to a high degree of standardization of all such phenomena. In the postwar era such leisure behaviors as television viewing, driving for pleasure, certain forms of outdoor recreation such as camping, some sport forms such as swimming or basketball and other leisure pursuits were participated in by vast segments of the population, sometimes even the majority.

The emergence of mass leisure did not mean that social class differences in the meaning, access to, style and use of leisure were eradicated. Such differences continued to exist. (See, for instance, White, 1955.) What mass leisure did mean was that the significance of class was much less and that, as Clarke (1956) observed: "In spite of much current research toward the delineation of different lifestyles, most investigations have largely overlooked the institutionalization of leisure." Leisure had become a separate social institution. This is not to argue that leisure was unaffected by work. Indeed, as many social scientists argued, the changing nature of work had an indelible affect upon the content and meaning of leisure. "To the exact end of greater productivity, capitalism, Protestantism, and industrialism have brought about a separation of work from all that is not work which is infinitely sharper and more exclusive than ever in the past" (Greenberg, 1964). Work was clearly at the center of life in the post-World War II era, but increasing affluence and a shortened workweek meant that the more sharply defined period of nonwork could be utilized for a wider variety of purposes.

The uses of leisure which were produced by this way of life did not produce a revolution in culture. Rather, "The highest level that humanist culture seems to be able to attain under this new kind of leisure is the middlebrow" (Greenberg, 1964). Indeed, it may be argued that the society which emerged after the war did not do away with work but rather rewarded it with more diverse opportunities for recreation and leisure. As Margaret Mead observed, recreation and work were tied together in a tight sequence in which one worked, then took recreation, then worked again. Leisure, which was not earned or which extended past the period necessary for "healthy recreation" continued to be suspect (Mead, 1957).

Critiquing Mass Leisure

The impact of mass leisure has been debated within various sociological and philosophical frameworks. Certainly, however, some issues are not too controversial. Leisure, since World War II, has become the basis for the development of many large industries. In some senses, this has led to the use of leisure becoming more standardized and vicarious. It has also meant, however, that many forms of leisure expression previously limited to an elite have become available in some form to a broader section of society. Even this, of course, may be doubted. The democratization of many forms of artistic expression, for instance, often means that what is produced by artists is changed in ways which make what they do more readily understandable to wider audiences. Mass leisure has had multiple effects on our society and the interpretation of such effects reflects the theoretical framework within which sociologists who study leisure and society operate.

Leisure as Commodity

Mass leisure brought about increasing commodification of leisure expression. That is, the use of leisure was associated with an ever-widening variety of products and services. As a newly privileged society emerged, new things were invented for them to do during leisure, from trampoline centers to inexpensive tours of foreign countries. Leisure experience, in effect, could be purchased. To the extent it could be purchased, it became yet one more commodity. Since the purchase of commodities in the era after the war was increasingly thought to be open-ended, and since people's wants and desires for such experience also were increasingly open-ended, there was a noticeable speed-up in the pace of life.

A number of factors accounted for this speed-up. The existential need to find the authentic was intensified. The new possibilities brought about by science and technology and the belief that "progress" was unlimited, opened new horizons. The expanded understanding, through the mass media, of the potential to participate in pleasurable activity, and the increasingly mobility which the automobile and expanded air travel brought about the desire to get more out of leisure. These and other factors set the stage for the speed up of life.

"Time deepening" (Godbey, 1981, p. 19) occurs when the individual, under the pressure of expanding interest and opportunity, attempts to increase the yield on time. Time deepening has three characteristics:

1) undertaking a given activity or behavior in less and less time, e.g., eating lunch at McDonald's in fifteen minutes or less;

2) undertaking more than one activity at a time, e.g., watching television while eating dinner; and

3) undertaking an activity more precisely with regard to time, e.g., knowing within fifteen minutes how long a 300 mile trip will take.

Time deepening was within the spirit of mass consumption and capitalism's divorcing both production and consumption from need. People, in the postwar era, began to buy and consume more things and to expect that they would continue to do so throughout their lives. This open-ended attitude toward things began to carry over into the realm of experience. If one leisure experience is good, two must be better. Time deepening was a style of life which sought to increase the yield on time for increasing pleasure and, for many, self-definition.

In effect, one could never own enough material goods or leisure experiences. The "experiential" component, as Toffler (1964) and others observed, was increasingly being built into a variety of products. Automobile dashboards looked more and more like cockpits of airplanes. Restaurants took on the motifs of factories, fishing docks and passenger trains. Travel agents promised, not so much transportation, but rather particular kinds of experiences on dude ranches, Caribbean islands or in "authentic' British pubs. The mass consumption of leisure experiences became the linchpin for hundreds of industries, along with those which manufactured things. Experience, American entrepreneurs began to understand, could be manufactured as surely as could material goods.

Attitudes in which leisure was equated with an act of consumption also carried over to public organizations which provided recreation, park and leisure services. According to Goodale and Godbey (1988), mass leisure produced a mentality in which leisure was thought of not as a state of mind but as a set of activities. Part of this transformation was in keeping with the desire of science to classify everything. Many recreation and park organizations began to take a "cafeteria" approach to their offerings. People were expected to choose leisure activities in much the same way as they chose food from a cafeteria. While these agencies originally promoted certain uses of leisure as being superior to others, gradually they began to promote the act of participation in and of itself.

The concept of recreation and leisure as a set number of units of human experience had the effect of making these units seem interchangeable. The format for the provision of such activities became increasingly standardized, as did the design of parks. As these units of leisure activity became increasingly similar and interchangeable, it was natural for people to seek more and more of them and for the emphasis to shift to the fact of participation and the amount of participation. As leisure activities became more interchangeable units or commodities, public and private leisure service providers began to assume there was a "standard" recreation program.

Normative Leisure

As leisure became a more important part of the economy, it "massified." Increasingly large numbers of people did the same or similar things during leisure, often with mass produced products and services. The mass production of table games, for instance, meant that rules tended to become standardized instead of differing from household to household and region to region. Mass tourism meant that the mode of travel, sight-seeing agenda, lodging, and even the souvenirs slowly became more alike. This situation has been criticized on many grounds.

According to Lasch (1979): "The appearance in history of an escapist conception of 'leisure' coincides with the organization of leisure as an extension of commodity production. The same forces that have organized the factory and the office have organized leisure as well, reducing it to an appendage of industry." Some variations of this point of view mark the critique of society developed by many social critics, such as de Grazia (1964). He claimed that rather than using leisure as a means of self-improvement, Americans have simply given in to consumption. Rather than use leisure as a liberating force to improve self-understanding, Americans have settled for ease and abundance. The religious significance has been sucked from leisure by the effective marketing of commercial forms of leisure expression which sprang from the same mentality which produced the factory. Taylorism, according to Goodale and Godbey (1988), which sought to remove the process of production from the hands of the worker in order to obtain greater efficiency, is every bit as much at home in Disney World as it is on the shop floor. Industrialism depended upon increasingly sophisticated machinery not only in cotton and textiles but also in basic commodity industries such as flour, meat packing, lumber and, eventually, the production of leisure experiences. Fredrick Taylor, in 1899, established a company whose product was advice on how to make enterprise more efficient. Among Taylor's services were time and motion studies of workers on the shop floor engaged in manufacturing processes. He called his system the "piece-rote" system, each man performing by rote in the most efficient manner. In serving the machinery of industrial capitalism, human beings had, themselves, been turned into machines, replaceable ones (Rifkin, 1987).

These principles were eminently recognizable in the emergence of mass leisure. Values such as rationality, efficiency, time-saving, division of labor and specialization were increasingly recognizable in leisure experience. Slowly but surely, as leisure became commodified it became more important that something be "produced" during leisure experience; that there be some demonstrable result and, finally, that such results be achieved as quickly as possible.

The process by which leisure became commodified is well-illustrated by the hobby of model airplane building, which went from being an activity which involved only a block of balsa wood, glue and a sharp knife to one in which a person, essentially, bought a preassembled kit with complete directions and plastic parts and glued the parts together. Similar cases can be found in a variety of leisure activities. Arts festivals slowly became buying festivals rather than the celebration and appreciation of art. Sports, such as tennis, had its very nature changed by high-tech equipment and indoor courts. Tourism experiences have been planned in such a way that they represent simply consuming in a novel location. Linder (1970) argued that the ways in which additional products are utilized in a leisure experience may include the consumption of more expensive versions of products and services, simultaneous consumption of products and services, or more rapid consumption. All of such approaches are designed to "increase the yield" on the experience. Ultimately, according to Linder, this approach to leisure consumption produced a situation in which the "marginal utility" of additional commodities on the pleasure derived from a leisure experience was less and less while at the same time the individual in question becomes more and more attached to the process of consuming goods.

Most elitist arguments against mass culture and mass leisure assume that the quality of culture or leisure will be debased when there is participation by the masses. According to traditionalist Ernest van den Haag (1957),

... the mass of men dislikes and always has disliked learning and the arts. It wishes to be distracted from life rather than to have it revealed; to be comforted by traditional (possibly happy and sentimental tropes) rather than to be upset by new ones. It is true that it wishes to be thrilled, too, but irrational violence or vulgarity provides thrills, as well as release, just as sentimentality provides escape (p. 59).

According to this point of view, culture and the uses made of leisure will be invariably "watered down" if the masses participate. If a museum wishes to accommodate the masses, for instance, it will make its displays and exhibits more easily appreciated and understood. Art for the masses will be less esoteric.

Such criticisms are in keeping with the ancient Athenian notion of leisure. Most people were assumed not to be capable of using leisure in ways which were worthwhile. Those who could required not only extensive education to prepare them for lives of leisure but also to be exempted from the mundane work of the masses.

Other arguments against mass leisure and culture, as identified by Kando (1980) simply use the past as a reference point and assume that the older culture was better than what has replaced it. In many instances, the dependence of the new culture or leisure forms on technology is thought to have harmed them. In tennis, for instance, while the elite argument might be that mass participation in the game has ruined the etiquette, sportsmanship, and grace which formerly surrounded the game, conservative arguments might center around the superiority of older rules and equipment.

Arguments against mass culture and leisure which sprang from the political left stress, to some extent, how the behavior of the masses has been manipulated by those in positions of power. "The real culprits are Madison Avenue, the mass media, irresponsible opinion and modern technology" (Kando, 1980), p. 54).

Marxist critiques of mass culture and leisure center around the belief that the elite supply the commodities needed for mass culture not only for financial profit but also to serve as an "opiate" which prevents the development of revolutionary consciousness. A variety of Marxist critical arguments assert that leisure in modern capitalist societies is an extension of alienation and a denial of authenticity.

Commodification of leisure is understood as a necessary element in the subordination of the entire social system to the reproduction of capitalism and its institutional structure. The consequence to the worker is surrendering to forms of leisure which turn away from self-defining, creative experience and, instead, consuming vast quantities of market-produced goods and services (see Chapter 25).

The commodification of leisure is often thought by Marxist and left-wing critics to be part of a larger process in which the mass media become powerful enough to shape the way life itself is interpreted. Fashion is communicated by the media as signifying meaning that can be obtained by purchasing the "right" item or engaging in the "right" activity.

The defense against Marx and other politically left critiques of mass culture and leisure is the argument that the system which is in place is passive, simply giving people what they want (Gans, 1974). According to this argument, the market-based economies do not essentially mold taste or preference. Rather, they respond to the cultural tastes and needs which people already possess. People would, for instance, generally prefer to hear "pop" music rather than classical. The market merely responds to this fact. Further, defenders of mass culture and leisure argue that there is no reason to assume that ballet, for instance, is superior to disco dancing. The elite should not be in a position of dictating cultural superiority since, in matters of culture and leisure, preference is an individual matter with no hierarchies other than those established by the majority.

In regard to elite and conservative arguments against mass culture and leisure, many are rooted in democracy. The assumptions of a democratic culture are that individuals have the freedom to decide for themselves what is worthwhile without having it imposed by an elite. If more people prefer square dancing to ballet, so be it. The public should get what it wants, rather than what some intelligentsia or other influential minority plans for it. "High culture" is, after all, primarily European culture and there is no objective way of determining that their uses of leisure are superior to ours.

It is also argued that mass leisure has brought an elevation in both taste and creativity among the public. Many poetry critics, for instance, have argued that hundreds of thousands of poets are producing poetry as good as that which was written by only a few individuals a century ago. Mozart recordings today sell in the millions; symphony orchestras flourish in countless communities. Mass culture, in other words, has democratized culture and our uses of leisure in ways which have expanded and elevated creative endeavors.

Mass leisure may also be thought to help create a strong sense of community based upon common experience during leisure. Class barriers to community are minimized when the majority of individuals share some common pursuit.

In a sense, most arguments for mass culture and leisure start from a standpoint of cultural neutrality. That is, it cannot be determined in advance what is a superior culture or use of leisure. That must be determined by the majority of individuals within a specific society.

The Democratization of Leisure

While leisure had become more standardized, it was also becoming more democratized. The democratization of leisure cannot be associated with any specific decade during the nineteenth or twentieth century but it was surely accelerated after World War II. There are several concepts which may be labeled as the democratization of leisure. According to Zuzanek (1975), the democratization of culture, and therefore of leisure, may have different meanings from a sociological perspective. In modern terms, the democratization of culture originally meant a lessening of the distance between the intellectual elite groups of society and other sectors (Mannheim, 1967). It may also mean a broadening of the audience for the arts and a profound change in its composition (Toffler, 1964). Not only does this notion assume that the audience changes but also the organization and control of culture.

The democratization of culture may also refer to the "mass distribution of the products of high culture at prices within the reach of all and in places where they were never available before" (Girard, 1972). Finally, mass culture may refer to the right to culture as a basic human right (UNESCO, 1972).

While these concepts are related, they are certainly distinct. Perhaps it may be said that the democratization of culture in North America after World War II was most evident in the mass distribution of products of high culture at prices which were affordable to the majority of the population. Mass production combined with rising incomes meant that the purchase of many of the products of high culture, from musical instruments to tickets to the symphony were within the financial means of an increasingly broad cross-section of the population. It may also be argued that, to a lesser extent, there was a broadening of the audience for the arts and that it involved a fuller cross-section of the public, perhaps primarily because mass education exposed a wider cross-section of the population to the arts.

While government did not assume that culture was a human right, the federal government became more involved in the arts and humanities, as did state government. This lead to the creation of the National Endowment for the Arts and the National Endowment for the Humanities, organizations which funded artists, community-based projects dealing with dance, music, the visual arts and other forms. This involvement increased until during the 1960s, when it reached its peak. It has been estimated that the public sector was funding almost one-half of artistic endeavor in many areas of artistic expression in the 1960s.

Critiquing the Democratization of Leisure

The democratization of culture and of the use of leisure, according to Zuzanek, (1975, pp. 7-8) has been justified on several assumptions. It has been assumed:

1) that all people should have similar access to the cultural resources of a community;

2) that the message of the arts can be communicated to the masses;

3) that the arts and culture represent "superior goods" which deserve dissemination; and

4) that arts and culture are a sufficiently high priority to be supported from public funds.

Against these arguments it has been argued that the democratization of culture and leisure endanger the base of the arts. Nietzsche (1883) even argued that: "The fact that everybody can learn how to read endangers for a long period of time not only literature but all intellectual development." Mannheim similarly argued that to make the arts accessible, one often has to translate them into simplified, more abstract, and more logical formulae, thus denying the very nature of the aesthetic experience.

It has also been argued that the democratization of culture imposes certain elitist cultural values on a total population which does not want them, and, perhaps, does not need them. This may be because, as de Tocqueville (1945) observed, democracy allows higher levels of education and culture while, at the same time, reducing the potential for exceptional talent. The democratization of culture, in other words, may produce a rule of mediocrity and a lowering of general standards.

In effect, it may be argued, the democratization of culture and the use of leisure produces a kind of crowd behavior in which people act at the lowest level of their impulses. The heterogeneity of individuals, in effect, gives way to the homogeneity of the crowd. (Zuzanek, 1975).

REFERENCES

Clarke, A. (June, 1956). Leisure and occupational prestige. *American Sociological Review, 21*(3):307.

de Grazia, S. (1964). *Of time, work and leisure.* Glencoe, IL: Doubleday and Co., Inc.

Gans, H. (1974). *Popular culture and high culture: An analysis and evaluation of taste.* New York, NY: Basic Books.

Girard, A. (1972). *Cultural development: Experience and policies.* Paris, France: UNESCO,

Godbey, G. (1981). *Leisure in your life: An exploration.* Philadelphia, PA: Saunders College Publishing.

Goodale, T., and Godbey, G. (1988). *The evolution of leisure: Historical and philosophical perspectives.* State College, PA: Venture Publishing, Inc.

Greenberg, C. (1964). Work and leisure under industrialism. *Commentary, 16*(1):57.

Kando, T. (1980). *Leisure and popular culture in transition,* 2nd Edition. St. Louis, MO: Mosby–Year Book, Inc.

Kraus, R. (1968). *Public recreation and the negro: A study of participation and administrative practices.* New York, NY: Center for Urban Education.

Lasch, C. (1979). *The culture of narcissism.* New York, NY: W. W. Norton and Co., Inc.

Light, P. (1988). *Baby boomers.* New York, NY: Norton, W. W. & Company, Inc.

Linder, S. (1970). *The Harried Leisure Class.* New York, NY: Columbia University Press.

Mannheim, R. (1967). Cited by Zuzanek, J. (1975) Democratization of culture in a sociological perspective. Waterloo, Ontario, Canada: University of Waterloo.

Mead, M. (September, 1957). The pattern of leisure in contemporary American culture. *Annals of the American Academy of Political and Social Science, 313.*

Nietzsche, F. (1883). Thus Spake Zarathustra. Quoted by Zuzanek, 1975.

Outdoor Recreation Resources Review Commission. (1962). *Outdoor Recreation for America.* Washington, DC: US Government Printing Office.

Rifkin, J. (1987). *Time wars: The primary conflict in human history.* New York, NY: Henry Holt.

Toffler, A. (1964). *Culture consumers.* New York, NY: St. Martin's Press.

Tocqueville, A. de (1945). *Democracy in America, Vol. 2.* New York, NY: Vintage Books.

van den Haag, E. (1959). "Of happiness and of despair we have no measure." In B. Rosenberg and D. White (eds.) *Mass Culture: The popular arts in America*. New York, NY: The Free Press.

White, R. C. (1955). Social class differences in the use of leisure. *American Journal of Sociology, 61*(2):145-150.

Zuzanek, J. (1975). *Democratization of culture in a sociological perspective*. Waterloo, Ontario: University of Waterloo.

Section Two:
Issues in The
Sociology of Leisure

CHAPTER 9

Stratification and Social Divisions

I n no society does everyone have equal access to resources and opportunities. In some social systems the variation is over a relatively narrow range. In Scandinavian countries, for example, few are "superrich" and few are really poor. Wage scales are high by world standards and the consequent economic differences real, but limited. In some developing societies, on the other hand, a very few may be extremely wealthy and most of the population at or below levels of destitution. The market economy of the United States, coupled with a political system that is not oriented toward equality and the redistribution of wealth, has produced pronounced societal levels when measured by wealth and income.

For example, in 1986 the lowest 20 percent of the U.S. population received 3.8 percent of the income excluding capital gains and the highest 20 percent received 46.1 percent. When government transfers are excluded and capital gains included the lowest 20 percent received 1 percent of the income and highest 20 percent received 52.5 percent of the income. Under that definition of wages, salaries, and investment income the distribution was as follows (Source: 1990 Statistical Abstract of the United States):

Quintile	% of Wages & Capital Gains
lowest 20%	1.0
2nd 20%	7.6
3rd 20%	15.1
4th 20%	23.9
highest 20%	52.5

Income varies according to a number of factors. African Americans are 3 times as likely as whites to have incomes under $5000 and Hispanics twice as likely. At the other end, whites are twice as likely as Hispanics to have incomes over $50,000 and 3 times as likely as African Americans. Households headed by the old (over 65) and the young (15-24) are most likely to have low incomes and least often have high incomes. Education, which provides the credentials by which workers enter the various levels of the economy, is also a major factor. About 15 percent of those with no high school have incomes of less than $5000 compared with about 3 percent of those with any college education. At the other end, less than 3 percent of those with no high school make over $50,000, but 20 percent of those with some college make over $50,000. Every factor that is significant in determining economic opportunity is part of the systemic differentiation of levels of income and wealth.

According to the Congressional Joint Economic Committee, the differences are increasing. In 1984, the wealthiest 40 percent of households received 67.3 percent of the income while the lowest 40 percent received 15.7 percent, the lowest share since 1947. The share of the middle 20 percent also declined to 17 percent. There are many indications that the "shape" of income stratification in the United States is changing. For most of the period since the industrial revolution, the society was said to be shaped like a *triangle* with a small number at the peak of earnings and wealth and the largest proportion at the bottom with low and insecure wage incomes. More recently that shape was seen as a *diamond* with a large middle class and relatively small numbers at the top and the bottom. Now that shape appears to be changing again. There are still the 5 percent or so of the really wealthy with assets that provide not only high incomes, mostly from investments, but also considerable power due to corporate ownership. In the new *snowman* shape, they combine with high-income professionals, managers, research-and-development technicians, and top-level finance and sales personnel to form the "new class" who receive high incomes, increase assets through investment, and have considerable discretionary income. This "head" of the snowman makes up about 30 percent of the total mass. The large "middle mass" is composed of the 50-60 percent who work in offices, factories, retailing, and other services on wages that sustain moderate standards of living. They are less secure, tend to have a series of jobs rather than a developing career, and often require two incomes to make house and car payments. The bottom layer, about 15 percent, are those who are marginal, in and out of employment, and who are never more than a few weeks from destitution if there are changes in income or expenses. They have entry-level jobs or exist on meager government support programs.

Further, some trend analysis indicates that the separation between each of the three groups is widening. The "new class," costly to replace in their economic roles, is gaining in income and in the lifestyle they believe they can afford. The middle mass reach the ceiling of their economic potential relatively early and, since they can be replaced with less cost, have considerably less economic security. The excluded at the bottom tend to be in and out of high-turnover jobs with low incomes and no security. Many are in areas of the inner city or rural backwaters where there is little opportunity for employment (Wilson, 1987). As a consequence, this society is "stratified," composed of layers that are largely defined by economic opportunity and reward.

Stratification: Class and Status

In sociological theory, two basic models of stratification have been employed to account for the "layers" of social division. The first is based on economic opportunity and the second on styles of life. Social class refers to differences in power; social status to differences in prestige. There is no disagreement that societies are differentiated in identifiable layers. Such identification, however, may be based on economic roles or on the way people live.

Social Class

The concept of social class is based on the theory of Karl Marx (1818-1883) who saw capitalist societies as divided between two classes: those who own and control the means of production and those who work for wages (Marx, 1867). Any concept of social class rests on economic criteria. Further, the capital-owning class and the proletariat of workers have different interests and unequal power to realize those interests. Those who control the means of production— land, machines, materials, and capital—are able to influence the institutional structure of a society in ways that consolidate their ownership, rewards, and power. They can shape the social system toward the primacy of return on investment capital rather than toward labor. Workers, on the other hand, a vast majority of the population, have relatively little influence or power. Even withholding their labor comes at high costs, loss of income and the potential loss of their niche in the economic structure.

From a Marxist perspective, history is fundamentally a struggle between those who control most resources and those who are dependent on them. It is primarily a struggle over power rather than rewards. In many cases, however, the proletariat are blind to their real interests and the ways in which they are controlled and exploited. This "false consciousness" is reinforced by the socializing institutions of the social system and reduces conflict. People are aware of differences in access to resources, political influence, and prestige; but not of conflicting interests or the profound division of the social system.

The system is constructed to perpetuate such differences. Taxation policies, property holding and protection, income sources, and institutional control are highly concentrated. Most estimates are that 80 percent of common stock (voting stock) in private ownership is concentrated in 1 percent of the population

(Lundberg, 1968). Highly rewarded in income are those who are essential to the interests of owners—managers, research technicians, and financial entrepreneurs. At the other end are marginal workers who can be replaced cheaply and quickly and whose skills are easily acquired (Braverman, 1974). Class is an economic classification that is based more on the source of income than its size.

Social Status

Max Weber (1958) distinguished social class and social status. Social class is economic and refers to the "life chances" of members of the class. Status is social and refers to the "lifestyles" of strata, the way they live. Always in conflict with Marxian ideas, Weber analyzed stratification in a more complex mode. Class is based on differential access to resources. Those with common access also have common contexts for their work, families, and leisure. Status refers to the level of esteem or prestige related to styles of life and social identification. Such status is more differentiated than class even though related to level of occupation and source of income. One important aspect of status is leisure (Veblen, 1899) in which individuals display styles of behavior and ownership symbolic of their presumed social level (see Chapters 8 and 25). Their "tastes" identify their social level and serve to consolidate their attachment to status groups.

Weber added that power was also more complex than the simple Marxist division. In various domains of social life, there are differences in the power to carry out one's intentions even against the resistance of others. People may seek effectual action in all realms of life, not simply the economic and political. Status is relevant to all the roles people take in a social system. All institutions including the school and the church are stratified. What one does for leisure, with whom one associates, and one's aims and values are all status-related. Inclusion and exclusion in social groups and organizations are status-based. Cars, clothes, sports, and even food are symbolic of status identifications. All the dimensions of action, interaction, and possession that make up our lives demonstrate status that is a pervasive element of what we do. Further, status is central to our identities, how others define us and how we define ourselves. As a consequence, status is a significant factor in determining the social environments and meanings of leisure.

Other Factors in Social Division

The most significant complementary factor in social stratification is ethnicity. As the proportion of peoples who are not of European origin grows and becomes a majority in some urban areas, ethnic identification and history will become an even greater element in social status and styles. At the present, ethnicity/race does more than identify cultural variations. Wealth, income, access to resources including education, and political centrality all vary for those of Northern European origin, Southern European origin, Asian derivation including the latest Southeast Asian immigrants in addition to those from China and Japan, the variety of Latin or Hispanic citizens, and those of African origin. Some ethnic groups have gained a foothold in American society relatively quickly while others have experienced more persistent discrimination and exclusion. For them, ethnic identity is compounded with poverty to produce patterns of social and economic exclusion. Ethnicity commonly intensifies the stratification system and, in some cases, effectively blocks upward mobility through access to education and economic opportunity.

A second reinforcing factor in stratification is gender (see Chapter 22). Women have consistently been denied access to opportunities that are reserved for men by men. High-prestige occupations have excluded most women. Law schools and medical schools admitted few women until the 1980s. Nomination to political office in the party system has been so gender-biased that many states have yet to elect their first women to statewide office. The invisible ceiling remains in place in many corporations that now employ women in management, but only up to a certain level. The school discouraged women from entering many fields, especially math and science. Even sociologists have until recently assigned social status to women based on their husband's or father's status. The dimensions and ramifications of generations of gender discrimination seem endless. Especially in a time when a large proportion of adult women are not married, the gender factor in access to opportunities and resources has far-reaching implications for the gender who are in numbers a majority in most societies.

Stratification has been approached with quite different premises in sociology. Those who take a systemic or functional view of the social system have argued that stratification makes the system work by assigning rewards and status to economic roles in ways consistent with the cost of preparation and value to the society. From this perspective, it is functional that physicians and productive research engineers receive incomes up to or exceeding ten times the national average while fast food counter help get a minimum wage. Some would question the high incomes of Wall Street salespersons or advertising executives and the low wages of nursing home caregivers and teachers' aides. It appears common to base income and other economic rewards on assessed contribution to corporate profit rather than social value. Nevertheless, no developed social system has been structured without some kind of stratification.

Critical theory focuses on the differential interests and power of stratified levels in the society. From a critical perspective, it is not the natural functions of the system but the protection of privilege that underlies stratification. Those who gain the greatest rewards in wealth and prestige also have the power to shape the institutional structure of the society. They lobby and purchase favor in government, control regulatory agencies, become the trustees of schools and universities, shuttle back and forth between Wall Street and the State and Treasury Departments, and at least exercise veto power in local politics. Such influence and control extends to the media, education, religion, and other socializing institutions. As a consequence, most citizens are taught to believe that such a stratified system is "right" in the sense of being in everyone's best interest. The ideologies underlying the system become the consensus beliefs that are taught, celebrated, and enforced every day of the week.

Whatever the theoretical explanation for stratification preferred, there is no question of its reality. Further, placement in the social system affects everything else. The doors that are open and closed for housing, education, leisure, transportation, religion, and market access are all differentiated by where one is in the stratification system. Leisure, the focus of the analysis that follows, is no less shaped by social level than other dimensions of life.

Different Resources for Life and Leisure

Insofar as both social status and class are based primarily on economic roles, they are central to access to resources for leisure. All activity that is accompanied by cost is sensitive to differences in income and wealth.

A Divided Society: Wealth and Poverty

There is a "poverty line" of income in relation to household size. Many government programs use this standard for eligibility for transfer payments. The percentage below that line varies according to the state of the economy, but generally runs about 15 percent of households. They are disproportionately located in inner cities and rural fringes. Most specifically, they are concentrated in urban and rural ghettoes where there are few opportunities for employment. Outside such areas, the official "poor" tend to be a transient population with most households shifting above and below the poverty level during a period of years. Employment, however, generally is at or near entry-level wages and offers no security. Last hired are usually first fired.

It is more accurate to measure poverty by security and assurance of resources for an adequate standard of living. If a household is said to be poor when they are no more than two weeks from exhausting their resources if there is an increase in expenses or a decrease in income, then the percentage of households would rise above 20 percent. Compounding their economic marginality is that those not on welfare but with uncertain incomes seldom have access to any health and hospitalization insurance despite high rates of illness and disability. As a consequence, adults and children in these households have little or no discretionary income to allocate to leisure. Both market and public resources that require fees, equipment, or transportation may be beyond possibility unless extraordinary sacrifices are made.

At the other extreme are those with income and wealth that are directed toward investment and leisure rather than "necessities." They can afford to travel great distances for short times, own resources that ensure access and privacy, belong to clubs that control other resources and limit access, and be entertained without concern for cost. They may demonstrate the "Engel curve" in which preferred goods, including upscale leisure, command a higher proportion of expenditures than the average because ordinary living expenses are not a concern.

In terms of resources for leisure, however, American society is not divided simply between the wealthy and the poor. Rather, about 75 percent of the population is somewhere in-between. As suggested above, there are still significant differences. At the top are the professional, managerial, and technical elites who are considered essential to a productive economy and expensive to replace. Increasingly, like the wealthy they may spend heavily for leisure. They engage in expensive activities such as Alpine skiing and travel to destination resorts. They gain the skills and experience to maintain involvement in upscale arts and sports. They eat in expensive restaurants, take mini-vacations on preplanned long weekends, and purchase tickets to expensive entertainment. They have the best equipment, the right clothes, and the budget priorities to purchase a variety of leisure resources and experiences.

Most of that 75 percent, however, is in the middle mass. They have "jobs" rather than a career, are more subject to loss of employment, and reach their occupational ceilings relatively early, often in their 40s. They work in the factories, offices, retail stores, and human services. Their skills have mostly been learned on the job and can be learned by others when they are replaced. More and more of them are in households with at least two limited incomes, making the house payments and meeting other expenses only by combining incomes and operating on a budget. They spend close to the average proportion of their household income on leisure and recreation, 6-7 percent. They travel, but usually in the a car and on a budget. They use public venues for sport, camp and stay at budget motels when they go to the great parks and forests, buy their equipment at discount stores, and seldom take expensive lessons to acquire skills for themselves or their children. They eat out at fast food chains and rely heavily on television and rented videos for entertainment. In general, their leisure styles are conventional, limited in cost, and employing resources that are available at a reasonable fee.

There are differences as well in resources other than economic. Those at the highest levels, the truly wealthy, tend to have considerable control over their time schedules. They are most able to stay over the weekend after a business trip to Tokyo or London, have second homes in which to escape the summer heat or winter cold, and plan regular trips to Aspen or Chamonix. The "new class," on the other hand, especially in their early stages of their careers often experience acute time famine. They may work 60-hour-plus weeks and take a lot of work home. They may trade higher costs for time efficiency in their leisure.

The new class and professionals are not the only ones to be impacted by time constraints. Those employed in the service sector of the economy, disproportionately women, may have to be on the job during any of the hours that hospitals or supermarkets are open. They may be at work nights or weekends on timetables that change from week to week. While they may coordinate schedules to share child care, they find it difficult to fit into the "normal" leisure activities that are scheduled for those who are on the Monday-Friday 8-to-5 shifts. Again, at the bottom are those whose employment, incomes, and schedules are all uncertain. When they have the most time, during periods of unemployment, they have little in the way of other resources. Even special consideration in costs may further stigmatize them and attack their sense of worth.

Styles and Stereotypes

One important point is that the activities in which people engage may not vary dramatically according to stratification factors. When the really poor are excluded from the analysis, surprisingly few significant differences in activity participation are found by levels of income or occupation. When the dependent variable is what people do rather than how they do it, there are great differences, primarily in cost-intensive activities.

For example, most people travel, but their styles of travel vary dramatically. The wealthy go first class, by air, and arrive at exclusive hotels and resorts as well as second and third homes. The middle mass go by car 90 percent of the time, stop at budget motels or with friends and relatives, and are usually limited to a single vacation trip each year. But both "travel for pleasure" and say they enjoy it. There are stylistic differences even in a higher cost activity such as golf. Getting a tee off time at a crowded and overused public course a few times a year is quite different from having a reserved time at a country club with luxurious facilities and a membership limited to a fixed number of white males who allow women or children to play only at off hours. Of course, the yearly cost is also different, by $20,000 or more a year. The same stylistic differences hold for eating out, going to the beach, swimming in pools, and even where one walks.

Early research in the 1960s was directed toward such issues as the determination of leisure by work roles, social status and class, and the unifying power of socializing institutions. Leisure was measured in terms of participation in lists of activities. Surveys often asked for some frequency measure while time-budget methods measured duration. Results were usually analyzed by correlating mean participation rates with socioeconomic and demographic indices. This method was supported by new computer technologies that facilitated dealing with large samples and multiple variables.

How well did it work? At first the method seemed reasonably successful as statistically significant correlations were found in most studies, especially with large samples. Other small studies compared and contrasted occupational groups (Smigel, 1963). When the activities measured were those based on social status, such as membership in community organizations, the results appeared to validate the assumptions of socioeconomic determinism. The correlations were not large except for a few selected activities. Since the likelihood of statistical significance is also correlated with sample size, an N of 1000 or so seemed to ensure probabilities of .01. Time-budget studies indicated small but consistent differences in average times spent in various kinds of activities in relation with gender, income, education level, and family composition. A few of the correlations were relatively strong: education level to the arts, age and gender to most sports, social status to community organization, and rural background to hunting and fishing.

In the 1970s and 1980s, however, the model has been subjected to considerable attack. One source was methodological. When multivariate analyses that measured the strength of correlations (the proportion of variance accounted for) were employed, the results were surprisingly unimpressive. One analysis of national outdoor recreation surveys found the variance accounted for to be less than 5 percent for most activities and to approach 10 percent for only a few special-resource activities (Kelly, 1980). The previously found relationships were there, but not with the predictive power presumed. Close to 20 such surveys were conducted in the 1970s with a variety of analyses. The results were much the same, mostly weak to erratic correlations (Snepenger and Crompton, 1985).

A second crack in the approach was produced by giving attention to social groups as agents and contexts of decision rather than to aggregate analysis (Field and O'Leary, 1973; Cheek and Burch, 1976). It was demonstrated that the immediate contexts of participation, especially family and friendship groups, differentiate participation more than income and occupational indices. A consensus began to develop concerning the determination of leisure patterns by stratification factors:

1) Socioeconomic and demographic factors are only moderately predictive of leisure participation rates.

2) Most of the variation found can be ascribed to certain constraints:
   • The poor are cut off from many kinds of participation, especially those that require travel and other costly investments.

- Racial and gender discrimination have long-term cumulative consequences that require generations of equal opportunity to erase.
- Ecological differences compound economic as the opportunities for some types of recreation are located nearest to those who can afford the most expensive housing.
- Excluding the very wealthy and the poor, commonalities of leisure participation appear to be far greater than differences.
- More immediate influences such as family composition and association patterns are combined with situational factors in actual leisure decisions (Kelly, 1978).

Such research on rates of participation have turned attention back to the question of style. Preselected lists of activities—fishing, reading, hiking, going to concerts, etc.—obscure the radical differences in ways of doing the activity. Leisure choices are not unrelated to social position, community and family roles, and the opportunities and expectations associated with social status. Those relationships, however, require a different approach in research.

Community and Occupational Studies

In the 1930s, there were a number of significant sociological studies of communities. One focused on leisure in a suburb (Lundberg et al., 1934) and others placed leisure in the context of community roles. No two were quite alike, but each found leisure to be embedded in the organization and stratification system of the community:

1) In a suburb of New York, George Lundberg, Mirra Komarovsky, and their associates (1934) did a pioneer study of leisure patterns of a community that was at that time more diverse than suburbs tend to be now. They used time diaries and interviews to investigate activities such as reading, visiting, entertainment, sports, media, motoring, and community organizations. They found that blue-collar workers had more time for leisure than managers, but that upper-level men and their wives were more likely to be involved in community organizations. In general, leisure patterns were conventional and tied to social status. Especially the wives, who were not in the paid work force, had routines of leisure that reflected their community status. Leisure reflected the value schemes of the managerial and working classes of the community.

2) In a midwestern town, Helen and Robert Lynd (1937) studied "Middletown" in 1924-25 and again in 1935. In the original study, Robert Lynd (1927) divided the population into two classes, "business" and "working." Leisure was found to be closely tied to work and family roles for both classes. Activities reflected differences in expectations as well as in opportunities and resources. Business class wives, accepting that homemaking afforded them little recognition, became the leisure leaders and innovators for the community. Men, on the other hand, were more oriented toward work and the associations that work status required. The home was the center of leisure for both classes, both in its space and the status afforded by its location and style. The business class, even during the depression of the 1930s, played golf, went to Florida in the winter, belonged to the country club, and were in the churches and other organizations befitting their status. Working class families on the other hand, hard hit by unemployment, had to trim their leisure to their incomes. They did not travel or belong to exclusive clubs. Rather, their leisure was low-cost, accessible, and based on the formal and informal association with other workers and their families. The family was a central context for leisure, but the proliferation of leisure-oriented community organizations gave support to the concept of Americans as status-based "joiners." From this perspective, leisure was something to buy and differentiated by income as well as the class-based social organization of the community.

3) Among later community studies that gave attention to leisure were the Midwest study of youth in "Elmtown" (Hollingshead, 1949) and of a changing small town in New York (Vidich and Bensman, 1958). Both found the styles of leisure to vary according to social status. Community organizations absorbed a major amount of nonwork time in the period before television. These organizations, for children, youth, and adults, had clearly demarcated membership sources. Children's organizations were not divided by activity interests, but by social class. Being on the "wrong side of the tracks" determined access and drove recruitment. In the New York study, the churches were central to leisure associations and had their status-based clienteles. Further, the decision-making structure of the community, both formal and informal, was determined by economic roles and the control of production and capital. The myth of being one happy and integrated community was belied by the realities of concentrated power intensifying the separated patterns of social interaction.

A number of studies also investigated the leisure styles of occupational groups (Smigel, 1963; Noe, 1972). Few of the comparisons were surprising. In general, those occupational groups with the higher incomes and educational backgrounds demonstrated the widest latitude of participation and met in environments that had attracted or were limited to others of their status. Attention was also given to the centrality of work in their lives with the commonplace finding that those with the highest rewards and greatest autonomy in their work most often placed greatest value on it. Factory workers, on the other hand, did not make work and work associations central to their life and leisure styles (Dubin, 1956).

1) Relative autonomy was the focus of an analysis of studies of executives and blue-collar workers (Noe, 1972). The most comprehensive study of executives (Hecksher and de Grazia, 1959) found that greater value was given to work than to leisure. Anticipating later research, executives reported putting in long hours on the job. Actual work weeks often exceeded 50 hours plus the thought, attention, and actual tasks that come home "after work." Counting business entertaining and work at home, some executives devoted 70 hours a week to their work. Leisure was curtailed, not because of assigned employment hours but because of the expectations of the work position. Nevertheless, the executive also has much more autonomy at work as well as a nonemployed spouse to arrange the home, family, and leisure aspects of life. Noe summarized that the executive had more "leisure within his work" while the blue-collar workers compensated with more autonomy in leisure that is separated from work.

2) A study that focused on blue-collar workers was completed in a "working-class suburb" in Northern California (Berger, 1969). The issue addressed was whether living in a suburb would be more influential in shaping lifestyles than the blue-collar work relationship. In general, Berger found that the workers did not become "joiners" or take on many new kinds of activity. Few engaged in any organizational participation at all. If any, they were most likely to be PTA or a church association. Visiting in each others' homes was also infrequent. Rather, family interaction and television seemed to occupy the most time. For men, westerns and sports were the preferred TV fare. There were no changes in tastes in food, reading, or entertainment. In general, Berger concluded that the styles of life and leisure in such a suburb still reflected blue-collar background and interests.

The strength of such studies is that they place leisure squarely in the context of life as it is lived. Leisure is not abstracted into a list of activities, scale of values or perceived outcomes, or any other preformed scheme. Rather, leisure is located in the midst of the context of life, family and community. Differences are found in how people act and interact as well as what they do. The focus is on context and style. The main weakness, on the other hand, is much the same. Concentration on the real lived context of life and leisure make it difficult to compare with those in other contexts. Further, it seems impossible to identify just which factors in that context are most influential in shaping those styles. Immersion in the community may also lead to a loss of cross-cultural and societal perspectives.

Stratification and Leisure Styles

Is there, then, any scheme for identifying the effects of class and status on leisure styles? Without giving quantitative comparative measures, there are a number of identifiable factors.

The first is clearly opportunity. The lowest class, the poor and disinherited, are cut off from the opportunities and resources that others take for granted. They have no discretionary income, little likelihood of developing skills and interests in educational settings, and no position that admits them to leisure environments. The wealthy, at the other extreme, possess position and resources that admit them to a world of private leisure in which cost is traded for access, opportunity, and quality of resources.

Most people, however, are in-between those extremes. They have multiple opportunities for leisure, but not those that are exclusive. If among the new class with relative high incomes, they can at least rent access to high-cost environments. They rent beaches and mountains by the week, travel in value-assessed packages, purchase good equipment, plan a variety of vacations and/or return to comfortable resorts when their children are young, and generally have enough discretionary income to take advantage of the opportunities in their home communities. They can pay the fees for public and many market-sector programs, join clubs, eat out where the food and service are a pleasant change, and place their children in a variety of programs to gain skills in the arts and sports.

It is the "middle mass" whose opportunities are most problematic. Everything they do has to be done in a cost-conscious style. They may, however, plan a special vacation trip to Disney World or the coast. They may make special leisure-based purchases—sports equipment, a gun for hunting, a video player/recorder, and even a boat or RV for weekend and vacation fishing trips. Like the more affluent, they depend on the market sector for many leisure resources, but always at a calculated price. Their opportunities are limited, dependent on resources that have mass markets and reduced production costs, and relatively conventional. On the other hand, many are in jobs that are limited in demands on time, imagination, or even energy.

The point is that opportunities and resources for leisure are available or not in ways that have economic bases. Especially in a society that depends heavily on the market sector to provide opportunities, economic reward level is one significant factor in leisure. On the other hand, just correlating socioeconomic indices against participation has produced only modest results. Differences in activity choices by upper-middle, middle, and working-class individuals in North America have not been dramatic. When education history is controlled, differences almost disappear. Rates of camping, listening to music, watching television, or engaging in sports are similar. What may differ is the place and style of participation. Only costly activities such as golf and downhill skiing have substantial variations (Kelly, 1980).

Leisure styles, however, may differ considerably according to social status as well as other factors. Going to concerts, a common category of activity in national surveys, is rather different for middle mass teens in a rock mob and elite adults at a symphony benefit concert. Further, there is a variety of styles within economic levels according to cultural factors that had led to different socialization histories. One problem is that there has been relatively little research on the "ethnicity of leisure," how leisure varies among cultures and subcultures.

In a stratified society, cultural elements are mixed with the economic to produce lifestyles. For example, the interaction patterns of poor urban white households, urban Italian families, Hispanic families, and others demonstrates how opportunity, immediate social context, and ethnicity combine to produce distinctive styles of entertaining, celebrating holidays, and including or excluding children in festivities. An event such as a family dinner may differ in how many are invited, the frequency and timing of such events, how the eating is sequenced, where people gather in subgroups formed according to gender, age, marital status, and family position, demonstrations of emotions and affection, topics of conversation, language conventions, and other elements that make up the event called simply a "family dinner."

There are many other examples of the compounding of stratification and ethnicity in leisure settings. Bar behavior differs by class, gender composition and preference, ethnic composition, location in a neighborhood or urban center, and other factors that make the category of "going to bars" almost meaningless stylistically. The danger is that leisure becomes subject to stereotypes that use ethnic identification to form inclusive and misleading categories. All factory workers do not stop at a blue-collar bar on the way home from work. All professors do not drink dry wine. All athletes are not "jocks" who read nothing but the sports pages. Rather, the leisure styles of most people are characterized more by diversity than a single theme.

The Hidden Costs of Class

There remain, however, significant ways in which social class impacts leisure. The first presupposes that leisure opportunities and resources are distributed unequally in a society because they are one means of control. The second argues that the impacts of social stratification are more subtle and more profound than can be measured by differences in income.

Leisure, Control, and the Reward System

The basic argument is relatively simple: Most economic roles provide little intrinsic satisfaction because there is little opportunity for self-determination or a sense of contribution to a worthwhile product or service. Nevertheless, the economy requires millions of workers who do their jobs with a minimum of resistance and a maximum of compliance. The reward system that keeps people at work presents an alternative. Do what is expected and receive an income that provides not only for necessities but for some leisure, time and income devoted to pleasure. Fail to do what is expected and the penalty is dismissal and exclusion from the rewards. In this approach, leisure becomes a commodity to be purchased on the market rather than self-determined action (see Chapter 25).

But that is not all. There are vast disparities in those rewards. Those at the top have not only great resources to buy leisure, but also considerable freedom in which to exercise their choices. Those in the middle, wage workers who can be replaced at minimum cost, have lesser resources and circumscribed opportunities. They are expected to conform in their leisure as much as in their work. Leisure, then, becomes an instrument of control (Clarke and Critcher, 1985). Most workers are expected not only to be compliant at work, but also to be predictable consumers for the leisure industries, thus providing markets for the leisure industries.

Critical analysis in Britain is based on class divisions in contemporary society. The history of leisure provisions and regulations in industrial societies is one of control. Workers are directed toward leisure that will support their productivity and away from activities that may render them less able to work. All sorts of laws have limited the hours of operation of working-class drinking establishments, outlawed various "unacceptable" leisure gatherings and ethnic festivals, and tried to substitute "healthy" physical and mental exercise under the watchful sponsorship of the factory owners and their minions. Most public recreation and community programs for workers and their families have been justified by their contributions to worker health, competence, and dedication to work.

Leisure has come to be defined as time earned by work. Holidays are for rest and recovery to prepare for a return to work. Vacations are purchased times and places. And all the purchases—time, space, symbols identifying the holder with a leisure activity, goods distributed on a schedule of planned obsolescence, and even packaged experiences at theme parks and other locales of entertainment—are to be taken as making any kind of work acceptable. Through the mass media, leisure is sold according to tastes that further divide the population. Advertising is directed toward market segments: beer and motorcycles to blue-collar males, beaches and resorts to more affluent young singles, wine and gourmet foods to status-conscious couples, and rock promotions to teens. Pleasure comes to be defined as consumption, not just of anything outside work but of the status-appropriate goods and services.

Leisure, like work, is stratified not only by economic function but also by gender, ethnic identification, race, and age. Income is a primary differentiating factor, but not the only one. As more and more leisure opportunities are provided by the market sector, provisions are designed to attract particular market segments and to extract the maximum profit from them. At tourist destinations, shops line the streets offering merchandise appropriate to the presumed tastes of the stratified clientele. Travel packages, holiday camps, beach resorts, and all the support system dependent on leisure travel are designed to capture markets differentiated by tastes that are learned in the families, neighborhoods, and schools in a society that segregates and separates residences according to income and wealth. In a society in which up to 80 percent have homes, refrigerators, and TVs, more and more it is in the realm of leisure that people try to find that "something more" that defines the "good life." And they are persuaded that leisure is for sale, or at least for rent. But there remain great differences between those who can buy a mountainside and those who rent a camping trailer in a crowded park alongside an artificial pond.

The Hidden Costs of Class

Differential access to opportunities and resources, however, are only the most manifest aspect of stratified leisure. In an influential study, Richard Sennett develops the argument that economic measures of social stratification are inadequate (Sennett and Cobb, 1973). Even analyses of the institutional ramifications of power and resource differences are only a starting point. Rather, urban industrial workers perceive threats to the fundamental context of their lives that are out of their control. The study probes the issue of how workers define their lives and what it means to have limited "life chances."

Sennett wrote of several dimensions of injury that underlie such indices as income, occupational status, and levels of education. The central issue is that of life in which basic directions and contexts cannot be self-determined. What does it mean to be channelled into life conditions in which there are few options for self-creating action? The "hidden injuries of class" that are identified include the acceptance of symbols of inability, the loss of dignity and a sense of accomplishment when sacrifice for others has been betrayed, and having to accept a social definition of always being replaceable. The deepest hidden injuries are the limited and defensive self-definitions that are fostered by conditions of relative powerlessness.

In a study of later-life adults in a medium-sized Midwest city (Kelly, 1987), many of the life stories told by women and men reflected such limited conditions and consequent views of life. Life for many is a struggle to avoid catastrophe. There were women who left school early to help support a family in which the father was shut out of work by illness, injury, or the economic failure of mines or factories. All their lives they worked for others—cleaning, washing, and doing the onerous chores of maintenance—while at the same time maintaining their own families. There were men who had a lifelong series of marginal jobs and who had to go on working through ill health in their 70s because they had no economic resources. In such cases, the injuries of class were quite clear, not hidden at all.

The manifest injuries of class have already been outlined: marginal levels of resources that allow for no sense of security or stability. A divorced black mother remembered the continual crises of "buying all those shoes" for her children. Her job was steady, but with a low ceiling income. For such people, the supermarket becomes a nightmare when they cannot afford most of the offerings. The opportunities taken for granted by those in the mainstream are outside their accessible world. Such people are the excluded, those whose life chances have always been just above subsistence despite histories of seeking and holding jobs. What is leisure for such persons in a market economy?

The hidden injuries of class are significant for leisure. The first is that the life journey is a continual struggle. Life is day-to-day, coping with the problems and traumas of life with a minimum of economic and social resources. The bare requisites for coping are always uncertain. "Life as struggle" can sound very existential connoting courage and strength in entering the storms of life and emerging on the other side. And for many of the marginal and excluded there is amazing courage and resiliency. But what if there is no "other side"? What if the struggle to survive just goes on and on, demanding and unrelenting? Leisure for such persons may consist of the meaning and joy that they can find or create in moments of playful exchange or imagination. But "discretionary income" and "free time" mean little to them in their struggle. The images of marketed leisure repeated by the media are unthinkable.

The second hidden injury is in the perspective of what is seen as possible in life. Just making it through the day and night is all that seems real. Planning the next holiday or vacation is not a consideration. What are the decisions, choices, options, and alternatives in such lives? What is the meaning of self-determination? The fact is that many of those with overwhelming limitations tell stories that include elements of finding, dreaming, and deciding even when excluded from most ordinary resources. Nevertheless, long-term investments in satisfying engagement, seeking new experiences, taking chances on something novel or challenging, or investing in a possibility for communicative interaction are not even in the world of possibility. The horizons of leisure as with the rest of life are close in, limited by all the dimensions of life that are out of control.

Even those somewhat above marginality and exclusion tend to have quite limited views of the potentials of life. Their goals are immediate and close, tied to homes and families, and without vistas of self-development or the exploration of the full dimensions of life. The point is that stratification impacts more than income and the price of the next car. It is all the cumulative resources and deprivations of the life course. It is life as lived.

Alienation: The Loss of Self-determination

What is the real condition of life? In a divided and stratified society, real conditions vary significantly. Not only access to resources, but the fundamental ability to assess alternative goals, develop lines of action, and become the person one would like to be is not equally available to everyone. The condition of being cut off from the possibilities of becoming is called "alienation." It means being separated from the dimensions of being human: self-determination, development, social worth, and community. From a sociological perspective, alienation is a condition of life, not a feeling or perception. When persons are cut off from possibilities of realizing their potential as human beings, they are alienated whether they feel bitter or contented.

Alienation is usually based in economic roles. Workers are said to be trapped in an "iron cage" of routinization (Andrew, 1981). The sole standard of work organization is productivity. In order to maximize production and minimize costs, work is "scientifically" designed. If such design produces a rationalized repetition rather than variety and a sense of craftsmanship, then the cost will have to be borne by the workers. The criterion of work organization is efficiency. The cost, however, may be in separating the worker from an actual sense of productivity, of doing something of value and worth to others. Quality control becomes a program of worker control rather than a commitment. And the end result in many cases is that computers and robots are found to be more efficient than people. The jobs remaining for human workers are then further routinized and dehumanized (Sheppard and Herrick, 1972). Such alienation is found both in the office and in the factory.

What are the consequences for leisure? It is not necessary to accept a work-determination model in order to identify a problem. It is true that leisure tends to be more associated with the institutions of the family and community than work. Life, however, cannot be totally segmented. There is evidence that those who have been denied opportunities for expressive and relational behavior on the job may be less able to recreate it off the job. Work is productive, but the workplace is also an environment for humanizing activity—for self-expressive play and community-building interaction. When those elements of life are truncated, then there are consequences for the rest of life. On the other hand, "when play is encouraged on the job, the job holder becomes more committed to his (her) job, more energetic in his (her) leisure, and a more effective contributor to the society in his (her) political activity and ideology" (Torbert, 1973). We might argue that the connections of work, family, leisure, and politics are not that simple and straightforward. Nevertheless, a denial of expressive and social activity for 40 or more hours a week for a lifelong worklife of up to 2000 weeks is unlikely to leave the rest of life untouched.

Human beings, whatever their work conditions, are too complex and their lives too complicated to easily identify clear lines of causality between work and the rest of life. Fundamental attitudes, however, may have some carryover. If one is primarily an instrument in one central realm of life, then it may be more difficult to engage in self-authenticating action and to relate to other persons in a noninstrumental mode. Critics argue that alienation in work produces people who lose the full dimensionality of being human. There is considerable evidence that a lack of self-determination in work results in inferior commitment to both the work product and the process. There is less evidence that alienated workers are more likely to treat other persons as things in home and community. Is work so basic to life that its alienation results in a "one-dimensionality" in the rest of life in which life comes to be defined primarily in terms of the things that can be possessed and used (see Chapter 25)?

Whether or not the "long arm of the job" is this powerful, it is clear that alienated work conditions can have either of two consequences for leisure. The first is that those who are treated as things on the job will treat others the same way off the job. The carryover is likely to be negative in its consequences for undertaking creative action or developing community in leisure. The opposite possibility is that of compensation. Those who are most limited at work will try to break free into leisure that is expressive and communicative. As suggested in the next chapter, the evidence does not clearly support either model. What is clear, however, is that a stratified economic system offers much greater opportunity for self-determination and autonomy for those near the top of the system than for those near the bottom. They are more often defined by those with controlling power as instruments of production than are those who are in charge.

Stratification: A Summary

Social stratification, then, is a matter of how power and rewards are distributed in a social system. Both life chances and lifestyles vary according to where one is in a layered system in which position is largely determined by economic role. Whatever the model of stratification that is most revealing of the nature of the society, there is no question that there are dramatic differences in the resources and opportunities for leisure. Further, those differences are demonstrated more in styles of behavior than in the activities themselves. Finally, there are more profound consequences of such social division including limited horizons of life's possibilities and an alienation from self-determination and community on and off the job.

REFERENCES

Andrew, E. (1981). *Closing the iron cage.* Montreal, Quebec, Canada: Black Rose Books, Ltd.

Berger, B. (1969). *Working-class suburb.* Berkeley, CA: University of California Press.

Braverman, H. (1974). *Labor and monopoly capital.* New York, NY: Monthly Review Press.

Cheek, N., and Burch, W. (1976). *The social organization of leisure in human society.* New York, NY: Harper & Row, Publishers, Inc.

Clarke, J., and Critcher, C. (1985). *The devil makes work.* Urbana, IL: University of Illinois Press.

Dubin, R. (1956). Industrial workers' worlds: "Central life interests." *Social Problems, 3*:3.

Field, D., and O'Leary, J. (1973). Social groups as a basis for assessing participation in selected water-based activities. *Journal of Leisure Research, 5,* 16-25.

Hecksher, A., and de Grazia, S. (July-August, 1959). Executive leisure. *Harvard Business Review , 6,* 156.

Hollingshead. (August, 1949). *Elmtown's youth.* New York, NY: John Wiley & Sons.

Kelly, J. R. (1978). Situational and social factors in leisure decisions. *Pacific Sociological Review, 21,* 313-330.

Kelly, J. R. (1980). Outdoor recreation participation: A comparative analysis. *Leisure Sciences, 3,* 129-154.

Kelly, J. R. (1987). *Peoria winter: Styles and resources in later life.* Boston, MA: Lexington Books, The Free Press.

Lundberg, G., Komarovsky, M., and McInerny, M. (1934). *Leisure: A suburban study.* New York, NY: Columbia University Press.

Lundberg, F. (1968). *The rich and the super rich.* New York, NY: Bantam Books, Inc.

Lynd, R. (1927). *Middletown.* New York, NY: Harcourt Brace Jovanovich, Inc.

Lynd, R., and Lynd, H. (1937). *Middletown in transition.* New York, NY: Harcourt Brace Jovanovich, Inc.

Marx, K. 1867 (1908). *Capital, Vol. 1.* Chicago, IL: C. H. Kerr and Co.

Noe, F. (1972). Autonomous spheres of leisure activity for the industrial executive and the blue-collarite. *Journal of Leisure Research, 3,* 220-248.

Sennett, R., and Cobb, J. (1973). *The hidden injuries of class.* New York, NY: Vintage Books.

Sheppard, H., and Herrick, N. (1972). *Where have all the robots gone?* New York, NY: The Free Press.

Smigel, E. (1963). *Work and leisure.* New Haven, CT: College and University Press.

Snepenger D., and Crompton, J. (1985). A review of leisure participation models based on the level of discourse taxonomy. *Leisure Sciences, 7,* 443-466.

Torbert, W. (1973). *Being for the most part puppets.* Cambridge, MA: Schenkman Publishing Company, Inc.

Veblen, T. (1899) (1953). *The theory of the leisure class.* New York, NY: Mentor Books.

Vidich, A., and Bensman, J. (1958). *Small town in mass society.* Princeton, NJ: Princeton University Press.

Weber, M. (1958). Class, status, and power. In H. Gerth and C. W. Mills (Eds.), *From Max Weber,* New York, NY: Oxford University Press.

Wilson, W. J. (1987). *The truly disadvantaged: The inner city, the underclass, and public policy.* Chicago, IL: University of Chicago Press.

CHAPTER 10

Work and Leisure

How do we know the difference between work and leisure? Both may be exciting or boring, solitary or social, routine or creative, sedentary or active. People work at home, at night, on weekends, and when they travel. They may play in the factory or office, in fugitive moments or organized events, in modes of intense engagement or relaxed disengagement. There is paid work, employment, and unpaid work such as housework and caregiving. In some societies people are paid not to work to reduce overproduction and encouraged to devote themselves to unpaid volunteer services. Both work and leisure may be easy or hard, enjoyable or a turn-off.

In fact, the lines of distinction may be somewhat blurred. Some activity may incorporate elements of each. There are those fortunate few who really mean it when they say, "I would do this whether I got paid or not." There are the unfortunate who look for some routine task on Sunday morning because there is nothing they really want to do. Both work and leisure may be more themes or dimensions of life than clearly differentiated activity (see Chapters 2, 36). Nevertheless, there are important defining elements of each:

Work is productive activity with predetermined outcomes of economic or social value. "Productive" denotes an outcome that is considered of social or economic value, that makes a contribution to the society. In work the products of goods and services are not incidental, but are the aim of the activity. It is socially necessary. From this perspective, making widgets, managing forests, or caring for children are usually work.

Leisure, on the other hand, has the central elements of being relatively free, expressive, and open. It may be significant, but is not required. It may be demanding and disciplined, but its meaning is focused primarily on the experience. It may produce something, an outcome or artifact, but the outcome is not predetermined or necessary.

This does not imply that all work is important and all leisure trivial. Producing one more brand of breakfast food or decorating a ski condo that will be occupied six weekends a year may be trivial. A creative idea or vision, the renewal of love and commitment in a shared experience, or a release from deadening routine may be highly significant. It surely does not imply that everything for which we are paid is valuable and activity we do out of love or enjoyment is trifling. In general, however, we usually know when we are meeting the requirements of work and when we have chosen activity mostly for the anticipated experience.

Of course, all employment is not work. Being paid and on a prescribed timetable may produce nothing of value to anyone except a profit on investment or filling a bureaucratic office. Nevertheless, either would be considered employment. Work and leisure, from this perspective, are both seen as dimensions of life while employment is a specified function. All jobs are not work, and all work is not employment. Ideally, people work because they want to be productive, useful, worthwhile, and socially engaged. Realistically, many people are employed because they are paid. Many who are employed more often "work to live" than "live to work."

Central Life Interests

How important is work in the lives of ordinary people? At one extreme are those who organize their entire lives around work that is absorbing and demanding. At the other extreme are those who treat the job entirely instrumentally, as a means to a necessary income that supports the aspects of life that are important. Further, it is hardly surprising that professionals, the "new class" of research and development technicians, and those who own their own businesses are most likely to find work central to their lives. It is equally predictable that those who are insecurely attached to jobs that offer no future advancement, only a wage for tedious tasks, care least.

There are two conflicting myths concerning the centrality of work for those in between, for the middle mass of ordinary people with ordinary employment. The "work ethic" myth proposes that most American workers find fundamental meaning for their lives in their work roles. They want to work, care about their work, and identify with it. The "alienation" myth argues that whatever minor satisfactions most find at the workplace, fundamentally workers are being used for the gain of others and know it. They have little sense of productivity, quality, community, or purpose. Most workers are manipulated, coerced, and evaluated to enhance the profit or prestige of owners, managers, and others with the power to shape work conditions.

Is either myth true? The answer is probably neither "yes" nor "no." Rather, an answer requires a second question: For whom? There may even be a third question: Under what circumstances?

In the 1950s, Robert Dubin inaugurated a research agenda on the "central life interests" of American workers. In a midwestern factory, he found that only 24 percent could be defined as job-oriented (Dubin, 1956). Three out of four preferred their associations and activities outside employment. Meaningful relationships, feelings of worth, and enjoyment were sought outside the job. Work was mostly a means to greater ends. Further research on this issue found that those with a "career" orientation, who connected their performance with possible future advancement, were twice as likely as the rest of the sample of managers and specialists to have their job as a central life interest (Goldman, 1973). In Britain, Stanley Parker (1971) asked simply, "What is your main interest in life?" Eleven percent of those employed in business replied "work" compared with 29 percent of those in human services.

Commitment has been defined as "the relative distribution of interest, time, energy, and emotional investment" devoted to work or other life sectors, especially family (Safilios-Rothschild, 1971). In this approach, some combination of family, home, and close relationships has generally been found to be more central than work in the value and action systems of most of those who are employed (Kelly and Snyder, 1991b). In a research design that does not require either/or choices, both meaning and satisfaction are common for men and women workers in family, work, and leisure. Family, however, is most often central to life investments and satisfactions. Further, leisure tends to be more tied to family and community than to work (Kelly and Kelly, 1992b). The "Protestant work ethic," which Max Weber (1958) argued was integral to the rise of capitalism, does not appear to be as dominant an ideology in industrial societies as once believed (Inglehart, 1990). Even a more modern secular work ethic hardly describes the habits of workers who hide out, stay away, maximize off-task time, look forward to Friday, and even sabotage the production process.

Do work roles shape timetables, determine economic resources, and provide some social identity? Of course. Do workers value associations expressed on the job, find ways to reconstruct their work to offer some enjoyment, and get caught up in particular projects? Frequently. Do they "live to work?" Not very often.

The second myth was partly introduced at the end of the previous chapter. Are most work roles characterized by "alienation?" Do workers have effective self-determination, a consciousness of producing something of worth, an attachment and a sense of solidarity with fellow workers? The evidence is mixed. In national polls, about three out of four workers usually respond that they are satisfied with their jobs. That seems to mean that they are willing to accept their employment out of the range of opportunities that might be realistically considered. Also, the proportion that indicate satisfaction does vary with the kind of occupation (Kahn, 1972): about 80 percent for professionals and managers, 60 percent of clerical workers, and 65 percent of unskilled workers. On the other hand, while 80-90 percent of professionals, scientists, and attorneys would choose the same line of work again, the percentage of unskilled auto workers is 16 percent, of textile workers 31 percent, and of white-collar workers 43 percent.

Analysts of alienation in work seem to select their evidence according to their aims and ideologies. There is no shortage of accounts of workers who take drugs on the shop floor, hide out in lofts during their shifts, resent their supervisors, and call in sick when they want to see a ball game. They report no loyalty to their employer, look forward to retirement fishing, and distrust the motives of management. Further, their lack of interest and challenge on the job is similar to leisure styles that exhibit no central commitment, seek no challenge, and are for the most part conventional and entertainment-ridden (Torbert, 1973).

At the other extreme are the organizational behavior specialists who are confident that devices such as "quality circles," shop-floor and office sharing of procedural ideas, diversification of tasks, and various education programs can significantly increase commitment to the company, the product, and to a sense of meaning and craftsmanship. At least, there is increasing acceptance of management principles and procedures that involve workers at all levels in development of production procedures and the work environment. At the same time, other studies find evidence of workers gaining enjoyment through playing with machines, interacting with each other, and introducing variety into what seem to be monotonous routines (Hollands, 1988). Some retirees, while happy to be relieved of many employment demands, also miss some of the banter with workmates and the sense of having a recognized economic role.

All this suggests that we cannot totally dismiss the concept of the work ethic. There are elements of meaning in producing, fabricating, managing, and developing, however limited, the conditions, that are central to being human. At least as an ideal, the ethic of work is more than a device of investors to get more profit out of the labor force. For some with high levels of satisfaction, there is significant meaning on the job. Most research indicates that they tend to be those with the greatest freedom to develop their own contexts of work and to have a sense of contribution to a recognized outcome (Kohn, 1990).

On the other hand, romantic dreams about some past idyllic time when workers entered the shop light of step and full of anticipation are probably nonsense, at least in industrial societies. In the United States alone, there were over 2000 strikes between 1880 and 1900. Studies of the work conditions of textile and steel workers in the last half of the 19th century do not suggest any likelihood of deep satisfaction or enjoyment in the 60-hour work weeks, high accident rates, and lack of any economic or health security. Labor-management relations are for the most part a history of conflict, not of common cause or interests.

In general, it appears likely that work is central to the organization of much of life, but not the highest value of many in the labor force. On the other hand, it is not unrelated or unconnected with the rest of life. It is the possible relationships that have attracted considerable attention among sociologists focused on work and leisure.

The Common Wisdom: Work Determines Leisure

Almost from the beginning, alternative possibilities have been recognized. Among them, the most commonly referred to have been those of Harold Wilensky and Stanley Parker. Both propose three possible relationships: identity, contrast, and neutrality. For sociologists who come to the study of leisure from the perspective of work, however, the underlying bias seems to be in favor of models in which work determines leisure.

Wilensky (1960) studied a variety of work situations and occupations in the Detroit area. His proposed model of the work-leisure relationship was mono-directional from work to leisure. Either the conditions and meanings of work would "spill over" into leisure or leisure would "compensate" for the conditions of work. The premise was that spillover would most likely characterize upper-level workers who found considerable satisfaction in their occupations, while leisure would be compensatory for those in routine jobs with little autonomy. Compensatory leisure was seen as a response to negative work situations high in boredom and low in challenge. Compensation was later called "the leisure solution" to the problem of industrial work. Wilensky also cited evidence of a fusion of work and leisure with a variety of on-the-job breaks and occasions of interaction that made a temporal and locational dichotomy unrealistic.

In Britain, Parker (1971) developed a threefold model that has captured the most attention. He also presupposes that the direction of determination or influence must be from work to leisure. His model has two levels and three kinds of relationship:

	Level	
	Individual	Societal
Identity	extension	fusion
Contrast	opposition	polarity
Separateness	neutrality	containment

The first two are essentially the same as spillover and compensation. The third logical possibility is that one is segmentation rather than determination. The "identity" or "extension" relation implies that work is central to life and provides for considerable self-determination, challenge, and collegiality.

"Contrast" or "opposition" is characterized by a separation of domains, limited or alienated work conditions, and a strong negative imprint of work on leisure. "Neutrality" suggests a weak relationship, less negative work conditions, and a separation of life domains and interests. All three, however, presuppose the primacy of work. Parker begins with work as basic even in the possibility of low-impact relationships. In a later revision, he admits the possibility that leisure may influence work, but does not pursue the logical possibility far.

One question is "What is the evidence?" Does one model represent most of the results of research directed toward the work-leisure tie? In the 1960s and 1970s, a sequence of studies addressed the issue. In the beginning, most of the research compared occupational groups (Wilensky, 1960; Parker, 1971; Smigel, 1963). The rather unsystematic studies usually found identifiable differences in activities and styles when comparing professionals and factory hands, social workers and blue-collar workers, and other groups. When occupational prestige was employed to distinguish occupational levels, significant differences were found in a survey design (Burdge, 1969). Soon, however, the relationships began to be seen as inconsistent and often weak.

Among the studies addressing the issue were the following: Wilensky (1960) claimed to have found some support among contrasting occupational groups for a spillover effect. Meissner (1971) did not find the "long arm of the job" to be determinative except for weak spillover in socializing preferences. Noe (1972) reviewed studies of executives and blue-collar workers and reported that executives had more freedom to pursue leisure at work ("identity") but less time off the job. Industrial workers, on the other hand, tended to separate the two. Torbert (1973) claimed that those with more challenging or creative opportunities in work carry these elements over into their leisure. Kelly (1976) found contrast or compensation to be a secondary element for blue-collar workers, especially older ones, but seldom the primary reason for selecting activity. Pennings (1976) reported weak spillover in both skills and attitudes. Staines and Panucco (1977) report correlations between objective and subjective involvement in work and leisure. In Australia, Kabanoff and O'Brian (1980) got inconsistent results including weak spillover in attitudes but also some compensation. In a survey design, Staines and O'Conner (1979) found that family is a priority in life and work is perceived to constrain both family and leisure activity. The "spillover" they measured was between family and leisure, not work and leisure. Most recently, Miller and Kohn (1982) found that complexity and intellectuality may be reciprocal between work and leisure supporting a "learning generalization" model.

In general, the relationships are less than consistent and never strong. Further, the methods employed in the studies are so different that it is impossible to attain any cumulative results. Also, the occasional inclusion of demographic variables has not seemed to strengthen the correlations. Some studies have concentrated on attitudes, some on the form of activities, and some on social or other characteristics of work and leisure activity. There has been little attention to the overall structural conditions that are the context of both work and leisure or on the characteristics of the workers themselves that may predispose them to certain kinds of work and leisure. Two general findings seem clear:

1) There is no persuasive evidence for the dominance of any single model.

2) Both work and leisure are too complex in motivations, styles, associations, and other factors to fit neatly into any circumscribed approach.

Note also that it is possible to place either a positive or negative spin on either spillover or compensation. Spillover may suggest that challenge, autonomy, community-building, and involvement may transfer from work to leisure. Conversely, spillover may denote that the boredom, conformity, separation, and lack of intensity of routinized jobs may carry over into leisure. In something of the same way, compensation may be viewed as a positive relief from stress in demanding or conflictual work situations or as a negative response to the lack of freedom and meaning in employment. If the ideal is autonomy, then identity or holism may be defined as control. If the ideal is involvement, then the relaxation of escapist compensation may be viewed as a failure to make leisure constructive and developmental. Valuation appears to depend on the starting-point of the analysis.

Some of the inconsistency may be due to misdirected or limited research designs. For example, steel workers are not likely to be attracted by three sets of tennis after eight hours near torrid furnaces. Simply being tired or satiated with a particular kind of activity does lead to situational leisure decisions that provide a change or even escape. The failure to locate compensation in general may reflect the fact that very little research on leisure choices and styles is situated. The level of analysis of all the studies referred to above is so abstracted from actual decisions that they may have little to do with actual Wednesday evenings or Saturday mornings.

Where does the issue stand then? One summary was developed by a sociologist and social psychologist in a joint analysis. They identify the state of the issues as follows (Zuzanek and Mannell, 1983):

a) There is some support for spillover at the structural level.

b) Spillover is most likely for workers who perceive work as important to them.

c) Support for compensation is weak except for some suggestions of motivational or attitudinal components for those in stressful jobs.

d) Work-leisure relationships seem to vary in different life and work conditions.

e) Segmental models are supported more by default than designed measurement.

f) Adding attitudinal dimensions to behavioral studies has not resolved inconsistencies.

g) There is not even a consensus on the level of support found for any of the models.

They conclude that the work-leisure relationship is multifaceted and multi-directional. Any simple model of determination of leisure by work is not demonstrated and rendered unlikely by the mixture of inconsistent findings from the variety of research designs thus far employed. A more useful and comprehensive model would expand the dimensions. From an institutional perspective, a life is engaged in multiple intersecting roles of which a primary economic role is only one. Those roles are shaped by culture, gender, status, age, and other factors that vary in their centrality and impacts through the life course. Work roles are central in determining levels of resources, social timetables, secondary role expectations, and other elements of the total social context. To divide life, however, into a simple dichotomy with a unidirectional power of determination is a gross violation of the complexity of life in society.

A Revised Approach to The Issue

What, then, is the relationship between work and leisure? To begin with, there are obvious and important contextual dimensions:

- Economic roles are basic to the allocation of resources, time and money.

- Leisure is learned in lifelong socialization that takes place in work in addition to other role contexts.

- Decisions are situational. In any actual decision about leisure, factors related to economic roles may well be salient. These factors may be as simple as being tired along with some carryover of work associations, expectations, and even skills.

- Leisure is only one element of life investment patterns that intersect at every decision point. Most commonly, family and other primary relationships provide both a setting and purposes for considerable leisure action.

Deterministic models of human behavior are for the most part giving way to those that are multivariate and interactive. Life is more of a process than a straight line. Neither economic nor technological determinism have proven adequate bases for predicting behavior. Nor have abstract psychologies of attitudes proven to predict actual choices well. Rather, the closer the investigation is to the concrete situation, the more complex and relevant the model of behavior. From a psychological perspective, the cognitive processes that connect work and leisure remain to be identified. From a sociological perspective, the level of analysis concentrating on conditions rather than persons has failed to produce consistent and cogent results. One sociological reason may be simply that socialization is complex and lifelong. Conversely, most research designs have at the same time been abstracted from real situations and based on simplified premises of determination.

To be more specific, a multidimensional model is needed. A useful model would include the following elements:

1) It would be multivariate to incorporate factors such as family status, age, gender, work history, job designation, ethnicity, and integration/alienation in the job context.

2) It would recognize that most leisure is actually a common "core" of accessible activity that does not distinguish occupational or any other groups definitively.

3) It would take account of the variations in intersecting roles through the life course. Developmental goals and processes are not the same for single young adults, parents, and preretirement workers in the same jobs.

4) It would recognize the legitimacy of segmentation rather than uncritically buy into the ideological premise that work "must" determine leisure and everything else be considered secondary.

5)   It would explore more relevant dependent variables, styles rather than activities and associations rather than locations.

Such a shift requires a fundamental reorientation in perspective. Leisure itself is understood as more than leftover and derivative. Rather, leisure is a dimension of life with its own meaning and integrity. It has its own place in the rhythm and flow of life. That place is neither separate nor determined. The failure of the deterministic model does not mean that it can be replaced with its opposite.

The replacement myth might well be one of containment. This model would be reinforced by much of the modern segregation of work and leisure. In metropolitan areas, workers leave residential areas that are selected according to criteria of cost and family lifestyle values rather than proximity to a lifelong occupational site. Workers drive off in every direction to jobs that may change from year to year and provide no regular off-site associations. Blue-collar workers commute to work from their neighborhoods and developments as do their white-collar counterparts. The dispersal of factories, shopping centers, warehouses, and other businesses throughout the megapolis and along the interstate highways separates work from leisure and family geographically. The American preoccupation with private space segregates family and leisure from work and community.

The separation model recognizes the variety of schedules, locations, expectations, and involvement in work. Some research locates connections between family and leisure rather than between work and leisure (Kelly and Kelly, 1992b). Work tends to be defined as instrumental by many even when there are enjoyable elements in the work situation. The assumption is that most people are primarily focused on the immediate contexts of their own lives. They have little sense of or commitment to larger issues and communities. The corporation is a paycheck. The government is a set of unreliable services and a tax bite. The school is a credential machine. The church is a service station. Leisure is entertainment. And even the family is a provider of care and security, a "haven in a heartless world."

Some have argued that such segregation has its functions. In the demands of many industrial occupations, workers may need some separation and relief (Goodale and Godbey, 1988). Holistic ideals that fuse work and leisure into a creative unity may be pipe dreams of those who have never degreased a machine or experienced aching arms and back from eight hours at a computer terminal. A lot of work has to be segmented if the rest of life is to have adequate vigor and challenge. In this alleged "postindustrial age," there are still thousands of jobs that are demanding in all the wrong ways. Constraints and routines may be required to get all the necessary work of the world done. Segmentalism in this context offers a necessary balance to such requirements. After all, in the world of production, structure and rationalization may be essential to produce goods or services that can command a market in the competitive world economy.

The Critical Rejoinder

Mainstream sociology often tends to assume the functionality of whatever is. The social system that has developed around industrialization is a functional response to what needs to be done. What exists "works" or it would not exist. Such an assumption has been challenged by critical analyses with roots in neo-Marxist cultural studies (Clarke and Critcher, 1985). In the area of leisure, historical analyses in both Britain and North America have begun to focus on power and the struggles of the working class against domination (Cross, 1990). Studies of both men and women wage workers demonstrate many ways in which even their leisure was a struggle between community control and attempts to break free into behaviors deemed a threat to the common order by mill owners and their representatives in church, state, and school.

The central theme of this critical challenge is that of social control by those who own and control banks, factories, and other corporate structures. Workers are kept in a state of insecurity to cement their dependence on their jobs. Their wages and other rewards are kept at a level that minimizes their ties to the job and cooperation on the job. The central criterion of all action that shapes the life conditions of workers is productivity. They are allowed access to education, housing, leisure, and other life chances in measures that keep them healthy, fit to work, and dependent on their allotted place in the economy.

What does this imply for leisure? It is not separate from work, but rather one manifestation of the control and reward system. Work in the sense of economic interests determines leisure in an essentially negative way. Leisure is determined for those with little economic and political power by those who have the power. The assumption is that work will be seen as instrumental by those in subordinate economic roles. Rather than reform work conditions toward self-determination, leisure becomes the gift and goal that makes work worthwhile. Leisure becomes a critical element in the control by the ruling class and the compliance of workers.

Leisure is, from this critical perspective, a market-mediated instrument that binds workers to the production process and to cooperation that supports the continuation of a capital-dominated social system (Kelly, 1991a). Leisure is defined as a commodity that must be earned and is indissolubly connected to what can be purchased and possessed. (See Chapter 25 for an expansion of this argument.)

A number of themes are gathered in this critique. The power to enforce compliance is masked behind an ideology in which "freedom" comes to be accepted as purchasing power in the marketplace of leisure. Such "commodity fetishism" (Marx, 1970) of attachment to things defines life and leisure in terms of possession. Work becomes instrumental, an "iron cage" in which the worker is alienated from satisfying engagement with production as well as solidarity with other workers. Absorption in mass media legitimates consumption-based values and world views (Habermas, 1975). What appear to be varying styles of leisure reflect profoundly different conditions of work, family, and leisure assigned by economic class, gender, and race (Clarke and Critcher, 1985). Access to leisure resources in a market economy differs by economic position and reinforces acceptance of one's "place" in the system.

Again, the underlying premise is one of the determination of leisure by work. Leisure is claimed to be as alienated as work, perverted by a preoccupation with possession rather than free and developmental action. In this perspective, however, there is much more than a neutral connection between work conditions and leisure activity. Rather, the determination is fundamentally control in which leisure becomes a means of exploitation. Further, the result is more than variations in leisure styles. The consequence is that leisure, like work, is deeply alienated. Rather than being a realm of relative freedom, leisure is seen as narrowed to consumption of what is provided by corporate interests with a central goal of return on investment capital.

Also, in this critical view, all kinds of other divisive designations are employed to differentiate opportunities for leisure. Women are more limited than men by access to opportunities, sex-role requirements, and lack of power to determine the conditions of their lives. Racial and ethnic definitions are arbitrarily enforced to raise thresholds and close doors to resources. Occupational groups learn "tastes" that keep them on the margins of the culture. And yet, amid all this, wage workers become convinced that it is all worthwhile because they can purchase leisure toys and are granted some time to enjoy them.

Leisure: A Social Phenomenon

The fundamental presupposition of any sociology of leisure is that leisure is a thoroughly social phenomenon. It is of the culture and a product of the social system. It is not separate and secondary, but embedded in the institutional structures, social times, and power allocations of the social system (Kelly, 1992a). As such, it is not unrelated to work; nor is it determined in a direct and simple mode. In a complex social system, both individual self-determination and institutional control vary by social and economic position. Leisure is not segmented, but woven into the system. In a dialectic between the decisions and orientations of social actors and the forces that shape and limit such action, leisure is neither separate nor totally determined. As a social phenomenon, leisure is subject to analysis from the perspectives of the economic base of resource allocation, the institutional base of its role intersections, the socialization base of its value and symbol systems, and the situational context of its actualization. In a real social context, leisure is both supported and blocked, provided resources and denied access, idealized and controlled, neglected and marketed. A dialectical approach to leisure and its connections with work raises a number of issues:

1) The first issue calls for sociologists and others to move beyond ideologies to the lived conditions of the full spectrum of social groups. On the one hand, the real conditions of the poor, excluded, and disinherited children, women, and men are at least in part a consequence of the economic system of a society. Their struggles for life in the present as well as for a future are reflected in what they do to express themselves, create community, fill ordinary hours and days, and seek new possibilities. Leisure is a dimension of that struggle in its constituent elements of expression, development, and community. For example, one study of unemployed ghetto youth found that recreation settings where there is some opportunity to demonstrate skill can help those excluded from economic roles to feel good about themselves (Raymond and Kelly, 1991). The issue isn't whether the unemployed have leisure, but how they cope with the everyday conditions of life.

   The same issue pertains to all other social levels and categories. To extrapolate from gross expenditure totals or regional tourism statistics the meaning of leisure in the day-to-day lives of executives, professionals, discount-chain checkers, seasonal farm workers, teachers, students, or any other occupational group requires great leaps of association. The lesson of the early community studies is that leisure takes place in real and multifaceted contexts. Ideologies may direct research to important questions, but are no substitute for immersion in real lives.

2) The second issue is to identify the ways in which economic roles provide contexts, resources, limitations, and orientations for the rest of life—family and community as well as leisure. Research design cannot assume some simple and direct determination of life and leisure by work. Rather, a central issue is how determinative definitions of both the self and society are learned in a power-differentiated institutional context. The socialization process for

everyone is lifelong and changes through the life course. What individuals want, see as possible, value, and risk are defined differently by men and women, wage workers and owners, Mexican Americans in Texas and fourth-generation Germans in North Dakota. Economic role is only one part of the total learning context.

3) The third issue is one of meanings. Just purchasing is not commodification and owning is not fetishism. What are the commitments, symbols, meanings, self-definitions, and value orientations that are the cognitive context of leisure decisions and actions? What are the meanings and outcomes of leisure-related spending, media use, packaged entertainment, and images of pleasure? Possession may be a way of life or an instrument for activity. Does leisure, in fact, reflect a culture of possession? One preliminary study suggests that adults do spend money on leisure, but most often see the goods and services as fostering an experience rather than as an end in themselves (Kelly, 1991a). Again, however, there is little carefully crafted research on the issue that delves into the real experiences that may vary by age, gender, and ethnicity as well as economic position. Further, there is the possibility of a deep cultural paradox between alienation and creation that permeates the society and renders problematic any single-issue research design.

4) The fourth issue revolves around time. Once misleading models focused on average work weeks are set aside, what are the actual patterns and varieties of time structure and allocation? How do work-determined schedules articulate and conflict with those set by other roles such as parenting and homemaking as well as leisure commitments and interests? Such schedule factors would appear to vary by gender as well as employment, life course period as well as income. Time remains a basic resource for leisure, one that not only varies widely but is one index of the possibility of self-determination. Economic timetables are basic to time allocation, but are not the sole factor in shaping leisure opportunity.

5) The basic issue of connection-separation between work and leisure may be more complicated than earlier models proposed, but the issue remains significant. There are a number of possibilities: Is leisure a small world of protection against the determinative and stifling forces of greater economic, political, and social powers? Leisure may be a privatized and compartmentalized segment of life that is related to others only in a defensive way. Or, at the other

extreme, is leisure a realm of creative possibility that provides a standard and a springboard for action in all other parts of life? Leisure may be at the center of becoming human rather than a secondary and leftover dallying with peripheral outcomes. The third possibility is that leisure is neither one nor the other, a limited box of activities or an actualization of creation and re-creation. It may be more mixed, related to economic and other roles and still a struggle for liberation. If so, then no ideology can capture the variety of its meanings or its multiplex resources and limitations.

6) The assumption that all constraint is negative, in work or leisure, ignores the necessary structure of any social action. Whatever people do together is in part shaped by rules, roles, expectations, and contextual factors. For example, coordinated activity requires some agreement on time that constrains individual action. Such structure is not in and of itself a negative element in life. Rather, the structures of work are part of its meaning and even of its satisfactions. In the same way, structured contexts of leisure are not simply "constraints," but are the agreed upon context that permits and facilitates common action. To divide life into work that is necessary and constrained and leisure that is free and open is to distort both. Some work, at least, has its elements of play and openness. Most leisure—all that involves other people—has elements of structure. For example, the role expectations and nurturing requirements that permeate the play of parents with children do not render such activity less important, satisfying, or even creative. All social life is structured by roles and resources. Any dichotomous model of life that identifies all structure with work and all freedom with leisure prevents a realistic analysis of both.

Work and Leisure: A Summary

There is more clarity about what does not seem to be true about the relationship between work and leisure than what is true. The early models are clearly inadequate because they all explicitly or implicitly are based on a bipolar division with monodirectional determination. A revised approach begins with a series of "nots."

- Life in society is not divided in a bipolar mode between work and leisure.

- Work does not determine leisure is a direct and simple way.

- Work is not just occupational level and leisure a list of activities.

Conversely, there has developed a basis for further exploration of the complex relationship:

- Leisure resources, both time and money, have an economic base.

- Both work and leisure are multidimensional as is their relationship.

- Other social roles such as family and community are part of the work leisure connection.

- Other factors including gender, age, and ethnicity are involved in the work-leisure relationship.

- The relationship is reciprocal or dialectical rather than having only one direction.

- Social stratification is basic to the work-leisure tie.

- Differences in leisure for those in different economic positions may vary more by style than by activity participation, especially when "core" activities are included.

- Leisure socialization contexts are multiple and vary through the life course rendering the total domination of any single factor problematic.

- Actual leisure decisions are more situational than any model can encompass.

- Value premises based on ideologies, whether from functional or conflict models, need to be subjected to critical analysis.

In general, what started out to be relatively simple as well as central to the sociology of leisure has developed into a formidable task with a multidimensional agenda. The relationship between work and leisure remains a central issue, but not one that can be adequately analyzed from the perspective of any simple theoretical model or ideology that substitutes facile claims for difficult research.

REFERENCES

Burdge, R. J. (1969). Levels of Occupational Prestige and Leisure Activity. *Journal of Leisure Research, 2*: 262-274.

Clarke, J., and Critcher, C. (1985). *The devil makes work: Leisure in capitalist Britain.* Urbana, IL: University of Illinois Press.

Cross, G. (1990). *A social history of leisure since 1600.* State College, PA: Venture Publishing, Inc.

Dubin, R. (1956). Industrial worker' worlds: A study in the central life interests of industrial workers. *Social Problems, 4,* 131-142.

Goldman, D. (1973). Managerial Mobility, Motivations, and Central Life Interests. *American Sociological Review, 38,* 119-125.

Goodale, T., and Godbey, G. (1988). *The evolution of leisure: Historical and philosophical perspectives.* State College, PA: Venture Publishing, Inc.

Habermas, J. (1975). *Legitimation crisis.* Boston, MA: Beacon Press.

Hollands, R. (1988). Leisure, work, and working-class cultures: The case of leisure on the shop floor. In H. Cantelon et al. (Eds.), *Leisure, sport, and working-class cultures.* Toronto, Quebec, Canada: Garamon Press.

Inglehart, R. (1990). *Culture shift in advanced industrial society.* Princeton, NJ: Princeton University Press.

Kabanoff, B., and O'Brian., G. (1980). Work and leisure: A task attributes analysis. *Journal of Applied Psychology, 65,* 596-609.

Kahn, R. (1972). The meaning of work. In A. Campbell, and P. Converse (Eds.), *The human meaning of change.* New York, NY: Russell Sage Foundation.

Kelly, J. R. (1976). Leisure as a compensation for work constraint. *Society and Leisure, 7,* 45-61.

Kelly, J. R. (1991a). Commodification and consciousness: An initial study. *Leisure Studies, 10,* 7-18.

Kelly, J. R., and Snyder, J. (1991b). Centrality and satisfaction: Work, family, and leisure. (Unpublished).

Kelly, J. R. (1992a). Leisure. In E. Borgatta (Ed.), *Encyclopedia of sociology.* pp. 1099-1107. New York, NY: Macmillan Publishing Co.

Kelly, J. R., and Kelly, J. (1992b). Dimensions of centrality and meaning in the domains of work. *Family and Leisure.* Sociological Quarterly.

Kohn, M. (1990). "Unresolved issues in work/personality." In K. Erikson & S. Vallas (eds.) *The nature of work.* New Haven, CT: Yale University Press.

Marx, K. (1970). *The economic and philosophical manuscripts of 1844.* London, England: Lawrence and Wishartt.

Meissner, M. (1971). The long arm of the job: A study of work and leisure. *Industrial Relations, 10,* 239-260.

Miller, K., and Kohn, M. (1982). "The reciprocal effects of job conditions and the intellectuality of leisure-time activities." Paper at the 10th World Congress of Sociology. Mexico City, Mexico.

Noe, F. (1972). Autonomous spheres of leisure activity for the industrial executive and blue-collarite. *Journal of Leisure Research, 4,* 220-249.

Parker, S. (1971). *The future of work and leisure.* New York, NY: Praeger Publishers, Inc.

Pennings, J. (1976). "Leisure correlates of working conditions." Paper at the American Sociological Association. San Francisco, CA.

Raymond, L., and Kelly, J. R. (July, 1991). "The leisure activities of unemployed black and hispanic youth." Paper at the World Congress of Sociology. Madrid, Spain.

Safilios-Rothschild, C. (1971). Towards the conceptualization and measurement of work commitment. *Human Relations, 42,* 489-493.

Smigel, E. (1963). *Work and Leisure.* New Haven, CT: University and College Books.

Staines, G., and Panucco, D. (1977). Work and nonwork, part II: An empirical study. In *Effectiveness of Work Roles.* Ann Arbor, MI: University of Michigan Survey Research Center.

Staines, G., and O'Conner, P. (1979). *The relationship between work and leisure.* Ann Arbor, MI: University of Michigan Survey Research Center.

Torbert, W. (1973). *Being for the most part puppets.* Cambridge, MA: Schenkman Publishing Company, Inc.

Weber, M. (1958). *The protestant ethic and the spirit of capitalism.* In T. Parsons (Trans.). New York, NY: Charles Scribners, Sons.

Wilensky, H. (1960). Work, careers, and social integration. *International Social Science Journal 12,* 543-560.

Zuzanek, J., and Mannell, R. (1983). Work-leisure relationships from a sociological and social psychological perspective. *Leisure Studies 2,* 327-344.

CHAPTER 11

Leisure Cultures and Ethnicity

The forms of leisure are almost infinitely varied. Games employ all kinds of implements, strategies, and settings. Arts take all sorts of shapes and materials to produce items both abstract and representational. Festivals may incorporate a variety of elements from the history, religions, arts, and common life of a culture. Sports have differences that are both subtle and dramatic. Even the common event of eating together has rituals and symbols as different as the foods themselves. Leisure incorporates elements of the culture of its time and place. Leisure, then, is thoroughly ethnic—of its particular culture.

At the same time, there may be parallels from one culture to another. Games may be cooperative, competitive, or even warlike. Arts such as music and dance have similarities of sequencing, rhythm, and coordination as well as cultural specifics. Festivals incorporate cultural uniqueness with blendings of mass movement, spectacle, and symbolism. Sports have common elements of antagonistic and synchronized action. Even eating has dimensions of inclusion and exclusion based on family and social structure, gender, and age.

All leisure, then, is specific to its culture. Yet, forms of leisure are often parallel from one society to another just because they are embedded in cultural forms and symbols. Anthropologists of play call attention to common forms, meanings for the society, and outcomes for individuals. All are, after all, behaviors learned in social contexts and have developed to make sense in and of that society. These forms serve both to introduce individuals to the nature of the culture, "socialization," and to reinforce its solidarity through common action. Play and leisure, from this perspective, are a significant part of learning and living in any society.

Play and the Culture

Anthropologists tend to use the term "play" rather than leisure. This usage reflects the focus on expressive or nonutilitarian activity in distinction to frequent sociological designations of a time-bounded life domain as "leisure." There seems to be little difference from the action perspective suggested in Chapter 2. One cogent summary of the relation of play to culture begins with the argument that play has biological as well as psychological and cultural dimensions (Sutton-Smith and Roberts, 1982). Play is not segmented, but is tied to economic, social interaction, political, domestic, and religious activity in relatively simple and in more complex societies. The games developed in a society may reflect the complexity of the social order even when focusing on physical skill, chance, or strategic action.

One significant approach to the relationship of play to the culture is from the life-course perspective. Play is usually a central medium of socialization of children toward the adult roles they will be required to assume later. Those roles are often differentiated by gender and may be oriented toward domestic maintenance, political argumentation, war, economic division of labor, family governance, or religious rituals. Social status based on family, wealth, skills, position in the family, or other factors may be enacted and reinforced in the games of children. Some games are well-defined and passed on from generation to generation. They tend to be closely tied to the socialization process. Others are more fluid and even allow for continual imaginative re-creation as children learn to deal with innovation and the "not yet." In any case, the materials and symbols of the play, organized or spontaneous, are those of the culture.

Several issues underlie this cultural basis of play or leisure:

1) To what extent are the play forms of children and adults fixed and ritualized and to what extent are they spontaneous? Only a careful analysis of the culture in which the play is embedded can reveal the correspondence with the fundamental nature of the culture. Common analysis would be that more traditional and rule-bound cultures foster more structured and less open play.

2) How is play related to cultural change? The "materialist" premise is that economic and technological factors determine all social and cultural change. The arrow of determination is one-way. Another possibility is that change is more complex. The arrows are bidirectional in a more dialectical process. Further, many aspects of a culture, including leisure, may be sources of change. This is especially likely when the focus is on ideas, values, and rituals. Innovation may take place in nontask behaviors that will alter even

economic tasks. Modes of interaction and decision making may develop in play that are transferred to the functional arenas of production and reproduction. From this perspective, there is no one cultural domain that propels all change. Rather, a culture is a complex, multifactorial process in which even play may lead the way to the new and different.

3) Are the functions that are carried out in play universal? The issue is whether there are common functions in any culture—biological reproduction, gender relationships, dealing with death, and the division of labor are examples—that are the basis for what appear to be quite different forms of play. If so, then the cultural basis of leisure can be analyzed from this functional perspective. How does the game reflect or prepare for actual participation in the social system? A stylized game may mirror a central religious ritual. A game with a ball or projectile and teams may prepare for the field coordination required for war. A toy is a miniature of an adult tool or instrument.

4) Is play always functional? That is, does play always serve to reinforce the norms, customs, and regulations of the social system. Does leisure reflect power differences based on age, gender, economic function, or kinship? Do the festivals of a culture always reinforce the value systems and institutional organization or are they sometimes subversive? For example, adolescent play may appear to challenge adult roles and norms when in reality what appears to be a challenge is just a way for youth to get such rebellion "out of their systems." If the latter, then rebellious behavior may be tacitly accepted as a developmental necessity. The other possibility is that in the relative openness of some play actors may learn that they can make changes in the given world. In enactments of rules and rituals, the innovative may try out change that undermines the old order. Are the limits of play as rigidly enforced as those of political participation?

5) To what extent is play distinct from other aspects of a culture? One perspective is that in simpler cultures, work and leisure tend to be less differentiated than in modern industrial societies. The times and places of play are mixed with those of work, family, and other institutions. The alleged clearcut separations of the industrial and urbanized society are melded into a more seamless fabric. This issue has now taken on new life in raising the possibility of a "postindustrial society." One characteristic of such a new social

form would be that work and leisure are again blended more than segmented. The same issue is raised in a different way in relation to gender with the argument that work and leisure never were as separate for women as for men in industrial systems.

The underlying theme of this approach is simple enough: leisure is *of the culture*. Its forms, instruments, symbols, and meanings can be understood only in their cultural context. Attempts to do cross-cultural and trans-historical comparisons can never lift play out of its contexts. Even football is more than a sport with a particular history. It reflects forms, values, and symbol systems of a specific culture. It is neither segregated nor unique. It, too, is ethnic—of the culture and tied to the power relationships, roles, values, and conflicts of that culture.

However, this is not all. Leisure is not only of the culture; it also creates culture. Leisure exists in the dialectic between the normative culture and the subcultures of the "small worlds" of individuals. Leisure has to do with culture on a macro scale and cultures on a micro scale.

The Cultures of Leisure

The significance of leisure in the creation and re-formation of culture is one central issue that will be explored further in Chapter 13. On a smaller scale, there is no doubt that subcultures are created in leisure. Not only are there immediate social groups that regularly engage in activity together, but there are small cultural systems that develop around such activity.

A number of terms have been used to refer to such subcultures. Each has a slightly different emphasis, but all refer to common elements of symbolic communication, interaction, commitment, activity form and locale, and social organization. At the heart of the subculture is regular common action. Such action may develop around events such as "anachronistic" festivals of mock medievalism, baseball card sales, or a softball league. It may involve travel to Native American archaeological sites, motorcycle encampments, or Bach festivals. The action may be localized into a dance group or stock investment club or nationalized with an annual convention and monthly publications. The organization may be quite simple in its localized form or complex as an international organization with staff, budget, and regular ritualized meetings. What is surprising to some is that the center is leisure action rather than economic, political, or religious activity.

Leisure may create a *social world* with a "unity of order," social structure, regularity of interaction, and boundaries that are set by symbolic communication (Shibutani, 1961, p. 566). Social worlds may be organized around common ethnic origin, formal organizations, or voluntary associations. It is voluntary associations that may develop around leisure actions and interactions. At the center is a common interest around which is created a system of behavior, communication, identification of membership, and means of continuation. Social worlds are units of organization that have been found to develop around such local activities as tennis, pub life, or softball; regional forms including taxi-dance halls and nude beaches; and diffuse activities of camping, fishing, sport parachuting, and motocross racing (Scott, 1990).

The term *subculture* usually focuses more on symbol systems than on organization. A subculture is a "set of understandings, behaviors, and artifacts used by particular groups and diffused through interlocking group networks" (Fine and Kleinman, 1979). In a subculture, there is regular sharing and communication of the common elements through an accepted system of symbols and values. In a leisure subculture the history of interaction creates a complex set of shared meanings for those that identify themselves as a part of the subculture. Those shared meanings may be based on central events, common technologies and techniques, rules and complex social norms, and a variety of identifying symbols of language, appearance, or behavior. In sum, a subculture is composed of all the elements that support sequences of interaction.

In studies of leisure-based subcultures, different elements have been identified as central including skills and techniques, social class origin, separating and identifying symbolic boundaries and rituals, histories of common action, integrated roles, space and locale, ethnicity, and forms of repression. Some have been directed at traditional recreational activities such as community theater or baseball and others toward more deviant lawbreaking or sexual behaviors. In all, however, members gain some sense of who they are and of belonging through leisure.

Investment and Identity

Robert Stebbins (1979, 1992) refers to members of skill-based leisure subcultures as "amateurs." The amateur, according to Stebbins, is to be distinguished from the professional whose work consists of the activity and from the dabbler or dilettante whose participation is occasional. The true amateur is, as the term connotes, a "lover" of the activity. The development of skill is prolonged and consistent with standards little or no different from those of the professional. At least three distinct elements characterize the amateur:

1) A high level of investment in skill development;

2) A personal identification with the activity; and

3) A community of co-participants.

Stebbins began his study out of his own commitment to classical music as an orchestral performer. For amateurs in such engagement, playing music well is usually a lifelong commitment. The investment in skill, instruments, and experience is consistent over many years and transfers from one locale to another. As a consequence, both personal and social identities come to be associated with the activity and performing ability. The leisure amateur can hardly imagine her life apart from the activity. The investment comes to be more than a decision or even commitment; it is central to selfhood. Finally, such sustained investment, also called "serious leisure," leads to community.

One fundamental sociological issue is how in massive and complex societies individuals connect with the whole. How can one connect, especially in a mass society in which corporations become larger and more complex, government is overwhelming in size, the media are standardized, and bureaucracy characterizes even service and religious organizations? Are the twin dangers of *anomie,* loss of norms and values, and *alienation,* separation from meaning and community, an inevitable result of size and complexity? As individuals, do we see ourselves as drifting in an indifferent world?

One answer to this problem is said to be in the mediating functions of more immediate associations (Bellah et al., 1985). Most important, the family provides a sense of solidarity and belonging while tieing individuals to the larger society through economic and social functions. The local church offers community and the celebration of a value system. Voluntary organizations are participatory contexts of activity and association that also yield a sense of identity. There are indications that increasingly the communities that develop around serious leisure are significant in meeting this need for mediation.

Leisure, then, provides more than activity. It may produce important social worlds, activity groups with histories, forms, and cultures. The activity may become the action focus of a *subculture* with its own symbol system and organization. In music, the activity group may be a string quartet, a chamber or full orchestra, or a school for skill development. The larger social world is one of such amateur musicians who have national and international organizations, conferences, and periodicals. The subculture that emerges includes the communicative media, the reflection of the highest levels of performance, and technologies related to dissemination such as recording, music publication and distribution, and festival scheduling. The localized manifestations of the subculture are the activity groups that regularly share in engagement.

The social consequences are manifold. People who play together tend to do others things together as well. The common engagement builds multifaceted relationships that may gain the attributes of sustained sharing that we call friendship. The sharing yields common histories, vocabularies, experiences, and even values. For example, who but the parent of a competitive swimmer can appreciate the significance of tenths of a second? Some experiences become too esoteric to be easily shared with those outside the subculture. Leisure subcultures, then, become communities of meanings and symbols that are not shared outside the group.

Stebbins goes on to describe and analyze other leisure commitments: theater, archaeology, and baseball. Each has distinctive emphases as well as the common elements of investment in skill and the building of a subculture. The nature of the activity has implications for the formation of the subculture. Theater has its diversity of tasks that have to be coordinated for a prescheduled event, the opening of the play. That deadline makes time a dimension that increases exponentially in impact as the fateful day approaches. Further, a hierarchy may develop based on the presumed importance of performance, organizational, and support functions. Even the growing stress surrounding the production may offer a sharing of experiences under pressure that are a factor in deepening the relationships of the amateur company.

Archaeology is less common as well as more dispersed geographically. Amateurs may strike out on their own to seek artifacts and join in organized "digs." Further, archaeology is unusual in being a scholarly discipline in which amateurs have made significant contributions. Therefore, the official journals in the field and the rigorous field research methods employed are more narrowly specified than for most leisure activities. Amateur archaeologists tend to have an educational background that enables them to cope with such literature, technical terminology, and training. It is a more knowledge-based activity than most. Also, the subculture includes considerable correspondence and informal communication as well as divisions among those who specialize in particular kinds of artifacts and cultures.

Perhaps at the other extreme in terms of intellectual requirements is amateur baseball. A seasonal sport that requires the organization of teams, leagues, schedules, equipment, and grounds, baseball tends to attract males with a history of successful sport participation in school and community leagues. The subculture of baseball also incorporates its own vocabulary, rituals, symbols, and even superstitions. Like theater, standards of professional excellence are available for comparison through television as well as live performance. And like theater and music, the availability of such performances on television competes for the time and support of audiences. Baseball differs in being more tied to age and the life course than music, theater, and archaeology. Relatively few compete past the age of 35 and almost none beyond 40. Rather, former competitors frequently become coaches, especially if their children are in Little League or other age-graded programs. Baseball also has a distinctively male subculture with its sex-segregated teams in which the history is not shared with the other sex. The vocabularies not only tend to be based on the form of the game, but also on masculine and often working-class cultures with images of conquest, strength, scoring, dominance, and aggression applied to both the game and to sexual interaction. Such elements have also been found in the subculture arising among rugby players in Britain (Sheard and Dunning, 1973) and are likely common to other sport groups. More recently Stebbins has gone on to investigate magicians and other practitioners of amateurism. In all cases, however, the common elements of skill, a symbolic subculture, and community are central.

Other Elements of Leisure Subcultures

Other investigators have focused more on locales such as bars with defined clienteles. In Britain, Smith (1985) was a participant observer in a "rough pub." There, almost all who came were "regulars" who had a place in the subculture defined by role, locational place for standing and interacting, and acceptance by other regulars. The patterns of interaction were relatively fixed and stable. Again, sex-role identities and appropriate vocabularies were crucial in gaining acceptance and a place in the patterned interaction and communication. Other studies of specialized bars that have clienteles defined by economic role such as businessmen or steel workers, sexual orientation, or social function illustrates the symbolic subcultural features of each. For example, a bar may be defined by economic status and function, such as a pick-up bar for white-collar office workers. In any such bar, failure to recognize and follow the subcultural norms will lead to some form of exclusion, however subtle or violent.

Another sport subculture, the world of Little League baseball, was studied by Gary Fine (1987). Here parental and child generations mix to form a subculture based on organized sport participation. The subculture is based on the ongoing interaction of players, coaches, parents, and officials. There is an organizational structure of the league and of age-adapted baseball. This structure continues as participants, especially players, pass through the system. Fine, however, focuses more on the situated interaction with its context of rules, negotiated applications, hierarchies of position, role-based vocabularies, and sequences of action. The organized games are understood as *performance* rather than play due to the social and spatial arrangements. Much of the culture of adult baseball is transferred and transformed in the Little League context. Slogans related to effort, team loyalty, and techniques of play are repeated and applied to the setting and occasion. Variations in skill are dealt with both by rules of participation and in more situational attributions and designations. As sport, the concern with winning may dominate the experience as defined by coaches, parents, and team leaders. The complex culture of baseball is imposed on children in ways that are filtered and adapted for their imputed cognitive and physical abilities.

The imposed structure is only one element of the social world. The network of communication is developed in the particular history of a team and league. Placement in the social hierarchy of the team is partly based on skill and position and partly dependent on other social elements. Fine distinguishes between the general Little League culture and the "idioculture" of a team with its specifics of past and present interaction and communication. From this perspective, there is a general subculture of Little League baseball that is carried out in the idioculture of the social group, the team.

Fine (1983) has also investigated the social world of fantasy games such as "Dungeons and Dragons" and "Chivalry and Sorcery." He finds that the groups that gather to play such games are composed primarily of late-adolescent and young adult males. The nature of the subculture reflects aspects of the games that highlight allegedly male role characteristics such as dominance, risk, aggression, and violence. The games and the vocabularies and behaviors of many players are overtly and subtly sexist. The game itself incorporates both structure and openness. A referee has considerable control over the contingent elements of the game. Players adopt roles and gain attributes through the rolling of dice. The shared vocabularies are derived from the history of participation and the given parameters of the game itself. Subcultural elements clearly differentiate those who have learned the vocabularies and roles and the rules from outsiders. Roles within the game are both cooperative and competitive, but the game, unlike sport, does not clearly identify winners and losers. Rather, the shared vocabulary and specialized knowledge create a temporary world in which there is action, outcomes, and yet a limited liability. Players are committed to the game and the group, but may take action and identity risks without jeopardizing their "real world" status and position. The shared fantasy creates a world of play with clear boundaries and an intensity of involvement in the experience. There are also formal and informal communication networks for each game. Unlike most leisure subcultures, however, interaction outside the game context appears to be limited.

Another predominantly male activity subculture is that of motocross motorcycle racing (Martin and Berry, 1979). This activity, however, combines motorized power with physical skill, risk, competition, and a "rough and ready" culture. Motocross bikes, unlike the road bikes associated with many motorcycle clubs, are "working" vehicles designed for speed and handling over the dirt course of hills, bumps, mud, and barriers. The club is a social group with its own culture. That culture, however, is embedded in the larger subculture of working class males. These men have grown up in a culture emphasizing speed, power, machinery, and demonstrations of masculinity. According to the analysis of the report, it is the experience of the track and the camaraderie that attracts and holds the commitment of the riders who are able to test their skill, strength, and selfhood against others. Unlike their jobs, in motocross they experience a world in which they demonstrate manhood and act out "aggressive activism" and individualism in ways impossible in the workplace. The small world of motocross is more than an exciting activity. It is a context for trying and testing meanings of selfhood that are learned in a larger subculture, but blocked in the worlds of work and family. The central instrument, the bike, along with all the symbolism of other equipment, clothing, and, most of all, the action itself form a significant social world.

A somewhat surprising slant on another leisure subculture was found in relation to sport parachuting. Such a sport is usually categorized as "high risk" by nonparticipants to whom the height and fall appear intimidating. A case study, however, reports that risk is claimed to be a minor factor in the experience by those who continue on beyond one or two jumps (Arnold, 1979). Rather, it is the skill mastery and technical development that are central to the exhilarating experience. In fact, the subculture of a parachuting club denigrates references to danger except in occasional jokes and stresses the advancement into higher levels of skydiving techniques. As with the other leisure subcultures, there is considerable emphasis on the development of specialized equipment and communication through personal exchange and published materials. Also, parachute club members commonly select costumes and badges that announce to the world the identity of skydiver.

A more ordinary activity has been studied from the interactionist perspective by Scott (1990). He argued that social worlds form around leisure interests in localized contexts that may be linked to wider associations and organizations. Contract bridge is an activity that may attain considerable centrality in the lives and schedules of "serious" players. The gradations of skill, vocabularies, action contexts, and social conventions are elements of the subculture in which serious players are distinguished from "social" bridge players. However, skill is not the only criterion of inclusion among the committed serious players. Giving priority to the particularities of scheduling in addition to association with structures of organization and symbols of skill identify those for whom bridge is more than just one activity among many.

There are any number of other examples that could be given of subcultures that develop around leisure activities. Some are related to animals such as the showing of dogs, cats, or horses. In western states, entire families devote high proportions of quite limited resources to the expensive activity of breeding, training, and showing or racing of quarter horses. Other social groups emerge around particular locations for rock-climbing, hang-gliding, or even panning for gold. Each subculture combines elements from a wider association of those engaged in the same activity with the possibility of a national organization, newsletters, journals, and meetings. The local manifestation, however, ordinarily will have some special characteristics based on history and composition. Such leisure is profoundly social and cannot be comprehended from any perspective that includes only individual experience.

Cohort Subcultures

Less attention has been given to leisure-related subcultures that are identified by age and cohort. Not only are pre-teens, teens, and other developmental designations identified partly by their leisure, but the patterns and symbols of those who are 14 today are different from those who were 14 in 1990 or 1980. "Cohorts," those born in the same period and who move through the life course experiencing the same historical events at the same age, are different from other cohorts at the same age. For example, the music and visual identifications of pre-teens must always be different from those of older brothers and sisters when they were the same age.

Age and cohort subcultures are further distinguished by social divisions, often based on family social status. Terminology changes, but most junior and senior high schools have a variety of subcultures. Studies of schools consistently find a mix of social groups that include the following:

- Elite conformists who dominate the reward structure of the school. They may be derived from the community status hierarchy and be distinguished by their social activities. They have been referred to as "socs" (soshes). In other schools, the athletic stars and their satellites are central and are referred to as "jocks" whether they are basketball players or cheerleaders. They have their own private parties, tacit rules of acceptability and exclusion, and high visibility in the school.

- Fringe nonconformists who are usually defined by the school authorities as "troublemakers." They may form gangs to organize their activity, both public and illicit. Often they have uniforms of jackets, hats, badges, and other apparel to identify them. Their regular activity is mostly away from school. They tend to be irregular or rebellious when engaged in school activity.

- Local culture members, sometimes referred to as "rednecks," who develop a subculture that contrasts with the elites. They reflect working-class backgrounds, are less likely to be college-bound, and also have distinctive country-style apparel and cultural interests.

- Counterculture students who have appearance styles that often come into conflict with school codes have more esoteric and unconventional tastes in music, and organize protests on political issues. These "freaks" form subgroups around particular interests in social issues, popular culture, and critical definitions of the school itself.

- Ethnic groups that are identified by race, language, or distinguishing cultural characteristics. They may be either conformist or nonconformist, engaged or resistant to academic norms, and organized or not.

Often forgotten in such typologies are the "ordinary students" who tend to blend more into the ongoing life of the school. Their subculture is more conformist, their tastes conventional, and their life styles inconspicuous. In many cases, they are the majority of students, but do not attract the attention of outside investigators and often not of the school's administrators and staff. They have no distinctive garb or vocabulary, outstanding behavioral customs, or distinctive values. They listen to "top 20 music," hang out a lot, go to class most of the time, and may have some special interest or activity that passes largely unnoticed by others. The mainstream cultures vary considerably from one region of the country to another, between urban and rural schools, and according to the economic status of the community. There are significant differences between schools from which 80-90 percent go on to higher education and those with dropout rates of over 50 percent. In general, however, there are a number of dimensions of such cohort subcultures that are common to most:

1) Their leisure styles are central to their group culture. Tastes in music, movies and videos, clothing, party environments, cars, and other leisure items vary in ways that clearly identify the subcultures. The specifics change from year to year and are often too subtle to be recognized from outside the culture. Fine distinctions among rock groups and styles may be highly significant for the social worlds of the school.

2) Symbols of inclusion and exclusion include what is worn, vocabularies and expressions, and where members gather. The school and its environs become a complex framework of bounded actions and interactions that have salient meanings both for the actors and for the excluded.

3) The gradations of conventionality and unconventionality are more than cultural preferences. They are a statement of identity that relates to the developmental concerns of the age. Social inclusion with peers, independence in relation to family and the adult world, and exploration of sexual identities are central, and not always consistent, aims for adolescent life. The subculture provides a primary context for the working out of these developmental processes.

What is distinctive about cohort subcultures is their transient nature. They are constantly changing, not in function but in form. The particularities are always in flux, partly due to the need to form and reform subcultures different from others that are similar and partly due to the changing environment. These subcultures are also markets for the business interests that target the enormous teen demand for popular culture: music, concerts, and other entertainment as well as precisely the "right" styles in clothing, sport equipment, and other leisure-related items. Obsolescence is the key marketing concept in replenishing the demand of teen markets. Promotion, especially via television, is designed to create continual demand. Such demand, however, is based on the identity symbols of the subcultures.

Ethnic Subcultures

There has been a distinct lack of attention to the factor of ethnicity in the study of leisure. Other than the sometimes published and sometimes suppressed results of national surveys that indicate racial variations in a few kinds of activity, the number of studies that focus on race and ethnicity is quite few. One study compares Mexican Americans to Anglo Americans in Texas (McMillen, 1983). Two dimensions of leisure are significant: participation and meaning. Activities with the same label may have somewhat different meanings from one culture to another. Several studies have indicated that Mexican American culture tends to be more family-oriented than many counterparts. Further, there is the issue of resources. Some ethnic groups have lower average incomes than national norms.

Surprisingly, McMillen, in a design consistent with most research in leisure participation, did not find significant differences between the ethnic sample of households and national survey results. Further, factors of social placement including family composition did not significantly impact participation. From this exploratory study, there comes a warning. We cannot assume that ethnic differences will be dramatic, at least as measured by frequency of participation in designated activities. An observational study of Mexican American use of Chicago parks found that the styles of interaction were based on the ethnic culture, especially kin ties of extended family and age and gender role segregation (Hutchison and Fidel, 1984). A comparison with African American and white patterns demonstrated that Mexican Americans formed larger groups based on extended family ties and engaged in activity with ethnic roots as well as mainstream sports (Hutchison, 1988). Again, the differences were in style more than in the activities themselves.

Several issues, however, have seldom been addressed in survey research. The first is that participation as numerical frequency may mask important differences in style. More recent research in the use of forest camp sites and picnic grounds by Hispanic groups has found a greater likelihood for relatively large family and friendship groups to use the site for family group activity of eating, games, and informal interaction. Second, so much leisure activity consists of informal interaction that significant differences based on activity lists are suppressed. And, third, the meanings of the activities may differ from one culture to another. For example, the value placed on extended family solidarity in Hispanic subcultures and the centrality of intergenerational loyalty may be obscured by an activity category of "visiting friends or relatives" or "picnicking." What seems indicated is that cultural factors can only be understood in a research framework that encompasses symbols, values, and meanings as well as counting behaviors.

A rather different example would be found in an ethnographic study of the leisure styles of computer technicians, marketers, and managers in Northern California's "Silicon Valley." In this subculture, education levels and incomes tend to be high. A high proportion of those in the upper-level subculture are relatively young, under 40, with family instability seen as a way of life. The environment offers an incredible variety of specialized restaurants with ethnic foods and obscure wines in dimly lit and rough panelled venues. Leisure styles include emphasis on the following elements:

- Eating out often in expensive small restaurants, usually with specialized menus and extensive wine lists.

- Considerable travel, often to Europe and the Pacific islands on holidays, but to nearer destinations on long weekends.

- An expenditure level close to total income with extensive use of "plastic money."

- "Sporty" clothing styles with recognized labels combined with cars, usually small and foreign, that symbolize more than transportation.

- Attention to appearance, not only clothes and hair, but also body contours enhanced by exercise programs in a multitude of establishments placed and priced for the target market.

The point is that ethnicity does not always indicate deprivation, minority status, or segregation. Rather, there are a variety of ethnic subcultures with distinctive leisure styles. The distinctions, however, are not found in studies that merely calculate frequency of participation in travel, walking, and attending concerts. Styles of travel as well the content of concerts from country western to Bach festivals vary widely.

The Web of Race and Ethnicity

Despite the growth of "minority" populations in the United States at a rate that will make the work force 50 percent of non-European derivation by the year 2030, very little attention has been given to the issue of cultural and racial differences in leisure. Even less attention has been devoted to the underlying causes of the differences that are identified. The fundamental issue is simple: what is the relative determinative force of culture and access to resources?

An early formulation of the issue was offered by Washburne (1978) in an analysis of recreation participation in California. The alternative suggested was that the primary cause of differences in activity choices was either economic marginality or ethnicity. African Americans were found to participate more than whites in team sports and less in wildland-based recreation. Controlling for socioeconomic factors reduced some of the differences, but others remained. Washburne concluded that ethnic differences are a factor in lower participation in outdoor resource-based recreation even though economic constraints are also relevant.

Other studies, however, have found significant differences based on socio-economic factors, especially in activities with high access and travel costs (Kelly, 1980). One analysis suggests that middle-class blacks may have patterns similar to middle-class whites, but that economic factors become primary for those who are poor and excluded from even modest-cost activities (Stamps and Stamps, 1985). Both ethnic cultures and economic deprivation may be salient, but with different activities and at different economic levels. At least, there is considerable doubt cast on the either/or formulation of the issue (Hutchison, 1988).

Again, part of the lack of clarity may be due to the oversimplified dependent variables of many of the studies. List of activities do not reveal profound differences in the ways in which different cultures eat together, form recreation groups, subdivide in leisure settings by age and gender, choose topics of conversation, and defer according to symbols of status and honor. For example, the place of children in adult interaction varies widely from one ethnic group to another. Some such factors have been suggested by earlier as well as more recent research.

A classic study of black culture in Chicago (Drake and Cayton, 1945) analyzed differences in social engagement within the confines of that expanding wartime ghetto. Perhaps the most enduring finding was that there were a variety of subcultures within the African American community ranging from the alienated to the conventional. At one extreme, a conventional middle class mirrored white social organization and styles. The black community, however, was found to be stratified with leisure styles that were anything but uniform. The very concept that there is a single ethnic culture designated by a racial label has been disproven over and over by black scholars from Franklin Frazier and W. E.

B. DuBois to William J. Wilson (1987). Further, the civil rights movement and the recognition of the positive significance of African American identity has added new dimensions to ethnicity with differential impacts in different strata of black society. Historical eras are not all alike.

Another Chicago study with a sample limited by its telephone directory base (Woodard, 1988) did not find strong race-based differences in leisure patterns, especially in informal kinds of activity. Rather, the "core" of activity remains central across ethnic/racial categories in an urban area. Seven of the eight most common activities were informal domestic engagements, mostly social and familial. Social class was more significant in differentiating participation in metropolitan activities that require travel and more expensive access. Age and gender are important for other kinds of urban engagement. The analysis provides evidence that a total focus on ethnicity as the determinant of leisure patterns is misdirected. Such other factors as age, gender, income, and education, however, may have somewhat different impacts in different cultures. Any design adequate to the task of understanding ethnicity should incorporate the interaction of such factors.

Another possibility is that both ethnicity and marginality have been over-simplified. On the one hand, all socialization is within a specific ethnic culture, be it black or nonblack, African American or North European. Current research indicating that there is no single "Hispanic" culture, but persons of Mexican, Cuban, Latin-American, and other origins, is one example of the need to specify cultures and subcultures. Cuban Americans in the United States, however, are also stratified by salient socioeconomic variables. Ethnicity is more than a label; it is a profound and complex context of socialization in which value systems and world views differ in ways that affect every aspect of life. Further, such socialization is both reinforced and modified from generation to generation. For immigrant populations, the separate identities of first-generation cultures seem to give way to assimilation aims in the second generation and then to attempts to recapture ethnic roots in the third and fourth. Conflicting trends such as intermarriage and religious identification are operative in the same subcultures. Socialization is, on the one hand, cumulative from generation to generation, and differential in the historical sequence of generations. At present, there is no study emphasizing leisure that even begins to encompass such issues.

Marginality, as well, is more complex than can be comprehended by a few survey indices such as income and education level. For example, a set of interviews of older African American men and women in a Midwest community found that they seldom engaged in water-based activities such as swimming and boating except for male engagement in stream fishing. The explanatory clue was that most had been children in the St. Louis area when public pools were closed to black children. They had no access to the places most urban children learn to swim. Such access remained closed to their families long enough that failure to be attracted to and comfortable with water built up over generations in those families. Today their grandchildren have access to a different socialization opportunity structure. For decades, however, the deprivation was cumulative. As a consequence, structural racism was a central factor in shaping attitudes toward a recreational environment.

Marginality is more than control of economic resources. Racism has meant physical danger as well as social rejection in some times and places. The territoriality of children, organized or not, had led to those who control areas to physically attack so-called invaders. This was true for Jews in Brooklyn, blacks in Montgomery, and Italians in South Chicago. Racial and ethnic identity in some times and places is *the* ruling dimension of access and exclusion, by law and by custom.

Social class is more than an index of classification. As analyzed in Chapter 8, it is a total context of life that shapes attitudes as well as resources. An oppressed minority culture is impacted in fundamental definitions of the world as well as in opportunities for social and economic participation. William J. Wilson's (1987) study of the "underclass" of the South Chicago ghetto area stresses that the context is more than a combination of poverty and race. Rather, the withdrawal of economic institutions and of the black achievers has left the area bereft of viable opportunity and of models of success. Only a fundamental restructuring of the entire area including economic enterprise and investment, schools, housing, transportation, and other basic institutions can turn walls into doorways. No one element of deprivation is the key to transformation; all are interconnected.

This does not mean that there is some sort of "culture of poverty" that dominates the minds of ghetto residents and renders programs designed to create opportunity meaningless. A study of unemployed black and Hispanic youth, also in South Chicago (Raymond and Kelly, 1990), found that most do find some sense of identity and ability in skill-based leisure activity. More important, however, was the consistent response that more than anything else they desired a chance to get past the barriers into some economic, educational, and social opportunity for life with a future. Despite local unemployment rates of over 50 percent, most had not lost their hopes and dreams. What they lacked was any idea of how to get over the thresholds and through the closed doors that blocked the way to meaningful engagement. Recreational opportunity helps, but is no substitute for opportunity beyond one more temporary fast-food job.

Further, in American society, race is something more than ethnicity. Race is an assigned social identification that cannot, for most, be altered. The historical assimilation of ethnic groups, the Irish and Eastern Europeans for example, into mainstream society is more a dampening than an acceptance of differences. Most Americans have opted out of any primary differentiating identification. Racial identification, on the other hand, is relatively permanent. Further, social definitions have assumed the differences of race to be greater and more enduring than those of language, culture, or religion. Race often totally excludes from interaction, determines residence, and remains central even to informal exchange. This remains a racist society, in structure as well as invidious attitudes. At the very least, racism remains an accentuating theme of the social structure and culture that compounds every other aspect of differentiation.

The earlier ethnicity vs. marginality formulation of the issue appears to be grossly oversimplified, even in the context of conventional survey research. Differences in leisure participation by racial designations and ethnic identifications compound reinforcing and conflicting cultural, economic, political, and social factors. Even regional variations are accentuated by racial discrimination formulas and ethnic solidarity. Being an Orthodox Jew is quite different in Brooklyn and in Des Moines, Iowa. Being an African American is different in Detroit, Selma, and Seattle. There are even some suggestions that race-designated subcultures are quite different in small Southern communities, Northeastern industrial cities, and in the West.

Further, ethnic cultures are stratified. There are significant differences according to economic resources, educational background, and social organization. In terms of orientations to the social system, economic marginality combines with social exclusion to produce subcultures that devalue long-term life investment for more immediate gratification. Integration and exclusion from social institutions are factors in conventional vs. alienated social patterns. Mixed through such social dimensions are the cultural symbols of language, dress, religion, and customs. How much difference is chosen out of perceived options and how much is determined by forces of exclusion? How can they be sorted out in an analysis that included historical change? Ethnicity is stratified, and marginality is cumulative and multidimensional. There are no simple models of explanation and no one-dimensional solutions to problems.

REFERENCES

Arnold, D. O. (1979). A sociologist looks at sport parachuting. In A. Yiannikis et al. (Eds.), *Sport sociology: Contemporary themes.* Dubuque, IA: Kendall/ Hunt Publishing.

Bellah, R. N., Madsen R., Sullivan, W., Swidler, A., and Tipton, S. (1985). *Habits of the heart: Individualism and commitment in American life.* Berkeley, CA: University of California Press.

Drake, S. C., and Cayton, H. (1945). *Black metropolis: A study of Negro life in a Northern city.* New York, NY: Harcourt Brace Jovanovich, Inc.

Fine, G. A. (1983). *Shared fantasy: Role-playing games as social worlds.* Chicago, IL: University of Chicago Press.

Fine, G. A. (1987). *With the boys: Little League baseball and preadolescent culture.* Chicago, IL: University of Chicago Press.

Fine, G. A., and Kleinman, S. (1979). Rethinking subculture: An interactionist analysis. *American Journal of Sociology, 85,* 1-20.

Hutchison, R. (1988). A critique of race, ethnicity, and social class in recent leisure-recreation literature. *Journal of Leisure Research, 20,* 10-30.

Hutchison, R., and Fidel, K. (1984). Mexican-American recreation activities: A reply to McMillen. *Journal of Leisure Research, 16,* 344-349.

Kelly, J. R. (1980). Outdoor recreation participation: A comparative analysis. *Leisure Sciences, 3,* 129-154.

Martin, T. W., and Berry, K. (1979). Competitive sport in post-industrial society: The case of the motocross racer. In A. Yiannakis et al. (Eds.) *Sport sociology: Contemporary themes.* Dubuque, IA: Kendall/Hunt Publishing Company.

McMillen, J. B. (1983). The social organization of leisure among Mexican-Americans. *Journal of Leisure Research 15,* 164-173.

Raymond, L. P., and Kelly, J. (July, 1990). "Leisure activities of unemployed black and hispanic urban youth." Paper at the World Congress of Sociology. Madrid, Spain.

Scott, D. (1990). An analysis of adult play groups: Theoretical and empirical considerations. Unpublished Ph.D. dissertation, The Pennsylvania State University, University Park, PA.

Sheard, K. G., and Dunning, E. (1973). The rugby football club as a type of male preserve. *International Review of Sport Sociology, 8,* 5-24.

Shibutani, T. (1961). *Society and Personality.* Englewood Cliffs, NJ: Prentice-Hall, Inc.

Smith, M. (1985). A participant observer study of a "rough" working-class pub. *Leisure Studies, 4,* 293-306.

Stamps, S. M., and Stamps, M. (1985). Race, class, and leisure activities of urban residents. *Journal of Leisure Research, 17,* 40-56.

Stebbins, R. (1979). *Amateurs: On the margin between work and leisure.* Beverly Hills, CA: Sage Publications, Inc.

Stebbins, R. (1992). *Amateurs, professionals, and serious leisure.* Montreal, Quebec, Canada: McGill—Queen's University Press.

Sutton-Smith, B., and Roberts, J. (1982). Play, games, and sports. In H. Triandis and A. Heron (Eds.) *Handbook of cross-cultural psychology: Developmenal psychology,* pp. 425-443. Boston, MA: Allyn & Bacon.

Washburne, R. (1978). Black under-participation in wildland recreation: Alternative explanations. *Leisure Sciences, 1,* 175-189.

Wilson, W. J. (1987). *The truly disadvantaged: The inner city, the underclass, and public policy.* Chicago, IL: University of Chicago Press.

Woodard, M. D. (1988). Class, regionality, and leisure among urban black Americans: The post-civil rights era. *Journal of Leisure Research, 20,* 87-105.

CHAPTER 12

The Functions of Leisure

T he government of France had, for a time, a Ministry of Leisure. Why? The statements of its Minister argued that leisure is both a human right and a significant element of the social system. He further contended that the allocation and distribution of free time and other leisure resources is a public issue. Why? The fundamental premise seemed to be that leisure is an essential part of the work-family-education-leisure balance of life. As a dimension of life, it is woven into the social system.

In the United States, on the other hand, no proposal for such a cabinet-level federal department has been offered by anyone in the political arena. Why not? In a different culture, productivity and national security are seen as paramount values. Most ideologies or value systems include leisure, if at all, only in a secondary place, contributing somewhat to what is "really important." Imagine the ridicule of the first senatorial candidate who might announce that the right to leisure was a central plank in his platform!

Nevertheless, leisure is frequently seen as contributing to the continuation and development of the social system. Not only has leisure become a major segment of the economy, but has important relationships to economic productivity, family formation and cohesion, and individual learning and development. From the perspective of the social system, leisure is said to be "functional;" that is, it contributes to the society.

The Institutional Framework

The basic hypothesis of the functional perspective is that the society is composed of an integrated set of institutions. The premise, generally taken for granted, is that the social system is worth preserving with no more than evolutionary and adaptive change. The model, called "structure functional," systemic, or institutional, views the society as a system of complementary institutions.

The social context of life is, for the most part, regular and predictable. While specific schools, families, or corporations may come in and out of existence, the system remains relatively stable. Even in a period of rising divorce rates, in some form or other most adults and children live most of their lives in families. The social system depends on the family system to provide for the reproduction and nurture of children, most housing and daily maintenance, sexual regulation, holding and transmission of property, a unit of consumption, and identification as well as a host of other functions such as being the most common environment for intimacy in relationships. The family is so central to the system that children are prepared for its roles and responsibilities, its forms are reinforced by law, and its norms are held to be sacred and above question in most religious contexts. As an institution, the family consists of a set of roles—father, mother, etc.—for which there are agreed upon expectations. Those roles are articulated into a consistent, if somewhat flexible, form.

Social institutions, then, are composed of regular roles and are organized into systems of normative behavior based on the functions or contributions to the society as a whole. While some variation is permitted in carrying out those roles, there are limits and sanctions for those who clearly violate the norms. Enforcement of the norms is partly a matter of consensus, partly of ideology, and partly of organizational rewards and penalties. Behavior in such a social system has regular and prescribed patterns based on an agreement as to what is right and what can be expected of others.

Each primary institution has one or more central functions. Those of the family, as outlined, revolve around children and day-to-day life. The economy produces the goods and services necessary for the maintenance of life. The polity provides regulation and national security. The school is responsible for preparing children for responsible adult participation, for learning and socialization. The church is said to give an aura of sacred reinforcement to the social value system. Together, they form an integrated system that as a whole provides a viable and stable context for life. From the functional perspective, each contributes in a special way to the survival requirements of the system.

Social solidarity or cohesiveness requires that the institutions be functionally interrelated in ways consistent with an overall value system that is learned and accepted by those living in the system. A society may change or evolve in response to external forces or internal factors such as new technologies. For example, industrialization and urbanization made former agrarian patterns of organization obsolete. Technologies such as the car, the telephone, or television brought about necessary changes in provisions and regulations of travel and communication. Such change, however, does not overthrow the system itself; there is no social revolution.

Life within such a system is not uniform. As introduced in Chapter 9, all complex systems are stratified in ways that are usually based on economic roles and some division of labor. The functional argument is that such stratification in functions and rewards is necessary to attract individuals into economic roles that are demanding, essential, and require arduous preparation. The result, whatever the basis of social divisions, is that some have greater access to and control of resources. Some have greater opportunities for self-determination than others. Often such stratification is based on factors such as age, gender, or race rather than economic function. The point is that social systems tend to work better for some than for others. In complex societies, there are all kinds of differentiating factors that operate to open and close opportunities throughout the life course.

In Chapter 19, the sequences of roles through the life course will be examined more closely. Here it is important to note that social institutions are the context for both continuities and changes in those roles. Life has a work career that begins in the preparatory institution of the school and continues through a sequence of positions in the economy until retirement or death. In each of our lives there is a family or primary relationship career that begins in one's family of orientation, usually continues through one or more families in which the individual takes adult roles, often including the rearing and launching of children, and frequently has a penultimate period of separation by widowhood. Community roles tend to intersect with work and family and be based on factors such as economic position and family composition. Religion may take a central, peripheral, or erratic place in the scheme of roles and commitment. Leisure, too, has a career that begins with the play of children with family and peers. It continues through school and the emerging independence of adolescence to adult engagements. These include the familial orientations of parents and later-life reinvestment to a final constriction in frailty. All these roles with their expectations, resources, and associations are interrelated. The life course is woven out of the threads of many careers that have institutional contexts. Life is not only social in terms of relationships, but is social in its ordered institutional context.

What is the place of leisure in this institutional framework? One possibility is that leisure is emerging in a new "postindustrial" social system to become an institution along with the economy, polity, family, and the others. That would require that leisure uniquely or at least centrally provide something necessary to the social system. Leisure would have to be an organized and identifiable sub-system in which something is accomplished that is required for the survival of the society. It would consist of a set of integrated roles, a recognized purpose, and the reinforcement of the fundamental ideology of the society.

It can be argued that leisure is a context for a number of useful functions such as recuperation for work, primary bonding, and individual expression that is crucial to learning and development. It is more difficult to support the argument that leisure uniquely provides for such functions. More important, each function seems to be secondary to that of another institution. Further, leisure in modern societies tends to be quite diffuse and varied rather than have a single organized set of institutionalized providers with a clearly articulated organizational structure. We speak of the school system, the family structure even though it is becoming increasingly varied, and the economic system. We seldom refer to a "leisure system" or a recognized set of consistent leisure roles. Leisure is characterized by its variability more than its regularity.

Nevertheless, leisure is frequently promoted as functional in contemporary social systems. In three areas, leisure is claimed to contribute significantly to the maintenance and development of the society. In simpler societies, leisure is often found to be so enmeshed in the ongoing round of life as to be difficult to identify and separate out from work, family, and community life. In more complex societies, work, family, school, church, and state tend to be more separated in timetables and interactions as well as organizations. In much the same way, leisure is seen as identifiable—distinguishable, if not always separate in time and place from other activity. Further, leisure is defined as valuable in the contributions it makes to the *basic* institutions of the social system. Leisure is integrated into the system.

The Economic Functions of Leisure

Modern economic systems are characterized by extraordinarily complex patterns of the division of labor. Most economic roles are highly specialized and articulated into large production and distribution systems. As a consequence, the degrees of authority, autonomy, skill utilization, academic and other preparation, specialized knowledge, mental and physical effort, routine, stress, environmental dangers, risk, and other elements vary considerably. Partly in correspondence to these factors and to demand and scarcity on the labor market, rewards also vary widely. The replacement value of some specialized and crucial workers is quite high; that of others extremely low.

In such a system, leisure has two main functions: the support of productivity and of consumption. Both are based on the activity of individuals in relation to their economic roles as producers and consumers. Leisure is seen as supportive of such economic functions rather than as fulfilling a function.

Production Roles

In economic analysis, workers are defined as "human capital." From this perspective, individuals gain through the acquisition of skills the abilities required to contribute to economic enterprise. These skills may be gained in education, some form of apprenticeship, or though other experience including leisure. Such skills form the human capital that matches other economic investment in the production process. In a perfect system, workers are rewarded in income, working conditions, and prestige in relation to the value and scarcity of their human capital. Further, economies grow and develop in relation to the investment of human as well as economic capital. For this reason, education is often held to be the critical factor in the development of an economy in world markets.

Through the developing period of industrialization, entrepreneurs discovered that there are limits to the ability of men, women, and children to work productively. Further, various technologies proved to be more efficient than people. As a result, some categories of workers—first it was children—were defined out of the work force. At the same time and partly due to labor organization and conflict, the hours of labor were reduced to increase human productivity in relation to capital and other investments in the process. Workers bargained and struck for, among other things, time for leisure—"8 hours for what we will." Owners and managers most often saw leisure from a different perspective, as a time for recuperation for higher productivity on the job. Owners attempted to provide and even enforce "constructive" leisure that would contribute to productivity (see Chapters 3 and 4).

In the contemporary economy, the same principle still applies. Leisure in the form of "constructive recreation" is promoted as necessary for economic productivity. There are a number of dimensions of this function:

- Escape, relief, and change are necessary as a contrast to the routines and requirements of the workplace. They provide a compensation for the necessary rigors and restrictions of work life (Wilensky, 1960).

- Leisure, especially activity that is regular and physically demanding, has health benefits that support productivity by reducing absenteeism and illness on the job and increasing strength, attention, endurance, and mental acuity. Studies indicate that workers who engage in regular physical activity are less subject to stress, cardiovascular problems, and a variety of other illnesses (Driver, Brown, and Peterson, 1991).

- Leisure may enhance the human capital aspect of a work force by yielding new or enhanced skills and abilities. This is especially the case for leisure that is devoted to adult education, formal or informal.

The focus is always on productivity. Some corporations may provide facilities and programs of recreation at no or subsidized cost for employees considered valuable. The convenience and reduced time and money costs are presumed to increase participation in activities that support economic efficiency. Promoters point to reduced absenteeism, health costs, and worker turnover as outcomes of such programs. Although it is difficult to measure results assigned to the multiple contexts of such activity or control for other factors, the economic function of leisure is presumed. Increasingly, recreation programs are combined with "wellness" programs that are more focused on health promotion and support.

From a human capital perspective, leisure is seen as one context for the gaining and support of productive economic *ability*. It provides needed rest and relaxation, a contrast to the presumed rigors of work. It enhances both mental and physical health in ways that may be returned to the workplace as increased efficiency.

Two additional comments are relevant. First, in the interests of the employer, such leisure should be constructive rather than debilitating. It should be *re-creation*, a replenishment of productive capacity rather than a depletion or loss. As a result, not only employers, but also public institutions, offer opportunities that are presumed to yield such positive outcomes. Consistently through history, activity that has been considered to be a negative factor in productivity has been restricted, regulated, and even banned by law. Second, social investments in leisure come to be justified and evaluated in terms of their alleged positive outcomes. The "benefits" of recreation come to be framed largely in terms of their functional contribution to productivity.

Leisure, then, is viewed as "useful"—not for its own sake or as a human right, but as complementary to what is really important. Leisure is secondary to work roles rather than a class of fundamental human activities. In this functional model, leisure is not an institution, but finds its meaning in the institution of the economy.

Leisure as Consumption

The second economic function of leisure is in consumption. The production and distribution segments of an economy require a market for their goods and services. In a society in which access to "necessities" is more or less universal and replacement only periodic, some other goods and services have to capture a market in order to maintain a return on investment. Further, as the production of goods becomes more efficient, new goods and services may make up the gap between capacity and consumption. Incentives such as obsolescence and style may provide some markets. But the proportion of the work force and of capital investment needed simply to maintain production for existing markets tends to be reduced by technology. New markets are needed to fuel economic expansion.

More and more, one of those expanding economic areas is in leisure. Over 90 percent of spending on leisure in the United States is in the market sector. Leisure is now at least the third largest sector of the economy. It provides investment opportunities and jobs in its multiplying and proliferating enterprises. Most of tourism, sport, the media, and popular culture as well as all sorts of equipment, apparel, space, and other facilities and support are provided by the market sector of the economy. Recreation is very big business in developed economies that have long since passed the point of scarcity of necessities. Also, the services dimension of leisure industry, which tend to be labor intensive and provide considerable employment, may expand even faster than manufacturing in a highly developed economy.

The other dimension of functional leisure consumption is in the economic reward system for labor. As analyzed from a critical perspective in Chapter 25, leisure increasingly has become central to the reward structure of the economy. When a high proportion of members of social system have access to housing, transportation, food, medical and educational support, and other necessities, then incentives to work productively may focus on "something more." What enhances the quality of life beyond basic existence? What, that is provided through the economy, is adequate incentive not just to show up at work, but to increase one's human capital? In short, how can the reward system draw workers to greater effort, skill, and loyalty?

One answer is clearly in leisure. Not only the vacation, the longer weekend, and the limited work week, but also in opportunity and resources, leisure is central to that "something more" that ties workers to their jobs. Failure to work productively means exclusion from the reward system. A higher level of preparation may yield disproportionate rewards. Workers can only sleep in so many bedrooms and drive so many cars. But, at least in theory, in leisure they may be insatiable. There is always a new or enhanced experience possible that may be offered by greater expenditure. The environment, implement, or even leisure-related ability may be improved through consumption. If there is time, we can always spend more on leisure that is marketed to suggest the possibility of infinite pleasure. In reality, we may settle for a new camper and a three-week trip, but we can always spend more on our hopes and dreams.

The truth is that the experience of work itself may be quite limited. The routines of many jobs are only marginally adjustable to yield richer experiences. But, in theory, the possibilities of leisure are almost without limit, especially if we are convinced that there is a direct correlation between spending and satisfaction.

Social Functions and Social Bonding

Leisure may also be seen as functional in relation to social institutions. As will be presented in Chapter 13, leisure is a context for the celebration of the culture in its communal or festival manifestations. Further, leisure is a context for the development and expression of social bonding. The building of relationships of trust and sharing, essential for meaningful human life, is more than a matter of common tasks. Relationships, at any age, are expressed in common play.

Community, Celebration, and Social Cohesion

The philosophical nuances of this argument will be developed in the next chapter. Here, from the functional perspective, it is important to note the sociological basis of the thesis. Societies may be totalitarian, ruled and held together by force. Or, more commonly, they are at least partly consensual, held together by agreement rather than by coercion. That agreement or consensus has to be taught, accepted, transmitted, and reinforced. It consists of a fundamental acceptance of the *rightness* of the system.

Any society has some sort of central value system. Sometimes it is relatively simple and taken-for-granted. Others may be officially promulgated ideologies in which the form and the substance are held sacred or above criticism. In any case, the value system is shared and taught through a set of symbols. Those symbols include vocabulary, concepts, signs such as flags and emblems, legends masking as history, and festivals. The values are transmitted not only in the school but also in the church, the family, and in play. Children's games reflect the set of symbols. Stories communicate the consensual ideas and ways of defining the world. And communal festivals dramatize and celebrate the basic values.

The examples are endless: Children used to play games like cowboys and Indians in which the cowboys were always the "good guys" and the colonization of Native American territory the assumed goal. Legends about major historical figures are repeated generation after generation until they become historical "facts." Flags appear everywhere, even in churches. Community festivals like the 4th of July literally parade the colors and call for patriotic response. In all such contexts, dissent and deviation are discouraged and sometimes punished by legal action. All in all, the symbols of the validity of the system are presented, reinforced, and celebrated. Even the supposedly transcendent aura of religion becomes one element in the scheme as "Gott mit uns" is translated into every language and culture.

The leisure dimensions of this celebration are manifold. As suggested, there are the community festivals—mass picnics with bands, flags, prayers, and parades. More subtle and probably more important are all the ways in which games and sports are devised to reflect the value system. The Super Bowl is not just a game; via the media it is a national celebration.

Again, the function is the support of social cohesion. A social system composed of diverse population segments may be divided by ethnic background and culture, language, economic strata, region, political power, religion, and myriad other factors. How, in a mass and diverse society, can it all be held together without tanks in the streets and thought-police in every institution? It is by agreement on the rightness of the system, a sharing of symbols, and a celebration of essential unity. Therefore, any game, story, contest, display, festival, or ritual that reinforces that unity provides a crucial function in a society in which individuals actually live most of their lives in small and bounded worlds.

The Family and Social Bonding

According to an analysis by sociologists Neil Cheek and William Burch (1976) the most significant function of leisure is related to social bonding. From this perspective, the nearby fabric of the social system revolves around the family and other face-to-face living groups. As outlined earlier, the family has multiple functions in the social system. No other institution takes on as many functions: reproduction, nurture, socialization, shelter, nourishment, property holding and transmission, consumption unit, and often production as well. Anything that supports the bonds of the family makes a significant contribution to the society. When "family" is defined more broadly to include all primary relationships of stability, intimacy, and sharing, then it is at the center of life throughout the life course. The family, however, is not the only important set of relationships. Neighborhood and school peers are vital for children and youth. Work companionship is a significant element in work environments. Communities are composed of smaller sets of organized relationships essential to fulfilling its common tasks.

The crucial issue concerns the nature of the relationships. Why doesn't each individual just act in his or her own interest? What is the nature of loyalty, responsibility, and caring even to the degree of altruism and self-sacrifice? Part of the answer has to do with the fundamentally social nature of the human animal. We learn that we are profoundly social, connected with others in ways that make life possible and meaningful, as we move along the path of life. Another part of the answer is that we develop such relationships in our common life, in its tasks and in its play.

Why play? Isn't it enough to work together, live together, and accomplish the tasks of daily life together? It would seem not. Primary relationships are more than concerted action. The dimensions of life together are expressive and purposeful, emotional as well as rational, spontaneous and regulated. Much of the richness of communication and sharing comes in off-task exchange. Relationships are more than a set of expectations and obligations. The caring and sharing frequently comes outside the requirements of survival.

The schema is reciprocal. On the one hand, we engage in play that adds dimensions to relationships that make them attractive, exciting, and even fun. On the other hand, relating to others in communication and action is itself satisfying. Leisure, as chosen and relatively open activity, allows for a focus on the relationships rather than on some external goal or outcome. Considerable leisure is "relational" (Kelly, 1983) in its focus on the expressing of the relationship more than the activity. All sorts of events are primarily environments of communication. Just as important, there are interstitial episodes of off-task interaction sprinkled through the day, even at work.

There have even been suggestions that women have, in Western cultures, become more oriented toward relationships than outcomes. Women may make decisions based more on the consequences for other persons than on abstract principles (Gilligan, 1982). Relational leisure that is directed more toward expressing and developing relationships than recognized outcomes may be a gender-differentiated style. If so, it would be consistent with the fact that in such societies women have been assigned primary responsibility for the maintenance of the family and other primary relationships.

A basic issue is whether primary relationships, family and friendships, can survive without the context of leisure. Is leisure essential to the survival of the family and other stable and intimate relationships? If so, it comes very close to having an essential function in the society.

Leisure and Human Development

The developmental dimensions of leisure will be examined in Chapter 19 on the life course and in Chapter 20. Here we will only outline the issues within the functional model.

Some slogans suggest that play is the work of children in the sense that it is their central developmental context. In play children learn motor skills, social skills, and coping skills. George Herbert Mead (1934) analyzed games as the context of learning about articulated social roles. Jean Piaget's (1952) theory of development holds play as central. Arguments for the importance of such organized play as Little League baseball are usually based on the learning that occurs as well as the experience of the game. Some even go so far as to suggest that children's play reflects adult culture in ways that prepare girls and boys for their differentiated adult roles.

After all, what are the central developmental tasks of human beings in this social system? And, relevant to the functional argument, where do they take place? The exploration and establishment of sexual identities, central for adolescents, takes place primarily in leisure. The finding and defining of dyadic relationships that lead to marriage are commonly in leisure. The nurturing and expressive play of parents with children is in leisure. The discovery of new domains of competence and of social integration for older adults is at least in part in leisure. As the previous section introduced, leisure is central to much social bonding throughout life.

The functional argument, then, contains a significant developmental dimension that will be detailed later. The point here is to recognize that dimension as a part of the analysis. Further, the implication is that leisure is not peripheral to human development. Rather, many essential learning and developing meanings of life are situated in leisure. Such development is not simply accidental or spontaneous. Rather, it is a recognized element of the organization of the social system. All sorts of opportunities and environments are supported that facilitate developmental activity, from the playground at school to the senior card club. Development is institutionalized in leisure contexts, organized for accepted social purposes. In short, it is deemed functional.

Critical Caveats

One basic criticism of the functional approach is that it appears to assume that the social system is functioning, that its maintenance is an accepted and acceptable goal. There is less than total agreement on this far-reaching premise in any society. Certainly there are questions to be raised in any contemporary social system—developed or developing, Eastern or Western, capitalist or socialist. These issues have been or will be dealt with more fully in other chapters of this book.

Here a summary of such critical questions will serve to place functional analysis in a more diverse context:

There is the possibility that leisure as actually practiced may be dysfunctional rather than functional. That is, it may contribute to the dissolution of the social system in some ways. For example, there is evidence that leisure in modern societies tends to become more and more "privatized." It draws people away from common and community-building activity to retreat into enclaves of their own entertainment. The home as electronic entertainment center attracts actors away from live action and interaction. The family as the social focus of leisure shields people from larger communities of concern and sharing. The market of leisure industry responds to and creates territories of separation based on economic resources and exclusivity. The social world of leisure may yield results counter to the building of a society of consensual responsibility.

Also, the economic systems of leisure are frequently based on possession and the purchase of entertainment. Not only may leisure bought on credit lessen the economic necessity of saving, but leisure images may misdirect economic resources away from the needs of some to the extravagances of others. Leisure, after all, when based on buying rather than acting always has an element of unfulfilled dreams.

Other critiques of the functionality of leisure are based on the fact of inequality within societies. A question seldom asked is "Functional for whom?" It would be difficult to sustain an argument that there is equality in leisure opportunity or resources. For example, functional leisure for women has commonly meant activity supporting family production. The limits and constraints are clear. For workers in routinized jobs, leisure may support an acceptance of alienated work rather than a constructive transformation of work conditions. For children, socialization in play may become in reality an oversocialization of conformity into roles such as those of war that are in the long term destructive. The household as a leisure consumption unit may become fixated on its possessions rather than the quality of its bonding. The critique raises the issue of differential interests. Leisure may be more accurately viewed in its variety as functional for those with power and a control of resources by truncating or limiting the potential of others with limited self-determination. Again, the question subverting the functional model is "Who benefits?" The assumption that what is good for the few is good for all is placed into question.

REFERENCES

Cheek, N., and Burch, W. (1976). *The social organization of leisure in human society.* New York, NY: Harper & Row, Publishers, Inc.

Driver, B. L., Brown, P., and Peterson, G. (1991). *The benefits of leisure.* State College, PA: Venture Publishing, Inc.

Gilligan, C. (1982). *In a different voice.* Cambridge, MA: Harvard University Press.

Kelly, J. R. (1983). *Leisure identities and interactions.* London, England: Allen & Unwin, Inc.

Mead, G. H. (1934). *Mind, self, and society.* Chicago, IL: University of Chicago Press.

Piaget, J. (1952). *Play, dreams, and imitation in childhood.* In G. Cattegno and F. Hodgson (Trans.), *Play, dreams, and imitation in childhood.* New York, NY: W. W. Norton & Co., Inc.

Wilensky, H. (1960). Work, careers, and social integration. *International Social Science Journal, 12,* 543-560.

CHAPTER 13

Creating and Celebrating the Culture

I n the most basic sense, sociological meanings of culture revolve around "the way of life of a social group" (Theodorson and Theodorson, 1969, p. 95). Since the use of leisure is part of this way of life, leisure may be thought of as part of the culture. Humans create their ways of using leisure no less than any other part of life. As Kando pointed out, culture may also be thought of as "the typical ways in which a society, or type of society, spends its time when not working" (Kando, 1980, p. 40). Here the term "popular culture" is sometimes used. While popular culture has no precise meaning, it may refer to middle-class culture, the most visible culture or the culture between the extremes of the elites of society and the poor, peasants or "folk culture." For the elites, the term "high culture" is often used, which may refer to the culture of the social elite, culture that is exploratory, revolutionary or creative, the repository of society's great cultural traditions or as excellent culture (Kando, 1980, p. 41). In many cases, high culture in North America refers almost exclusively to European culture. Thus, "classical" music refers primarily to the music of Germany, France, Austria and elsewhere rather than the most important music of India or China.

Finally, it is sometimes said that our own society has a "mass culture," which refers to "Elements of culture that develop in large, heterogeneous societies as a result of common exposure to and experience of the mass media . . . The emergence of mass culture is a part of the process of the development of common unifying cultural values and attitudes in the new and vast population of modern national social units (Johnson and Johnson, 1978, p. 53).

All of these kinds of cultures may be said to owe their existence to the leisure which humans make.

The Role of Leisure in Creating Culture

In the ancient Athenian culture which produced Plato and Aristotle, leisure was thought to be of a higher order of work and was closely associated with learning.

Leisure was a way of life devoted to self-understanding and perfection. Those who had the privilege of leading such lives, supported by slaves and women who did most of society's work, were expected to behave in ways which would literally create the culture of the society. It was those who had leisure who would write the important poetry, discover great philosophical truths, contribute to art, drama and religious understanding. Thus, the link between leisure and culture was a direct one from the first conceptualization of leisure.

The Swiss philosopher Josef Pieper argued that leisure is the basis of culture. For Pieper, culture " . . . is the quintessence of all the natural goods of the world and of those gifts and qualities which, while belonging to man, lie beyond the immediate sphere of his needs and wants" (Pieper, 1952, p. 17). Celebration was the root of leisure, and such celebration was a way of joyfully affirming ones place in the universe—divine worship. Leisure was also closely linked to contemplation and passive receptiveness which was thought to be important to the development of philosophical truths and establishing an understanding necessary for true celebration.

Rather than being a period of time or a form of activity, Pieper conceived of leisure as an attitude of the mind, and such an attitude was not the inevitable result of a holiday or vacation. It also was not, strictly speaking, susceptible to the human will. People could not obtain leisure simply because they wanted it. In particular, Pieper believed some people were simply incapable of accepting their lives in the world with joy and were, therefore, incapable of accepting all the good things to be found in their culture or of experiencing leisure. Leisure was thus linked directly to spiritual faith as was the development of culture.

In the modern world, leisure continues to be the realm in which "high culture," "popular culture," and countless subcultures are defined and expressed. Many sociologists have advanced the argument that leisure increasingly serves as the realm in which modern culture is created and maintained. Kaplan (1960), for example, has argued that leisure has become the medium in which members of the nuclear family relate to each and express how they feel toward one another. As the family has become less a unit which is maintained for economic purposes and as work has become specialized and done outside the home, parents and children know less about the work or school lives of others within their family unit. It is the world away from work in which the family comes to define itself.

MacCannell (1976) argued that leisure is displacing work from the center of social arrangements in the modern world. Life itself is supposed to be fun. This removal of culture from workaday activities forms the central crisis of industrial societies. Creativity, he believed, lies almost exclusively in the province of cultural, rather than industrial, productions. Intimacy and spontaneity are preserved in social arrangements away from work. Cultural experiences are now valued in and of themselves and have become the ultimate repository for values in society.

As leisure has become the realm in which culture is produced, it is not surprising that the production of leisure experiences has become both an industry and a part of the value associated with the purchase of many material goods. Toffler (1980) and others have written of the manufacturing of experiences which takes place in the modern world, from the design and operation of restaurants to guided tours to vacation packages to theme parks. There has also been great concern that this production of vicarious experiences makes the line between the real and the unreal less certain. The emerging modern mind, it is argued, is bent on expanding its repertoire of leisure experiences, increasingly adapting the same open-ended notions toward the collection of experiences as formerly existed toward the ownership of material goods.

MacCannell thought that culture is "produced" in modern societies. First, there was the representation of an ideal, a model for something, such as a fashion model. Then there was the influence of the model on other people. Next, a process was developed to link the model and its influence with a wider audience and commercial distributors. Such production both organized the attitudes we have toward the model and toward life as well as provided a base for the modern community. Cultural productions also give rise to a modern form of alienation— individuals interested only in the model or life-style, not in the life it represents.

The Role of Play in Creating Culture

Play is often thought to create culture. The Dutch historian Johan Huizinga, (1950) for instance, thought that every aspect of culture: language, law, war, art and others, arose from the play spirit within a society. Culture was, in effect, played from the very beginning. Play, Huizinga thought, was older than culture, since animals were capable of play, although their play patterns were not as complex as those of humans. Play was not rational and served its own ends. It was characterized as being outside of ordinary life, limited in time and space, bounded by rules which players voluntarily accepted, had something at stake and an outcome which was in doubt, and was characterized by exaggeration, illusion, and secrecy. There was no moral content to play, save the rules established for it. Above all else, play was limited in its aims, although it utterly absorbed the player. Thus, it was characterized by being both frivolous and ecstatic.

Early in the development of a culture, the play spirit was most highly evident in every aspect of daily life. Thus, for example, law and the justice system were characterized by contests which did not so much seek to determine scientifically the guilt or innocence of an accused party but rather to play a game and see who won and lost. Winning at play was, in effect, a sign of the will of the gods.

As a culture grew older, much of the play of everyday life diminished or became more highly institutionalized. Industrialism, in particular, produced a culture in which seriousness and importance were thought to be synonymous.

Utility and efficiency slowly became the ascendent values, and activities were increasingly done as means to ends. If one did play, he or she played "in order to" not merely because it was natural to do so. The line between play and ordinary life almost disappeared and the overseriousness of play forms such as sport destroyed the limitedness so crucial to their nature. War lost all elements of the play spirit in the twentieth century with disastrous results.

These changes, for Huizinga, signaled the decline of culture since " . . . real civilization cannot exist in the absence of a certain play-element, for civilization presupposes limitation and mastery of the self, the ability not to confuse its own tendencies with the ultimate and highest goal, but to understand that it is enclosed within certain bounds freely accepted" (Huizinga, 1950, p. 211). For culture to exist, humans had to maintain the ability to play, and to play in the same way as do children and animals. Culture was dependent upon both limitation and upon the recognition of the nonrational nature of human beings. Science, technology and materialism have sought to create a world without limitation and to use wholly rational means to produce irrational ends, to the detriment of both the play spirit and the culture.

The Role of Culture in Shaping Leisure

While leisure and play appear to be of great importance in the development of culture, the existing culture, in turn, shapes leisure expression. As sociologist Bennett Berger (1963) observed, leisure behavior, like work, is part of the social structure and is, therefore, not "free" but is constrained by the norms and values of society.

Thus, it makes little sense to suppose that leisure expression emerges without regard to the characteristics of a particular culture. While such cultural differences cannot be dealt with in a comprehensive manner, Kaplan (1960) identified differences in leisure expression in terms of central tendencies, using the ideal type Gemeinschaft-Gesellschaft devised by the German sociologist Tonnies (1940) (See Table 13.1, page 183). This division distinguishes between societies which are rural and simple in their social organization and those which are socially complex and urban. As may be seen, leisure in rural societies is likely to be classless, group-centered, spontaneous and useful while, in urban societies, leisure is characterized by specialized activities, fads and a wide range of choices.

Godbey (1990) similarly sought to identify such tendencies by differentiating between cultures of postindustrial societies which were more pluralistic and cultures which were less pluralistic, containing a single dominant culture (See Table 13.2, page 184). As may be seen, degree of cultural pluralism may have a great impact on almost every aspect of leisure expression. Cultural pluralism emphasizes the role of leisure as anything the individual wants to do

TABLE 13.1
Characteristics of Leisure

Gemeinschaft	Gesellschaft
Outdoor More use of large yards, streams, outdoor games.	*Indoor* More use of special buildings or rooms in the home; indoor games.
Participation More self-reliance in leisure; more talk and visiting.	*Observation* More reliance on entertainers; more mass media; more reading.
Noncommercial More activities in schools, homes, and community buildings.	*Commercial* Willingness to pay for entertainment; theaters and other establishments.
Group-centered Family activity; church groups; leisure close to group norms.	*Individual-centered* Tolerance of individuality; less dominance by family.
Few choices Relatively small range of interests among residents.	*Many choices* Larger variety of interests and types of persons.
Generalized activities Less opportunity to develop or use special play skills.	*Specialized activities* More specialized training and outlets.
Utilitarian orientation Leisure as outgrowth of household or work skills.	*"Cultural" orientation* Wider interest in artistic activities.
Spontaneous Little need for formal organization of play-life.	*Organized* Dependence on recreational specialists.
Body-centered Games of strength; play in setting of physical work (communal home building or harvesting).	*Mind-centered* More reading; creative activity.
Classless Activities cut across social stratification.	*Classbound* Leisure as symbol of status.
Conservative Slow to change play-ways.	*Faddish* Follows newest fads and crazes.

Source: Kaplan, M. (1960). *Leisure in America: A social inquiry.* New York, NY: John Wiley and Sons (pp. 113-115).

TABLE 13.2
Leisure in Singular and Plural Culture Societies

	Plural Culture Society	Single Culture Society
Concept	Leisure is anything the individual chooses to do which he/she finds pleasurable; leisure is unlimited, an end in itself.	Leisure is a set of identifiable experiences which the individual is taught to enjoy; leisure is limited, a means to an end.
Variation in behavior	Range of acceptable behavior wide.	Range of acceptable behavior narrow.
Standards to judge behavior	Laws set limits; no universally accepted mores by which to judge leisure behavior.	Mores and folkways set limits of behavior; universal standards for leisure based upon perceived cultural necessity.
Role	Individual and subcultural identity linked to leisure behavior.	Tribal, local or national identity linked to leisure behavior.
Role problems	Difficult to judge leisure ethically; dispute over leisure values; lack of meaning.	Lack of experimentation or alternatives; persecution of that which is foreign; easy to use leisure as a means of social control.
Government's role	Identification of recreation needs difficult; may provide only selected kinds of services or serve certain subcultures or groups disproportionately.	Identification of recreation needs easy; may provide services which act as a common denominator.
Commercial organization's role	Commercial sector has more diverse opportunities; can cater to individual or subculture's tastes; easier to create needs.	Commercial sector has more limited opportunities; more difficult to create needs or cater to individual's or subculture's tastes.

Source: Godbey, G. (1981). *Leisure in your life: An exploration.* 2nd Edition. State College, PA: Venture Publishing, Inc. (p. 115).

for pleasure. The limits of such behavior are established more by laws rather than mores or folkways. Fads and rapid change in leisure activities are characteristic. For single culture societies, leisure is more rooted in tradition and the range of acceptable behaviors is considerably smaller.

Thus, leisure and culture may be thought of as mutually reinforcing concepts. Culture is created out of leisure and reshaped by it. Leisure, however, even its very meaning, is correspondingly shaped and limited by culture.

■ REFERENCES

Berger, B. (1963). The sociology of leisure. In E. O. Smigel (Ed.), *Work and leisure.* pp. 21-40. New Haven, CT: College and University Press.

Godbey, G. (1990). *Leisure in your life: An exploration* (3rd ed.). State College, PA: Venture Publishing, Inc.

Huizinga, J. (1950). *Homo ludens: A Study of the play element in culture.* Boston, MA: Beacon Press.

Johnson, A., and Johnson, O. (September, 1978). In search of the affluent society, *Human nature,* pp. 50-59.

Kando, T. (1980). *Leisure and popular culture in transition* (2nd ed.). St. Louis, MO: C.V. Mosby Co.

Kaplan, M. (1960). *Leisure in America: A social inquiry.* New York, NY: John Wiley and Sons.

MacCannell, D. (1976). *The tourist: A new theory of the leisure class.* New York, NY: Schoken Books.

Pieper, J. (1952). *Leisure: The basis of culture.* New York, NY: New American Library.

Theodorson, G., and Theodorson, A. (1969) *Modern dictionary of sociology.* New York, NY: Thomas Y. Crowell.

Toffler, A. (1980). *The third wave.* New York, NY: Morrow.

Tonnies, F. (1940). *Fundamental concepts of sociology.* New York, NY: Harper & Row, Publishers, Inc.

CHAPTER 14

The Experience of Leisure as Flow

I f leisure is conceptualized as "free time," and participation is comparatively voluntary, then the commonality of the experiences which take place may be that participation is deliberate and thus deemed worthwhile by the participant. Such uses, however, may reflect alienation or ignorance and may be harmful to the individual instead of beneficial. In other conceptualizations of leisure, however, the experience itself is thought to be characterized by numerous emotional and intellectual states. While many different researchers and theorists have analyzed such states, to a remarkable extent there is a convergence of opinion concerning what constitutes a certain kind of leisure behavior. While psychologist Mihaly Csikszentmihalyi (1975) has identified what he calls the "flow" state to characterize meaningful action during either leisure or work, this concept is consistent with a long line of inquiry by sociologists, social psychologists, philosophers and others. The following represent some of the major attributes of the leisure experience which are in keeping with the concept of flow. Many of these attributes are not unique to leisure, since it is assumed that an individual may experience them in work or leisure. Csikszentmihalyi, for example, found that these attributes were sometime attained in activities as diverse as rock climbing, playing musical instruments or performing surgery. Perhaps the importance of identifying leisure as a milieu in which these attributes can be found makes it clear that work is not the only arena for important, satisfying or meaningful behavior.

The Leisure State is Different From Ordinary Life

People pursue leisure experiences because they provide opportunities which are unique from the rest of life. While there may be a tendency to think that work and leisure were indistinguishable in preindustrial societies, it is much more reasonable to assume that even within tribal cultures, individuals knew when the experience in question was outside the ordinary. As work became more ordered during industrialization, a routine of work and other obligated activity became the basis of daily life and leisure became, in some senses, in opposition to such routine.

The Leisure State is Autotelic

Csikszentmihalyi used the term "autotelic" to describe the flow experience, which he defined as the "psychological state, based upon concrete feedback which acts as a reward in that it produces continuing behavior in the absence of other rewards" (1975, p. 23). Other researchers have described the leisure state as being autotelic or characterized by feedback which is rewarding. London, Crandall and Fitzgibbons (1977), for instance, identified the needs fulfilled by leisure experience compressed into three dimensions. One of these dimensions was "feedback," which included having knowledge of the results of your performance, seeing results, knowing how well you are doing without hearing it from others, hearing how well you are doing from other people and pressure to do well (London, Crandall and Fitzgibbons 1977). The motivation for leisure behavior is thus intrinsic rather than extrinsic. It is the "doing" of the behavior which is rewarding in and of itself, even if such doing may result in an end product, such as occurs when one paints a picture. Many social psychologists have observed that such intrinsic motivation may actually be harmed by introducing substantial extrinsic motivations. Thus, someone who, for instance, ice skates simply out of love for activity may lose some of that love if someone begins paying him or her to ice skate. This is not to argue that leisure can never have any extrinsic rewards, only that to the extent that they become an important motivating factor, the behavior in question may cease to be leisure.

The Leisure State is One in Which the Participant Trusts the Process

There are different ways in which an individual demonstrates the trust of the process involved. It may be that the individual has developed skills which allow for the challenge to be successfully met. This doesn't necessarily mean that the outcome is known in advance, rather that the individual has a level or range of skills which are in harmony with the type and magnitude of challenge inherent in the behavior. As Csikszentmihalyi (1975) observed, the "flow" state occurs when there is a close match between challenge and skill. When the challenge far exceeds the individual's skill, anxiety will result. When the skill of the individual far exceeds the challenge, boredom will result. If an individual's skill level rises greatly in relation to the challenge, an activity which previously may have produced flow will begin to produce boredom. If a teenager who enjoyed a certain video game becomes skilled enough to almost always win, for instance, the game may become a bore and will no longer be of interest unless the challenge can be raised through some handicapping system.

The trust of the process can also be evidenced in other ways. In contemplative uses of leisure, it is sometimes the whole world which must be trusted. As the philosopher Josef Pieper (1952) stated, leisure involves "letting go." Leisure, he thought, is similar to going to sleep. You can't force yourself to sleep, nor can you force leisure to occur. In both cases it involves an act of trust which allows the individual to let go so as to be able to give him or herself to the behavior in question.

Finally, the trust for the process may have to do with other individuals involved. In such cases, the motivations or intentions of others involved in the behavior must be trusted. Thus, it may be more difficult to experience leisure while in the company of strangers unless there is some reason to believe they have similar goals or intentions.

In leisure behavior the trust is a necessary component of loving the behavior in question. As Godbey (1985) observed, leisure involves acting "from internally compelling love . . . " Stebbins (1979), too, pointed out that the amateur is, first and foremost, someone who "loves" to do the activity in question. Love involves trust. Another way of conceptualizing trust in regard to leisure experience is to think of it as faith. People come to have "faith" in a certain leisure activity such as camping, which means they no longer have to logically justify their participation in the activity in terms of assessing costs and benefits. Social exchange theory, which assumes that humans act after a logical assessment of costs and benefits of participation, may not apply to leisure behavior, at least when a given leisure behavior is well-established. Pieper argued leisure involved an act of faith, Godbey thought leisure activity provided a basis for faith since it served as symbolic evidence of the meaningfulness of existence. It is not surprising, therefore, that terms such as the "born again runner" have entered our vocabulary. Leisure experience is often religious in the most fundamental sense.

In the Leisure State There is a Refocusing of Attention on Either a Very Limited Stimulus Field or a Greatly Increased Stimulus Field

During leisure one's attention is likely to be changed from nonleisure either by centering attention on a limited stimulus field, in effect narrowing one's consciousness, or by broadening one's consciousness to seek to take in the totality of existence. In "flow" experience, the consciousness of the participant narrows to concentrate on the activity at hand. In some cases, competition, danger, or the opportunity for material gain (such as in gambling) may cause this constriction of consciousness. Conversely, leisure behavior which revolves around contemplation and tranquility results in an emptying out of the mind so as to be receptive to the whole of creation. Such contemplation, for the ancient Athenians, constituted listening to the universe. It produced a kind of learning—"intellectus"—which could not be obtained through work-like effort.

In both these cases, leisure results in a refocusing of attention and an emptying out of the mind and the normal state of consciousness produced by the world of work and obligation.

The Leisure State Involves Loss of Ego, Self-Consciousness and Sense of Time.

During leisure, one's awareness of self is minimized, since they have given themselves to the behavior at hand. There is, in effect, a merging of action and awareness. You become the game of chess. The game of chess becomes you. In such situations, people temporarily surrender much of their identity, temporarily forget their ego needs. Self-consciousness is minimized, particularly where the behavior has rules, such as a sport or game, or where the participant can act with assurance. This is particularly true, as mentioned earlier, when the challenge of the behavior is closely matched to the skill of the participant.

Not only is there a lessened sense of self during leisure, there is also a lessened sense of time. The individual, in effect, loses him or herself in the behavior and, thus, also loses sense of time to some extent. People enjoying themselves at a party or "all wrapped up" in a game of tennis are less likely to be aware of time's passage than they would be in other situations. Perhaps as the party or tennis match is ending they may suddenly realize more time has passed than they were aware of.

Because leisure behavior tends to lessen awareness of self and of time, it is deeply refreshing in the most fundamental sense. The temporary escape from the pressures of time and the burden of self-awareness, for many, produces a relief from stress which is literally re-creating.

This lessening of self and time awareness is often considered an attribute of play. Huizinga (1950) characterized play as "utterly absorbing" and such absorption led to play possessing a unique reality which was clearly different from ordinary life. So may it be said about the flow state and about many conceptualizations of leisure. In all cases the human will is positively activated toward some behavior whose meaning is contained within the experience itself. Leisure may, therefore, be thought of by the participant as "intuitively worthwhile" (Godbey, 1985). That is, the giving of the will to the behavior in question is not merely a rational calculation of costs and benefits, it involves some act of faith, since, compared to instrumental activities, it is both a more total giving of self and a voluntary giving of self.

The Leisure State is Temporary—Limited in Time and Space

From what has previously been said, leisure, at least as it relates to the flow experience, is, by definition, temporary. That is, it is in contrast with that which is normal and ordinary. The flow state occurs when challenge and skill are balanced and such balance is the exception rather than the rule. Flow assumes a change in attention from what is "normal" and normal attention states characterize everyday ordinary life. While the ancient Athenians may have viewed leisure as a permanent condition in which one experienced the absence of the necessity of being occupied, leisure, conceived as a psychosocial state, is temporary.

The Leisure State Involves Learning

All leisure behavior involves some degree of learning, according to the previous analysis. If leisure behavior is to result in flow there must be some degree of challenge and therefore some degree of skill involved and such skill involves learning. For the flow experience to continue, the challenge may increase thus increasing the skill necessary. If we accept this proposition, then some forms of behavior, such as television viewing, possess much less potential to serve as leisure experience than others, such as reading, playing a musical instrument or mountain climbing. Ironically, television viewing, from the standpoint of time spent, is often described as the most time-consuming leisure activity in North America. According to the descriptions of leisure in this chapter, television viewing rarely constitutes flow experience and, from this perspective, may not be a leisure experience.

Maximizing Flow During Leisure

There are numerous ways in which the flow state can be maximized during leisure. The easiest and most important has already been mentioned—flow is most likely to occur when individuals perceive opportunities for action as being evenly matched with their abilities. Flow will most likely occur when the individual is provided with optimal challenges in regard to their skill. Flow is also more likely to occur in behavior which have unreachable ceilings. That is, activities such as piano playing, writing poetry or golf where there is always the potential to improve. Flow also is more likely to occur when the behavior contains noncontradictory demands for action and provides clear, unambiguous feedback in response to the individual's actions. Harmony and order are present in ways which may be absent in the ordinary world. For this to happen, the individual delimits reality, controls some aspect of it, and responds to feedback with a concentration which excludes anything else as irrelevant. As skill increases, the individual goes further into the activity and, thus, accepts larger and more complex challenges. Thus, flow is in keeping with the concept of specialization in leisure activity discussed in Chapter 18. That is, there is the possibility for a continuum of involvement within a given leisure behavior which occurs only as the individual becomes more skilled in it.

Csikszentmihalyi used examples of activities which had a high potential to produce flow experience such as making music, rock climbing, dancing, sailing, and chess.

What makes these activities conducive to flow is that they were designed to make optimal experiences easier to achieve. They have rules that require the learning of skills, they set up goals, they provide feedback, they make control possible. They facilitate concentration and involvement by making the activity as distinct as possible from the so-called paramount reality of everyday existence. For example, in each sport participants dress up in eye-catching uniforms and enter special enclaves that set them apart temporarily from ordinary mortals. For the duration of the event, players and spectators cease to act in terms of common sense, and concentrate instead on the peculiar reality of the game (p. 72).

These activities do not "expand the consciousness" of the participant, rather they provide, or may provide, a sense of discovery, transporting the person to a new reality. The individual is pushed to higher levels of performance and new states of consciousness. "In short, it transformed the self by making it more complex. In this growth of the self lies the key to flow activities" (Csikszentmihalyi, 1990, p. 74).

It is easy to see the compatibility of the theory of flow with the stimulus seeking or optimal arousal theories of play. Humans, in both cases, are thought to desire to process information and do so more pleasurably when there are rules established which allow for the interpretation of information of stimuli in a limited and specified frame of reference which has a defined goal. In both play and flow there is an understanding in advance of what constitutes a positive outcome, although the extent to which the outcome can be positive is open-ended.

It may be argued that flow is evident, to some degree, in many forms of leisure behavior as well as many forms of work. Those leisure experiences in which flow is most evident may sometimes be referred to as "peak" experiences. Such activity is among the most deeply satisfying and refreshing of human experiences.

The sense of flow within a leisure behavior may be impossible under conditions of anomie or alienation. Anomie, a term coined by the French sociologist Emile Durkheim, referred to situations in which there is a lack of rules or in which the norms of behavior have become so unclear that an individual no longer knows what is permitted or what do to (Durkheim, 1951). Alienation occurs when people are forced by the social system to go against their own personal goals. "At the individual level, anomie corresponds to anxiety, while alienation corresponds to boredom (Csikszentmihalyi, 1990, p. 87).

Flow, then, as well as many forms of meaningful leisure and play, are dependent upon the social system as well as the capacities of the individual.

REFERENCES

Csikszentmihalyi, M. (1975). *Beyond boredom and anxiety.* San Francisco, CA: Jossey-Bass, Inc., Publishers.

Csikszentmihalyi, M. (1990). *Flow—The psychology of optimal experience.* New York, NY: Harper & Row, Publishers, Inc.

Durkheim, E. (1951). *Suicide.* New York, NY: The Free Press.

Godbey, G. (1985). *Leisure in your life: An exploration.* (2nd ed.) State College, PA: Venture Publishing, Inc.

Huizinga, J. (1950). *Homo ludens: A study of the play element in culture.* Boston, MA: Beacon Press.

London, M., Crandall R. and Fitzgibbons, D. (1977). The psychological structure of leisure: Activities, needs, people. *Journal of Leisure Research*, *9*(4) pp. 252-264.

Pieper, J. (1952). *Leisure—The basis of culture.* New York, NY: New American Library.

Stebbins, R. (1979). *Amateurs—On the margin between work and leisure.* Beverly Hills, CA: Sage Publications, Inc.

CHAPTER 15

Leisure in Ordinary Life

R esearch designs always have a set of premises about the nature of what is being studied. In most fields those assumptions are repeated over and over until they tend to be taken for granted. The problem is that in the cumulative process of "normal science" (Kuhn, 1970) alternative premises and approaches are forgotten. When those alternatives contain significant dimensions of whatever is being studied, then research may be deceptive and informative.

Based on the assumptions of most social science research on leisure, the findings are deceptively limiting. In North America, most research has been funded by agencies that manage land and water resources used for recreation. As a consequence, as with a recent Forest Service study, leisure is defined as activity that requires a trip. In much the same way, research designs are based on lists of activities that can be designated by form and by place as well as time. They tend to be *events* located in weekly timetables and designated by place. That is, they have identities such as "softball at the park on Monday evening" or "rafting on the river Saturday morning." Leisure and recreation become tacitly defined in those terms.

Why is this a problem? Simply because most ordinary leisure not only doesn't require a trip, but is not an event at all. Most leisure in ordinary life is woven into the process of the daily round, neither special nor clearly differentiated. In leisure styles there are special punctuating events, highlights amid the ordinary. Such events may be important and highly valued. But most leisure is quite ordinary. And it is "ordinary leisure" that consumes the most time for most people.

Leisure and Special Events

One problem with designing inclusive research on leisure is that many people overlook ordinary leisure unless they are reminded. We tend to think in terms of special identifiable events and activities when asked about leisure and recreation. Even the chapters of books on leisure designate sports, the arts, travel, outdoor recreation, and sometimes mass media as though together they make up the bulk of leisure activity. In fact, extremely low percentages of adults engage in any of them outside the home in any given week. Except for television and some reading, they fill relatively little off-work time. When weekends come, many adults eat out but relatively few attend special events. When vacation time arrives, people tend to get outdoors, go somewhere, and even try unfamiliar activities. But the most common vacation trip remains a family journey by car.

Why is such disproportionate attention given to special events? First, they involve special resources, public and market, that must be managed for occasional use. National Park overlooks, Forest Service campgrounds, and Corps of Engineers waterways require management for just that seasonal and special use. Predicting use patterns and the consequences of management strategies calls for focused research. The funding of such research attracts attention. Second, leisure events are a major part of the market sector of leisure provisions. Financial investments are based on estimates of potential demand for the goods and services. Although there are also major markets for home electronic entertainment, reading material, and gardening supplies, events such as eating out and destination travel are the basis for considerable business investment. Third, event-scheduled leisure is most visible and attracts the most media attention. Events are news just because they are special rather than ordinary.

A more fundamental reason for such attention is that special events claim an importance beyond their frequency. It appears to make sense that people will spend the most time and money on those activities that are most important to them. The single study that has directly tested this assumption found no correlation at all when activities were ranked by importance, frequency and duration of participation, and money spent on the activity (Kelly, 1973). Further research has suggested an explanation for this surprising inconsistency among indices of leisure investment. The two kinds of activity that adults value highest or would least want to give up are:

1) interaction with the persons most important to them; and
2) "high investment" activity in which there is a sustained development of skills.

The first, social interaction with friends and family, tends to be frequent but low cost. The second, sustained engagement in which one develops a sense of selfhood and competence (see Chapters 11 and 18) may require financial expenditure but less time. It is important partly because it is special rather than common.

Special events are important just because they are less common and ordinary. They provide a change, a punctuation in the ongoing and ordinary round of life. They offer heightened meaning and focused experience. They are special, by definition and in their place in the balance of leisure styles and patterns. As such they may attract disproportionate financial expenditure in relation to the time they consume. They are important in overall lifestyles partly because they are occasional.

This chapter, however, will focus on "ordinary leisure"—on what most people do most of the time. Of course, the major time uses outside of employment are sleep, personal and household maintenance, getting to and from work for many, child care for parents, and watching television. Ordinary leisure tends to be related to those activities as well as fill in the cracks and gaps in daily schedules. It is "ordinary" not only because it is common but also because it is connected to the tasks and routines of daily life. As such, it is both important and easily overlooked.

"Core" Leisure

Again, the focus on events in most leisure research has led to a neglect of the mundane. Part of the inattention is a matter of interest on the part of students of leisure and those who fund their programs. Another part is related to the aims and tools of research. Most social research is oriented toward identifying *differences*. How do leisure participation and meaning differ by age, gender, educational background, family status, region, or socialization history? Which population aggregates are most active physically, most likely to travel overseas, or to drop out of various kinds of activity? Research designed to answer such questions statistically compares categories of people and their rates of engagement. Little attention is given to what is common across such categories.

What gets lost in such approaches is what most people do most of the time throughout their lives. If that sounds contradictory, prepare to be surprised. A review of a series of studies intended to identify styles of leisure engagement (Kelly, 1983) found an unintended result. The statistical method employed in six studies was "factor analysis." This method groups items, in this case types of activity, into factors that are different in participation levels. No two studies identified the same clusters of activities, but some appeared in more than one study. For example, intellectual or cultural activities, team sports, outdoor resource-based activity, or motorized activity sometimes formed a group of activities in which participation in one often overlaps with others. Engagement in such clusters differentiated those studied and were often referred to as "leisure styles."

Several problems, however, emerged. One was that the combinations and clusters differed when the samples or the activities studied differed (Schmitz-Scherzer et al., 1974; Kelly, 1983). The styles may be produced, at least to some extent, by the choices of the research designer. A second problem was that correlations with differentiating factors tended to be modest. Most important, however, was that most of the analyses omitted most of the activities that people do most often. The reason is simple: the technique is devised to identify factors by which people differ, not what they have in common. Activities that most people do cannot differentiate factors or styles. Therefore, they have often been omitted from the analyses. The result has been identification of so-called leisure styles that do not include watching television or after-dinner conversations.

Out of this inverse analysis came the concept of the "core" of leisure activities. The core consists of those accessible things that most people do most days. The core is relatively informal and inexpensive. Socially, it consists of all the informal interactions with those in our households and in other locales of frequent exchange, such as the workplace. It is mixed with responsibilities and tasks: play with children is both nurturing and expressive. It is accessible, with television in 95 percent plus of American homes, and reading such as magazines and newspapers readily available. It may involve walking, going shopping, meeting friends, and other activity around the home. Such core activity is common to the lives of children and the old, the employed and the retired, those who left school and those with Ph.D.s, the rural and the urban, as well as those of differing ethnic backgrounds. It is often of low intensity and taken for granted. Like air, it is so common—and perhaps necessary—that we seldom think of it.

The Locales of Ordinary Leisure

The Home

The primary locale of core leisure is, of course, the residence. It is where those in the most pervasive and stable relationships are likely to gather. It is also increasingly a locale for a variety of on-call entertainment: not only television but also recorded music, videos, stocks of reading material, and now the home computer.

In a three-community study of adults, the activity ranked first was "sexual activity and expression" (Kelly, 1978). The most common relationship for the sexual interaction of adults is that of marriage and the most common place is the residence. For the more affluent, the bedroom has become a multidimensional recreation center with the bed, television and video players with remote control, mini-bars, jacuzzis and spas, and a selection of other instruments and resources. Even for those of modest means, the bed remains the place to go for most sexual encounters. While frequency and intensity of sexual activity varies, it remains a significant form of "relational leisure."

A New York Times poll (December 5, 1990) found that 80 percent of adults with children usually eat dinner together as a family. Follow-up interviews revealed that despite conflicting schedules and the time pressures on single parents, families go to great lengths to eat dinner together. Not only is the meal a symbol of the cohesiveness of the family, but it is the primary time for the exchange of information and concerns. For a majority of the 550 parents polled in a national sample, the "family dinner" is an opportunity for conversation with the television switched off. When the mother is employed, the food may be simple or even purchased and brought in, but the meal retains its meaning of communicative sharing. Coordinating times, especially with older children and varied employment schedules, is a priority even when it requires a struggle.

Specific patterns of interaction differ, but the centrality of home and co-residents is common across socioeconomic and ethnic lines. In the same three-community study, the "ten most important" nonwork activities for most adults, men and women, were:

- two kinds of personal interaction with spouse and/or children;
- two kinds of family activity including travel and games;
- one or two home activities such as reading, watching television, or music;
- one or two special recreational activities, often sports or outdoor activity;
- a home maintenance activity; and
- something idiosyncratic that is important to the self and done for its own sake (Kelly, 1978).

Note again the centrality of the family, informal interaction, and the home. Time diary research finds that informal interaction follows only television watching in the amount of time not devoted to sleep, employment, and household and personal care (Robinson, 1977).

Patterns and meanings of social interaction as leisure will be explored in the next chapter. Three points are relevant in this focus on ordinary leisure:

1) often leisure activities are primarily social contexts in which the sharing and communication are the primary meaning of the action;
2) such interaction takes place in the ordinary times and places of life, in the daily round of life; and
3) such interaction is not separated from the web of primary relation-ships, but is embedded in the context of social roles.

What are examples of such ordinary leisure in and around the home? Other than electronic media and the common meal, many vary according to the composition of the household and period in the life course:

Parents play with children in and around yard maintenance tasks.
Children have regular expectations of playing catch when a parent gets
    home from work.
Small children are read to each night.
Sisters and brothers share experiences of the day.
Adults reminisce over coffee or wine.
The Sunday paper is shared and discussed.
A vacation trip is planned.
The week's events are shared while driving to another home for dinner.
A small child demands that a parent join in play with a toy.
The entire household joins in planning, celebrating, and remembering
    a holiday.

A widow watches the news on TV and calls a friend to discuss it.
A retired couple exchange ideas for presents for a grandchild.
Gardening is a source of pride as well as of shared action.
A video is jointly selected for Friday night.
Carwashing becomes a playful shared task.
A woman visits her frail sister and makes coffee.

Friday dinner is preceded by some wine and cheese.
There is a chat with neighbors in the midst of Saturday's lawn chores.
Walks are common after dinner during the summer's longer days.
Mystery novels are read, shared, and discussed.
The family goes to the library together to bring books home.

The possibilities, of course, are endless. The point is that all sorts of activity
takes place in and around the home that is hardly recognized as leisure. It is so
much a part of ordinary life that it is taken for granted. Further, it may be just
the expressive behavior that gives some joy and flavor to life. The home is more
than shelter and the family more than an organization fulfilling necessary
functions. Much of the richness and warmth of life is in its daily play.

Leisure at the Workplace

Much the same kind of informal interaction characterizes many places of
employment. A study of shipyard workers in Britain describes their "occupational culture" on the job (Brown et al., 1973). The routines and tasks of
shipbuilding become a context for all kinds of joking, personal exchange, and
even manipulation of the tasks themselves to afford some variety and meaning.
An observational study of a private school in the same country discovered a
multifaceted culture of playful exchanges that took place in the halls, common

areas, dining hall, and grounds as well as playing fields and other recreational sites (Woods, 1979). It is suggested that such off-task behaviors and communications are an integral part of the institution, a dimension that lightens mood and constructs relationships with emotional dimensions.

The general topic of leisure in the workplace merits more study than it has received. A preoccupation with productivity seemingly biases research toward attention to tasks rather than toward inattention and escape. Nevertheless, the assumption that play is a negative factor in productivity is more an article of faith than a demonstrated fact. It may well be that the coffee room, the informal exchange, and even some daydreaming is characteristic of the most productive rather than least valuable workers in many settings.

In any case, there is no question that only a work routine that figuratively chains the worker to a segregated machine or terminal can prevent leisure at the workplace. Sneaking off to a secluded area for some dope or booze has been found in steel mills. Less attention has been given to work sites such as engineering departments that have their formal and informal play. In one such office and laboratory setting, the noon bridge game was followed by discussions of critical hands throughout the afternoon. Early morning golf dates seemed most likely to occur when the department head was out of town or on vacation. Most important, however, was the continual flow of jokes, heckling, kidding, jibes, cracks, and other disrupting communication that was mingled minute-by-minute with the exchange of assistance, ideas, questions, and other task-related talk. One possibility would be that such productive exchange was lubricated and facilitated by the flow of playful commentary.

It might be illuminating to keep a diary of such behaviors in other work settings such as schools, garages, stores, and offices. More important, the connections between such play and productive enterprise could be examined. Does kidding around in a research laboratory lead to collaborative ideas and lateral problem-solving? Do jokes among teachers and students broaden and deepen relationships? Does the male vocabulary of the garage or service station serve to build single-sex bonding? Do the casual flirtations of the office tend to lower barriers to communication across gender and status barriers? Do playful remarks provide a fuller dimension of office relationships that might otherwise be limited to orders and instructions that come to be resented? Whatever the outcomes, positive or negative from the perspective of productivity or community-building, such behaviors are the stuff of workplace interaction.

The Fabric of Ordinary Life

One minority approach to sociology has special relevance for the study of ordinary life. Proponents of this approach refer to their work as "existential sociology" (Douglas and Johnson, 1977). While it touches existential philosophy in its attention to the ways in which human actors construct their lives in decision and action, it is more inclusive than the philosophy. Rather than some determinative model in which individuals are seen as simply the products of social forces, human life is viewed as a dialectical process in which social factors mix with directed action. The social environment is not just a "structure," but is produced in the dialectic in which the actor both acts and is acted upon. The "social experience of daily life" (Douglas and Johnson, 1977) is said to be the focus of sociological enterprise.

Further, this enterprise includes dimensions of emotion and feelings as well as reason and analysis. Models of social interaction and action that exclude emotion and mood as though every decision were some calculation of weighted factors in a purely rational procedure are rejected in favor of a less sequential or structured process. The presumption is that considerable social life is more a matter of emotional reaction and unexamined action than any analytical research models recognize. Any theory of "reasoned action" has limited application.

For example, academic social psychology has wrought a kind of "bloodless revolution" that has come to account for human behavior in terms of rational thought, information processing, and evaluation. People interact without emotion. There is no anger or fear, no desire or repulsion. Freud and all the evidence of the significance of the nonconscious and irrational in shaping behavior are ignored. In research designs, such elements are inconvenient or inadmissible. Presumed dictums of science do not admit data that cannot be replicated and interpretations that are singular and not "objective." Therefore, all the unique and problematic elements in social interaction are abandoned in favor of patterned assimilation and evaluation of information that are assumed to be much the same from one episode to another.

Existential sociology begins at a different point with the question "What is human action?" (Douglas and Johnson, 1977). Actors take intentioned action in concrete daily life in which many elements are not repeatable. They are made out of an assessment of what is possible as well as desirable. This experience includes feelings and emotions. Any understanding of daily life, from this perspective, begins with actual situated experiences rather than with abstract principles. Generalizations are built out of multiple and varying examinations of the real and concrete. Analytical observation and participation are valued research methods. Statistical analysis is seen as only one tool among many. There is no objective knowledge in a positivist sense, but all knowledge is interpreted in the research process.

There are a number of theoretical foundations of this "down-to-earth" approach to sociology. The first is the concept of Max Weber (1964) in which he distinguishes between understanding (*verstehen*) and explanation (*erklaren*). *Verstehen* is an imaginative reconstruction of the thought and experience of other persons to discern the crucial elements in their decision and action processes. The assumption is that human action is "meaningful" and complex.

The second foundation is the symbolic interaction model of behavior developed by George Herbert Mead (1934). Mead stressed the symbolic dimension of the social order as well as its learned content. Generalized expectations are abstracted from the symbol systems associated with action contexts such as games. From this basis, functional analysts have stressed role-learning and personality development. Interaction theorists focus more on the problematic nature of the society, that it is constructed and redefined in symbolic exchange. What appears to be "given," the institutional structure of a social system, is actually a learned set of symbols that are reinforced in common action.

The third foundation is the "phenomenology" of everyday experience (Shutz, 1972). Without ever knowing what is "real" and what is only appearance in the world "out there," social actors attempt to make sense of the world they perceive and experience. They become attached to particular symbols out of which they create a structure of meaning. In the social sharing of these creations, we come to generally agree on what exists and how we can respond. We behave "as if" we can rely on the regularity even when we recognize that our social worlds are being continually renegotiated. Hidden in our regularities of interaction are a number of taken for granted rules and regulations (Goffman, 1967). Even in leisure we take intentioned action based on how we define both the particular situation and its more regular context. Reality, then, is not a given something "out there," but is the construction of a dialectical process in which common symbols mediate between the actions of individuals and the social context (Berger and Luckman, 1967). The social consensus consists of a shared universe of meanings that are both pervasive and fragile. The fundamental self-definition is one of the possibility of action in this symbolic world, of "I can" or "I am able" rather than "I am" (Merleau-Ponty, 1964).

This existential view of social action and interaction stresses decision in a problematic context defined by shared symbols. The process of perception, interpretation, and evaluation that leads to action is complex. It includes elements of reasoned analysis, emotional response, learned patterns of behavior, and the acceptance of implicit rules and roles. In everyday life, we interpret, respond, act, react, redefine, revise, and renegotiate. Action is neither simple nor linear.

Leisure in Ordinary Life

Leisure, from this perspective, is found in the midst of the process. It is not simple or monodimensional. It is not *just* attitude or decision, mood or behavior, reasoned action or emotional response. It is the process of action in a perceived world of possibilities. Leisure is found in the action, not the locale or time. It must be enacted in order to be. And it takes place in a problematic world of symbols and meanings that are continually being interpreted and revised.

Leisure, then, is everyday action as well as singular event. It is ordinary as well as extraordinary. It is a dimension of life. The question is, "What is that dimension?" What is the experience? Situated in the push and pull of social interaction, is leisure really anything identifiable and distinctive? The question is critical when an existential perspective is adopted. Leisure is then caught in the midst of the often confusing stream of life as it is lived rather than as an abstracted ideal.

In a concrete sense, what is being identified as leisure? Douglas (Douglas and Johnson, 1977) is explicit that leisure may be authentic and creative action. It may play with ideas, materials, and relationships in ways that express respect, love, and even an awe of the potential of life. It may involve mind and body, reason and emotion. In authentic act, whether it involves rebuilding a carburetor or creating a sculpture, building a farcical line of conversation or reading Dickens, in at least a small way it creates a new self and a new world. The point is not the time, place, or material; but the enactment of possibility.

On the other hand, Douglas reminds us that leisure may be oppressive, insidious, and fraudulent. It may be a mindless escape into television, movies, spectator sports, drug use, the violence of pornography, and other forms of indulgence. Such experiences are designed to produce a feeling of gratification without the cost or risk of real action. Just because they may offer a feeling of freedom, they may stand in the way of the exercise of freedom. They are inauthentic because they are deceptive. Play becomes an escape rather than initiative and action. Leisure reduced to mental state may be the the basis of self-deception and bondage rather than an act of freedom.

Everyday leisure, however, from this perspective includes both the authentic and the fraudulent. Leisure is all kinds of action and interaction, however creative or inhuman. When it is reduced to escape and predefined activity, to pseudo-decision and sham, then both the self and the world are reduced in scope and meaning. When leisure takes the risk of open-ended play, then the self and the world are at least slightly redefined. When we go on to examine day-to-day leisure, it will encompass both the existential and the fraudulent, the authentic and the inauthentic. The difference is defined by the nature of the action, not by the form of the activity.

The Construction of Everyday Leisure

Much of life consists of routines. What is the meaning of leisure amidst those routines?

Leisure as a Context of Interaction

Chapter 16 will explore in more detail the nature of social interaction as leisure. Here the focus is on how the activities of leisure provide a context for the day-to-day interaction of regular relationships. Examples are literally endless:

- The young mother expresses love, teaches motor and social skills, develops vocabulary, delights in her child's spontaneity, and enjoys the interaction itself in a few minutes following breakfast in the kitchen and before the trip to day care.

- Friendships are made and expressed in the locker room, on the bus, in hallway conversations, on the bench, and in the experience of the game itself among members of a high school baseball team. The jokes, cracks, silliness, and put-downs are as much a part of the social fabric as exchanging plans, hopes, sexual experiences, and classroom frustrations.

- The picnic, organized with some effort primarily by the mother, allows the two employed parents to take direct parenting roles that are more emotional and bonding than didactic and regulatory. The beach volleyball is not a contest, but a relaxation of role hierarchies and a playing out of role reversals, suppressed antagonisms, and even aggressive independence in engagement rather than withdrawal.

- A retired couple, both having left the work force voluntarily in their late fifties, now spends some time almost every day with friends who have retired in the same satellite town or with their adult children and teenage grandchildren. They have no major hobby investment outside the home and yard, but meet others for shopping, meals, walks, high school basketball games, church meetings, and just for coffee at the local cafe.

In a study of adults age forty and older in Peoria, Illinois, leisure was found to be one resource among others in coping with later life change (Kelly, 1987). For some, leisure engagements were primarily an environment for social exchange. Who was present was clearly more important than the nature of the activity. In fact, one downtown cafeteria had become a noon meeting place more because of price and the relaxed atmosphere than because of the acceptable quality of the food. Many kinds of activity participation were strongly and inversely correlated with age, especially activities that required strenuous physical exertion (exercise, sports, and outdoor recreation) and higher costs (travel in retirement). Informal interaction, however, remained central to life patterns for those who were physically and mentally able to meet and communicate. The contexts varied, some formal and some informal, but the centrality of "core" associations remained.

One important element of leisure through the life course is providing a context for relationships to be developed and expressed. One Peoria retired teacher had been part of a "music club" since high school. The friendships of that group had sustained her through a series of life changes and traumas as a kind of quasi-family. A widower went to a community recreation exercise program to be with people, although he disliked the program. Churches and activity-based organizations provided opportunities for regular associations that were not age-segregated. Leisure is not just social interaction, but the social dimensions are central throughout life for most people. Further, the times and places of such interaction may be scattered through the day rather than reserved for designated set-apart times and places. Leisure is, among other things, a *social space.*

Leisure and Emotional Expression

What psychologists call "affect," the emotional elements of life, is also a significant part of everyday leisure. A number of examples have already been given: the young mother, the baseball players, the retired grandparents, and others. The expression "lighten up!" is based on the premise that we can't endure hour after hour of solemn and serious mood. In all sorts of ways, life incorporates the humor of parody and the grotesque, the exchange of personal affirmations and symbolic recognition, and the acting out nonproductive meanings. We often respond more to mood than to meaning, to signals than to statements. Symbolic communication includes affective signs of body language and facial expression.

Life is affect at least as much as so-called reasoned action. Affect is the emotional component of action and interaction. It is the feeling dimension of joy, the warmth of relationships, and the excitement of risk. And a great deal of such affect is found in play. Puppies frolic and professors become silly with their children (and sometimes with each other). Why do we repeat nonproductive and economically unrewarding activities over and over and often with great enthusiasm and at high cost? At least part of the satisfaction found in most activities can never be measured fully by any multiple item scale: it is in ineffable emotion. What, after all, is the rational meaning of great music?

Another central dimension of ordinary leisure is in the imagination. No kind of leisure is as common, recurrent, persistent, and perhaps as necessary as day-dreaming. Further, no leisure may be as free of constraint or uplifting to the spirits as such imaginative wandering. In day-dreaming we transcend many of the boundaries of ordinary life without leaving the times and places to which we are attached. We engage in action, feel, think, relate, and love in ways that we cannot manage in real life. We go to distant places, communicate with inaccessible people, attempt unrealized skills, and become undeveloped selves. And yet in all this, we remain identifiable selves.

Daydreaming may help us get through the tedious task, the boring class, and the repetitive conversation. Some imaginative flights take only seconds; others may weave their fantasies for hours. Some produce innovative connections and ideas that prove to be of value later; others are so fanciful as to be little more than escape. Whatever their form and orientation, they are surely leisure: free, focused on the experience, and with primarily intrinsic meaning. In most daydreams, there is an imaginative blending of the openness of freedom and the reality of selfhood. There is a mixture of experiential transcendence and concrete history. We are ourselves and yet more. We remain what we have been and become something more. We recognize real others and yet know them in unrealized ways.

Like emotions, the imagination is at the very center of ordinary leisure. It seldom appears on activity lists or is probed in interviews. Yet, along with informal interaction, it is more common, found in more times and places, and perhaps more important that anything we usually refer to as leisure. In terms of real life as we live it, mood and imagination are the stuff of the seconds and minutes of the day if not always the hours and days.

The Substance of Ordinary Leisure

So much of the study of leisure concentrates on the extraordinary. And there is good reason to give attention to meaningful and significant actions and interactions. Resources, relationships, and sustained investments are punctuating highlights of the round of life. This attention does not, however, offer an excuse from recognizing the ordinary.

The substance of ordinary leisure is just that—very much immersed in the fabric of daily life as we live it from minute to minute. It is available media and accessible entertainment. It is exchange with those we see every day and to whom our lives are bound. It is moments of emotion and lightness in the midst of tasks and roles. It is play without purpose and that somehow is very important to our relationships. It is imaginative flight and fantasy very much in the middle of the routine and humdrum. It is escape as well as attention, relaxation as well as directed action. There are, after all, 24 hours in the day. Some are filled with responsibilities, some with rest, some with directed action, and some just filled. "Anomic leisure" that has no particular purpose or fulfilling outcome (Gunter and Gunter, 1980) may have a place in ongoing life, too.

Again, the possibility is raised that leisure is not so much a designated domain of life as a theme wound through all the elements of life. Further, in ordinary life, leisure may not be so much a clearly defined dimension as a mixture of meanings. If leisure is to encompass daydreaming as well as gymnastics and goofing off as well as producing Shakespeare, then no simple conceptualization is likely to be adequate. Further, leisure from this perspective is emotion and action, mood and meaning. In subsequent analyses of interaction, satisfactions, personal development and other issues, it is important not to forget how leisure is often part of everyday life and ordinary experience.

REFERENCES

Berger, P., and Luckman, T. (1967). *The social construction of reality.* New York, NY: Penguin Books, Inc.

Brown, R., Brannen, P., Cousins, J., and Samphier, M. (1973). Leisure in work: The occupational culture of shipbuilding workers. In M. Smith, S. Parker, and C. Smith (Eds.) *Leisure and society in Britain.* London, England: Allen Lane.

Douglas, J., and Johnson, J. (1977). *Existential sociology.* New York, NY: Cambridge University Press.

Goffman, E. (1967). *Interaction ritual.* Garden City, NY: Anchor Books.

Gunter, B. G., and Gunter, N. (1980). Leisure styles: A conceptual framework. *The Sociological Quarterly, 21,* 361-374.

Kelly, J. R. (1973). Three measures of leisure activity: A note on the continued incommensurability of oranges, apples, and artichokes. *Journal of Leisure Research, 5,* 56-65.

Kelly, J. R. (1978). Leisure styles and choices in three environments. *Pacific Sociological Review, 21,* 187-207.

Kelly, J. R. (1983). Leisure styles: A hidden core. *Leisure Sciences, 5,* 321-338.

Kelly, J. R. (1987). *Peoria winter: Styles and resources in later life.* Lexington, MA: Lexington Books.

Kuhn, T. (1970). *The structure of scientific revolutions.* Chicago, IL: University of Chicago Press.

Mead, G. H. (1934). *On social psychology.* Chicago, IL: University of Chicago Press.

Merleau-Ponty, M. (1964). In J. Wild and J. Edie (Trans.), *In praise of philosophy.* Evanston, IL: Northwestern University Press.

Robinson, J. (1977). *How Americans use time.* New York, NY: Holt, Rinehart and Winston.

Schmitz-Scherzer, R. et al. (1974). Notes on a factor analysis comparative study of the structure of leisure activities in four different samples. *Journal of Leisure Research, 6,* 77-83.

Shutz, A. (1972). *The phenomenology of the social world.* Evanston, IL: Northwestern University Press.

Weber, M. (1964). In A. Henderson and T. Parsons (Trans.) *The theory of social and economic organization.* New York, NY: The Free Press.

Woods, P. (1979). *The divided school.* London, England: Routledge & Kegan Paul, Ltd.

Interaction as Leisure

What is usually the single most important factor in being satisfied with leisure? On a given occasion, it may be the weather, the final score, or the attention demanded by the activity. Most often, however, the most significant factor in the ordinary round of leisure is who else is there. As suggested in the previous chapter, special events are important to highlight the ordinary. As will be examined in the next three chapters, intensity and involvement are central to finding extraordinary meaning. But day in and day out, the quality of interaction is foremost.

How do we decide what to do Saturday night? The event schedule of the community provides a set of possibilities. Cost and personal financial circumstances are a factor. Location, crowding, and other access elements are involved. First, however, is usually whom we want to be with. Then there is typically a negotiation over the particulars of time, place, and the composition of the party. Whom we are dancing with is more important than the quality of the music. In fact, the right quality of interaction can turn a B-movie into a memorable evening or make the walk home more important than the concert. At least within some limits of awfulness, the "whom" seems more important than the "what."

Why is this usually true? In many leisure settings, the central action is actually interaction. Few remember who won the beach volleyball game, but we remember how we met an exciting new friend. The numbers on the scorepad are soon forgotten when an evening of bridge is an excuse to be together with people we enjoy. Even a long anticipated trip to Spain can be thrilling when shared, and miserable when conflict with companions intrudes on the experience.

Some leisure is solitary. Some is emotionally intense. Some is detached entertainment. Some is challenging. But often, *the interaction is the action*. The activity and the environment are primarily a setting for communication, sharing, and articulated action. One danger of a preoccupation with psychological meanings is that the social nature of much leisure experience is overlooked. A focus on the nature of the activity obscures its common contextual nature. The central meaning is in the sharing. The challenge is in the communication. The risk is in self-disclosure. The creation is of community.

Of course, most interaction is part of the day-to-day round of life. As leisure, it is part of the "core" of ordinary and accessible activity. We enter into innumerable exchanges with others at work, school, and, most of all, around the home. Some are pointed and specific, related tasks and routine responsibilities. Some are ephemeral with little meaning more than a recognition of the existence of another person. And some are play, the creation of lightness in the midst of life's heaviness.

Leisure Interaction Settings

Georg Simmel (1950) called it "sociability." In such interaction, the focus is on the intersecting lines of action. Each person remains an actor, perceiving the context, interpreting the situation, taking some action, reading the responses, reinterpreting the situation, and revising the line of action. It is a process that retains some fluidity even in the most rule-bound and regulated circumstances. There are errors in interpretation, misreadings of the actions of others, and outright errors in judgement. On some occasions, we simply fail to comprehend how our actions, the verbal and nonverbal signs of meaning, are being received by others. "What we have here is a failure to communicate" most often refers to conflict emerging out of misreadings and misperceptions. It is a dialectical process, not just a matter of vocabulary or syntax.

In sociability, the primary meaning of the process is the process itself. The process is more important than who wins the game, scores the highest, or receives the award. In fact, many leisure events are constructed so that participation is the primary end. Differentiated outcomes are downplayed in favor of a concentration on the interaction. In sociability, the primary aim is the creation of synergistic mutual pleasure.

The social space may be defined with sociability central. The social space is deliberately defined as separate from the "serious" worlds of work, religion, and even family. In the games, there is no record of scores. Celebrations are designed to include everyone regardless of skill or status rather than singling out a few elite players. In such a separate social space, there is greater freedom to focus on the relationships. The aim is social expression, the playing out of the personal meaning of relationships. In some more exploratory situations, the aim may be to try out new possibilities of relating to others. In any case, the interaction process itself is primary. The spectacle, trip, game, or event becomes an environment for communication and sharing. Not only just "hanging out" but also scheduled events may have their primary meaning in the process of social exchange that develops.

The ordinary contexts of everyday leisure were introduced in the last chapter. The special point here is that playful interaction may take place anywhere. Computer keypunchers interrupt their monotony to kid about the disruptions that might be caused for unknown and distant clients if a decimal were misplaced. Truck drivers analyze yesterday's football game at the loading dock. Teachers flirt in the coffee room. And soldiers joke about casualties as they wait to load into a helicopter bound for a combat zone. As many have remarked, "It's what gets you through the day."

What may not be recognized is that such play does not just happen. It is a construction of deliberate action as well as spontaneous reaction. The kidding reflects the frequency of error amid repetition. The concern with football may compensate for the long hours of lonely boredom on the highway. The flirtation communicates real interest as well as social constraints. And the possibility of death is no joke even when serious discussion is unacceptable. Playful exchange mixes the realities of the situation with the nonserious and the nonconsequential.

There are also the designated locales of play. We expect to play at a party and serious conversation may be rebuffed as out of line. In leisure settings, however, a wide variety of play may be taking place at one time. Think of all the actions and interactions at a high school basketball game. How many personal agendas being played out have nothing to do with the game? How many histories are reenacted or protested at a family reunion? Just because the interaction is playful and without designated outcomes doesn't mean that the process is disconnected from the real world. We bring our identities, our histories and our hopes, even into leisure events.

One example of the mixture of actions and interactions in a single setting is the swimming pool (Kelly, 1987, pp. 130-131):

"What actually happens at a public swimming pool on a summer afternoon? There are various styles of behavior—from lounging near the fence and maintaining a convenient distance from the water to exhibitionist diving, a boisterous ball game, or solitary swimming of fifty laps. The variety is more than preferences for different degrees of physical exertion. Rather, it reflects both sides of a dialectic. On the one hand, the actors are presenting different identities through the media of the action. They are playing to selected observers and seeking to be defined as 'cool,' competent, risk-taking, sexy, or friendly. On the other hand, the styles of action are signs of how interaction is desired and implemented. Frolicking children, card playing students, self-conscious and posing teens, caretaking young mothers dividing their attention between conversation and protection, and lap-counting fitness seekers are all doing more than pursuing individual aims. They are entering and responding to social groups with particular modes of interaction. The leisure environment, the pool, provides a physical setting for the varieties of self-presentations and social styles. Further, the social world of the pool with its agreed-on customs and values enables actors to play out the identities and engage in the social interactions that express something of who they want to be and become. The pool is a kind of stage on which a variety of parts may be played and social exchanges negotiated."

What is different about the leisure setting? First, it may be more open than the work or family setting. The official agenda, for the most part, is expressive behavior. The roles are less rigid and the outcomes less predetermined. There is more openness for interaction focused on itself. Second, there is more of an expectation of play. In a work setting, the signal that what follows is not serious may have to be loud and clear or risk leading to misunderstanding. In a leisure setting, the opposite may be the case. We are expected to keep it light and keep external agendas out of the exchange. The primary meaning is more likely to be assumed to be the interaction rather than the outcome.

Second, the shared definitions are that the interaction is constructed for intrinsic rather than extrinsic reasons. Work colleagues who meet in a pub or rooftop lounge after employment hours on Friday are there to relax, have fun, and, perhaps, to make arrangements for some event during the weekend. At a cocktail party the aim is to facilitate conversational interaction. The expectation for relatively self-contained interchange is prior. Playful conversation, joking, story-telling, fantasizing, and other conversational modes intended to develop enjoyable rather than informational exchange can be inaugurated most easily. On the other hand, in a nonleisure environment, signals have to be given and acknowledged to change business into a playful transaction.

Relational Leisure: Family and Friendship

Then, what about all the playful interaction among those with highly consequential relationships? What about the situations in which roles cannot be abandoned? There are few situations in which parents and children are together in which fundamental role expectations are abandoned. Parents still act to protect children on a picnic or a bike hike. Children may "test the limits," but in the end usually defer to the authority of parents in leisure settings. Even a game such as "you be me and I'll be you" is a temporary suspension of authority that can be reestablished with an announcement that the game is over.

In such settings, there is almost always some attenuation of freedom. The responsibilities of being a mother are not set aside when mother and child play a game. The history of a relationship does not disappear when husband and wife take a walk or play golf. All the themes of complex role histories are still present when adult children play cards with their parents. The paradox, however, is that such leisure engagements that are usually lower on perceived freedom tend to be highly valued. The reason is simple: "relational leisure" is important to the development and expression of those relationships that are central to the meaning of our lives.

Interaction as leisure is more than sheer activity. It is a context for the expression of bonding (Cheek and Burch, 1976), for the development of intimacy. Relationships are more than authority, common action on required tasks, and meeting obligations and expectations. There is also the expression of the meanings of the relationship, of emotion and information, intimacy and agendas. Relationships need to be expressed in multifaceted ways. Any relationship has its own trajectory, its ups and downs, ins and outs. In a marriage there is a legal contract. There is also an implicit contract of mutual expectations and obligations. Far beyond the contract, however, there is a web of spoken and unspoken elements that change over the years and often build on each other. That web is spun in leisure, in expressive behaviors, as well as in doing what needs to be done to maintain the family. In fact, it might be argued that the expectations of a modern marriage call for the relationship to go far beyond maintenance requirements to a complex sharing of intimacy.

Again, the possibilities of such relational expression are almost endless. A young mother is cleaning up after her two-year-old's breakfast and preparing her to get ready for delivery to day care in a half-hour. In a few minutes, there is play with a toy on the floor, reference to a favorite book, delight over a new word or phrase, promise of a trip to the zoo on Saturday, and a series of smiles, giggles, and other affective exchanges. Amid the tasks surrounding eating and dressing, there are multiple levels of play, response, and interpretation. Would the period of time be listed as leisure in a time diary? More likely it would appear as task-oriented morning preparations. Is there play scattered through the time? Of course, and on a number of physical, verbal, emotional, and nurturing levels. Is it important? Probably most mothers would rate it higher than many events labelled "leisure." Relational leisure tends to be woven into the ongoing round of life with its responsibilities and tasks in addition to providing the central meaning of special events. Some now suggest that this relational and embedded quality differentiates much of the expressive behavior of women from that of men. If so, it is a matter of roles at least as much as orientations and values.

How are friendships made and expressed? In a social world in which workers seldom live in ethnic neighborhoods around the workplace with a thick network of interrelationships, many friendships are developed around leisure. Friends entertain and go out to eat together. They share cabins on vacations. Men fish together. Teens water-ski together. Grandmothers share pictures together. Neighbors exchange tools and talk. What is surprising is that increasingly friendships are inaugurated and developed in leisure. After work, women and men who have been engaged in various levels of communication and concerted activity scatter 360 degrees and do not meet again until the next workday.

One study of just-retired workers from a food processing plant in the Midwest (Kelly and Westcott, 1991) found that most had settled into retirement without trauma or major disruption. They had anticipated retiring. This pattern of "ordinary retirement" was characterized by considerable continuity with previous patterns of life. Some postponed tasks around the house and a trip or two were completed in the first few months. Then life usually settled into a set of routines in which the family was the center of the social world. Timetables, organized meals, entertainment, trips, social events, dropping in, exchanging assistance, holiday festivities, and other aspects of daily life were shared first of all with spouses, adult children, and other kin. Friends of long-standing, however, also took a significant place in such ordinary interactions. Activity patterns tended to revolve around the core of relatively accessible and low-cost activities. As one man said, "I just do what comes along." Most of what comes along is with family and friends. In fact, studies of older adults find that informal social interaction retains its centrality through the period when other kinds of activities are being abandoned. This was supported in the retirement study with the addition that many activities that were continued were done with established groups of friends.

The freedom-salience paradox is found most acutely in intimate relationships in which there is deep and sustained trust, sharing, interaction, and communication. Such relationships may be in the legal, economic, and social context of a marriage contract or in some other form. They may or may not have a central sexual component. Whatever the particulars, intimate relationships are absolutely central to life, to satisfaction, and to coping with the events of the life course. Such relationships combine the most profound and powerful expectations and the most far-reaching obligations. They are composed of such a vast history of entanglements that one analyst defined marriage as "what we've been through together." On the other hand, when asked questions such as "When do you feel most free to be yourself?," the most common answers do not refer to a time or place but to the presence of one or more intimate other persons. It is precisely in relationships that are deep and complex that we most often experience trust and acceptance. Wives, husbands, lovers, and other intimates are the most common companions in leisure. In those primary relationships, with all their strands of history, we also tend to feel most free and most expressive. From this perspective, leisure is more a quality of relationship than a feeling or a type of activity.

Relational leisure has its intrinsic meanings and satisfactions. There may be a high level of perceived freedom. Yet this does not occur apart from the necessary routines of life, but in the midst of them. Even in the special times separated from tasks in which behavior is primarily focused on the experience rather than an outcome, the chosen companion is most often one to whom we are most bound. Freedom is not always found most fully in segregation from central roles. Rather in the acceptance of intimacy, we may be most free.

Occurrences of Leisure

The times and places of activity remain important. Just who else is present is always a significant element of the meaning of any experience. However, as suggested in the previous chapter, considerable leisure is not in clearly defined and separated environments. Especially relational leisure may occur in the interstitial "break" as well as the special event. As with the mother preparing her child for the journey to day care, it may be very much in the midst of the daily tasks of ordinary life.

Such interstitial occurrences are not always brief and simple. Rather, there may be an intricate set of taken-for-granted rules that underlie a complex process of interchange. There may be considerable ambiguity that renders outcomes problematic and also inserts risk and uncertainty into the episode. One kind of engagement that calls for careful signaling and testing of meanings is in the common play of flirtation. The implicit ground rules, that may or may not be agreed upon by all participants, usually specify whether or not the episode is strictly limited to that moment or can have implications for further involvement. Usually a careful testing and reading of responses is required unless the flirtation is a routinized game in which the ground rules are well-established. Nonserious flirting is a common form of the "let's pretend" game that takes infinite forms in social settings. Gestures of affection, questions, and symbols of the unknown and untried are kept within the agreed upon definition of the situation. However, there is always the possibility of a shift in meaning when one person uses the playful definition to explore breaking through the limits to further engagement. If such a redefinition is understood and accepted, then all the symbolic communication, verbal and other, is subtly altered so that the new line of exchange can be developed. "No way" exchanges are turned to "what if?" In all this process, relatively fixed or changing, the interaction is the meaning of the episode.

In such episodes, there is the presentation, reception, and verification of identities. Participants are continually communicating who they are as well as who they might like to be if the interchange continues in a particular direction. Further, in all exchanges with sexual components there is the element of differential power based on factors such as gender, social status, organizational role, and presumed attractiveness (Rubin, 1990). In some situations, the game takes on goal-directed form as one actor attempts to gain compliance from another. Such compliance may range from a smile or momentary touch to intercourse in the game of "coquetry" (Simmel, 1950:50-51). In some games no outcome is attempted beyond the immediate response. In others the half "yes" and half "no" become a signal for advancing the game into a mode with outcomes beyond the immediate. Sometimes all that is sought is that the other offer a sign of sexual acceptance, that the actor is "attractive" as a woman or man. Some communication of placement on the "sexual hierarchy" (Zetterberg, 1966) of the situation is enough. The real meaning is acknowledged placement in some implicit ranked order of how one rates as a man or woman. Sexual identity is renegotiated in the play process with the meanings being entirely symbolic. In other cases, the compliance sought is more than symbolic as one actor seeks to "score" with a sexual response from the other.

This is only one illustration of the complexity of the social interaction process. Often there is more going on than a simple exchange of information, stories, or gestures. Rather, into interaction we bring our identities that have been developed over the years in a variety of settings and yet remain somewhat fragile and open to renegotiation. We are always becoming, in a process of self-definition that is advanced or retarded by our line of action and the responses we receive. In a social interaction setting, all the identities are presented in some situation-specific form. But the actors are not dolls or toy soldiers lined up in fixed positions. Rather there is always some fluidity to the process that takes on a life of its own. Seldom can any one actor fully manipulate the process unless there is a tremendous imbalance of power. There are multiple layers of meaning that are dynamic rather than static. And no two episodes have precisely the same pattern or outcome. Again, it is this multifaceted and problematic dynamic that *is* the interaction. Off-task interaction, leisure in the sense of being focused on the experience rather than a predetermined outcome, in all its complexity is the action. The setting, an activity or event, is often only the context for the real action.

All sorts of games may be played in such interaction. Community may be broken as well as built. Identities may be shattered as well as developed. Open play may turn into closed manipulation when one or a group of actors orchestrate the process for their own ends. There is always the possibility of fraudulent lines of action. Games may be used to seek advantage. Episodes may be staged to embarrass, trick, or otherwise put others at a disadvantage. Communication may be distorted to obscure intentions. A prerequisite of real play is honesty of presentation. When games are played to gain particular outcomes rather than to be involved in the process, personal agendas destroy play. More important, they may also destroy valued identities and an accompanying sense of worth. A mode of interaction may be designed to control rather than exchange. Differential power may be exercised to coerce outcomes. When this occurs, then the very nature of leisure—activity for its own sake—is violated. Yet, considerable interaction that passes for leisure because it takes place in designated settings—bars, health spas, or dances—is just such behavior.

Communication as Leisure

Any social world has its communicative conventions. Language and the metalanguage of communication about the nature of the conversation (Bateson, 1972) are understood as bearers of meaning. Examples from leisure settings illustrate how communication becomes the substance of leisure in interaction. In an urban establishment in which eating and drinking become a context for meeting other persons, there are multiple levels of rules. Communication is more than the exchange of identification, stories, and interest. It becomes part of the dance of negotiating the future, whether that future is one more drink, the evening, the night, or much more. First-level rules cover such matters as seating, paying for drinks, tipping, courtesy, verbal loudness, physical maneuvers, and other public conduct. Second-level conventions regulate more site-specific behaviors. For example, there are "wine bars" designed as settings to facilitate the inauguration of relationships among young office workers. Gestures, body posture, direction of attention, eye contact, level of conversation, and other behaviors are interpreted as signs of inclusion and exclusion. How one sits at a bar is communication. Sitting square may signal serious drinking. An open posture may signal receptivity to conversation. Conventions of introduction vary from one bar to another. And a clear violation of the unspoken conventions will usually lead to exclusion from the action.

The point is that there are many layers of communication. We may think of telling stories as the most common form of communication at a party. Yet, those stories are articulated into an agreed-on format for exchange. Further, verbal and body language signifies whether a current story is acceptable and entertaining or should be brought to swift completion. As skilled actors in social situations, we assimilate, interpret, and respond to multiple clues and signs of meaning simultaneously in ways that generally further the line of interaction. There is metacommunication, communication about the nature of the exchange, as actors signal that what is going on is acceptable or should be diverted. All sorts of conventions of deference and authority are mixed into what appear on the surface to be self-contained stories. All of this is incredibly complex, sometimes fascinating, and often intimidating. Yet, it is what we do in social interaction.

Constructed Events: Rules, Roles, and Conventions

Events tend to be planned and defined and usually occupy a defined social space. Leisure may occur in episodes that are more ad hoc and occur in the midst of almost anything else. Leisure also consists of events that are constructed primarily for enjoyment rather than extrinsic production. Such constructed leisure events are commonly located at sites with a designated leisure purpose. Such a location, however, does not make the events either pure or simple.

For example, camping may be understood as a drama of social roles (Burch, 1965). The drama is carried out on the open stage of the campground. The camp site may be a staging area for a number of activities such as hiking, fishing, swimming, or birdwatching. At the site itself, there is the possibility of group activity such as card games, volleyball, or singing around the campfire. Some activity is sex-segregated when the "men"—males age 10 and above—leave together for some foraging game with the aim of reinforcing traditional male images and identities. Normal roles, however, carry over from home as younger children are left with female caregivers who are expected to be responsible for organizing the campsite tasks. In fishing, woodchopping, and other "provider" tasks, adult males are able to demonstrate to the family roles that are normally hidden because of the separation of home and work site. Camping becomes an open stage for the reinforcement of engendered family and social roles.

As suggested in Chapter 11, the identities based on gender, economic position, and education may be dramatized in leisure cultures. Leisure events are often constructed to provide a dramatic social world in which identities stifled in the ordinary routines of life may be highlighted and developed. The dullness of everyday work, sex, or other experience is transformed in the artificial environment that offers a pretense of risk, domination, and effectual action.

One frequently studied site of such action and engendered bonding is the traditional poker group (Crespi, 1968; Zurcher, 1970; Kelly, 1983). A regular game of poker among players who may have some other social connection is structured for the single purpose of the game. That structure may be deceptively simple: a table, cards, and the official rules of the game. Systematic observation reveals a complex layered structure for what appears to be an informal evening. Several analyses agree on this complexity and the taken-for-granted nature of many of the binding rules and conventions. Such card playing most often takes place in a home that is cleared for the action of the evening. The groups meet with regularity. Members seldom miss even though Crespi found that most do not include poker among their favorite activities. Zurcher's analysis clearly reveals the various levels of structure that govern the interaction. The general rules of poker prevail, but are augmented by "house rules" that govern the amounts of money that can be bet, the range of games permitted, and responsibilities for banking the chips, providing refreshment, and inviting guests.

Second-level rules also provide a rigid structure for the repetitive event. Betting stakes are high enough to be consequential, but not high enough incur serious losses. Players should care whether they win or lose, but should never risk family maintenance, carfare, or tuition. In some groups women are not permitted in the room during play. In other they are allowed to observe quietly and serve refreshments. In none of the groups studied do women play poker with men. Further conventions regulate keeping the table clear for the game, quitting times and announcements, withdrawing a dime from each pot for beer, and the topics of conversation permitted. Such second-level rules are usually demonstrated most clearly in the rituals of recruitment and exclusion. Usually a guest is invited and "tried out." The house rules are explained. However, the alertness of the potential initiate on picking up on the taken-for-granted conventions and in responding to cues when violations take place largely determine whether or not he will be invited back. Sanctions for violations include subtle cues, informational suggestions, joking, ridicule, and, ultimately, exclusion. Core players expect neophytes to pick up on the clues and cues quickly and generally without comment or criticism.

What is going on in such an interactional leisure event? The scripts depend on the nature of the action as well as factors such as the external relationship of players. Work-based groups differ from neighborhood groups with their different histories of association. Nevertheless, Zurcher (1970) identifies a number of meanings for such groups. Some clearly refer to the presentation and confirmation of masculine identities. The "scripted competition" allows for self-testing without long-term consequences. Risk is real but limited. Opportunities to demonstrate skill are coupled with emotional control and mastery. What Goffman (1967) terms the "action" of the measured contest provides an excitement and experience of participating in an event in which something appears to be occurring. It may be a contrast from much of life in which activity leads to no clear outcome and action is rendered ineffectual. Poker yields outcomes that are signaled and recognized, for each hand and the evening. The subtleties of learning to interpret the gaming styles of others—their likelihood of taking risks, bluffing, and attempting to deceive—call for acute perception and interpretation of all kinds of signs and symbols. The evening also includes some retrospective analysis, consideration of missed opportunities, and announcements of event-bounded success.

Poker has problematic outcomes. No two nights end alike. Every event begins anew with each player equal no matter what the cumulative results of the past. The rules, conventions, and social rituals provide a clearly communicated and agree upon structure for the event. These permit concentration on the game itself. As Huizinga (1950) suggests, the play is set apart, not only in its results, but also in the parameters of the drama. Within this structure, two kinds of interaction are going on simultaneously: the game itself and the conversational exchange that is blended into the verbal communications that carry forward the action. With all the layers of rules, the event is also a context of informal interaction.

Leisure events tend to combine the two elements: interaction, informal or more orchestrated, and communicative exchange. That is, people play the game and they talk. In some events, the conversation is primary and the activity more of a context. In others, talk is not allowed to interfere with the "action" that may involve risk, gain and loss, and a high level of intensity. The focus may be first on the action or on the interaction, on the contest or the conversation. In the real setting, however, the distinction may be lost. The event is identified as a time and place of play. The action is real just because its consequences may be limited to the event. The self may be tried and tested in ways that are too costly at work or at home. Routines may be set aside or broken. For a time, life may seem more the way it was intended to be—action and interaction, relating and doing, in a structured context that facilitates the combination.

The Significance of Interaction

One form of leisure is social interaction. No focus on individual experience should obscure the pervasively social nature of leisure. Throughout the life course, interaction itself is a central component of leisure. Further, leisure provides a context in which significant relationships are inaugurated, developed, expressed, consolidated, and extended. This dialectic of leisure action and interaction is fundamental to the social nature of leisure.

Further, such interaction is embedded in the combinations of roles that we take through the life course. However defined a leisure event may be, we engage in its action as individuals who are students, parents, workers, and the players of other roles. Differentials of power, authority, status, resources, and skills come with us into leisure settings. Leisure is not "free" in the sense of being totally separated from the rest of life. Who we are in work, family, community, and other institutions impinges on leisure interaction. In some cases, actions are severely constrained by the intersection of such roles. Leisure may, in some cases, allow us to set aside many of those identifications to construct a largely self-contained event, but complete separation is unusual.

Who are the most common leisure companions? Of course it is those with whom we live and share multifaceted relationships. Considerable leisure is "relational" in the sense of expressing significant relationships. Such expression becomes the central meaning of the interaction, whatever its setting. Other interaction is bound by reciprocal roles that can never be fully transcended in any game: parent-child, foreman-mill hand, doctor-patient, mate or lover. The deference patterns of relationships of unequal power are never fully left behind. The histories of relationships are never totally absent. The agendas of work or family are never irrelevant to leisure exchange.

Out of this connected independence of leisure come a number of issues:

- Just how free is leisure when interaction cannot be wholly separated from other ongoing roles and relationships?

- To what extent can the rules and rituals of a leisure event provide a secluded context for riskful action that does not impact nonleisure roles?

- Are the taken-for-granted social norms of many leisure interaction settings a denial of the freedom of leisure or a basis for concentration on the action?

- Do the identity agendas and aims of social actors become the fundamental meaning of leisure occurrences and events? Is the play or game a singular environment for action or a stage on which we act out who we are and want to be? Are the two in conflict?

- How can the dialectic of leisure interaction best be interpreted? Do research designs all have to begin on one side or the other, with the individual or the organization?

- Just how significant are the interludes and interstitial episodes of playful interaction in nonleisure contexts? Are they really what "gets us through the day?"

- When interaction is fully incorporated into models of leisure, what remains of definitions and approaches that stress intrinsic motivation and freedom?

Whatever the answers to these questions, there is no question that interaction and leisure are central to one another. As such, leisure is not segregated from the ongoing processes of life together, but is woven through the entire texture of life.

REFERENCES

Bateson, G. (1972). *Steps to an ecology of mind.* New York, NY: Ballantine Books.

Burch, W. (1965). The play world of camping: Research into the social meaning of outdoor recreation. *American Journal of Sociology, 69,* 604-612.

Cheek, N., and Burch, W. (1976). *The social organization of leisure in human society.* New York, NY: Harper & Row, Publishers, Inc.

Crespi, L. (1968). The social significance of cardplaying as a leisure time activity. In M. Truzzi (Ed.) *Sociology and everyday life.* Englewood Cliffs, NJ: Prentice-Hall.

Goffman, E. (1967). *Interaction ritual.* New York, NY: Anchor Books.

Huizinga, J. (1950). *Homo ludens: A study of the play element in culture.* Boston, MA: Beacon Press.

Kelly, J. R. (1983). *Leisure identities and interactions.* London, England: Allen and Unwin.

Kelly, J. R. (1987). *Freedom to be: A new sociology of leisure.* New York, NY: Macmillan Publishing Company, Inc.

Kelly, J. R., and Westcott, G. (1991). Ordinary retirement: Commonalities and continuity. *International Journal of Aging and Human Development, 32,* 81-89.

Rubin, L. (1990). *Erotic wars.* New York, NY: Farrar, Straus, Giroux.

Simmel, G. (1950). In K. Wolff (Trans. and Ed.) *The sociology of Georg Simmel.* New York, NY: The Free Press.

Zetterberg, H. (1966). The secret ranking. *Journal of Marriage and the Family, 28,* 134-142.

Zurcher, L. (1970). The friendly poker game: A study of an ephemeral role. *Social Forces, 49,* 173-186.

CHAPTER 17

Satisfactions, Motivations, and Outcomes

F or decades almost all research attention was on the question of "What?" What do people do that may be labelled leisure or recreation? The secondary questions were "Where?" and "Who?" The location was important to those managing land, water, and other resources. Identifying the population segments most likely to engage in particular activities was important to those predicting demand or identifying markets. But underlying all attempts to explain leisure behavior is the question of "Why?"

The composition of the question varies. It may be couched in terms of anticipation: "What are the motivations for future behavior?" It may be immediate: "What are the experiences of an episode or event?" It may be a matter of perceived outcomes: "What are the satisfactions derived?" The focus may be on the decision process as in marketing research. It may be on summated outcomes as with research designed to predict future participation in types of activity. It may focus on selected kinds of outcomes—physical, emotional, social, or developmental—to the exclusion of others. In any case, exploration of the "Why" question requires dealing with the consciousness of individuals.

Early Investigations

This requirement kept the issue of motivations and satisfactions on the periphery of sociological research through most of the earlier period of development. The most distinguished exception was the Kansas City Adult Project developed by Robert Havighurst (1957, 1961) and his University of Chicago colleagues. Their design sought to identify patterns of meaning as well as likelihoods of participation. The methods employed were complex and rendered replication unlikely. Not only why do people choose their activities, but how is leisure related to family, work, and community roles? Do leisure patterns differ significantly for different groups who have varying opportunities, resources, and cultural values? And how is leisure tied to psychological factors and mental health functioning?

From this sequence of studies came the first inclusive view of the several dimensions of leisure meaning. The elements of relaxation, social engagement, and self-expression were all found to be part of adult leisure orientations. This was a dramatic advance over previous explanations that had tended to stress single themes.

Scales were developed and applied to specific activities to examine their multi-dimensionality. Dimensions of meaning identified were autonomy vs. other-directedness, enjoyment vs. time killing, instrumentality vs. expressivity, gregariousness vs. solitariness, service vs. pleasure, relaxation vs. arousal, and ego-integration vs. role diffusion. Other dimensions found were creativity, development of talent, future potential, physical energy input, status and prestige, and work complementarity (Havighurst, 1957). These meanings were attached to specific kinds of activity, not to a vague domain of "leisure in general." Further, the contextual factors of resources and social role relationships were related to combinations of meaning for the individual. As such, the design was thoroughly social as well as psychological in a model of the bridge discipline of social psychology. It may have been the comprehensive and interdisciplinary nature of the research, however, that prevented it from being a replicated approach.

A much simpler approach in the 1970s reflected some of the issues, but not the methods, of the Kansas City project. In a series of studies in three communities, a brief satisfaction scale was developed with as few as 18 items rated in salience for up to six "most important" activities by adult samples (Kelly, 1978 a,b). Many kinds of activity were found to be primarily social in meaning with satisfaction found in expressing and strengthening relationships and in companionship. Other kinds of activity had meanings more focused on the experience with its excitement, challenge, and physical, mental, or emotional intensity. Most leisure activities were done first of all for enjoyment, but the enjoyment might be intrinsic to the activity or to the social context. Further, many activities rated important had elements of role expectations since they were usually done with family members or other intimates. Like the Kansas City analysis, activities were found to be multidimensional in meaning with the form of the activity as well as the social context relevant to the nature of the outcomes experienced.

Both of these approaches were based on sociological premises and grounded in the social context of decisions and engagement. Neither, however, took advantage of methods being developed by social psychologists who had a background in research psychology. Therefore, the major shift in the field came when those with training in psychology departments entered the field.

Early Psychological Approaches

At the University of Illinois, research in the early 1970s introduced social psychology to the study of leisure. Survey methods were enriched by the inclusion of meaning-indexing statements that could be reduced to factors amenable to classification. These meaning factors were then analyzed along with social placement variables to add a new dimension to the explanation of leisure participation (Bishop, 1970). The three main types of leisure were labelled "active-diversionary, potency, and status." These categories joined the nature of the activity with its meaning to the participant. The presumption was that individuals could be categorized in their leisure patterns by these activity-meaning combinations. Other uses of similar factoring approaches produced sets of activity clusters, sometimes labelled "styles." A comparative study of the results, however, indicated that the activity-meaning factors varied with different sample characteristics, lists of activities, and details of analysis (Kelly, 1983).

Nevertheless, the joining of measures of meaning with types of activity and characteristics of participants began a new agenda for leisure research. In the early period, the issue was addressed by those with both sociology and social psychology backgrounds. Attention to meanings in the form of motivations and outcomes, however, more and more became the province of psychologists. One of the most significant lines of research was inaugurated by B. L. Driver of the U.S. Forest Service and extended by a number of his students and colleagues. Their attention was focused on forest and other outdoor resource-based recreation (Driver, 1976). The methodologies developed were subsequently picked up and applied to other types of leisure activity.

In a summary of a conference held at the University of Illinois, seventeen meaning factors were identified that had been found consistently using these methods (Crandall, 1980). Even this early list demonstrates the multidimensional nature of the meanings of leisure to individual actors:

1) Enjoyment of nature, escape from civilization
2) Escape from routine and responsibility
3) Physical exercise
4) Creativity
5) Relaxation
6) Social contact
7) Opportunities to meet new people
8) Heterosexual contact
9) Family interaction
10) Recognition and status
11) Social power

12) Altruism
13) Stimulus seeking
14) Self-actualization, self-improvement, and feedback
15) Achievement, challenge, and competition
16) Way to kill time and avoid boredom
17) Intellectual aestheticism

Vocabularies differ from one study to another as do the ranking of the importance of the meaning factors. Modes of intensity vary from relaxation to challenge. Social distance varies from escape to intimate involvement (Iso-Ahola, 1989). The nature of the action includes physical and mental, competition to time filling, status achievement to altruism, and self-development to service. Again, some elements are primarily related to the form of the activity and others to the social context or natural environment. Later research would produce different patterns of style and specification of motives and satisfactions. The significant advance, however, was that a viable general approach was being developed to address the important issue of meanings. This approach called for participants to recall one or more experiences with a type of activity and to summarize the outcomes in preformed categories in the form of scales.

The time frame of this approach was recollective rather than immediate (Kelly, 1987: Chapter 2). The actual process of action and interaction was not segmented. The variations through the process of a leisure event were ignored in favor of a summation expressed in scaled responses. Nevertheless, if the aim was to add to the understanding of the likelihood of individuals repeating an activity or experience, such a decision would usually be based on a recalled summary rather than an analysis of the moment-by-moment experience. In any case, the approach was demonstrated to be viable and presumed to be useful. It was then extended through a number of variations.

Satisfactions: Positive Outcomes of Leisure

One common bias of the method was to include only positive outcomes in the scales. A dual presumption underlay this bias:

1) Individuals would not choose activities with negative outcomes; and

2) Positive recollections would draw them back to the same activity or environment.

The most extensive line of research from this perspective has been that sponsored by the U.S. Forest Service. Over decades of research in a variety of settings, participants in outdoor activities filled out schedules with scales. Instruments were completed in the environment, at trail heads and boat landings, at home and in groups. The scales were repeatedly analyzed and revised. In time a general pattern was established that could be summarized. Again, the multiple elements of meaning were demonstrated. Some outcomes were conflicting as well as complementary. All varied according to the activity engaged in, the nature of the environment, and the social setting. Overall, the "experience preference domains" could be reported in a systematic format (Schreyer and Driver, 1989):

1) Enjoy nature
    a. Scenery
    b. General nature experience
    c. Undeveloped natural area

2) Physical fitness

3) Reduce tension
    a. Tension release
    b. Slow down mentally
    c. Escape role overloads
    d. Escape daily routine

4) Escape noise and crowds
    a. Tranquillity/solitude
    b. Privacy
    c. Escape crowds
    d. Escape noise
    e. Isolation

5) Outdoor learning
    a. General Learning
    b. Exploration
    c. Learn geography of area
    d. Learn about nature

6) Share similar values
    a. Be with friends
    b. Be with people having similar values

7) Independence
    a. Independence
    b. Autonomy
    c. Being in control

8) Family kinship

9) Introspection
    a. Spiritual
    b. Personal values

10) Be with considerate people

11) Achievement/stimulation
    a. Reinforce self-confidence/self-image
    b. Social recognition
    c. Skill development
    d. Competence testing
    e. Seeking excitement/stimulation
    f. Self-reliance

12) Physical rest

13) Teach/lead others
    a. Teaching/sharing skills
    b. Leading others

14) Risk taking

15) Risk reduction
    a. Risk moderation
    b. Risk prevention

16) Meet new people
    a. Meet new people
    b. Observe new people

17) Nostalgia

These are not in order of importance. Eleven of the seventeen domains break down into subscales with identifiably different components. Further, as complex as this set of scales is, it is based on outdoor recreation experiences with little or no attention given to a range of activities and settings such as cocktail parties, movies, television, reading, dancing, listening to music, in-home interaction and conversation, sexual activity, or a thousand other forms of activity that may be leisure. Note as well that the social and experiential scales are all designed to measure satisfaction. Dissatisfaction may be registered only by giving a low score to an item or domain of items. The conflict among some factors, however, requires that experience high on one dimension would be low on others. In no case does this approach produce responses that claim that damage has been done by engaging in the activity.

A different analysis of this line of research has produced a somewhat neater framework for the analysis of experiential outcomes (Driver and Brown, 1987):

Probable Personal Benefits from Outdoor Recreation Opportunities

- Personal development
- Social bonding
- Therapeutic/healing
- Physical fitness/health
- Stimulation
- Independence/freedom
- Nostalgia
- Commodity-related

Again, even the summary list suggests that recreation is not generally a simple experience. No attempt is made in this research to develop one overriding theme or explanation of outdoor recreation. Rather, the greater the variety of participants and environments studied, the more complex the pattern of perceived satisfactions.

This complexity is not reduced by a second line of psychological research that incorporates a fuller range of activity. In this case, the aim was more directed toward possible uses in counseling than toward recreation resource planning. Further, the range of activities studied included many that are more ordinary and everyday rather than requiring special arrangements.

Two issues are addressed in the second line of research. The first concerns the psychological properties of leisure experiences. The second is how those properties are related to particular activities. In research with student and other populations, 45 properties of leisure experiences were identified from an omnibus scale with from two to eighteen items indexing each property. The 45, in alphabetical order are (Tinsley and Kass, 1978):

- abasement
- ability utilization
- achievement
- activity
- advancement
- affiliation
- aggression
- authority
- autonomy
- catharsis
- compensation (Freudian)
- counteraction
- creativity
- diffidence
- deference
- dominance
- exhibition
- getting along with others
- harm avoidance
- independence
- infadvoidance
- justice
- moral values
- nurturance
- order
- play
- recognition
- rejection
- relaxation
- responsibility
- rewards
- security
- self-control
- self-esteem
- sentience
- sex
- social service
- social status
- succorance
- supervision/human relations
- supervision/technical
- task generalization
- tolerance
- understanding
- variety

Note that all are not positive. There is a recognition of some negative elements in leisure experiences. The problem with such a list, however, is that experience elements become so narrowly defined that it is difficult to get a concept of the overall nature of experience. Further, instrumentation for 45 elements is prohibitively complex for many research situations.

In an extension of the approach, Tinsley has grouped many of the elements and related them to particular kinds of activity. The argument is not that an activity has only one meaning or dimension, but that there are consistent connections between the form of an activity and predominant outcomes. The clusters of activities with their meaning categories is as follows (Tinsley and Johnson, 1984):

1) Intellectual stimulation: working crossword puzzles, watching television, going to movies, reading fiction

2) Catharsis: watching basketball, bicycling, jogging, roller skating, swimming, playing tennis, playing volleyball

3) Expressive compensation: canoeing, camping, vegetable gardening, hiking, lake fishing

4) Hedonistic companionship: attending popular musical performances, drinking and socializing

5) Supportive companionship: picnicking, visiting friends and relatives

6) Secure solitude: collecting autographs, collecting stamps

7) Routine, temporary indulgence: shooting pool, playing cards

8) Moderate security: playing golf, bowling, playing guitar

9) Expressive aestheticism: playing chess, raising house plants, baking and cooking, woodworking, photography, ceramics, painting

The list of activities is, of course, still very partial. What is more surprising is the categorizations such as watching television as intellectual or collecting as solitude. The multi-dimensionality of activity meanings is recognized in the research, but lost in the categorization. In general, it is important to accept that the nature of the activity is one major factor in its meanings and outcomes. Further analysis, however, indicates that many activities have significant scores on more than one of the nine dimensions. The classification system fails to deal adequately with multidimensionality or with variability when situations change. One question is whether the complexity of leisure experience can be reduced to one or a few themes. At one extreme is an attempt to identify two dimensions, stimulus-seeking and engagement vs. escape and avoidance (Iso-Ahola, 1989) and at the other an approach that subdivides into forty or more categories. Are there other possibilities in the structure of experience?

The Structure of Meaning

One approach to simplification is to assume that there is a general identifiable category of behavior called "leisure activity." This approach avoids the differences in motivations and satisfactions related to the form and environment of the activity. The components are abstracted from experiences with specific activities and episodes into a domain referred to as "leisure activity" (Beard and Ragheb, 1980). Six components of meaning have been found to factor together:

1) Psychological: a sense of freedom, enjoyment, involvement, and challenge

2) Educational: intellectual challenge and knowledge gain

3) Social: rewarding relationships with other people

4) Relaxation: relief from strain and stress

5) Physiological: fitness, health, weight control, and well-being

6) Aesthetic: response to pleasing design and environmental beauty

Such a list tends to confuse longer-term outcomes such as educational and physiological factors with immediate experience. The most serious question is whether or not there is a commonly understood realm of behavior called "leisure." Any list of generic meanings and outcomes would encompass rigorous activity such as mountain climbing and competitive sport along with dozing in front of the television and daydreaming. The likelihood of agreement on what different respondents include as leisure would seem to be low indeed.

Nevertheless, a more recent attempt has been made to develop a scale that focuses on "perceived freedom" as the defining theme of leisure activity. This "Leisure Diagnostic Battery" is composed of a number of scales developed and refined in a series of studies. The allegedly simple concept of "perceived freedom" is called into question by the process. (How would an individual actually perceive "freedom" except in a definitional process?) In this case, five major dimensions are composed of numerous subareas. Again, the complex nature of leisure experience, even when divorced from specific activity, is revealed (Ellis and Witt, 1984):

Scales Composing "Perceived Freedom"

1) Perceived leisure competence: cognitive, social, physical and general competence;

2) Perceived leisure control: effecting positive outcomes;

3) Leisure needs: relaxation, surplus energy, compensation, catharsis, optimal arousal, gregariousness, status, creative expression, skill development, self-image;

4) Depth of involvement in leisure experiences: centering of attention, merging of action and awareness, loss of self-consciousness, control of self and environment, action with immediate feedback; and

5) Playfulness: cognitive, physical, and social spontaneity, manifest joy.

This set of subscales combines multiple elements that may, in some cases, be contradictory. There are psychological elements such as loss of self-consciousness and sociological elements such as status. Action elements such as producing outcomes and feedback and emotions such as joy are incorporated. The sources of the items are as varied as ancient psychological theories and contemporary concepts of Csikszentmihalyi's "flow" and Leiberman's playfulness. "Perceived freedom" comes to involve almost any perceived meaning from any source with a reliance on statistical sorting techniques to make some sense of the results. This scale may be applied to a particular setting or set of experiences as well as to "leisure in general." The intention is to identify the themes that are present or absent in the experience of an individual to provide a basis for diagnosis and remediation. To connect the results with a program, however, requires a clear delineation of how particular settings and activities yield degrees of the multi-dimensional psychological outcomes. Further, there are no measures of "actual" outcomes, only of abstracted perceived evaluations.

Also, underlying such psychological approaches is the concept of "need satisfaction" (Mannell, 1989: 289). Are there identifiable human needs that are satisfied by leisure activity? In fact, there are two related questions:

1) Are there any requirements of human existence that are met only by leisure? and,

2) Is there any evidence of requirements for human existence that are met partly by leisure?

An affirmative answer to the first question would require identification of an essential human need that is met in no other way. That might be an impossible task. An affirmative answer to the second question would require comparative research into the nature and functions of leisure in multiple cultures over periods of historical change. No psychological scale administered in a single society and historical epoch can address the issue. Further, an unexamined assumption of need satisfaction approaches to leisure is that the outcomes are positive rather than destructive, alienating, or wasteful.

Nevertheless, in the research introduced above and in other lines of study, there are a number of persistent themes. Most focus on the nature of the experience for the individual actor or on social relationships. The overriding dimension continues to be freedom in some form or guise. Other elements are involvement in the experience, beneficial personal outcomes such as development and learning, and a reinforcement of social bonding. Mingled with all such meaning dimensions is a vague but persistent theme usually called "enjoyment."

Dimensions of Meaning

Scales are not the only means of investigating the meanings of activity. A set of self-reports of actual experiences that individuals had found to be "memorable" and others that were ordinary or more "everyday" were analyzed. This approach has the advantage of not preforming the categories by which the experience is described. In this study, the most frequently reported characteristics were (Gunter, 1987):

1) a sense of separation from the everyday world;

2) freedom of choice in one's actions;

3) pleasurable involvement in the event;

4) spontaneity;

5) timelessness;

6) fantasy (creative imagination);

7) a sense of adventure and exploration; and

8) self-realization.

Note that again there are elements of action, heightened experience, involvement and challenge, personal development, and a special environment. Leisure is not just time and space, activity, or state-of-consciousness. It is all three and more.

In a combination of time diary and interview methods, Shaw (1985) also identified major themes of leisure:

1) freedom of choice;

2) intrinsic motivation;

3) enjoyment; and

4) relaxation.

Again, the common elements are choice, focus on the experience for its own sake, and enjoyment with the perennial relaxation demanding a place in the spectrum. As previously introduced, the challenge vs. relaxation dimension continues to suggest that no monothematic approach to leisure is possible.

This denial of simplicity is further elaborated in a model that is based on a review of other studies rather than empirical research (Gunter and Gunter, 1980). A significant addition, however, is that each of the properties may be absent or present. As a consequence, leisure may be alienated, separated from personal development and social engagement, or anomic, unconnected and aimless. The positive bias of most psychological research is countered in a model that includes activity that may even be destructive of self and community. The dimensions to be found in leisure, according to the literature review, are familiar ones:

- Choice: at least selected from alternatives

- Self-containment: action with an integrity of meaning

- Intense involvement and enjoyment: fully occupies the actor

- Timelessness: a suspension of awareness

- Fantasy: separation from ordinary routine

- Creativity: the possibility of novelty

- Spontaneity: openness

- A sense of exploration, curiosity, and adventure

Much ordinary activity, on the other hand, is characterized by an absence of all or most of these elements. Activity may be restricted, time-killing, routinized, and destructive of self and community. In a normative sense, such activity is not leisure. It may, however, occupy nonwork time; take place in parks or theatres; and have no end outside the experience. It may be a response to a condition of alienation rather than community (see Chapters 9 and 25).

Motivations for Leisure

Do the analyses and typologies presented offer a basis for understanding the motivations for leisure activity? Iso-Ahola (1989: 268) argues that intrinsic motivation is "the heart of leisure behavior." This is because activities done primarily for their own sake are most likely to stimulate optimal arousal and be enjoyable. The focus is then entirely on psychological factors. The findings, from psychological studies, that the nature of the activity and the social environment impact the emotions, consciousness, and enjoyment are rendered peripheral. Iso-Ahola goes on, however, to propose that a control of conditions and an enhancement of immediate and positive feedback enhance the likelihood of intrinsic motivation.

One problem with this approach is that "motivation" becomes confused with outcomes, satisfactions, and all the elements of the immediate experience itself. Motivation usually refers to factors in undertaking action. In a rational choice model, motivations are reasons. In a model that includes emotions, motivations may involve feelings, dreams, and other nonrational elements. Motivations, however, are made up of recollected outcomes in addition to anticipations. In the actual condition of decision-making, motivations become a weighted evaluation of the recollected past and the anticipated future. It becomes difficult to distinguish motivations for future action from satisfactions in current action and outcomes from past action.

The fundamental question of "Why?" remains. In an actual decision context, there is likely to be a highly situational jumble of factors. We do not, after all, decide to go on a picnic in general. The real question refers to a picnic at a local park on Sunday afternoon. Research has demonstrated that situational factors may be primary in the decision. Weather, the schedules and availability of particular companions, potential crowding of the site, the condition of transportation, recent history of familial or group interaction, and possibilities of alternate times and places are woven into the decision (Kelly, 1978b). Previous satisfaction with such picnics are relevant to whether the possibility is even considered. Costs and availability of alternative activities along with conflicting alternatives are factored in. A measured hierarchy of perceived outcomes such as developed in the research described above is only one part of the process. More pressing factors, including perceived role obligations, may take priority in the decision process. Further, the process may be a negotiation among several people rather than an individual response. In short, actual decisions are social as well as psychological in composition.

There is clearly a danger in any models of motivation and satisfaction that become too narrow and focused. For example, an experience sampling study of adolescent activity found a variety or "balance" in their activity patterns (Kleiber, Larson, and Csikszentmihalyi, 1986). Free-time activities were most likely to be enjoyable, pleasurable, and "feel free." Productive activities such as work, school or other, yielded more challenge and concentration which in Csikszentmihalyi's flow model are attributes of optimal experience. Particular kinds of nonwork activity, such as sports, games, arts, and hobbies, however, were rated highest on concentration and challenge. Students devoted the most time, on the other hand, to activity such as watching television and informal socializing that were found to be relaxing. The "affect balance" model of activity selection is supported by such research. Individuals seek some activity contexts that are challenging and demanding, that call for high levels of effort and concentration. They tend to evaluate such experiences as high on enjoyment, personal development, and other aspects of satisfaction. Conversely, they also seek some disengagement in relaxing and undemanding activity, some of which is informal and social. They anticipate a low level of demand and arousal in such contexts. They seek a "balance" in activity and in outcomes.

The point is that there is no single pattern or model of leisure in general. Rather individuals recollect past outcomes and anticipate future satisfactions in different combinations in different times and places. Leisure consists of both engagement and disengagement, both high levels of involvement and low levels of concentration and effort. The challenge and demand that lead to the optimal experience of flow (Csikszentmihalyi, 1990) are a significant element in the balance of leisure styles, but are not the essence of leisure. Rather, flow is found in conditions of high obligation and low choice as well as in states of perceived freedom and intrinsic motivation. Leisure has no monopoly on optimal experience of any kind. A sense of closeness and community may be associated with role obligation. Challenge may be found in the requirements of work. And leisure is actually most likely to be boring (Csikszentmihalyi, 1990). Being disengaged and entertained may also be perceived as free and for its own sake. Further, individuals may seek experiences of high or low involvement at different times and for quite different reasons.

The Multidimensional Nature of Leisure

The psychological approaches to the motivations and satisfactions of leisure outlined in this chapter underscore the complexity of the phenomenon. As has been presented throughout this book, leisure has many dimensions of meaning as well as many forms, locales, social settings, and degrees of intensity. Leisure takes place in actual contexts of time, place, activity, culture, and associations. Every attempt to abstract the action from its realities, from the concretion of actualization in ever varying situations, surrenders something essential to its meaning and dynamic.

On the other hand, leisure is psychological and social, a matter of consciousness as well as action and interaction. One striking aspect of the research approaches from psychological perspectives is that they tend to reinforce rather than conflict with the sociological. Social psychologists have found leisure to be varied on forms and meanings, multidimensional, and contextual. Disconnecting leisure from its actual forms and settings may be operationalized into a reliable scale, but is also abstracted from its changing diversity. When the psychological outcomes are tied to types of activity, the variations in meaning become evident. From no perspective can leisure be demonstrated to be simple, monothematic, or invariant.

However useful and informative the abstracted scales of attitudinal social psychology in revealing the diverse themes of leisure, they also present a clear danger. As lived experience, leisure is a process, not an undifferentiated abstraction. Leisure as action and interaction is dynamic, not static. The dimensions of experience rise and fall in salience. Within a single episode there may be concentration and inattention, challenge and boredom, communication and separation, high and low intensity. We may recall the peaks or the valleys, the highs or the lows. We may return to the action, the environment, or the relationship drawn by the highs and disregarding the lows. Or, we may seek to avoid adversity by deciding on different possibilities. We may focus on rational long-term outcomes or immediate emotions. Our attention may shift from the self to others and back, from action to evaluation, and from involvement to self-consciousness. And all of this dynamic is *the* leisure experience.

REFERENCES

Beard, J. G., and Ragheb, M. (1980). Measuring leisure satisfaction. *Journal of Leisure Research, 12,* 20-33.

Bishop, D. W. (1970). Stability of the factor structure of leisure behavior analysis of four communities. *Journal of Leisure Research, 12,* 55-68.

Crandall, R. (1980). Motivations for leisure. *Journal of Leisure Research, 12,* 45-54.

Csikszentmihalyi, M. (1990). *Flow: The psychology of optimal experience.* New York, NY: Harper & Row, Publishers, Inc.

Driver, B. L. (1976). Quantification of outdoor recreationists' preferences. Proceedings of a symposium on Research, Camping, and Environmental Education. The Pennsylvania State University, University Park, PA.

Driver, B. L., and Brown, P. (1987). Probable personal benefits of outdoor recreation. In *President's commission on Americans outdoors: A literature review*. Washington, DC: U.S. Government Printing Office.

Ellis, G., and Witt, P. (1984). The measurement of perceived freedom in leisure. *Journal of Leisure Research, 16,* 110-123.

Gunter, B. G. (1987). The leisure experience: Selected properties. *Journal of Leisure Research, 19,* 115-130.

Gunter, B. G., and Gunter, N. (1980). Leisure styles: A conceptual framework for modern leisure. *The Sociological Quarterly, 21,* 361-374.

Havighurst, R. (1957). The leisure activities of the middle-aged. American *Journal of Sociology, 63,* 162-182.

Havighurst, R. (1961). The nature and values of meaningful free-time activity. In R. Kleemeier (Ed.) *Aging and Leisure.* New York, NY: Oxford University Press.

Iso-Ahola, S. (1989). Motivation for leisure. In E. Jackson and T. Burton (Eds.) *Understanding leisure and recreation: Mapping the past, charting the future.* State College, PA: Venture Publishing, Inc.

Kelly, J. R. (1978a). Leisure styles and choices in three environments. *Pacific Sociological Review, 21,* 187-207.

Kelly, J. R. (1978b). Situational and social factors in leisure decisions. *Pacific Sociological Review, 21,* 313-330.

Kelly, J. R. (1983). Leisure styles: A hidden core. *Leisure Sciences, 5,* 321-338.

Kelly, J. R. (1987). *Freedom to be: A new sociology of leisure.* New York, NY: Macmillan Publishing Company, Inc.

Kleiber, D., Larson, R., and Csikszentmihalyi, M. (1986). The experience of leisure in adolescence. *Journal of Leisure Research, 18,* 169-176.

Mannell, R. (1989). Leisure satisfaction. In E. Jackson and T. Burton (Eds.) *Understanding leisure and recreation: Mapping the past, changing the future.* State College, PA: Venture Publishing, Inc.

Schreyer, R., and Driver, B. (1989). The benefits of leisure. In E. Jackson and T. Burton (Eds.) *Understanding leisure and recreation: Mapping the past, changing the future.* State College, PA: Venture Publishing, Inc.

Shaw, S. (1985). The meaning of leisure in everyday life. *Leisure Sciences, 7,* 1-24.

Tinsley, H., and Kass, R. (1978). Leisure activities and need satisfaction: Replication and extension. *Journal of Leisure Research, 10,* 191-202.

Tinsley, H., and Johnson, T. (1984). A preliminary taxonomy of leisure activities. *Journal of Leisure Research, 16,* 234-244.

CHAPTER 18

Specialization and Serious Leisure

The rise of specialization and professionalization in work has been paralleled by a similar phenomenon in leisure—the rise of the specialist. Many other explanations have been given for the rise of the specialist in leisure activity. It has been argued that higher levels of formal education combined with increased economic resources and increases in nonwork time have allowed individuals to go further in appreciations, skills, knowledge of and commitment to a given leisure activity. It has also been argued that much work today is being "deskilled" and that highly educated people are now using leisure as a means of obtaining satisfactions formerly found in work. The similar notion of "amateurism" as defined by Stebbins (1979, 1992), assumes that the rise of professionalism in work has given rise to a parallel phenomenon of serious leisure.

The Elements of Specialization in Leisure Activity

Specialization in leisure activity may have many elements. It may involve increasing sophistication in regard to skills, appreciations, equipment, commitment, language, and the selection of environments and other people with whom one participates. Specialization, according to Bryan, involves: "a continuum of behavior from the general to the particular, reflected by equipment and skills used in the sport and activity setting preference" (Bryan, 1977).

From studying fishing, Bryan identified four stages of participation in which increasing levels of specialization were evident. These included an initial stage in which the participant is a beginner with few expectations concerning the activity, a second stage in which the individual wishes to document his or her success and accept bigger challenges, a third stage in which technique, equipment, protocol, aesthetics and association with other similarly specialized individuals becomes important and, a fourth stage in which the individual may build his or her identity around the activity. Other researchers have found more stages in the specialization process, such as Hamilton-Smith's (1985) study of cavers (spelunkers) or fewer stages, such as Scott's (1991) study of bridge players. In Scott's study, bridge players could be classified as either "social" or "serious." Social players consciously resisted specialization while serious players actively sought it. Additionally, researchers have found that some forms of a leisure activity lend themselves to specialization more than others. Donnelly, Vaske and Graefe (1986), for instance, found that one form of boating, sailing, had a greater range of specialization than motorboating. Within both kinds of boating, they found that there was a hierarchy of specialization from day boaters, to overnight cruisers, to racers. The most specialized participants were those who raced sailboats with crews.

While Bryan's original research concerning fishers may not be applicable to all leisure activities, several conclusions of his research have formed the basis for subsequent theory and research concerning leisure specialization. Among these conclusions are:

1) that fishers go through a predictable cycle of angling experiences, usually moving into more specialized stages over time;

2) that specialized fishers have in effect joined a leisure social world —a group of fellow sportsmen holding similar attitudes, beliefs and ideologies, engaging in similar behavior and having a sense of group identification;

3) that attitudes and values associated with fishing changed with increased specialization from the consumption of fish to preservation and emphasis upon the nature and setting of the activity; and

4) the values attendant to specialization are inextricably linked to the properties of the resource on which the sport is practiced (Bryan, 1979, p. 174-175).

Thus, increased specialization in a leisure activity may involve a complex of changes which involve the individual becoming more knowledgeable, more judgmental, more identified with a group of similarly specialized individuals and more interested in the behavior for its own sake rather than a means to some other end. While specialization is a relatively new concept in the sociological examination of leisure behavior, several studies have examined specialization in regard to each of the areas previously discussed. In regard to the relation of specialization to the leisure environment or setting, for example, research has found that level of specialization is related to how participants perceive their leisure setting and is also useful in understanding the attachments formed to these settings.

The Amateur

Another way to view the process of specialization is that of the "amateur." Sociologist Robert Stebbins (1979, 1992) has studied people who go through a progression of increasingly serious involvement in activities from which they do not make their living. When an individual begins participation in a leisure activity, according to Stebbins, he or she is immediately confronted by professional standards. As professionalism has grown, beginners in many leisure activities are confronted with standards which make their own accomplishments seem insignificant by comparison. The beginning tennis player, for example, may watch professional players on television. At this point, the beginners must choose between starting a "career" as participants which will involve increased learning and identification with the activity or remaining a "dabbler," restricting identification with the activity and participating in a nonserious manner. If the participant begins the process of becoming an amateur, however, they move away from play and toward serious commitment. The "amateur," a term which in its most basic sense means one who loves, is more and more prevalent in society, according to Stebbins, because technology has closed most avenues for fulfillment in work. Work motivations, therefore, are sought outside of work through leisure activities which will lead to attractive identities. Amateurs, however, are confronted with many problems. They are serious about some form of leisure and are misunderstood by their friends, who often participate in the same activity just for fun. The avocation may get out of hand for the amateur, interfering with other duties. Amateurs get all wrapped up in their activity and may neglect duties to families or friends. They also have the problem of being outsiders in the professional world relating to their activity and must make their living elsewhere.

Leisure Experience as Career

The increase in the extent to which individuals specialize in various forms of leisure behavior has caused some sociologists to think of such behavior as leisure "careers." That is, there is a . . . "socially recognized patterned sequence of (leisure) roles, often with increasing prestige and rewards . . . " Additionally, individuals " . . . in a particular society tend to follow the same or one of a few standard patterns of role progression" (Theodorson and Theodorson, 1969, p. 37). Thus, while specialization in various leisure behaviors may differ in the amount of specialization possible and in the ways in which one follows the path of specialization, leisure "careers" may parallel careers at work. That is, in both instances there is a great range of meaning that the behavior may have for the individual, from relatively little to serving as a central source of identity. Additionally, in both work and leisure careers, the paths by which one may attempt further specialization are largely defined.

Another parallel in leisure and work careers is the concept of commitment, involvement or ego involvement. While not fully defined, these closely related constructs all deal in some way with the amount of importance and pleasure an individual associates with an activity as well as the level of "costs" of participation which an individual will pay in order to participate. A generally accepted definition of involvement is as follows: "Involvement is an unobservable state of motivation, arousal or interest. It is evoked by a particular stimulus or situation and has drive properties. Its consequences are types of searching, information-processing and decision-making" (Rothchild, 1984, pp. 216-217). Thus, as leisure behavior becomes more specialized, the individual may not only become increasingly interested in the behavior but also increasingly discerning in the "particular": qualities of the situation which are associated with this increasing interest.

While involvement is not yet a fully defined construct among recreation and leisure researchers, it has been defined as " . . . a psychological state of motivation, arousal or interest between an individual and recreation activities, tourist destinations or related equipment, at one point in time, characterized by the perception of the following elements: importance, pleasure value, sign value, risk probability and risk consequences" (Havitz and Dimanche, 1990, p. 175). Sign value refers to self-expression, the extent to which the behavior allows for expression of " . . . one's status, one's personality, or identity" (Kapferer and Laurent, 1985, p. 50). Selin and Howard (1988) identified five subcomponents of ego involvement: centrality, importance, pleasure, interest and self-expression. A situation or stimulus elicits high ego involvement when an individual finds it central to his or her personal values or important in terms of either salient enduring or situational goals. Ego involvement is related to feelings of pleasure and enjoyment and amount of interest shown in the situation or object. Finally, they found that ego involvement involves self-expression or the extent to which individuals express their self-concept or individuality through the situation or object.

Commitment has been used by sociologists as a means of explaining consistent patterns of behavior over time. Buchanan (1985) suggested that commitment has three major components:

1) consistent or focused behavior while rejecting alternative behaviors;

2) the presence of a side bet; and

3) the presence of affective attachment.

Consistent or focused behavior may relate to frequency of participant and specialization while a "side bet" refers to the involvement of other interest (such as purchasing related equipment or investing in practice time) to support the behavior. Affective attachment refers to "the specific mechanism underlying commitment (which is) dedication, inner conviction, or a moral imperative" (Scott, 1990). Thus, the activity is "personally pleasing" and "intuitively worthwhile" (Godbey, 1985). The consistent or focused behavior exhibited by committed persons is thought to be the result of a process and not a trait. While the concept of commitment to leisure activity is not the same as specialization or involvement, all three are closely related. If one becomes more highly committed to a given leisure behavior, he or she is likely to become more highly involved and specialized.

The dimensions which determine the degree of involvement or commitment of a participant in a recreation or leisure activity may be the attributes of the activity, the other individuals involved, the equipment or the setting in which the behavior takes place or some combination of these.

The Blurring of Work and Leisure Priorities

As the range of specialization, commitment or involvement in given leisure activities has increased for many people in modern societies, priorities between work and leisure are in a state of flux. It should not, therefore, be surprising that a Roper Poll (1990) found that, for the first time, a higher percentage of people (41%) thought leisure was more important than work than those who thought work was more important than leisure (36%) (American Enterprise Institute for Public Policy Research, 1990, pp. 118-120).

The Dutch historian Johan Huizinga, in discussing play, stated that "Frivolity and ecstasy are the twin poles between which play moves" (1950, p. 21). So it is, increasingly, with leisure expression. It may range from a pleasant diversion with little consequence for the individual to the central source of self-definition and life satisfaction.

In examining any given form of leisure expression, therefore, it is not surprising that there has been greatly increased differentiation in both forms of the activity and in its meaning. In regard to sport, for instance, it is difficult to find any single criterion to distinguish sport from nonsport which always applies to what we currently define as "sport." While sport may be defined as play, much of today's sport is in the realm of business and part of ordinary life. While sport is often thought to involve "physical prowess," surveys tell us that most participants today in given sports activities participate only a few times a year and thus are unlikely to have developed such prowess. While competition is thought to be inherent in sports, the New Games movement and other forms of cooperative sport purposely remove competition. While sport may be thought to involve a code of "sportsmanship," this code is massively violated at every level of organized sport. While sport may be thought to develop character or have a positive effect on potential juvenile delinquents, many collegiate and professional athletes have very high rates of criminal arrest. Sport, then, like other categories of leisure expression, is a term which has little inherent meaning until the level of specialization is described such as "pick-up basketball" or The Olympics.

In many other forms of leisure expression, the range of involvement is so great that it no longer makes sense to assume the activity in question has any inherent meaning.

REFERENCES

American Enterprise Institute For Public Policy Research. *American Demographics.* May/June, 1990(3): 118-120

Bryan, H. (1977). Leisure value systems and recreational specialization: The case of trout fishermen. *Journal of Leisure Research, 9*(3), 174-187.

Bryan, H. (1979). *Conflict in the great outdoors.* University, AL: The University of Alabama Press

Buchanan, T. (1985). Commitment and leisure behavior: A theoretical perspective. *Leisure Sciences 7*(4), 401-420.

Donnelly, M., Vaske, J., and Graefe, A. (1986). Degree and range of recreation specialization: Toward a typology of boating related activities. *Journal of Leisure Research, 18*(2), 81-96.

Godbey, G. (1985). *Leisure in your life: An exploration* (2nd ed.). State College, PA: Venture Publishing, Inc.

Hamilton-Smith, E. (1985). Personal interview. The Pennsylvania State University: University Park, PA.

Havitz, M. E., and Dimanche, F. (1990). Propositions for testing the involvement construct in recreational and tourism contexts. *Leisure Sciences, 12,* 179-195.

Huizinga, J. (1950). Homo ludens: *A study of the play element in culture,* p. 21. Boston, MA: The Beacon Press.

Kapferer, J. N., and Laurent, G. (1985). Consumer involvement profiles: A new practical approach to consumer involvement. *Journal of Advertising Research.* 25(6), 48-56.

Roper Organization, quoted in *The American Enterprise, 1*(3), May, 1990.

Rothchild, M. L. (1984). Perspectives on involvement: Current problems and future directions. *Advances in Consumer Research, II,* 216-217.

Scott, D. (1990). *An analysis of adult play groups: Theoretical and empirical considerations.* Ph. D. Dissertation. The Pennsylvania State University, Department of Leisure Studies.

Scott, D. (1991). A narrative analysis of a declining social world: The case of contract bridge. *Play and Culture, 4,* 11-23.

Selin, S., and Howard, D. R. (1988). Ego involvement and leisure behavior: A conceptual specification. *Journal of Leisure Research, 20* (3), 237-244.

Stebbins, R. (1979). *Amateurs—On the margin between work and leisure.* Beverly Hills, CA: Sage Publications.

Stebbins, R. (1992). Amateurs, professionals, and serious leisure. Montreal, Quebec, Canada: McGill-Queen's University Press.

Theodorson, G., and Theodorson, A. (1969). *Modern dictionary of sociology,* p. 37. New York, NY: Thomas Y. Crowell Co.

CHAPTER 19

Leisure and the Life Course

T he metaphor is that of "life as journey." Beginning with birth and ending with death, life is seen as a progression in which the self has continuity of identity along with developmental changes of competencies, interests, aims, and modes of behavior. In the life journey, there are sequences in the fundamental contexts of life—family, friends, locale, institutional roles, and resources as well as how we define ourselves. There are both continuities and changes in every aspect of our selves as well as in the contexts of our lives. We have a sense of who we are and might become that is always tempered by how others define us. We are existential beings who take consequential action and social beings who have learned everything from others.

The Life Course Model

The life course consists of *transitions,* changes such as finishing high school that are anticipated and accomplished at about the same time as our age peers. Those who move through the life course in the same time periods are termed a "cohort" as in the military metaphor they march together. They experience the same historical events at the same ages. Almost every life course also includes *traumas,* changes in health, family, or work that are unanticipated and require significant reconstruction of life. One study of adults age 40 and over found that most had experienced at least one major trauma and many had met a series of such losses and disruptions (Kelly, 1987).

Further, there are major role-based strands to the entire web of life course sequences. The first to be identified and employed as a model of analysis was the "family life cycle." Early versions presented "stages" of life, from the family of nurture through the formation of a family of procreation, with the assumption that each was different and identifiable. Later revisions more often referred to periods rather than stages and continuities through transitions through the life journey (Rapoport and Rapoport, 1975). The model identified central tasks and expectations associated with being in sequence an infant, young child, launched child, courting young adult, newlywed, childbearing parent, child-rearing parent, launching parent, postparental adult, grandparent, and widow. The assumption was that most individuals completed the sequence in order and in time. Contemporary use of the FLC model has been revised to take into account the increases in single adulthood, single parenting, divorce, remarriage, reconstituted families, aging alone, and variety in women's roles.

The life course, however, is not based on family alone. Rather, the economy, the school, the community, and other contexts are also the basis for sequences of roles. Each role sequence incorporates its own set of resources, expectations, associations, and tasks. When a sequence develops in a predictable and regular course, it may be said to have a "career." Many careers, however, start, stop, and restart in a pattern that is more zigzag than linear. From this perspective, there may be careers of family, community, leisure, and education in addition to work. Further, changes in any one career may impact the others. For example, unemployment affects every other element of life, as does becoming a parent, beginning or ending a marriage, or committment to a demanding "serious leisure" investment. Through all such change, however, individuals develop characteristic modes of behaving, interacting, problem-solving, and preparing for the future that provide continuity across career sequences and through time. One very sketchy framework for life course analysis would consist of parallel and intersecting role sequences as follows:

Figure 19.1
The Life Course: Intersecting Careers

Birth...Death

Themes: PREPARATION...............ESTABLISHMENT..............CULMINATION

Work: Skill learning.....Entry.....Career or series of jobs.....Withdrawal....Retirement

Family: Childhood...Launching...Marriage...Parenting...Launching...Postparent...Grandparent...Widow

Education: Play...School...College...Return education...Parallel learning...Other

Leisure: Play...Recreation...Family.....Reconstituted......Reevaluated.....Limited

---

For any individual, the sequences are likely to be revised by any of the events that may disrupt the career of predictable transitions. Fundamental losses of health, intimate companions, or economic opportunity impact every element of the life journey. For example, having to leave school before finishing secondary school to help support a family that has lost its primary income-producer will affect everything else throughout life. Every life course is unique. The framework is just that, a heuristic approach to systematic analysis, not a fixed formula for the prediction of any individual life.

Role Careers: The Social Context

The life course model is one extremely useful approach to understanding leisure. Leisure is, after all, not disconnected, but thoroughly embedded in the social contexts of relationships, resources, and requirements. Every major element of life has a *career,* however zigzag or uneven. The work career may be a series of mostly unrelated jobs. The family career may be disrupted by divorce or never include marriage at all. The education career more and more involves various returns to educational experiences rather than so-called "terminal degrees" and a permanent farewell to school. The leisure career may be diverted by a move from the sunbelt to the snowbelt or the activity history of a new life companion. Nevertheless, it is possible to trace connections through both the continuities and changes. Further, roles intersect so that a change such as becoming a parent has enormous impacts on all the other role trajectories.

The framework of the life course role careers includes the following:

- Both continuity and change characterize the individual. The shift from one period to another is most often a transition anticipated, prepared for, and taken in company with cohorts who share the experience.

- Both continuity and change characterize the social context. Old roles are left behind and new ones assumed. However, the social skills, intimate associations, developed interests and abilities, and resources tend to be at least partly cumulative and carry through the transition.

- The historical context is also significant. Major events such as wars and recessions and social changes such as shifts in sexual patterns and expectations affect the lives of each cohort at a particular time in the life course. There are differences in the Great Depression, World War II, Baby Boom, and Viet Nam generations.

- Most lives contain traumatic events. Only a minority of people move through the life course experiencing only predictable transitions. Disruptive events have powerful affects on both the resources and personal development of most individuals. The measured impacts of such disruptive events alone are sufficient evidence that there is no inevitable and immutable scheme that determines everything important in anyone's life.

- As roles change, so individuals change as well. There is an ongoing dialectic between contextual factors such as role expectations and related resources on the one hand and personal actions, aims, self-definitions, and dreams on the other. We are both products and producers in the dialectic of self and society that goes on throughout the journey of life.

Leisure and the Life Course

Two themes are intertwined in a life course approach to leisure. One is the trajectory of participation that is based on abilities, opportunities, and resources that change through the life course. What we do as leisure is related to the full context of role sequences, especially when there are major shifts in context such as leaving school or retirement. The second theme, the focus of the next chapter, is that of *development*. What happens to individuals, especially in relation to leisure, as they move through the sequence of life course periods? We are, after all, in the process of "becoming," of continuity-based change in who we are. Here, however, primary attention will be on what we do; the following chapter will add the dimension of who we become.

The three major periods of the life course—preparation, establishment, and culmination—do not divide neatly into equal numbers of years. In a social system, however, in which schooling is prolonged and earlier retirement is combined with longer life spans, the three periods are becoming more equal in length. Many do not leave school for the work force until their mid-twenties or later. Retirement in the mid- or late fifties is becoming more common with more life spans extending past the mid-eighties. As the day can be divided roughly into a 8-8-8 pattern of work, sleep, and leisure/maintenance, so the life course can be divided roughly into 20-30 years of preparation, 30-40 years in the work force, and 25-35 years of "official" later life. In fact, the divisions are fuzzy and blurred for most individuals as various parallel roles are begun, developed, revised, reconstituted, and left behind.

The Preparation Period

"Preparation" is that period of life in which much of the meaning is anticipatory. Children and youth are being prepared to assume adult roles in the economy, polity, family, and community. They are being "socialized" by learning the skills, values, world views, and habits necessary to participate fully in the culture and society. While the family is the primary agent of socialization, special institutions such as the school take a central place in the process. The period has a forward orientation, with at least some of the meaning of most experiences and learning directed toward the future. For a child, a play experience may have all its meaning in the moment. A child does not play a game to learn about generalized role expectations. A teen does not "hang out" with a crowd after school to explore the dilemmas of sexual identification and intimacy. The social system, however, organizes and provides for such experiences because they are part of the preparation process.

The descriptions and analyses that follow are in no way exhaustive, but are intended to illustrate how leisure and play behavior shift in form, meaning, and contexts through the life course. Such shifts are in part developmental as each person takes on the tasks of becoming appropriate to mental, emotional, and physical abilities. They are also in part social as expectations, requirements, and resources change in an age-graded progression.

Infancy: 0-12 Months

The play of infants is primarily response to environmental stimuli. Both the recognition of stimuli and the responses rapidly become more and more complex. Recognizing others (Peek-a-boo) may be simultaneous in age with an aimless manipulation of crib toys. The infant seeks sensory gratification in warm contact and increasingly in acting on touchable things that yield perceivable outcomes. Things move, make noises, and impact other things. As the infant develops, symbols become important and language usage begins. Words have meaning as designations and become part of play with parents and others. Play is very immediate and time periods for any action tend to be brief. Interpersonal bonding and effectual action have only immediate meaning at first. In later infancy, however, repetition widens into exploration. Simple symbolic designation ("mommy," "truck," or "bottle") allows for the beginning of patterns of action and communication. Play in infancy is *the* form of action by which the infant tries out possibilities and recognizes outcomes. In such play, the infant is also developing motor control and the bare beginning of social skills. Pleasure tends to be immediate and sensual, rather than laden with meaning.

Early Childhood: 1-2 Years

The learning dimension of play becomes more explicit, especially as parents and other caretakers make consistent connections between actions, implements, outcomes, and responses. The security found in parental bonding, usually with a primary nurturing caregiver, becomes reinforced by a variety of material and psychic rewards. Play becomes more oriented toward efficacy, getting results from actions. At the same time, symbolic connections with the "real" world emerge as toys are associated with larger versions. Play may also gain both the excitement and frustration of elementary problem-solving. Less and less movement is aimless. More and more is social, simple and short interactions, and the deliberate manipulation of play instruments (Piaget, 1952; Sutton-Smith, 1971). The child may combine imagination with action ("This rock is a bear. It's running.") Play involves gaining a sense of the self acting on the environment with some consistency of response. Pleasure is associated with efficacious action and with affectionate responses from playmates, whatever their ages. Both motor and social skills become more precise, accurate, and complex. At the same time, however, limits and negative outcomes are experienced in both the physical and social environments. Some things just don't "work" and produce frustration.

Later Preschool and Complexity: 3-5 Years

The child is becoming more self-interpreting. The social environment becomes more complex and differentiated with peer playmates in structured and unstructured settings. The family, however, remains a primary context of play, especially when there are siblings. Other children become more individually differentiated by gender, but also by consistent play characteristics. More and more the playing child creates situations that test anticipated outcomes (Erikson, 1963). Play becomes more complex in form as well as in social context. Institutional settings such as day care, preschool group learning programs, and organized recreational opportunities combine consistent adult expectations and even rules with larger and more varied peer interactions. Language becomes more central to play. The child continues to be expressive and seek immediate pleasure, but also has more complex and sustained instrumental aims. The world of play becomes more problematic and less reliable. Play combines imagination with design in imitative responses to the fantasy world of television and reading as well as the real world of observed adult behavior. Previous gender differences of restricted physical exertion for girls are probably reduced as expectations become less gender differentiated. Nevertheless, the toys and games offered and encouraged for little boys and girls still reflect anticipated adult roles. Few girls are given footballs and few boys have their own baby carriages. Norms of what is appropriate require more symbolic discrimination by the child. The rules and roles of games offer both excitement and learning about the regularities of organized social life (Mead, 1934; Opie and Opie, 1969). There appear to be significant differences in the more regulated and learning-oriented play situations dominated by adults and those that children organize for themselves. Even self-organized play, however, increasingly mirrors the adult world of work and of the play of sports and games. Social structures and symbolic meanings in play are increasingly in touch with the world of the future. That is, play is preparation as well as immediate.

Later Childhood: 6-11 Years

Gender becomes increasingly significant in allocating resources and shaping expectations. More organized recreation, especially team sports, are either sex segregated or gender biased. Children are graded in cognitive, motor, and social abilities in ways that open and close doors to recreation opportunity. Further, a child's evaluation of self may depend heavily on rated competence in organized play. Now, due to the school schedule, play has more designated times and places rather than being *the* main activity of life. Schools take a greater place in providing opportunities for learning and participating in various activities, especially sports and the arts. Comparative skill becomes a central issue in life. Being included or excluded may be decided by adults as well as by peers.

In this period, the power of the media, mostly television, comes to have a powerful influence on styles of behavior. Heroes from entertainment and sport may become fashionable. Children negotiate rather complex social situations, not always with success. While the family remains an important venue for leisure, various peer groups take on greater salience. They are not only contexts of activity, but teachers and reinforcers of values and tastes that may conflict with the family. There are also other adults of significance in the school and recreation contexts. In organized activities, children learn that all evaluation is not personal, but may be based on generalized sets of standards.

The consistent findings of gender differences (Lever, 1978) in group composition and orientation and in the activities themselves suggest that social norms and values are learned differently by males and females (Gilligan, 1982). For girls, affective bonding provides a basis for judgement different from the negotiated action system more common for boys. One current issue is the extent to which activities stressing competition and power negotiations are being offered and rewarded more for contemporary girls than for previous cohorts. The play of school-age children reflects the value orientations, anticipated roles, and organizational norms of the society. The reward systems of the school and organized recreation reflect the particular culture into which children are being socialized and that permeates every aspect of their lives.

Early Adolescence: 12-15 Years

This is a period of great change. The issue of sexual identity is compounded by bodily changes that more powerfully mark differentiation. Sexuality becomes more central to identity and choice, but is as much a source of bewilderment and confusion as identification and integration (Csikszentmihalyi and Larson, 1984). Social groups often consist of a small circle, usually of the same sex. The school, however, is escalating the evaluation of performance and differential selection for opportunities and rewards. Team sports, for example, become increasingly exclusive as participants are winnowed out of the competitive contexts. More leisure is informal, "hanging out" and consuming targeted media, than directed and organized. A number of themes are mixed into patterns of leisure in this critical transition period of development:

- Symbols of leisure engagement, especially music and clothing, provide statements of peer identification, independence from parents, and even rebellion.

- The peer group, increasingly differentiated by social status and stylistic symbols, specifies just how and where leisure will be engaged. Resistance to the family is more common, but varies widely among younger adoles cents.

- There is a fascination with the forbidden that may lead to exploration of sexual intimacy and of prohibited locales and substances.

- Often young teens experience conflict between their own orientation toward the immediate and the pleasurable, and adult insistence in preparing for the vague and distant future. This may be focused on a conflict between the school and leisure.

- Also, activities that are primarily expressive and immediate may be favored over those, such as sports, that are evaluative. Conversely, there is also a pull toward activities that confer peer prestige.

- Leisure has a primary function in providing opportunities for exploring heterosexual attachments. Being defined as acceptable and attractive may become a preoccupation for those socialized toward social group status. Again, there is ambivalence toward the fearsomeness and desirability of developing relationships with sexual dimensions.

For some younger teens, a performance-oriented activity may become central. For others, the family remains significant. In most cases, leisure becomes a social space for peer relationships. The activity may be less important than its social meaning in the peer culture. There is also the greater likelihood of restrictions on female leisure than male due to differences in sex roles that emerge most powerfully in this period. The concepts of power for males and danger for females is a theme of greater salience.

Later Adolescence: 16-18/20 Years

In some ways, this period accentuates the themes of the previous one. In this period there is considerable variation. In inner city areas, an economic abandonment augmented by the retrenchment of older industries has reduced employment opportunity. Teens who leave school may have few legitimate work opportunities or resources to escape the area. In other areas, entry-level jobs attract many who do not have the motivation or resources to enter higher education. At the other extreme, are those who plan four to twelve more years of education after completing high school. In between are those who combine community college study with jobs. The educational and economic position of the family combined with gender-differentiated expectations and role learning lead to a variety of education/work trajectories. In some circumstances education is valued as the pathway to later opportunities; in other situations, it is not.

Adolescence itself is a term that would be rejected by most in this age category. The immaturity and lack of sexual competence connoted would be countered by assurance of sexual experience and exploration. Most older teens are at some time "sexually active." Leisure means times and places for sexual interaction for most. Only a minority engage regularly in sports or other organized recreation. However, in both the games of sexual experimentation and those of physical skill, what is provided for, expected of, and permitted for young women and men varies widely. Most "games" have contrasting— sometimes complementary and sometimes competing—gender roles.

In this period, teens devote the most time to informal interaction—"hanging out"—and to the consumption of pop culture in the forms of music, television, and videos. The forms of group events, parties and less formal gatherings, varies according to socioeconomic status and neighborhood cultures. Further, status groups form cliques that exclude and include with sets of symbols that include activities and locales as well as clothing, cars, cassettes, and other consumer items. Some groups are formed around activities of school and community organizations in sport and the arts, but their adherents are always a minority. Small towns, suburbs, urban neighborhoods, and other settings may have quite different resources and activity patterns. Being African American in a Mississippi Delta town, a San Fernando Valley Mexican American, and a Scarsdale executive's teen headed for a Ivy League university are almost incomparable.

Yet, there are also parallel factors. The desire for peer acceptance takes on a more heterosexual cast for most. Institutional evaluation and achievement become more salient as doors to college and the work force loom ahead. It is a time of transition in leisure and in school:

- The sociosexual meanings of leisure are predominant for most.

- Experimentation with intimacy, independence, and even rebellion may become a central theme.

- Opportunities to demonstrate competence are significant for some, perhaps a minority, who are focused on the future.

From this time on, it becomes difficult to define periods of the life course by age. In this period, some are becoming parents and others remain tied to their own parents. Some have clear views of the future and further years of educational preparation. Others have no clear vision of the future and identify no doorways to anywhere. The variations in life course careers and trajectories become quite differentiated in this period. As a consequence, leisure patterns are also incredibly varied. They take place everywhere from the streets to churches, every time from after school to 3 AM, with adult mentors and with rebellious peers, in organization and disorganization. And the paths taken in this period may be highly consequential for future careers in family, work, and leisure.

Establishment: Production and Position

Two themes predominate in this central period of the life course: *productivity* and *placement* in the social system. Both themes provide the fundamental meaning of work, family, leisure, and community roles. Life is presumed to be *now,* not primarily in the future. The first transition, then, is leaving school, whatever the age. The second is the beginning of a new family unit, usually with marriage and at least the expectation of children. It should be noted, however, that the likelihood of marriage in the society is dropping from the previous 95 percent toward an 80+ percent level, almost half of all marriages end in divorce, and many children never or seldom have two resident parents. Nevertheless, life is clearly different for establishment adults.

The Transition to Establishment

Simply leaving the school behind has enormous impacts on leisure. All the programs and facilities are no longer available. Such a loss is especially acute when the student is leaving a college or university where sports are organized and facilities are free, entertainment offerings respond to the concentrated markets, and most schedules permit regular involvement. The degree to which leisure is centered on school programs varies more for those in public high schools. In any case, the former student now has to seek opportunities, pay for resources and facilities, and juggle a schedule that is not designed for regular leisure.

As opportunities are left behind, so new roles intersect to place new demands and expectations on those entering the establishment period. Work timetables provide a framework for the time available for everything else. Increasingly those timetables are variable rather than fixed for the year. Family roles, especially becoming a parent, impact all resources for leisure, especially time and money. Now that a majority of women remain in the work force during childrearing years, most take on the "second shift" of home and family maintenance before and after the employment day. Increased participation by males and lowered expectations for household tasks only partly offset the doubled roles (Hochschild, 1989). "Establishment" means a centrality of work and family in ways that reform the meanings and the practices of leisure from the preparation period.

This does not mean that leisure disappears while the "serious business" of productivity and placement is begun. Rather, leisure is changed in orientations and settings to complement the new roles. In an intensive study of former university students making the transition, six themes were identified (Kelly and Masar, 1980):

- The extra-residential leisure of students was largely moved to at-home entertainment and interaction.

- The sexual exploration of late preparation turned to commitment to a new nuclear family. This family then became the focus of most leisure.

- Becoming parents had the most dramatic impact on both the resources and aims of leisure, especially when the mother relinquished her work role.

- Some leisure was oriented toward social placement in joining status-appropriate organizations or activity contexts.

- For some with a strong work career orientation, leisure that conflicted with employment requirements or expectations was laid aside.

- Leisure priorities reflected intersections of resources, associations, and timetables related to work, family, and leisure. Previous leisure interests and investments were adapted to the new circumstances with some continuity as well as change.

The social context of the establishment period changes significantly as school roles are replaced by work, the centrality of the parental family gives way to the formation of a new intimate community with or without children, and the temporary community and residence of school years becomes a new series of locales. In intimate relationships, most often family, there is acceptance, social position, immediate interaction, residence, economic consumption and management, and gender-role investment. The "family" is the most common social base for leisure. The residence is the central place for leisure. Building, developing, and expressing relationships is a primary purpose for leisure. Even when relationships are tenuous and conflictual, they are central to the allocation of time and other resources.

The action theme is that of productivity. The entire positioning, reward, and sanctioning system of the society is based on that value. How we are valued, rewarded economically and in prestige, and given access to all kinds of resources depends on economic evaluation of the worth of our productive efforts. Differential rewards in work are based on the replacement costs and presumed value of economic functions. Even children may be rated and valued according to standards of present and future productivity. And leisure is commonly justified in terms of its contribution to economic productivity, as "re-creation" for work. In the transition to establishment, more is changed than places and schedules.

Young Adulthood: 19/21-29 Years

More commonly today, young adults enter the work force, but delay taking on marriage and parenting roles. This subperiod, then, has characteristics of both preparation and establishment. It is a time of crossing multiple thresholds into adult life. Fundamental to the other role transitions is the economic. Failure to gain a start on an economic pathway usually cuts young adults off from progress on family, community, and leisure careers. On the other hand, leaving the educational escalator this early may mean a lifetime spent in jobs that have little intrinsic excitement or trajectory of opportunity. Independence at this age often entails an income.

Young adults use leisure as a primary venue for meeting and developing relationships with others who are potential intimate companions. Places for activity are expected to be places of meeting. Clubs, bars, and neighborhood hangouts as well as churches, festivals, concerts, dances, and athletic events become gathering places. Those who are still students find numerous such environments in and around the school. They are in a longer period of preparation that may extend through several years of graduate or professional education.

For other young adults, however, this is a time of radical change. Starting work is more than gaining an income. This change is usually accompanied by other transitions. Moving from the parental home or campus housing to a private residence and taking on the consumer role with a car, appliances, clothes, some leisure instruments, entertainment fees, and perhaps a vacation trip transforms almost every aspect of life. The world of consumer credit opens a range of possibilities for leisure in addition to a world of long-term financial obligations. Income is more than spending money; it is the possibility of a new life style. In this new life, leisure is both symbol and substance in a revised investment of economic, personal, and social resources.

Nothing, however, changes life as does the marriage/parenthood package. Now that marriage is increasingly predicated on a decision to become parents rather than gaining regular sexual access, the two roles become more closely related. Not only do the contexts and resources, but also many of the aims for leisure change. Within marriage, activities and settings for exploring and expressing the relationship may take priority. Joint leisure at and away from home becomes more central along with parallel activities such as home improvement and watching television. The companionship of a premarital "courting" period that may or may not involve living together is intensified for some who place explicit value on enhancing the relationship and decreased for others who come to take the relationship for granted.

In any case, the birth of the first child changes everything. If the mother leaves the work force, her income is lost at the same time that the expenses of providing for an infant arrive. Most couples quickly settle into a pattern in which primary responsibility for the day-to-day and hour-by-hour care for the child devolves onto the mother. Pregnancy and childbirth precede this time of extreme demand on the energy and attention of the mother, usually partly at the expense of the marital relationship. Some fathers take a full share of parenting and even insist on reconstituting meaningful leisure for their wives. Most do not and may even reestablish premarital patterns of external engagement. There is, of course, continuity of interests and associations for young parents, but changes in time allocations, resources, and priorities are dramatic. Especially mothers of preschool children are more likely to refer to a "struggle" for leisure than to a reasoned "balance."

On the other hand, both women and men frequently attempt to maintain contact with earlier leisure engagements. Especially when there have been years of investment in gaining skills and when significant relationships are formed around the activity, young adults may try to reserve some time and energy to continue an important activity. More leisure takes place in and around the home.

Playing with children comes to be so mingled with care and nurture that both the meanings and satisfactions cannot be designated as free or required, leisure or responsibility. Nevertheless, there are also attempts to engage in activity that provides not only a break from work and parenting roles, but also its own intrinsic meaning and satisfaction. Leisure in this period is re-formed, but it is not annihilated.

Early Maturity: 30-44 Years

For most adults, this period continues parenting roles with children living at home. Childbearing is completed and offspring are being evaluated in school and other social contexts. Children become increasingly independent from family care and more tied to their own roles in school, as part-time and summer employees, and in community organizations. The parenting role gradually becomes less that of a caregiver and more one of support and even companionship. The eventual "launching" when the child leaves home is anticipated by a series of moves toward relative autonomy and independence. In terms of leisure, the great change is the child's acquisition of a driver's license.

In the economic sphere, in this period careers demonstrate at least promise of advancement or probably never will. Many jobs are recognized as "dead end" and may be left in lateral moves to more intriguing or rewarding environments. For most in the work force, there is a series of jobs rather than the articulated progress of a career. This might be seen as the central period of life in which productivity and position are achieved or not. For some, it is a time of striving and progress. For others, it involves coming to terms with many of the limits of life. Such recognized limits may produce a profound dissatisfaction and desire to make a fundamental change, in work, marriage, or even leisure. There is a tension between stability that leads to acceptance and accomplishment that leads to change.

In stability-oriented lives, leisure tends to be rather conventional. The husband-father devotes time and attention to consolidating his position in work and to family support. The wife-mother, more often now also in the work force, deals with complex household management tasks and child support and nurture within continual time constraints and conflicting role expectations. Leisure is defined primarily in terms of family cohesion, child development, and community solidarity. Leisure tends to be home and family-centered and vacations organized for common family participation. This integrated lifestyle may be described as "balanced" when the components of work, family, and leisure are in a relatively stable framework.

More and more, however, this stability is disrupted by events that alter the role intersections and unbalance their relationships. Divorce, loss of employment, or other traumas require more than psychological adjustment; they require reorganizing the structure of life. Environments may be altered by moving from one neighborhood or community to another. Women often reenter the work force if they have left it for childrearing or now have economic demands requiring a regular income. In such change, more people adjust than revolt. Part of the adjustment may be in leisure. Leisure may provide security amid change as activities and relationships are retained. Or leisure may provide new and renewed opportunities for developing relationships, demonstrating abilities, or even risking innovation. Physical fitness, competence in an artistic discipline or craft, travel, or immersion in an activity-based organization may become more central to both time allocations and self-definitions.

Whether or not life is radically reevaluated and restructured in later middle years, there are common changes even in the context of continuity:

- Childrearing changes from primary care through support to launching. Both constraints and contexts of leisure change as children become less a central focus.

- Launching together with work roles that are continued or redeveloped provides many women with more resources, both time and money, for leisure reinvestment.

- Single-parent families are highly constrained in both time and economic resources, especially when the mother assumes multiple roles with multiple children.

- Leisure may be one aspect of life that is reevaluated during the shifts in role expectations that occur during the transitions and traumas of mid-life.

- Leisure may be a dimension of stability amid change or an arena of exploration when novelty is missing in other domains.

Later Maturity: Age 45 to Retirement

This is the period often referred to as "postparental" even though most adults find that parenting concerns change rather than disappear. Nevertheless, the number of years between launching and retirement is now the longest in the life course for many. That is startling when it is remembered that in the 1890s, in most families a parent had died before the last child left home. The age of 45 is probably arbitrary. This establishment period may begin in a family sense when children are launched, in economic terms when careers reach a recognized plateau, or in a personal dimension when meanings are reassessed. It is a time in which individuals begin to recognize that life is more than half over, that whatever it means or is worth has no undefined future in which to achieve value.

For some, this realization provokes a crisis of meaning in which intimate relationships as well as work are evaluated and may be found wanting. For others, the change is neither dramatic nor reflective, but is more a matter of responding to altered sets of possibilities and expectations.

For many, this is the period of maximum resources for leisure. Despite the fact that participation in most physically demanding activities has lessened for most and disappeared for many, peak earnings coupled with reduced parenting demands tend to increase both discretionary time and income. Further, a career advancement orientation toward work is frequently stifled by a realization that current levels are about as far as one is likely to go. Even when the associations and routines of work are valued, its meaning comes to be more instrumental and defined in terms of the financial support of home, family, and leisure. Time to visit grandchildren or go fishing may be more valued than overtime income.

There have been significant cohort changes. More women are in the work force in this period, whether or not they have been during parenting years. More women will have had experiences of relative independence, both economically and socially. Up to half of the adults no longer have an intact first marriage. Further, every cohort entering this period in the twentieth century will have more education than previous ones. More will never be married. More will live alone. And more will expect to have an interesting and regular set of leisure engagements.

Leisure travel in this period continues to be mostly by car and commonly directed toward visiting kin. Mid- to later-life adults are increasingly being targeted as a major market for many kinds of travel packages, however. Former focus on those in their 20s and 30s is changing as the numbers in younger age groups are reduced and the resources of second-half adults for leisure increased. Although golf is the only sport that does not have a rapid decline in participation by those over 40, more men and women in their 50s and 60s now expect to maintain some level of physical activity. Noncompetitive activities such as swimming, cycling, and walking attract considerable interest.

The possibility of reinvestment in leisure is a recurrent theme. Especially women who have concentrated on childrearing may believe that now is the time to invest in some leisure oriented to their own development and expression. For many men and women, this time of later maturity may involve a shift away from the priority of work and the constancy of parenting, to activity that reflects greater value placed on the self and on intimate relationships. However, the later maturity period is also one in which adults tend to seek a balance among the life investments of family, work, leisure, and self (Kelly, 1987). Both self-expression and the "generativity" of contributing to the lives of others emerge as goals.

The place of leisure in this time of consolidation and review varies from person to person. Some look back, settle for where they have been and what they have become, and seek security and acceptance. Others want something more in the time ahead that is seen as limited. They may make changes in their priorities and allocations. Leisure may then rise in salience as options in other roles are closed. When employment is largely playing out the string and children are preoccupied with establishing their own lives, leisure may be the area of life most open for reinvestment. Waiting to be a grandparent and weeding the lawn may not be enough. The quality of intimate relationships is critical. Communication and sharing with family and friends is a major element in selecting activities and investments when such relationships are available. Some argue that in this period men may shift their values more toward such intimacy while women, preoccupied with nurturing earlier, may focus more on their growth and accomplishments (Ryff, 1985).

Culmination: A Time of Consolidation

The final major period of life is usually divided into two periods: "active aging" and frailty. More accurately, there might be three: the active period, a transition time, and the final loss of independence and crucial functional abilities. The trends seem clear. More adults enter each later life period in relatively good health, with viable financial resources, and with a personal history of varied engagement. The education levels of each cohort are higher than previous ones. Overall, the resources of each later-life cohort are fuller. Each cohort is expected to live a little longer. The issue, however, is the quality of life, not the length of life.

Leisure has an important place in addressing this issue. Research into satisfaction in later life had found that there are two prerequisites: functional health and financial viability. When older adults possess these, then two factors distinguish those who are most satisfied with their lives: engagement with regular, challenging activity (Palmore, 1979; Mannell, 1988) and quality relationships with primary others (Kelly, 1987). When work is laid aside, leisure becomes the primary social space for both meaningful activity and relationships.

The "Young Old"

Later life does not begin at any set age. From a psychological perspective, it begins when an individual accepts that life will come to an end and that the time remaining to make it worthwhile is limited. The reassessment begun in midlife takes on a greater temporal urgency. Physiologically, it begins when the ongoing processes of aging place constraints on activity that require significant adaptation. Economically, it begins when the work career is defined in terms of years left to complete rather than as a time of greater opportunity. Socially, later life is characterized by a gradual constriction rather than expansion.

The fuzziness of this definition is compounded by a number of social trends. Men are now retiring at younger ages, often in their late fifties. Sometimes this is by choice, sometimes due to employer action, and sometimes for health reasons. There is, however, no mandatory retirement age in most occupations, and some prefer to remain in the work force. Women are more likely to work on into their sixties, especially if they have not had a work trajectory that permitted them to put together an adequate financial package for retirement. Market providers are increasingly trying to appeal to older adults with advertising images of activity, especially in modes that require expenditures. The emphasis on health supports various kinds of physical activity. The new image of the "young old" is one of engagement rather than withdrawal.

There is evidence that older adults have lower rates of participation in some kinds of activity: sports, physical exercise, outdoor recreation, and travel. Cultural activity, family and other social interaction, community organizations, and many home-based activities decline little with age or only in the final years of frailty. Affective involvement with friends and family remain central to leisure styles (Kelly, 1987). Expressivity in personal relationships may involve both companionship and helping. Most of the "young old" now have some caregiving responsibility for parents or others entering frailty. When close to their children and grandchildren, they commonly combine the sharing of activities with various modes of helping.

In a study of the ordinary retirement of blue-collar workers (Kelly and Westcott, 1991), the most common leisure companion was the spouse. Travel was usually directed toward other family. Informal interaction with friends was combined with occasional events such as entertaining, eating out, and sometimes activities such as card games, fishing, or a organizational event. None, however, had any connection with age-segregated "senior" programs. Rather they found their lives relatively full and satisfying in activities with continuity from earlier years. They enjoyed their freedom from work schedules and demands. In general, they believed they had earned their new status that enabled them to do more of what they wanted when they wanted. There was little evidence of dramatic changes or taking on quite new activities or relationships. Life remained profoundly social, tied to other persons with whom the past years had been shared. Activities were most often social spaces for those relationships. Nevertheless, there were special activities that held interest: from fishing and rebuilding cars for men to more social events for women.

A reassessment of resources, abilities, and satisfactions may lead to a voluntary disengagement from some previous engagements and commitments. It may also lead to a concentration on those of highest priority. For the most part, however, the later years are characterized by continuity in values, lifestyles, and patterns of life even through the transitions of retirement. Most retired adults remain in the same community interacting with much the same family and friends in the same places (Atchley, 1989). Schedules are reconstituted in ways that cause many to claim, "I don't know how I had time to work!" Leisure is one dimension of life in which meaning is found. It is not separate, but tends to be integrated with the full set of relationships and responsibilities.

Leisure for some affords an opportunity for continuing and exploring self-expressive activity (Gordon et al., 1976). It can provide a context for trying activity requiring blocks of time not previously available. There is always the possibility of recapturing a commitment abandoned in the pressure of earlier years or even taking up something new. Investments in productive engagement may be replaced by activity that offers an opportunity to demonstrate competence (Kelly, 1987). The balance of life investments may shift more toward leisure and bonding with significant others. Such a shift is less marked for those who were already family focused or with central leisure investments.

Frailty: The Final Years

The last period of life is marked by a constriction in abilities, social bonds, and activities in addition to geographical range. Frailty, the loss of the competence of independent living, may come suddenly due to a health trauma or be a gradual decremental process. For married women, there is usually widowhood, the loss of a spouse with all the change and adjustment entailed. Giving up driving a car is a major loss in independence in our society that is so dependent on private transportation. Formal and informal supports may enable the increasingly frail adult to remain in her own residence and resist institutionalization for longer period. In the end, however, almost half of those over 80 will spend some time in care facilities, usually due more to the loss of mental than physical ability.

One function of leisure is to support all the competencies—mental, physical, and social—that delay frailty. Another is to provide a context for maintaining as many meaningful relationships as possible. Leisure, more and more in and around the home, also serves to provide interests and routines for those who become unable to go anywhere without aid. Shared activities become more with family and neighbors. Distance becomes an enemy. It is those who take the time and effort to come to the frail person, often those who are also caregivers in some ways, who are the remaining companions of the last period of life.

Again, one aim is to enhance continuity. Any activities that provided a sense of self-expression and ability in earlier years may be adapted and supported. Nevertheless, the process of entering frailty is one of loss in every dimension of life.

The Life Course and Leisure Issues

The life course framework views life as a process, changing and yet with significant continuities. The intersecting role sequences provide a social context for the life journey that incorporates resources, expectations, requirements, and self-concepts. All of these factors have their impacts on leisure, not only what is done but also how, why, and with whom. As will be explored in the next chapter, there are also developmental dimensions to leisure in this life course context.

This perspective is yet another affirmation that leisure is not a separate domain of life, but is closely connected with family, work, and community. Further, those connections shift as we move through life, sometimes with predictable sequences and other times disrupted by traumatic events. Leisure may provide continuity through such change, or it may offer one resource for dealing with the impacts of change. There are a number of themes that appear and reappear even in such a sketchy approach to the life course:

- Leisure is always tied to the immediate communities of the life course period, family and peers with whom we interact regularly.

- Leisure also provides opportunities to develop and demonstrate competence in activities that have a career over the years.

- Leisure may rise and fall in salience through the life course amid the full set of commitments and obligations associated with family, work, and other roles.

- The play of childhood, the exploration of adolescence, the intimacy building of young adulthood, competence and reexamination in midlife, and social integration in later years are only a few of the central themes that are developed in leisure. The life course metaphor provides further evidence that leisure may be central rather than peripheral to life's central concerns.

REFERENCES

Atchley, R. (1989). A continuity theory of normal aging. *The Gerontologist, 29,* 182-190.

Csikszentmihalyi, M., and Larson, R. (1984). *Being adolescent.* New York, NY: Basic Books.

Erikson, E. (1963). *Childhood and society.* New York, NY: W.W. Norton.

Gilligan, C. (1982). *In a different voice.* Cambridge, MA: Harvard University Press.

Gordon, C., Gaitz, C., and Scott, J. (1976). Leisure and lives: Personal expressivity across the life span. In R. Binstock and E. Shanas (Eds.) *Handbook of aging and the social sciences.* New York, NY: Van Nostrand Reinhold.

Hochschild, A. (1989). *The second shift.* New York, NY: Viking Penguin, Inc.

Kelly, J. R. (1987). *Peoria winter: Styles and resources in later life.* Lexington, MA: Lexington Books.

Kelly, J. R., and Masar, S. (1980). *Leisure identities in the student- establishment transition.* Champaign, IL: Leisure Research Laboratory, University of Illinois.

Kelly, J. R., and Westcott, G. (1991). Ordinary retirement: Commonalities and continuity. *International Journal of Aging and Human Development, 32,* 81-89.

Lever, J. (1978). Sex differences in the complexity of children's play. *American Sociological Review, 84,* 471-483.

Mannell, R. (1988). Leisure and non-leisure states during the daily life of older adults. Paper at the Research Symposium of the National Recreation and Parks Association. Kansas City, MO.

Mead, G. H. (1934). *On social psychology.* Chicago, IL: University of Chicago Press.

Opie, I., and Opie, P. (1969). *Children's games in street and playground.* London, England: Oxford University Press.

Palmore, E. (1979). Predictors of successful aging. *The Gerontologist, 19,* 427-431.

Piaget, J. (1952). *Play, dreams, and imagination.* In G. Cattegno and F. Hodgson (Trans.) *Play dreams, and imagination.* New York, NY: W.W. Norton.

Rapoport, R., and Rapoport, R. (1975). *Leisure and the family life cycle.* London, England: Routledge and Kegan Paul.

Ryff, C. (1985). Adult personality development and the motivation for personal growth. In D. Kleiber and M. Maehr (Eds.) *Motivation in adulthood.* Greenwich, CT: Jai Press.

Sutton-Smith, B. (1971). Children at play. *Natural History,* Special supplement on play. (pp. 54-59).

CHAPTER 20

Leisure and Personal Development

T he previous chapter examined play and leisure activity from a life course perspective. As role sequences unfold through life's journey, the resources, associations, contexts, and aims of leisure change. There is continuity as individuals recognize abilities, develop interests, and seek to repeat and enhance satisfactions. There is also change, both predictable transitions of age-related roles and disrupting traumas that alter the most fundamental elements of building a life. Through this process, leisure possibilities and investments shift in response to changing conditions. Chapter 19 focuses on what people do and the social contexts of their engagement.

This chapter takes those life course shifts in leisure meanings and engagements as the basis for asking a different question: "What happens to those individuals in their leisure careers?" Underlying this deceptively simple question is a second theme of the life course. The *developmental* metaphor is based on a variety of analyses of continuities and changes in the individual through life. Further, there are a number of analytical frameworks that attempt to demonstrate that each period of life has fundamental developmental requirements. Not only do we change through life's journey, but we *must* change to cope with the realities of life in that period. Behaviors, values, and self-definitions that work quite well for teens fail to provide an adequate basis for life in establishment or culmination periods. Rather, each period of life has its characteristic *developmental tasks* as well as resources, roles, relationships, and requirements.

The developmental metaphors are not rigid and invariant schemes through which all persons progress in the same way and at the same rate. They vary in different cultures, by gender, and often by social strata. They describe a process rather than dictate an unvarying ontological order. Nevertheless, each framework offers one perspective on how we change from one period to another in a process in which each task builds on those that went before. Further, there is the suggestion that a failure to accomplish the developmental requirements of one period leave us unready to move on in the growing and maturing cycle.

Models of Human Development

Probably the most renowned formulation of such a life span developmental progression is that of Erik Erikson. He argues that there is a basic conflict at each major stage of life that must be met and reconciled before moving on to the next. His major focus in his earlier work was on childhood and adolescence with Freudian themes central. His analyses (Erikson, 1963) of development include the possibility of crises when the conflicts become particularly acute or difficult to resolve. The progression may be summarized as follows:

Period	Developmental Conflict
Infancy	Trust vs. mistrust
Early childhood	Autonomy vs. shame, doubt
Play age	Initiative vs. guilt
School age	Industry vs. inferiority
Adolescence	Identity vs. identity confusion
Young adulthood	Intimacy vs. isolation
Maturity	Generativity vs. self-absorption
Old age	Integrity vs. despair, disgust

(Source: *Psychology Today,* May 1987)

In later years, Erikson expanded the concept of the developmental crisis to encompass more of a sense of the significance of continuities of action by the individual and by giving more attention to the second half of life. The issue of inevitability vs. a more existential approach in which individuals act to construct their lives was raised by Erikson's own changes in analysis. Nevertheless, the premise is that maturing is more than getting older; it involves significant change in who we are and how we interact with our environments. We have to become different as we deal with fundamental issues of life.

A similar, but somewhat different, scheme is more explicitly related to expressive action. As Erikson's scheme tends to focus on self-acceptance in earlier years and in the final period of old age, the developmental dilemmas proposed by Chad Gordon and colleagues (Gordon, Gaitz, and Scott, 1976) are more social in character and oriented more toward action that encompasses the life spheres of work, family, and leisure:

Life Course Development and Dilemmas

Period and Age	Developmental Dilemma Security vs. Challenge
1. Infancy: 0-12 months	affective gratification vs. sensorimotor experiencing
2. Early childhood: 1-2 yrs.	compliance vs. self-control
3. Oedipal period: 3-5 yrs.	expressivity vs. instrumentality
4. Later childhood: 6-11 yrs.	peer relationships vs. evaluated abilities
5. Early adolescence: 12-15 yrs.	acceptance vs. achievement
6. Later adolescence: 16-18/20 yrs.	intimacy vs. autonomy
7. Youth: 19/21-29 yrs.	connection vs. self-determination
8. Early maturity: 30-44 yrs.	stability vs. accomplishment
9. Maturity: 45-retirement yrs.	dignity vs. control
10. Retirement: to disabling event	meaningful integration vs. autonomy
11. Disability: to death	survival vs. acceptance of death

(Revised version—source: Kelly, J. R. *Freedom to be: A new sociology of leisure,* 1987)

The fundamental dilemma of development, according to this model, is between security and challenge. There is the possibility of existential action that strikes out into territory that is at least in part unsettled and unknown. Such action always entails risk to whatever of the self is secure and settled. Against this challenge oriented toward growth, there is always the possibility of security. Such security may be found in primary social relationships, in the accomplishment of role expectations, or in self-definitions that are closed to new potential. In early childhood, this dilemma is perhaps least acute as developmental action is encouraged by the significant others of family and nurturers. Independent expressive action becomes more channelled and sanctioned even in early childhood. In adolescence, emerging independence and sexuality commonly place the individual in dilemmas of adult vs. peer acceptance as well as personal vs. social definitions of the self. In maturity (called Establishment in the previous chapter), social institutions of work, family, and community become more centrally the context of the dilemma between security and risk. In later years, however, there may a turning back to self-acceptance and the integration of values with actions.

Throughout such a developmental cycle, play and leisure offer a context for action with immediate feedback, identity expressing investments, social contexts of both acceptance and experimentation, and alternatives to the work-family roles. Leisure tends to fall more on the action/challenge side of the dilemma. As such, it may provide a critical context for seeking challenge as well as working out developmental tasks crucial to the period. Note that play and leisure are central to the developmental agendas of the first 20 or 30 years, depending on the time of the transition to establishment roles, and again to the reintegration of later maturity and retirement.

One further generalization about developmental models is significant. Note that they are phrased in terms of conflict and dilemmas. To summarize, "Whoever said that life was easy?" The developmental cycle is not a simple, linear path from birth to death along which individuals stroll together with their cohort companions. Not only are there disrupting societal events such as wars, recessions, and social conflicts precipitating change, but each developmental journey has its own setbacks, failures, and deep conflicts. Orientations toward action and growth are blocked by the organized agendas and interests of parents, teachers, employers, and other social gatekeepers. Orientations toward security and acceptance are thwarted by the insecurities and self-interested aims of those with entrenched powers of inclusion and exclusion. Even the institutions of the social system operate in ways that keep many individuals unsettled and on the margins of integration.

Learning in Leisure

In leisure, as in all of life, we are in the process of becoming—sometimes in deliberate ways and others in ways that we do not recognize at the time. Csikszentmihalyi (1971) has argued that in leisure experiences we are most likely to develop criteria for the rest of life. Expressive activities may be those in which experiences of the highest quality become the standard by which we judge other experiences from work or education. Gratification in the event, environment, or interaction may be highest in those times in which we have exercised the fullest choice. Work enrichment, for example, often involves enhancing the leisure-like elements of the work setting by increasing control over the environment or immediate feedback from the process.

One possibility is that leisure is chosen because of intrinsic interest and meaning in the experience itself. In such events, we learn that it is possible to become engrossed in some kinds of action processes rather than have entirely instrumental meanings. This may place many expected life tasks in a negative light. For teens, dull educational experiences are expected to be endured even though they fail to stimulate anything close to the excitement of many leisure settings and entertainments. Repetitious routines at work are accepted because the income supports the family and leisure even when they fail to offer any challenge.

At least as important is the educational principle that we learn best in conditions that maximize choice and offer a stimulating experience. Choice maximizes the probability that we will find that companions, environment, and action yield meaning then and there. There is most likely to be significant learning in such "high" and intrinsically involving experiences. When we are fully caught up in the action and receiving significant feedback reinforced by affective components, we are compelled by who we might be and become.

There is much more to learning in leisure than the enjoyment of the moment. Intrinsic meaning is developmental. When we devote high energy and attention to a situation, we are most likely to receive high-impact response. In games with measured outcomes, we learn on the spot how well we are doing. With significant companions, we receive symbolic responses that tell us just how we are doing with those who count. Competence is given an instant rating. Initiative is tried and evaluated. Children try out their abilities in play. Adults seek to demonstrate what they would like to be in the relatively open context of leisure. When the action works, self-definitions may be changed. The nature of leisure is developmental just because it is focused on the experience.

Throughout the life course, we learn interpersonal skills in leisure. In many institutional settings, interaction styles are prescribed and set. Many roles permit only a narrow latitude in their enactment. Leisure, however, may be less rigid. In general, parties are more varied in interaction possibilities than sales meetings, vacations than production lines, and games than driver training. The options for trying out variant portrayals of selfhood may be greatest in leisure. Therefore, the learning potential is also the greatest. Lines of action or self-expression found viable in leisure may be transferred to other roles and settings. Chapter 23 will develop further the critical issue of leisure as a context for identity development. Here the main point is that the relative openness of leisure allows for crucial developmental learning.

Four Themes of Life

The premise is that life is not all work, all community, all development, or all anything else. Rather, the journey of life mingles and intertwines a number of themes that together make up the meaning context of life. These themes may be in conflict at some times and be complementary at others. Further, each theme may have greater or lesser centrality to the construction of a life at various periods of the life course. Each theme is, however, fundamental to the multi-dimensional development of the individual who is simultaneously a social creation and a self-creating actor.

Four Themes of Life

Theme	Primary Institutional Context	Designation
Productivity	The Economy	Work
Bonding	The Family	Community
Learning	The School	Development
Expressivity	Leisure	Play

The common view has been that each of these themes has primary periods of life. In those periods, the theme is dominant, but still secondarily significant in others. Work would be seen as central to the maturity (or Establishment Period), development and learning to childhood and adolescence, and play to early childhood and retirement. Bonding and community shift meanings through the life course from dependence to sharing and care giving and back to dependence. Immediate communities, especially the family, are central throughout the life course as bonding is central to all social beings.

Another view would be that all four themes are significant throughout the life course, but in different ways and with varying centrality. Further, while there are evident conflicts, the themes tend to be complementary in an integrated or balanced life. From a developmental perspective, all four are necessary in every period. Nor is one necessarily dominant in the balance. For example, in retirement, leisure is a context for intrinsically satisfying experiences, meaningful social integration with immediate communities, the reconstitution of competence, and the possibility of valued contributions to the lives of others. Central identities related to work and family continue to be significant to self-presentations to others in community and leisure settings. Life, then, incorporates all four themes in varying combinations and contexts.

The review that follows will illustrate how the theme of play and the context of leisure contribute to development through the life career. It should be recognized, however, that in actual life situations, more often than not all four themes have some interconnected place in the action and interaction. The focus on leisure and learning should not be read as an assertion of their primacy in the scheme of life.

Childhood Play and Development

Even the most circumscribed focus on education and learning includes the context of play among children. Some even repeat that "play is the child's work." Such a view takes the perspective of childhood as preparation and tends to ignore that children play for the present experience, not future developmental solutions and outcomes. Nevertheless, play and development are closely linked.

Early Childhood

Different examples of the contributions of play to development among young children tend to concentrate on one aspect at a time. For example, motor control is developed in play that requires more and more complex and precise manipulations. The almost random movement of infants soon becomes refined as toys yield a reaction of effectiveness for the infant. Graded toys and self-constructed play implements become more complex and demanding in gross and fine motor control. In play, arms, hands, and legs are not just exercised; control is learned and developed.

Accompanying such motor learning is a wide range of affective gratifications. Just moving with control feels good. Further, the central other persons in the life of a small child express their approval with emotional responses, bodily and verbal, as well as specific rewards. The child learns to associate such positive affective responses with particular kinds of actions. Insofar as the basic developmental dilemma is that of compliance vs. self-control, play becomes the arena for trying out a variety of actions. Compliance involves the child "testing the limits" of action and learning the boundaries of acceptable and safe behavior. Self-control involves constantly trying out all sorts of physical, communicative, and emotional acts to demonstrate self-directed action within the contexts of acceptance.

Up to the age of 3, most interaction is at home and under the supervision of one or more caregiving adults. The mother figure is most often the central provider of both limits and contexts of action. More and more, however, the social context of self-directed action becomes more complex with the addition of other nurturing figures, siblings, and other playmates. Play is usually not organized. The responses are largely from a single individual to the child rather than generalized.

Play also provides the context for the development of the imagination, cognitive skills, and communication. More complex play requires coping with symbols that may be quite abstract. The toy is not really an airplane, but may be played with in ways that represent flying. Dinosaurs are not out there on the street, but have a kind of reality even before concepts of time are mastered. In play, even the beginning of humor may be comprehended and appreciated

(Lieberman, 1977). In general, it is the parents who set the context of play as oriented toward exploration and experimentation or toward repetition and conformity. Also, it is usually parents who have clearly gender-differentiated approaches to the toys and modes of play appropriate for little girls and boys or who encourage a full range of behaviors.

In general, in young childhood the child moves from the "autosphere" of self-exploration to the "microsphere" of external manipulation (Erikson, 1963). In the second year, the "macrosphere" of the larger world is opened in play with the gaining of social skills, ability to use symbols, and motor development. According to Erikson (1963), "Child's play is the infantile form of the ability to deal with experience by creating model situations and master reality by experimenting and planning" (p. 222). A further element in the environment of most young children now is television, bringing other symbols that increasingly capture the attention of the small child. In this period, play is closely tied to bonding within the family and to emotions of expressivity. Perhaps most central, however, is the child learning the possibility of effectual, although limited, action.

Middle Childhood

The period from age 3 to 5 used to be labelled "preschool." Now children of this age are commonly enrolled in a variety of semistructured programs that involve social interaction with nonsiblings, interactive play, and eventually activity directed toward learning. The consequences of this earlier introduction of social complexity in play are only beginning to be studied. Along with exposure to more complex media through cable television, the world of the playing child has become more diverse, more structured, and perhaps more advanced developmentally.

The developmental dimension of compliance takes on a more social form. Children learn to recognize a greater diversity of expectations and behaviors from other children. They also learn that few of their self-initiated actions will pass without some response from others. Sanctions may be from peers, parents, or other nurturers. Communicative skills are advanced as the child leaves the home environment in which private signals are accepted and interpreted. Videos designed for children offer a fuller set of learning experiences than the gross entertainment marketing of Saturday morning cartoons.

Play still involves learning the limits of compliance as well as the possibilities of self-control and directed action. Every element, however, becomes more complex and diverse. During this period abstract concepts such as time take on salience. Symbol systems become more complex and abstract. In many families, books excite the imagination with a variety of stories that allow the child to empathize with unseen characters and situations. Study of play in the forms of drawing and stories indicates that creativity develops rapidly up to the time of entering school and then slows dramatically (Gardner, 1980). Play awakens innovation that may be stifled by the routines of school and adults who reward conformity (drawing within the lines). The key seems to be play that is self-directed and open rather than oriented toward prespecified outcomes.

Some play roles and implements are clearly designed for preparatory role learning. The child wants in some distant day to become a fireman or even a doctor. Gender becomes more directive and specific. The child comes to know her or his gender as well as those of others in pervasive ways that shape every action and interpretation. Greater latitude for girls does not always yield a similar widening of activities encouraged for boys. Play involves identification with adults in imagined contexts of work and the "out there" world. The dilemma of expressivity vs. instrumentality permeates play. How much play can be open and freely expressive? How many actions must be calculated in terms of their results for the self and others? This period involves a great deal of trial and error as the child learns to look ahead in addition to the immediate. Competence is a constant issue. Learning that "I can" involves both "I am able" and "I am permitted." Even in play, children develop agendas with all the interpretation and evaluation involved.

Later Childhood

Now the context of life becomes increasingly institutionalized. Games may become organized sports. Learning is placed into the evaluated and routinized context of the classroom. In this larger world, the developmental dilemma is said to be peer relationships vs. evaluated abilities. It is more than a play vs. school division. Adult evaluation impinges on organized play, especially sports. Peer acceptance is relevant everywhere. The major shift, however, is toward the more consistent role structures of social institutions. The family remains central, but both competes and cooperates with the school and the role-laden world of recreation.

The school becomes a major context of informal interaction along with sport and arts activity. More computer learning may lead to electronic games. The skills for play, from reading to sport-specific practices are increased rapidly. At the same time, however, results are being evaluated—institutionally by adults and informally by peers. Self-definitions of competence and inability are being learned and then become central to choices and dreams.

Evaluated development through play may anticipate adult roles (Sutton-Smith, 1971). Social roles involve relative power based on abilities and gained social status. Fantasy and daydreaming become ways of projecting the self into an unknown future. In all such contexts, the child is learning how to take roles and enact them in ways that are both acceptable and personal. Games involve generalized roles and positions with their own prescribed expectations that are one way of learning about the social world (Mead, 1934). Some games foster innovation and others obedience in forms that reflect the adult society. Games may stress strategy, physical power, independence, leadership, accommodation, conformity, or flexibility. All are related to the abilities and values of later work and community roles. Further, learning itself is not only promoted but tested, judged, and ranked. "Better than" and "worse than" become central operating rules of action and interaction.

Again social skills are learned through the variety of settings and interactions of play that brings together directed action with the regularity of structure. The child becomes a more and more sophisticated actor and interpreter, or suffers the consequences. Gender differences in playground behavior reflect and prepare for later productivity and bonding (Lever, 1976). Negotiation and strategic competence in male play in larger organized groups and affective and communicative competence in smaller female play groups are connected with gender divided adult roles and orientations.

Sports are less likely to be sex-specific than even a decade ago. Girls are more often encouraged to engage in competitive team sports rather than take secondary, cheerleading roles. The learning that takes place in sport varies widely—from emphasis on obedience and conformity in team organization to opportunities for risk-taking, acceptance of positive and negative public outcomes, and handling pressure and stress. Organized sport, however, with its focus on results and ability, may leave behind more losers with negative self-definitions than winners who gain acceptance and courage. Further, the trend toward adult-organized sports for young children may lessen the self-organization and negotiation values of games that children organize for themselves (Kleiber and Kelly, 1980). The quadriplex ball field may not substitute fully for the old vacant lot. In the same way, performance-oriented arts programs may have quite different developmental outcomes than previous family-centered musical gatherings.

The dilemma of the period may have shifted away from peers and play to adult-evaluated performance (Elkind, 1981). Rigidity may dominate exploration. Judgements may supersede experimentation. Children may come to fear trying anything at which they may not excel. Pressure supplants spontaneity. In short, organized play may become too developmental and lose the values of its immediacy. In any case, play is clearly not a side issue in the development of children.

Adolescence and Youth: Independence and Acceptance

The teen years may be *the* critical transition period of life. Erikson has referred to it as a crisis period. It is a time when the themes of productivity, bonding, learning and expressivity take on new forms, social contexts, and urgency. Again, leisure is critical for development. Life becomes more complex. Leisure takes place in a greater variety of settings, especially as the driver's license opens a new world of mobility. Sexuality is the great and mysterious attraction that dominates the world of fantasy even more than of action. Identification involves specific peer groups with their symbols of clothing, music, and activities. Sometimes adult disapproval is reason enough to try almost anything.

Early Adolescence

The early teens are perhaps the most uncertain of life's periods. Peer culture rushes young men and women beyond familiarity and security to risk and experimentation. Adult authorities and gatekeepers try to hold back the tide and, as a result, are frequently quite out of touch with reality. Sexual identity becomes acute, but is also fearsome. Peer acceptance is often focused on a small group of intimates even when social status groups become models of behavior. In the school and other adult-organized settings, however, performance is evaluated according to adult rules and standards. The conflicting pressures for conformity to peer and adult tyrannies deepen the dilemma.

The themes of life are also conflicted. Bonding is torn between friends and family. Productivity is found in the measured adult contexts of school and sport. Expressivity takes the varied forms of peer culture with its mixtures of conformity and rebellion. Development takes place everywhere, but not in consistent directions. The venues are not just school and playing field, but include the halls, sidewalks, and meeting places for "hanging out," informal meeting without specific aim or agenda.

In this period of sexual change and awakening, everything changes. Gender becomes charged with sexual meanings and overtones. Beginning to establish the meaning of becoming a woman or a man now becomes explicitly sexual, not just a matter of gender. Establishing a sexual identity, not in the abstract but in the reality of relationships, becomes the central developmental preoccupation. And, for the most part, the context of the project is in leisure. Formal and informal interaction settings exist in and around various events, some of which are actually designed by adults to provide an alternative to sexuality. Watching, meeting, exploring, and experimenting are levels of interaction that are tried out on the streets and at parties, at church and at ball games, and in class and in the car.

Teens spend about 40 percent of their waking time in some kind of leisure activity: informal socializing with friends, watching television, in sports or hobbies, listening to music, or just letting the imagination roam (Csikszentmihalyi and Larson, 1984). They tend to be least happy when doing schoolwork, jobs, and chores and most happy when with their friends and away from adult control. The deepest satisfactions, however, come from accepting the discipline and risks of challenging activity and becoming deeply involved in the action. It is in such activity, whether in school or play, that a new sense of competence and purpose may be awakened and solidified. Development takes place everywhere, but there are significant difference between those that demand action and those that just entertain.

Later Adolescence

The study was repeated when some of the same students were high school juniors and seniors. Appreciation of family had increased. Most found life more satisfying as identities were more developed and some of the acuteness of earlier conflicts and uncertainties reduced. Some, however, tend to split work and play, productivity and enjoyment, effort and entertainment, in ways that promise poor preparation for adult roles (Csikszentmihalyi and Larson, 1984). Leisure is the primary context of peer bonding, both same and other sex, but often is based on artificial stimulants and amusements rather than sustained investment in either abilities or in relationships.

The dilemma may become more focused on a conflict between intimacy and autonomy. The desire to be close to one or more significant others conflicts with the exercise of independence and self-direction. As a consequence, many have a series of relationships that are characterized by both intimacy and resistance. Social acceptance remains a central preoccupation, but may be altered to incorporate more independence as life moves closer to the transition to college or the world of work. In areas where youth unemployment is high, inner cities and rural fringes, alienation in school and confusion as to where economic opportunities can be found may lead to anomic or even destructive leisure.

Investment in athletic and arts skill now tends to involve specialists who are a distinct minority. Adult-directed organizations and activities remain significant for a minority, but structures of exclusion along with disenchantment rule out the majority. Opportunities to experience demonstrated competence and meaningful engagement are often left only for the adept and those with special opportunities for support. At the same time, experiences of significant bonding and action may be found in a variety of marginal and even countercultural contexts. Both bands and basketball may be self-organized and provide important alternatives to school and community programs. In any case, most still seek enjoyment primarily in leisure and respond more to entertainment than challenge.

Development and Establishment

There is a tendency to assume that development is for the young and that all important personal characteristics are set in childhood and adolescence. While there are some for whom the life course is smooth and predictable, they are a minority. Significant change and even crisis lie ahead for most. The problem for summary analysis is that the adult life course becomes so varied and complex that only illustrations of developmental tasks and dilemmas can be given.

Young Adulthood—the Transition

The dilemma may be between connection and self-determination. As preparation orientations turn to entry into establishment roles in work and family, every element of life is transformed. Productivity is a goal for work and family, but also for leisure that takes on an "adult" aura of being constructive and appropriate. Considerable leisure may be directed toward what used to be called "courting," exploring and establishing a significant and central relationship. The old tasks of choosing a "life work and life partner" may seem more problematic and less final than for previous generations, but at least a beginning on those life dimensions is a central preoccupation.

For those embarking on the beginnings of employment and family careers, there are evident shifts to leisure that is more home centered, oriented toward an "intimate other," responsive to work role expectations and to a new social status configuration, and, in time, related to the opportunities, requirements, and meanings of parenthood. For some the transition from teen entertainments is difficult. For others new roles and contexts facilitate the shifts. The predominant developmental orientation of leisure may be toward intimacy and social position, but the urge toward self-determination and a personal identity may also lead to some special leisure investment. Again, for some a sport, artistic skill, cause, or even travel may take a high priority in the new balance of productivity, bonding, expressivity, and learning.

Mid-life Maturity

The most consistent leisure development for parents is the focus of leisure on the nurture and development of children. The forms and contexts change as children move through their own family based journey, but the centrality is almost universal. Performance orientations may shift to nurture and experimentation to consolidation. Most may not have an articulated work career, but most adults do have a family career in which the birth of children and launching are only two of the several significant markers.

The dilemma is said to be that of stability vs. accomplishment. Most often, there are salient changes in midlife that precipitate reorienting responses. In all of life's spheres—work, family, and leisure, there are transitions and traumas. Further, midlife often involves at least the beginning of a reevaluation of relationships, meanings, and priorities, even to the level of a "midlife crisis" (Levinson, 1978). Each of life's themes may be an arena for struggle between stability and change. The change may be forced as relationships, opportunities, and abilities are lost or altered. The developmental task is to reform life, preferably in a scheme that offers adequate promise of satisfaction and identity for the future. The balances of productivity vs. expressivity and community vs. self-determination may be reformulated by revised priorities. Leisure may be more expressively individual or more relational, depending on both life conditions and amended value systems. The aim is both to form a foundation for the remainder of life and to make changes that promise a full measure of satisfaction. Leisure may express both sides of the ongoing dilemma between security and challenge.

Culmination and Reintegration

When does "culmination" begin? Not with an age category, but when an individual looks ahead to recognize the limits of life and engages in a process of bringing it all together. Surprisingly, it may be a period of change in selfhood and commitments as well as stability.

Later Maturity

The dilemma of dignity vs. control is more individual than social. The context, however, is thoroughly social. Work roles are winding down and often completed in the mid- or late fifties. Parenting is turned to adult support, grandparenting, and often to caring for surviving and frail older parents. Development may be more directed toward the "meaningful integration" of relationships and of life investments.

The current surprise, however, is in the dimension of leisure (see Chapter 27). Those in their 50s and 60s are increasingly being found to be the "active old" who take advantage of their time and financial resources to travel, renew former activity involvements, and even take on new possibilities. Control of one's life may lead to an investment in activity believed to be satisfying in a condition in which productivity and bonding themes may lessen in importance. Leisure leads to a sense of "dignity" or meaningful identity when economic roles no longer promise advancement and family roles are less commanding. Personal competence and social connections may become more central to leisure as individuals reevaluate what is most worthwhile in the period of life remaining. There may be withdrawal from commitments found to be less central to selfhood or less satisfying as well as a reinvestment in relationships and activities that yield the greatest sense of being a worthwhile and able person. The conflict between security and individuality becomes less acute in later life so that leisure may be even more of an integrating factor in life.

Retirement - Later Life to Frailty

The dilemma of meaningful integration vs. autonomy may not be as conflictual as in earlier life. Integration is of meaning as well as relationships. More commitments and resources are directed toward social integration. The reciprocities of life are based more on bonds that can be relied on. Yet, they are being broken by frailty and death. Most women become widows. Health becomes more problematic. Leisure is a context for expressing and consolidating bonds that incorporate shared histories and future commitments of community. It may be less exploratory and more oriented toward solidarity, but is no less important. Further, in some cases, leisure is a major remaining opportunity to demonstrate productive ability and personal self-determination.

One study of "ordinary retirement" (Kelly and Westcott, 1991) found leisure to be thoroughly embedded in the daily round of life. Along with some travel that was usually family-related, life without the demands and routines of employment composed a fabric of interactions with friends and family that was marked by its commonplace character. Some older adults may integrate a major commitment to self-expressive and autonomous activity into the balance of later life, but for most leisure is a relatively satisfying set of engagements with significant social meanings. Those who maintain a commitment to challenging activity, however, are most likely to find life full and highly satisfying (Palmore, 1979).

Leisure and Development

The major theme of this cursory analysis is that leisure is quite central to the developmental requirements of the life journey. Rendered quite absurd is any view of leisure as residual or secondary activity. Many of the crucial elements of being and becoming human through the changes of life are found, expressed, and worked out in leisure. Further, from this developmental perspective, leisure is profoundly related to all the major themes of life. Actual investment in activity varies greatly from the play world of children through preparation and establishment roles and preoccupations to the reintegrated play world of later life. Nevertheless, activities have long-term implications as well as immediate meanings as social actors are engaged in a lifelong process of becoming. Who we are is expressed and developed in the intersections of expressive, productive, and relating action and interaction.

REFERENCES

Csikszentmihalyi, M. (1971). Leisure and socialization. *Social Forces, 60,* 332-340.

Csikszentmihalyi, M., and Larson, R. (1984). *Being adolescent: Conflict and growth in the teenage years.* New York, NY: Basic Books.

Elkind, D. (1981). *The hurried child.* Reading, MA: Addison-Wesley Publishing Co.

Erikson, E. H. (1963). *Childhood and society.* New York, NY: W.W. Norton.

Gardner, H. (1980). *Artful scribbles: The significance of children's drawings.* New York, NY: Basic Books.

Gordon, C, Gaitz, C., and Scott, J. (1976). Leisure and lives: Personal expressivity across the life cycle. In R. Binstock and E. Shanas (Eds.) *Handbook of aging and the social sciences.* New York, NY: Van Nostrand Reinhold.

Kelly, J. R. (1987). *Freedom to be: A new sociology of leisure.* New York, NY: Macmillan Publishing Company, Inc.

Kelly, J. R., and Westcott, G. (1991). Ordinary retirement: Commonalities and continuity. *International Journal of Aging and Human Development, 32,* 81-89.

Kleiber, D., and Kelly, J. (1980). Leisure, socialization, and the life cycle. In S. Iso-Ahola (Ed.) *Social psychological perspectives on leisure and recreation.* Springfield, IL: Charles C. Thomas.

Lever, J. (1976). Sex differences in the games children play. *Social Problems, 23,* 479-488.

Levinson, D. (1978). *The seasons of a man's life.* New York, NY: Alfred C. Knopf.

Lieberman, N. (1977). *Playfulness.* New York, NY: Basic Books.

Mead, G. H. (1934). *On social psychology.* Chicago, IL: University of Chicago Press.

Palmore, E. (1979). Predictors of successful aging. *The gerontologist, 19,* 427-431.

Sutton-Smith, B. (1971). Achievement and strategic competence. In E. Avedon and B. Sutton-Smith (Eds.) *The study of games.* New York, NY: John Wiley and Sons.

CHAPTER 21

Sex and Sensuality

While sex and sensuality have long constituted an important part of leisure expression, most sociologists interested in leisure behavior ignored them. Consequently, more attention has been given to comparatively rare forms of leisure behavior such as outdoor recreation, while little attention has been given to an almost universal form of leisure expression.

In this chapter, we will examine what justification can be made for the sociological examination of sex and sensuality as leisure behavior, some forms and meanings of such behavior in historical context, and current issues concerning such behavior.

Sex and Sensuality As Leisure Behavior

Various forms of sexual behavior have much in common with leisure behavior. First, all sexual behavior, even intercourse, is learned. Human beings are not born knowing how to kiss or have intercourse, nor do we have any fixed definitions of what is erotic, although we do develop sexual needs without being taught. Humans learn how to express these needs by seeing other people (or other animals), by experimentation, by reading or observing pictures, or by formal instruction. If none of these learning devices are utilized, the individual in question remains ignorant. Researchers at sex clinics have found that many childless couples were not able to have children because they didn't know how to have sexual intercourse. They hadn't learned how. "Going to bed" had not been sufficiently explained.

Also, as sociologist Nelson Foote has observed, the stimuli which cause sexual desire among males and females are primarily symbolic rather than physiological (Foote, 1954). That is, the things which stimulate us sexually are not fixed by our body's chemistry as much as they are learned symbols. In some societies, for instance, a woman's breasts may be considered sexually arousing, while in another society, women go bare-breasted. Large biceps and chest may make a man more sexually appealing in one era but not another. Consequently, we are not compelled by heredity to respond in fixed ways to certain sexual stimuli (although we may be highly conditioned by our culture). A related circumstance is that the human female, unlike other mammals, potentially will accept intercourse at any time. Therefore, humans develop longings for or aversions to sexual activity quite apart from instinct. Anthropologists have observed that in societies in which children are permitted to observe the sexual intercourse of adults, they may become active participants in full sexual relations several years before puberty. Freud contended that sexual energy (libido) was not a product of puberty but a basic life force from birth to death (Freud, 1938). How this energy is expressed is determined more by family relations and social experiences than by biological factors.

In modern societies, sexual behavior may be thought of serving three functions. According to Comfort (1976) sexual behavior may be categorized as:

1) procreational sex—for the purpose of producing children;

2) relational sex—total intimacy between two people; or

3) recreational sex—sex as physical play.

While some organized religions in our society haven't traditionally accepted pleasure as a legitimate motive for engaging in sexual activity, many have recently tried to head off the movement toward recreational sex by asserting that worthy sexual activity must be relational.

Recreational sex, of course, is nothing new. In even the strongest kin-based cultures, the gap between relational sex and sex designated to produce offspring has been filled by recreational sex. While some forms of sexuality expressed total involvement between two people, others reflected "an old human pattern in which sexual contacts were permitted between a woman and all her husband's clan brothers or a man and all his titular sisters (Comfort, 1976). Today, many in our society are beginning to believe that procreational, relational and recreational sex all have a role to play. The advent of HIV-AIDS, of course, makes such attitudes increasingly dangerous.

Forms of Sexual Expression in Historical Perspective

Sexual activity has always had the potential to be a form of leisure behavior, and the beliefs of various societies and the difficulty with which they struggled for survival have greatly influenced that potential. The earliest influences upon attitudes toward sexual behavior in the Judeo-Christian world were the Talmud and the Old Testament (Jahusz, 1973). Marriage and children were of the greatest importance to the ancient Hebrews, and all men, including priests, had to marry. A woman could be divorced for failing to have children.

In Greece's Classical Period, the main function of women was still childbearing. The Greek gods and goddesses were believed to have active sex lives and, perhaps because of this, many prohibitions against sex were absent in Greek society. The double standard was accepted in regard to sexual behavior. It was expected that married men would have sexual relations with women other than their wives, but this freedom did not apply to women. Marriage in Greece, Rome and other ancient societies typically was not based upon love, especially not upon romantic love. Since love was not part of marriage, men sought amorous activity outside of marriage. Women, other than prostitutes, were prevented from doing so by their home-based existence and second-class status in society. Finally, since homosexuality was more acceptable than in many other societies, it was common for older men to have sexual relations with young boys, and provisions were made for them to meet, both in temples and in private residences. The Greek island of Lesbos, which was believed to be inhabited by a number of female homosexuals, gave rise to the term "lesbian."

The emergence of Christianity reinforce women's second-class status. Man was considered superior, and woman was thought to be the cause of his downfall and misfortune since Adam and Eve. Even the institution of marriage was not made one of the seven sacraments until the sixteenth century. The worship of the Virgin Mary in the Middle Ages was responsible for the development of the code of chivalry by the aristocracy. According to this code, women were to be idolized for their character and, originally, sexual relations had no place in this concept. It was the beginning of romantic love, full of emotion and longing. Virginity was a virtue and a sign of women's moral superiority. As with many ideals, the reality of sexual relations during this period was far different; rape was common, and adultery flourished among nobility and peasant. While the church may have had strict prohibitions against many forms of sexual expression, priest themselves often used their religious authority to seduce women. Also, as historian Barbara Tuchman has observed: "While the cult of courtly love supposedly raised the standing of noble ladies, the fervid adoration of the Virgin (Mary) developed as a cult ... left little deposit on the status of women as a whole (Tuchman, 1978). Women were commonly considered inferior to men, and this belief was reinforced by the all-male clergy.

During the Reformation, Martin Luther and other religious leaders began to recognize the sexual needs of men and women, declaring that intercourse between men and women was normally permissible, and that frigidity and impotence were grounds for divorce. As the concept of chivalry spread to the middle classes, love became the basis for many marriages.

The Puritans who arrived in the New World were trying to keep their own way of life, which included the belief that sex except within marriage was sinful. The Calvinist belief in thrift, salvation through work, and the distrust of pleasure and idleness became part of the American character. Even in the mid-1800s there was shocked criticism concerning the introduction into society of dances such as the waltz and the polka. A member of the clergy complained of "the abomination of permitting a man who is neither your lover nor your husband to encircle you with his arms, and lightly press the contour of your waist" (Dulles, 1965). Nevertheless, these dances became very popular. Even prejudice toward mixed swimming gave way, although very slowly.

Victorian England maintained a double standard in regard to sex. A "lady" was expected to be ignorant about sex, acting as if she did not even know of its existence. Brewer has referred to her male counterpart as the boozing,whoring, one standard for me, another for my wife, typical Victorian male (Brewer, 1962).

Such attitudes are still found in our society, reflected in our beliefs and in the laws concerning what we may do in our leisure time. There are still laws against adultery in some states today, although they are increasingly unenforceable. In the early 1900s, such laws brought severe consequences to offenders, as the Chicago Code of Ordinances of 1911 demonstrates: If any man and woman live together in an open state of adultery or fornication, every such person shall be fined not exceeding $500, or confined in the county jail not exceeding one year (1925).

The revolution in sexual mores and behavior which has occurred, however, has blunted our distrust of sexual pleasure. Fewer laws exist governing sexual behavior, and those which do are often not enforced or are not enforceable.

Some forms of sexually-related activity, such as pornography, prostitution and sexually-related games and contests have existed in most societies in some forms since ancient times and continue today.

Pornography

Pornography may be considered a use of leisure in that it is a use of free time for purposes which the individual voluntarily and pleasurably chooses. Pornography is as old as humans, although the definitions of what is pornographic have varied greatly within different cultures. The art that is sacred in one culture may be considered lewd in another; one society may require that women cover their breasts in public, while another require that they cover their faces. Not all obscene displays that serve as leisure activity are so considered because of their sexual content. Our own society, for instance, bans certain forms of entertainment that were popular in other times and cultures. Such pursuits as bull and bear-baiting, in which large dogs were set on a bull or bear with a bloody fight ensuing, are not permitted because the cruelty to the animal is considered obscene. It should be noted, however, that our society does not seek to ban fictionalized violence as it prohibits fictionalized sex. Thus, a child watching television may watch one person murder another but may not watch them have sexual intercourse or even swim in the nude.

Leisure activity that could be considered pornographic may take many forms. The Report of the Task Force on Pornography and Obscenity has classified types of pornography in contemporary society as

1) book and manuscripts;

2) film and plays;

3) the spoken word;

4) art, pictures, and music; and

5) advertising (1970).

The Yale Law Review has provided a list of 68 methods of dissemination that have at one time been banned or prohibited by the courts of some states when they were thought to transmit obscenity (1966). Such methods include dancing, photographs, records, statues and drawings.

Books and magazines cover a wide range of written material of various quality, style and intent. Serious literature, such as James Joyce's *Ulysses,* has sometimes been held to be obscene. Other books are intentionally written without "socially redeeming value," primarily to arouse the sexual interest of the reader. (Sexual arousal is not generally considered to be a socially redeeming value, although some social scientists feel it has a positive effect upon behavior.) Many such books seek to use the frankest possible language. Some magazines, such as *Playboy,* have enjoyed huge success by combining sexually-oriented material with other articles and features not related to sex.

Films and plays may be classified as those which exist primarily in order to exhibit sexual activity, as opposed to those in which such activity is a natural occurrence in the development of the story line. As movies have become more explicit, the film industry has developed a code to distinguish the degree of sexual frankness or level of maturity for which the film is appropriate. This, of course, has also made it easier for those who want to attend sexually explicit films to do so by looking for the X-rated ones. Television, which is presenting more sexually explicit material, has sometimes also begun to inform viewers about the "mature" nature of certain shows. The issue of how far television should go in presenting sexually explicit material is an explosive one. To some extent, rental of X-rated video tapes, which have become available in most communities, allows adults to view sexually-oriented programming without children doing so.

Most societies consider certain words to be obscene, and therefore seek to curtail or limit their use. Part of the negative reaction presumably caused by such words is based upon linguistic and tradition. A word such as "shit," therefore, has a different value than a word such as "feces," even though they are synonymous. Such linguistic values are constantly changing; it is hard for us to image how Clark Gable shocked the nation in *Gone With the Wind* when he said "... I don't give a damn."

One form of leisure activity that often uses words considered to be obscene is graffiti, written slogans and risque or obscene comments in public places. In many ancient cultures, there is evidence of graffiti of the same type found today on the walls of public rest rooms and the outside of buildings in our urban areas.

In some societies, the visual arts may be considered simply by revealing the human body. The Report of the Task Force on Pornography and Obscenity, for instance, in 1970, bemoaned a "disturbing tendency of religious greeting cards to expose areas of cherubim's bodies which are best left private" (1970). Erotic art is found in most societies and attitudes toward it vary; from the extremes of considering it to be of religious significance to imprisoning those who produce it. Music and advertising usually are considered pornographic only in a subliminal manner. Such music motifs or rhythmic patterns are considered to be sensual or suggestive. Advertising often implies sexual rewards for those who use a certain product, or associate its use with sexually attractive people.

What is pornographic and what is not are often analyzed in our society on the following basis. Is it offensive? Does it incite lust? Is it repulsive and without redeeming value? In a multicultural society such as the United States, however, the range of opinion concerning what is offensive, repulsive and without redeeming value is extremely broad. This has made it quite difficult to interpret the test of pornography as stated by Judge Alexander Cockburn in England in 1868, which was used in this country until the late 1950s. The test was "whether the tendency of the matter charged as obscenity is to deprave and corrupt those whose minds are open to such immoral influences, and into whose hands a publication of this kind may fall" (1966).

The relationship between exposure to material considered to be obscene and the committing of sex crimes is not yet clearly understood. There is evidence that viewing sexual material does cause an erotic response in some people, but so does daydreaming. The effect of this erotic response, which is more prevalent in males than females, is subject to question. Some scholars have argued that pornography acts as a substitute for antisocial sexual behavior; others have contended that it stimulates such behavior. Perhaps the most disturbing finding concerning pornography, particularly sexually violent pornography, is that it tends to desensitize those who view it.

Today the U.S. Supreme Court leaves judgements concerning obscenity as a matter to be interpreted according to local community standards. Two difficulties arise from this approach. First, there may be great variation of opinion and attitude among those of the local community. Second, many materials in question are distributed nationally through the mails or produced for a national reader or viewership. Differing local standards make such undertakings difficult.

Pornography in all its forms is primarily a product of the male imagination. There is little history of pornography designed for females, except that produced for lesbians. The women's liberation movements, which have sought to make the roles of men and women more equal in society, may be partially responsible for the beginnings of a pornography industry aimed at women. *Playgirl* magazine, "beefcake" calendars, and male exotic dance revues represent a counterpart to many institutions designed for males.

It may be argued that pornography should be distinguished from erotica. Erotica is merely material which is sexually explicit. Pornography is the perversion of the erotic which involves degradation or violence. Understood in these terms, it is natural that many women's groups (and some men's) have fought pornography since women are the target of most degradation or violence depicted in pornography. The fear is that viewing pornography may desensitize the viewer to such acts viewed. There may be some basis for this belief. One study of college students found that 70 percent of males who viewed films of rape reported that they would be capable of rape (Pittsburgh Post Gazette, 1984). This disturbing finding also raises the larger question of viewing violence or degradation in nonsexual contexts. While women are the victims of most degrading or violent pornographic material, men are the victims of most violence depicted in the media. How are we harmed by viewing countless television murders, both real and fictitious?

Today there is evidence of an even wider range of opinion concerning pornography. While pornography is increasingly an issue for many women's movements, it is also increasingly available to the public at video rental stores. The content of television is increasingly sexually suggestive. MTV, a cable channel aimed at teenagers, is concerned almost solely with rock videos whose theme is sexual intercourse.

It is difficult to predict the future of pornography. There is some evidence that after the initial exposure to pornographic films, many viewers do not attend others. Pornography is ultimately repetitious, since the number of sex acts and displays is limited. Some observers believe that the widespread availability of pornography is one more indication of the extent to which sex has become shallow or meaningless in our society, with a corresponding loss of the capacity for deep love. Others, however, feel that pornography may help free individuals from puritanical inhibitions and disgust with our own bodies, and may actually enhance our capacity to love. In nearly all forms, pornography represents sex as a consumable item.

Prostitution

Prostitution has always been dependent upon men choosing to use their leisure time for sexual activity outside of marriage. In early Greece, where the double standard existed for men and women, two types of prostitution flourished. Since the Greek male believed that sexual intercourse not only was his right but was also essential to his health, prostitutes were considered necessary and were expected to accompany men in public, where wives were forbidden. Such courtesans were usually well-educated. The second form of prostitution began as a means of worship, since money paid to certain prostitutes was used for the upkeep of temples. Some of these "love goddesses" were slaves in supervised brothels, while others were women who voluntarily sacrificed their virginity to the gods and goddesses. Male prostitution also existed, since homosexuality was accepted.

Prostitution was evident in Christian societies in the Middle Ages. Although Christian emperors tried to abolish it, prostitution was finally accepted as a necessary evil in order to control adultery and rape. Prostitutes were sometimes organized into guilds and lived in designated houses in special districts. Unlike the Greek courtesans, however, they were often abused by their masters.

In industrial nations, prostitution became a byproduct of urbanization. It was reported that there were 80,000 prostitutes in London in 1800, even though the entire male population numbered only 1,300,200. In the United States, every large city had its red-light district, where men could gamble, drink and hire the services of prostitutes (Jahusz, 1973).

Increasing sexual permissiveness is thought to have caused some decline in prostitution during the last few decades. Today, however, prostitution is legal in several counties in Nevada and illegal, "free-lance" prostitutes are making a comeback in American towns and cities. Additionally, male homosexual prostitution is flourishing. Pittman (1971) described such male houses of prostitution, which exist in every major city, as ones in which a number of male "models," managed by a male "madam," perform sexual acts for homosexual and bisexual customers. The homosexual market values novelty and youth above all else. The advent of AIDS, of course, has made this and all other forms of prostitution a life-threatening behavior.

Prostitution is a way of life for many who are forced to live on the streets of our urban areas, when they are runaway or "throw-away" children, drug addicts, or the mentally ill. Such prostitution exploits the powerless and is dangerous for all concerned.

Prostitution is also being used as a basis for tourism. Many organized tours of Southeast Asian countries, often aimed at businessmen from Japan, Germany and elsewhere, feature prostitution as the main attraction. HIV-AIDS, of course, has made all forms of prostitution extremely risky for all concerned. This is made an even bigger problem due to the link between prostitution and drug addiction.

Sex-Related Games and Contests

Many forms of sexual behavior have qualities associated with play. That is, they have specific rules and require skills, knowledge and endurance on the part of players.

There are, for example, games and contests related to courtship. Traditionally, adolescent males have engaged in competitive games and contests with each other for the right to court or receive the affection of a female of their choice. Many such events, from the jousting of knights to high school football, are based upon the traditional notions of aggressive males and submissive females.

The New England custom of bundling represented a kind of courtship contest in which a girl and her suitor were allowed to get into bed together, keeping their undergarments on, after the girl's parents had retired for the night. Although the practice of bundling came about so that the courting male would not have to walk home on a freezing night, the sexual overtones were obvious. In some cases, parents provided obstacles such as a board fitted into a slot which divided the bed in two, encasing the lower parts of their bodies in tight garments, or even tying the girl's legs together. The degree of freedom parents gave such couples was often related to the desire for their daughters to be married.

Kissing games represent a form of courtship behavior which continued in this country after the more formal elements of courtship had been largely abandoned. A study by Avedon and Sutton-Smith (1971) of adolescents in rural Ohio found three distinct groupings of such games:

1) chasing kissing—games usually played out of doors by younger children;

2) mixed kissing—games of junior and senior high school students in which couples do not pair off before the game but pair off momentarily once the game has started; and

3) couples kissing games in which the pairing occurs before the game, which permits them to continue to enjoy their interest in each other.

Such games provide a kind of bridge in the social development of teenagers by allowing them the expression of individual impulses while simultaneously safeguarding the players by placing limits on the expression of such impulses. Sexually-related games, of course, are play and like all forms of play have rules. Today, many of the rules of courtship, as well as other playful ways of learning about and containing sexuality, seem to have disappeared.

All sorts of leisure, of course, have sexual dimensions. Not only is sexual action and interaction a major form of leisure, but there are sexual meanings and overtones in engagement in the arts, sport, and even walking in shopping malls.

We are such thoroughly engendered beings that all that we do is based on sexual identification. We present ourselves as engendered beings. We offer portrayals of femininity and masculinity learned in our cultures and social groups. For example, a high-school basketball game is more than an athletic contest; it is also an arena for the presentation of sexual identities and of sexual encounters. Events of mixed genders are quite different from those involving only one sex. In fact, both women and men sometimes seek to exclude the other sex in order to minimize the games that are common in mixed-sex environments. In fact, it is difficult to imagine any kind of recreation and leisure activity in which sexuality is not, in some degree, a factor. Sexuality is not segregated into any particular time, place, age, or type of activity.

Trends in Sexual Behavior

Sexual behavior has been reshaped during the last few decades by a variety of influences, including more effective means of birth control, changes in attitudes toward premarital sex, changes in women's roles, the advent of HIV-AIDS, and others.

Increases in Premarital Sex

There is little doubt that technology has been responsible for the leisure potential of much sexual activity. Effective means of contraception have drastically reduced the incidence of procreation in sexual intercourse. Kinsey et al. (1953) reported that the ratio of sexual intercourse to pregnancy in a sample of over 2,000 women was approximately 1,000 to 1. Other significant findings included increased premarital intercourse among females at rates closer to men, an increasing percentage of marital copulations leading to orgasm, an increase in extramarital intercourse, and declining insistence by males of premarital female virginity. Psychiatrists at some universities report that students who are virgins feel insecure and hurt because of their lack of sexual experience and peer group pressure to become sexually active. Other students embrace a "secondary virginity" in which the individual becomes celibate after a disillusioning period of sexual promiscuity.

There is reason to believe that the "sexual revolution" has had much more to do with changes in females' sexual behavior than males.' It has been argued, for instance, that males' premarital sexual behavior has changed little during the last century but that a larger percentage of females have become involved with them. Sexual historian Vern Bullough (1984) argued that there has been basically no change in the sexual behavior of men in the twentieth century. Premarital sexual rates for women, however, more than doubled between the 1930s and the 1970s.

Recognizing Sexual Needs

One of the most far-reaching trends affecting current sexual behavior is the increasing recognition of the sexual needs of many segments of society, for whom it was frequently thought that sex was inappropriate. Such groups include the elderly, the physically handicapped, prisoners, and the developmentally disabled.

In terms of the elderly, for instance, there is increased recognition that sexual behavior is no longer justified solely in terms of child-bearing and that the elderly continue to have both sexual interest and capacity. One study found the majority of men and women from ages 60 to 93 to be sexually active (Comfort, 1976).

Society increasingly believes that the physical and mental condition of a person does not and should not cause the removal of sexual expression, although such attitudes are by no means universal. In some cases, authorities responsible for the management of prisons, schools for the developmentally disabled, hospitals, and other institutions have sought to liberalize regulations in ways which allow for greater sexual expression. In some prisons, for instance, conjugal visits allow prisoners to visit with wives or lovers in private quarters on the prison grounds.

A Blurring of Distinctions Between the Sexes

In the United States there has been a blurring of distinctions between the sexes in the last several decades leading to an increase in the range of acceptable behavior of males and females. Since participation in many forms of leisure behavior is directly relate to gender, changes in the concepts of masculinity and femininity may alter future leisure patterns radically. A number of factors have changed the images of males and females from polar extremes to a continuum, with very few individuals at either end. Much of this change has resulted from a new societal permissiveness and emphasis upon achieved status rather than ascribed status. Furthermore, today's society is more accepting of a variety of sexual pattens. Indeed, with the development of effective contraception, movements such Gay Liberation and women's liberation, bisexual social functions, sex-change operations, sex therapy, and increased pornography, it has become increasingly difficult to determine which sex patterns can be termed "deviant." While by no means a settled issue, there is increasing evidence linking homosexual behavior to biological factors rather than lifestyle or environmental factors.

As the potential of sex to become leisure activity has increased, its practice has become more diverse. In such a period of change, the link between politics and sexual behavior is becoming stronger and stronger. The Gay, Lesbian, and

Bisexual Liberation movements, for instance, have concentrated on protecting rights under the law and developing a political power base. In cities such as San Francisco, this political power is already a reality.

While a strong backlash, often from fundamentalist Christian denominations, is occurring against more diverse forms of sexual expression, it remains to be seen whose viewpoint will capture political power.

Constraints on the Sexual Revolution

Three types of constraints will counter the sexually more liberal society which has emerged in North American culture. First, as mentioned previously, the reemergence of fundamental religious groups has meant that liberal attitudes toward premarital sex, pornography, prostitution, sex education, abortion and assertive sexual behavior by women are being fought in the courts and in the media. Additionally, many in the holistic health movement have stressed taking responsibility for one's own body, which includes responsibility for sexual behavior. Finally, there is increasing concern over the economic consequences of children born out of wedlock. Among African Americans, for instance, currently over one-half of all children are born to single mothers. There is no national consensus on any sexual issue, nor is there likely to be in the foreseeable future.

A second reason for constraints is that, for many, the sexual revolution has trivialized sex. Leonard (1989) has argued that recreational sex has become an activity "in which sexual intercourse becomes a mere sport, divorced not only from love and creation, but also from empathy, compassion, reality, responsibility, and, sometimes, even common politeness" (Leonard, 1982, p. 72). The sexual revolution has reshaped American life but today the search is for ways to integrate sex into life, rather than approach it with the mentality of a consumer.

A final and fundamental constraint on the sexual revolution is HIV-AIDS. This sexually transmitted disease, in the words of Robert Ornstein and Paul Erlich, "clearly has the potential for decimating the human population" (Ornstein and Erlich, 1989, p. 95). AIDS flies in the face of sexual promiscuity. Having multiple sex partners, for both homosexuals and heterosexuals, may risk one's life. Much of the consumer approach to sex which has characterized the sexual revolution has become highly dangerous behavior. Abstinence and monogamous relationships have more to recommend them. While evidence is mixed on the extent to which sexual behavior is being changed by the AIDS virus, such behavior is likely to be increasingly changed as an increasing percentage of the population contract the disease.

REFERENCES

Avedon, E., and Sutton-Smith, B. (1971). *The study of games*. New York, NY: John Wiley and Sons.

Brewer, L. (1962). *The good news*. London, England: G. P. Putnam's Sons.

Bullough, V. (April 9, 1984) The revolution is over. *Time Magazine*. pp. 75-83.

Comfort, A. (February, 1976). Future sexual mores: Sexuality in a zero growth society. *Current,* pp. 29-34.

Do we need a sex-bias pornography ordinance? (July 5, 1984). *Pittsburgh Post Gazette,* p. 12.

Dulles, R. A. (1965). *History of recreation: America learns to play*. New York, NY: Appleton-Century-Crofts.

Foote, N. (1954). Sex as play. *Social Problems, 15,* 159.

Freud, S. (1938). Three contributions to the theory of sex. In A. Brill, (Ed.), *The basic writings of Sigmund Freud*. New York, NY: Modern Library.

Jahusz, A. (1973). *Sexual development and behavior: Selected readings*. Homewood, IL: Dorsey Press.

Kinsey, A. et al. (1953). *Sexual behavior in the human female*. Philadelphia, PA: W. B. Saunders.

Leonard, G. (1982). *The end of sex*. New York, NY: Doubleday & Company, Inc.

Ornstein, R., and Erlich, P. (1989). *New world: New mind: Moving toward conscious evolution*. New York, NY: Doubleday & Company, Inc.

Pittman, D. (March-April, 1971). The male house of prostitution. *Transaction,* (pp. 21-26).

The obscenity report: The report of the task force on pornography and obscenity. (1970). New York, NY: Stein and Day, (pp. 27-34, 80).

Tuchman, B. (1978). *A distant mirror: The calamitous fourteenth century.* New York, NY: Alfred Knopf, (p. 215).

Yale Law Review, (1966), pp. 1409-1410.

CHAPTER *22*

Gender and Leisure Experience

From the earliest conceptualizations of leisure in the Western World, it was clear that leisure was primarily for males. The Athenian ideal of leisure, as conceptualized by Aristotle, when put into practice, required that women as well as foreign-born slaves do the mundane work of everyday life in order to free native-born males for a lifetime of attention to the more fundamental issues of life. Women in Athenian culture as elsewhere, were simply thought incapable of benefiting from leisure or, in turn, of benefiting society from obtaining it.

The homebound existence of most women not only precluded leisure in the sense of a lifetime of pursuing serious activity undertaken without the pressure of necessity, but also meant that distinctions between work and leisure were far less absolute; perhaps even irrelevant.

Industrialism's Role in Segmenting Work-Leisure Relations

While men and women often shared agricultural work more equitably in peasant life prior to industrialization, child-rearing and domestic life were still the primary responsibility of the female. Most leisure activities were sex segregated. The process of industrialization reinforced the distinction between the sexes in regard to work and leisure. Money gradually replaced land as the basis of power, as factory work slowly replaced agricultural work. Men were the earners of money and parceled out to their wives and lovers as they saw fit. While many male peasants at first sought to undertake the dual tasks of working in the factory and then farming after they returned from their first job, gradually they became the labor force for those who owned the means of industrial production. Only about fifteen percent of females were in that labor force at the beginning of the 19th century. As leisure came to mean "free time," the time left over after industrial work, and as society was gradually reorganized so as to accommodate the leisure needs of the industrial worker during his free time, leisure increasingly corresponded to the lives of men but not women. The public house or bar, for example, replaced many rural forms of recreation for the male factory worker. Such places were almost exclusively for men and no equivalent facilities were available to females, although for some the church may have fulfilled a similar role in terms of socialization. Even the "Rational Recreation" movements which had sprung up in Europe and then North America, seeking to reform the leisure habits of the working class, concentrated mainly on men.

For women, the emphasis was upon teaching working class women to be better homemakers and mothers. The behaviors in which women engaged that might be considered leisure continued to have a decidedly domestic flavor, such as quilting bees. In almost all leisure contexts, women were subservient to men and only rarely did they leave the role of supporter and caregiver. In these few instances, they often served as entertainers or decorations. This is not to imply that women had no free time, rather that their generally inferior social status denied them most free time opportunities available to men. Their time was much more permeable than men's since they continually adjusted their schedules to the needs of husbands and children and their mobility was generally less than men's. What leisure expression they had was frequently tied to their role as caretaker for husbands and children. Women, after all, were considered first and foremost the bearers of children. In 1800, females gave birth to an average of eight children during their life, five of whom survived until maturity (Hochschild, 1989).

The split in the work roles of men and women which industrialism produced was changed temporarily by wars or other emergency situations. Women were temporarily pressed into the labor force of factories, for instance, during both World Wars. It was not until the end of World War II, however, that women began to stay in the labor force or enter it in significant numbers. Gradually the percentage of women in the labor force has increased until it is now approximately sixty percent. Moreover, such work is increasingly more likely to be career-seeking behavior and to be undertaken for longer periods of a woman's life. Whether the work roles of women will become the equivalent of men's remains to be seen, but the gaps in both income and level of education are closing rapidly. As this has happened, a primary trend and a secondary one have emerged with regard to leisure. The primary trend is that the leisure behavior of women is beginning to more closely resemble that of men. Women have become more involved in travel, sport, outdoor recreation, and attending commercial establishments where alcohol is sold than previously. A secondary trend is that men's lives are gradually including some of the responsibilities which were once almost exclusively the province of women, such as household maintenance and childcare. It may be generalized, however, in regard to leisure that gender continues to be of central importance in both predicting and explaining leisure behavior.

Different Developmental Trajectories

That men and women develop differently in modern societies comes as no surprise. Developmental theories assume that behavior is the result of accumulated experiences, attitudes and beliefs, individual personal and social development, current situations and the individual's perception of these factors. Surely men and women can be expected to differ on these variables.

In spite of this, developmental theories have been challenged by Henderson et al. (1989) and others as being based primarily upon the experiences of men. Erikson (1963) for example, assumed that development consisted of a series of psychosocial issues which have to be resolved. For the adolescent, the major issue is forming a separate identity. Forming intimate relations is primary for young adults, while in middle adulthood the ability to guide and nurture succeeding generations in their development is of primary importance. Older adults face the challenge of integrating their successes and failures and finding meaning in life.

Each stage of life has developmental tasks (see Chapter 20). Tasks of young adults include selecting a mate and learning to live with a marriage partner, starting a family and raising children, managing a home, starting an occupation, finding satisfying social groups and taking on civic responsibility. For middle adulthood, these tasks include achieving adult civic and social responsibility, establishing and maintaining an economic standard of living, assisting teenage children in becoming adults, developing satisfying adult leisure activities, and adjusting to the physiological changes of middle life. In older adulthood, the tasks include adjusting to deceasing physical strength and health, adjusting to retirement and a reduced income, adjusting to the death of a spouse, affiliating with one's age group, meeting civic and social obligations and establishing satisfactory living arrangements. Growth and personal well-being were found through the achievement of these tasks.

Women's lives, it may be argued, are less uniform and predictable than men. Their progression through various stages of life is therefore likely to be much less uniform than men's. Reproductive and family roles affect women in different ways from men and, since women are more socialized into an ethic of responsibility than men, they are more likely to adapt their roles to meet the needs of others. Adaptability, in fact, is a major theme in the development of women (Henderson et al., 1989). This process of adaptation allows women to adjust more easily but makes long-range planning more difficult. It may be less likely, therefore, that women will have opportunities to become highly specialized in forms of leisure expression which require high levels of skill, continuous practice, or commitments of time over many years.

Many developmental psychologists have argued that women develop and resolve issues surrounding their identity later in life than men. For men, identity is likely to precede intimacy while the female comes to know herself through relations with others. Male identity is thought to be contingent upon separation from the mother while, for the female, identity involves an ongoing relationship with the mother. Women may, therefore, not differentiate themselves from others as much as males and they may be more likely to feel a sense of responsibility or guilt over meeting the needs of families and friends. These characteristics are reinforced by socialization processes which stress achievement and self-reliance for boys and nurturing and responsibility for girls.

Women and men also often vary in regard to what may be termed generational or cohort effects. That is the circumstances and events which shape the behavior of a given generation or cohort of individuals. While we may say that one generation lived through the "Vietnam Era" or the "McCarthy Era," such eras may have very different meanings and importance to men and women. The very events which define a generation may be quite different, and their influences upon the future lives of men and women correspondingly differ.

Amounts and Meanings of Leisure

Almost all the research done dealing with work and leisure from historical and sociological perspectives has concerned itself with men's work (Deem, 1988). Little attention has been paid to the work and leisure patterns of women. Some sociologists have argued that leisure has different meanings for women than for men, the differentiation between work and leisure is less clear cut for women than for men, and typical leisure activities are defined as such based upon the role the male traditionally plays in such activities (Deem, 1988). Most major studies of leisure, while examining differences in participation between men and women, start with definitions and assumptions which are based upon the experiences of males. Labeling outdoor activities like camping as leisure, for example, ignores the role that many married women with children will fulfill in a camping trip—preparing meals, cleaning and looking after the children.

There is also evidence that many homemaking and childcare activities have elements of both work and leisure for those involved. Cannon (1978) found that housewives rated activities such as watching television, reading the newspaper, visiting with friends as leisure, and activities such as washing dishes, making the beds, cleaning the bathroom and dusting as work. Other activities, such as childcare and meal preparation were thought of as having elements of both work and leisure. Additionally, some surveys have found that shopping has mixed meanings.

When men and women undertake joint leisure activities, evidence suggests that women are likely to adjust much more easily than do men, reflecting a pervasive power differential. The female is more likely to become a part of the male's group of friends, to give up time with her friends in order to spend time with the male, and to become involved in his leisure interests than vice versa.

This is particularly true in working class or lower socioeconomic groups. After marriage, "Men are far more likely than women to maintain the patterns of leisure established before marriage and parenthood" (Woodward and Green, 1988, p. 133). While there is evidence that woman who enter institutions of higher education after high school and remain single show increasing similarity to males in terms of their leisure patterns, the importance of gender roles becomes much more pronounced with marriage or living together.

Because leisure often has different meanings for men and women, it may make little sense to seek to determine whether or not men and women have similar amounts of leisure or free time. One large-scale time diary study which was undertaken in 1965 and replicated in 1975 and 1985 found that, while women historically have done the vast majority of household work and childcare, men are becoming increasingly involved as women move into the labor force in record numbers. While women still do the majority of housework, men's share of such work has grown as measured by time, on average, from 15 percent to 33 percent between 1965 and 1985. In 1985, men spent 10 hours a week in household duties and women about 20. Married men spent about three hours a week more on household chores in 1985 than did single men, although a decade prior men spent no more time on such chores after they married than before. Overall, Robinson's research found that women spent 7.5 fewer hours per week doing housework in 1985 than they did in 1965, while men spent 5.2 more hours. In terms of child rearing, similar findings were evident, with women spending about three times as many hours as men in such duties.

While men and women may be moving toward a model closer to equality in regard to work and leisure, numerous sociologists have argued that the revolution in women's roles has stalled. The changes which have taken place in the last few decades, it is argued, have been triggered by the decline in purchasing power of male wage earners, a decline in male blue-collar jobs and the rise of female jobs in the service sector. According to Hochschild (1989), women who now work outside the home experience two situations which make them less likely to push for more male help in homemaking and child rearing duties. First, women make less money than men and, second, marriage is much less stable than previously. Women who do get divorced are hurt considerably more in economic terms than are men and are less likely to remarry. This means that many women who are married and in the labor force work up to one extra month per year compared to their husbands (Hochschild, 1989). Women therefore increasingly defer marriage. It is among women who are not married or who are in the later stages of a "traditional" marriage that equality with men in amount of leisure time has become a reality. For those who are married, there is a high likelihood of continuing to do a disproportionate amount of second shift work.

Other time diary research found that in the early morning hours, the work status of the wife makes no difference in what activities men undertake. "Rather, whatever contributions they make in response to the time constraints of their employed wives occurs after the husbands return home in the evening" (Berk and Fenstermaker-Berk, 1979). Men were found to be most likely to take on household chores when the wife was at work or simply not available.

Social class appears to have an important effect on the amount of time men spend in childrearing and household maintenance activities. Numerous studies have found that men in upper social classes are likely to spend significantly greater amounts of time in such activities compared to their counterparts in lower social classes (Stone, 1972; Robinson, 1989). There is also evidence that men's role in such behaviors varies greatly by country.

Overall, however, if examined throughout the life cycle, studies from earlier periods which have used traditional definitions of leisure for both men and women have often found that women not employed outside the home have about as much leisure time as men. Lundberg et al. (1934), for example, undertook one of the first large scale time diary studies in Westchester, New York. The study considered leisure time to be all activities except "sleep, paid work, care of household and children, care of self, transportation, and other items which the record indicates are primarily instrumental or incidental to the other activities rather than ends in themselves" (Lundberg et al., 1934, p. 89). The average number of leisure hours was found to be 7.4 for men and 7.2 for women. Housewives had the highest number of leisure hours, 9.2, while laborers had the lowest, 6.2. Similarly, a time diary study undertaken for the Mutual Broadcasting Company in 1954 found that on weekdays men spent 3.6 hours on leisure activities while women spent 4.7. On Saturdays men spent 5.5 while women spent 5.3 and on Sundays the time spent was 4.5 hours for men and 5.1 for women.

These findings came at a time when women had not entered the labor force in large numbers and, while studies of the entire population still find little difference in average amounts of leisure time between men and women, for women in the process of pursuing a career, raising children and being a homemaker, time for leisure is at a premium. It is not so much in the amount of time for leisure that males and females differ in modern societies as it is in differences in access to resources and freedom to use them.

Differences in Access to Leisure

Men and women vary systematically in their access to leisure, the types and degree of constraints which inhibit participation, and in their rates of participation in various leisure activities and motives for participation. These differences are themselves shaped by a myriad of intervening variables. For instance, in modern societies, women are less likely to have access to automobiles during adolescence and, often, during later life. They are therefore less likely to participate in some forms of leisure expression which involve travel. Perhaps partially as a result of this and partially as a result of greater parental supervision of female teenagers, they are likely to spend more time on the telephone than adolescent males, in effect visiting friends by telephone rather than driving to their houses to visit. Women in the past had lower levels of formal education than men and were therefore less likely to have been exposed to many forms of leisure which additional years of schooling might provide. Women who work outside the home for pay have salaries which are approximately two-thirds those of men and thus often have economic limitations which are greater than those of men. Therefore, gender is often compounded with poverty in limiting the lives of women.

In addition to these differences, secondary institutions often provide differently for males and females with regard to leisure, both in amount and in the content of what is provided. Public schools, for instance, have historically spent more money supporting sport and athletic activity for males than for females, although federal law now requires that opportunities be more equal. Public recreation and park departments are historically more likely to provide services to adolescent males than to females. Many public institutions plan leisure services which do not recognize the female's greater role in childcare and thus make female participation more unlikely.

It is, therefore, not surprising that most large studies of participation in many forms of recreation and leisure which take place outside the home find that females are less likely to participate and, when they do, to participate less often than do males. This is generally true in participation in most forms of outdoor recreation and sport.

Many studies which examine adult men and women now use three categories to describe most of their subjects: employed male, employed female, and homemaker. These designations recognize that, from a standpoint of behavior and social roles, employed females may be placed between homemaker and working male. That is, employed females often show time uses and participation rates which are midway between those of working males and homemakers (Robinson, 1977).

Perhaps the most central issue in terms of female's access to leisure is that of patriarchal control. Male power has a strong influence on women's leisure opportunities, friendships, and social networks throughout their lives (Wimbush and Talbot, 1988). Males exert such power in a variety of ways. For instance, "A considerable body of evidence points to the fact that both the regulation of women's access to public places and their behavior once they gain entry, are grounded in the question of women's right to occupy particular spaces" (Middleton, 1983, quoted by Woodward and Green, 1988, p. 134). Males exert many forms of social control over a wide variety of public and private spaces used for leisure from bars and pubs to athletic facilities and outdoor recreation sites. A woman entering a tavern alone may be subject to ridicule or harassment. Many golf courses and tennis clubs still have "ladies" day or special hours for women to participate. Outdoor recreation areas are managed largely by males and the design and management of the area is likely to have sprung from the desires of males. Thus, for instance, states are far more likely to provide for hunting and fishing opportunities on public lands than for bird watching.

In some cases, partially in response to such situations, women have historically formed gender segregated groups for purposes of socialization and other forms of leisure.

> This category of female leisure groups is commonly based on the assumption that women's 'spare time' should be filled by learning or elaborating aspects of domestic ideology like 'homemaking,' the care and nurture of others, 'good works,' and improving one's physical appearance. Activities tend to be presented as expressive rather than productive, and voluntary rather than committed. While they may serve as useful support systems for many women, they also serve to perpetuate and preserve the hegemony of patriarchal relations in leisure and in society in general (Talbot, 1988, p. 172).

Such groups may ultimately represent a response to limited access to other forms of leisure resources, which men control through a variety of strategies.

"Strategies of control exerted by male groups in leisure venues are ultimately just one expression of a process of social control which is constructed with reference to dominant forms of masculinity, and 'acceptable levels of violence.'" (Woodward and Green, 1988, p. 134). Not all social control comes from violence or its threat, of course. Often it is simply a disdain which tells the female she is not welcome or that her behavior is naive or inappropriate.

Perhaps in summary it should be noted that sociologists concerned with leisure and, indeed, many other areas of social inquiry are just beginning to pay serious attention to women. Most of the sociology of leisure has been about males or about models which are largely based upon males. Some sociologists believe that women must be studied separately to avoid this problem. There is also an attempt to understand women's use of leisure in historical perspective, using the limited means available to understand women's lives such as personal diaries. Feminists argue that women's leisure roles will be understood only when both gender and gender relations are systematically examined as primary variables, rather than merely one among a handful of social and economic statuses.

Further research will be needed to understand what "leisure" means to women and the extent to which it is being redefined by their changing roles.

REFERENCES

Berk, R. A., and Fenstermaker-Berk, S. (1979). *Labor and leisure at home: Content and organization of the household day.* Beverly Hills, CA: Sage Library of Social Research, (p. 230).

Cannon, R. L. (1978). *The private sphere: How women feel about the work they do.* Master's Thesis, Department of Sociology, University of California at Santa Barbara, CA.

Deem, R. (1988). *All work and no play? The sociology of women and leisure.* Milton Keynes, England: Open University Press.

Erikson, E. H. (1963). *Childhood and society.* New York, NY: W. W. Norton.

Henderson, K. M., Bialeschki, D., Shaw, S. M., and Freysinger, V. J. (1989). *A leisure of one's own: A feminist perspective on women's leisure.* State College, PA: Venture Publishing, Inc.

Hochschild, A. (1989). *The second shift: Working parents and the revolution at home.* New York, NY: Viking.

Lundberg, G. A., Komarovsky, M., and McInerny, M. A. (1934). *Leisure: A suburban study.* New York, NY: Columbia University Press, (p. 92).

Robinson, J. (1977). *Changes in Americans' use of time: 1965-1975.* Cleveland, OH: Cleveland State University.

Robinson, J. (December, 1989). Who's doing the housework? *American demographics,* (pp. 24-28).

Stone, P. (1972). Child care in twelve countries. In A. Szalai (Ed.), *The use of time: Daily activities of urban and suburban populations in twelve countries.* The Hague, The Netherlands: Mouton.

Talbot, M. (1988). "Their own worst enemy? Women and leisure provision." In E. Wimbush and M. Talbot (Eds.), *Relative freedoms: Women and leisure.* Philadelphia, PA: Open University Press, p. 172

Wimbush, E. and Talbot, M. (Eds.). (1988). *Relative freedoms: Women and leisure.* Philadelphia, PA: Open University Press.

Woodward, D., and Green, E. (1988). "Not tonight dear!" The social control of women's leisure. In E. Wimbush and M. Talbot (Ed.), *Relative freedoms: Women and leisure.* Philadelphia, PA: Open University Press.

CHAPTER 23

Leisure Identities and Roles

The "Who am I?" question is always important. There is continuity in how we define ourselves and present ourselves to others from one event and environment to another. Life is not composed of discrete incidents with totally self-enclosed meanings. Rather, despite variations, we tend to be much the same person from one time and place to another. The ways in which we define ourselves are central to how we direct our lives, respond to events, and allocate our resources. Leisure, as demonstrated through most of the previous analysis, is one integrated dimension of life, not a separate or residual category. Individuals define themselves in and through leisure engagement as well as in their work, family, community, and other roles. For some, an arts or community engagement is central to personal and social identities. They are truly violinists who teach math in a public school or actors who work in a bank. For most, leisure is one dimension of life that contributes to identities that have several components.

In the study of Peoria adults (Kelly, 1987), there were a number of women who were "balanced investors." Membership in women's organizations was an important realm of the overall meaning of their lives. Especially for those who had no work career or family, such organizations provided opportunities for investment that yielded definitions of identity and worth. They defined themselves as women working with other women in organizations that provided a sense of purpose in addition to a community of congenial and like-minded associates. Active involvement in projects was more than something to do; it was an integral part of who they are.

One perspective on the journey of life focuses on the sequences of roles that define opportunities, resources, and expectations. A second perspective stresses development, the requirements for growth and change based on the kind of person we need to become as those sequences unfold. A third approach concentrates on the self-defining and self-directing person who is constructing a life. The basic premise is that no matter how much of who we are is learned from others, we are always reflexive in setting out the course of our lives.

Composing a Life

The sequences and developmental tasks of life are not invariant or predetermined in some all-encompassing order. The life cycle is an ordered framework for analysis, but for most people takes unexpected turns and reversals. Rather, there is always a good deal of improvisation as women and men make their way through the unanticipated and expected events of the life course. Some persons are quite existential, self-directive and goal-oriented in shaping their lives. Others are more responsive and malleable as they allow events to shape and redirect their journeys. In all cases, however, we are acting and defining beings who are in the process of "composing a life" (Bateson, 1990).

Bateson has woven together the narratives of five women who "are engaged in that act of creation that engages us all—the composition of our lives. Each of us has worked by improvisation, discovering the shape of our creation along the way, rather than pursuing a vision already defined" (p. 1). In the weaving together of the life course themes that follow, however, it is clear that the improvisations are more than random occurrences. Rather, there are numerous ways in which each woman meets new and often unexpected challenges, opportunities, losses, conflicts, and gratifications that call for reconstituting fundamental relationships, competencies, and even values. Through the reweaving, however, there is a sense of integrity. Each of the five demonstrates not only resiliency and strength, but also a coherent sense of self that builds, develops, and sometimes surprises.

Life, then, is not bound to the rails of a track that permits only occasional switches and alternative routes. Life is a composition, with structure and order along with variations and idiosyncrasies of performance. Yet, through the journey, there is a center, not fixed but ever changing. One metaphor for that center is identity.

Personal and Social Identities

"Identity" is definition. Yet, it is more than that insofar as that definition becomes operative in the social world. Identity is self-definition, yet learned in relation to others. It is styles of interacting with others, yet reflexive in how we see ourselves, self-image as well as the presentation of self. Identity has consistency and integrity, yet may change from one situation to another. Identity is always being revised by how others respond to presentations. It is role-based and subject to alteration as roles change through the life course. Identity has a foundation in childhood, yet is subject to age-appropriate development. Identity is, then, dialectical—central to how roles are enacted and responsive to how those enactments are received. Identity is always fluid, in process rather than fixed and immutable.

This complex concept may be partly clarified by the following distinctions (Kelly, 1983):

Personal identity is one's self-definition in a role context.

Social identity is the definition by others of how one takes a role.

Presentation (Goffman, 1957) is the mode of enacting a role in order to receive social definitions of an intended personal identity.

Role identity (McCall and Simmons, 1978) is how a role is consistently enacted, a style of behavior.

In this metaphor, an individual in an accepted role (social identity) behaves (presentation) in such a way that the consistent enactment (role identity) reinforces his or her self-definition (personal identity). There is almost always some discrepancy between the personal identity and social identity that may require a revision of the presentation to reestablish the desired role identity. Further, in many social situations, the response is mixed and the task of interpretation a matter of selective perception and weighted evaluation.

All of this seems quite complicated. In fact, it is. Social action is a skilled behavior that involves sophisticated interpretive reading of symbolic actions and gestures as well as words. Even within the boundaries of an interaction episode, meanings change in ways that may be cumulative or may be conflicting. And leisure episodes are no exception. Some are clearly defined with rules of timing, action, and communication as in a board game. Others are defined in the process of their occurrence as in a surprise encounter at a party. In either case, the real meaning of the event may well be in the process of identity presentations and counter-presentations, responses, interpretations, revisions, and, eventually, terminations. The role, of player or guest, may be only a general behavioral expectation for the working out of personal identities and altering or reinforcing social identities.

The Role Context of Leisure

In almost any situation, there are general behavioral expectations based on role designations. As already outlined, these roles change through the life course in each institutional context—school, work, family, and leisure. Seldom are we fully detached from one or more of these roles. Even in leisure, we are still students, mothers, supervisors, instructors, or beginners. In a given situation, one role may be dominant. Usually, roles are reciprocal. In the classroom, one acts the role of instructor and all others that of student. What is expected in each role requires at least an approximate fulfillment of the reciprocal expectations. The instructor cannot lecture if no one listens and vice versa. In other situations, however, an individual may enact multiple roles. At an office party, a conversation group may include a boss, a spouse, a subordinate, a stranger, a sex interest, a sailing companion, and a professional rival. Managing all these relationships in a many-directed conversation is a difficult feat requiring advanced arts of communication and complex strategies.

The point is that we *enact* roles. There is always more to interaction than just obeying the rules or even meeting the expectations. To begin with, in many groups there is no consensus on what is expected. Often we are unsure. Frequently expectations are in conflict. And many situations are complex. Yet, even in such conflict and complexity, we engage in interaction as persons with some identity. We have self-images that we want to project. We define ourselves in each role in a special way that we have found effective, comfortable, or exciting. In every episode we are our selves, with some consistency of identity that shapes how we take the role.

This identity or self-definition provides stability to our enactments. We have a composite sense of our abilities, limitations, histories, and characteristics. We play every role and present ourselves in every situation with some consistency. Our base of experience and knowledge is presented in the embodied person we have come to know as our selves. Further, we have a long history in which some identities have been affirmed by others and some have been rejected. We have a sense of what "works" in a variety of circumstances. We draw on a practiced repertoire of presentation skills and styles to meet the occasion. And we do this in a mix of self-awareness and taken-for-granted customs. Postures, vocabularies, affective responses, and gestures are only the communicative beginning of the entire portrayal of who we are in that time and place. Further, this identity is social; it is how others have come to know us and anticipate our actions. In some contexts, identities are assigned for us. In others we may choose what we believe to be most appropriate to advance some line of action.

In such identities, however, there is also variety. We are not exactly the same person in every situation. We may be more emotional at home, more brisk and brusque at work, more lively at leisure, and more relaxed with friends or lovers. Some roles are segmented and allow us to switch presentations. We can be more openly competitive on the racquet court than at the office, more aggressive at a business meeting than at the dinner table. In our identities, then, there is both consistency and variety. Whether or not there is a "real self" hidden under all the portrayals may be an issue for debate. Usually we believe that there is a self underlying our presentations that has value and stability. In practice, however, there is variety.

One metaphor for all this is that of the theater. In any drama, there are the limitations of the stage, the composition of the audience, and, as always, time. There is a script that moves the action forward and provides the basis for the interaction of the drama. No two actors, however, play a part in the same style. Each places her own stamp on the part and makes it her own. And there are "good" or responsive audiences and "bad" or cold ones. So no two performances are just alike.

Identities and Leisure

One meaning of any leisure event may be that it provides a setting in which to offer or advance an identity. When we value a particular identity, it is satisfying to have it expressed and even more gratifying when it is affirmed by others. If it is important to be physically competent, then a sport may offer the best opportunity for the expression and demonstration of that identity. Other kinds of competence may be best expressed in a challenging activity, whether at work or at leisure. Identities of nurturing are most often expressed in the family, but may also be affirmed in volunteering or community organizations. Being a decisive leader may find reinforcement in political activity.

Of course, each of us has a history in which we have developed our identities through action and learned them through interaction. We have received feedback, not always positive, everywhere we have done anything. Our self-definitions and our skills have been learned through a lifetime.

Leisure, however, has some special affinities to identity. To begin with, in leisure we are most likely to be able to select activities in which we are or may become competent. Further, we can most often choose companions who provide positive reinforcement to valued identities. Our jobs often involve criteria for evaluation that are standardized and do not fit our aptitudes well. Our intimate relationships involve such deep and complicated mutual understandings and interpretations that change is difficult. In leisure, we may be able to try out new variations on old themes, play the part somewhat differently, and receive immediate feedback.

This focus on identity provides a basis for understanding an anomaly in leisure experience. From one perspective, optimal experiences are character-ized by a loss of awareness of time, the environment, and the self in the immersion of "flow" (Csikszentmihalyi, 1990). A recent study (Samdahl and Kleiber, 1989), however, found that self-awareness was associated with feeling good, especially in leisure. It seems that being aware of the self, of who we are and what we are doing, is part of the meaning of many situations. Especially in social interaction, some of the satisfaction is in presenting ourselves, expressing identities, and receiving some positive response. Meeting the challenge of an activity may lead to flow, but awareness of the self as acting is not in conflict with feeling good about the action.

Such a focus on identity is expressive, part of the immediate experience of the action. It is also developmental, a sense of *becoming* someone more able or with a new dimension of selfhood. Again, we do not go through the life course simply as pawns on the chessboard of life. Rather, we are, with greater or lesser autonomy, composing a life.

Identity and the Life Course

Who we are is always in the middle of who we have become and who we want to become. A case study of off-road motorcycle racing illustrates how the past, present, and future come together in the commitment to an activity (Martin and Berry, 1979). In a mass society in which individuality is not always easy to accomplish, commitment to the organization, skills, and community of a particular activity may provide a distinguishing personal and social identity. In this case, a young man may define himself and announce to others "I am a motocross rider." As introduced in Chapter 11, dirt bike riders form a subculture with their events, symbols, performance norms, equipment, and modes of communication. The commitment to such racing also provides what is often a central identity (Kelly, 1983).

For men from working-class backgrounds, their childhood and youth have been among males who stressed machinery, speed, and competition. Mechanical skills and masculine competition are a fundamental value. Driving and working on cars and bikes are anticipated in teen years and made a central element of life when the treasured drivers license is attained. Motocross racing in young adult years combines the preoccupation with mechanics, speed, male camaraderie, and competition. It is an extension of earlier socialization. As the sound of the engine conveyed feelings of independence, control, and control of power, direction, and motion in teen years, so now the dirt bike provides an even more vivid experience of the same dimensions. At the same time that country club youth are traveling with their families, practicing golf, or going to dances, the working-class youth are in the streets with their engines and transmissions.

There is always the factor of access. Bikes require payments, but not wealth. The necessary knowledge and skills are familiar and available. The transition from cars to motocross is a relatively easy one. Once the commitment is made, motocross offers a context to express, develop, and receive confirmation of a valued kind of identity. Being a bike rider, especially a successful one, is an identity consistent with values adopted much earlier and still central. When the realm of work offers little except routine obedience and occasional breaks of fellowship, motocross is an arena of effectual action as well as identity. In a mass society in which the ordinary worker receives little feedback or recognition, this leisure investment becomes the basis of a valued identity. The bike, protective clothing, jackets with patches, and other symbols mark the rider as someone who is more than just another factory hand. Further, that identity can be demonstrated and enhanced in the development of physical control and strength, acting out aggressive activism and individualism, and self-testing in a competitive man's world that rewards stamina, courage, and tactical skill. It is a social space in which a personal identity can be presented and receive social validation.

Motocross illustrates how orientations, values, and skills learned in childhood and youth can be transferred and transformed for an adult setting and performance. Such continuity can be found in a wide range of leisure activities. The key may be to gain a reinforcement of competence in earlier years that becomes the basis of a later identity. The context may be sport, the arts, social settings, sexual warfare, or anything else that requires aptitude and skill. Further, the activity requires a consistent context in which competence based identities can be recognized, reinforced, demonstrated, symbolized, and developed further. That is, identities require a role context in which performances can be built, evaluated, and reconstituted. The context may be that of the corporation or bureaucracy in work, the association or competition in leisure, the reward system of the school, or some kind of family or peer group. What is necessary is enough structure for the presentation and validation of identities. Symbolic attachment to an activity and its culture makes the individual someone special amidst the mass.

Elements in Identity Development

Almost any kind of game, sport, performance, or play can become a critical context for identity development. These contexts always reflect their specific culture and its value systems. Identities are always learned in the particular setting, not in general. That is why especially significant other persons, gatekeepers and judges, can make such a difference in risking a consistent portrayal. For children it is parents, teachers, and coaches in addition to peer leaders. For adults it may be other kinds of leaders who open and close the doors to activity and recognition. In any social context, however, there is the person— acting, interpreting, and going ahead to compose a life. In this process of identity formation, a number of elements are usually salient:

Competence: The first question is "Can I do it?" When entry-level competence has been demonstrated, then the level of competence becomes central to an identity. For children, there are multiple mechanisms of inclusion and exclusion in any activity. All sorts of feedback on ability are given in being chosen or left out. Fundamental to persistence in an activity, however, is the self-evaluation of ability. "I can do it" becomes a question, "How well?" The limits of the environment and resources become internalized into self-images of ability. Always central to identities, then, is the question of competence. Performance is central to identity. The demonstration of ability is more than a show; it is at the center of the self-definition and its meaning.

Indeterminacy in leisure: One element of many kinds of leisure that makes the development and evaluation of competence possible is indeterminacy. Unlike many work and school situations, there is a relative openness in leisure as to outcomes. Scores are only one kind of result that provides feedback on ability. Even a card game has its totaling of points, chips, or money to measure the result for the event. In leisure, there are frequent and often direct measures of skill learning. They are not so consequential or final that the risk of trying is completely inhibited. On the other hand, the more central an identity, the more outcomes matter to the individual.

The self-containment of play: The measured outcome is possible because leisure episodes and events are largely self-contained. Games of all kinds have endings and then begin again. One essential element of sport is that every contest begins with the score even. Further, play results generally do not have major impacts on work rewards or roles. The world of play tends to have its own boundaries. Nevertheless, anyone can invest that world with a high level of significance. When a leisure based identity becomes central to one's sense of selfhood, then the outcomes take on greater salience. Further, the outcomes may be more cumulative than segmented. For central identities, there is a sense of performance over time of which each incident is only one bit of evidence among many. Some leisure may even be like the out-of-town tryout or preopening preview of a new play in which evaluation is sought and revision expected. The tryout is an experimentation with the "real thing" in the future when the play reaches New York or London. There is continuity to leisure identities that may be built up out of single low-consequence events. Competence is tested over time and leisure based identities revised or reinvested accordingly.

Signs of identity: What does it mean when a young mother does her shopping in the supermarket in her tennis togs? Similarly a production line foreman drives into the company parking lot in a pickup truck rigged for hunting expeditions. A high school student wears a sports letter jacket to history class. University students plaster Greek letters and insignia on a variety of locations of their informal clothing. On the backs of cars there are stickers proclaiming that "I'd rather be flying/sailing/riding/skiing." All are symbols of a valued identity, of how individuals want to be defined by others. They don't proclaim they work in an advertising agency or sandwich shop; they want to be seen as a skier or hunter or athlete.

Appearance is not peripheral to social interaction (Stone, 1962). It inaugurates exchange by announcing critical items about the self to others. We dress "toward" a presumed audience in a preassessment of social occasions. What we wear, along with symbols of identification, is more than obeying norms or meeting expectations. It is saying something, sometimes dramatically and sometimes delicately, about ourselves. A trucker may wear a cap identifying the brand of his truck. A business man or woman carries the "right" briefcase. But there are also bowling shirts, fishing hats, football jackets, and other signs of leisure orientation. There is a symbolic ethnicity of leisure in which actors seek not only symbolic identity, but also to signal others about something important.

Leisure settings: Many leisure locales offer especially open settings for the presentation and validation of such identities. Analyses of poker games have stressed the centrality of role portrayals consistent with their male constituency and competitive system (Kelly, 1983). In many leisure events, there is a fundamental "action" with agreed upon limits of time, space, and meanings. This "frame" enables the action to have outcomes that are limited in their consequences (Goffman, 1974). The campground, gym, or playing field is a setting in which the action becomes a mini-drama with interactive performances and contained meanings. In some leisure, rules and roles are clearly defined. In others, there is more a process of building the meanings of the episode. In either case, however, the reciprocal presentations are interpreted and built into a framework of meaning in which the "action"—whether a context or a conversation—has outcomes that strengthen or weaken the identities offered.

The point is that even events with limited consequences have outcomes that may be significant for self-definition. Especially when a leisure based identity is highly valued, responses and symbols of evaluation may be taken quite seriously. The outcomes are of consequence for identities if not for segmented roles. Again, the concepts of investment and "serious leisure" are pertinent. In various phases of the life course, an individual may place greatest value on a leisure identity. When years of commitment and effort have been directed toward a particular activity, then results are not trivial. The so-called "pastime" is an investment in and of the self. The previous life course analyses suggest numerous concrete ways in which leisure identities are critical to selfhood.

Again, the issue is not so much what we do as who we are. Life is process. In that process, there is the dialectic between action and context. We follow our sequences of roles, but not as robots. We accept limits on our resources, but not without adaptation and amendment. We look forward to predictable life journeys, but are also composing life as we go.

Leisure, from this perspective, is more than a set of activities that change as our roles and opportunities change. It is more than doing what is expected on time: rock music in teen years, zoos when we are parents, and travel after launching. Leisure is a varied and diffuse set of action contexts in which we express who we believe we are and seek to become something more. In this process, there is both continuity and change. There are consistencies and openness, familiarity and novelty. Insofar as the risks and seeking to become of an existential orientation become basic to leisure. It is a primary dimension of development.

Role Identities

Who are we in this mass society? Is it enough to be digits in the computer, coded files in the office, and predictable targets in segmented consumer markets? We are surrounded by sameness: mass transit, mass media, mass marketing, and all kinds of symbols that deal with us as less than individuals. We gain our knowledge through impersonal television, identify with corporations and professional sports teams, and sit through routined religious rituals. Brands of anything mean less and less; only the labels differ. We buy, use, and discard without long-term commitment to anything.

In the midst of such anonymity many adults turn to home and family. There, at least, we are known and perhaps appreciated. What we do has some impact. Who we are has meaning. There is even the possibility of doing something that lives on after us. But even those central roles change. Marriages wax and wane. Parenting involves letting go as well as holding fast. In all roles, work and family, there are disappointments, ruptures, disillusionments, losses, and outright failures. In the midst of all this, then, leisure is one aspect of life that offers opportunity. Of course, leisure may fail, too. But at least it is one more chance, often one in which there is some response to what we do and who we are. In some cases, especially when the limits of other roles are recognized, leisure may be quite central to who we are and hope to become. Being a woman or a man in this mass society is more than having a job and a home, however important they are. It is also being our distinctive selves, to others and to ourselves.

Of course some leisure is leftover, low priority, and peripheral to anything important. Some is low impact, low intensity, and segmented. Nevertheless, there are also leisure investments that are quite central to the process of weaving together the strands of life's tapestry. They are, at least, part of the balance of life. There is, however, another side to this possibility. It is that leisure is not wholly free and disengaged; rather it has roles and identities.

The concept of "role identity" suggests both consistency and salience. It is who we are in a role, how we enact the role. It incorporates self-defining action with the context of regularities and expectations. And it has implications for leisure. If leisure has roles, then it is not fully free and detached. Rather, there are carryover principles and conditions from one occurrence to another. If there are identities in those roles, then the process and outcomes have persistent meaning. How well we do is important.

Leisure, then, like action in family, work, and community, has meanings beyond the immediate experience. It has structures as well as openness. It is like the rest of life at least as much as it is distinctive. As actors, we come into and leave the environments and events of leisure with identities that have been impacted. We are always learning who we are, in leisure no less than in school. We are always dealing with the expectations of others. We always have some agendas for selfhood, however vague and partial. In leisure, we are selves in process, composing a life in the symbol systems of our minds as well as in the courts and studios of our play.

The role identity model offers alternative approach to two critical issues: The first is that of motivation and satisfaction. Why do people consistently choose particular leisure activities, environments, and social settings? One approach focuses on the experience. Another concentrates on the expectations and resources associated with social positions. But why is there so much variety among individuals coupled with consistency in individual choices? One possibility is that identities differ. Who we are and seek to be in leisure varies widely. On the other hand, there is consistency in our self-definitions that directs us to venues that provide opportunities for identity expression and development. Much of the meaning in an experience is more than immediate; it is in how our identities are expressed and reinforced. Identity may be a central element in the meaning of a series of experiences that we choose and repeat.

The second issue is that of personal fulfillment. Life is more than a series of discrete occurrences found pleasurable or painful. Rather we develop lines of action that build on the past and are aimed toward the future. These lines of action have as a goal a state of being that we may call "fulfillment." It is more than fleeting pleasure, although philosophers have termed the state "happiness." Such a state of relative fulfillment presupposes that there is a self with some continuity of self-interpretation. We are selves, reflexive in our self-defining and evaluating. We have personal and social identities. The state of happiness, then, may be at least in part a result of how well we are able to create and actualize desired identities. Fulfillment is personal in its foundation in who we are and become. Conditions of our lives make a difference, but so does our directed action. We make our lives as well as endure them. In the self-interpretive process in which we take the themes of life and compose, self-concepts or identities are one way of putting together actions, values, and results. We have a sense of who we are and at least a little dream of who we might be. From this perspective, leisure is more than seeking pleasure. It is seeking ourselves, in actions and events with their own meaning and integrity.

Leisure is, then, both personal and social in meaning. We present ourselves in a role, develop and establish an identity, receive confirmation or correction on our performance, and evaluate the process. We enjoy successful role enactment on both the central and secondary levels. Creating our portrayals of identities has its own satisfaction at the moment and in the development of selfhood.

REFERENCES

Bateson, M. C. (1990). *Composing a life.* New York, NY: Penguin (Plume).

Csikszentmihalyi, M. (1990). *Flow: The psychology of optimal experience.* New York, NY: Harper & Row, Publishers, Inc.

Goffman, E. (1957). *The presentation of self in everyday life.* Garden City, NY: Doubleday Anchor.

Goffman, E. (1974). *Frame analysis: An essay on the organization of experience.* New York, NY: Harper & Row, Publishers, Inc.

Kelly, J. R. (1983). *Leisure identities and interactions.* London, England: Allen and Unwin.

Kelly, J. R. (1987). *Peoria winter: Styles and resources in later life.* New York, NY: The Free Press.

Martin, T. W., and Berry, K. (1979). Competitive sport in post-industrial society: The case of the motocross racer. In A. Yianakis (Ed.), *Sport sociology: Contemporary themes.* Dubuque, IA: Kendall/Hunt Publishing.

McCall, G., and Simmons, J. (1978). *Identities and interactions,* revised edition. New York, NY: The Free Press.

Samdahl, D., and Kleiber, D. (1989). Self-awareness and leisure experience. *Leisure Sciences, 11*:1-10.

Stone, G. (1962). Appearance and the self. In A. Rose (Ed.), *Human behavior and social processes.* New York, NY: Houghton Mifflin.

CHAPTER 24

Time In and Time Out

I n many languages, there is no word for "leisure." There is, however, some variation on "free time." We may argue that there is little or no time that is really free and that time itself provides nothing distinctive to the concept of leisure. Nevertheless, there is a long historical connection between time and leisure that transcends language and culture. The long assumed coming of an "age of leisure" was based largely on the historical trend of a reduced average work week.

Fundamental approaches to time have changed. When the economic base of the society was agricultural, time was seasonal and cyclical. The school year began after harvesting and ended before planting. Religious services were scheduled for 11 AM on Sunday after the daily chores were completed. Farm cycles of work and rest were based on daylight hours in addition to the requirements of tending to crops and animals. Agricultural time was work based, but not a rigid clock time.

The industrial revolution reformed social time to meet the requirements of the factory. Machines not only paced the production process, but also the lives of their tenders. Shifts were reduced to 12 and eventually 8 hours a day. The work week was reduced to 6, 5 1/2, and eventually 5 days. Schedules were invariant through the year because machines know no season or cycle. Only a loss of markets would shut them down. Workers had to adapt to the costs of keeping the factory productive. At the same time, the necessity of intercommunication held offices to fixed hours. Retailing was slow to adapt to this rigid schedule until World War II put the primary shoppers, women, into the factories and offices in numbers that required expanded sales schedules. Industrial time was by the clock, invariant, and production based.

A current proposal is that developed societies have now entered a "postindustrial" era. Evidence is mixed. The fact that over 50 percent of employment is now in services rather than production is the most common element. Social time is said to be altered in this new era. Social timetables are now characterized by greater openness and flexibility. Services, especially retailing, are available almost any day and any time of the day or night, at least in metropolitan areas. The fixed 8/9 to 5, 5-day-a-week schedules of offices and factories now characterize a minority of workers. Seasons are reemerging as a factor in social time, now because of leisure rather than agriculture. Vacations, minivacations, early retirement, and various means of "time shifting" have broken the lock of the factory on household timetables. Time for leisure is now more varied and fragmented.

The Question of the Declining Work Week

In the 1960s, it was taken for granted that work hours would continue to decline and there would be a resulting increase in leisure time. Predictions of 32-hour and four-day workweeks were commonplace. Leisure was seen as a "problem" by the sophisticated who were concerned that common people would be unable to fill all that time. Answering the question of what has happened since then is extremely complex. The following summarizes what seems to have happened:

1) People think they are working longer hours during the last few decades;

2) There is a higher percentage of people in the labor force;

3) As measured by time diary studies, people are working about an hour less per day then twenty years ago;

4) The pace of life continues to speed up; and

5) Retirement has lengthened for millions of Americans and now represents where our society has made provision for a "society of leisure."

The current debate is partly a matter of time perspective. Since the Civil War, average hours of industrial employment have dropped from about 70 in 1850 to 65 in 1870, 62 in 1890, 55 in 1910, and 45 in 1930—a 35 percent reduction in 80 years (de Grazia, 1964). A continuation of this proportional trend would have brought the average to 42 hours by 1950, 40 by 1970, and 37 by the year 2000. Or, more dramatically, the steady rate of a five hour reduction every two decades would reduce the average from 45 in 1930 to 40 in 1950, 35 by 1970, and less than 30 by 2000. Of course, neither rate was realized. In fact, the average workweek has more or less leveled off at just over 40 hours. According to the Bureau of Labor Statistics, there was a one hour decrease in the 1980s to 43.8 hours per week. This figure, however, refers to full-time workers covered by the Fair Labor Standards Act. Many other workers are either part-time or do work not covered by that legislation. When the average work week of all adult workers is measured using time diaries, Robinson (1989) found that unmarried men worked an average of 41 hours per week, married men worked 42 hours, unmarried women worked 33 hours and married women worked 30 hours. There is, of course, considerable variation around the mean number of hours worked—from families where both husband and wife work fifty hour weeks to couples who live together with the female working part-time and the male unemployed to people who live alone and have two part-time jobs.

In terms of all work done for pay by adults in our society, Robinson's replicated time diary studies, using nationally representative samples, found that, among those who work at least ten hours per week, men worked seven fewer hours per week in 1985 than they did in 1965—42 hours versus 49 hours. Employed women work eight fewer hours a week in 1985 than in 1965—31 hours versus 39 hours, largely due to limited-hour jobs in retailing.

It is in the period of life known as retirement that the largest gains have been made in amount of leisure available throughout our life span. Today, the life expectancy of a male who reaches 65 is 79.8 years while for females who reach age 65, the corresponding life expectancy is 83.7 years. On average about twelve of these years will be in relatively good health. Since less than one worker out of four waits until age 65 to retire, many retiring in their late fifties, this means millions of Americans live from twelve to twenty years in good health with little or no time spent in paid work. This represents a major trend in increasing nonwork time. Our society has been organized in ways which provide for vast quantities of time apart from work during the last decade or two of life, but much less in all other periods, such as for two-worker families with young children.

During that same period, vacations were obtained by a larger proportion of the work force and those vacations have lengthened. Three-day weekends have revised holiday timing to yield blocks of weekend time several times a year. In general, there are more time spaces through the life course that offer possibilities for leisure.

Other projections are based on the changing nature of work. Production industries and offices are being invaded by the computer. As automated assembly, accounting, and record-keeping machines are replacing many factory hands, office bookkeepers, and clerks, drastic reductions in those segments of the work force have been predicted. Estimates are that it would be technologically possible to replace 70 to 90 percent of workers in some factories and offices through automation. Of course, everything technologically possible is not economically feasible or socially desirable. Thus far predictions of mass unemployment have been tempered by a number of other factors including investment costs, labor costs in less developed economies, and higher expectations for information gathering and analysis and product diversity. Employment has shifted to services. There has been selective structural unemployment, but not a mass exodus from employment. There will continue to be significant losses and dislocations, but computers create as well as eliminate jobs. In the integrated world economy, there is far-reaching change that will continue to impact work opportunities and schedules. However, that change does not mean the end of work or its time requirements.

The Case for Relative Stability

As indicated, the current trend is for a slight decline in the average employment week. The average of 44 hours prior to World War II, jumped to 46 due to wartime pressures, and has stabilized at just over 40 hours in the decades since, if part-time workers are excluded. Just as important, however, is the fact that the "average work week" figure is probably more misleading than revealing. For example, the proportion of males in the work force decreases from about 90 percent for those age 25 to 54 to less than 75 percent for those age 55 through 64. Some are forced into retirement by health, company cost-cutting policies, or industry failures. Others choose to leave full-time employment. Further, employed women seem less likely to retire "early," partly due to economic necessity. Many such women, however, work part-time or seasonally.

Also, the majority of adult women—married or single, childless or mothers—are now in the paid work force. This closes some second-job or "moonlighting" opportunities to men. Second incomes in households are now more likely to be from the employment of women. Such employment is largely in services including health and retailing. Such services tend to require longer hours and irregular work schedules. All gains in employment since 1960 have been in services such as government, education, health care, retailing, finance, and recreation rather than in production. These are the jobs that are most likely to require the longest hours, often outside the 8 to 5, Monday through Friday schedules.

At the same time, the hours of many professionals, managers, and technical personnel who carry heavy responsibilities and have a career orientation of expected advancement are unlikely to decline. At one end of the employment spectrum are those workers who are easy to replace in jobs that require little preparation or specialized skill. Their hours may be irregular, but demands on their time are limited by corporate aims to keep wages and benefit costs low. At the other end are those workers with hard-to-replace technical skills who may be pressured to work longer hours for employers striving to keep a competitive edge in world markets. The outcome is considerable variation in work weeks and in incomes. Some "replaceables" are limited to irregular timetables, fewer hours, and periods of unemployment ending with early retirement. Those who are costly to replace—professionals, managers, and technical experts—may actually work longer hours in conditions of high pressure.

Unemployment also impacts time availability and allocations. Not only does unemployment rise in periods of economic recession, but there are always some patterns of localized unemployment. When an industry is unable to compete on world markets, cutbacks or closures may produce high unemployment in a particular community or area even in times of general prosperity. A mill town or inner city area may have unemployment rates over three times national or even state averages. Most serious is the concentration of joblessness among inner-city youth (Wilson, 1987). Jobless rates of 50 to 80 percent are found among inner-city youth who are out of school. The underlying problem is similar to the mill town dependent on a failed industry, employment opportunities have moved out of the area leaving only a few entry-level service jobs. In any case, unemployment removes both resources for leisure and a time structure in which to develop a balance of activity.

The most inclusive economic trend related to time, however, is the growth in the employment of women. This long-term trend (Fuchs, 1983) is measured by the increase of women age 25 to 45 in the workforce from 15 percent in 1890 to 60 percent in 1980. More women are self-supporting and/or the sole economic provider for a household. Most of this employment, however, has been in the service sector of the economy. Women are most of the immediate-care staff in nursing homes, most of the checkers in the 24-hour supermarkets and discount stores, and most of the staff in restaurants and lounges open late into the night. In terms of time availability and allocation, such employment has two primary implications. Women tend to have the most irregular and fragmented employment hours, a fact often obscured by figures on "average work weeks." Second, most women come home to the primary responsibility for household maintenance and child care. As a consequence, it is not surprising that employed single parents, usually mothers, have the least discretionary time.

The point is that "postindustrial time" is far from an unmitigated dawn of freedom and leisure opportunity. There are some new possibilities, especially in the last third of the life course. For many, however, leisure time remains a struggle, a matter of allocation according to priorities rather than great stretches of "free time" remaining after all life's responsibilities and requirements are completed. Further, there is great variation in time pressures and openness indexed by type of employment, gender roles, age, and family composition.

Quantities of Time: Time Diary Studies

In the 1960s, the time diary method of studying time allocations was employed in a twelve-nation comparison (Szalai et al., 1972). Usually referred to as the "international time budget study," it set the course for subsequent studies of variations in the amounts of time given to work, household maintenance, personal care, and leisure. The results, hundreds of pages of tables of average time per day and per week, have become a benchmark for later comparisons. For example, in some nations the study was prior to the mass introduction of television.

The method requires participants to complete a form dividing the day into periods, usually 15 minutes, and asking for primary and secondary activities, place, companions, and sometimes other information. This demanding assignment has been widely used despite problems associated with accuracy, high refusal rates, and analysis limitations. Its greatest values lie in the production of quantitative measures that can be compared across cultures and social systems.

One critical issue is how time allocations have changed over time. John Robinson's "Americans' Use of Time Project" has produced analyses that permit general comparisons from three times a decade apart: 1965, 1975, and 1985. The following table gives average times for a number of activities for men and women age 18 to 65 in those three decades.

Table 24.1: Average Time in Activities (in Hours)

	Total			Men			Women		
	1985	1975	1965	1985	1975	1965	1985	1975	1965
Total	40.1	38.3	34.5	41.1	38.6	34.4	39.6	38.3	34.4
TV	15.1	15.2	10.5	15.7	16.2	11.7	14.5	14.1	9.3
Visiting	4.9	5.5	6.6	5.0	5.1	5.8	4.8	5.7	7.5
Talking	4.3	2.3	2.6	3.5	1.9	1.6	5.1	2.7	3.6
Traveling	3.1	2.6	2.7	3.4	2.8	3.0	3.0	2.4	2.4
Reading	2.8	3.1	3.7	2.7	3.0	4.2	2.9	3.3	3.3
Sports/ Outdoors	2.2	1.5	0.9	2.9	2.3	1.4	1.5	0.8	0.5
Hobbies	2.2	2.3	2.1	1.9	1.6	1.4	2.6	3.0	2.8
Adult Education	1.9	1.6	1.3	2.2	2.1	1.6	1.6	1.3	0.9
Thinking/ Relaxing	1.0	1.1	0.5	1.2	1.0	0.2	0.9	1.2	0.6
Religion	0.8	1.0	0.9	0.6	0.8	0.7	1.0	1.3	1.0
Cultural Events	0.8	0.5	1.1	0.8	0.3	1.3	0.8	0.6	0.9
Clubs/Org.	0.7	1.2	1.0	0.8	0.9	0.8	0.6	1.5	1.2
Radio/ Recording	0.3	0.5	0.6	0.4	0.6	0.7	0.3	0.4	0.4

(Source: Americans Use of Time Project, University of Maryland. (*American Demographics*, November, 1990)

Overall discretionary time has increased in the two decades as measured by this diary method. Since 1965, the greatest use of that increase has been in watching television. There is also an increase in time devoted to talking (and possibly listening) and sports and outdoor activities. That time increase varies, however, with middle-aged two-income families reporting a decrease. Parenting and employment remain the greatest impediment to discretionary time. This gain in discretionary time does not come from a reduction of work time as much as greater efficiencies in household maintenance and a reduced number of children being cared for. Families are smaller, childrearing years more compressed, and childless adults more common.

Robinson's comparative studies are augmented by his analysis of national recreation surveys that show surprising age differences. For most activities, increasing age has indexed declines in participation in almost all recreation activities, especially those requiring physical exertion and travel. Even allowing for cohort differences in resources and education levels, the overall relationship has seemed secure. Comparing studies from 1965 and 1982, however, indicate that older Americans report more participation in recreation and those under 25 report less. Further, the outdoor activities in which increases are greatest tend to be among the less common: skiing, sailing, and jogging. Higher levels of education suggest that participation will increase in the future for each age cohort, especially if smaller households, shorter work weeks, and flexible work schedules increase. The actual conditions in which time is available and allocated, however, involve multiple factors.

Probably the most salient is parenting. No other factor has as much impact on time available as well as the choice of activities and their meanings (see Chapter 19). A study at the University of Michigan examined how childrearing families use their time (Timmer, Eccles, and O'Brien, 1985). The most common activity for families together is watching television. Children of employed mothers watch TV an estimated 6 hours 40 minutes a week with one or both parents as compared to over 8 hours for the children of full-time homemaker mothers. That is about half of the children's total time watching television. "The most striking finding was the relatively *small* amount of time parents in either type of household spend in 'quality time' activities." Employed mothers spend an average of 11 minutes a day reading, talking, or playing with children and about 30 minutes a day on weekends. Homemaker mothers average 30 minutes a day during the week and 36 on weekends. Fathers spend even less time in such enriching activity, 8 minutes a day on weekdays and 14 on weekends. Most of the time parents and children spend together is at mealtimes or watching TV.

The gender difference in over 900 households was also striking. Homemaker mothers have an average of nearly 5.25 hours of recreational activity a week and those in the work force just over 3.1. Employed fathers, however, average an hour a week more recreational time than their employed wives. This is consistent with all other comparative studies. Of course, time alone is only one measure of opportunity. Even vacations away from home may be quite different for the father who drives the car and the mother who tries to entertain, feed, and manage the children.

Such time diary research has a number of values. It uses a universal quantitative measure enabling comparisons. There is a basis for analysis of changes over time. The data are relatively contemporaneous with the activity and in a format that promises to be more accurate than general recollections and estimates. It is unquestionably one valuable approach. Its limitations are also significant. Reports of averages conceal variations within population categories as well as from day to day. Activities are categorized as maintenance, work, leisure, etc. simply by their form with no recognition of differences in meaning or orientation. There is no sense of directed action, schemes of meaning, the importance of companions, or even sequences of activity. Time is time, eating is eating, and golf is golf . . . without variation. Nonetheless, time is also a significant category of resources, allocation, and meaning to social actors.

Time for Leisure: Feast or Famine?

There is a strange contradiction in the study of leisure time. On the one hand, comparative time budget studies report a consistent increase in time available for leisure over the past 20 years. This time is not leftover when everything else is completed, but is mostly achieved by spending less time on homemaking and maintenance and having fewer children. Further, this trend is counter to that of the increase of women, especially mothers of younger children, in the work force.

On the other hand, there are also consistent reports by adults of perceived decreases in discretionary time. The Harris poll reported in 1988 (New York Times, March 16, 1988) is only one example of such a "time crunch." According to the 1988 analysis American adults report that the time free for leisure has declined from 26 hours a week in 1973 to 19 in 1980 and 16.6 in 1987. The report suggest that pressures on the daily and weekly schedule from work, household, and family may be increasing, especially for employed women. The 1987 Harris survey reported that men averaged 20.3 free hours a week and women only 15.6. Others have proposed that the larger proportion of the population living in metropolitan areas may be impacted by the hassles and inefficiencies of urban congestion.

There are two kinds of data mixed into the contradiction. Time diary data is relatively concrete, but is subject to the limitations outlined above. Estimates, however, are influenced by how respondents feel about their time. Some kinds of activities may feel less open and free, less leisurely, than previously. Further, if people believe that they are under time pressure, they may underestimate the amount of time they actually have available. Finally, if most of that time is given to low impact activity such as watching (or at least sitting before) a television set, then it may not feel like much time at all. Perceptions of time duration vary under different conditions (McGrath and Kelly, 1986). The lack of highlights of involvement and intensity in much of so-called "leisure time" can lower estimates of its quantity as well as quality.

One argument is that ours is a "time famine" culture. Steffan Linder (1969), a Swedish economist, has proposed that for an increasing number of affluent upper and middle class adults the great shortage is now time rather than money. The really scarce resource is time to do what one wants to do. This is supported by a number of studies of adults of all ages that have found that the major impediment to engaging in valued activities is a shortage of time. As a consequence, in leisure as in work, there is pressure to get as much done as possible in the time available. Linder argues that this pressure is intensified by the need to "do it all" and "have it all" in a consumption-oriented society. Driving all the cars, playing with all the toys, and experiencing all the entertainment produces a response of "so much to do and so little time to do it." Leisure seems less leisurely, even if more time is available. This pressure may be intensified by status pressures to engage in leisure that symbolizes how well one has made it in life (Veblen, 1899). Consuming the "right" meals, wines, vacation trips, and electronics fills a lot of time, especially if they have to be orchestrated to appear before the right viewers.

When time is perceived as both critical and scarce, then the consequence may be an attempt to pack more experience in the time available. This "time deepening" in leisure (Godbey, 1991) stresses maximizing the results of every time investment rather than concentrating on an immersion in the experience of the moment. Recreation equipment and programs and vacation packages that promise the most in the least time prosper as people are ready to trade more consumer dollars for a promised return in time use. There may be a recognition that time cannot be "saved." Once it is passed, it is lost and cannot be recovered. Leisure time, when perceived as precious and scarce, may be subjected to higher expectations. When coupled with a highly commodified definition of leisure (see Chapter 25), the pressure to maximize experience may result in spending more money in a time-efficient leisure package.

Note the social class bias in this analysis. The assumption is that those experiencing a time famine are affluent in the sense of having ample discretionary income. They are not marginal in terms of affording housing, health care, or retirement income. "Time famine" may be mostly an experience of the "new class" of technicians and professionals whose income is ample for both investment and leisure. The life conditions and pressures of those employed in service industries at low wages and without security are less likely to consistently lead to valuing consumption time over income.

What is more common is the reality of time as a scarce resource, a limit on leisure as well as an opportunity. This scarcity is partly a matter of the life course, impacted especially by parenting. It is also affected by work timetables and expectations, efficiencies of home and self maintenance, and all the contingencies of health and resources. The time crunch is exacerbated by the "double shifts" of employed mothers and the demands of caregiving for frail or ill family members in addition to crowded highways and longer lines at the checkout. The prices to pay for having more discretionary time are clear: be an unmarried nonparent, have a job that is regular and limited, avoid the crowds of the big city, have relaxed homemaking standards, and retire relatively young.

Implications for Leisure

What does all this mean for "leisure time"? Does the term have valid contemporary meaning? Does having leisure mean being disengaged from those other dimensions of life—work and relationships—that are usually considered to be important dimensions of life? In that case, leisure might not be worth the cost.

First, it is clear that for most people most of the time, leisure does not mean leftover time. The premise of any analysis that assumes that reductions in the workweek are automatically translated whole into leisure is false. Rather leisure is carved out of time that has social structure, related to economic and family roles. Further the possible implementation of those roles is seldom if ever complete. Leisure requires a decision to allocate resources, including time, to a particular activity in the midst of other possibilities and even demands. Leisure is more of a struggle for those with multiple role responsibilities than a residual gift. In this sense, there is always a time scarcity, although "famine" may be too strong a term.

Second, leisure time is tied to the larger timetables of the social system. For most, weekends are different from weekdays. School and work schedules provide the context for time that is relatively discretionary. Juggling the time demands and opportunities of multiple roles requires synchronization of schedules. For leisure events that are scheduled on a one-time basis such as a dinner party, other engagements have to be cleared or adjusted. For regularly scheduled events, a music series or basketball schedule, times such as Saturdays or second Wednesdays are set aside. In other cases, priority is given to family dinners or religious observances. The larger and more complex the household, the greater the task of timetable reconciliation. This management task has traditionally been assigned to the wife/mother even when the power to decide priorities is reserved. All of this complicated leisure and community scheduling takes place within the framework of work and school schedules. As a consequence, any significant change in the framework such as a child beginning public school or a job requiring being at the work site on Saturdays or evenings disrupts the entire delicately woven fabric of synchronization. For example, an adult taking a job in health services with variable hours impacts the social time framework for the entire household. It used to be assumed that financial budgets reflected family and individual priorities; it may be the time budget that is the best index of values.

Third, perceived scarcities of time, whether actual or not, lead to attempts to maximize the return on the time investment. There may be the pressures of "time deepening" in which effort, attention, planning, and money are put into an event to gain the fullest experience possible. There may be a reevaluation of priorities to eliminate less satisfying or lower quality experiences or environments. There may be an attempt to get more by spending more. There may be life course changes when the opportunities unique to an age are given special attention. There may even be a form of selfishness in which individuals seek their own pleasure without regard for others. A recognition of a personal time famine, however measured, may lead to higher expectations for leisure.

Fourth, changes in the structures of time and in perceptions of time may precipitate alterations in allocations. For example, those who work longer and irregular hours may arrange long weekends in order to engage in activities that require a block of time. In fact, both official and self-constructed three-day weekends are emerging as a more common pattern for leisure. Mini-breaks are a priority, especially for those who work under high pressure and do not believe they can wait for that two weeks in August. Two-income households may go to great lengths to fabricate periods of mutual time off to compensate for the daily and weekly conflicts in schedule. In general, possibilities of schedule flexibility in employment have led to a new trade-off, longer work days in exchange for longer weekends. In fact, the old time-income tradeoff is no longer automatically decided in favor of income. More workers are now choosing free time rather than money (Best et al., 1979).

Fifth, time thus becomes more than an invariant measure with every minute and hour having the same value. Rather, the quality of time is integral to personal calculations and allocations. Some break time may be of low value with disengagement and relaxation the primary outcome. Other nonwork time may be set aside and given a high valence because its exercise is critical to a valued relationship, personal development, or even health. The quality of the experience or the value placed on an outcome makes some minutes, hours, and days precious. Some time is fiercely guarded while other time is let go with little thought. Time as an index of value, then, is more than a number to be applied universally and without weighting. Time has quality as well as quantity.

Nevertheless, time analysis remains a useful instrument for beginning to examine variations among cultures including similarities and differences according to age, gender, resource level, family configuration, and work conditions. As the structures and value systems of a society change, they will at least in part be reflected in allocations of time. Whether or not time defines leisure, it is a necessary resource.

REFERENCES

Best, F., Bosserman, P., and Stern, B. (1979). Income-free time trade-off preferences of U.S. workers. *Leisure Sciences, 2*: 119-142.

de Grazia, S. (1964). *Of time, work, and leisure.* Garden City, NY: Doubleday & Company, Publishing, Inc.

Fuchs, V. (1983). *How we live: An economic perspective on Americans from birth to death.* Cambridge, MA: Harvard University Press.

Godbey, G. (1991). *Leisure in your life: An exploration* (3rd ed.). State College, PA: Venture Publishing, Inc.

Linder, S. (1969). *The harried leisure class.* New York, NY: Columbia University Press.

McGrath, J., and Kelly, J. R. (1986). *Time and human interaction.* New York, NY: Guilford Publishing Company.

Robinson, J. (April, 1989). Time for work. *American demographics,* (p. 68).

Szalai, A., et al. (1972). *The uses of time: Daily activities of urban and suburban populations in twelve countries.* The Hague, The Netherlands: Mouton.

Timmer, S., Eccles, J., and O'Brien, K. (Winter, 1985-86). How families use time. *ISR Newsletter.* Ann Arbor, MI: Institute for Social Research, University of Michigan.

Veblen, T. (1899) (1953). *The theory of the leisure class.* New York, NY: New American Library.

Wilson, W. J. (1987). The truly disadvantaged: *The inner city, the underclass, and public policy.* Chicago, IL: University of Chicago Press.

CHAPTER 25

Today's Leisure as a Market Commodity

I ncreased reliance on the market sector to provide recreation opportunities and resources is a pronounced trend today in all developed societies. The evidence is overwhelming. Leisure based industry is a growth area for economic investment. Destination resorts, water parks, tourism facilities, sport and fitness clubs, equipment manufacturing, retail sportswear boutiques, and many other kinds of businesses are being developed. At the same time, the funding for public recreation is shifting toward cost-recovery fees and memberships with as little as 15 percent of some community programs being supported by tax revenues. As much as half of some people's discretionary time is spent before that great advertising medium, television. Travel and tourism is growing into one of the top two or three international business segments. Multinational corporations are moving into the leisure business with massive infusions of capital and the expectation of reliable profits.

When we examine the leisure patterns of most adults in modern societies, the centrality of market provided opportunities is evident. First, of course, is the omnipresent television. But there are also the media of paperback books, thousands of magazines, tapes and compact disks, and now home video with choreographed musical offerings, movies, and speciality shows. For the vacation there are a multitude of packages for both travel and destinations. What isn't for sale is available for rent. Every kind of eating and drinking environment is available in urban areas with the varieties spreading to the hinterlands and especially to resort areas. Specialty boutiques market to leisure oriented clients with ever new fashions in clothing, shows, equipment, and symbols of affiliation. Swimming pools are transformed into water parks with the energy provided by slides and wave machines rather than by the swimmers. The mode of engagement is not action, but consumption. Sport is a spectacle. Sunsets are a photo opportunity. And shopping becomes the main activity for travellers. The dominant mode of most market provided leisure is consumption.

Leisure Choice and the Marketplace

So, what's the problem? The leisure marketplace is offering a greater and greater variety of possibilities for the consumer. In a market based economy, the main way in which goods and services are distributed is through market mechanisms. The premise is that of the "sovereign consumer." In classical economic theory, demand rules the market. Sooner or later, the economy will provide what the consumer desires and can afford. Decisions as to what is to be available are not made by some "higher authority" of government or social agency, but by the individual and the household. Priorities are set by those who allocate their resources toward the goods and services they most need and value. Priorities for investment, then, are based on the assessment of anticipated markets. Profit is based on meeting demand.

According to most economic analyses, the household—whether or not a family—is the locus of decision. Choices are made in some process, democratic or authoritarian, among members of the household. The value placed on life-sustaining goods and services may claim priority. For economic resources above and beyond such requirements, tastes and preferences vary widely. A flexible and responsive market system measures those preferences and provides goods and services for which there is the greatest effective demand. Choice resides with the consumer, not with any command center designated by those with political power. Choice is maximized by the market. In the 1990s, the collapse of command economies in Eastern Europe and elsewhere and the turn toward market systems provides strong evidence that there is more than rhetoric underlying such an ideology.

Further support comes from the results. It is evident that market systems are productive. In developed societies, the extent and variety of resources offered for leisure is overwhelming. It would appear that the greatest latitude is provided for the choices to be made by individuals, families, and households. For example, travel destinations once available only to the affluent are now opened to the middle mass with chains of budget motels, low-cost equipment in discount stores, and the possibility of renting items and venues with prohibitive owner-ship costs. The variety of possibilities offered by the market is expanding each year.

Then, is there a problem? In fact, two critiques have been developed. The first questions the validity of resource distribution that relies primarily on the market. The second is both more profound and subtle. Does leisure, and life itself, come to be defined in terms of consumption? Does the market system do more than distribute goods? Does it also shape and alter human consciousness?

Leisure Resource Distribution and the Market

The critique begins with the assertion that a market system is inevitably biased toward certain kinds of provisions and investments. That bias is based on the unequal distribution of wealth and income in capitalist economies, especially the United States, and on the investment imperative.

Differential Purchasing Power

The exact figures are not as important as the relative proportions of wealth and income among the top and bottom of the economic pyramid. In income, the highest 10 percent receives over 25 percent of the income while the lowest 12 percent receives less than 2 percent of the total national income. In wealth, the discrepancies are even greater with 5 percent controlling over 20 percent of assets and owning about 80 percent of the common stock in private hands. Further, the trend in the '80s was toward a greater concentration of wealth. Most disturbing may be that the relative earnings of the top 40 percent are increasing at the same time that both the middle 20 percent and the bottom 30 percent are decreasing. In terms of market purchasing power, the U.S. society is developing greater inequality (see Chapter 9).

The point is that the upper 5 percent of the population is literally looking for ways to spend money on leisure. They give lavish parties, own several homes in a variety of environments and climates, and travel first class or by private jet across oceans and continents for weekend romps. At the other end, as much as 20 percent of the population has no discretionary income at all. Any expenditure for leisure comes out of meager allotments for food, housing, clothing, and other necessities. In fact, a much larger segment of the population, probably over 30 percent, is less than two weeks from destitution if either income or costs of living change radically.

Insofar as the society relies on the market to provide major resources for leisure, then a few have almost unlimited opportunities. Businesses will respond to their every desire and even whim. They are that desirable upscale market for whom price is of minor importance. They can purchase privacy, space, service, and convenience. They can purchase access to the private beach, the exclusive resort, the expedited travel, and the second and third leisure-located home. Just behind the truly wealthy are the professionals, financial managers, and the "new class" of valued research and development designers who are expensive to replace. They, too, can purchase access to the special places, opportunities, and resources both in their expensive urban environments and at a distance.

At the other extreme are those whose incomes are near or below the poverty line. They outnumber the truly wealthy nearly 10-1. For them the economic dimensions of life are a daily struggle for survival. They live in the margins between public-aided housing and health care and market provided resources they cannot afford. Any unexpected financial demand obliterates that narrow margin. And they have children! Now children, not the aged, are the population segment most likely to live in poverty. Who pays for their educational toys, music lessons, sports equipment, books, and other developmental resources that most take for granted?

The Investment Imperative Bias

At least as important is the investment bias built into a market system of resource allocation and distribution. The salient fact in market-sector investment is the necessity of securing a return. Money can always gain guaranteed interest. To lure capital to risk, it is necessary to gain a return in excess of interest; that is, a profit. The higher the risk factor, the greater must be the rate of return. This investment imperative directs market-sector capital toward those enterprises that have the highest likelihood of maximum profit.

What are the markets that attract risk capital? For the most part, they are those with established or potential markets that are cost-intensive. Considerable leisure is cost free or low cost. Some activities that require costly resources are usually low return. For example, programs directed toward children are often costly in personnel resources, but limited in price structure. Activities that require urban space, such as softball, have not usually attracted participants with the income to rent such land. Much use of wilderness, except for travel costs, requires personal rather than financial investment.

On the other hand, the affluent can and will pay for leisure opportunities. Especially they will pay for access to scarce resources such as beaches or the green grass of urban golf courses. They will invest thousands in private club memberships, hundreds of thousands in private resort residences, and hundreds of dollars a day for luxurious travel and destinations. As a consequence, market leisure investment is skewed toward the "high end" markets.

Even for the much larger middle mass, investments are directed toward resources with relatively high fees and costs. A new resort in Las Vegas will cost $700 million because it can vacuum cash from occupants through housing accommodations, meals, shows, and, most of all, gambling. A Disney World is expanded in billion dollar increments because every aspect of the operation is designed to extract money from vacationers for whom the trip is a major and rare venture. At the other extreme, there is little potential profit in bike paths, hiking trails, and children's art programs.

The consequences are more far reaching than just a bias toward cost-intensive programs and resources. For example, the barrier islands off the southeastern coast of the United States are ecologically fragile. Many are protected by inaccessibility or protective ownership. The scarcity of island beaches has placed enormous pressure on those available for development. On many such islands there is little or no public access to beaches and the ocean. All is controlled by resort and residential development. Further, such development is almost entirely designed and marketed for upscale buyers and renters. In fact, the local populations are cut off from this resource that is so central to their culture. In thousands of cases all over the world, the investment imperative has directed development to the affluent and excluded not only the poor but also those of moderate economic resources.

The examples of this bias toward investment return are too numerous to even begin to outline. Sport becomes a spectacle redesigned for huge stadiums and for advertising supported presentation on television. The entire organization of sport has at its apex the corporate ownership of legally protected monopolistic franchises. Players become commodities and bodies are written off like obsolete machines. Golf courses forbid walking and require the rental of carts that increase the number of paying players the space can accommodate. Choice locations go to the most expensive hotels and condominiums, not to those that will maximize enjoyment of the resource. Tax breaks are given to businesses that attract high spending clients and visitors. Even "public" recreation programs dedicate scarce land and indoor space to programs that promise the highest return rather than the most developmentally valuable engagement.

Both income inequalities and investment bias in a market system distribute resources in ways that maximize opportunities for a minority, limit them for a majority, and exclude a significant number at the bottom. Cost-intensive activities are promoted. Consumption is primary. Styles of participation are directed toward using the right equipment in the right place wearing the right apparel. And "right" means expensive. The more it costs, the greater the potential profit.

The Second Critique: Definitions of Life and Leisure

Even more profound than the economic critique, however, is the one that is usually labelled "commodification." It argues that leisure that is primarily consumption leads to life that is actually dehumanizing. Leisure becomes a matter of possession rather than action, of being entertained rather than engaging in activity and with other persons. Underlying the argument is a normative view of what it means to be human. Human life is believed to be defined by dimensions such as freedom which is expressed in self-determined action and community which consists of fundamental relationships of sharing and commitment. From this perspective, life cannot be purchased, meaning is not for sale, and things are only instrumental.

Leisure, in a market system, may come to be defined in terms of purchasing and possession rather than action and community. The basic act comes to be consumption. Freedom is a market choice. And the outcome sought is possession. Further, although few individuals would admit to such a set of values, many are caught in what Marx (1970) called "false consciousness," a failure to identify one's real interests and buying into a system that exploits the many to benefit the few. The overall argument includes at least the following six sequential elements:

1) Leisure becomes a symbol of social status. Thorstein Veblen (1899), as discussed elsewhere, developed this argument 100 years ago in his "theory of the leisure class." He argued that leisure had become a symbol differentiating the upper class from those of the common masses who were required to work. The wealthy elites exhibited a calculated lifestyle of extravagance and waste to demonstrate that they possessed wealth that lifted them above necessity. Their "conspicuous consumption" was a lifestyle that symbolized their superior status.

   The masses, on the other hand, also had leisure styles that corresponded to their place in the status hierarchy. They learned tastes appropriate to their status. Such tastes supported markets for the goods and services appropriate to their place in the society. At the same time, their leisure style was also based on consumption to the extent that leisure became a reward for their work. Leisure is then purchased by labor that may itself be routinized, stultifying, and alienating. Status based tastes provide markets for the economy, separate elites from the rest of the society, and bind workers to their economic roles. For the worker, leisure becomes something that must be *earned* through work. Further, similar leisure tastes bond workers to their status groups and serve to "keep them in their place."

   The details of Veblen's argument reflect that period of history. For example, elites now seem to exhibit lifestyles that symbolize that they are "productive" rather than idle even when their leisure may seem extravagant. Many elements of the critical argument, however, retain their bite. Affiliations such as churches, country clubs, and voluntary organizations such as symphony guilds retain their high status inclusion and exclusion patterns. Elite sports have high access costs. Fashions, especially in clothing, change so that keeping in style requires replacing goods that are hardly worn. Engaging in activities with exclusionary costs demonstrates to the world that personal wealth has reached a level at which normal standards of use and waste can be disregarded.

Basic to Veblen's analysis is the assumption that the market delivers leisure goods at a price. These goods—activity locales, equipment with a continual obsolescence of technologies and styles, and distinguishing apparel—signify both social status and level of market power. The stylistic rigor that accompanies upscale activities excludes those who cannot afford that level of leisure. Downhill skiing at exclusive resorts, for example, involves donning fashionable togs both on the slopes and in the lodge, using the latest equipment, high rent accommodations, and full attention to factors of fashion rather than the experience of skiing. Lower cost styles of skiing tend to be segregated by location and even by the quality of the resource. Leisure travel, toys, and togs all serve as crucial symbols of social status. And such status based leisure is oriented to consumption rather than the experience.

2) Such consumption is more than taste; it is a central reward for docile participation in the economy. Any economy requires an adequate number of workers to produce goods to compete on national and international markets as well as services to support the standard of living of the society. Many of the necessary tasks are less than fulfilling. Someone has to clean offices, shops, and even hotel rooms. Someone has to run or watch the repetitive operations of the machine. Someone has to type data into the computer files, refill the discount store shelves, and change the bedding in nursing homes. Further, the rewards for such tasks tends to be relatively low in comparison with the salaries, bonuses, incentives, and packages of managers, research staff, professionals, and even key sales personnel. Yet, there has to be some incentive to make such workers willing if not eager to come to work and perform adequately.

Leisure has become central to the economic system as reward. According to this definition, leisure is not a right but must be earned. Time for leisure is granted by the employer or the system in general. Purchasing power to acquire market distributed leisure opportunities is given according to economic criteria. Income is claimed to be based on productivity, on the value of the product and the rate at which it is produced. Great differences in purchasing power are supposed to draw workers into the effort and preparation that yields the greatest rewards.

The system has become both differentiated and complex. Lifted above survival, workers are to strive to gain a wider range of consumer goods. The credit system serves to intensify the ties to jobs when vacations and "big toys" such as recreation vehicles are purchased on credit and with "plastic money." As the bumper sticker proclaims: "I owe, I owe. It's off to work I go." Failure to perform required tasks and to meet the timetables of the workplace are met with the ultimate sanction, dismissal and loss of purchasing power. Beyond necessity, workplace sanctions mean a loss of leisure insofar as it is defined as consumption.

3) Recall that Veblen also argued that leisure is central to the tastes that divide the society into status groups. There is no difficulty in characterizing the leisure of the superrich. A birthday party that involved flying hundreds of people to a specially prepared grounds in North Africa costs more than most people earn in thirty years. And the significant factor was not the party, but the social status of being included!

We also make casual references to other status based styles of leisure. Motorcycle groups tend to be "blue-collar." Country and western music fans are also usually wage earners with limited economic possibilities. Symphony concerts draw adults with higher education. Their children go backpacking or ride to the hounds while the factory hands have tents or campers and ride trail bikes. Such taste preferences not only keep people with similar styles together . . . and separated from other classes, but provide the varied markets for leisure goods and services. Leisure as marketed commodity provides the demand for an increasingly important segment of the economy. Over $300 billion a year in the U.S. economy alone for *direct* spending on recreation is not peripheral.

Further, leisure, a market beyond necessity, is especially subject to the dictates of fashion. For the teens, the latest tape or disk is required in devotion to the highly promoted group or performer to whom one pledges allegiance. Entertainment goes out of style monthly. For the sport enthusiast, the market offers newly designed equipment every season. For those who frequent elite venues, be they white in winter or green in summer, last year's jacket simply cannot be worn. The market dictates that fashion, not function, must rule the purchasing cycle in leisure. Leisure, then, is not only tied to the consumption of things, but to the latest thing.

4) From this perspective, the "good life" comes to be defined in terms of such consumption (Miller, 1987). In a system in which most households are raised above the level of economic necessity, new expectations take precedence. What is it that defines life that is more than adequate, that is worth the effort and compliance that characterizes the world of work for most? It is no longer food and

shelter or even school for children and basic levels of transportation and clothing. It is that "something more" that makes life special and that gives at least the feeling of freedom and choice.

That "something more" can be more concrete than an inner sense of meaning, more lasting than a transitory experience, and more measurable than a changing relationship. It can be parked in the driveway, worn where others will notice, recorded on videotape, and symbolized with the right labels and insignia. It can be a possession, remaining to be grasped when the experience of its use is a dim memory. And, unlike an experience, its value can be measured directly by its price. Quality equals cost.

The consequence may be that higher cost comes to be associated with preference and value. For example, some kinds of entertainment are quite pricey in admission fees. Conversely, an evening walk costs nothing but time and a little effort. Distant travel costs more and may be valued more than a nearby environment that yields a different set of delights. The crux of the matter is equating price with worth. The "good life" becomes the more costly environment, event, or even relationship. Further, insofar as the demonstration to others of that cost becomes integral to its meaning, then the meaning of life itself becomes commodified, something to be bought and displayed.

One influential exposition of this commodification of life is that of the counter-culture critic, Herbert Marcuse. His analysis was that life could become "one dimensional," limited to the ownership and control of things (Marcuse, 1964). He argued that any social system requires a certain amount of regulation that results in the repression of order-destroying actions by individuals or groups. Contemporary capitalist societies, however, have gone beyond necessary order to "surplus repression" that limits legitimate freedom. One element of this repression is found in defining life solely in terms of the material things that can be owned and controlled. Success is not found in personal development or social contribution, but in the single dimension of things. A second element, based on a neo-Freudian perspective, is that this repression also limits the sensual nature of humankind. Rather than being open and expressive in the physical and emotional aspects of relationships, strict limits are placed on such expression. Even intimate relationships may come to be defined in terms of control and symbolic possession rather than expression and intimacy.

Alienation for Marcuse is more than a loss of control of work conditions. It permeates the entire society including leisure and community. Preoccupation with things, "commodity fetishism," turns people away from their own natures to the alienated and alienating theme of possession. The full dimensions of action and interaction are reified into price and symbols of ownership. Communication—bodily, emotional, and intellectual—is reduced to manipulations in which others become objects to be used. Leisure, then, becomes another commodified domain of having and holding rather than expressing and creating. It is a social space cut off from its own meaning of openness and relative freedom. Work, too, becomes instrumental rather than the production of goods and services of value to others.

5)   Leisure, like work and the family, can become commodified. It may be defined as consumption. The freedom of leisure becomes the exercise of market purchasing power. It is entertainment, not action; preoccupied with the self rather than extended to others. Leisure becomes alienated: directed toward control rather than freedom, things rather than experience, and the routinized rather than the creative. It is, in short, a package to be purchased.

Examples are too numerous to even begin to list. The two new hotels in Las Vegas are the Mirage with a fake jungle and artificial volcano that erupts every thirty minutes and the Excalibur with a medieval castle, moat, drawbridge, and jousting court. Anything to lure people into the real action, risking that symbol of commodified selfhood, money. Las Vegas is not just a strange gambling den in the desert, but now markets itself as a destination with entertainment for the entire family. The package of glitter and glamor now includes sport and exercise, sun and sand, as well as the familiar gambling, food, shows, and legalized prostitution.

In the media, Sunday supplements now promote a variety of leisure commodities. Travel packages predominate with their promises of sun, sand, sea, and sex. For the most part, "leisure" sections are promotions rather than journalism. On television, watched up to 50 percent of leisure hours by some, the linking of leisure with marketing is commonplace in advertising. It is also more subtle in the drama and comedy programs in which leisure locales, eating in expensive restaurants, travel, sports cars, and other commodities are the usual environments of pleasure. The message, direct and indirect, is that spending money to be in the right places wearing the right clothes and mingling with the right people is the key to happiness. The "good life" is a commodity intensive life.

6) Such market focused definitions of life and leisure lead inevitably to a similar definition of the self. In a switch on the philosophical premise, "I think, therefore I am," a contemporary French painting proclaims "I shop, therefore I am." The meaning of life comes to be defined in terms of the market. The signs of a successful life are easily measured in the accumulation of possessions. In another switch, we learn to love things and use people.

The life of the mind is reduced to pieces of paper announcing the acquisition of academic degrees and credentials. Even in the university, success is measured by income. For a woman success in marriage is measured by the attraction and retention of a man controlling financial assets. For a man success in marriage is measured by acquiring a physically attractive woman and the production of children who "do well." Even the body becomes a commodity with the prescribed gender-appropriate shape becoming a fixation leading to diet and exercise regimens and even to several hundred thousand below-the-neck cosmetic surgeries each year.

The critical question of "Who am I?" is not answered in existential terms but in terms of possession. "Development" refers to the location of the four-bathroom home. The "journey of life" means flying first class. Community is at the exclusive club. Growth refers to investment portfolios and risk to common stocks. Exploration is in a new German sport sedan. Taste refers to gourmet cuisine and excitement to a wine vintage. And nurture becomes the most expensive and competitive preschool program.

What is the Issue?

Again, what's the problem? If it works, if people are happy with their measurable definitions of life and leisure, why not leave well enough alone? It is true that most of the people in the world cannot afford a possession saturated lifestyle. However, there is ample evidence that such a life is just what most desire. Have-nots seek to become haves. Governments are overthrown and economies junked because they do not provide a standard of living that measures up to that depicted on American television. In developed countries people make their choices for leisure. More and more of those choices reflect commodified values. At times it appears that the very act of spending money is the most satisfying activity in the leisure styles of many people. No one is forced to live this way. If consumption produces satisfaction and people direct their lives toward even greater consumption, isn't this exercise of freedom their right?

There are two responses to this acceptance of commodification: the first is that there is evidence that it doesn't really work all that well. The second is that it may not be as accurate an assessment of contemporary leisure as its critics assume.

The Basis of Satisfaction

What is it that is truly satisfying in leisure? Is it entertainment, consumption, and entertainment? Or is there evidence that something different yields the greatest happiness?

To begin, there is general agreement as to the kinds of leisure that people value most highly, that they are least willing to surrender (Kelly, 1983). The first is the "serious leisure" described in Chapter 18. It is "high investment" leisure in which there is a sustained commitment to the development of skills and knowledge. Such leisure becomes central to an individual's personal identity. Often significant participation communities are formed around common action. In such serious leisure there is the development of a sense of ability, the risk of trying to do something well, and the recognition of personal development.

Mihalyi Csikszentmihalyi (1990) has analyzed how such an investment in challenging and skill-based activity leads to "optimal experience." He argues that it is such experience that gives meaning to life. It is the core of satisfaction. In his research on everyday experience, however, there is a surprise. Thousands of respondents have reported that they are twice as likely to have such deeply satisfying experiences in their work as in their leisure. That does not mean that work is so wonderful, but that leisure is often a disappointment. The reason is clear from the data: most leisure consists of being passively entertained rather than taking action. Optimal experience is rare when sitting before the television or aimlessly filling time.

The second kind of leisure that is most satisfying involves communicative interaction with the people most important to us. It is leisure that explores, builds, and expresses community. It is a context for the development of relationships of trust, sharing, and intimacy. Such leisure also involves risk, the risk of relationships. Its freedom is expressed in commitment to others rather than in openness and indeterminacy. Note also that both serious leisure and relational leisure include structure and action.

The problem with commodified leisure is that it lacks both those elements of satisfaction. It is based on being done to rather than doing, possession rather than sharing, things rather than people, and instrumental behaviors rather than intrinsic meanings. Optimal experience, according to Csikszentmihalyi, involves challenge, investment, risk, and community. Things may be used, but they are never ends. Such leisure is existential rather than commodified (Kelly, 1987).

Ordinary Leisure: Things and Meanings

Further, there is some evidence that the commodified view of leisure is one-sided. One effort to examine the evidence indicates that people may not be as caught in the trap of things as the critics argue (Kelly, 1991). The evidence on commodification tends to be macrosocial, resting on such items as the growth of leisure industries, cost-intensive leisure provisions, shifts away from the public to the market sector, the growth of leisure providing corporations, and the significance of mass media. On the same level in an analysis of marketing and participation data in the United States, there is considerable counter evidence:

1) Cost-intensive activities are not increasing in participation faster than those that are relatively cost-free. The trend picture is quite mixed.

2) The activities that people do most are relatively cost-free: entertaining friends at home, informal interaction with other household members and workmates, watching television, listening to music, walking, and reading for pleasure. More adults cook for pleasure than gamble, more garden than go to clubs and discos, and relatively few engage in such chic activities as Alpine skiing (4.2 percent) or going to fitness clubs (7.7 percent).

3) Expenditure trends in the United States indicate that the percentage of household income spent directly on recreation has remained relatively stable since 1970 at about 6.5 percent. Gross expenditures in most leisure categories increased somewhat more than the rate for durable goods between 1970 and 1977. The total amount of growth between 1970 and 1980 was about that of the total economy, 34 percent in constant dollars.

4) Proportions of those owning leisure equipment who purchased new goods during 1983 ranged from 20 percent to 50 percent depending on the replacement needs of the items. Purchases were more related to durability than fashion.

5) Most leisure trips are still by car (85 percent) and on a budget.

6) The kinds of activities that adults consistently rate most important, as described above, are not cost-intensive.

7) The diverse studies of anticipated outcomes from leisure experiences suggest multiple meaning and satisfactions. Use and display of equipment has not been found to be a dominant factor in outdoor recreation.

In general, the evidence seems mixed. Certainly purchase and possession are characteristic of some leisure styles. Display and status symbolism are evidently a part of some choices of activities, locales, and related equipment and clothing. On the other hand, to expand that linkage into a total commodification of leisure would require a different kind of evidence. It would be necessary to examine the overall patterns of participation of a variety of individuals and the meanings they ascribe to their choices and actions.

Only an exploratory study has been attempted to explore the issue of commodification in the consciousness of adult leisure participants (Kelly, 1991). This study with a sample of adult women and men found that purchasing things is an element in some leisure. However, such market participation is defined primarily as instrumental rather than as an end for most activities. Even for travel, the relatively high costs are said to be required to secure the real satisfactions of companions, activities, and environments. Favorite day-to-day activities that produce the highest satisfaction and "good times" do not tend to be commodity-intensive. Even the majority that went shopping "for the fun of it" as often as once a week claim that the main meaning was not the actual act of purchasing. An analysis of overall styles by interviewers indicated that commodities were central to the leisure styles of only 5 percent of the sample, one element among others for 36 percent, and of little importance to 59 percent. Of course, commodification may have become so fundamental to the culture that people are not aware of its power. The case for its total domination of leisure in developed economies, nevertheless, is yet to be made.

On the other hand, the significance of owning, possessing, and displaying in leisure styles, especially those of the affluent, cannot be quickly dismissed. At the very least, there is considerable evidence that most leisure is privatized rather than communal, dependent on markets and media for many resources, consumptive rather than vitally active, and of low rather than high intensity and commitment. Nor can it be denied that leisure is big business, a major and growing segment of Western economies. Further, the likelihood is high of more sophisticated and differentiated marketing in the future. Tourism provisions are offering more variety, especially for the rental markets. It is also evident that market sector investment is drawn by the promise of profits in ways that will shape what is available and promoted as leisure opportunities for men, women, and children of all ages and social levels. The focus will be on cost rather than the quality of experience.

REFERENCES

Csikszentmihalyi, M. (1990). *Flow: The psychology of optimal experience.* New York, NY: Harper & Row, Publishers, Inc.

Kelly, J. R. (1983). *Leisure identities and interactions.* London, England: Allen and Unwin.

Kelly, J. R. (1987). *Freedom to be: A new sociology of leisure.* New York, NY: Macmillan Publishing Company, Inc.

Kelly, J. R. (1991). Commodification and consciousness. *Leisure Studies 10,* 7-18.

Marcuse, H. (1964). *One-dimensional man.* Boston, MA: Beacon Press.

Marx, K. (1970). *The economic and philosophical manuscripts of 1844.* London, England: Lawrence and Wishart.

Miller, D. (1987). *Material culture and mass consumption.* New York, NY: Basil Blackwell, Inc.

Veblen, T. (1899) (1953). *The theory of the leisure class.* New York, NY: New American Library.

CHAPTER 26

Constraints on Leisure Expression

I t makes no sense to think of leisure apart from constraint. Freedom and pleasure must be thought of in comparative rather than absolute terms. All humans are constrained by both the physical and social environment as well as their own physiological constraints. Leisure expression represents not so much the absence of constraints but rather a lessening of constraints, greater perceived freedom and, sometimes, a voluntary acceptance of a new set of constraints such as the rules of a game or the folkways of a different culture during a tourist experience.

In many cultures, as we have previously seen, leisure was the prerogative of an elite. Additionally, in most traditional cultures, individuals did not make leisure choices so much at an individual level but rather as a member of a group. There was, for instance, a certain way to celebrate the harvest and everyone obeyed those folk ways. It is only during this century that a wide range of alternatives of leisure expression have become available for those residing in industrial democracies.

Early Research on Leisure Constraints

The first examination of leisure constraints was often undertaken as part of larger studies. These studies were concerned with the provision of recreation, park and leisure services or else were part of larger community studies. Individuals were simply asked about any recreation or leisure activities in which they wished to participate but could not. Respondents who desired to participate in some activity but said they were prevented from doing so were then asked what prevented them from doing so. Often the questioner presented a list of alternative reasons for the respondent to consider. Such questioning assumed that the individual first developed a desire to participate and then either participated or was prevented from doing by some barrier or constraint. Several studies, often done to determine the use of public recreation and park services, have asked people about reasons for their nonuse of such services. Table 26.1 (Howard and Crompton, 1984) shows such a listing from one such study. It lists responses which individuals typically give if they are simply asked for reasons why they don't participate in particular leisure activities or use certain leisure services or use them more frequently. Figure 26.1 (Godbey, 1985) shows an attempt to identify all residents of a given community with regard to their participation status in a given leisure activity. As may be seen, of those who do not participate, some are constrained by lack of awareness of the opportunity, some are aware of the opportunity but do not wish to participate, some wish to participate but are constrained by circumstances which the agency sponsoring the leisure activity could respond to and some are constrained by reasons which are beyond the control of the agency.

While of some use, asking individuals why they did not participate in a leisure activity in which they expressed the desire to do so has some severe limitations. First, some answers, such as "lack of time" or "lack of money" may simply indicate that the individual was not very interested in the leisure activity in question. Second, since leisure activities are loaded with status connotations, many individuals may feel pressured to say that they would, for instance, like to visit the local art gallery but simply don't have time to do so (even though they watched four hours of television every day).

Perhaps the most basic problem with this approach is that it assumes that individual preferences for leisure, constraints and participation patterns are separate from each other rather than interactive. Individuals may overcome constraints in order to engage in valued activity.

The Interactive Nature of Constraints, Participation and Motivation

The process by which an individual participates in a leisure activity or experiences constraints which prevent this from occurring involve the motivation or desire to participate, the existence or nonexistence of a constraint and the act of participation or the prevention of participation. While most of the early research cited above assumes that constraints occur only after the desire to participate, (Crawford and Godbey, 1987) theorized that constraints may enter this relationship not solely by intervening between a preference for an activity and participation in that activity, but also by their influence on establishing preferences. Desire to participate, constraints and the act of participation, they assumed, are mutually influencing and in a dynamic relationship. A person who participates in the game of chess, for instance, and finds it very enjoyable may experience fewer constraints to participation, such as lack of time, since his or her desire to

Table 26.1
Reasons for Nonparticipation in Specific Leisure Services in City A by Rank and Frequency*

Rank	Reason	N
1	Site location inconvenient	47
2	Lack of sufficient interest	43
3	Lack of time	40
4	Personal health reasons	37
5	Use alternative facility or program	32
6	Fear of crime at site	28
7	Lack of skill—don't know how to do activity	18
8	Site too crowded	16
9	Lack of transportation—no car	15
10	Lack of money	12
11	Lack of public transportation	9
11	Fear of crime traveling to from site	9
13	Site poorly maintained	8
14	Don't know enough about site	7
14	Too old	7
16	Site hours of operation inconvenient	4
17	Site polluted	3
17	Don't know anyone at facility or program	3
17	Don't have other people to do activity with	3
17	Don't like program leader or staff	3
21	Activities not interesting	1

* Reasons given by those respondents who knew of the existence of the specific leisure service in question, indicated they wished to participate but were prevented from doing so. More than one reason could be given.

Source: Howard, D. and Crompton, J. (July 1984). *Journal of Park and Recreation Administration, 2*(3):44.

Figure 26.1
A Model of Nonparticipation in Leisure Services

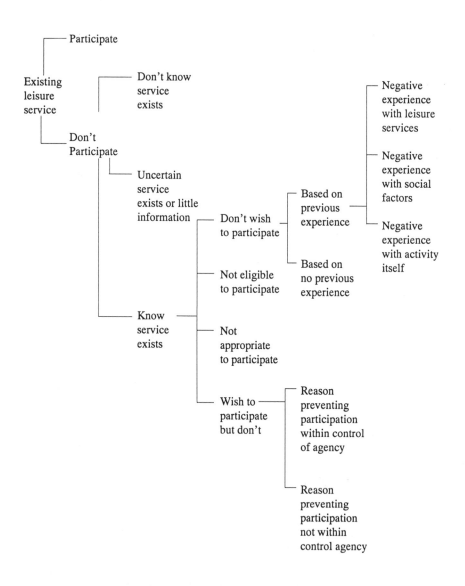

Source: Godbey, G. (Second Quarter, 1985). *Journal of Park and Recreation Administration*, 3(2):4.

participate is now stronger. Another person who wishes to play chess but is continuously unable to find a partner to play with is likely to find that his or her desire to participate is diminished.

Crawford and Godbey identified three types of constraints to leisure behavior: intrapersonal, interpersonal and structural.

Intrapersonal Constraints

These constraints involve individual psychological states and attributes which interact with leisure preferences rather than intervening between preference and participation. Examples of intrapersonal constraints include stress, depression, anxiety, religiosity, kin and nonkin reference groups, attitudes, prior socialization into specific leisure activities, perceived self-skill, and subjective evaluations of the appropriateness and availability of various leisure activities (Crawford and Godbey, 1987, p. 122).

Interpersonal Constraints

These constraints are the result of interpersonal interaction or the relationship between individuals' characteristics. Constraints of this sort may interact with both preference for, and subsequent participation in leisure activities. One might, for instance, not be able to find a suitable partner or group for a leisure activity and thus find the preference for participation diminished.

Structural Constraints

These represent constraints as they have typically been conceptualized in past research. They are commonly conceptualized as intervening constraints or barriers between leisure preference and participation. Examples of structural constraints or barriers include family obligations, financial resources, season, climate, the scheduling of work time, availability of opportunity, transportation and knowledge of opportunities.

The Hierarchical Nature of Leisure Constraints

The process of participating in a given leisure activity, according to Crawford, Jackson and Godbey (1991) involves the successful negotiation of these three kinds of constraints, which are encountered hierarchically. That is, an individual first encounters intrapersonal constraints and, if such constraints are negotiated, a leisure preference is formed. This may be done when such constraints are absent or when their effects have been confronted through some combination of privilege and exercise of the human will. Next, depending upon the activity, the individual may encounter constraints at the interpersonal level. Only when these two types of constraints are overcome are structural constraints encountered.

An example of this hierarchical model would be a sixth grade girl who wished to learn to wrestle. Most other girls did not "want" to wrestle, perhaps because they had been taught that it is not an activity they "ought to do." For them, this intrapersonal constraint was the most powerful deterrent to participation. In the absence of intrapersonal constraint, the girl who wanted to wrestle was faced with the interpersonal constraint of finding people with whom to wrestle. If this obstacle were overcome, then the structural constraint of finding a place and time would be encountered.

It is assumed that intrapersonal, interpersonal and structural constraints are also aligned in a hierarchy of importance, with intrapersonal being most important, interpersonal next and structural least. This proposition is supported by the notion of "psychological orientations" (Huston and Ashmore, 1986). Psychological orientations serve to predispose individuals to behave in certain ways, and consist of at least three subjective evaluations:

1) the beliefs a person has about what he or she ought to do;

2) what the individual likes or wants to do; and

3) the extent to which the person has the competence or the ability to perform a particular behavior (Huston and Ashmore, 1986, p. 15).

The subjective evaluations inherent in psychological orientations are important because they may prevent individuals from testing the extent to which "higher level" interpersonal and structural constraints exist. Those individuals who are most affected by intrapersonal constraints, then, would be unlikely to enunciate the desire to participate in a given leisure activity. As a result, they would not reach the stage of encountering higher order constraints. Conversely, those who overcome intrapersonal and interpersonal constraints are likely to experience and identify more structural constraints.

A Hierarchy of Social Privilege

From the previous, it may be seen that social class may have a more powerful influence upon leisure participation and nonparticipation than the analysis of socioeconomic variables in leisure activities has typically demonstrated (see, for example, Kelly, 1980, 1989). This influence is not direct, however. Rather, it is channeled through variations in the ways in which people perceive and experience constraints and opportunities.

The results of several empirical studies support this interpretation (Kay and Jackson, 1990; Searle and Jackson, 1990; Robinson, 1977; Searle and Jackson, 1985a; Washburne, 1978). Income and education frequently exhibit strong relationships with the perceived intensity of constraints, but the direction of the relationship is dependent upon the type of constraint. Thus, it has been demonstrated that the tendency to report the effects of structural constraints increases with income and education, but so does the desire to increase the range of participation. If, as Jackson (1990) has proposed, this expressed desire is interpreted as evidence of the absence or weakness of antecedent constraints, then better educated and higher income individuals are subject to fewer and weaker intrapersonal and interpersonal constraints on participation than their less privileged counterparts. They may have more resources to battle and overcome barriers.

There is also evidence that gender is a critical variable in terms of this hierarchy of constraints. Raymore, Godbey and Crawford, for example (1992), in a study of 350 Canadian eleventh graders, found that females not only scored lower on a self-esteem test than did males but also identified more intrapersonal constraints to their leisure participation

Given that social class has typically been operationalized by social scientists as income and education together with occupation, the previous model may be said to reveal a hierarchy of social privilege. This would mean that those whom researchers have assumed to be the most disadvantaged, those who report the highest level of structural constraints, may in reality enjoy an overall level of access to leisure services that is not available to others. It would also seem to indicate that the notion of open-ended consumption of leisure experience will lead to more structural constraints and fewer intrapersonal ones.

Some studies have, in fact, found little relation between reported constraints and participation or a positive relation between number of reported constraints and participation. Shaw, Bonen and McCabe (1991) for example, found that level of participation in physically active forms of leisure was generally not related to perceived constraints. Kay and Jackson (1991) found that participants often identified more constraints than those who did not, presumably because those who participated could identify not only actual constraints but also potential constraints which they were able to overcome. It should not be surprising that participants may be able to identify more constraints, particularly of a structural nature, since they are likely to have a greater level of knowledge about the activity in question. They are also often likely to have higher levels of formal education and simply be more verbal than those who don't participate. The more important question, however, may be the kinds of constraints identified. Those who are higher in terms of social privilege may identify as many or more constraints but they are less likely to be intrapersonal constraints.

It may also be argued that this hierarchical model of constraints applies to an individual's likelihood of specializing in a leisure activity. For instance, a male college student might casually participate in modern dance and wish to specialize more, but be intrapersonally constrained from doing so by the perceived attitude of his peers. Only when such perceptions are successfully negotiated are issues of interpersonal constraints, such as finding others who wish to specialize in modern dance, encountered. If these constraints are negotiated, then structural constraints, such as finding a dance studio and appropriate music, will become a salient issue.

As a further example of how the previous typology of constraints affects a person who is already participating, let us consider the situation identified by Stebbins (1979) that may confront a "beginner" in many leisure activities (see Chapter 18). Upon beginning to participate in an activity, the individual is immediately confronted with professional standards. At this point, what the beginner has achieved seems insignificant by comparison, and a decision is made either to divest his or her ego from the activity and become a "dabbler" or to begin a process of learning and skill acquisition.

At this critical juncture some individuals will simply prefer not to begin specializing in the activity. Of those who might wish to do so, however, some will be constrained by intrapersonal factors (e.g., the belief that females should not be highly competitive in a sport). If these constraints are overcome, there will still be interpersonal constraints, finding other players with similar skill levels, interests and aspirations. Should such interpersonal constraints be negotiated, there remain the structural constraints of money for equipment, access, lack of time and so forth.

Among participants in certain activities, one type of constraint, talent or skill, may become particularly important. This may be treated as a structural constraint. That is, it intervenes between the desire to participate and actual participation for the nonparticipant, while for those who participate, the level of talent or skill intervenes between the desired level of specialization and the attainment of that level. The tennis player who wishes to become highly specialized and who has overcome intrapersonal and interpersonal constraints may simply find that he or she cannot, for instance, return hard serves hit to the forehand with any degree of accuracy. Such constraints, however, become apparent only for those who have successfully negotiated other constraints at an earlier stage. Participation continuation in sport, for example, may be blocked by a competition ethic that defines losing as unacceptable.

Constraints and Ceasing Participation

Constraints to leisure also occur after the individual has been participating, perhaps over a number of years. People may stop participating for reasons which are voluntary or involuntary. That is, they may choose, for instance, to quit playing bingo because they simply have lost interest or because they no longer can get a ride to the bingo game or because their eyesight has become too poor to see the cards. Ceasing participation may be divided between those who merely quit participating in an activity and those who replace the leisure activity with another. As Jackson and Dunn (1988) found, using data from a household survey in Alberta, Canada, when respondents were asked about their leisure behavior during the year, 51 percent of the sample said that they had ceased participating in some leisure activity during the year. Of those, 23 percent were "Quitters" who did not replace the activity with a new one and almost 28 percent were "Replacers," who added some new leisure activity during the year. Forty-nine percent of the sample had not ceased participating in any leisure activity during the year and of these, 20 percent were "Adders" who added one or more new leisure activities without dropping any and around 29 percent were "Continuers," neither dropping or adding activities. Respondents were more likely to drop exercise-oriented activities than others.

A study of retirees who had moved to a retirement village (Morgan and Godbey, 1978) examined the total number of leisure activities individuals participated in before and after moving to a retirement village. It was found that, overall, there was a slight decrease in the total number of leisure activities participated in but an increase in the frequency of participation of those in which respondents continued to participate. Many of these changes in participation were attributed to changes in the availability of leisure resources rather than the act of moving or of retirement.

One other interesting aspect of increasing participation or beginning it in later life is that older adults frequently begin an activity which they had discontinued for several years, sometimes in a new format (see Chapter 27). Thus, many activities which are "added" are not necessarily new ones but old ones which have been rediscovered.

Change in participation in leisure activities, we may summarize, is usually incremental unless there is some traumatic event, such as the death of a spouse or a pronounced change in health. The cycles of participation in leisure activity are likely to show more differences among individuals as the "mass society" created by the Baby Boom Generation is reformed by the next generation.

REFERENCES

Crawford, D., and Godbey, G. (1987). Reconceptualizing barriers to family leisure. *Leisure Sciences, 9;* 119-127.

Crawford, D., Jackson, E., and Godbey, G. (1991). A hierarchical model of leisure constraints. *Leisure Sciences, 13;* 3.

Godbey, G. (Second Quarter, 1985). Non-use of public leisure services: A model. *Journal of Park and Recreation Administration, 3*(2):4.

Howard, D., and Crompton, J. (July, 1984). Who are the consumers of park and recreation services? *Journal of Park and Recreation Administration, 2*(3):44.

Huston, T., and Ashmore, R. (1986). Women and men in personal relationships. In R. Ashmore and F. Del Boca (Eds.), *The social psychology of female-male relations.* New York, NY: Academic Press, Inc. (pp. 167-210).

Jackson, E. (1990). The operation of leisure constraints. Leisure challenges: Bringing people, resources and policy into play, Sixth Canadian Congress on Leisure Research, Ontario Research Council on Leisure. Ontario, Canada, (pp. 352-356).

Jackson, E., and Dunn, E. (1988). Integrating ceasing participation with other aspects of leisure behavior. *Journal of Leisure Research, 20*(1):31-46.

Kay, T., and Jackson, G. (1991). Leisure despite constraint: The impact of leisure constraints on leisure participation. *Journal of Leisure Research, 23*(4), 301-314.

Kelly, J. (1980). Outdoor recreation participation: A comparative analysis. *Leisure Sciences, 3;* 129-154.

Kelly, J. (1989). Leisure Behaviors and Styles: Social, Economic and Cultural Factors. In E. L. Jackson and T. L. Burton (Eds.), *Understanding recreation and leisure: Mapping the past, charting the future.* State College, PA: Venture Publishing, Inc, (pp. 89-111).

Morgan, A., and Godbey, G. (1978). The effect of entering an age-segregated environment upon the leisure activity patterns of older adults. *Journal of Leisure Research, 10*(3):177-191.

Raymore, L., Godbey, G., and Crawford, D. (March, 1992). The relation of gender and self-esteem to leisure constraints among adolescents. Submitted to *Leisure Sciences.*

Robinson, J. (1977). The 1977 nationwide outdoor recreation survey: Some results and conclusions. The Third Nationwide Outdoor Recreation Plan, Appendix II, Survey Technical Report 4. Washington, DC: U.S. Department of the Interior.

Searle, M., and Jackson, E. (1990). Recreation non-participation and barriers to participation: Considerations for the management of recreation delivery systems. *Journal of Park and Recreation Administration, 2;* 23-35.

Searle, M., and Jackson, E. (1985). Socio-economic variations in perceived barriers to recreation participation among would-be participants. *Leisure Sciences, 7;* 227-249.

Shaw, S., Bonen, A., and McCabe, J. (1991). Do more constraints mean less leisure? Examining the relationship between constraints and participation. *Journal of Leisure Research, 23*(4), 286-301

Stebbins, R. (1979). *Amateurs: On the margin between work and leisure.* Beverly Hills, CA: Sage Publications, Inc.

Washburne, R. (1978). Black under-participation in wildlife recreation: Alternative explanations. *Leisure Sciences, 1;* 175-189.

CHAPTER 27

Leisure and Retirement

The stereotypes of retirement are almost all negative. And for the most part, they are wrong. The first is that many die when they retire. The truth is that some retire due to health problems. Health aside, there is no relationship between retirement and death. The second is that most people dread retirement. The truth is that most workers look forward to the relative freedom of retirement. In fact, the average age of voluntary retirement has become lower in the last decade. The third is that the retired become "roleless" with no real place in the society. The truth is that one role changes, from worker to former worker. All other roles remain much the same. Retirement does require some reallocation of resources, both money and time, as well as some reevaluation of priorities and possibilities. It is not, however, a time of unrelieved loss of self or social connection.

Perhaps the most common stereotype is that retired older persons have *nothing worthwhile to do*. The assumption is that in a production-oriented society dominated by a work ethic, retirement is little more than a prelude to death. Further, in order to mitigate this sad state, it is necessary to provide a special set of time-filling activities in segregated places to fill the void. Note the assumptions of this view: first, most adults centered the meaning and the timetables of their lives around their jobs; second, they have no other significant commitments or relationships; third, they have been forced out of the stimulating environments of employment; and fourth, they lack the flexibility to adapt to change.

What Do Most People Do In Retirement?

Fortunately, relatively few retired men and women fit the sad stereotype. Almost everyone has seen or read of the marvelous "old folks" who are organizing multicultural festivals, starting innovative pollution-free businesses, and snowshoeing across the Himalayan tundra at age 84. Few retired adults recognize anything relevant to their lives in those tales either. Nor do most retirees find that upscale retirement resorts in glamorous locales are a remote possibility for their budgets. In between the 5-10 percent who can afford expensive options and the 15-20 percent who are severely limited by poverty are the mortal majority of ordinary folks for whom retirement is one more phase in the self-propelled journey of life during which most have already had to cope with a series of transitions and traumas (Kelly, 1987). Retirement is one more change, generally foreseen and usually anticipated.

What do they do?— these ordinary people in retirement. An interview study of the twenty-five men and women who had retired from a food-processing plant in the Midwest focused on their own accounts of activity as well as their resources and relationships (Kelly and Westcott, 1991). These women and men had left routine jobs and were without the special resources of a college education or financial affluence. Except for the few who had health problems or had recently suffered the loss of a spouse, they were getting along reasonably well. Life was full and viable, if not spectacular. For most, a common story emerged from the interviews, a general profile of ordinary retirement for unexceptional people.

A Profile of Ordinary Retirement

What do ordinary people do on retirement? A profile from the same study begins with a decision to retire several years before the age 65. They are "aging in place," in the community and home that were their preretirement physical and social environment. The overall image is one of continuity—in relationships, values, and patterns of activity. The blocks of time opened by retirement afforded the opportunity for a planned car trip or two and the completion of a couple of projects. "At first I did a lot of work around the house" was a common description of the first months. After the completion of that initial agenda, they settled into routines that were built around relationships, interests, and commitments that had paralleled work for years, often for most of the adult life course.

Positive elements include a sense of freedom, blocks of time for travel and other activity, not having to get up early in the morning, and reduced pressure. One man specified relief from "setting the clock at 5:30." Another asserted that "It's good just not to be so tired so much of the time." A relatively active man summarized the freedom by saying, "I can do what I want when I want to do it."

For the retired workers in this case study, there has not been quite as much travelling as anticipated. Plans for becoming active in one or more community organizations have not materialized. The activity picture is one of continuity, doing the kinds of things done before retirement with the addition of days and weeks free for things that take a chunk of time. There are not many plans unfulfilled because most plans were rather vague to begin with.

With only a high school education, the range of leisure interests seldom extends far beyond the immediate. For those with intact marriages and other family members accessible, the family is the center of the social world. This is reflected in their value priorities. Family and home in some combination are first in importance. Men are more likely to be engaged in projects around the residence. Women spend more time in family interaction. Both, however, are generally "family-focused" in their orientation and values. Trips are usually family visits. Family celebrations punctuate the yearly schedule. For those who are married, the husband or wife is the usual companion for most activities and the main confidant. Other kin are also important. A recent widowed woman referred to her precious "grandchildren" just one state away. If nearby, children and grandchildren are a regular part of the social routine and the most common destinations for trips if distant. Distance is the main factor in patterns of extended family interaction.

Financial conditions are neither lavish nor extremely limited. For those who lived their entire lives on modest incomes, a modest retirement is not a great change. For most, life is a good as it has ever been, if not quite all that had been hoped. Unlike many whose work had greater elements of autonomy and variety and who were forced out of high status positions, for these retired factory hands leaving the workplace is final with no desire for part-time employment, even for those who left the plant in their mid-fifties. Their jobs were routine and demanding and defined instrumentally, primarily as a source of necessary income.

Activity patterns revolved around a core of relatively accessible and low-cost engagements. The ordinary retired watch television, regularly if not always intensively. They talk to others in their household and get together with immediate family and friends. They do some entertaining, usually informally. Get togethers with friends may involve card games, eating out inexpensively, or just spending the evening together. As one man said, "I just do what comes along."

Around the home, most do some reading, at least newspapers and magazines. Gardening and yard work are common in the summer, sometimes as a satisfying commitment and sometime as a chore. Men usually had some little project in the offing. Women more often sought out conversation with family and friends. Religious activity is the most common organizational activity outside the home and is significant for the minority of the retired. Most women have a hobby, usually a traditional women's handcraft. Almost half the men go fishing regularly in season, although several admitted they did less fishing than they had anticipated. Special engagements for half a dozen include regular square dancing or bingo. Men are somewhat more likely to head out in the car and women to talk on the telephone. Going shopping is common for all. And *none* participate in any age-designated "senior" activity. Why not? They report that their lives seem fairly full.

What takes the place of the structuring of work schedules and the everyday-ness of work associates? For the most part, new routines are constructed around a core of companions and activities. The regularities are punctuated or highlighted by occasional special events, often involving some travel. Routines, however, are synchronized with television schedules, regular involvement with other family, and just the everyday tasks of living. Ordinary retirement seems rather predictable. Are there no surprises or idiosyncratic patterns? Of course there are exceptions. Three blue-collar men play golf regularly in season. One woman is involved in a special volunteer program in a nursing home, and a man in prison tutoring. A man with a college education is working on a crossword puzzle book. Another builds radio-controlled airplanes, but does not fly them himself. No two retirees are just alike, but the similarities seem to overshadow the differences. The stories told by this small number of retired workers are consistent with other research (Kelly 1987). For those with intact families and viable health, their core of activities is focused on home and family, even when the quality of the relationships is less than perfect.

These men and women are in early retirement. As each year passes, more will experience losses in their social networks and in their own abilities. The "active old" will enter a period of transition that requires more and more adaptation to limits. Nevertheless, any approach to activity in retirement begins with the fact that most men and women are at least relatively engaged, satisfied, and going on with most of the things they did before retirement. Whatever the losses related to leaving their work roles, they seem to be more than compensated by the release from routines and demands.

Continuities of Retirement

There are individuals so invested in their work that life loses meaning without it. There are some who have to reinvest in activity that resembles work to cope with retirement (Ekerdt, 1986). Maintaining a sense of worth and even productivity is a central theme of satisfying retirement, even when the context of activity yielding such a self-definition shifts away from the workplace. The old image of the trauma of retirement has given way to one that stresses the normal transition that is expected and taken in company with cohort compan-ions. The new image is that of the "active old" who have to make time in their schedules for anything new or extraordinary. "Continuity theory" (Atchley, 1989) has replaced models of disengagement as well as those that focus on activity itself. Continuity encompasses who people are in addition to what they do.

The journey of life has had its zigzags. Some directions have been blocked, some surprising opportunities opened, and some lines of action diverted. Through that journey, however, there are the continuities of the self who has learned a variety of skills, social repertoires, and self-definitions that carry over from one situation and time to another. As social actors, we become largely consistent in who we are and how we act, in our identities and styles of behavior.

In the same way, there is consistency over time in our relationships and activities. Death, divorce, geographical moves, and other events disrupt our social tapestries. We add and subtract activities as resources, opportunities, associations, and interests change. Nevertheless, there are commitments—to others and to activity investments—that persist through the years. Especially in relationships and activities in which there is a sustained commitment, we tend to manage our lives toward continuity. When skill-based activity such as fishing or chamber music is central to a sense of life's meaning, then the retired usually sustain involvement. Further, such activities continue as the basis for companionship and friendship.

Any perspective that assumes that at some magical or cataclysmic time, age 65 or any other, we become different persons is quite false. For the most part, even when recognizing incremental and inevitable change, we see ourselves as the same person who was 55 a few years ago and 45 only a decade before. We do not categorize ourselves by age, but know ourselves in the continuity of an "ageless self" (Kaufman, 1986).

The implications of this continuity of selfhood for leisure and recreation are manifold:

- First, there is the likelihood that most older adults will go on doing most of the things they have done before with most of the same associates.

- Second, while revised activities are not precluded, the likelihood is that changes will build on previous satisfactions, associations, and skills rather than leaping into something entirely new.

- Third, any opportunities that require a radical redefinition of the self are unlikely to attract much interest. This is especially true when the redefinition involves a category with negative connotations such as "old" or "senior." The self that is getting older, especially in the relatively active early retirement years, is the same person as before, more "ageless" than primarily defined by age.

Is There "Extraordinary Retirement?"

People, however, are characterized by their diversity. The error of accepting negative stereotypes about "retirees" should not lead to the inverse mistake of defining almost everyone as "ordinary." Economically, there are the up-market affluent as well as the disinherited marginal and poor. Culturally, there are those bound into prescriptive lifestyles and those who are experimental, the conventional, and the risk takers. There are even a few whose lives revolve primarily around their work or their leisure.

There are extraordinary retirees who have the financial means and initiative to move to a friendlier climate for all or part of the year. At the upscale end of the market are those with the wealth to purchase condominiums or homes in richly appointed communities that are usually on water and offer private golf courses and other recreational facilities. Restricted by the cost to the affluent, they attract those accustomed to country club amenities and social life. They continue to travel, often spending part of the year in former environments and in travel. They are able to purchase a full set of opportunities for leisure as well as the privacy of a recreation-based residential enclave.

More common are the "snowbirds" who move to Florida or the Southwest on a budget. Some may choose a locale with a number of retirees from their snowbelt community. Others take advantage of the concentration of the active old to form new friendships in activity-based groups. They tend to redevelop activity patterns that are responsive to the opportunities of the new environment. Such retirement areas and developments have their own life cycle as the initial settlers age, become frail, and die or move nearer to family caregivers.

At the other extreme are the retirees who struggle to survive due to histories of irregular or low-income employment. They have no pensions or savings, only the limited income of low-level social security. Their lives are dominated by the problems of the bills already on the table and the devastation that can be wrought by acute health costs. Their lives also demonstrate continuity in their day-to-day strategies of survival.

The affluent are important markets for upscale provisions. The poor are significant targets for life-sustaining programs. Most retirees, however, stay in the communities and neighborhoods where they have lived before. Further, their values and routines reflect their histories despite some reorientations related to preparations for retirement. In a study of preretirement and retired older adults in the protypical community of Peoria, Illinois (Kelly, 1987), two lifestyles were found to be far and away the most common. The first type was composed of "balanced investors" who found significant meaning in a combination of family, work, and leisure. They found at least two of the three aspects of life important enough to take some priority in the allocation of resources. Their identities were not limited to a single role, but took on a balanced configuration appropriate to their period in the life course. The second common pattern was the "family focused" who tended to organize their lives around the central commitment of family roles. Usually with less educational background, they defined their lives primarily in terms of home and family. Work and leisure were valued in terms of their contribution to the expression and strengthening of family bonds.

The retired replaced work demands and opportunities by expanding their other commitments, especially those of the family. Retirees with a balanced investor type of lifestyle characterized those whose lives include somewhat greater resources and variety than the "ordinary" retired factory workers. They are more likely to allocate financial and time resources based on an articulated set of values. Further, although their lives are seldom spectacular in unusual commitments, they have made decisions about activities and relationships that are worth maintaining, cultivating, or renewing. When they achieve a balance of caring and sharing relationships and meaningful activity, they are most satisfied with their later years.

However striking later-life continuity, it does not preclude shifts in emphasis or even a resocialization into new roles and commitments. There are radical changes in the life course of many adults, but life tends to be more a matter of building on foundations and composing with familiar themes than turning to the utterly new. As a consequence, those with the fullest and most diverse base on which to build are the best able to respond to the opportunities of retirement.

Retirement is a significant change, all emphasis on continuity notwithstanding. The most obvious change is in the structure of time. The week is no longer dominated by employment obligations. This opens blocks of time to be reallocated for new routines or special events. While travel is the most obvious possibility, new commitments of meeting friends, caring for grandchildren or neighbors, or redeveloping a demanding skill are not unusual. Also, there is a flexibility in timetables that permits more spontaneous response to unplanned opportunities.

For leisure, two parallel possibilities may be developed. The first is to utilize leisure to reconstitute a fundamental structure for time. Freedom from incessant demand does not imply a total lack of regularity. Most retirees rebuild some structure in their timetables. Complete voids are no more satisfying than demand saturation. New commitments to leisure activity and groups may be combined with a reengagement with former skills and identities. The second possibility is to retain enough openness that it is possible to respond to the immediacy of a lovely afternoon, an unexpected invitation, or a random impulse.

As a consequence, extraordinary retirement is partly a matter of recognizing the opportunities that are released by the new life situation. Further, if ordinary retirees tend to be relatively satisfied with their lives, then what is special about being more than ordinary? The answer may be surprising.

Requisites and Prerequisites of Satisfying Retirement

What characterizes those who are doing more than getting along reasonably well in their later years? Are there marks of extraordinary retirement?

The "prerequisites" are almost self-evident. They are functional health and economic viability (Palmore, 1979). Without those fundamental conditions, everything else is difficult or impossible. No community program, service, support, or association can replace the prerequisites. The issue is what is most significant when those two conditions are met. In a longitudinal study, group and physical activity for both men and women and solitary activity for women were the most salient factors distinguishing those with a higher level of satisfaction in later life (Palmore, 1979). A causal model of analysis identified health, socioeconomic status, and activity as the three primary factors (Markides and Martin, 1979). In a review of thirty years of research, Larson (1978) found that the following health conditions, social activity accounts for between one and nine percent of the variance in life satisfaction.

Other research has identified some refinements in the importance of activity (Kelly, 1992). Especially among older persons, the quality rather than the quantity of relationship is most significant (Tobin and Neugarten, 1961; Conner, Powers, and Bultena, 1979; Kelly, Steinkamp, and Kelly, 1986, 1987). One issue is the extent to which leisure and social activity make a direct contribution to life satisfaction rather than as a context for social interaction and integration. This question was addressed directly in a study of women who had retired from employment or had always been homemakers (Riddick and Daniel, 1984). Leisure activity was found to have the strongest direct effect on life satisfaction, followed by income and health. In a different study, leisure activity level accounted for 6.2 percent of the remaining variance in life satisfaction after the 11.8 percent of health, occupational status, educational level, age, gender, and marital status were entered (Kelly, Steinkamp, and Kelly, 1987).

A number of explanations have been offered for the consistent finding that social and leisure activity make an independent contribution to well-being in later life. One holds that engagement in activity itself is important to a balanced and satisfying life (Cutler and Hendricks, 1990; Longino and Kart, 1982). Lemon, Bengtson, and Peterson (1972) suggest that informal leisure provides a context for significant social interaction. They further argue that frequent participation in fewer salient activities contributes more than does a wide range of activities. Atchley (1989) proposes that leisure enables retired persons to continue roles that they have valued earlier. This approach of engagement in meaningful activity defines leisure as an arena for the development and expression of valued identities in which some competence, achievement, and recognition may be gained (Havighurst, 1961; Rapoport and Rapoport, 1975; Gordon, Gaitz, and Scott, 1976; Kelly, 1992).

In summary, there seems to be ample evidence that leisure and recreation are important elements of the quality of life in retirement. Further, there are indications that some kinds of activities contribute more than others and that quality is more important than quantity. A summary of the early findings of the Yale Health and Aging Project (Elder, 1991) points to the importance of genetic endowment and then adds: "But if staying involved with other people and keeping up your tennis game turns out to be even part of the answer, it just may be the closest humankind will ever get to the fountain of youth."

Alternative Theories of Activity

In the 1961 volume edited by Robert Kleemeier, *Aging and Leisure,* a number of authors went beyond presentations of what older people did to analyze the relationship of changes in economic and family roles in retirement to the meanings of nonwork activity. Especially the chapter by Robert Havighurst on "The Nature of Value and Meaningful Free-time Activity" which examined the dimensions of values found in a range of leisure engagements. He and others in the Kansas City Study of Adult Life found that leisure is multidimensional in meanings, varied in forms, and interwoven with family and community roles. Lifestyles of "balance" and "home-centered" at high, medium, and low levels of activity were in part indexed by social status measures.

The Reduction Model

From the same study, Cumming and Henry (1961) proposed their "disengagement theory" that has usually been placed in opposition to views of aging that stress activity and continuity. Disengagement is based on the dual findings that older people tended to be less involved than younger in activity outside the home and that both tended to be relatively satisfied with this situation. The argument was then developed that some withdrawal from activity is functional for older people who need to concentrate their resources and energies on activity that is appropriate and satisfying for their stage in life.

It is certainly true that advancing age is correlated with lower rates of activity and even a constriction of interests (Havighurst, 1961). In a more recent study, lower rates of participation were found for each older age category in travel, outdoor recreation, and exercise and sport (Kelly, Steinkamp, and Kelly, 1986). For those over 74, the rates were lower also for participation in community organizations, cultural activity, and even home-based activity. There appears to be a constriction process that narrows the range of activities in spatial location as well as number in later life. However, two kinds of activities—social activities and family leisure—remain relatively high in participation. Continuity is demonstrated in the "core" of relatively accessible and informal leisure that makes up the ongoing, day-to-day center of activity.

This constriction in the range of activity was also reported in a time-diary study (Lawton, 1987). Increasing age was associated with more time spent alone eating, resting, and relaxing, and engaging in at-home religious activity rather than in more active engagement outside the home. In a Houston area study, the pattern of constriction associated with age held for such activities as dancing, movies, sports and exercise, outdoor recreation, travel, reading, cultural production, and spectator sports to a greater degree than for social interaction, entertaining, voluntary organization, and cultural consumption (Gordon, Gaitz, and Scott, 1976).

The Engagement Model

Constriction, however, may be an adaptation to conditions rather than a preference. Gordon, Gaitz, and Scott (1976), for example, suggest that energy reductions and the relinquishing of some social roles lead to some constriction in frequency and range of activity participation, but that the "meaningful integration" of sharing and interaction remain central for those in retirement years. Further, self-definitions with valued identities are significant and often supported by leisure engagement.

Maddox (1968) reports on a longitudinal study in which declining health reduced capacity to engage in many kinds of activity. The decline, however, tends to be gradual for those without traumatic loss in ability. Further, the declines are more gradual for activities such as reading, culture, entertaining, conversation, home enhancement, and other in-home and social activity than for events that are physically demanding (Gordon, Gaitz, and Scott, 1976; Kelly, Steinkamp, and Kelly, 1986). Even travel and community organization participation are markedly lower only for those in the age categories associated with frailty. Older people continue to engage in activity that brings them together with valued other persons and in which they feel comfortable with their abilities. The stability of golfing rates suggests that even outdoor activity can continue to attract those with the developed skills, resources, and companions.

The Continuity Model

The reduction model, then, is supported when the sole measure is frequency of participation by activity type. A life course approach that is based on continuity, however, suggests an engagement model of adaptation and choice (Kelly, 1992). With activity associated with perceived quality of life, older persons are more likely to focus on those activities and relationships that they believe contribute most to their lives. Those most satisfied with their lives in later years are those who have maintained engagement with meaningful activities and associations. Overall age-related lower rates of participation in many kinds of recreational activities obscure the relative stability in rates for activities that are appropriate, possible, and satisfying. Activities are selected rather than simply reduced, at least until the time when frailty severely limits the possibilities.

Leisure That Makes A Difference

The approach toward leisure in retirement being developed here has the following themes:

1) The activity patterns of retired men and women are characterized by considerable continuity with the activities and relationships that have been meaningful to them in their preretirement years.

2) Retirement, then, involves a reconstruction of patterns of involvement based in previously established competence and associations to accommodate the new freedom from demand.

3) The image of the "active old" is more accurate than one of voids of time and commitment, despite a pattern of age-related constriction an activity.

4) Retired adults are social actors who are selecting valued engagements that have proven satisfying rather than disengaged pawns sliding into voids of meaningless and low life satisfaction.

A primary issue, then, is that of resources and opportunity. What do retired men and women need in order to develop a satisfying lifestyle with adequate levels of engagement? What are the factors that really make a difference?

In general, the two complementary elements of satisfying retirement, beyond the prerequisites, are activity and community. They are regular and meaningful engagement with doing things that are satisfying and sharing life with people through interaction and involvement. For most older persons, both the activity and the relationships are an extension of histories that have been developed through the life course.

Retirement Activity

Does it make any difference what kinds of activity older adults do? Is bingo as satisfying as volunteer service, television as golf, or gardening as travel? One approach would be that almost any pattern of regular action and interaction that provides a sense of meaning and brings retirees into association with friends and family would fulfill the requirements. Some research, however, indicates that for those with the highest levels of satisfaction, certain kinds of activity have a place in the spectrum of participation. In the Peoria study, there were significant age differences (Kelly, Steinkamp, and Kelly, 1986). For those age 40 to 64, regular travel and participation in the arts and other cultural activity distinguished those with the highest level of perceived quality of life. Social and travel activity marked those age 65 to 74 with the highest satisfaction. For those 75 and older, family and home-based activity were most salient. What is suggested is that the activity should be whatever provides the greatest stimulation and social involvement within the pattern of constriction that develops in later years.

In the longitudinal Duke study, activity outside the home, social and physical, marked the retirement-aged men and women highest in life satisfaction (Palmore, 1979). The two dimensions seem to be challenge and social integration. In addition for women, more likely to live alone, solitary activity that is involving is significant. Another approach identified the kind of activity often referred to as "serious leisure" (Stebbins, 1979). This activity that is demanding of skill, attention, and commitment. Serious leisure has a career of inauguration, development, and demonstrated competence. It usually involves its devotees, "amateurs," in regular interaction with groups in which association is built around common action. Those engaged in serious leisure make this commitment a central element of their identities. In retirement, these identities may claim even greater centrality. A Canadian study of time use and associations in later life found that those who were extraordinarily satisfied with their lives were those engaged in serious leisure (Mannell, Zuzanek, and Larson, 1988). They experienced both the sense of community with their companions and the sense of competence produced by meeting the challenge of the activity (Csikszentmihalyi, 1990).

Again, the two critical elements seem to be challenge and community. Challenge is stimulating, involving, and even exciting. Facing a challenge—physical, mental, or social—requires concentration and effort. Meeting the challenge requires a demonstration of skill. The outcome is two-fold: the immediate involvement and the consequent sense of ability and worth. Community is commonly developed in the process of such engagement. Bonds are formed not by mere proximity or being entertained, but in common action; especially activities that require exchange and reciprocity to form relationships of communication, sharing, and trusting.

The forms of activity that combine the two elements are almost infinite. They may focus on physical, mental, aesthetic, or social tasks and challenges. They may involve outcomes that can be seen and appreciated, that are shared or more individual, that are of recognized social value or more private. They are commitments that become central to life's meaning over time. They are the "extra" that may lift retirement above the ordinary.

Examples are endless. Retirees run, dance, fish, play softball, produce plays, counsel, teach, write, experiment, explore, learn, and organize. They sculpt in metal or wood, throw pots or create stained glass, rebuild old cars or train dogs, landscape or decorate, coach or provide care. The keys are that the engagement is regular, demanding, and involves some kind of community. It calls for continued learning and development, for assessment and commitment. And usually it has some connection with previously valued identities.

Such "serious leisure" is not the whole story of anyone's retirement activity. In the balance of a leisure style there is also disengagement and relaxation, low-intensity as well as demanding activity, appreciation as well as creation, being alone as well as sharing. The ordinary patterns of living are there as well, especially in the day-to-day associations of home, family, neighborhood, and friends. But the extraordinary is the something more that highlights the ordinary, that makes the self someone special—a person of ability sharing with others. And it is the highlights that produce extraordinary enjoyment in the routines of retirement.

Programs and Resources

First, it is evident that the world of retirees is not waiting around out there for just about anything to fill their time. In an analysis of those 13,000 individuals age 60 and over in the 1984 National Health Interviews, the proportion who participated regularly in "senior center" programs was quite low (Kelly and Reis, 1991). The percentage who never go to senior centers was 86.9 and who never eat at centers 92.7. In general, the percentage of those over 60 who are regularly engaged in any specific type of age-designated program is about one percent. If there was ever an accepted myth that desperate retirees would flock to just about any program, that presumption has been exploded. The issue to be resolved concerning such programs is the extent to which they serve and support those most bereft of economic and social resources rather than the more resourceful "active old."

Second, the reasons given for not participating in age-designated programs are consistent with the engaged image of ordinary aging. The most common explanation older persons offer is that they are too busy (McGuire, Dottavio, and O'Leary, 1986). Additionally they testify to the negative images of "senior" activity programs as of low quality attracting individuals of low ability who would not be interesting companions. For the most part, in order to attract older participants, programs must project a quite different image—one of quality, interest, and value. Just filling time is not attractive to most retirees. Even ordinary retirement is too full to be devoted to boredom. Most retirees have to make a place in their schedule for any activity.

Third, the negative image is related to the requirement of a redefintion of the self. Even though they recognize the reality of age and loss, in general older people do not reclassify themselves as "old," "senior," or "golden." They are the same persons who guided and taught children, improved a home, fulfilled the demands of a job, and shared life with friends. Any program that requires the negative redefinition of age runs counter to continuities of identity. When such a program also requires entering an age-segregated and unfamiliar environment, the psychological price of admission is too high. This resistance also reflects a common confusion between service and activity programs that is intensified by locating them in the same place.

Fourth, a pilot study of those who were participating in a number of recreational programs for older adults found that they were primarily attracted by a reputation of high quality (Schneider, 1989). They were willing to cross the barriers of age and place segregation because the leadership of an exercise, arts, or educational program was known to be excellent. Most participants had personal histories of community activity and had often been brought along by friends. This emphasis on quality may also account for the rapid growth of the Elderhostel program that offers educational stimulation, travel, and companionship at a reasonable price. The appeal is not the "elder" designation or the age-segregation, but the combined quality and budget.

What seems to be suggested by this analysis is that the "senior" market for activity opportunities is much more diverse than many programs have acknowledged. There are many retirees who seek travel opportunities in a variety of cost levels and in a variety of social contexts. Some want to be led and protected; many do not. Some travel on a budget while others are expanding the upscale travel market. Styles of travel differ for retirees as they do for their children and grandchildren. The business term is "market segmentation," not by age alone but according to social and economic resources and developed lifestyles and tastes. Increasingly travel businesses are identifying diverse market segments *among* later life adults.

The same diversity is demonstrated by responses to public programs. As distinct from service and support programs, there are many indications that over-50 softball and "century" doubles tournaments in tennis are expanding, but relatively few adults are active in sports past the age of forty. Bach choirs and festivals attract older persons with developed skills and tastes, but there is a demand for singalongs as well. Duplicate bridge attracts some and bingo others. Continuity with previous patterns of participation is one clue to attracting participation. Recognized quality is another. The criterion of success is not percentages of participation in uniform programs, but providing unique opportunities that draw consistent engagement out of the diversity of personal histories.

One community response to all this would be to recognize that retirees are still people who will direct their lives in a balance of engagement that is at least relatively satisfying. Why not just accept ordinary retirement as it is? The problem is that "ordinary" is not all that it might be. Those who are more than doing OK are those involved in communities of challenging activity. They have more than routines that fill the day; they have commitments that yield a sense of competence and community. They have that "something more" that transforms the ordinary into the extraordinary. The process of constriction that characterizes later life may at least be delayed by opportunities that are both possible and satisfying.

In the life course studies of leisure, two main dimensions of motivation have been found. The first is more individual: action contexts that offer the opportunity to develop, build, and demonstrate competence. People want to relax, rest, escape, and withdraw at times. But the engagement they find most central and valued offers the challenge of action. The second theme of motivation that draws consistent engagement is social, the expression of community. To be able and to be related to others, these are the elements that most often draw people of any age into consistent activity. And it is such activity that makes the difference later in life.

REFERENCES

Atchley, R. (1989). A continuity theory of normal aging. *The Gerontologist, 29,* 2, 183-89.

Csikszentmihalyi, M. (1990). *Flow: The psychology of optimal experience.* New York, NY: Harper & Row, Publishers, Inc.

Conner, K., Powers, E., and Bultena, G. (1979). Social interaction and life satisfaction: An empirical assessment of later life patterns. *Journal of Gerontology, 34,* 116, 121.

Cumming, E., and Henry, W. (1961). *Growing old: The process of disengagement.* New York, NY: Basic Books.

Cutler, S., and Hendricks, J. (1990). Leisure and time use across the life course. In R. Binstock, and L. George (Eds.) *Handbook of aging and the social sciences,* 3rd edition. New York, NY: Academic Press, Inc.

Ekerdt, D. (1986). The busy ethic: Moral continuity between work and retirement. *The Gerontologist, 26,* 239-244.

Elder, S. (1991). The secrets of (successful) aging. *Yale Alumni Magazine,* April, 24-29.

Gordon, C., Gaitz, C., and Scott, J. (1976). Leisure and lives: Personal expressivity across the life span. In R. Binstock and E. Shanas (Eds.) *Handbook of aging and the social sciences.* New York, NY: Van Nostrand Reinhold Company.

Havighurst, R. (1961). The nature and value of meaningful free time activity. In R. Kleemeier (Ed.) *Aging and leisure.* New York, NY: Oxford University Press.

Kaufman, S. (1986). *The ageless self: Sources of meaning in later life.* New York, NY: New American Library.

Kelly, J. R. (1987). *Peoria winter: Styles and resources in later life.* Lexington, MA: Lexington Books.

Kelly, J. R. (Ed.) (1992). *Activity and aging.* Newbury Park, CA: Sage Publications, Inc.

Kelly, J. R., Steinkamp, M., and Kelly, J. (1986). Later life leisure: How they play in Peoria. *The Gerontologist, 26,* 531-37.

Kelly, J. R., Steinkamp, M., and Kelly, J. (1987). Later life satisfaction: Does leisure contribute? *Leisure Sciences, 9,* 189-200.

Kelly, J. R., and Reis, J. (1991). Identifying senior program participants. *Journal of Park and Recreation Administration, 9,* 55-64.

Kelly, J. R., and Westcott, G. (1991). Ordinary retirement: Commonalities and continuity. *International Journal of Aging and Human Development, 32,* 81-89.

Kleemeier, R. (1961). *Aging and Leisure.* New York, NY: Oxford University Press.

Larson, R. (1978). Thirty years of research on the subjective well-being of older adults. *Journal of Gerontology, 16,* 134-143.

Lawton, M. P. (1987). Activities and leisure. In M. Lawton and G. Maddox, (Eds.) *Annual Review of Gerontology and Geriatrics.* New York, NY: Springer Publishing Company, Inc.

Lemon, B. W., Bengtson, V., and Peterson, J. (1972). An exploration of the activity theory of aging. *Journal of Gerontology, 27,* 511-523.

Longino, C., and Kart, C. (1982). Explicating activity theory: A formal replication. *Journal of Gerontology, 37,* 713-722.

Maddox, G. (1968). Persistence of life style among the elderly: A longitudinal study of life patterns of social activity in relation to life satisfaction. In B. Neugarten (Ed.) *Middle age and aging.* Chicago, IL: University of Chicago Press.

Mannell, R., Zuzanek, J., and Larson, R. (1988). Leisure and 'flow' experiences. *Journal of Leisure Research, 20,* 4, 289-304.

Markides, K., and Martin, H. (1979). A casual model of life satisfaction among the elderly. *Journal of Gerontology, 34,* 86-93.

McGuire, F., Dottavio, D., and O'Leary, J. (1986). Constraints to participation in outdoor recreation across the life span. *The Gerontologist, 26,* 538-544.

Palmore, E. (1979). Predictors of successful aging. *The Gerontologist, 19,* 427-431.

Rapoport, R., and Rapoport, R. (1975). *Leisure and the family life cycle.* London, England: Routledge and Kegan Paul.

Riddick, C., and Daniel, S. (1984). The relative contributions of leisure activity and other factors to the mental health of older women. *Journal of Leisure Research, 16,* 136-148.

Schneider, C. (1989). *Senior Program Participation.* Unpublished M. S. thesis. University of Illinois at Urbana-Champaign.

Stebbins, R. (1979). *Amateurs: On the margins between work and leisure.* Newbury Park, CA: Sage Publications, Inc.

Tobin, S., and Neugarten, B. (1961). Life satisfaction and social interaction of the aged. *Journal of Gerontology, 16,* 344-346.

Section Three:
Forms of Leisure

CHAPTER 28

Organized Recreation and Leisure Services

T he widespread emergence of organizations devoted to the provision of leisure services is primarily a phenomenon of the twentieth century and is associated with industrialization and urbanization. These organizations today provide a vast array of services. Sessoms (1984) divides such services into public, private and commercial. As may be seen in Table 28.1, these various services differ in philosophy, objectives, administrative organization, finance, program, membership, facilities, and leadership.

In modern nations, it is difficult to imagine all the ways in which leisure service organizations shape our leisure behavior or to imagine their sheer size. The market sector is by far the most pervasive. North Americans spend more of their free time with the products and services of the commercial sector than without them. Television and other mass media, travel and tourism, theme parks, commercial sport facilities for both spectators and active participants in sport and many other commercial ventures occupy, in some manner, the majority of our leisure. The impact of such commercial outlets on our daily lives is enormous. Commercial leisure resources have been developed to a particularly great extent in the United States. More tourists, for example, visit Disney World than visit the United Kingdom.

Commercial leisure services are often high-risk ventures, since it is difficult to determine on what people will spend their money and time. Interest in many leisure activities may rise or fall rapidly. Enthusiasm for such activities as bouncing on trampolines at trampoline centers, miniature golf, cross-country skiing, bungee jumping or aerobic exercise may change rapidly, making it difficult for organizations to plan for future development. Consequently, commercial organizations often try to diversify their activities and products. They also use extensive advertising to try to create a favorable image with the public.

Table 28.1
Comparison and Contrast Study of Public, Private (Voluntary Agencies), and
Commercial Recreation

	Public	Private	Commercial
Philosophy of Recreation	Enrichment of the life of the total community by providing opportunities for the worthy use of leisure. Nonprofit in nature.	Enrichment of the life of participating members by offering opportunities for worthy use of leisure, frequently with emphasis on the group and the individual. Nonprofit in nature.	Attempt to satisfy public demand in an effort to produce profit. Dollars from, as well as for, recreation.
Objectives of Recreation	To provide leisure opportunities that contribute to the social, physical, educational, cultural, and general wellbeing of the community and its people.	Similar to public but limited by membership, race, religion, age, and the like. To provide opportunities for close group association with emphasis on citizenship, behavior, and life philosophy values. To provide activities that appeal to members.	To provide activities or programs which will appeal to customers. To meet competition. To net profit. To serve the public.
Administrative Organization	Governmental agencies (federal, state, and local).	Boy Scouts, Settlements, Girl Scouts, Camp Fire Girls, "Y" organizations, and others.	Corporations, syndicates, partnerships, private ownerships. Examples: motion picture, television, and radio companies; resorts; bowling centers; and skating rinks.
Finance	Primarily by taxes. Also by gifts, grants, trust funds, small charges, and fees to defray cost.	By gifts, grants, endowments, donations, drives, and membership fees.	By the owner or promoters. By the users; admission and charges.

Table 28.1 (Continued)
Comparison and Contrast Study of Public, Private (Voluntary Agencies), and
Commercial Recreation

	Public	Private	Commercial
Program	Designed to provide a wide variety of activities, year-round, for all groups, regardless of age, sex, race, creed, social, or economic status.	Designed to provide programs of a specialized nature for groups and in keeping with the aims and objectives of the agency.	Program designed to tap spending power in compliance with state and local laws.
Membership	Unlimited – open to all	Limited by organizational restrictions such as age, sex, and religion.	Limited by law (local, state, and federal), social conception regarding status and strata in some places, economics—those who have the ability to pay.
Facilities	Community buildings, parks (national, state, local), athletic fields, playgrounds, playfields, stadiums, camps, beaches, museums, zoos, golf courses, school facilities, etc.	Settlement houses, youth centers, churches, play areas, clubs, camps, and others.	Theaters, clubs, taverns, night-clubs, lodges, racetracks, bowling lanes, stadiums, and others.
Leadership	Professionally prepared to provide extensive recreation programs for large numbers of people Frequently subject to Civil Service regulations.	Professionally prepared to provide programs on a social group-work basis. Employed at discretion of managin gagency.	Frequently trained by employing agency. Employed to secure greatest financial returns. Employed and retained at the discretion of the employer.
	Volunteers as well as professionals. College training facilities growing.	Volunteers as well as professionals.	No volunteers.

Source: Sessoms, H. D., Meyer, H., and Brightbill, C. (1975). *Leisure services: The organized recreation and park system.* Englewood Cliffs, NJ: Prentice-Hall, pp. 13-15.

According to Munson (1978), these organizations may be categorized as:

1) an individually owned enterprise, such as a dude ranch;

2) a local corporation, such as a ski resort;

3) a large nationwide corporation such as a chain of fitness clubs;

4) a concession operation in which a campsite or other facility is operated on public property under a contractual agreement; and

5) a manufacturer-operated enterprise, such as a bowling alley, which is operated by a manufacturer of bowling equipment.

Government involvement in recreation, park and leisure services includes municipal recreation and park departments, which have become a typical service during the last fifty years. These local agencies provide a number of services including planning, acquiring, developing, and maintaining park land and recreation areas and facilities. They provide services for groups or individuals with disabilities or special needs; educate for specific leisure skills, sponsor special community events, and celebrations as well as sponsoring social, cultural, and athletic programs on a continuing basis.

At the state level, governments in both the United States and Canada perform a number of functions directly related to recreation. Each of the 50 states, for instance, has an agency or subdivision whose primary responsibility is outdoor recreation. Additionally, other state agencies dealing with youth, the aged, education, conservation, planning and other functions usually provide recreation services to their clientele. Each state has developed a network of areas and facilities for recreation, including parks, forests, game preserves, conservation areas, historic sites and monuments, and beaches and marinas.

At the federal level, there is involvement in many forms of recreation and leisure services, particularly outdoor recreation. Since the federal government maintains one-third of the landmass of the U.S., many government agencies are involved in land management. While most federal land management agencies were not created to do so, most are now involved in outdoor recreation management. Such agencies are primarily within the United States Departments of Agriculture and the Interior. The U.S. Forest Service, for instance, was formed in 1905 to protect and develop forest reserves in the public domain. The increasing use of these areas for camping by the public and the resulting forest fires brought about the agency's involvement in outdoor recreation management. In 1960, the Multiple-Sustained Yield Act recognized recreation as a legitimate management purpose. Other land management agencies include the following:

- Bureau of Land Management, which conserves, manages, and develops 470 million acres in the western states and Alaska;

- the Bureau of Reclamation, which is involved in the development of water resources;

- the Fish and Wildlife Service, which is responsible for wild birds, mammals (except certain marine mammals) inland sport fisheries and fishery research activity;

- the Army Corps of Engineers, which undertakes civil works such as the improvement of rivers, harbors, and waterways for navigation, fish and wildlife, and shore protection; and

- the Tennessee Valley Authority, which conducts resource development for economic growth in the Tennessee Valley Region through the development of a system of dams providing outdoor recreation along with flood control and electric power.

Even the National Park Service did not originally recognize recreation to be a sufficient reason for the development of a national park. Today, however, it administers 30 million acres which are of historical, cultural, natural and recreation significance.

Many private, nonprofit organizations as well as government sponsored ones have emerged to meet the needs of special subsections of the population. Therapeutic recreation, for instance, refers to both direct and indirect recreation or leisure services provided to special populations such as the developmentally disabled, emotionally disturbed, physically handicapped or other groups whose special needs limit their recreation opportunities. Organizations providing these opportunities include not only residential institutions like state schools for the developmentally disabled, but also community organizations such as municipal recreation and park departments and transitional organizations for example "halfway houses," sheltered workshops and others. They also include commercially managed services such as centers for treatment of drug addiction.

Many private, nonprofit organizations provide leisure services primarily for youth. Such organizations sprang up in the early twentieth century out of concern for children of the urban poor. Many have been concerned, in some way, with "character building." These organizations, according to Farrell (1978) may be religious oriented, such as the Catholic Youth Organization or YMCA, or social service oriented, such as the Police Athletic League. They typically involve a central national office with a specialized professional staff, regional offices, and local or neighborhood associations made up of volunteers.

Another type of leisure organization concerned with a special clientele is the employee recreation organization, which typically provides athletic programs, social and educational activities, and other leisure services to employees and retirees. Such programs often represent an attempt to improve employees' health, productivity and loyalty to the company.

Finally, many private, nonprofits are interested in the promotion of a given leisure activity, such as camping or golf, and seek to promote the activity to those who do not presently participate. Such organizations range from Ducks Unlimited, which serves duck hunters, to the United States Yacht Racing Union.

There has been a rapid increase in private, nonprofit organizations which provide leisure services (Szwak, 1989). Such growth probably reflects greater numbers of people with specialized leisure interests as well as means to pursue such interests.

Roles of Leisure Service Organizations

Leisure service organization in the public, private, nonprofit and commercial sector may be identified by their role or roles (Godbey, 1990). Most such organizations fulfill one or more of the following roles:

Promoter of Specific Leisure Activities and Facilities

Many leisure service organizations seek to interest people in participating in specific recreation and leisure activities. In some cases, this is done in the belief that the activity being promoted is "superior" to other choices of activity which the individual might make. Many outdoor recreation organizations act on the assumption that the activities they promote are more worthwhile than other activities

Bowling centers, for instance, sponsor advertising promoting the joys of bowling. Some state or provincial leisure service organizations promote various sports and athletic activities in the hope that, if people become involved in such sports, they will become more physically fit, both for their own betterment and that of society. In some mental hospitals, therapeutic recreation workers encourage emotionally disturbed patients to grow plants, whether or not the patient has such an interest previously, in the belief that it is a valuable step in learning to accept responsibility. In all these cases, the agency wants the person to modify his or her behavior to include certain forms of leisure activity. The leisure service organization serves as a stimulus to awaken this interest. Since a given leisure activity is often valued only after some form of exposure to it, the organization justifies its approach by saying that the individual may not appreciate the happiness found in sailing, for instance, because he or she has never been exposed to it. A child playing basketball all summer in a ghetto area may not desire to go camping until exposed to a camping program and may need to be introduced to such a program one step at a time or on a number of occasions before he or she can decide whether or not it is worth doing.

Culturally Neutral Provider

When acting as a neutral agent, the leisure service organization seeks to provide or sponsor whatever leisure activities, facilities or services in which its clients express interest. In this role, it is assumed that the agency has no right to impose its own values upon the client, and should cater to existing leisure interests rather than attempting to create new ones. The chief task of the agency is to identify accurately and supply those leisure experiences in which people wish to participate. The determination of leisure desires may involve surveys, boards and councils, public hearings, or the collection of information concerning participation in a variety of activities.

Social Change Agent

Some leisure services attempt to change people's behavior or social condition through the use of leisure activity. Such change goes beyond creating interest in a specific leisure activity. In such "social engineering," the leisure activity serves as a means to an end; it is a technique or tool for change aimed at benefiting the individual and society. Some real estate developers use golf or tennis as a means of interesting people in purchasing condominiums. Boys' Clubs sponsor after-school programs for teenage boys in the hope of averting delinquent behavior. Nature programs in county park systems may be initiated to change the attitudes of young people toward the outdoors and to foster an attitude of stewardship toward the land. Employee based recreation programs are often sponsored to attract potential employees and to improve the morale of those already employed in order to enhance company productivity. For a leisure service agency to act effectively as an agent of change, however, there must be an ideal situation articulated by the agency as a goal.

The recent interest in "leisure counseling" reflects the belief that people can be helped to use their leisure in more satisfying ways. However, leisure service agencies that sponsor such programs often find that counseling leads to the agency making judgements for the client about which activities are potentially more worthwhile.

Coordinator of Leisure Opportunities

As a coordinator of leisure opportunities within a community, a leisure service organization seeks to maximize citizens' opportunities to participate in a wide variety of leisure activities. The organization, in this role, takes the initiative in bringing together representatives of commercial, private and public leisure service agencies in order to share information, avoid duplication of services, and plan ways to allow joint cooperative use of each agency's programs and facilities. As a coordinator of leisure opportunities, the leisure service agency tries to make them familiar with the total range of leisure opportunities within the community. Often, particular attention is given to informing new community residents about such opportunities.

In many cases, the citizen is primarily interested in a given leisure activity rather than its sponsor. A swimmer, for instance, may be interested in swimming in a clean, well-maintained pool at a nominal cost regardless of the organization managing it. It is conceivable that many different leisure service organizations could provide for this service successfully—commercial neighborhood pools, YMCAs, municipal recreation and park departments, public schools, and so on. Therefore, it would appear desirable for all the organizations who could provide this service to consult with each other to avoid duplicating services. This belief, however, is by no means unchallenged. Grodzins (1966), for instance, has argued that an overlapping of functions by leisure service agencies is actually desirable.

Provider for the Recreationally Dependent

Here it is assumed that the leisure service agency should direct its major effort toward providing services to those who are highly dependent upon the agency for meaningful leisure experience or who have a minimum of alternatives to the use of these services. Some people are fortunate enough to have a wide variety of leisure opportunities to choose from because of their relatively good health, income, mobility, education and so forth. While these individuals may depend upon leisure service agencies for some of their leisure experiences, they are not dependent to the same degree as those who are in poor physical or mental health or who have less income, mobility, or education. The leisure service organization may attempt to compensate for this inequity of opportunity in regard to play, recreation, open space, and related areas. There are, of course, no absolute guidelines as to those characteristics that constitute a high degree of recreation dependency. Many would argue that it is possible to be poor and still enjoy a rewarding variety of leisure experiences. When dealing with an issue as basic as where children can play, however, it quickly becomes apparent that in urban poverty areas where the apartments are small and overcrowded, children's play opportunities are very limited unless some organized effort is made to provide parks, playgrounds and leisure activity programs. People with physical handicaps may likewise enjoy a variety of leisure activities with the support of interested organizations, but such help is not always forthcoming. The rationale for a public leisure service organization to provide services for the recreationally dependent is that it should be a "provider of last resort," responsible for helping meet the leisure needs and desires of those for whom no one else can, or will, provide. Much the same argument has been made concerning the responsibility of government to provide employment for those who cannot find work during a recession or depression.

Enhancement of the Physical Environment

Many leisure service agencies have, as a primary role, the protection and improvement of the environment. Many types of leisure activities are dependent upon certain environmental features or conditions which most people cannot supply individually in urban or suburban areas. In addition, the quality of the leisure experience may be highly dependent upon environmental conditions. Boating in a polluted lake is a markedly different experience from boating in a clear, clean one. A number of these leisure experiences are referred to as "land based" and include boating, camping, hunting, backpacking, and mountaineering. Leisure service agencies maintain a variety of areas and facilities to accommodate such activities.

Some leisure service agencies also perform services that contribute to the "quality of life" of a community, such as planting shade trees, acquiring stream valley parks, preserving historical sites and unique natural areas, and protecting wildlife.

Health Promoter

A variety of leisure service organizations provide services aimed at improving or maintaining the health and wellness of those they serve. Employee leisure services, for example, often organize activities aimed at improving the physical fitness of their workers. Also, leisure services may organize social events, festivals, guided tours, or other events in such a way as to stress healthful living.

Provider of Leisure Education and Counseling

In many cases, organizations concerned with leisure provide information to those they serve about a wide variety of leisure opportunities. Skills and appreciation of specific leisure activities, from karate to flower arranging, also may be taught.

In both community and clinical settings, those who provide leisure services may be involved in counseling individuals who have a disability or problem which interferes with their satisfying use of leisure. Those in the therapeutic recreation profession provide such services to the physically and developmentally disabled, the emotionally disturbed, the drug dependent, prisoners and parolees, patients in hospitals and hospices, and many others.

Adjustment to Institutionalization

When people move from private residences to large, group-living situations, their leisure resources and, sometimes, their leisure needs change. The institutions served by recreation, park, and leisure service professionals vary widely, but may include: colleges and universities, the armed forces, nursing homes, prisons, hospitals, and other group living situations. The mere fact of moving to or from such a living arrangement causes change, and often problems, in one's ability to engage in recreation. Leisure services help to overcome such problems.

Promoter and Facilitator of Tourism

Many leisure services are involved with promoting and managing tourism and other visitation. They may be primarily involved in promoting an area as a tourist destination, coordinating conferences and conventions, managing tourist attractions or resorts, leading recreation activities for visitors, or serving as a retail travel agent. All these services, and others, are necessary to the well-being of what may be the world's largest industry.

Recreation and Leisure as a Function of Other Organizations

As recreation and leisure have become a more important part of everyday life, many organizations which historically have had no interest or mandate to involve themselves in recreation and leisure provision now find that they are becoming involved. In the public sector, for instance, those who plan highways increasingly concern themselves with the relaxation needs of the traveler, providing rest stops, picnic areas, and information centers about nearby tourist attractions. Most natural resource agencies now understand that leisure activity is an important use of the land and waters they administer.

Criticisms of Government Involvement in Recreation and Leisure

Although governments have become highly involved in a variety of undertakings in regard to recreation, leisure, sport, tourism, and related endeavors, there are numerous criticisms of such involvement. A central criticism is that government will seek to use leisure as a means of social control. This, of course, is both a criticism and a legitimate matter for government involvement, depending upon one's sociological perspective. Most governments, for instance, sponsor programs of sport and socialization aimed at male youth who have a high probability of delinquency. While such programs attempt to socially control such youth, they also seek to protect potential victims of their crime. Perhaps a more fundamental use of leisure as social control is the close link between sport spectacles and loyalty to the government in power. Sport celebrations and contests become a spectacle sponsored by the state and are used in order to create and reinforce loyalty to the state.

Government also seeks to persuade people to undertake certain activities during their leisure and avoid others. Most modern governments, for instance, promote physically active forms of leisure for its citizens. Most seek to discourage gambling unless that gambling is sponsored by the state itself—often in the form of lotteries. In many Communist countries, vacations, often taking place at government run spas or resorts, were used to reward loyal, productive workers. Elite summer camps were reserved for the children of party members or for children who appear to have the potential to be loyal party leaders.

In spite of these extremes, it seems logical that government involve itself in some forms of manipulation and social control pertaining to leisure. If government acts as the manager of public forest land, for instance, some control must be exerted on the public's recreational use of such areas. The alternative has proven to be a continuous round of forest fires. In local parks, government may either provide or not provide picnic tables, tennis courts, or separate sitting areas for older people. These decisions, regardless of what they are, will shape and control behavior. The more logical question may be the areas of behavior which should be controlled and the degree of such control.

If government seeks to promote the performing arts, some forms and types of artistic expression are likely to be promoted at the exclusion of the others. This, in turn, may begin to shape the direction of artistic endeavor.

Reynolds (1980) has suggested that the following steps would help return control of public leisure services to the participant and minimize social control:

1) encourage development of leisure lifestyles which are consistent with the financial means of people and therefore under their control;

2) broaden the educational base of leisure service professionals so they can deal with people's leisure needs as a whole rather than dealing only with compartmentalized activities or with the provision of traditional recreation facilities;

3) recognize that participants themselves are the only relevant judges of how effective leisure services are; and

4) help individuals develop independent leisure skills.

If such changes were effected, government might take more of an educating, facilitating, and counseling role, with a greater degree of direction from those they serve.

Certainly government is not alone in its use of leisure as a means of social control. Corporations sponsor recreation, doing so in an attempt to improve the "morale" of their workers and job performance. Youth-serving organizations, such as the YMCA, Boys' Clubs, or Girl Scouts also seek to change the behavior of those who participate in their programs. Often such agencies will define their ideals in terms of behavior or attitudes, and then will sponsor programs they believe will help meet or help foster these ideals. Commercial recreation, through the use of massive advertising, seeks to control the behavior of people by creating a need for their services or products in the mind of the individual. Thus, all types of leisure agencies may seek to use leisure as a form of social control.

A second criticism of government involvement in leisure is simply that government has no way of determining what people want to do during their leisure. That is, it isn't possible to identify what people really want to do during their free time. This inability may stem both from government's inability to measure or monitor leisure needs or from the inherently pluralistic nature of recreation or leisure needs themselves.

The federal government of the United States, in undertaking three nationwide outdoor recreation plans during the nineteen sixties and seventies, was largely unable to control the measurement process or to keep it from falling into partisan political hands. Thus, different measures of participation were used for each plan and many agenda were inserted in the plans by bureaucrats which had little to do with the conclusions based upon the research. To date, the Federal Government has not been capable of monitoring outdoor recreation behavior or other forms of leisure behavior for planning purposes. "Trends" in leisure behavior, which require the replication of a measurement of participation at least once, can thus only be determined by private research organizations.

A more basic problem in determining the need for recreation and leisure is what Mercer (1973) and other referred to the "pluralistic" nature of recreation and leisure need. That is, such needs are capable of being conceptualized and acted upon within more than one value framework. Table 28.2 demonstrates the diverse frameworks within which recreation need may be measured. As may be seen, such need might be based upon people's actual recreation activity patterns, the relation between available recreation resources and socioeconomic statuses, reactions to the introduction of new recreation opportunities, "objective" standards established by experts, or expressions of desire to participate in certain activities.

As may be seen, the values inherent in these conceptualizations are in conflict. If it is assumed that what people currently do for recreation should provide a planning basis, then established standards of experts may not apply. Also, what people feel or believe they would like to do for recreation or leisure may be very different from what they are actually doing. These and many other conflicts are evident among these diverse concepts of need.

Thus, in the public sector, there is no agreement upon assumptions about how to measure leisure needs. How a public agency measures leisure need will have a direct relation to how the agency serves the public. For example, if the agency uses only an "expressed need" model, it may assume that only those who "need" or "demand" to go camping are doing so. Future generations of campsites, therefore, may be targeted to those who already use them. If the same agency used "felt need" as a basis for providing campsites, however, it would attempt to provide them for those who said they "wanted" to go camping, whether or not they were actually doing so. Many public leisure service agencies recognize the multiple nature of recreation need and try to gather information which measure these diverse concepts.

In private, nonprofit and commercial leisure service organizations, determining recreation or leisure service demands assumes different dimensions. Private, nonprofit organizations make assumptions about what changes should be made in society and use leisure activity as a means of bringing about such change. Commercial leisure service organizations may seek to create a market through advertising or by teaching people how to participate or to enjoy their services. They also often try to measure felt and expressed demand more precisely to determine more exactly who uses the types of services or products they provide and who would like to.

Perhaps in summary it should be stated that need for leisure services can never be measured completely in a scientific way, nor can any other broad human need.

A third criticism of government involvement in leisure services is that government will be reactionary in its provision. That is, government will not sponsor many leisure activities in which people are obviously interested if they are controversial or experimental. One example of this would be government's failure to sponsor activities like bowling or pocket pool in the 1940s even though these activities had become very popular. Both these activities had a negative connotation in many communities and were thought to attract the "wrong

Table 28.2
Recreation Needs

	Conceptualization of Recreation Need	Definitions of Recreation	Value Assumptions	Information Needs
Expressed Need	• Individual's need for leisure is determined by individual's current leisure activity patterns.	• The expression of individual values through participation in freely chosen activities.	• Government should be a culturally neutral provider. • There is a relatively just distribution of recreation resources. • Individuals have a relatively easy and equal access to recreation resources. • Individuals don't have a similar need for publicly sponsored recreation services. Variation in need is expressed through differences in participation rate.	• Determining what people do during leisure; activities participated in, duration, frequency, sequencing, and scheduling.
Comparative Need	• Need for leisure services of government as systematically related to both supply of leisure resources available to an individual and his/her socioeconomic characteristics.	• High autonomy in nonwork activity which is the perogative of an elite; a right to pursue happiness which is systematically inequitably distributed.	• Government should not be a culturally neutral provider. • People do not have similar need for public recreation resources. • Those with low socioeconomic statuses have higher need. • There may not be relatively just distribution of recreation resources. • Individuals may have relatively difficult and unequal access to public recreation services.	• Studies of participation and nonparticipation and relationship to socioeconomic variables. • Studies of relationship of supply of recreation resources to socioeconomic status. • Case studies examining reasons for participation among various subcultures.
Created Need	• Leisure need is determined by individual choosing to participate in activity after being taught to value it.	• Any activity in which, after sufficient introduction, an individual will freely and pleasurably participate.	• Government should not be a culturally neutral provider. • Individuals often don't know what they want to do during leisure and are happier if given guidance. • Leisure activities are substitutable since the individual seeks certain environmental conditions, not specific activities. • It is legitimate to use recreation to promote the desired goals of the state.	• Pre- and posttesting of behavior and attitudes as a result of participation in public recreation services.

Table 28.2 (Continued)
Recreation Needs

	Conceptualization of Recreation Need	Definitions of Recreation	Value Assumptions	Information Needs
Normative Need	• Experts can establish precise, objective standards to establish desirable minimum supply in quantitative terms. Implies physiological need for leisure.	• A set of physiologically necessary yet pleasurable activities undertaken during nonwork time which restore and refresh the individual and prepare him/her for work again and otherwise contribute to his/her well-being.	• Government should not be a culturally neutral provider. • Individuals have similar need for public recreation. • Certain well-established kinds of recreation resources are inherently in the public interest. • Recreation resources should be equally distributed through space.	• Testing of assumptions of standards; e.g., accuracy of service radii. • Testing relationship between perceived satisfaction and social quality indicators; e.g., crime rate, and having met standards.
Felt Need	• Individual's need for leisure activity as a function of individual belief, perception, and attitude.	• What an individual would choose to do given a minimum of constraints or high autonomy. It is a set of personally ideal activities in the mind of the individual which, given the opportunity, he/she will undertake.	• Government should be a culturally neutral provider. • Many individuals desire to participate in activities which they currently do not. • There may not be a relatively just distribution of recreation resources. Individuals often have legitimate reasons for not using public recreation resources. • Individuals may not have relatively easy or equal access to public recreation resources. • Individuals will be happier participating in what they "perceive" they want to do than in what they are currently doing.	• Attitudinal research concerning people's desire for recreation experiences and environments and intensity or desire.

Source: Mercer, D. (1973). The concept of recreation need. *Journal of Leisure Research, (Winter), 39* and Geoffrey Godbey.

element." In art, sport, and other forms of leisure expression, it is argued, government will never sponsor new forms of expression until it is politically safe. This argument, however, appears to hold less weight now that many government agencies involved in leisure services have taken a "marketing" approach to the provision of their services. This approach has meant that if people want a given leisure activity, and are willing to support it financially or politically, government is much more likely to respond. Thus, we find Federal land managing agencies sponsoring bungee jumping, hang-gliding, motocross, nude beaches and other forms of leisure expression which would have been unthinkable a few decades ago. The same may be said for the National Endowment for the Arts and the National Endowment for the Humanities, public museums and art galleries and other public repositories of culture. These organizations have been so willing to risk controversy that members of the U.S. Congress have condemned their operations.

Government's Unique Contributions to Leisure Expression

In spite of the difficulties of government involvement in leisure mentioned above, government remains uniquely qualified to provide some leisure services. Consider what would be missing if government were not involved. One of the greatest contributions made by government is the provision of leisure resources which are not economically feasible for the private sector to provide. Large parks in urban areas, for instance, require large expenditures for acquisition and development, as well as maintenance. Government leisure service organizations help mobilize the resources of a community in a way that could not be done without them, because of the sustained effort involved. In some instances, for example, government leisure service agencies have had more success in opening public swimming pools for recreational use than have private citizen groups.

Some art forms are partially dependent upon the government for their survival. The government serves as patron of such art forms as ballet, opera, sculpture, and poetry, providing financial assistance and promotion. The National Endowment for the Arts, for example, makes financial grants to small publishers to enable them to produce books of poetry which, even though written by talented poets, would not make a profit as a commercial undertaking. Additionally, government preserves areas of historical importance or unique physical characteristics for the public.

The provision of leisure services to segments of the population with special needs or disabilities, such as the emotionally disturbed, the mentally retarded, the physically handicapped, the aged, and prisoners, is also largely by government, although special-purpose organizations also make important contributions.

Government also promotes tourism and provides for many tourism services, such as tourism promotion campaigns which promote an entire region, state or country, which private sector entrepreneurs are usually unwilling to finance. Government likewise collects numerous forms of information of use to those in the tourism business as well as in other recreation and leisure enterprises.

Government also regulates a wide variety of leisure services in an attempt to ensure that issues of public safety and welfare are addressed. While the quality of most of the offerings of the commercial sector have been improved by such regulation, it has also resulted in shaping leisure behavior more to the ideals of government.

REFERENCES

Farrell, P. (1978). Recreation youth-serving agencies. In G. Godbey, *Recreation, park and leisure services: Foundations, organization, administration.* Philadelphia, PA: W. B. Saunders, (pp. 187-20).

Godbey, G. (1990). *Leisure in your life: An exploration.* State College, PA: Venture Publishing, Inc.

Grodzins, P. (1966). Sharing of functions: The national recreation system. In *The american system: A new view of government in the United States.* Chicago, IL: Rand McNally & Company, pp. 125-152.

Mercer, D. (Winter, 1973). The Concept of Recreation Need. *Journal of Leisure Research, 39.*

Munson, K. (1978). In G. Godbey, *Recreation, park and leisure services: Foundations, organization, administration.* Philadelphia, PA: W. B. Saunders Company, pp. 133-175.

Reynolds, R. (1980). Leisure services and social control. In T. Goodale, and P. Witt (Eds.), *Recreation and leisure: Issues in an era of change.* State College, PA: Venture Publishing, Inc., (pp. 246-260).

Sessoms, H. D., Meyer, H., and Brightbill, C. (1975). *Leisure services: The organized recreation and park system.* Englewood Cliffs, NJ: Prentice-Hall, pp. 13-15.

Szwak, L. (1989). The non-profit sector as recreation suppliers. *Trends, 26*(2):36.

CHAPTER 29

Tourism

W ithin the modern world, tourism has become a widely shared experience, an identifiable form of leisure behavior with characteristics which allow it to be analyzed like other forms of leisure behavior. It is an industry of huge economic consequence. As tourism has become more a part of our popular culture, due to increases in discretionary income, increases in the technological sophistication of our methods of travel and widespread marketing of touristic opportunities, sociologists, along with other social scientists, have begun to examine it.

There is no agreed upon definition of tourism. The term may refer to anyone who travels or it may specify reasons for traveling such as sightseeing, visiting friends, educational or cultural trips, participating as visitors at special events, shopping expeditions, rest and relaxation or others. Tourism professionals may consider it tourism only if there is overnight stay and/or if the travel is of a specified distance from the traveler's home, such as fifty miles. Generally, there is also the implication that such travel is not part of a daily routine.

The study of tourism, from a sociological perspective, is in its infancy. Most of the research concerning tourism has been market driven and has not started with any theory of human behavior or theory of tourism. Nevertheless, as we will see shortly, a few theories have been developed and examined during the last few decades.

The Rise of Tourism

Tourism as we commonly think of it, mass tourism, may be traced to Thomas Cook, an Englishman. In 1841 Cook, a deeply religious man who believed in temperance, organized a train to carry 540 people round-trip to a temperance convention. Four years later, he had become a full-time excursion organizer (Lundberg, 1974). Cook saw this as more of an opportunity for people to further their education than a business. He eventually became a tour operator, a retailer of tours, and the inventor of traveler's checks. From these beginnings, other travel organizations emerged which increasingly enabled the common person to travel with greater safety, predictability and at a more affordable price. Mass tourism exploded at the end of World War II due to rising discretionary income, improvements in transportation and the advent of the professional tourist agent, all of which allowed for more people to be moved through time and space at a cheaper price. Thomas Cook and his successors gradually democratized tourism until today, within modern nations, it is a part of the expectation of the good life.

Tourism had existed previous to the advent of mass tourism but in more limited forms. It was usually the prerogative of the elite. Travel was limited and often done as a religious pilgrimage, as exploration or, for a limited number, to visit the seaside, baths or shrines. In Europe, beginning during the Renaissance, the "Grand Tour" became popular among the wealthy. Such tours were considered part of a proper education and sometimes involved study at a university as well as extensive travel on the Continent. It was a rite of passage for those who could afford it.

Theories of Tourism

No single theory of tourism has emerged which has been universally accepted by tourism researchers. Indeed, it could be argued that tourism is such a diverse phenomenon no single social theory could explain it. Nevertheless, a handful of theories have been developed which appear to be useful.

Many sociologists, such as Buck (1978) have argued that tourism, if is conceptualized as a process rather than an event or series of events, may be understood by viewing it as play. Tourism would seem to conform to virtually every characteristic of play as identified in the seminal work of Huizinga (1950). It is voluntary, outside ordinary life, limited in time and space, surrounded by an air of mystery, utterly absorbing yet recognized as being somewhat make-believe, has something at stake, an outcome in doubt and may promote the formation of social groups. Graburn (1977) suggested that antecedents to the anthropological study of tourism are evident in earlier analyses of human play. Manning (1973) has described tourism as representing a form of play in his study of Bermudian social life and Lett (1983) has analyzed charter yacht tourism in the Caribbean using several of Huizinga's identified characteristics of play.

Tourism may also be explained psychologically as a form of play by explaining it in terms of stimulus-seeking behavior (Berlyne, 1960; Ellis, 1973). According to such explanations, humans have a need to process information or knowledge. Berlyne believed a relation existed between information flow and various elements of uncertainty. When a person is faced with a stimulus where he or she is unable to predict the outcome of an event, a conflict is created which promotes the processing of information to reduce uncertainty. Theoretically, each individual has an optimal information-seeking level for each stimuli. "Berlyne distinguishes between two kinds of exploration: (a) specific exploration aimed at finding a single answer to a problem or challenge and (b) diverse exploration aimed at finding in the environment elements which can produce excitement or distraction" (Bishop and Jeanrenaud, 1980).

The complexity of the play thing or situation determines how much it will be explored. Exploration is encouraged when the object or situation has many things which can be seen, heard, touched, smelled, tasted or manipulated. Such exploration may lead to assimilation in which there is a repetition of behaviors, often with subtle transformations in the play or or in the play situation so the individual gains some proficiency. Finally, there may be creativity—". . . the production of novel responses that have an appropriate impact in a given context" (Bishop and Jeanrenaud, 1980). Conversely, assimilation may lead to the environment or play object losing its distinguishing novelty. When this happens, the situation may return to what Huizinga referred to as "ordinary life," thus causing the player to either withdraw from the situation or object formerly used for play or to begin behaving toward it as one would toward ordinary life.

When tourism is viewed as play which is stimulus-seeking behavior, social psychologists have generally assumed that there will be a cycle of involvement on the part of the tourist rather than a static kind of experience. That is, the level of arousal that is optimal will likely change with experience, causing changes in the tourist's behavior to achieve the optimal level.

Tourism has also been conceptualized as the search for the authentic. That is, the tourist wants to find what is real, pure, good or meaningful in the world. MacCannell (1976) has argued that, within the modern world, tourism represents the quest for the authentic. According to MacCannell, modernity is characterized not only by expanded literacy, generalized health care, rationalized work arrangements and geographic and economic mobility, but also by a mentality which sets modern society in opposition both to its own past and to underdeveloped nations. Since, in modern nations, work is replaced by leisure as the center of social arrangements and of creativity, tourism becomes a vehicle by which the individual from a modern society tries to find some overarching system in the world which can make sense of it. The tourist at first may simply visit the artificial attractions which those in the tourism industry have developed for profit. But, as the tourist's understanding increases, he or she is motivated to find the "back region" of the tourist area as opposed to the "front" region, for the back region is where real life is unfolding, where the real site may be understood and appreciated. Generally, the commercial segment of tourism seeks to keep tourists away from the back region and to distract them with the manufactured sites which make a profit. Thus, the commercial sector is the cause of inauthenticity in tourism experience and only locally controlled tourism which springs from a consciousness of the uniqueness of the area in question can provide the tourist with the authentic.

This interpretation has been criticized not so much for being wrong, but for pertaining to only a segment of the tourist population. There is some question as to whether all tourists' understanding develops with increased tourist experience in such a way that they seek the authentic. Some, for example, may be content with fun and sun year after year with little increase in their understanding or curiosity concerning the area in which they vacation. Cohen (1988) has also argued that authenticity can emerge. That is, an area such as Disney World, can, over time, come to be the "authentic" in the minds of tourists who visit it even though it was originally just a manufactured tourist site.

While tourism may not always represent the search for the authentic, certainly it appears that concepts of tourism are being more frequently explored today which seek to minimize the commercialization and inauthenticity of much mass tourism experience. Such tourism may be labeled "Green Tourism," "Eco-Tourism," or "Alternative Tourism." Generally, it seeks to integrate the tourist more directly into the life of the community visited, and to incorporate tourism planning with other forms of community planning. It also attempts to keep local people in control of the tourism development process, and to gain an understanding of the unique character of an area from those who reside within it.

Alternative tourism represents, in many ways, a basic alternative to the concept of mass tourism. Under various conceptualizations of alternative tourism, tourists are more highly integrated into the host culture rather than remaining outsiders. They live very much like the natives do during their stay. Krippendorf (1987) stated that "Green Tourism" is based upon planning before development takes place with regional coordination of district plans. Tourism schemes spring from a concept and use concentrated development within existing settlements rather than developing new ones. Green tourism protects the fine landscapes of the area, reuses existing buildings, and sets limits on the amount of development in an area. Only natives of the area serve as developers. The economic, ecological and social issues surrounding tourist development are all considered rather than just the economic ones. Traffic plans favor public transportation. Developers are required to bear the social costs of their development, and the architecture, historical sites, and natural sites are retained even if they serve as an obstacle to tourist growth.

This vision of alternative tourism assumes, first and foremost, that tourism can be controlled by local citizens and that their way of life can be maintained even with a high level of tourist visitation. As Butler (1989) has observed, however, alternative tourism may actually cause a greater impact on the area in question. Under alternative or Green tourism, for instance, tourists may penetrate further into the personal space of residents and involve residents to a much greater degree. Additionally, it may expose fragile resources to more frequent visitation and cause greater leakage of expenditures out of the local community. Confining tourism to a tourist district, it is argued, may actually do less damage to the way of life of residents than alternative tourism. Certainly what Green or alternative tourism provides, a closer association with local life, allows the tourist to penetrate the front regions of tourism and potentially gain a more profound understanding of the local culture and environment. To the extent that tourists seek the authentic, alternative tourism may flourish.

Those sociologists, such as Buck, who view tourism as a form of play, disagree that the tourist is seeking the authentic and believe that the manufactured front region is what most tourists want. In studying tourism in Amish Country in Pennsylvania, for instance, Buck found that the built up tourist region with its commercial attractions provided a region in which tourists were happy to shop and sightsee while the real Amish were protected from them. Other studies have argued that the establishment of tourist districts within cities or regions both keeps the tourists happy and keeps their impact upon the local people minimized.

Many anthropologists and sociologists view tourism as imperialism, a process by which one group comes to dominate another. This interpretation is made most often where there are great differences in the power, economic resources, and degree of modernity between the guests and the hosts. According to such thought, tourism represents an expansion of a society's interests abroad which are imposed upon or adopted by the guest culture which result in the ebbing of power in the host community and the gaining of power by the guest culture (Nash, 1977). Many sociological case studies have sought to document this process. According to Machlis and Burch (1984), tourism should be thought of as a specific, intense form of relations between strangers. When tourism occurs between individuals from technologically inferior and superior cultures there is a cycle which leads to imperialism. In the early phases of contact, the local, technologically inferior guests are dominant over the guests whose very incompetence convinces the locals of their own social values' goodness and makes them even more insular. Gradually, however, the locals adopt some of the tourists' technology and exploit them to obtain an economic surplus. With the growth of such efforts, lack of production capacity makes the locals more dependent upon the foreign economic system. Gradually, the locals become more dependent upon tourists. The technologically less advanced locals eventually become completely dependent upon the actions of their metropolitan centers, which the guest's culture now dominates.

The determining variable in any relations between strangers, Machlis and Burch argued, is relative power. As the dominance of the guests slowly asserts itself, the means of stabilizing relations shifts in predictable ways. The ratio of decisions made by guests and locals shifts until the guests dominate, the socioeconomic status of the guests goes from heroes to travelers to settlers to independent tourists to packaged tourists and finally to social workers who arrive at government request to try and help the locals who are now disproportionately urban poor. Transactions change from barter to gifts to cash to personal credit to standardized credit to subsidies. In every realm, the changes which take place destroy the culture of the locals and make them subservient to the guests. From this perspective, tourism is based on the exploitation of local environments and local low-wage workers, disproportionately women, who provide most direct services.

While much tourism is exploitive, MacCannell and others have argued that some methods of managing tourism by locals can minimize the negative impact of guests. It has also been argued that, in many cases, the host culture wants the changes that are brought about by adopting the guests ways of life; that there is a tendency to romanticize the lives of native peoples who, given a chance, will voluntarily share the technological benefits to which the guests have access. Others argue that, lacking political and economic power, locals have no choice.

Cycles of Tourist Involvement

A major theme of the tourism literature is that every aspect of tourism may be understood in terms of predictable cycles. Such cycles include the motivations of tourists who successively visit an area, the development of the tourist site or environment, the cycle of individual involvement with a given area and others. These cycles tend to be highly interdependent. The typology of tourists developed by Plog (1972), for instance, is based on the amount of novelty sought. Initially, small numbers of adventuresome tourists (allocentrics) visit an area. As the area becomes more accessible, well-known and better served, those tourists seeking less adventure and contrast (mid-centrics) begin to dominate. Finally, as the area becomes older and less different from the visitor's area of origin, a declining number of tourists who seek even less variation and novelty (psychocentrics) will visit. Butler (1980) identified the factors which bring about changes in tourist sites as: changes in the preferences and needs of visitors, gradual deterioration and possible replacement of the physical plant and facilities, and the change or disappearance of the original natural and cultural attractions which were initially responsible for the site's popularity.

In terms of individual cycles of involvement, many studies have shown that increasing familiarity of a tourist site or area for an individual tourist is characterized by an evolution in motives, behaviors, satisfactions and understandings. In many cases, the findings of such studies suggest that with repetition, tourism becomes increasingly less distinguishable from everyday life. That is, tourists act more like they do in everyday life, spend less money and spend it more carefully and for items they would purchase in their everyday routine (Godbey and Graefe, 1991). The vacation home represents an example of an experience which, for many owners, gradually goes from a touristic experience to everyday life. While initially, vacation or second home owners are likely to act as tourists and are primarily interested in recreation activities, with time this orientation changes as the second home becomes increasingly familiar.

For some owners, the transition to ordinary life is completed when they retire to the vacation site, thus making it their home and making themselves residents instead of tourists (Robertson, 1977; Godbey and Bevins, 1987).

Tourism—The World's Largest Industry

The futurist Herman Kahn predicted that tourism would become the largest industry in the world in the near future. Some analysts think it already has. Within the United States, tourism is the third largest retail industry, the second largest private employer and directly employs more than five million people (U.S. Travel and Tourism Administration, 1988). Such claims, in one sense, are difficult to substantiate since the component parts of the tourism industry are subject to question. They may include transportation, lodging, restaurants, attractions and other components. Certainly, many of the economic systems which serve tourists also serve resident populations. While it is estimated that more than one-third of the days spent in hotels and motels in the United States are spent by tourists, many trips are for mixed purposes and have components of both commerce and vacation or play. The huge appeal of conferences and conventions, for instance, is based on this mixture of work-related obligation and play.

Since tourism is often viewed by planners and managers in both the public and private sector as being primarily an economic phenomenon, it is not surprising that numerous studies attempt to document the economic consequences of tourism. A primary concern of many of such studies is the extent to which revenues generated by tourism are recycled within the community or geographic area being studied. This is often called the "multiplier effect." In some studies it is found that much of the money generated by tourism "leaks" out of the local tourist area. This is particularly likely to occur when the tourism infrastructure has been developed by outside corporations or when there is a large difference in the level of technology between the guest culture and the host culture.

While tourism is an increasingly significant part of the economy of nations and of smaller geopolitical units, it often receives far less government support than industries of comparable size such as agriculture or manufacturing. There are many reasons for this. Tourism is often associated with seasonal, low paying jobs which are subject to rapid change. Tourists are often viewed negatively by indigenous populations. In many instances, the existence of tourists leads to increasing local prices for food and other commodities and a reshaping of local life to fit the needs and preferences of the tourists.

In seeking to understand the economic consequences of tourism, there is a need for more realistic methods of calculation. The great division among tourism researchers is between those who study only direct economic impacts and those who study behavior or the environment. This has resulted in economic impact studies often failing to consider consequences which have enormous economic impact upon a community such as changes in the level of pollution, in the level of formal education attained by the local population, access to technology or the development and maintenance of transportation systems. Economic impact studies, in short, have usually confined themselves to precisely what multinational corporations have been criticized for confining their interest to: direct, short-term profit.

◢ REFERENCES

Berlyne, D. E. (1960). Determinants of subjective novelty. *Perception and Psychophysics, 3*(6):415-425.

Bishop, D., and Jeanrenaud, C. (1980). Creative growth through play and its implications for recreation practice. In Thomas Goodale and Peter Witt (Eds.), *Recreation and leisure: Issues in an era of change.* State College, PA: Venture Publishing, Inc., (pp. 81-99).

Buck, R. (1978). Toward a synthesis of tourism theory. *Annals of Tourism Research, 4*(1), pp. 110-111.

Butler, R. (1980). The concept of a tourist area cycle of evolution: Implications for management of resources. *Canadian Geographer, 24*(1):5-12.

Butler, R. (1989). Alternative tourism: Pious hope or trojan horse? *World Leisure and Recreation, 31*(4), pp. 9-17.

Cohen, E. (1988). Authenticity and commoditization in tourism. *Annals of Tourism Research, 15*(3):71-386.

Ellis, M. (1973). *Why people play.* Englewood Cliffs, NJ: Prentice-Hall.

Godbey, G., and Bevins, M. (1987). The life-cycle of second home ownership: A case study. *Journal of Travel Research, 25*(3):18-23.

Godbey, G., and Graefe, A. (1991). Repeat tourism, play and monetary spending. *Annals of Tourism Research, 18*: 2, pp. 213-226.

Graburn, N. (1977). Tourism: The sacred journey. In V. Smith (Ed.), *Hosts and guests: The anthropology of tourism*. Philadelphia, PA: University of Pennsylvania Press, (pp. 17-31).

Huizinga, J. (1950). *Homo ludens: A study of the play element in culture.* Boston, MA: Beacon Press.

Krippendorf, J. (1987). *The holiday makers.* London, England: Heinemann.

Lett, J. (1983). Ludic and liminoid aspects of charter yacht tourism in the Caribbean. *Annals of Tourism Research, 10*(1), 35-36

Lundberg, D. E. (1974). *The tourism business,* Third Edition. Boston, MA: CBI Publishing Company.

Nash, D. (1977). Tourism As a Form of Imperialism. In V. Smith (Ed.), *Hosts and guests: The anthropology of tourism*. Philadelphia, PA: University of Pennsylvania Press, (pp. 33-49).

MacCannell, D. (1976). *The tourist: A new theory of the leisure class.* New York, NY: Schocken Books.

Machlis, G., and Burch, W. (1984). Relations among strangers: Cycles of structure and meaning in the tourist system. *Sociological Review, 31*(1):666-689.

Manning, F. E. (1973). *Black clubs in Bermuda: Ethnography in a play world.* Ithaca, NY: Cornell University Press.

Plog, S. C. (1972). *Why destination areas rise and fall in popularity.* Unpublished paper presented to the Southern California Chapter, Travel and Tourism Research Association.

Robertson, R. W. (1977). Second home decisions: The Australian context. In J. T. Coppeck (Ed.), *Second Homes: Blessing or Curse?* New York, NY: Pergamon Press, (pp. 119-138).

CHAPTER 30

Sport

Sport is a common part of life for most people in industrial societies. Sporting events are routinely reported in both newspapers and on television to a greater extent than any other form of leisure. On many local TV "news" shows, sport reporting constitutes one sixth to one fourth of the entire program. No other form of leisure expression can be said to receive such wide coverage.

Sport has found its way into the public schools as well as colleges and universities. Professional sports events have become critical parts of many holidays and weekends for millions of Americans. Retirement communities have been built around golf or tennis. Debt-ridden cities often spend millions for new stadiums to keep a professional team or attract one. Involvement with youth sports is a common experience for millions of boys and, increasingly, girls. Sport is analyzed and reanalyzed by both participants and by spectators in gyms, in bars and on the subway.

If sport is analyzed from the perspective of the social sciences, it may be considered to be a game occurrence, an institutionalized game, a social institution or a form of social involvement (Loy, MacPherson and Kenyon, 1978). As a game occurrence, sport is thought to be playful, involve competition, and have outcomes which are related to physical skill, strategy and chance. Sport is distinguished from other games by the physical prowess of participants. As institutionalized games, sport involves teams, sponsorship, codified rules and regulations which are typically enforced by some governing body. It is a technical sphere which consists of intrinsic aspects such as physical skills, knowledge and equipment required for a given contest and extrinsic aspects which include the playing field or area, the physical skills and knowledge possessed by coaches, groundskeepers, cheerleaders, team physicians, fans. As an institutionalized game, sport is a symbolic sphere which may involve display and ritual, and an educational sphere which involves the transmission of skill and knowledge by those who have them to those who lack them (Loy, MacPherson and Kenyon, 1978).

If sport is analyzed as a social institution, it implies a sport order ". . . composed of the categories of primary, technical, managerial and corporate social organizations which arrange, facilitate and regulate human action in sport situations" (Loy, MacPherson and Kenyon, 1978, p. 15). Finally, sport may be analyzed as a form of social involvement with behavioral, cognitive and affective dimensions.

Sport, then, may be viewed as a continuum based upon how much formal organization is involved. At the least formal level, it may be thought of as being synonymous with play. Next, there is informal sport, semiformal sport and finally, formal sport which may be called "athletics" (Snyder and Spreitzer, 1989). Edwards (1973) placed play and sport at opposite ends of a continuum and thought play became sport under the following circumstances:

1) the activity became less subject to individual spontaneity and discretion;

2) rules, regulations and roles became central; as the activity became less separated from the routines of daily life;

3) individual accountability for quality of performance is emphasized;

4) motivation for participation becomes extrinsic;

5) the activity becomes more serious and requires more time and effort; and

6) winning and losing have consequences which extend beyond the participants.

Sociological Themes in the Study of Sport

Certain themes have dominated the study of sport from the perspective of sociology and related social sciences. Among such topics has been social stratification in sport, particularly based upon race, social class and gender. In many traditional cultures, most forms of sport have been almost exclusively the prerogative of males. With the advent of industrialization and eventual mandatory attendance at public schools, females have become more widely exposed to sport, although usually in more limited ways than males. As women have entered the labor force in large numbers, the variation in sport participation between males and females has become increasingly less, although still distinct. Sport is today often one of the issues of women's movements. Such issues are as diverse as equal funding for women's sports in secondary and higher education, equal prize money for professional female tennis players, the issue of whether or not girls should be allowed to compete in Little League and other organized forms of age-grouped sport, the extent of television coverage of female collegiate basketball teams, and the use of female cheer and dance squads to increase the "sex appeal" at sports events.

In terms of social class, many analyses of sport participation show that, in almost every sport, the likelihood and extent of participation in various sports increases as social class does. While it is popularly thought that participation in sports such as basketball and football is dominated by those from the lower social and economic classes, such is generally not the case. Reasons for this include the fact that those with higher levels of formal education are more likely to be exposed to such sports, have easier access to playing fields and courts, be in better physical health, have money for equipment and lessons, and have access to transportation.

The role of sport within educational institutions has been examined extensively, particularly within higher education. Since the United States, unlike many other countries, does not maintain government sponsored amateur sport systems to serve as training grounds for elite athletes, colleges and universities often serve as the main setting within which elite athletes can perfect their skills and/ or prepare for professional sport. This situation often works at cross purposes with other objectives of institutions of higher education. It also accounts for the endless studies of the academic attainment of athletes in postsecondary institutions and of the ways in which such athletes are treated differently from other students.

In terms of more highly institutionalized athletics, management, political economy and mass media coverage have been dominant themes. In all sport, violence among both players and spectators has been examined. In Britain, for instance, football (soccer) "hooliganism" has been analyzed as a phenomenon of working class culture, as an expression of alienation and as a logistical problem of sport management. Similarly, sport participation across the life cycle has been examined. In spite of some broadening of participation in later life, to a great extent participation in most sport forms occurs during the first three decades of life. Even in the so-called "lifetime sports," there is a decline in participation during each ten year period of life from the age of twenty. Golf represents the exception, which is one of the reasons why participation in golf is growing in aging societies such as Japan or the United States. Some of the reasons which are thought to account for the decline in participation with increasing age include not only physical limitations but also lack of role models, discrimination or lack of promotion by institutions which sponsor sport and lack of appropriate modification of equipment, rules and playing areas. While sport has been extensively modified for youth along these lines, there is much less attention to the modification of such conditions for older adults, although progress is being made.

In the sociological examination of all of these issues, the conceptual framework within which issues are examined is critical. Sport, perhaps more than other forms of leisure, has been interpreted through the use of diverse ideologies and social theories. Thus, concepts such as "amateurism" may be interpreted as a positive means of keeping sport from being subverted and losing its playful character by not allowing athletes to be paid for competing. Alternatively, however, it may be viewed as a means by which upper-class British males kept sport their exclusive province since only the wealthy could afford to spend the time in practice needed for high levels of achievement without concern about earning a living.

Snyder and Spreitzer stated that four sociological perspectives guide the study of sport. These include a functionalist perspective which focuses upon the way society and groups are composed of interrelated and interdependent parts and ways in which each part functions to support the goals of the group or society (Parsons, 1971). Conversely, sport can be examined from the standpoint of conflict theory, which assumes that social order is imposed upon those people who have little power by others who have great power. The interests of these two groups are, therefore, in conflict. Human needs, rather than social stability, is emphasized by this perspective. Exchange theory, as mentioned elsewhere, focuses upon the ways in which people exchange social and material goods such as favors, recognition, material goods, assistance, promotions and other rewards (Homans, 1961). Finally, the symbolic interactionist perspective is concerned with the way in which everyday interaction is based upon symbols people use to label and classify the world around them (Blumer, Mead and Blumer, 1982).

The research questions asked about sport change for each of the topics mentioned previously depending upon which of these four sociological perspectives is adopted. Even the orientations toward the study of sport would vary greatly. As Snyder and Spreitzer observed, functional theory might focus on how sport was related to other social institutions, conflict theory is concerned with whether sport promotes or deters social change, exchange theory deals with ways in which sport is a source of rewards and sanctions, and symbolic interaction with how involvement in sport is influenced by interpretations.

The Democratization of Sport

There are numerous indications that sport has democratized during the last fifty years. As this has happened, participation in sport has increased, there has been an increased diffusion of sport through society. Differentiation in the form and meaning of sport, and "sport" has become a concept which is less clear, perhaps even less meaningful. In the last five to ten years, there has been some decline in active sport participation due, among things, to the aging of the population.

Increased Participation in Sport

While exact numbers are hard to come by, it would appear that during the last fifty years sport has become a more pervasive form of American life, even though television is the only contact for most adults. Certainly it can be argued that a higher percentage of the population is involved in sport and voluntary physical exercise. The reasons for such increased participation include a greater awareness of and belief in the physiological benefits of sport, increased discretionary income, increased instruction in sport through public school physical education courses, more liberal attitudes toward women's participation in sport, and more public and private provision of sport equipment and facilities.

It is difficult to determine the exact magnitude of this increase both because there is no standardized way to measure participation in sport and also because there is some evidence that individuals tend to exaggerate their participation in sport and athletic activities. A study by Godbey and Chase (1983), for instance, found that individuals overestimated the number of times they went swimming or played tennis at clubs to which they belonged by an overage of almost 100 percent. Analyses of private sector data by Warnick and Howard (1985) indicated that sport participation is lower than commonly believed. Further, most sport participants, usually about 75 percent, engage in the sport irregularly (Kelly 1987). Nevertheless, there seems little doubt that active participation in sport has risen dramatically during the last fifty years.

Increased Diffusion of Sport Throughout Society

There is also evidence that sport is much more widely diffused through society than ever before. While variables such as age, social class and gender are still important in predicting sport participation, their impact has lessened greatly. While those with higher levels of education are more likely to participate in most sports, males are more likely to participate than females, and young more than old, the differences in participation are not as great as previously. Age may still be the best single predictor of participation in sport and the relation of participation to age is almost always negative, declining consistently during each decade of life past twenty. There is only one clear exception to this: golf. Even the so-called lifetime sports such as tennis decline in participation with age.

While during the 1930s and 1940s there was great concern by numerous social critics that "Spectatoritis" (Nash, 1953) was occurring in society, a malady in which people watched sports events rather than participated in activity, the relation between viewing sport and participating is not necessarily an either/or relationship. Godbey and Robinson (1979) found that those who are most likely to attend a sporting event are also the most likely to be active participants in the sport. The relation between televised viewing of sport and active participation is also likely to be more complex than an either/or relation-ship. Regular adult sport participation is, however, generally quite low, usually in single digits.

Increased Differentiation in Form and Meaning

Just as leisure has differentiated in form and meaning during the last decade, so too has sport. This differentiation of form reflects not only a greater expression of cultural pluralism but also greater diversity in the meaning of sport and its role in people's lives. Professional sport has become such a pervasive form of entertainment that top athletes have signed multi-year contracts for huge amounts of money. Sports reporting now covers labor-management disputes and corporate aspects of sport as well as what happens on the field. The sport of boxing has been almost single-handedly revived by a cable TV network—ESPN. Made for TV "junk sports" have invented sports or staged events to fill programming voids.

Sports such as running, rock climbing, triathlon, and other "ultra sports," those which are either high risk or require great physical and mental preparation, have increasingly become a direct expression of spiritual life.

The identity-seeking behavior of sports fans is such that whole lives may be built around athletic teams or events. Many sports fans exhibit the characteris-tics of a cult. Mass sport participation may signal something ominous in our society. As Morris Berman stated in *The Re-enchantment of the World:* "We are haunted by our phoniness, our playacting, our flight from trying to become what we truly are or could be. As the guilt mounts, we silence the nagging voice with drugs, alcohol, spectator sports—anything to avoid facing the reality of the situation (Berman, 1984). Sport, then, may have the same narcotic function it has sometimes been thought to combat.

For millions, however, sport is a casual encounter with mildly physical activity done a few times a year with little meaning in their lives. Numerous surveys demonstrate that the vast majority of those who have participated in most sports have done so only occasionally during the last year.

Sport may also be thought of as an important component of the economy. One study, for instance, found that residents of Pennsylvania spend about $1000 per person per year on sporting goods. This does not include the cost of attendance at sporting events, fees for participation and the huge percentage of mass media expenditures which are sport related, to say nothing of sport-centered vacations, instruction and so on.

For some Americans, sport is viewed as a component of a physically-fit style of life. The wellness movement has not often distinguished between "sport" and "exercise" since both are presumably undertaken for the purpose of fitness.

Campaigns launched by the President's Council on Physical Fitness and Sports as well as the "Life. Be in it" campaign which the National Recreation and Park Association launched in the early 1980s promote sport almost exclusively to help achieve the end product of better health. More recently the Canadian government has begun to promote active lifestyles. All these campaigns view sport as a means to the end of better health.

Originally, much sporting activity in this country was attributed to the instinct for play. This instinct for play was exhibited in the rural play of small communities as well as the more serious play of an emerging urban elite. Much sport behavior, which was loosely organized and inconclusive, would appear to meet Huizinga's criteria for play (see Chapter 13). Today much sport behavior seems outside the realm of play. That is, it has become a part of ordinary life, reported along with the weather and the stock market on the evening news. Sport, for many, is a means to an end rather than an end in itself and the ends to which it claims to be a means include money, access to education, diversion, weight loss, spiritual salvation, and even self-definition. It is increasingly difficult to determine what are the time and space limitations of sport. Football and tennis, for instance, are now played indoors, at night and year round. Sport for many is "serious business" and sport instruction, using cinematography, reflects the same ethos that time and motion studies of the industrial work place did a few decades ago. Every attempt is being made to rob sport of its mysteries.

As sport has democratized in form, function and diffusion among social classes it has become increasingly problematic to know what the term "sport" means. In today's existential world of sport, it is difficult to determine the characteristics, if any, that different sport situations have in common. While some sport has often been thought of as play (Loy, McPherson and Kenyon, 1978), much sport activity today would not, as previously mentioned, meet most criteria of play as defined by play theorists. Sport has also been defined as involving "physical prowess"—"the use of developed skills and abilities" (Loy, McPherson and Kenyon, 1978)—yet the bulk of participation in most sports today is by those who participate only a few times a year. The increasing fad-like nature of many sports and the tendency for those with high levels of education to be exposed to many sports intensifies this trend.

Competition, too, may be thought of as inherent in sport, yet today we see a full spectrum of positions in sport with regard to competition, from the cooperative sports and games movement (Orlick and Botterill, 1975) where challenge without competition is central, to professional sports. This includes the Olympics, where children are prepared for competition from early childhood and hundreds of thousands of dollars may be spent redesigning the helmet of a luge sled driver. Organized sports for children has pushed in opposite directions at once, ranging from world-level competition in the Little League World Series to co-ed baseball leagues where everybody plays and scores aren't recorded.

If sport is thought of as emanating from a code of sportsmanship or as developing character, surely we are on shaky grounds. Athletes reflect a diverse spectrum of ethical and unethical behavior. They may be hardened criminals, drug addicts, or the moral leaders of the community.

Sport may be thought to involve rules which participants readily accept but there is mass violation of sport rules at all levels of sport. With some regulatory bodies, such as the National Collegiate Athletic Association, it is difficult even to understand the rules.

Sport in today's society, then, appears to have almost no fundamental nature. Because of this it is increasingly unclear how to judge sport. Nineteenth century notions of "amateurism" and "character building" are of little value. While "play" remains, for many, an important ideal for sport, organizational attempts to promote sport in the twentieth century have very often killed the potential for play.

In the seamless web of postindustrial society, the democratization of sport has paralleled the democratization of leisure in general. The concepts and assumptions about sport which developed during the industrialization process are increasingly irrelevant. The concept of "sport" therefore, must be rethought.

REFERENCES

Berman, M. (1984). *The re-enchantment of the world.* New York, NY: Bantam Books, (p. 7).

Blumer, R., Mead, H., and Blumer, B. (1982). "The convergent methodological perspective of social behavioralism and interactionism," *American Sociological Review, 45,* 409-419.

Edwards, H. (1973). *Sociology of sport.* Homewood, IL: Dorsey Press.

Godbey, G., and Chase, D. (1983). The accuracy of self-reported participation rates: A research note. *Leisure Studies, 2,* 231-235.

Godbey, G., and Robinson, J. (Summer 1979). The American sports fan: 'Spectatoritis' revisited. *Review of Sport and Leisure, 4,* (1).

Homans, G. (1961). *Social behavior: Its elementary forms.* New York, NY: Harcourt, Brace and World.

Huizinga, J. (1950). *Homo ludens: A study of the play element in culture.* Boston, MA: Beacon Press, (p. 13).

Kelly, J. R. (1987). *Recreation trends toward the year 2000.* Champaign, IL: Sagamore Press.

Loy, J., MacPherson, B., and Kenyon, G. (1978). *Sport and social systems.* Reading, MA: Addison-Wesley Publishing Co.

Nash, J. B. (1953). *Philosophy of recreation and leisure.* St. Louis, MO: Mosby.

Orlick, T., and Botterill, C. (1975). *Every kid can win.* Chicago, IL: Nelson-Hall.

Parsons, T. (1971). *The social system.* Glencoe, IL: The Free Press.

Snyder, E., and Spreitzer, E. (1989). *Social aspects of sport,* (3rd ed.). Englewood Cliffs, NJ: Prentice-Hall.

Warnick, R., and Howard, D. (1985). Market share analysis of selected leisure services from 1979 to 1982. *Journal of Park and Recreation Administration 3*(4), 1985, pp. 65-76

CHAPTER 31

Outdoor Resource-Based Recreation

More than 260 million acres of federal land are available for recreation use. States offer another 42 million acres and local governments about 10 million. These areas include forests, mountains, lakes, rivers, deserts, beaches, trails, prairies, and other terrains. In some areas wildlife is protected; others are managed for hunting and fishing. Of the total about half is forest, nine percent wilderness, ten percent fish and game preserves, and six percent designated parks and special recreation areas. Federal land in the coastal and mountain West, not including Alaska, comprises about 75 percent of the total.

On these public lands and in areas privately held, people hike, fish, hunt, climb, sail, camp, swim, canoe, raft, tube, run, play games, sun, ski, drive motorized vehicles, soar, and enjoy innumerable other kinds of activity. In some locations, management agencies offer parking, access roads and trails, camping sites, parking, lookouts, safety protection, ski slopes, harbors, docks and launching ramps, and other facilities that make recreation participation possible. At other sites the provider does nothing except allow access.

Along with the resource provisions, businesses on site or at a distance provide equipment such as boats, boots, casting rods, tents, and a variety of speciality items. They offer transportation, marinas, cabins and camping sites, ski lifts, guide services, rafting trips, sightseeing flights, repair services, canoe rentals, and a host of other facilitating resources for rent, lease, or sale. They teach beginners how to boardsail or scuba dive, climb sheer rock faces safely, survive in wilderness areas, and ski steep slopes with minimal risk to life and limb. There is a critical complementarity between public and market providers, in mail and community retailing as well as with businesses located at or near the outdoor recreation environments.

Lakes, rivers, ocean beaches, forests, and mountains have a special appeal as leisure environments. Some kinds of activity require particular outdoor resources. Fishing, backpacking, water and snow skiing, camping, boating, and even hiking draw people to sites that are the basic resource for the activity. Outdoor recreation, however, is more than just doing the activity. There is something special about being *in* the environment that is crucial to the meaning of the experience. Therefore, the quality of the environment is significant. Degraded conditions, crowding, standing in line, and pollution at one location may drive users hundreds of miles in search of a better environment. Across the country, highways in and out of urban areas become bumper-to-bumper "parking lots" on high season weekends as people seek that special place. As a result, management *for* recreation as well as protection of the resource become a complex balancing act of providing and restricting.

Environmental Conflicts

Public management of outdoor environments involves more than clearing roadways and parking areas. Conflicts have been acute over land and water that may be utilized in more than one way. For example, a forested mountain slope may be managed for sustained yield timber harvest, bulldozed for a ski run, or preserved in a natural state for a vista or conservation purpose. Timber interests and recreation developers may both want to cut trees, but using different rates and methods. Preservation interests may want to preserve a critical environment for an endangered species of plant or animal life. Tourism interests may be divided between winter ski development and summer highway travelers.

The three interest groups are the developers, recreation users, and conservationists. In some cases, coalitions may be formed. The economic enterprise may be a recreation based resort, lumber, or mineral extraction. Conservation interests usually argue in terms of the scarcity or uniqueness of the resource and the irretrievable character of most use or development. Some recreation users call for development and others for preservation through limited access. Backpackers may conflict with businesses that offer horseback trips, cross-country skiers with snowmobilers, birdwatchers with trail bikers, sailboaters with powerboaters, and so on. Conservation organizations confront the lobbies of business associations in legislative halls and chambers. Low impact recreation enthusiasts meet the trade associations of high-impact equipment manufacturers and distributors. Recreation users may disagree with some supporting development and others conservation. The managers, charged with upholding the public interest, are torn by conflicting interests and manipulated by differential power.

Of course, long-term comprehensive planning would appear to be the required strategy for public agencies. Such planning, however, calls for a research knowledge base that can forecast the outcomes of interventions and policies on elements as diverse as water quality and regional economies or wildlife habitats and boater safety. Further, priorities tend to be established in the political process rather than by science. Political influence may be based on factors other than the size of constituencies or campaign contributions. The goal oriented interventions of users and developers necessitate integrated and comprehensive management plans if the natural resources are to best fulfill their sustaining potential for life. Plans however, in and of themselves, do not resolve conflict when interests and values differ. And those most seriously affected by management plans and decisions may not have the greatest political clout.

Recreation in Natural Environments

From a recreation perspective, we tend to focus on what people do rather than on the environment. This ignores the symbiotic relationship between the two. What people do and how they do it are based on the nature of the environment and in turn have impacts on that environment. The 1987 report of the President's Commission on Americans Outdoors suggests the relative magnitude of outdoor recreation by adults:

Table 31.1
Percentage of Activities Participated in Often or Very Often by Adults

Walking for pleasure	50%
Driving for pleasure	43
Swimming outdoors	43
Sightseeing	34
Picnicking	28
Fishing	25
Camping	21
Bicycling	17
Running or jogging	17
Birdwatching, nature study	15
Motorboating, water-skiing	15
Day hiking	12
Hunting	11
Off-road vehicles	11
Backpacking	5
Downhill skiing	5
Cross-country skiing	3

Source: Report of the President's Commission on Americans Outdoors, Washington, DC: Island Press, 1987.

What such lists obscure is the wide variety of styles in which most activities can be done. For example, downhill skiing may be at lavish upscale resorts or on local hillsides. Styles of camping vary widely, partly due to differences in life course period as well as the opportunities afforded by the site. Families with young children on a time-limited vacation trip camp differently from retired couples following the seasons. The range of resource opportunities varies from highly developed campgrounds adjacent to a lake or in a national park to designated but undeveloped areas several days hike into the mountains. The general labels such as "camping" or "boating" include such a variation in activity and motivations as to become almost meaningless. Other than a floating craft, what are the similarities between white-water kayaking and weekending on a 60-foot motor launch in a yacht club marina?

Nevertheless, there has now been enough research on resource based outdoor recreation to make a number of generalizations about the interplay between resources and behavior. What follows is based primarily on the hundreds of studies of recreation in public natural areas rather than on market research. Although the variations are considerable within generic activity categories, recreation in parks, forests, sea and lake shores, river, deserts, and other environments has been subjected to considerable investigation producing in excess of 100 published papers a year. Further, this is a period of theory development. More and more studies are explanatory or issue-directed rather than only descriptive. Those funded by government agencies are almost always tied to some management problem.

What, then, do we know about people who come to natural environments for recreation? Who are they? What do they do? And, what do they want?

Who Are They?

Demographics are only the beginning of an answer to this fundamental question. To begin with, those who visit natural resource areas are those who can afford to get there, but cannot afford private preserves. That is, they are neither the poor nor the very rich (Cichetti, 1972). They tend to be above average in education level. The most significant demographic finding, however, is that within the parameters of financial and physical ability to travel, there are few distinguishing factors in either forest or water-based outdoor recreation (Kelly, 1980). Gender, age, family life cycle, income, race, occupational level, and education together account for less than eight percent of the variance in whether or not people participate in resource-based outdoor recreation.

What may be more useful is to examine population trends in relation to participation trends. Two stand out:

1) The "middle mass" of the population is more and more likely to engage in recreational travel—almost always by car (85 percent) and often to special destinations.

2) That "middle mass" is aging so that styles of recreational travel
    associated with postparental and early retirement life periods will
    be more common.

Other trends include smaller families with compact childrearing periods,
more families with single parents, the majority of adult women in the work force,
and more adults not living in a family unit. Together, these suggest that the
formerly standard style of camping and resource use—the family with children—will be less common. Nevertheless, a general summary is that a wide
spectrum of individuals can be expected to engage in outdoor recreation even
though fewer will be in two-parent, childrearing families.

More specifically, who are they? Most often they are persons on holiday or
vacation. Especially those visiting destination attractions are investing a block
of time in a "punctuating" special event that is different from their weekly round
of leisure. Such events are in the "balance" rather than the day-to-day "core" of
activities, important partly because they are extraordinary. Like core activity,
however, such events may be important partly because they provide an opportunity for interaction with significant other persons. Most people come to the
forest or the shore in groups. Most groups are not occasional, but are preformed
family and friendship associations that change through the life course. The
relationships, then, are almost always central to the experience. The environment is, among other things, a different and distant locale that affords opportunity for the expression of relationships that are different from the ordinary round
of life.

Nevertheless, most recreation visitors to outdoor resources are limited in
both time and money. Most are middle income, requiring that they do almost
everything on a budget, with some sense of maximizing the experience and
minimizing expenses. In economic terms, their outdoor recreation is price-
elastic, to some extent a calculation of obtaining the fullest experience within the
limits of financial and temporal expenditure. They may budget time even more
carefully than money. Those who specialize in a particular activity or seek
specific environments will design a trip to maximize the time for a trout stream,
rock face, or wilderness trek (Buchanan, 1985).

It would be neat and useful to profile the "typical park visitor. "On-site
research, however, demonstrates that there is considerable variety in styles of
recreation, even in similar environments. For example, an observational study
of those camping at developed sites in the Pacific Northwest produced a number
of varied camping styles.

They include:

1) "Budget campers" using the campground as a low cost base for
    access to resources.

2) "Travellers" for whom the campground is a cheap overnight accommodation.

3) "Sportscar couples" with minimal tents and equipment, short stays, an itinerary, and a suitcase full of dress clothes for stops in a city every fourth or fifth night.

4) "Student campers" of two varieties:
   (a) the "explorers going where no one has gone before" and,
   (b) "party campers" using the campground as a place to celebrate school holidays.

5) "Family campers" of several varieties:
   (a) "Expressive nurturers" who use the environment to foster communication and learning with their children,
   (b) "Role players" with a father doing provider tasks, going fishing, and leaving maintenance and caregiving to women,
   (c) "Staging area campers" with children old enough to peel off and find peers for family-independent activity, and
   (d) many combinations of the types.

6) "Breakaway campers" for whom the central aim is to get as far away from others as seems safe and viable.

7) "Comfort campers" who bring along every possible home device and change as little as possible from home conveniences. A variation are the "power campers" whose goal seems to be to live a fully electrified life in the woods. "V campers" are a variation of comfort campers who combine RVs and TVs and may even rent the third V, videos.

8) "Toe-in-the-water campers" who aren't sure they like all the outdoor stuff, but give it a try for the sake of significant companions.

9) "Extractors" who use the campsite as a base from which to forage for fish, game, or anything else that can be legally removed.

No doubt there are other styles as well, especially in more densely populated areas where camp site use is more focused in a particular activity or resource. Recently, different styles have also been identified based on cultural or ethnic background as well as commitment to a specific activity. Overall, the spectrum of resource based recreators may be identified by activity, group, or age cohort.

1) There is a continuum of resource visitors from those who come to engage in a particular activity to which they have a long-term commitment, "specialists" in the activity (Bryan, 1977), to those who just want to be in a different environment for a change. Frequently those with a particular activity commitment such as fishing or geological exploration, will form a group that develops timetables, interaction rituals, and spatial designations.

2) Others vary according to the kind of group to which they are attached (Dottavio et al., 1980). Families with young children, families with teens, couples exploring a relationship, couples with a long-established relationship, groups of families, activity based groups, single-sex groups seeking a change from back home associations, retirees without a deadline, and many others come to the resource with recreation aims that are social as much as environmental.

3) Further, current age cohorts may differ from the way that older cohorts came to the same resource before. Those who are 40-50 today tend to be more educated, more concerned about the natural environment, and have smaller families and more discretionary income than did those of the same age 20 years ago. Now the "active old," persons in their 50s, 60s, and even 70s, are more likely to engage in active and even strenuous encounters with the environment than previous generations. Expectations along with resources change from decade to decade.

No simple set of factors can delineate either group composition or activity styles. Rather, they are a response to multiple elements of opportunities, interests, histories, relationships, roles, and resources that shift through the life course. Some outdoor recreation is accessible to home and can be inserted into weekly schedules in season. For most, however, gaining access to a special resource is a punctuating event, a change from the ordinary habitats of urban living to the special meanings of the natural resources.

What Are They Doing?

There is, of course no simple answer. Those who come to the forest, mountain, desert, and water have a variety of motivations. They want to be together and get away, find excitement as well as relaxation and a reduction of stress, involvement and disengagement, change and yet predictable limits. Their patterns of activity, then, may reflect this lack of consistency.

Again, they usually come together. The composition of the group is a central factor in what they do (Field and O'Leary, 1973). The activity oriented party may shape their schedules and provisions around the activity—river rafting, back-country hiking, fishing, or making the round of major "sights." Others use the activities as contexts for interaction. The life course approach is a useful framework from which to analyze variations in group composition and activity:

- A group of students will see a park as a party environment with activities oriented toward interactive "fun," many of which are simply transferred from back-home patterns.

- A couple exploring an intimate relationship may use the site to be "alone together" and do almost everything together.

- Parents of young children have concerns for safety and bedtime quiet as well as for activities that maximize familial interaction.

- Parents of older children often seek environments for shared learning experiences as well as possibilities for activity that separates children off with their peers.

- Single parents, usually mothers, may see the outdoor locale as a special opportunity for sharing responsibility with children in the process of camping.

- Older couples are more likely to plan trips with designated stopover points and to define the trip as just as important as the destinations. They may also be most open to interaction with others having similar interests and relaxed timetables.

A central factor in what people do is whom they are with. Further, most often, the group originated in an urban area. The natural resource presents opportunities quite different from the concrete, small apartment, telephone, shopping mall, and even the swimming pool or tennis court. The groups seek environmental change as well as common activity. They are in a strange place even though usually with familiar companions. Home routines, if not roles, have been left behind.

They both adapt to the new environment and adapt the environment to themselves. Familiar patterns of privacy, communication, time allocation, and task assignment have to be renegotiated for the changed spaces and amenities. At the same time, they may turn the campsite into a comfort zone resembling a California patio, cut firewood beyond possible use to dramatize competence as a provider, and build symbolic barriers against neighbors. Outdoor recreation, like the rest of life, involves a negotiation between the self and the environment.

Some write about "the wilderness experience" as though it were singular and undifferentiated. Actually there are innumerable kinds of natural environment experiences with dimensions of appreciation, escape, social involvement, and learning. The intent of all, however, is to combine the resource opportunities, companions, and their own action into an enjoyable set of experiences.

There is considerable research indicating that for most vacationers activities come in bundles or packages (McCool, 1978). These clusters more or less fit the opportunities (Ditton et al., 1975). There is a "fit" between the setting, its resources, and the aims of participants. Sites are selected because of that fit between resources—rock faces, stocks of fish, graded hiking trails, or beach access—and the histories and intentions of the group. In the bundle, there are three components: the group and its commitments, the space and its resources, and time with its articulated allocations. Preferred locales offer opportunities for activities that cluster together for the preformed groups.

The styles of camping listed earlier suggest that broad categories of activity may be quite deceptive. Even such a typology obscures the nuances with which every individual and group compose their particular matrix of activity. For example, in breaking away from normal routines and locales, many hope to engage in some exploration. They may be more likely to "try it out" than at home. Such an approach is developmental, using the special opportunity to be and become someone a bit different from ordinary life. So many of the identities of life are routinized into situated roles that the challenge of the outdoor environment becomes a moment of relative openness.

Both the challenge and the change are significant elements of outdoor recreation. Physical challenge is coupled with challenges of coping and the exercise of skill in the rapids, the surf, the trail, or the mountainside. The concept of *specialization* (Bryan, 1977; also see Chapter 18) suggests long-term commitment to skill development. It may also orient activity choices to particular environments that offer the appropriate challenge. Hiking into a secluded trout stream is required when a placid river or lake will not provide the special experience.

Probably more common is *diversity* within recreation groups. Seldom is there total agreement in priorities for time and resource allocation. Age differences divide families. Personal recreation histories include negative as well as positive experiences. Gender may differentiate both back home roles and socialization (Shaw, 1985). The common support and nurture roles assigned to women may be resisted when expected in the campground or on the trail. The bundle of activities and tasks developed by a family may reflect patterns of power and decision making as well as the preferences of different members.

Most often the total recreation event is characterized by combinations of change and carryover, escape and responsibility. One trip may be designed to incorporate specialized fishing for some, relaxed interaction and task sharing for others, a reduction of stress and the high exertion of a hike, forgetting schedules and meal planning, getting away from some and close to others. The implications are manifold: For a group, it means that an event requires accommodation of a diversity of aims, hopes, and requirements. It means that flexible and varied environments that support a diversity of activities tend to be most desirable and likely produce the maximum total satisfaction. And it means that narrow stereotypes of visitors are more often wrong than right.

What Do They Want?

Amidst all this diversity, are there any clear patterns of what those entering natural environments for recreation want? Action and anticipation are not separable, but are united in every stage of a recreation event. One summary of motivations lists three kinds of reasons for participation (Schreyer, 1986): social interaction or "sharing enjoyment," escape or change, and the development of self-worth. In most situations, an event combines all three of these generic experiences.

The special time and place of outdoor recreation, for a day or weekend or vacation, provides an opportunity for both the social and action dimensions of leisure. The special environments offer opportunity for kinds of activity not possible, at least on the same level, in more mundane settings. They also offer separation from the ordinary and the enrichment of contact with their special resources. No scale of satisfactions can adequately capture what is unique about water rushing through down a rocky canyon, a sunset over a fir-circled lake, or a glacier-clad mountain. The experience is always something more than any analytical recollective summaries.

Nevertheless, there are some patterns found in resource based outdoor recreation meanings. One is that expectations tend to be high. When a precious time is set aside for a once-a-year event, both the direct costs and the other possibilities foregone heighten the perceived value and hopes. Further, those meanings tend to be diverse. The experiences are, as already suggested, multidimensional. A complex event such as a park visit has combinations and sequences of outcomes, both positive and negative.

Research tied to activity in resources suggests the following guidelines:

- Individuals bring their own aims and agendas to the resource that shape choices and what is sought in the event.

- The type of environment and provisions from the highly developed to the primitive is only one factor in determining outcomes. Social environments, who you are with, may be more salient than where you are (Knopf et al., 1983).

- An event such as camping is not really an activity as much as a context for action and interaction. Further, an event that takes place over time is inevitably quite varied in outcomes and satisfactions with its own "career" of ups and downs (Schreyer, 1984).

- An event may have polar as well as complementary meanings. A single forest visit may include excitement seeking and relaxation, solitude and togetherness, security and self-testing (Wahlers and Etzel, 1985). Such diversity in meanings is reinforced by the common diversity within recreation groups.

What do people want in their special-environment experiences?

1) They want to escape, to get away;

2) They want to escape together, to foster intimacy and enhance communication with valued and enjoyed other persons;

3) They want to "let go" in emotional release and expression, to know different affective responses in the different environment;

4) They want to "be themselves," to break away from the rules and roles of everyday life and seek a fundamental authenticity that may be denied in ordinary routines; and,

5) They want an experience that is based on the special environment, an immersion in the natural that provides a balance to the usual built and artificial locales of everyday life. Such an experience is partly a matter of space and openness, partly of scope and variety, and partly of aesthetics and beauty.

Who comes to these special places? Except for the urban poor, almost all kinds of people, with a diversity of hopes and histories. For them the forest, water, mountain, or historic site are contexts for action and interaction. They come seeking and creating an experience that has many elements, both familiar and unique to the time and place.

They come to nearby sites on hurried day trips, often with a specific activity purpose. They fish, sail, hike, or picnic in a limited time and then leave. More and more, they come on a mini-vacation, an extended weekend that allows for somewhat more travel, fuller escape, and more of a sense of a resource based event. And, of course, they come on the traditional vacation, trying to create an experience and a memory that will highlight the other 50 or so weeks of the year.

In every case, however, they are combining their own purposive action with the opportunities of the resource, a resource valued enough to warrant the investment of self and those scarcities of time, money, energy, and imagination.

REFERENCES

Bryan, H. (1977). Leisure value systems and recreational specialization: The case of trout fishermen. *Journal of Leisure Research, 9*(3), 82-91.

Buchanan, T. (1985). Commitment and leisure behavior: A theoretical perspective. *Leisure Studies, 7,* 401-420.

Cichetti, C. (1972). A review of the empirical analyses based on the national recreation surveys. *Journal of Leisure Research, 4,* 90-107.

Dottavio, D., O'Leary, J., and Koth, B. (1980). The social group variable in recreation participation studies. *Journal of Leisure Research, 12,* 357-367.

Ditton, R., Goodale, T., and Johnson, P. (1975). A cluster analysis of activity, frequency, and environmental variables to identify water-based recreation types. *Journal of Leisure Research, 7,* 282-295.

Field, D., and O'Leary, J. (1973). Social groups as a basis for assessing participation in selected water-based activities. *Journal of Leisure Research, 5,* 15-25.

Kelly, J. R. (1980). Outdoor recreation participation: A comparative analysis. *Leisure Sciences, 3,* 129-154.

Knopf, R., Peterson, G., and Leatherberry, E. (1983). Motivations for river floating: Relative consistency across settings. *Leisure Sciences, 5,* 231-256.

McCool, S. (1978). Recreational activity packages at water-based resources. *Leisure Sciences, 1,* 163-174.

Schreyer, R. (1984). Social dimensions of carrying capacity: An overview. *Leisure Sciences, 6,* 387-394.

Schreyer, R. (1986). Motivations for participation in outdoor recreation and barriers to participation. Review papers for the report of the President's Commission on Americans Outdoors. Washington, DC.

Shaw, S. (1985). The meanings of leisure in everyday life. *Leisure Sciences,* *7,* 1-24

Wahlers, R., and Etzel, M. (1985). Vacation preference as a manifestation of optimal stimulation and lifestyle experiences. *Journal of Leisure Research,* *17,* 283-295.

CHAPTER *32*

The Arts as Leisure

T he histories of leisure and the arts are intertwined in any culture or sequences of cultures. We marvel at the intricacy and subtlety of graphic arts produced in relatively isolated island cultures of the South Pacific. The small sculptures and vessels from China are breathtaking in their own right and surprising when we realize they may be thousands of years old. In Greece the performance of original music and poetry was considered to be the height of social grace among the privileged elites. The explosion of the arts in the European Renaissance transformed the culture in its glorification of the human mind, body, and spirit. The architecture of the great Gothic cathedrals with their spires and spaces reflect a culture dominated by religious devotion and ecclesiastical power. The revival of the Japanese tea ceremony dramatizes a grace and precision characteristic of classical themes in the arts of that culture. And the 20th century music of Mahler, Stravinsky, and Ives blends new harmonics with folk tunes and tonalities.

In retrospect we tend to judge the worth of an historic culture more by the remaining evidence of its artistic works than by its mundane products. Even in contemporary societies with their technological preoccupations and economic imperatives, art is often viewed as the acme of the culture, the dimension that draws life above the repetition of drab functions and indistinguishable products. Those who reach the pinnacles of popular and commercial success in many performing arts are rewarded richly, often extravagantly, in popular arts of music and film. For the most part, however, those who engage in artistic production have only modest or even submarginal economic rewards. For most there is a central element of leisure, engaging in the activity primarily for its own sake, for the experience. Most artists, by necessity as much as by choice, are amateurs. Both producing and appreciating artistic performance is leisure for most, despite the constant tie between quality and the experience.

The arts as leisure take the related forms of performance and appreciation, of production and consumption. The performance may be highly professional, whether the performers are among the few "stars" who are highly paid or the vast majority who are paid below the levels of most sales or midmanagement personnel in business. The appreciation may involve a high level of knowledge and discrimination, usually based on a personal history of involvement, or may be more a matter of untutored enjoyment. On a given evening, professional levels of performance may be mediocre or worse and amateur offerings be superb in quality. On the other hand, for a decade the most often produced amateur, usually school, play was "Aaron Slick from Punkin Crick" and the best-known theme from classical music, from the William Tell overture,was heard weekly on the "Lone Ranger" radio program. The arts are not just rarefied symbols of high social status; they are woven into the commerce of life in ways often taken for granted.

Sociological analysis of the arts includes a number of interrelated issues: What are the institutional foundations of artistic production and consumption? How are production and consumption related? What are the symbolic meanings of the ways arts are displayed and disseminated? Is art used to reinforce social divisions in a stratified society? Is art relatively autonomous or bound into the institutional reward and control structures of the society? What are the conditions that foster artistic innovation or enforce conformity? And, perhaps most difficult, is the evaluation of quality internal to the art or an extension of fundamental power perpetuation in a social system? The large question would appear to be something like: Are there social conditions that produce or stifle great art?

From a leisure perspective, the issues are a bit more narrow: What is the nature of art and especially the relation of the so-called "fine" and "folk" arts? As leisure, arts participation may be divided into the reciprocal elements of appreciation and creation. Both involve social and economic support. This chapter, then, will address in order: arts appreciation, social and economic support of the arts, and creation in the arts.

What Are the Fine Arts?

To begin with, it is evident that almost anything can be considered an artistic product. A pot may be art when it is unique and characterized by a grace or embellishment given by the potter. A simple tune may be classic in its lack of elaboration. A wordless mime may infuse an ordinary action with singular poetry of motion. The variety of art forms and styles cross cultural and historic barriers with similarities and discontinuities. In fact, the lack of continuity and consensus in contemporary art as well as thought has been given the label of "postmodernism." Some argue that any former standards of what is "classical" and even what is art have been dissolved into a bewildering diversity without shape and coherence.

Sociologists studying art have usually taken an inclusive perspective (Zolberg, 1990). Further, they have often been relativistic in dealing with standards of quality. One problem with this approach is that it fails to deal with an art as "discipline." As in any discipline, there are forms and criteria, however loose and even contradictory, that are utilized by those who practice the art. Even those who choose to violate ordinary canons of quality do so as a deliberate act of innovation or even revolution. A comprehensive sociology of the arts will incorporate the history and structure of those internal vocabularies, criteria, and forms as well as the social contexts of production and consumption.

As to forms, the so-called fine arts tend to blend into the more common or ordinary forms in ways that defy clear distinctions. Classical music weaves in folk themes. Sculpture utilizes ordinary materials and even items of "junk." Poetry incorporates slang and regional idiom. Painting blends in oblongs of photography or is created with the new palette of the computer. An untutored "primitive" artist is recognized as a special talent when well-trained professionals are discarded as derivative and without creative ability. The traditional "fine" and "folk" distinction is more ignored than honored. A distinction that remains salient, however, is that of marketed "popular culture" with its transient orientation toward target markets and mass distribution.

One typology of the arts illustrates the common distinction:

Figure 32.1 Types of Art

	Fine Art	Popular Art
Original or Live Work	Symphonic music, chamber music	Popular music, folk music
	Opera	Musical comedy
	Serious contemporary music	Jazz
	Public monumental art	Works sold at stores or art fairs
	Ballet	Show dance
	Modern dance	Modern dance
	Serious drama	Serious drama
	Experimental theater	Experimental theater
Reproduced Works	TV—educational channel	TV—light programming
	Art and classic films	Popular films
	Serious novels/nonfiction	Mass market books
	Specialized periodicals	Mass circulation periodicals
	Poetry/literary criticism	Advertising
	Art comic strip books	Mass circulation comics

(Source: V. Zolberg, *Constructing a Sociology of the Arts*, p. 144)

Distinctions may be between "serious" and "light" in the demands made on both the producer and consumer. Yet, this seems to be contradicted by placing all jazz in the popular category. Russell Lynes (1949) divided arts into "highbrow," "middlebrow," and "lowbrow" suggesting that consumer tastes reflect the general cultural divisions of the society. He argued that there are accepted "tastemakers" who assign levels that come to symbolize cultural strata. Conversely, contemporary sociologist Herbert Gans (1974) believes that there are "taste cultures" that cut across social strata and that defy evaluations of quality. For him, taste is a matter of choice, whatever the learned contexts and symbolic functions of "youth cultures" or ethnic styles. In a more negative approach, Pierre Bourdieu (1984) argues that artistic tastes are used to perpetuate social inequality. So-called high culture not only identifies the social elites, but becomes a symbol of social inferiority among those who come to define themselves as of lesser status and worth. Art and its appreciation becomes symbolic capital in the serious status game that marks those who are deserving from lesser beings. One danger is that sociologists reinforce such uses of the arts for social ends by their hierarchical categorizations and ignore the leisure element in which arts participation is primarily for the immediate experience, not the social payoff.

In any case, the distinction between appreciation and creation is fundamental to any analysis, whatever the theoretical framework. The arts as leisure clearly includes both. As such, it also includes the businesses that market artistic products, governmental actions that support some arts and censor others, and both professionals and amateurs.

The Arts as Appreciation

Attendance at arts performances is a major element of arts engagement as leisure. Further, the likelihood of such participation is related to education and especially to experiences of higher education (see Table 32.1).

In 1985 about 23 million people attended at least one classical music concert, 30 million a musical play, 21 million live drama, and 39 million visited an art museum or gallery. As arts supporters are fond of pointing out, more people visited a museum than a professional baseball or football game. Education level has more of an effect on arts participation than any other kind of leisure. In an earlier study of attending performing events, those with some graduate school education made up more than 50 percent of the male and 30 percent of the female audience although they were then less than 5 percent of the population (Baumol and Bowen, 1966).

It is significant to note the interaction of gender and education history. Women are slightly more likely to attend arts performances than men despite the greater proportion of men with graduate school education. In projecting future

Table 32.1 Participation Percentages in Appreciative Arts Activity

Activity		Total	Male	Female	H. S. Grad.	Coll. Grad.
Attend	Classical music concert	13%	11%	14%	7%	29%
	Opera	3%	2%	3%	1%	6%
	Plays	12%	11%	12%	6%	26%
	Ballet	4%	3%	5%	2%	9%
	Jazz concert	10%	10%	9%	7%	18%
	Musical plays	17%	15%	19%	12%	34%
Visit art museum		22%	21%	23%	14%	45%
Read books		56%	48%	63%	52%	78%

(Source: Statistical Abstract of the United States, 1988)

attendance at the performing arts, both factors are important. First, the percentage of adults with graduate education is increasing, especially among women. At the same time, the proportion of women in the work force has risen dramatically in the last decades. Women, then, may have more financial resources under their own control, but significantly less time available.

Although there are some levels of the performing arts available in most communities, metropolitan centers are the focus of high level arts appreciation opportunities. There appears to be a cosmopolitan lifestyle associated with urban centers that includes discretionary income, higher education, and affiliation with organizations that support performing groups. Those styles, however, vary. There are younger and less conventional supporters of off-Broadway, side-street, and experimental theater. There are those who frequent jazz clubs. Social status, on the other hand, appears to be a factor among the more conventional members of symphony and opera guilds for whom "opening night" is a major social occasion.

Receiving less attention, but woven into the lifestyles of many outside the great cities and distant from the "Big 5" symphony orchestras or even regional opera and ballet companies, are community and school productions. Colleges, high schools, community theaters, volunteer community orchestras and choirs, outdoor summer performances, and a variety of organizations offer the performing arts on some level of skill to localized audiences. Summer festivals are tied to tourism programs and become destinations for those planning vacations. Some musical programs establish long traditions and attract visitors from across the country and abroad. Symphony in the Grand Tetons of Wyoming, Bach in central Oregon, international music camp in Michigan, opera in Santa Fe, and Shakespeare in Ontario are among the offerings that combine natural environments with the performing arts and become vacation meccas for many who seek both. Further, national services organize tours of individual performers, groups, and even entire productions that cross the country bringing the arts to school and community auditoriums in areas that cannot support local productions of quality. Statistics are unreliable, but a considerable proportion of those millions of attendances are to such local and regional productions.

Public television, specialized cable channels, and occasionally the major networks also bring fine arts performances into the home. Previously, seeing and hearing the best performers was denied to most people and might be a once-in-a-lifetime event for others. Now the legendary performers of the past and the present sing, dance, act, and even create before the camera. Children and youth may experience the highest quality, even if the small screen is only a shadow of a live performance. Their standards and their visions are raised to new heights never demonstrated by the local dance instructor or musical aggregation. Although viewer ratings may seem small alongside those for Sunday football or a top-rated sitcom, they are there to be chosen by those who value the experience. And those who watch dance and opera on television are far and away most likely to go to live performances (Robinson, 1987). Also, at home individuals read poetry and listen to classical music on the radio or on their own sound systems. Investments in high-fidelity music systems with the new technologies of compact disks are already challenged by other digital systems of reproduction range from $100 to several thousand dollars. Music becomes for many as continual a part of the life-supporting atmosphere as sunlight and oxygen. The vast markets for high-fidelity units in cars is based on classical as well as popular music tastes.

One other factor in arts appreciation is worthy of attention. First noticed in relation to those who attend dance performances, there is also a relationship between a history of participation and later appreciation. Those who have studied dance, usually as children or youth, are most likely to attend ballet or other dance performances as adults. While the relationship is not as strong for music and drama, the most discriminating and loyal supporters of the performing arts are often those who have been producers at some time and at some level. As a consequence, more than any other kind of leisure, there is a connection that can be traced between school and later life. Opportunities to create music, art, theater, or dance in school are significant springboards to adult support and appreciation. Of course, arts programs of a high quality are most often found in the schools of communities with high income levels and whose children are most likely to attend quality colleges and universities. Despite the evident tie between social status and arts engagement, other related factors make those of higher social status most prepared to be discriminating supporters and appreciators.

Household studies of leisure participation also suggest that attendance at performing arts events may be highly correlated with education, but not age

(Kelly, 1987a). There is no significant decrease in attendance at live theater or concerts by age from the twenties through the period of "active" aging and until the onset of frailty limits getting out of the house and access to most public buildings. As a consequence, the aging of the population does not pose the same kind of threat to arts appreciation that it does to participation in sports or more demanding outdoor activities.

In the United States in 1985, about $2 billion was spent on arts performances, just a little less than on sports events. Adjusted for inflation, however, this figure has changed little in the past two decades (Robinson, 1987). Robinson argues that the elite nature of performing arts audiences may be exaggerated despite the significance of educational background. His analysis is that the average attendee is middle-income with some college education and in a nonprestige white-collar occupation. Over one-third of those who go to jazz concerts have not been to college. Further, there are two population groups that have high levels of performing arts attendance regardless of education. One supports the social status position; it is those with incomes above $50,000. The other, however, supports the socialization analysis; it is those in occupations related to social science and teaching. Women's participation is higher for ballet, musical theater, and classical music, supporting the importance of prior experience and socialization. And, of course, the life course factor has some influence with the middle-aged somewhat more likely to attend than those in the childrearing period.

Arts supporters are not narrow in their tastes, according to Robinson (1987). Those who attend sports events are 2.4 times more likely to attend musical theater than those who do not attend sports events, 2.2 times more likely to visit museums, and 2.6 times more often at jazz performances. There are, however, certain stylistic patterns that suggest that appreciation of the arts is part of an overall style. Attendance at concerts, for example, is strongly associated with gourmet cooking; but it is also related to the ordinary activity of gardening.

Tastes are acquired, after all. That is the basis of the education appreciation connection. Being part of a family or social group that makes the arts a central part of life is the foundation of appreciation. Both educational opportunities and a history of performance, however, can counteract limitations in family background or interest. More than any other leisure activity, appreciation and creation in the arts are based on both the quantity and quality of education.

Support of the Arts

In 1986, there were more than 1600 community orchestras in the United States with budgets of almost a half billion dollars. More than 1100 companies were producing opera. The 170 professional companies had budgets of about $170 million. Libraries are usually tax-supported; but theater, dance, museums, orchestras, and opera companies have to raise most of their own financial support. Some comes from admission receipts. The remainder, however, has to be sought from public and private sources.

The National Endowment for the Arts, while a significant presence in the field, operates on a very limited budget and has had to cope with reductions. Along with some state agencies, the NEA supports organizations and individual artists who apply for support and are selected by committees that represent both the arts and political interests. As in any such competition, the organizations and individuals who are established and in the mainstream of styles and tastes tend to have a considerable advantage in the process. Other financial support is given by foundations that allocate all or a part of their incomes to the arts. Local or regional foundations join with corporations to underwrite programs in their areas. Perhaps the most consistent support has come from educational institutions that not only have their own performance programs, but subsidize and provide a performance location for external groups.

National and state support always has a political dimension. Members of commissions are usually chosen as an honorific return for political favors or campaign financial contributions. As a consequence, they tend to represent establishment perspectives and tastes. The accusation of censorship occasionally is leveled at such official funding bodies when an art exhibition or performance is denied funding or support is withdrawn after objections are raised. Complaints may be based on alleged violations of community standards in relation to sexual norms, religious customs, or political ideologies. The fundamental freedom that is presupposed in artistic creation comes in conflict with the social conventions and political divisions when public funding is at issue.

Just as significant are the more subtle pressures and limitations placed on the arts in relation to private support. Foundation boards, corporate officers, and individuals who donate to professional, semiprofessional, and amateur performing groups tend to support those who demonstrate a faithfulness to their own tastes and interests. While some foundations appoint advisory boards of artists and experts, they also usually represent relatively conventional perspectives in their fields.

It is the market, however, that may be the most significant force determining what is performed, by whom, and how. Paintings are purchased through dealers who select for display what is most likely to sell. Music directors of mid-level orchestras recruit "name" guest performers, advertise "pops" concerts with programs designed to attract the so-called "middlebrow" audience, and even sprinkle their standard programs with tried-and-true selections. Anything innovative has to be rationed carefully and over-balanced with standard repertoire. For dance companies, holiday Nutcrackers pay the bills for the remainder of the season. Theater companies seldom produce anything radically critical of the accepted values of the society and most often have schedules dominated by plays and musicals with well-known reputations for entertainment. The arts depend on the audience, especially those who will pay for the privilege. It is no wonder that experimental theater is seldom found outside of major cities and the departments of universities and colleges.

Two issues are relevant here: The first is the recurring one of the relationship of the arts to social status. The second is that of social control of the arts through the funding and sanctioning mechanisms of the society.

Especially local arts organizations—community symphony orchestras, theater and opera, and museums—depend on the local sources of financial support. The "guilds" that are founded to provide that support tend to enlist the social elites of the community. In fact, the annual symphony guild dinner dance, usually at the country club, may be *the* major social event of the year. Social status depends not only on being seen there, but in being listed among the donors. Programs with categories designating the level of financial contribution are published and distributed so there will be no mistake about responding on a scale commensurate with presumed status. Dinners before the opening nights of the premiere events or visits by prestige performers are implicit symbols of the social hierarchy, often with status inherited from two or more generations of community status. Such symbolic connections of status and the arts not only reinforce the image of the fine arts as being only for a self-selected minority, a matter of special taste, but also tend to exclude those whose status does not measure up. Zolberg (1990) argues that the audience is a social construction tied to the symbolic culture and institutional divisions of a social system. An exclusive focus on differential tastes obscures and audience pleasure-seeking ignores all the ways in which appreciation and support of the arts are produced by the socializing and stratifying institutions of the school, the economy, and even the polity.

Social control is more than selecting audiences according to price and acquired taste. In totalitarian systems the arts are often directed to provide direct propaganda supporting the ideologies and even practices of the regime. Ancient Rome was not alone in providing mass entertainments for those excluded from political power. The former Soviet Union consistently supported film-making that glorified the mythical socialist worker and banned music considered to represent the "decadent West." Eastern bloc arts festivals had to submit their programs to Soviet censors. Even composers went in and out of favor with changes in ruling elites.

In the United States where most citizens support conventional ideologies and related vocabularies and symbol systems, the arts are regulated more by the market than by state intervention. Nevertheless, as outlined in the historical chapters, all sorts of policies of taxation, licensing, and direct financial subvention shape what is available, especially to the masses. The very fact that the arts require an audience means that they require space, means of public notice and promotion, and the ability to carry out financial negotiations. All kinds of barriers can be placed, directly and bureaucratically, in the way of launching anything new. Media policies may prevent announcement, and banks may refuse a line of credit. In general, those renderings that celebrate the accepted value systems tend to be enabled, and those that are deemed critical or even subversive have to surmount a variety of formal and informal barriers. Outright censorship is seldom necessary to keep things in line.

Creation in the Arts

From a leisure perspective, creation is primary. On all sorts of levels and with a full range of formal training, people of all ages are *doing the arts*. The venue may change through the life course, like sport especially when leaving school. Nevertheless, small children draw, act, sing, and dance their way through the day. Performance is not an alien activity that must be inculcated in children; it is expression that creates form as well as responds to the performance of others.

Some have developed theory and research based on the premise that creation is an unusual and esoteric activity, that there is something different and special about artistic production. If so, it is due as much to stifling and truncating the natural as it is to the difficulties of being a viable artist. There is a playful and imaginative impulse in children. Some argue that the adult institutional world tends to inhibit that impulse. If so, then the issue is not why people try to create, but how some make it through the filters of conformist society to continue to try. Further, what are the sources of real innovation, of artistic endeavor that breaks through the merely competent?

Howard Becker (1982), a sociologist, argues that artists live in small "worlds" of interaction that shape and support their efforts. Total focus on the individual artist misses the ways in which artistic subcultures provide an interactional context for mentoring, leadership, deviation, and even eccentricity. Bourdieu (1980) adds that the subculture of artists provides the primary set of standards that artists accept as relevant. Art may then be innovative or traditional. In the end, however, there are the institutionalized gatekeepers in the schools, museums, agencies, galleries, and endowments that offer or withhold recognition.

For example, an experimental theater group can exist at a subsistence level with only mutual support and a minimal dedicated audience. To not only survive but develop, however, some more established theater organization will have to recognize and appropriate the creative director, designer, or performing personnel. Then, that established theater provides the springboard to wider acceptance and support. What begins in a loft may end with national awards, visiting professorships, and foundations seeking to lend support. This is, in the end, a social process in which immediate interactional communities are the basis for commitment and risk-taking that becomes incorporated into the institutional-ized system. This process, abstracted from actual cases in contemporary Chicago theater, is paralleled in other arts.

There is, of course, also the individual question. What distinguishes those who become creative artists (and perhaps scholars) from the run-of-the-mill who add little to the development of the art or discipline? Sociologists might argue that factors of time and place, being in the right institutional milieu with the right sponsors, are always relevant. Psychologists have not offered any definitive answer, perhaps recognizing the variety in temperaments and personalities accepted as creative. One basic approach, however, suggests that those who are creative are "problem finders" rather than just "problem solvers" (Getzels and Csikszentmihalyi, 1976). They are risk-takers who have the courage or the assurance to do more than follow the agendas of others. The stereotype of the artist as having the capacity for divergent thinking and a certain "inner-directedness," to use the Riesman term, is fairly accurate.

Two other aspects of creativity merit attention: The first is to dispel the myth of seclusion. Those who are not productive often ascribe their failures to external conditions. They believe that if only they could be separated from the ordinary pressures and demands of life, they, too, could be creative. The problem with this defense is that too many of the world's most creative artists have lived very much in the world of demand and even conflict. Mozart was preoccupied with economic survival. Bach had his children and his weekly performances. Charles Ives managed an insurance business. Leonard Bernstein withdrew from the New York orchestra in order to be more productive as a composer, but never matched the creativity of what he had produced when caught in the midst of timetables, pressures, and deadlines. Despite the dream of creative locales or protected leisure times, there is no evidence that there is any perfect environment that will ensure production. For the most part, artists have to manage conflicting elements of life that seeks some balance as do ordinary people.

The second issue is that of freedom. Certainly freedom is central to creation in the arts, perhaps the freedom for action more than freedom from constraint. Dance is limited by the capabilities of the body as well as the forms of music. Painting is limited by the dimensions and textures of materials and theater by language and the stage. Yet, even within traditional forms, art has a dimension of newness. However conventional, any work of art is something that has not existed before, an offering of the artist that adds to the world. The freedom to choose and the satisfaction of production are united in artistic work. What is most contemporary in the arts is the inclusion of new media and forms. Traditional limits are always being pushed outward in the act of creation.

On the one hand, the artist works with limiting materials. The poet uses the language even when inventing new terms and twisting old forms. The painter may incorporate three-dimensional materials, but still has limits of size and shape as well as verticality. Fantasy and play are a part of the innovative element of creation, yet involve form and discipline. Even though the artist is always working toward a new future, the "not yet" of life and existence, there are recognizable skills and forms in the product. The arts, then, combine discipline and freedom. In fact, in most cases, the greatest powers of innovation are exhibited by those with the fullest mastery of technique. A high level of creation, then, calls for commitment to skill in addition to some innate ability. There is craft in molding a delicate platter of pottery, flowing through the lines of a Bach aria, or immersion in the dimensions of an O'Neill play.

As leisure and as creation, doing the arts involves both learning and producing. Innovation involves disciplined skill as well as risk. Creation in the arts may bring into the world something new and expressive, intensely personal; and yet is based on an investment of the self in the craft. At the center of art is the paradox of freedom and discipline. From a social perspective, the paradox requires that any art have an infrastructure of learning, places to learn and demonstrate the craft in a climate that permits and even encourages freedom of expression. In a totalitarian context, art requires rebellion and even revolution. In a repressive condition, at the very least art involves resistance.

Who Is Doing the Arts?

Two trends in arts participation seem in opposition. The first is the indication of a short-term decrease in arts participation during the 1980s (Kelly, 1987a). The reason is simple to locate. Women have been most likely to engage in the arts, especially women with some higher education. With a higher proportion of those women in the work force, time available for demanding arts participation is reduced. In fact, the reductions in engagement in activities such as painting have been less for men than for women, somewhat reducing the gender gap. The problem of time compression for employed women seems to have taken its toll.

The counter trend is based on the consistent relationship between participation in the arts and higher education. Each cohort of men and women in the population has higher rates of higher education background than the older cohorts. At a consequence, it would be reasonable to project a long-term increase in engagement in arts production, especially by amateurs. The key is not vague interest or occasional dabbling. The close tie between satisfaction and skill development suggests that commitment is central. Schools may offer opportunities to gain interests and develop abilities. However, without enough commitment to continue development, arts engagement will either fade or have cycles of participation.

In a national survey of 20,000 households, variations in commitment are indexed by the regularity of participation (see Table 32.2).

Table 32. 2 Frequency of Participation in Cultural Activity

Activity	Total	Days in the past 12 months			
		Under 11	11-23	24-41	42+
Adult education	14.7%	6.2%	2.5%	1.6%	4.4%
Attending music/dance	15.7%	13.9%	1.1%	0.4%	0.2%
Live theater	16.1%	14.9%	0.9%	0.2%	0.2%
Listening to music	46.4%	13.8%	2.2%	2.9%	27.5%
Painting/drawing	5.5%	3.2%	0.6%	0.7%	1.1%
Reading	47.1%	13.1%	3.4%	4.2%	26.4%
Sculpting	0.3%	0.2%	0.0%	0.0%	0.0%
Weaving	0.3%	0.2%	0.0%	0.0%	0.0%
Woodworking	5.7%	2.7%	1.1%	0.7%	1.2%

(Source: Mediamark 1984 national survey)

Note two seemingly contradictory dimensions. First, in most arts appreciation activities, those who participate very seldom are the majority. The exceptions are listening to music and reading, both accessible, home-based activities. Second, those who engage in productive activity quite regularly are commonly the second largest category. As with other activities, doing the arts includes a minority whose commitment and regularity make it central to their lives. They are those whom Stebbins (1992) refers to as "amateurs" who love the activity and have high standards of performance. Artistic production may be quite central to the resource allocation and identities of a minority who are not professionals. Artistic engagement is for them a "high investment" activity around which they tend to build significant self-images and relationships.

Stebbins began his line of research on amateurs with his own commitment to playing in classical music groups. Along with sports, he has examined amateur theater and other arts organizations. As introduced in Chapter 18, such "serious leisure" combines an acceptance of high standards of performance and a devotion to skill development with the likelihood that the activity will provide a primary community of friends who share the experience. Amateur theater, for example, requires such a demanding schedule of preparation and performance that it becomes difficult to maintain other leisure investments. Further, the actor, chamber music player, or dancer often comes to define his or her life as much or more in terms of that leisure commitment as in terms of work or even family.

Again, there is a bond between production and consumption. Some response is expected from those who watch and listen and is part of the meaning of doing the art. There is the dimension of public offering in arts production, even when localized and limited. Further, the feedback that is most valued by the performer is from informed consumers. Those best able to appreciate the quality of a work are those who have been producers themselves. As a consequence, there is a symbiosis between doing the arts and appreciating what others do. Empathy with what has gone into the production—in theater, music, or any other art—is most complete when one has had the experience oneself.

The Arts and Leisure

In an influential essay, Josef Pieper (1952) developed an argument that "leisure is the basis of culture." His argument was based on a view of leisure as an inner condition of openness and receptivity, a "mental and spiritual attitude." Leisure is more than filling time with activity; it is engagement with meaning and with community. The arts are forms of communication that fulfill and reveal a culture. They do not simply reproduce, but make a statement about the themes and meanings that underlie the forms. They express some meaning, emotion, and coherence of a facet of existence.

The deep connection between leisure and creation is perhaps more evident in the arts than in any other form of activity. Insofar as leisure is the "freedom to become," (Kelly, 1987b), it is directed toward the "not yet" of personal and social existence. For Aristotle *(Poetics, Chap. 26)*, art not only imitates life but creates what "might be" or even "ought to be." It is always playful rather than being limited to accepted existence. What is necessary for such art? Is it not leisure, not only as time but as a total environment that enables playful action? Schiller (1954) believed that persons are human only when they play, when they engage in creative activity for its own sake. Creative activity, from this perspective, is not a luxury, but is at the center of what it means to be human.

The aesthetic for Schiller is both a response and a heightening of existence. The arts are more than personal performance; they are at least a glimpse of the harmony and beauty that life might be. Creation is not for the sake of possession, but is a shared vision necessary to the creation of a more human and humane tomorrow. Art exists in a dialectic of what is and what might be, of being and becoming. And leisure is the context of such creative activity. It is the orientation of creation for its own sake and the condition of relative freedom that makes action possible. Play is the action dimension of leisure. Creation is the producing element of play. Leisure is the possibility of both.

REFERENCES

Baumol, J., and Bowen, W. (1966). *Performing arts—The economic dilemma.* New York, NY: 20th Century Fund.

Becker, H. (1982). *Art worlds.* Berkeley, CA: University of California Press.

Bourdieu, P. (1980). *Questions de socologie.* Paris, France: Editions de Minuit.

Bourdieu, P. (1984). *Distinction: A social critique of the judgment of taste.* Cambridge, MA: Harvard University Press.

Gans, H. (1974). *Popular culture and high culture: An analysis and evaluation of taste.* New York, NY: Basic Books.

Getzels, J., and Csikszentmihalyi, M. (1976). *The creative vision: A longitudinal study of problem finding in art.* New York, NY: John Wiley, Inc.

Kelly, J. R. (1987a). The arts in the United States of America. In L. Hantrais and T. Kamphorst (Eds.), *Trends in the arts: A multinational perspective.* Amersfoort, The Netherlands: Giordano Bruno Press.

Kelly, J. R. (1987b). *Freedom to be: A new sociology of leisure.* New York, NY: Macmillan.

Lynes, R. 1949 (1980). *The tastemakers: The shaping of American popular taste.* New York, NY: Dover.

Pieper, J. (1952). *Leisure: The basis of culture.* New York, NY: New American Library.

Robinson, J. (1987). The arts markets. *American Demographics,* September, 42-46.

Schiller, F. (1954). In *On the aesthetic education of man.* R. Snell (Trans.). New Haven, CT: Yale University Press.

Stebbins, R. (1992). Amateurs, professionals,nd serious leisure. Montreal, Quebec, Canada: McGill-Queen's University Press.

Zolberg, V. (1990). *Constructing a sociology of the arts.* New York, NY: Cambridge University Press.

The Mass Media

O n a given day, most American adults do not participate in sports or the arts. They do not exercise, engage in disciplined contemplation, or travel to a forest, mountain, or seashore. Most do, however, watch television and quite often read part of a newspaper and listen to a radio, often in a car. "Mass" denotes general availability and connotes a level of content and style of presentation that is inclusive. "Media" denotes communication of a message. Only a few decades ago "mass media" meant newspapers, radio, popular magazines, and even billboard advertising. Today mass media means television with every other form secondary, residual, and even peripheral. Television dominates mass communications by any measure of time use, information transmitted, or attention given. Not since the invention of printing has a communications technology revolutionized a culture as has television. Any study of leisure, family life, time allocation, or day-to-day life in any context that was completed before the advent of television is of only historical interest.

What do men, women, and children do with their discretionary time in every modern society? More than anything else, they watch television. The most recent Gallup Poll estimates an average of about 2 1/2 hours a day for adults, but that figure obscures considerable variation. Certainly people still talk to each other, read, and engage in a number of purposive nonwork activities. But when it comes to daily, time-consuming, and even habitual engagement, television watching is in a class by itself. Why? It is available. It is inexpensive. And, if we are to believe most self-reports, it is enjoyable.

Television is *the* mass medium. Radio sets are available in 99 percent of homes and in most cars. Newspaper reading has declined and many cities are faced with the problem of having only one. The loss of contrasting perspectives in news selection, communication, and interpretation is a political issue of significance. Many papers are now owned and controlled by large media corporations that claim local control, but still have general policies for the entire corporate enterprise. But most people get their news primarily from television.

Magazines are relatively narrow in their appeal and intended markets. They are based on interests segmented by age, gender, lifestyle, education level, region, leisure investment, products, professions, and a host of other factors. They are financed more by advertising than subscriptions or single purchases and are designed to deliver specified market segments to their advertisers. Further, they are often dependent on particular leisure interests, product lines, or differentiated lifestyles to attract and retain a readership.

Radio, too, has become highly specialized. The "all news" format is primarily an urban phenomenon and is aimed at those who want to "catch up" in a limited time and on demand. Most stations play music all or most of the time. The music is selected for highly differentiated tastes, often reinforced by age and ethnicity. The division is not just "classical" and "pop," but reflects generations in playing "golden oldies," easy-listening, hard and soft rock, blues, jazz, and all sorts of fine-tuned styles. Like the magazines, they are able to sell their advertisers access to specified market segments. Programmers and advertisers alike target listeners with great accuracy.

There are also the live performances of popular culture that are well-targeted. The demographics of an area in age and education distributions are only the beginning of identifying local tastes for hard rock, teen idols, old balladeers, country and western, and all the musical styles. Further, there is a synergy between live performance and recorded music in which albums and singles are tied to tours and highlight concerts. The new element, however, is the connection of live performance with recorded videos and promotion on cable television. The music video is a new art form combining the music with visual imagery. At first the videos were primarily of the live performances themselves. Now, however, they are composed of quick flashes of imagery often only symbolically related to the music itself. The promotion of these videos with their short marketing life is highly dependent on free and cable television and especially MTV-type channels that specialize in such videos and are dependent on their promotional programs.

Even motion pictures, once the epitome of mass culture, have become targeted and specialized. During the first half of the twentieth century, the urban movie palace and the small-town theater became the primary entertainment locale for most men, women, and children. Although teens were always the most reliable audience with about half the movie clientele under the age of 20, the movies were for just about everyone. Motion pictures stars were celebrities across social and cultural divisions. The movie theater was a central leisure meeting place, usually eclipsing the older dance halls and social clubs. Further, it was "respectable" as the halls, clubs, and bars never were.

In the television era, the motion picture industry suffered a 65 percent decline in attendance since 1950 and over a 25 percent loss in the number of theaters. Over 11,000 enclosed theaters shut their doors between 1950 and 1965, a loss not offset by the temporary phenomenon of the drive-in open air theater.

These teen oriented "passion pits" have now almost disappeared. The new movie theater format is the multiscreen theater in which selection is maximized. The mass appeal of films has been replaced by segmented markets: sophisticated and educated adults, adolescent "horror," violence and crash features, children's entertainment, and all the other specialized genres of film. A few films attain mass markets, but most audiences are segmented. The new theater offers films simultaneously for a variety of tastes and makes most of its profit at the refreshment counter. Further, the "after-market" for videos, subscription television, and eventually free TV is a major part of the total financial package for motion pictures. Theater revenues, while sometimes substantial, are only the beginning. It is no surprise, then, to discover that the old motion picture studios are now part of international media conglomerates that operate in all the visual media and distribute to worldwide markets.

Even the popular media of music and film lead back to television. Along with the major networks, local independent stations, subscription cable, extra-cost movie, sports, and other segmented cable outlets and producers, video purchase and rental, and new technologies on the horizon, some form of television—the in-home entertainer—is at the center of the matrix of visual entertainment. Even live performances are advertised primarily on television and depend on TV to promote the career trajectories of their stars. In the business network as well as in the time allocation of individuals, television is central.

Popular Culture and the Life Course

Television is at the center of the complex offerings of popular culture that are interwoven into lifestyles throughout the life course. Some elements are symbols of age, culture, and social group. They differentiate groups and provide ways of identification. Television, for example, changes in content and styles for children, teens, and adults; and yet as a medium remains the predominant entertainer. What follows is only a bare outline of media and popular culture through the life course (Kelly, 1990):

Children—Television and all the clothing, games, and toys modeled on popular television programs; the rise in wartime and fall in peacetime of war toys; comic books, uniforms, games, and TV cartoon themes; the use of TV and comic characters to sell vitamins, breakfast food, shoes, and toys. More than at other ages, children seem to be passive recipients of the media.

Youth—Rock groups with their recordings and videos, dancing and clubs, concerts and television specials, cable and MTV, transistor radios in miniature and "boom boxes," tapes and CDs, stereo and quad—

nothing characterizes and bonds teens as does their music. However, teens are less passive than children. They respond to marketing and promotion, to fads and symbols; but they also choose what they like. Teens are the largest part of the movie market and a prime target for TV programming. Identification is vital so they gather at the right places, wear the right clothing, drink the right beverages, and, most of all, attach themselves to the right media symbols. In a sense, teens are popular culture—in ways that are constantly changing and yet continue to form behavior styles with identifiable character.

Adult singles—Most adult singles do not fit any image of the playboy and playgirl with 2000 recordings, a sports car, designer labels, and a trip to Club Med every other month. Beginning incomes and the demands of starting a career make that level of consumption only a dream for most. More are at home in front of the television than the stereotypes suggest. But the transition from teen to establishment adult often includes a period of experimentation and courting of lifestyles as well as partners. Targeted periodicals, nonfamily cars, and weekend entertainment are part of the singles culture outside the small town and urban ghetto. The culture symbols, often picked out of the TV series and ads, are employed to present an image that will be accepted in the social milieu where hoped-for relationships can be formed.

Parents—The more home-centered leisure of parents shifts media interests to "family" programs and videos that may give way to more "adult" entertainment later in the evening. Identities are developed utilizing symbols of social and economic establishment as well as "couple" contexts of activity. Pop culture tends to be replaced by conventional culture. An evening out is more likely to mean McDonald's with the kids than a rock concert and 4th of July picnics and parades more than the urban scene "where a lady may buy a gentleman a drink." Two incomes tend to be directed toward home and family. Convenience is a factor in leisure, especially for women who come home to the "second shift."

Older adults—Media are giving increased attention to post-launching adults and the "active old." Advertising-driven programming responds to recognized markets. Media tastes may reflect those acquired in earlier periods. Radio has its "easy listening" and "oldies." Magazines focus on financial investment, home, and garden. Television retains formats of the old variety specials as well as stars who have lasted over decades and provide identification objects for those in mid-life. Reinvestment in more demanding leisure is not uncommon, but accessible entertainment takes most "discretionary time."

By listening to the music, assessing clothing fashions, classifying vocabularies, and identifying the cultural symbols, an age cohort can be targeted, attracted, and influenced in the market-driven media. Why? Because mass media are a major element of what people do in their everyday lives.

Table 33.1 Everyday Participation in Common Activities

Activity	Teens	Singles	Age 65+	Parents One-Income	Dual-Income Parents	Single Parents
Watch television	89%	67%	81%	74%	72%	62%
Read newspaper	49%	62%	87%	65%	68%	66%
Listen to music	78%	76%	20%	42%	46%	50%
Talk on phone	62%	50%	47%	48%	40%	65%
Exercise	54%	48%	34%	35%	30%	39%
Talk with friends	34%	32%	30%	32%	29%	37%
Read books	20%	18%	35%	17%	27%	25%
Read magazines	34%	21%	20%	14%	14%	12%
Hobbies	39%	29%	39%	14%	19%	13%
Gardening	11%	6%	30%	34%	24%	9%

(Source: *Where Does the Time Go? The United Media Enterprises Report on Leisure in America.* New York: Newspaper Enterprise Association, 1983)

Table 33.1 does not specify the amounts of time given to common activities. In general, other research indicates that television captures the most time with no other activity even close. It is important to note, however, that people still read, talk with each other, and even, in some way, get some exercise. Television has not eradicated all other action and interaction, but it does occupy a major segment of waking hours.

Reading books, as reported in the previous chapter, is a common activity for about a quarter of the adult population. Like other cultural activities, it is more common for women than men and for those with some college education. Books, however, range in a wide spectrum from those read primarily to gain knowledge and for self-development to mass-produced formula books sold in the supermarkets. Reading may be demanding and require a high degree of attention and mental exertion, or it may be little more involving than a TV sitcom. Books may be a high art form or one more form of mass entertainment. In either case, reading is portable and can be begun and stopped on demand.

The remainder of this chapter will focus on television, the dominant medium. It is important, however, to recognize that television is tied to several other media and offerings of popular culture. Live performances, movies, mass and specialized magazines, and even popular books are interconnected with television in the marketplace and in the home. The international corporate conglomerates that produce and distribute so much mass entertainment are only the economic peak of a complex industry.

Television—The Transforming Technology

There is some disagreement on the extent and nature of television viewing. Television sets may be turned on—estimates are as high as six hours a day, but that does not mean everyone in the household is watching. Television may be on in the background while vacuuming the house, bathing the baby, or even reading. Sitting in front of the screen may induce sleep or intense excitement in the final minutes of a close basketball game. Further, those with the most unobligated time—teens and the retired—tend to watch the most. The "second shift" parent probably watches the least.

Current time-diary studies indicate that on average adult Americans watch about 15 hours of television a week or between 2 and 2 1/2 hours a day (Robinson, 1990). This figure is about the same for 1975 and 1985, but is almost a 50 percent increase from 1965. Again, however, this raw number yields no information about the intensity of viewing or the character of the experience. Older people living alone are known to carry on a running argument with television commentators and hosts. Children may appear to be giving rapt attention to a targeted program only to volunteer that it's all "make believe." Those who work under considerable stress during the day confess that they almost always fall asleep in front of the TV in the evening, even during a selected and rented video movie.

Gross numbers can be staggering. One estimate is that the people of the world spend 3.5 billion hours watching television every day. It would be hard to support that number as necessary to re-creation (Kubey and Csikszentmihalyi, 1990). In another estimate, at the rate of 2 1/2 hours a day, an adult who lives 70 years will spend seven of forty-seven waking years in front of the screen. It is true that people walk and talk, read and daydream, fiddle around in the home and garden, shop for fun and eat out with friends. Nothing, however, matches the time consumption of television through the life course. Variations (Table 33.2) are important, but the totals are staggering:

Table 33.2   Hours Watching Television and Hours Available for Leisure

Activity	Mean Hours per Day Watching Television	Mean Hours Available for Leisure
Teens	3.97	5.85
Age 65 and older	3.50	6.18
Singles	2.89	5.45
Parents of grown children	2.78	4.44
Single parents	2.68	3.64
One-income parents	2.52	3.41
Married without children	2.42	5.22
Two-income parents	2.24	3.25

(Source: *Where Does the Time Go? The United Media Enterprises Report on Leisure in America.* New York: Newspaper Enterprise Association, 1983—National sample of 1000+)

Note that single parents, often most limited in discretionary income, give the highest proportion of their meager leisure time to television, reinforcing the argument that low cost and easy access are important factors in TV watching. Also, those who are married but have no children, often younger and more career oriented, watch the least out of their discretionary hours. The variations are clearly embedded in life circumstances, other opportunities and obligations that change through the life course.

Television programming is not just a matter of routine, more of the same day after day. There are highlighted events that capture the attention of a culture. Some are periodic sports spectacles such as the football Super Bowl, the baseball World Series, or the Olympic Games. Networks bid billions to carry these events, and then spend more to promote them. They become almost national festivals that capture an inordinate amount of everyday conversation in the workplaces and neighborhoods. On occasion, special programs such as Alex Haley's *Roots* also become landmark events that reverberate throughout the culture. More often, however, attempts to manufacture programs that do more than shift viewing percentages a few points are a failure. Habit, loyalty, and indifference rule program selection in many homes most of the time.

Dramatic events may also turn attention to television as the primary purveyor of the news. Such a classic event was the assassination and funeral of President Kennedy. Other dramatic events such as a space launching tragedy or an election may rivet attention to the screen. The progress of a war or other longer event may shift viewers from network programming to the CNN all-news format. The immediacy of television coverage, however regulated and limited, brings home the reality of a war, hurricane, or plane crash as nothing else has or could. In a sense, TV brings the world into living rooms in color imagery to heighten awareness of a world larger than seen before. All media events are not constructed by the media. They are, however, selected and edited for acceptable consumption.

Television in all its forms is a product of the market economy. Exceptions are those in which it is used and controlled by a totalitarian state. Major network television is supported by its advertisers. Programs are designed to attract particular market segments. Their content is not permitted to offend those targeted viewers. Within the drama, situation comedy, or made-for-television movie, there is often a series of hidden commercials. The principal characters drive luxury models of sponsoring car manufacturers, while the products of competitors are wrecked in the big car chase scene. Brand names are casually pronounced and associated with glamorous settings and people . . . for a fee. Labels are displayed. Airlines, hotel chains, and vacation destinations are woven into the scenario. The promotion of products is both direct and indirect. More significant, however, is the covert censorship by sponsors. Controversial issues are ignored or treated with careful "fairness." Controversial actors or directors are bypassed in favor of media "personalities." Serious dilemmas are treated as comedic dialogue: Race becomes "cute" and divorce is sexy. The end of it all is not art, drama, or even entertainment. It is the attraction of potential customers and clients. Even the news is subjected to the scrutiny of ratings first and content afterwards.

The central fact of television is that it is *there.* In at least 90 percent of American homes, there is at least one set. In many there are two or more, not in the same room but in the kitchen, the bedroom, and the playroom. Access is immediate, requiring no more than pushing a button or flipping a switch. Remote controls are so standard that it is no longer necessary even to stand up to turn the set on, switch channels, or adjust sound. It is so easy! At the same time, it is also inexpensive. The per hour cost of television, depreciation of the set and the cost of power, is pennies per hour. Nothing in history has offered so much attraction for so little! All the viewer has to do is endure or ignore the commercials; or be entranced by their exciting formats and images.

All of this has overwhelmed modern societies in a few decades:

Table 33.3   Television and Radio Ownership: 1950-1987

Households with	1950	1970	1987
Radio sets	92.6%	98.6%	99.0%
Average number	**2.1**	**5.1**	**5.4**
Television sets	9.0%	58.5%	87.4%
Average number	**1.01**	**1.39**	**1.86**
Cable	0%	0%	48.7%
VCRs	0%	0%	48.7%
(Source: Statistical Abstract of the United States, 1988)			

The 1990 Gallup Poll found that 77 percent of the households had VCRs. Cable use has also grown, although at a slower rate. As a consequence, studies of time use prior to the almost universal availability of television in any society are now only quaint. Rich and poor, educated and illiterate, across all the dividing categorizations of the society, there is television available and often on.

In a survey of their readers, Consumer Union (*Consumer Reports,* September, 1991) found a steady increase during the 1980s in the proportion who are subscribers to cable and who watch it regularly, paralleling national figures. Satisfaction, however, was the lower than for any other services rated including insurance, hotels, airlines, and even movers. Further, subscribing to cable has brought about changes in viewing choices: more news, nature programs, movies, science programs, sports, and educational programs and fewer soap operas, drama series, cartoons, and talk shows. Whatever its failures to provide reliable service, the cable franchise does have an impact on what is available and what is watched.

It is no wonder that there is concern over the impact of this highly commercial medium on both individuals and on the society. Are children seduced into consumerism and accustomed to violence? Are women depicted as objects to be used and controlled by men? Does sex become a contest rather than communication, a barter more than intimacy? Is the "good life" defined by possessions, being the right place with the right apparel and car? Is leisure reduced to being entertained with a loss of the dimensions of developmental action and community building interaction? Are deep divisions and conflicts in the political and economic world ignored or transformed into tame and innocuous curiosities? Does the visual nature of television change the ways in which we learn and encounter the world? These and similar questions raise the issue of how people watch television.

Intensity and Interaction

How do people usually watch television? A recent study employed the "experience sampling" method in which "beepers" are used to signal subjects at random times. They then fill out a survey form about what they are doing and how they feel about it. Different from interviews and more traditional questionnaires, on-site and at-the-time responses are gained. Along with time diaries, a picture of TV viewing is beginning to be filled in.

The study (Kubey and Csikszentmihalyi, 1990) finds variations in how people watch TV, but also ventures a number of generalizations:

1) Television viewing is passive and relaxing. It employs a low level of concentration. Watching television is, then, low on both challenge and anxiety.

2) Television may increase the time families spend together. That time, however, is lower on attention and taking action even though positive in general feelings.

3) Television viewing may follow feeling lonely or having other negative emotions. It is an escape from being down, partly because it provides some structure and diversion.

4) After watching TV, viewers tend to feel more passive and less alert. The extent to which this is related to the time of day rather than the medium is unresolved.

5) Satisfaction declines the longer television is watched.

6) Those who watch more television tend to enjoy it less and be less satisfied with their lives in general.

In general, watching TV is found to be low in activation and moderate in both affect and intrinsic motivation. Clearly most TV programming is intended to be entertaining rather than challenging. Watching the medium is relaxing rather than demanding, passive rather than active. Insofar as the overall balance of leisure includes relaxation and low intensity in its rhythm, TV provides the easy and accessible opportunity. Further, for the most part, viewers report that they enjoy it, even though not thrilled or engrossed.

One approach to television viewing is that of the "active audience" (Altheide, 1985). In an interactional perspective, television is seen as a stimulus that is interpreted, defined, discounted, and even rejected in some circumstances. Viewers are presumed to be able to do more than passively receive the messages

Chapter 33 • The Mass Media   465

of the medium; they turn it off both mentally and physically (especially with the remote control). There is resistance as well as response. The extent to which viewers engage the screen in some kind of dialogue is unknown. What is known is that all cognition is a process that involves interpretation and evaluation, however uncritical.

There is a critique in the Kubey and Csikszentmihalyi study, even though the authors suggest no allegiance to formal critical theory. Television is said to structure life, not only time but also definitions of life. Its reliable formats and messages give an overall reassurance that life is reliable and manageable. Problems are defined as personal rather than structural, amenable to adjustment rather than requiring social change. The market system that both supports and is the implicit message of most television is shown to supply the good things of life reliably. Life's problems are subject to remedy within the system and most directly in marketplace consumption. Even home, family, and education are treated as goods that can be purchased with a correlation between price and quality. Homes are a purchase, not a creation; and a "good education" is measured by cost rather than effort.

New Technologies and Increasing Choice

One element of the persistent criticism of television has been that there is little choice. Three commercial networks, each with programs similar to the other two, dominated the channels. Even local independent stations would usually fill their hours with network reruns. That limitation has been challenged by new technologies, especially cable transmission and the video cassette recorder (VCR). Both are now found in a large majority of American homes, close to 80 percent for the video player and a large majority for cable.

Cable, despite concern that many of the additional channels are just replay repetitions of the networks, does offer greater variety. Programming includes all-sports channels, performing arts programs, Disney children's selections, round-the-clock news, all movies, and a variety of local programs. The sports may include monster truck mud racing as well as international sports and the news may become trivial or repetitive. Nevertheless, cable offers more choice. For added fees on top of the basic charge, relatively recent movies, pop music videos, major sports events, and other special programs are available. The new technology of fiber optics will increase the possibility of special programming directed, for a fee, into the home. Commercial-free first-run movies, Broadway plays and musicals, opera from La Scala and music from the Concertgebouw, and other offerings will be available with decoding devices and credit card billing. Legislation is also under consideration to increase competition in major cable market areas.

The VCR offers, at modest cost, another set of choices. "Time shifting" is possible by recording programs and viewing them at a time chosen by the viewer rather than the network. Commercials can be "zapped" out during recording or "zipped" through by using the remote control and the fast forward. Movies and other programs can be rented or purchased at speciality stores, supermarkets, gas stations, and libraries for viewing on demand. Favorite programs can be recorded to be seen again. The video technology adds considerably to the control of the viewer over the medium. It retains the easy access of the medium, but increases choice and control at a modest price. The number of households that will rent four or more movies for the weekend is surprising, even when some are for children or adults to view separately and on age-graded schedules.

Even the little remote control device, now standard on most new sets, adds to choice. Commercial sound can be muted and ignored. Dull programs can be abandoned with the press of a button. Cable subscribers can jump from one possibility to another in split seconds rather than remain with one program through inertia. More sophisticated devices even offer a split screen for those who want to watch two programs at once.

These and other technologies increase the ability of the viewer to resist the programming design of the networks and to "deschedule" according to individual preferences and commitments (Altheide, 1985). Previously, the television enforced a relatively rigid sequencing of events. Now the household with multiple sets and control devices can "play" with the medium. Time itself becomes more open and less tightly structured through such technological additions.

Critiques of Mass Media in Contemporary Culture

Those who defend the right of the individual to choose argue that television is the ultimate democratic medium. No one has to turn it on, selection is widening, and it can be turned off at will and with little effort. It is there at low cost. Further, most programming, just because of the advertising base, is responsive to the behaviors of the viewers. They "vote with their seat."

On the other hand, nothing that consumes as many hours of waking life as does television can remain immune from evaluation and analysis. Its availability and attractiveness demand that its impacts be subjected to careful scrutiny.

The fundamental element of most critiques is based on the economic structure of the medium. Television, as developed in the United States and with the exception of public broadcasting, is first of all an advertising medium (Ewen, 1976). As such, its entire economic structure is based on securing the attention of market segments for those who pay the bills. As a consequence, programming is designed to attract buyers, those with the purchasing power to make a market for the specified goods and services. Drama is not an expression of the developing nature of the art, but sets market attracting characters in settings that promote purchasing. Sport becomes a mass spectacle with even the rules changed to enhance the excitement that a small screen can transmit. The "bottom line" is not quality but sales. Risk in programming is rare, and tried-and-true formulas abound.

The enormous investment in production and distribution does not find its return in critical acclaim, but in the various "ratings" services that utilize electronic set monitors or daily viewing diaries. It is not just a matter of numbers. An advertiser of upscale cars or vacations buys time during programs with high income audiences and space in specialized periodicals. The sales pitches to the massive teen market, to mothers for home products, and to men for beer are an intricate blending of ad style, timing, and association. Then, within the programs themselves, products are displayed and promoted by association with the right people and places. Programs that pretend to offer information and even news are actually a stringing together of promotions of travel destinations, entertainment, and leisure based products. The cumulative message is consistent: buy and be happy! The right purchase can ensure sexual, economic, and social success. Failure in the marketplace, on the other hand, engenders feelings of inadequacy, inferiority, and anxiety. The images of the "good life" are heavily laced with material goods. Owning is power. Buying is satisfying.

The second element of the critique has more to do with the actual use of the medium. When two to three hours a day are devoted to such entertainment, the time is lost for other possibilities. Television may well be central to the fund of conversation at work or at school, but even there it directs attention to its artificial world of sound and color. It is, for the most part, the easiest thing that people do. Even allowing for some "active audience" engagement, it is watching, not doing. TV time is time lost to action and interaction, to the excitement of real involvement and the community of real relationships. What are the consequences for personal development of devotion to this entrancing medium rather than to developing some skill? What are the impacts on family communication of eating most meals to the accompaniment of a TV game show or sitcom rerun? Can students no longer give attention to any mode of communication that does not employ flashes of visual brilliance and episodes of action? How may a commitment to a television schedule preclude regular engagement in something more involving? Some TV viewing is needed relaxation and disengagement. Yet, there may be a price for being entertained too easily and too well.

Whatever the concerns, television is there and will not go away. It gives structure to the timetables of life. It reinforces conventional values and mainstream ideas. It presents images of market dependent lifestyles and the lure of leisure just beyond our economic reach. It devours incredible amounts of time and fills voids of loneliness and boredom. It is in the middle of leisure and of life, day after day.

REFERENCES

Altheide, D. (1985). *Media power.* Beverly Hills, CA: Sage Publications.

Ewen, S. (1976). *Captains of consciousness: Advertising and the social roots of the consumer culture.* New York, NY: McGraw Hill.

Kelly, J. (1990). *Leisure,* (2nd ed.). Englewood Cliffs, NJ: Prentice-Hall.

Kubey, R., and Csikszentmihalyi, M. (1990). *Television and the quality of life: How viewing shapes everyday experience.* Hillsdale, NJ: Lawrence Erlbaum.

Robinson, J. (1990). Americans' use of time project. In B. Cutler. Where does the free time go? *American Demographics.* November.

CHAPTER 34

Addiction and Artificial Experience

S ocial critics have long feared that the combination of affluence, increasing time away from work and a market economy would lead to the use of leisure in vicarious ways and in ways which altered the senses. Both were considered misuses of leisure which could be overcome with proper preparation by many who have sought to reform or improve society. Historically, the "Rational Recreation" movements fought against the working man's use of leisure for heavy drinking in the pub by promoting alternatives such as brass bands, organized sport and reading. In the United States, social reformers sought alternatives to "spectatoritis" and urged Americans to be active during their leisure. The alleged enemies of the "worthy" use of leisure have included alcohol, the theatre, television, professional sport, marijuana, cocaine and other "drugs," and a host of other evils.

In spite of such efforts, mind altering drugs and vicarious experiences of many types have formed a central part of modern leisure experience in industrial nations. To Marx, such behavior might represent a manifestation of the "false consciousness" engendered in the working class. Conflict theories of society would explain the emergence of a mass entertainment industry and of a drug culture as an important method by which those in power keep those who might threaten them from taking action. The prevalence of drugs in ghetto areas, televisions and VCRs in working-class apartments and the endless parade of collegiate, amateur and professional sport which pervades every sector of society may be seen as evidence of how successfully the public can be diverted from using leisure to understand and take political action concerning the problems of the day.

These behaviors may also be seen merely as the commodification of leisure and the emergence of an efficient market economy to supply those commodities. Drug use is nothing new; nor is entertainment. What is new is the extent of access. While Veblen (1899) mentioned drug use as part of the conspicuous consumption that characterized a gentleman of leisure—today a vast array of mind altering drugs are within the economic reach of most of the population, as is the ability to undertake behaviors which may be defined as addicting if done in excess. Alcohol, of course, which costs little to produce, has almost always been available to all social classes. Within many traditional cultures its consumption served purposes other than inebriation. Wine, for instance, was often a safe substitute for water when pure water was a rarity. Beer and ale in medieval Europe served as a readily available source of nutrition. Every village had its brewmaster who produced a highly caloric, carbohydrate rich mixture for the consumption of the locals. In modern societies, however, the purposes of wine, beer and spirits have less to do with sanitation or nutrition than with socialization or intoxication.

Addictions and Use of Leisure

Historically, the concept of "addiction" was not applied especially to narcotics or alcohol. It simply referred to liking, to engage in a habit, ". . . and the term was applied equally to all popular medicinal bromides, as well as to habits unconnected with substance use" (Peele, 1989, p. 22). During the last century, narcotics, along with cocaine, were indiscriminately dispensed and, for the most part, such drugs were not considered dangerous or addicting. Coca-Cola,® for instance, contained a dose of cocaine until 1906. Today, we apply the term "addiction" to a variety of behaviors and believe it to be an illness over which the individual has no control. Also, there is increasing reason to believe that use of leisure and addictions are related. As addictions expert Stanton Peele (1989) argued, many parents are no longer trustful of their children, having lost the idea that children can learn and grow from exploration, independence, risk and adventure. "Yet the abilities to manage oneself, to accept the responsibility of independence, and to generate adventure and excitement without behaving antisocially are skills that enable people to avoid drug or alcohol abuse and other addictions" (Peele, 1989, pp. 251-252). Leisure activity which is vicarious, in which the individual is passively entertained, does not produce the ability to manage oneself, accept responsibility or become independent. Indeed, the individual in question is likely to become more dependent upon outside sources for stimulation rather than develop the ability to entertain him or herself. Perhaps such abilities are related to the concept of self-efficacy. Self-efficacy is the feeling that one can control the outcomes in life which are important (Bandura, 1989). Those individuals with low levels of self-efficacy would seem to be less likely to seek to control their own use of leisure and more likely to rely on vicarious experience. While leisure behavior, in both the ancient Athenian sense and in the concept of "flow" is self-regulating, in addictive behaviors there is no self-regulation. Such self-regulation is related to self-regard or self-esteem. That is, an individual with higher self-esteem is more likely to be self-regulating.

Not only is individual self-efficacy important in how leisure is used, so, too, is community efficacy. In communities which appear to be powerless, unable to control outcomes which are important to successful community life, there is a greater tendency toward passivity.

Where self or community efficacy are low, leisure behaviors are more likely to be passive, and such passivity is related to addictive behavior. Television viewing, for example, among children is positively related to obesity since it interferes with burning calories through active play. Like excessive eating, drinking or drug taking, it is a passive, consumer-oriented form of entertainment. "The link between watching television and obesity and other addictions is that watching television depletes the child's resources for direct experience and interaction with the environment in favor of vicarious experiences and involvements" (Peele, 1989, p. 254).

Television viewing, for people who are alone, may, like drugs, keep the mind from having to face depressing thoughts. According to Csikszentmihalyi, (1990) " . . . what drugs in fact do is reduce our perception of both what can be accomplished and what we as individuals are able to accomplish, until the two are in balance" (p. 169). While drugs may produce an alteration of the content and organization of consciousness, they do not add to our ability to order them effectively.

Sexual activity, too, may simply be used as a way to impose an external order on our thoughts, of killing time " . . . without having to confront the perils of solitude" (Csikszentmihalyi, 1990, p. 170). It is, therefore not surprising that television viewing, sexual activity and drinking are relatively interchangeable behaviors within many households. What such activities do is focus attention naturally and pleasurably, but what they fail to do is to develop attentional habits which might lead to a greater complexity of consciousness. Addictive behavior, then, is undertaken to relieve the pain which may creep into the unfocused mind. Note how this idea is in keeping with optimal arousal theories of play.

Addictive uses of leisure may also be a way of coping with change or of seeking to reduce information overload. Toffler discussed one response to the shock of rapid change as seeking a unitary solution. "Thus, the bewildered, anxious student, pressured by parents, uncertain of his draft status, nagged at by an educational system whose obsolescence is more strikingly revealed every day, forced to decide on a career, a set of values, a worthwhile lifestyle, searches wildly for a way to simplify his existence. By turning on to LSD, Methedrine or heroin, he performs an illegal act that has, at least, the virtue of consolidating his miseries" (Toffler, 1970, p. 361).

Socialization Into Potentially Addictive Behavior

In most behaviors which involve the use of mind altering drugs, there is a process of socialization which is not uncommon from the socialization process which takes place with other uses of leisure. Such socialization, among other things, teaches the novice to experience the activity as pleasurable. The use of alcohol, tobacco, LSD and a variety of other drugs is not inherently pleasurable to the beginner, who, without the positive reinforcement of the social group as well as instruction, would often find the experience completely negative. Many beginners, for instance, become ill from a first cigarette and find the experience of LSD terrifying.

While many individuals begin the use of some potentially addictive behavior for social reasons, there is evidence that, for the person who is further along in the continuum of addiction, individual rather than "social" reasons explain the behavior. Thus, heavy drinkers are more likely to give individual reasons for drinking, e.g., feeling good or becoming relaxed, than to give social reasons, e.g., to be sociable or because of a special occasion (Riley, Marden and Lifshitz, 1958).

British sociologist Kenneth Roberts has observed that both alcohol and tobacco in modern times have become an accompanying activity to many other forms of leisure expression:

> Why do we allow ourselves to be persuaded to spend so much smoking ourselves to death and drinking our minds to oblivion? This is the reality of Britain at leisure more frequently than healthy outdoor pursuits. Many smokers are addicted, but few "drinkers" are physically dependent on alcohol. . . Different people use alcohol in different places for different reasons. Most visitors to pubs name the human company, not the beer, as the main attraction. Alcohol's appeal can only be explained once we realize that it has become a companion to so many other recreations, and that to describe alcohol as the object of expenditure is often misleading (Roberts, 1981, p. 41).

Certainly similar claims could be made about other forms of drug use, such as marijuana, coffee or heroin. Much of such behavior is not by those who are addicted and it often is accompanying behavior to social visitation, conversation, or other social purposes.

Perhaps part of the explanation for the increase in the use of mind-altering substances is the tendency for modern societies to become increasingly rational and devoid of nondrug experiences which are, literally, intoxicating. In festivals, rituals and other forms of ceremony, many preindustrial cultures produced the hallucinogenic qualities which, for modern societies more often require drugs. In discussing primitive societies, Caillois mentioned the "shared vertigo" which was the climax of many festivals in which the rules of everyday life were turned inside out. Belief in the supernatural also caused such altered states of consciousness.

> The invasion of ghosts, the trances and frenzies they cause, the intoxication of fear or inspiring of fear, even if they reach their peak in the festival, are not absent from ordinary life. Political or religious institutions are frequently based upon the awe engendered by just as overwhelming a phantasmagoria (Caillois, 1961, p. 89).

This, of course, does not imply that primitive cultures did not use any mind-altering drugs; they did. What is implied, however, is that primitive societies, in becoming modern, gradually change the form of games and rituals they undertake from those which Caillois termed "mimicry" and llinx to those of "alea" and "agon." In primitive cultures, play often involved becoming an illusionary character by forgetting, disguising or temporarily shedding one's own personality in order to become someone else—mimicry. They also participated more frequently in games and ceremonies which were based upon the pursuit of vertigo, consisting of efforts to "momentarily destroy the stability of perception and inflict a kind of voluptuous panic upon an otherwise lucid mind" (Caillois, 1961, p. 23). While modern society is not devoid of such games and rituals, they are largely replaced by games of chance, such as gambling "alea," and games which are competitive contests involving skill and rules— "agon." Perhaps as this change takes place in society, the desire for magic, the supernatural and the alteration of the senses is more frequently sought with the help of mind-altering drugs.

Positive Addictions

During the last few decades, as the concept of addiction has spread to a wider and wider range of behaviors, the term "positive addiction" has been coined. Basically, a positive addiction is one which produces positive rather than negative results for the addicted individual in question. It has sometimes been argued, for instance, that the "addicted" runner will be better off physiologically as a result of his or her addiction. In spite of such arguments, the individual who is addicted to any leisure activity, be it television, running, sexual behavior, or eating may be said to be using the behavior to avoid confronting him or herself. Just as the so-called "workaholic" may hide in his or her work, so may the addicted runner or TV viewer hide through and in that behavior. Similarly, there is evidence that many "workaholics" are actually quite well-adjusted and have found meaning in life through their rather singular preoccupation with work. Perhaps the same may be said for some individuals who during their leisure pursue a positive addiction.

Vicarious Leisure as an Extension of Vicarious Work

As mentioned previously, the design of much modern work is attributable to "scientific management" of the workplace. The design of many leisure facilities and services has also been undertaken from the same perspective. That is, a system has been planned which individuals are not free to alter to any great extent. While scientific management started with the principle that planning the process of work must be taken away from the control of workers so that they would fit into a rigidly predesigned system which stressed efficiency, much the same could be said about Disney World. The experiences of Disney World have been structured in such a way that the individual has little opportunity to shape or organize the leisure experiences available. The same kind of time and motion studies Taylor used to make the workplace efficient and maximize profit have also been used by Disney to maximize profit. In essence, in neither situation is it possible for the individual to have much "effect" on the environment. While some explanations of children's play stress the importance of the child exerting an "effect" on the environment, in much of the vicarious leisure experience available in our culture, it is not possible for the individual "consumer" to have any effect on the environment. Just as the use of drugs, according to Csikszentmihalyi (1990) reduces both our perception of what can be accomplished and what we, as individuals, can accomplish, so too does the planned leisure environment. While creativity during play, as discussed previously, requires making a response which is both unique and has appropriate effects within the context of the situation (Bishop and Jeanrenaud, 1990), few such opportunities exist in most commercial amusement parks, guided tours, television programming or other highly planned leisure enterprises. In all such instances, individualism must be minimized in order to fit into a preexisting structure which defines the experience, in advance, in ways which limit initiative. While what is experienced may be pleasant, diverting and interesting, it involves much less of the individual's own uniqueness and provides little basis for self-understanding or perfection—the goals of leisure for the ancient Athenians.

Thus, it may be argued, much of modern leisure may be thought of as highly vicarious. Big-time college football games are highly "programmed." So are many tourist experiences, mass media use and a host of other leisure experiences. The advent of the computer has contributed to the extent to which such experiences are vicarious. As Rifkin observed, the computer has great potential to be used as an instrument of social control, because it can dictate the sequence, duration, tempo and coordination of activities in ways not previously possible. Once programmed, the future unfolds according to the dictates of the computer while society becomes voyeurs watching the future unfold.

It is not just in the commercial sector that the vicarious nature of much modern leisure experience may be found. Many forms of public recreation, park and other leisure services may be said, in many instances, to provide leisure activities in which the individual is a mere observer or has little opportunity to invest his or her own uniqueness in the situation. Social critic Paul Goodman (1956) argued that the increased extent of the organization of all aspects of our society made it increasingly harder for one to grow up. This was most evident in urban areas—" . . . concealed technology, family mobility, loss of the countryside, loss of neighborhood tradition, and the eating up of the play space have taken away the real environment" (Goodman, 1956, p. 76). While urban areas organized recreation and park departments, departments of public housing and others, Goodman stated, these bureaucracies did not coordinate what they did and dealt with people in regard to only one aspect of their being.

Perhaps it may be said that, if the division between vicarious and nonvicarious leisure is the difference between having the design and meaning of a leisure experience planned for you by others as opposed to planning it yourself, vicarious leisure appears to be on the increase in modern life. As such, it reflects many of the values inherent in scientific management and the modern corporation. Certainly people often find ways to counter vicariously planned leisure experiences so that they may participate more actively or according to their individual interests. They may, for instance, do "the wave" at a highly planned football event or reorganize a play area for their own uses. In regard to playgrounds in public housing areas, for instance, Goodman observed that "At first, urban boys shunned the official playgrounds, but now, driven by necessity, they have agreed to take them over and turn them to their own uses, games, adventure, necking and battle" (Goodman, 1956, p. 78). Such efforts, however, are often doomed to failure since they do not reflect the "proper" uses of the vicarious leisure environment.

Certainly, vicarious leisure and addiction must both be thought of as continuums rather than absolute conditions. Certainly, too, they are related concepts which are a significant part of modern leisure experience.

REFERENCES

Bandura, A. (1989). Quoted in S. Peele, *Diseasing of America: Addiction treatment out of control.* New York, NY: Lexington Books.

Bishop, D., and Jeanrenaud, C. (1990). Creative growth through play and its implications for recreation practice, In T. Goodale, and P. Witt (Eds.), *Recreation and leisure: Issues in an era of change.* State College, PA: Venture Publishing, Inc.

Caillois, R. (1961). *Man, play and games.* Glencoe, IL: The Free Press.

Csikszentmihalyi. M. (1990). *Flow: The psychology of optimal experience.* New York, NY: Harper & Row, Publishers, Inc.

Goodman, P. (1956). *Growing up absurd.* New York, NY: Vintage Books.

Peele, S. (1989). *Diseasing of America: Addiction treatment out of control.* New York, NY: Lexington Books.

Rifkin, J. (1987). *Time wars: The primary conflict in human history.* New York, NY: Henry Holt.

Riley, J., Marden, C., and Lifshitz, M. (1958). The motivational pattern of drinking. In E. Larrabee and R. Meyersohn (Eds.), *Mass leisure.* Glencoe, IL: The Free Press, (pp. 327-335).

Roberts, K. (1981). *Leisure*—(2nd ed.). London, England: Longman.

Toffler. A. (1970). *Future shock.* New York, NY: Bantam Books.

Veblen, T. (1899). *The theory of the leisure class.* New York, NY: B. W. Heubsch.

Section Four:
The Future

CHAPTER 35

Social Change and Leisure

T he rate of social change in our society and, indeed, much of the world today is truly staggering. By social change, we mean " . . . any modification in the social organization of a society in any of its social institutions or patterns of social roles. Usually social change refers to a significant change in a social behavior or a change in some larger social system rather than to minor changes within a small group" (Theodorson and Theodorson, 1969, p. 384). Whether or not leisure is considered a social institution within modern society, it is shaped by social change within other institutions such as family, education, and work and, in turn, shapes them. In this chapter we will consider a few aspects of social change and ways in which they may reshape our use of leisure.

The Aging Society

Virtually every modern nation has experienced an aging of its population, both because people are living longer and because birth rates decline with modernization. Since age has historically been one of the more powerful predictors not only of what people do during their leisure, but also of the motivations and satisfactions they seek from such experience and the style in which they participate, the rapid aging of the population has profound implications for leisure. Accompanying the aging of the population has been a change in the economic well-being of older people. Today, individuals between the ages of 55 and 64 are the most economically privileged group in society. While those who are 65 and over are often poor, they are no more likely to be poor than any other age group. The official poverty rate among the elderly is 12 or 13 percent, the same as for society as a whole. The rate is now highest (21 percent) for households with children under the age of eighteen. Thus, older people have more financial resources for leisure than they did a mere two decades ago when old age was much more likely to be associated with poverty. Children and adolescents, however, in many ways constitute the new underclass.

The "Baby Boom" generation, born between 1946 and 1954, may or may not move into their fifties and sixties with the same economic resources as their predecessors, but they will certainly be highly socialized into a wide variety of leisure experiences, in better health than their predecessors, and less likely to view old age as a time in which activity should automatically come to an end. Women in this group are more likely to have been employed in the labor force and to have levels of education similar to males. Thus, gender differences may be somewhat lessened.

While the significance of age may change, there will still be massive change in participation due to aging. For example, large declines in participation in sport can be expected, particularly team sports, contact sports and ice and snow sports (Foote, 1990; Naisbitt and Aburdene, 1990). While outdoor recreation activities which are physically demanding may decline in participation, other forms of outdoor recreation, such as bird watching, may experience sharp increases (Foote, 1990).

Retirees currently watch more television per week than those in the work force. It may be expected, therefore, that TV viewing will increase and that television programming will reflect the interest of older people to a greater extent than previously.

Such changes indicate the need for what might be called a retrofitting of leisure environments, facilities and services to meet the needs of an older population. Older people using parks have often been found to be very interested in issues such as safety, contact with the natural environment, socialization, predictability, and cleanliness (Godbey and Blazey, 1983). Facilities such as swimming pools, for instance, in the future will be designed and managed in ways which make them more "user friendly" for older people. That means that it will be possible to enter the water gradually, find a place to sit down while in the water, have shaded area outside the pool to avoid prolonged exposure to sunlight, have a snack bar with food more appropriate to older people and other changes. This type of retrofitting will also take place in parks, where campers are likely to need more of a built environment. Guided tours may reflect a greater interest in history. Sports are more likely to be modified to the same extent that they are modified now for children and youth. Even what constitutes "popular" music is likely to change. Markets will be increasingly segmented and age and generational effects will contribute to such segmentation.

The aging of society may be the most important demographic change affecting leisure in our society. Today's older people may be poor predictors since tomorrow's "active old" will have higher levels of formal education and many are likely to be in better health.

Changes in Women's Roles

Broad changes in the roles of women are reshaping leisure behavior in a variety of ways. The movement of the majority of women into the labor force and slow trend toward closing the income gap between men and women suggests that the leisure patterns of men and women will become more and more similar. Additionally, the fact that people are spending more years in educational institutions, with women now enrolled at about the same rate as men, has meant that men and women have more similar access to leisure facilities and opportunities to learn leisure skills. In many cases, differences between free time use is greater between homemakers and employed women than between employed women and employed men. This is not to argue that any form of equality in terms of leisure values, patterns or resources has taken place, only that differentiation is declining.

Many of the differences in the leisure of men and women historically have been partially explainable by great differences in their income levels, mobility and legal rights. Many have also been understandable in terms of what mores and folkways existed in society concerning appropriate leisure behavior for women. All of these factors are in a state of change. The basic issue is the extent to which the power of men is being replaced by greater autonomy and self-determination, as well as resources, for women.

While issues surrounding women and leisure have generally been ones of equality during the last few decades, such as the desire to have public schools spend equal amounts of money for sports for women, these issues are changing. It is likely that such issues increasingly will deal with women's identities— the visions women have for the use of leisure (Godbey, 1989).

Changes In Work

Massive changes in the conditions and meaning of work, taking place in industrial societies as well as in the composition of the labor force, have great implication for leisure. Perhaps several generalizations can be made. First, the vast majority of jobs today are in the provision of services rather than the production of goods and that majority continues to get bigger. Today over four of five workers are involved in the production of services, including retailing, rather than material goods. Cybernated systems increasingly are capable of producing most material goods with only a few human monitors and labor-intensive production is being transferred to low-wage areas of the world.

Within the "professions," requirements for continuous learning are increasing, making it more expensive to prepare such workers. Since most postindustrial societies are living far above their economic means, there is every reason to believe that there will be fewer and fewer such professionals. They will enter the labor force later in life after expensive education, work long hours for high pay and retire or change occupational directions much earlier. These will be what business analyst Charles Handy (1990) called the "core workers," one of three types of workers in organizations of the future. While core workers will shape the organization, much of the actual work will be contracted out to workers outside the organization who will be paid for the results they produce, not the time they put in. They will be paid in fees, not wages. Finally, there will be workers in the flexible labor force who work in temporary positions or part-time. They are now the fastest growing part of the labor force in most industrial societies. They are disproportionately female. They may have more than one job and, in some sense, might better be thought of as self-employed. Many of them are young people who move through a variety of work experiences.

The fourth kind of work which will be done in society, according to Handy, is work done by the customer. Customers will assemble and finish more of the furniture they buy, bag their own groceries, pump their own gas, put more toys together and otherwise contribute their labor to the things they buy.

Perhaps a fifth type of work should be added to Handy's list—the volunteer. The volunteer will increasingly be treated like a paid employee in society. They will be recruited, "hired," trained, evaluated, "fired," rewarded symbolically, and promoted. Volunteers will replace paid workers to a great extent in a variety of social services and other workplaces. The ratio of volunteers to paid workers will change as many "retired" workers remain or come back into the workplace as volunteers.

Workers will become more diverse in the future in terms of education, income, their ability to pursue a single career, and the meaning of work to them. More work will be done outside of organizations. More work may be done within homes, since telecommunicating allows many to work at home much more efficiently than they could in the office.

Not only are the conditions and organization of work in a state of change, so are the characteristics of the workers. The majority of new workers entering the labor force during the next decade will be women and members of ethnic minority groups. Their preparation for work will largely determine the competitiveness of the United States' economy in global markets. Additionally, work will change to suit their needs, from worksite day care to greater use of flexible hours to remedial education for those whose education was insufficient to prepare them for tomorrow's jobs. As the population of postindustrial nations continues to age, many industries will face a shortage of workers. This is already resulting both in attempts to get previously retired workers back into the labor force in some capacity as well as changes in immigration policies to make it easier for younger workers to enter the country.

The number of hours an individual puts in during his or her lifetime will be dependent upon the extent to which corporate capitalism, which increasingly appears to dominate in much of the world, is contained and controlled by the state. The economic dominance of Japan suggests to many analysts that hours of work are likely to increase in other postindustrial nations in response. Economists such as Schor (1991) have argued that the amount of leisure is decreasing and may continue to do so due to the demands of employers, the preference of workers for more money as opposed to more time away from work, and the addictive nature of consumption.

Such arguments ignore the huge increases in life after retirement, which is where increases in free time have come during the last few decades. While workweek length may or may not have increased slightly during the last decade, the more significant trend is the strong likelihood that the total percentage of the hours of one's life devoted to work have declined and will continue to do so. According to Handy (1990) the hours worked during a lifetime are likely to decline from 100,000 to 50,000. Such a reduction will occur within four options. A first is one in which one assumes a job in a core profession, after many years of education, and works long hours, but for fewer years than others. Thus, they may work 45 hours per week for 45 weeks per year for 25 years. Second and third options are ones in which people work outside of organizations as either part-time or temporary workers. They will work 25 hours per week for 45 weeks (part-time workers) or 45 hours a week for 25 weeks (temporary workers) for 45 years. In a fourth option, individuals may be able to work full-time for ten years, then take ten years out to raise a family, then return to the work force at 45 hours a week for another fifteen years. All of these options add up to 50,000 hours of work over a lifetime—thus cutting the hours of lifetime work in half! Of course, such a reduction would require an increase in productivity rates, so that an economy would be competitive on world markets. Only an adequate return on investment can pay workers at rates that will maintain a viable material standard of living. The alternative is to exclude a large proportion of the population.

Whether such a change is realized depends on a variety of factors, including the extent to which workers continue to consume material goods at higher and higher levels, the degree to which such consumption is taxed, the amount to which work is made more meaningful and the depth to which the desire for more leisure exceeds the desire for more money. While no definitive answers can be given here, there is evidence that Americans' desire for more leisure is increasing. As mentioned earlier, the majority of Americans, for the first time, recently stated that leisure was more important to them than work (Roper, 1990).

These changes indicate that time available for leisure will likely increase dramatically and that the stage of life and the way in which individuals experience leisure will be increasingly different. So, too, will be the satisfactions sought. Our mass leisure culture will likely be more diversified by such change. Leisure's role in people's lives will be increasingly diverse and planning leisure services in both the public and the market sector will require more knowledge about the specific lifestyles of potential participants. Market segmentation for leisure products and services will become even greater.

Economic Constraint

Many social critics and futurists argue that much of the economic affluence found in North America during the 1950s and 1960s was a result of a temporary situation which occurred after World War II. As previously discussed, this temporary period in which North America had little economic competition in the world produced a mentality in which consumption became thought of in open ended terms. This period is largely over. Both the United States and Canada, as well as many other modern nations find themselves in great debt. For the United States, its continued massive military spending has been thought by some historians to risk a decline in both living standards and economic power (Kennedy, 1987). The end of the "Cold War" may now turn considerable military spending toward rebuilding the infrastructure, health care and other purposes with greater economic benefits. Given massive federal deficits, however, part of any "peace dividend" may have to help make up the ballooning debt.

The aging of the population, corruption on Wall Street and in the banking industry, the internationalization of the economy and many other issues have produced new forms of economic constraint. In 1990, U.S. corporations spent almost sixty cents on every dollar to amortize debt—the highest percentage ever. Federal deficits, while presented by government as being in the range of 18 or 19 percent, are more likely 30 percent when all costs are included. The United States has the largest trade deficit of any nation and household savings rates are among the lowest in modern nations. Federal debt service now surpasses defense spending. These issues among others, e.g., spending to replace urban infrastructure, HIV-AIDS costs, care of dependent and frail older persons, delayed costs of environmental pollution, and the bailout of the banking industries mean that economic constraint will likely be a reality, at least compared to the lifestyle our society came to expect in the 1950s and 1960s.

These changes suggest that Americans will not be able to afford such costly consumptive leisure and will be more critical consumers of the leisure products and services they *do* purchase. Further, the material standard of living in any economy depends upon the strength of its production industries in competitive world markets. An economy cannot survive on services.

A More Educated Society

One of the changes within our society during the last two decades and in those of other industrial nations is that the percentage of people attaining higher levels of formal education has continued to increase. While there is much criticism of the quality of such education, this change is likely to reshape leisure behavior in a variety of ways. Increasing levels of formal education means that individuals have been exposed to a wider range of leisure activities and generally have acquired more diverse leisure skills. It may also mean that they are more likely to specialize in given forms of leisure behavior, acquiring more knowledge about a given leisure pursuit and undertaking it for reasons other than diversion or refreshment. People with higher levels of education are likely to be more demanding of those who provide leisure services, more interested in the quality of the environment in which leisure activities take place, and more interested in forms of leisure expression which may be called cultural.

The Decline of the Linear Life Plan

Another important form of social change within modern nations is the break-up of a linear life plan; that is, a way of life in which people undergo highly similar experiences during the same periods of their lives. In the linear life plan, people spend the first few years of their lives at home, and their later childhood and adolescence attending school, then enter the labor force as a "full-time worker" or homemaker and finally retire. All this is changing. Today, there is great variation in such life patterns. People may begin schooling at two (day care), stay in school until they are thirty, enter the labor force at sixteen or after their children are grown, retire at age 55 or not retire at all, begin higher education in their thirties or forties, marry at 15 or 65 and go through three or four cycles of marriage or no cycle at all.

The decline in the standardization of life stage and experiences is likely to be accentuated in the near future because of increased immigration, increased differences in educational attainment, broader variation in the roles of women and of minority groups, the proportion of broken marriages, and reaction to the accelerating rate of change. The effect of this decline of the linear life plan may be increased variation in the meaning, use of and access to leisure for people who are of similar age. Age is likely to be an increasingly weak predictor of leisure behavior while variables such as personality, lifestyle and education level may become even more important. This will make planning for leisure even more difficult, in both public and private sectors.

The Postmodern Era

All the previous changes suggest that our very definition of self is in a state of flux. We are entering, according to Gergen (1991) the "postmodern era." The technological achievements of the last century have produced a radical shift in our relations to each other. Advances in radio, transportation, telephone, computers, and satellite transmission have produced ". . . an enormous barrage of social stimulation. Small and enduring communities, with a limited cast of significant others, are being replaced by a vast and ever-expanding array of relationships" (Gergen, 1991, p. xi). This radical increase in social stimulation moves us toward a state of saturation and sets the stage for "an unbridled relativism" within all spheres of life. All beliefs are thrown into question.

Romantic and modernist viewpoints of the world are falling into disrepute. The romantic view of life, a product of the 19th century, attributed to each person characteristics of personal depth, passion, soul, creativity and moral fiber. Such a view was consistent with "deeply committed relationships, dedicated friendships and life purposes" (Gergen, 1991, p. 6). The modernist view, which rose at the beginning of the 20th century, held that the chief characteristics of self were contained, not in the domain of depth of feeling, but in the ability to reason. "Modernists believed in educational systems, a stable family life, moral training and rational choice of marriage partners" (Gergen, 1991, p. 6).

In the postmodern era, however, as emerging technologies saturate us with multiple voices of humans, we become part of the voices we hear and the increased range of relationships we share, and they become part of us. "Every reality of self gives way to reflexive questioning, irony, and to the playful probing of yet another reality. The center fails to hold" (Gergen, 1991, p. 7).

Our true and knowable selves are therefore in a state of chaos. Our definitions of self are based increasingly upon relationships and less on a consistent self-concept. Our personality becomes a pastiche, borrowing bits and pieces from whatever sources of stimulation flood our minds from day to day. All human acts, Gergen believes, become instrumental. The definitional boundaries of humans are challenged, and nowhere are such boundaries challenged more than during our leisure. Female bodybuilders, "Deadheads" who build their lives around following an aging rock group, androgynous entertainers such as Michael Jackson, bungee jumping, "virtual reality" and other forms of leisure expression emerge from the postmodern consciousness. Social norms surrounding leisure mean less and less. The historically oldest notion of leisure, in which activities were done as an end in themselves, is itself called into question. Leisure and its use become means for shaping and reshaping identities.

Leisure and Cultural Development

While leisure is being reshaped in the postmodern era of so called "developed" nations, leisure within "developing" nations is likely to be reshaped by their own progression of cultural development—one that will move them into closer association with the postmodern world. If three subsystems of culture are recognized—informal contacts with family and friends, local cultural institutions and national or global mass media, (Wnuk-Lipinski, 1981), then historical evolution consists of the transition from informal contacts to local cultural institutions to national media outlets to supranational and global media outlets.

This is not to argue that all cultures evolve in similar fashion. The transition from traditional to modern to postmodern culture is sometimes challenged by new patterns which emerge in individual countries, such as urbanization without industrialization in developing countries such as Brazil, rapid transition from traditional; to modern societies without the elimination of preindustrial structures or the rise of individualism (Japan and other Southeast Asian countries) or the return, perhaps temporarily, to some form of religious or cultural fundamentalism in many "modernizing" countries.

While it would be a mistake to assume that modern nations ever fully assimilate into indistinguishable cultural units, a number of strong forces within postmodern nations both encourage homogeneity among such nations and draw nonmodern nations into the postmodern world. Computers in all countries work basically the same and "Bureaucracies and computers have much in common: both must work reliably by fixed laws and without ambiguity. Because they share these talents, computing machines and bureaucratic people can be easily combined" (Fraser, 1987, p. 327). Computers have become international bookkeepers and, within a global economy, their use will be pushed onto business in developing nations.

Television also contributes to the homogenization of both postmodern and developing nations. Since the program producing capacity of the United States surpasses all the rest of the world, much of what the world sees on television are portrayals of American life.

A similar case can be made for tourism. Tourism, as discussed in Chapter 29, may be understood as a special instance of relations among strangers, often involving guests from postmodern cultures visiting host communities which are less modern. This process tends to bring increased control by those of the postmodern, guest culture.

Finally, the internationalization of economies has produced greater interdependence and has a homogenizing effect upon all nations' products and services.

These changes mean that developing nations are increasingly aware of the leisure patterns and products of modern nations. According to Godbey and Jung (1991), while the leisure practices of postmodern nations are an inappropriate model for the rest of the world because they consume so many material goods, the leisure styles of such nations are appealing to developing nations. "The sense of individual freedom, mobility, style, and relative independence of church, state and family are widely admired" (Godbey and Jung, 1991). Additionally, developing nations desire to consume goods at the same level as residents of postmodern nations. It may be said that the "strength" (but not necessarily goodness) of leisure culture in postmodern nations is greater than that in developing ones. That is, having been exposed to modern leisure culture, those in developing nations may come to prefer them to their own.

Postmodern nations, because they will increasingly recognize that they serve as a model for the leisure customs of developing nations, may therefore seek to modify their own leisure behaviors by taxing consumption and other means. This will happen primarily because postmodern nations will recognize that the environmental consequences of having the majority of the world's people emulate their extremely material intensive style of leisure expression would produce environmental chaos. If the Chinese, for example, owned automobiles at the same rate as do North Americans, the polar ice caps would melt, producing havoc to the low lying coastal areas of the world. Postmodern nations may also try to prevent developing nations from following their example by "cultural barter" (Godbey and Jung, 1991). In exchange for the developing nations agreeing not to emulate the postmodern nations' most consumptive forms of leisure expression, developing nations would be provided with "...various types of widely conceived cultural assistance, such as free access to satellite television, to music and video tapes, various forms of cultural exchange, assistance in preservation of cultural and historical heritage, free technological transfer, and/or joint production of consumer durables serving leisure needs, with emphasis on collective, rather than individual forms of consuming leisure" (Godbey and Jung, 1991, p. 44). Postmodern nations may also seek to promote a phenomenon in the poorest of nations which Sahlins (1976) refers to as high leisure preference at low levels of income. This entails keeping work minimal while using leisure in nonconsumptive ways, such as resting, talking with neighbors and taking walks. Again, such strategies will represent a change for postmodern nations which presently seek to expand markets into developing nations. It will be based on increasing recognition that the nonsustainable lifestyles of postmodern nations cannot be shared by the rest of the world without huge increases in pollution and environmental degradation at present levels of technology.

Perhaps in summary it may be said that such a reorientation in leisure patterns among both developed and developing nations is dependent upon establishing a more common view of social, economic and ecological ideals based upon an increased recognition of interdependence. Such a recognition may result is a first step toward a philosophy of leisure appropriate to nations with vastly differing means.

REFERENCES

Foote, D. (1990). *The age of outdoor recreation in Canada.* Toronto, Ontario, Canada: Ministry of Tourism and Recreation.

Fraser, J. (1987). *Time—The familiar stranger.* Redmond, WA: Tempus Books.

Gergen, K. (1991). *The saturated self-dilemmas of identity in contemporary life.* New York, NY: Basic Books.

Godbey, G. (1989). *The future of leisure services: Thriving on change.* State College, PA: Venture Publishing, Inc.

Godbey, G., and Blazey, M. (1983). Old people in urban parks: An exploratory investigation. *Journal of Leisure Research, 15*(3), 229-245.

Godbey, G., and Jung, B. (1991). Relations between the development of culture and philosophies of leisure. In B. Driver, P. Brown, and G. Peterson (Eds.), *Benefits of leisure.* State College, PA: Venture Publishing, Inc.

Handy, C. (1990). *The age of unreason.* London, England: Arrow Books.

Kennedy, P. (1987). *The rise and the fall of great powers: Economic change and military conflict from 1500 to 2000.* New York, NY: Random House.

Naisbitt, J., and Aburdene, P. (1990). *Megatrends—1990. Ten new directions for the 1990s.* New York, NY: Murrow.

Roper Organization, quoted in *The American Enterprise, 1*(3), May, 1990.

Sahlins, M. (1972). *Stone Age Economics.* New York, NY: Aldine Atherton., p. 72.

Schor, J. (1991). *The overworked American: The unexpected decline of leisure.* New York, NY: Basic Books.

Theodorson, G., and Theodorson, A. (1969). *Modern dictionary of sociology.* New York, NY: Thomas Y. Crowell Publishers.

Wnuk-Lipinski, E. (1981). *Time budget—Social structure—Social policy.* Poland: Wroclaw-Ossolineum.

CHAPTER 36

New Orientations to Leisure

T he traditional sociological approach to leisure has been one of segmentation. Leisure was defined as the time left over after work and necessary
maintenance were completed. As such, it was not only separated from the
essential domains of life, but also secondary in meaning and importance. An
inability to define precisely what was necessary or to assess when the undefined
necessities were accomplished did not prevent sociologists from retaining a
derivative view of leisure. The alterative for some was simply to reject any study
of leisure because it was undefinable and amorphous.

Economists were not as hesitant to deal with leisure. Leisure in economic
terms was the opposite of work: Work can be assigned a dollar value in wages
or other income. Leisure was defined as time for which one is not paid, for which
the value is intrinsic. As such, leisure has an opportunity cost in foregone
income. Time is allocated to work or leisure with an economic value of income
for one and unrealized income for the other. Again, however, the meaning of
leisure was derived from work and activity necessary to permit one to work.

As a consequence, there has been a simple taken-for-granted model in which
any time released from work has been assumed to be available for leisure.
Decreases in average work hours were said to signal a "new age of leisure" as
though there were nothing in life but these two segmented domains. Further,
leisure was quantified as hours and minutes as though its nature were transparent
and self-evident.

An Alternative Model

A different approach involves more than a different definition of leisure. It
involves a different and multidimensional view of life. As argued in Chapter 10,
life is not divided into a simple dichotomy of work and leisure. First, work and
leisure are not that separable in terms of activity, time, place, association, and

even effort. Second, there is more to life than those two domains. In fact, the primary locus of value for most adults in Western societies is neither work nor leisure. It is primary relationships, a bundle of social ties to family and friends and centered around the home (Kelly and Kelly, 1992). At the very least, life is composed of the domains of work, family and community, and leisure. It contains the dimensions of productive endeavor, bonding, and expressive activity. Further, necessity may entail enjoyment, and fun has its required elements. Meaning can be, and to some degree usually is, found in a full range of the domains and dimensions of life.

Leisure is not as separable, nor as secondary, as traditional models demand (Kelly, 1992). Since most of the chapters preceding this one have presented some parts of that argument, only a summary will be offered here:

- Elements of leisure, expressive activity in which the primary meaning is in the experience, are found at the workplace, in the home and school, and just about everywhere else. Much leisure is interstitial, moments and minutes of off-task "fun" or play found or created in the midst of the ongoing round of life.

- At the same time, there is no fully separate realm of leisure in which who we are, how we have learned to define ourselves, our primary roles and relationships, our personal histories, and our access to resources are irrelevant to our choices and styles of leisure. The real lived conditions of our lives have their impacts on what we want, see as possible, and can accomplish in leisure.

- Leisure, then, is complex and multidimensional. It includes a diversity of forms of activity as well as social contexts with a wide range of meanings. It is engagement and disengagement, directed and aimless, structured and spontaneous, imaginative and physical. It is the moment of fantasy in the middle of the workday and a carefully planned and long anticipated vacation. It is a context for the building and strengthening of our most significant relationships, for exploring and developing central expressions of what we may be and become, and the variety that makes life's routines bearable. It is acting, communicating, bonding, learning, creating, and withdrawing (Kelly, 1987). Its importance is based at least in part on its complexity.

In this alternative model, life is not divided into two or three domains, each with a distinct and unique function. All productive endeavor is not limited to work, bonding is not limited to the family and other primary relationships, nor expressive and free action to leisure, nor learning and development to education. Rather, there are at least the four dimensions of life that may be found to a greater or lesser extent in each domain, in any institutional setting. They are:

1) Productivity, activity of recognized social worth and usually associated with the economic sphere of work;

2) Bonding, the communication and commitment of primary relationships and commonly focused on the family;

3) Free expression, action undertaken primarily for the experience and assigned to leisure; and

4) Learning, the personal development of becoming a person of greater ability usually associated with eduction.

In this approach, all four dimensions can at least potentially be realized in any domain of life. There may be productivity in the family, bonding in leisure, learning at work, and expressive behavior almost anywhere. In fact, in a study of employed men and women (Kelly and Kelly, 1992), none of the four dimensions was found to be absent from work, family and community, or leisure. Family/community and leisure were closely associated with bonding central to the meanings of leisure and leisure an important context for exploring and building relationships. Work was the most defined domain, and yet included elements of learning, community, and expression.

Leisure, then, may be seen as a dimension of life that can be found and realized in the midst of life rather than only in segregated times and places. The relative openness of leisure allows for the exploration of new and different actions and identities. The essential self-determination or freedom of leisure opens the possibility of existential, self-creating action. The focus on the experience permits a communication and sharing that make relationships primary rather than some external outcome or product. Leisure is the spontaneity of play, the exhilaration of action, the refreshment of disengagement, the authenticity of honesty, and the optimal experience of involvement for its own sake. The various components of leisure experience may be discovered in moments at work and interludes at school as well as in specially designated and constructed events. As such, leisure is central to life, not peripheral; woven into the day and week, not segmented. It is part of the rhythm and balance of life's meanings, relationships, endeavors, and diversions.

One problem with this model, however, is that leisure may disappear into the complexity of life. What is distinctive, even definable, about leisure when it may be encountered almost any time or anywhere? The leftover time definition, whatever its limitations, was at least clear and even quantifiable. Leisure as a dimension of life may be lost in a sociological focus on the more concrete institutions of the economy, polity, church, school, and family. If leisure can be identified as a separate domain, it may have measurable parameters of time, economic costs, organization, and function. It might be secondary, but at least it can be defined, studied, and measured.

The most viable response is based on a dialectical analysis. Life in society can indeed be divided into domains that have central functions and identifiable organizational structure. Leisure, too, has its designated off-work and off-task times, however they may be scattered in an postindustrial society. It has its public and market sector provisions, its organizational components, and its economic costs and benefits. There are activity forms that are not product-determined for most participants, events for which the experience is the main meaning, and even legally mandated periods in which work cannot be required for most in the labor force. Recognizing the fuzzy boundaries, irregularities, and exceptions does not obliterate such structure and regularity.

The other end of the dialectic, however, recognizes the pervasive nature of leisure as action. It is act and meaning that is inseparable from the contexts of work and family, from sets of social roles we all play, and the long- and short-term intentions of our actions and interactions. Leisure as a dimension of life stresses the interwoven process of life in society, the connections and overlapping meanings. Leisure as a dimension of life focuses on agency, on the interpreting and acting person who makes a zigzag course through the journey of life. When the focus is on agency, then play is endemic to all of life rather than a separable domain.

Leisure in Life

In this dialectic, leisure is both agency and structure. It is simultaneously a dimension and a domain. This view may not lend itself to analytical simplicity, but it does more justice to the nature of life in society. A research design may deliberately oversimplify in order to obtain measurable outcomes. Explanatory theory, however, must incorporate a full range of experiences, meanings, and contexts.

In the study of leisure, the term "holism" has been essentially negative. It proposes that leisure cannot be segmented by timetable or location. That denial is now taken for granted. The dangers of the old work-leisure dichotomy are also taken for granted. Life is not as dualistic as that model presupposed. The more current issue, then, is what leisure *is*, not what it is not.

"Play" is action, even a style of action. It is the action dimension of leisure. As such, it is surely not limited to a few select contexts. As actors, we may be playful almost anywhere. One way of dealing with the tragic and the ultimately consequential is to treat it in a playful mode. There is play in the surgery theater, in the strategic bomber with its nuclear payload, and in the face of death. A certain "lightness of being" can be created anytime and anywhere. Conversely, seriousness can be introduced into any game and flight of fancy in a way that destroys its playfulness. Play is not just in designated times. It may well be the transcendence of the routine that gets us through the day.

From this perspective, leisure is profoundly human and humanizing. Much of modern life seems out of control. In a mass society, the actions of the individual often seem limited to choices among packaged products and ideas. In bureaucratized institutions, rationalized procedures and routines require conformity, sometimes even cheerful conformity. Amid economic forces that operate on a world scale, there seems no action to take that alters the wasteful affluence of the few and the literal destruction of so many. Leisure can be an escape from this loss of autonomy and control. If it dominates all of life, it can be dehumanizing. If it provides a realization of action in the midst of so much control, it may be necessary. Life that is constantly product directed and on task may stifle human capacities to love, to create, to express, and to grow. It might be ideal if all life could be free and authentic; it may be more realistic to hold out for leisure as a dimension and a domain.

Leisure in this perspective is autotelic action that finds its meaning in involvement in the experience. It is action that expresses and develops the self and that creates community with other selves. It is not free in the sense of being without structure or even limitations, but it is free in the sense of being fundamentally self-determined. It may be argued that through the continual lifelong processes of socialization, no action is really free. Certainly none is devoid of social and cultural learning. Yet, it may be a necessity of human existence to live in a faith that action may be real and consequential, that there is a real existential dimension to life.

Still in this perspective is the view of Aristotle and Josef Pieper (1963) that such action is necessary for the continuation and development of a culture and a social system. Some transcendence of the realm of sheer necessity, however and wherever it may be achieved, is the basis for the creation of the dialogue of ideas and the creation of beauty on which a culture is built. Some time of celebration is required to bring peoples together into a sense of unity and mutual responsibility. Leisure, then, is not trivial and residual; but is essential to the actualization of life together.

It is also essential to moving into the future with flexibility and openness. At the heart of leisure, according to Huizinga (1950) and a host of others (Kelly, 1987), is the creativity of play. Play is action that explores the possible and invades the "not-yet." It is play as the action dimension of leisure that creates the forms and images, the concepts and techniques, that enable humankind to cope with change and move toward the future. Leisure, in its freedom, is in the middle of that most necessary function of creative action.

What does it mean to be human? Certainly it means to develop, to engage in a lifelong process of becoming. Being human involves ties to others, action that is of worth to others, and accepting being a part of the society with requirements as well as opportunities. It also means being a unique individual with a life course not quite like that of anyone else. The journey of life is more than reading the road signs and obeying traffic rules; it is setting out to go somewhere and coping with all the barriers and detours. Routes are recreated and redirected in the changing contexts of life and as we change ourselves. Along this journey, leisure is at least a bit of open space, occasional opportunities to enter and even recreate new environments. Leisure is a dimension of becoming in the midst of directions and frameworks set by others.

As such, leisure is a human dimension. It is the possibility and sometimes the actualization of freedom. It is the aim of becoming and the accomplishment of being. It is authentic action amid alienation. Life is more than leisure; but in this human and humanizing sense, there may be no authentic life without leisure.

Value Systems and Leisure

Leisure has been viewed in a variety of ways through the history of Western societies. There have been contradictions and conflicts in these views. Any assumption that leisure is always positive, a "good thing," is contradicted by its place in some value systems.

For example, leisure may be seen as waste. If the sole value is productivity, then any resource committed to unproductive activity is waste. Re-creation can be justified if it is demonstrated to increase productivity. According to the Protestant Ethic thesis of Weber (1958), life in this world is the arena of divine and human action. At the center of the human action required by the deity is work, responsible and productive effort rationally designed to maximize outcomes. Leisure as a sphere of life is of no intrinsic value. Only rational recuperative activity can be justified on the basis of its contribution to work. From a different perspective, Veblen (1899) argued that leisure is nonproductive activity that symbolizes wealth at a level transcending any necessity. Leisure is conspicuous waste that symbolizes membership in an elite social class.

Leisure may also be accepted as a reward for productive work. Leisure time is earned by work time. It is realized only after work time is completed and work obligations are fulfilled. Leisure in economics is relegated to the realm of consumption. The resources for leisure, time and money, are earned through compliance in the workplace in productive engagement. From a critical perspective (see Chapter 25), leisure has no value of its own, but becomes an instrument of social control that binds laborers to their work roles and to the system that gives them the reward of leisure. Leisure is the "dessert" at the end of the meal. It also becomes a segment of the economy that provides a market for goods and services that yield a return on investment capital.

Leisure is sometimes viewed as neutral, a time that can be used for constructive or destructive activity. Sociologists who adhere to value neutrality prefer to pass no judgements on the worth of various kinds of activity. Photographing birds and constructing shelter for the homeless may be leisure when a free choice in nonwork time. Gang violence and drug use may also be leisure when chosen as a preferred way of life. No value judgement is levied on either the nature of the activity nor its outcomes for value free purists. A more moderate position would render negative judgement on activity that harms others or destroys the viability of the social system, but not on the individual motives or experiences.

As with the waste and reward views, leisure may be considered secondary as a part of the balance of life. It is recognized that it is difficult to remain on-task all the time, that some lightness and diversion are an important part of the balance of life. Activity that focuses on the experience, that is primarily expressive, serves a purpose for the individual who needs a balance to concentrated and demanding roles such as work, parenting, homemaking, or even community responsibilities. "All work and no play" has negative consequences that may feed back into more important roles and responsibilities. Leisure is recuperative, off-task minutes and hours that provide a necessary balance to the real engagement of the world. It is also possible to suggest that the various elements of a balanced life—work, leisure, family and community, and development—can be more or less equally valued. The balance may shift as we move through the life course, but all dimensions are important to a fulfilled and balanced life, to the realization of humanity.

The focus may be on the action dimension of leisure, on its existential dimension. Leisure is action done primarily for its own sake, for the meanings of the experience. Those meanings may be at the center of the action, the involvement and meeting of challenge (see Chapter 14). They may be in some composite of enjoyment that involves communication and sharing in an action context. The meaning, however, is primarily in the state of consciousness of the actor. The individual takes action because of what he or she is and becomes in the process. Even more, what we are is at least in part created in that action.

Leisure is also social in its nature. There is the fact that what we do, how we do it, and what it means are all learned in our social contexts. There is the persistent element of the social in activity, who is there and the quality of interaction is integral to the meaning and satisfaction of the episode. There is the importance of bonding, of the relationships themselves that tie leisure so closely to family, friendship, and other relational commitments. Leisure is not detached, but takes place in the midst of social contexts with histories, expectations, and taken-for-granted definitions. Leisure is social in context and intentions, in communicative action and mutual interaction.

Leisure, then, is both existential and social. It is *social expression* in which we take action with and for each other that is focused on the experience. In such action we realize what we are. At the same time, action may be directed toward becoming, toward what we might be. Leisure as action, then, is both immediate and future-oriented. In fact, it may be creative just because of the focus on the present rather than on defined outcomes. It is existential in the sense of decisive action that is developmental, not by intention but by being real action. It is social in the sense of involving other people and their definitions of the situation, but also at the center of the meanings of the experience. As suggested in the previous section, leisure is both existential and social because human beings are both. It is a dimension of human life—complex because life is complex and dialectical because life is dialectical.

Leisure and the Quality of Life

What is the place of leisure in personal and social value systems? As just outlined, there are many possible approaches. Some define leisure as secondary to greater values. Some locate leisure in the midst of a full set of values as one among many with its own meaning and integrity. A few have even held leisure to be the highest value, the end for which other aspects of life exist.

One approach is to value leisure as integral to a greater value, the quality of human life. Human life, from this perspective, may be seen as special, but still a part of the total ecosystem, of the interrelated global and galactic fabric of existence. Leisure is not ultimate or final as a value, but has an essential place in the overall meaning and context of life. Incorporating several of the previous perspectives in a complementary model, it is part of the individual and social balance of life. It is expressive action that realizes individual action and social interaction that expresses the social nature of being human. It is personal and social expression that lifts life beyond survival to the creation of self, of community, and of culture. It is beyond requirement, action in the middle of life that at the same time transcends necessity. As play, it does more than reproduce the past and the present; it is open to and even creates a future that may be at least a little new and different.

What is the future of leisure? Of course that depends on all sorts of factors—economic, social, political, and ecological. But it also depends on the value systems that develop in modern societies. Leisure may take a greater place in the economy of consumption. It may become more important to individuals who crave some freedom and autonomy in the midst of structured demand and even repression. Or, it may come to be valued as essential to the overall quality of life.

There are, in fact, some indications of just this development of a new value system (Inglehart, 1990). It does not disvalue production and the material, bonding and the social, or the varieties of learning and personal development. There is, however, in North America and Western Europe a measurable shift away from granting primacy to material values and physical security to a greater concern with self-expression and the quality of life. There is evidence of the growth of an ethic that stresses the quality of life's experiences and environments rather than possessions and prestige. It suggests that a postmaterialist world view is developing, especially among the young with university education, that places a premium on self-creating action and the quality of human relationships. In such a new world view, the existential and social elements of leisure have more than a secondary place. Leisure may become a valued and accepted dimension of human life.

REFERENCES

Huizinga, J. (1950). *Homo ludens: A study of the play element in culture.* Boston, MA: Beacon Press.

Inglehart, R. (1990). *Culture shift in advanced industrial society.* Princeton, NJ: Princeton University Press.

Kelly, J. (1987). *Freedom to be: A new sociology of leisure.* New York, NY: Macmillan.

Kelly, J. (1992). Leisure. Chapter in *the encyclopedia of sociology,* E. Borgatta (Ed.), pp. 1099-1107. New York, NY: Macmillan.

Kelly, J., and Kelly, J. (1992). Centrality, commitment, and satisfaction in three life domains. (under review).

Pieper, J. (1963). *Leisure: The basis of culture.* New York, NY: New American Library.

Veblen, T. (1899). *The theory of the leisure class.* New York, NY: Macmillan.

Weber, M. (1958). *The Protestant ethic and the spirit of capitalism.* T. Parsons (Trans.). New York, NY: Scribners.

CHAPTER 37

From Consumption to Action

The rise of science and technology has led to an ordering of the world in more absolute ways than humans thought possible. While this has brought about miracles of production and has reshaped the material standard of living for millions in ways unimaginable to previous generations it has also led to a ordering of life which is alienating. "Human institutions—the state, the government, the civil service, the party, the factory—have become impersonal and anonymous powers of enormous strength which the individual tries in vain to master. Thence arises the growing sense of frustration, anxiety and despair which pervades the Western hemisphere. At the back of it all is man's (sic) estrangement from nature" (Heinemann, 1953, p. 168). Simultaneous with the rise of science and technology has been a philosophical revolt against the dark side of what it has brought. This revolt may be called Existentialism.

> The essence of the existential protest is that rationalism can pervade a whole civilization, to the point where the individuals in the civilization do less and less thinking, and perhaps wind up doing none at all. It can bring this about by dictating the fundamental ways and routines by which life itself moves. Technology is one material incarnation of rationalism, since it derives from science; bureaucracy is another, since it aims at the rational control and ordering of social life, and the two—technology and bureaucracy—have come more and more to rule our lives (Barrett 1958, p. 269).

In a world in which technology, bureaucracy and rising affluence provided more opportunities for leisure but increasingly defined in advance the ways in which those opportunities would unfold, the existential search for the authentic was a natural consequence. The line between work and leisure became artificial for those who viewed the world in existential terms. If there is no "human nature," if we must define or seek to define ourselves through authenticating acts, if we must literally bring ourselves into being on an individual basis without the comfort and guidelines of tradition or religion, then the line between work and leisure is meaningless. All activity, whether "work" or "leisure," can potentially contribute to a fundamental task: the task of defining who one is.

While the rational side of humans is viewed as being capable of infinite development by the logical positivistic view of the world often found in science and technology, existentialism sees it as only one facet of our being. In a world in which any concept of God is peripheral, the notion of "self" is abstract and in need of further definition. Such a need the individual must meet through his or her own actions. As the philosopher Kierkegaard wrote in the middle of the 19th century, "When I behold my possibilities I experience the dread which is 'the dizziness of freedom' and my choice is made in fear and trembling" (Kaufmann, 1956, p. 17). Freedom, without the comfort of theological and ethical systems, can produce terror and absurdity.

It is small wonder, then, that many people reject freedom at an individual level during their leisure. In an abstract world in which our lives are highly programmed, many will suffer alienation. Such alienation may lead to leisure being used simply as an arena for consumption of the products and services which have been planned for them. Indeed such a course of action appears to have taken place within highly industrialized societies. Leisure is used to watch television, for shopping, for mass-produced tourism "packages," for mass-produced films, magazines and newspapers. The forms of most leisure activities are increasingly shaped by the products and services produced by huge organizations.

This mass consumption of both material goods and experiences is not part of a sustainable culture for several reasons. First, the volume of goods produced has had fundamentally negative effects upon the human habitat. For example, the ozone layer surrounding the earth, on which our lives depend, is disappearing at the rate of two to four percent per year. Second, the population of the world is doubling and our highly consumptive society does not provide a useful model for such a world. Third, Western societies suffer from a profound loss of sense of community and of spirituality which harm our sense of well-being and our contentment. Fourth, levels of formal education are increasing at a great rate, and we are at the forefront of developing models of lifelong learning for the majority. Such a situation means that leisure must increasingly serve as an arena for both learning and the exercise of knowledge.

Changing Leisure from Consumption to Action

If leisure as alienating mass consumption is to change as rapidly as is necessary, many alterations must be made in society. While it is not possible to consider all of them here, the following appear to be some areas in which such change is critical.

Recognizing Leisure's Relation to Health

One force in our society which is working toward the transition of the use of leisure for purposes other than consumption is the changing notions of health and wellness. While there has historically been a tendency to believe that "health" is a service which is "delivered" by those in the medical profession and industry, in reality, the rise of the medical model of practice has had little to do with our health. Noted scientists Robert Ornstein and Paul Erlich (1989) stated that, to logically approve the huge amounts our government spends for "health care," one would have to believe that such service is important to people's health. "It is not. To justify such a massive social investment, one would also have to believe that the entire medical enterprise including all the accumulated medical research evidence and training of the past century, has provided a meaningful extension of life. It has not" (Ornstein and Erlich, 1989). We live only four or five years longer than those in Britain did a century ago, and most of the advance in longevity has been due to advances in sanitation such as the purification of water, better sewer systems and improved hygiene. Epidemiologists John and Sonia McKinley (1989) pointed out that medical intervention played an extremely small role in the containment of communicable diseases " . . . medical intervention in infectious diseases such as tuberculosis, diphtheria, whooping cough, influenza and the like are responsible for only 3.5 percent of the total decline in mortality since 1900." The major elements in enhancing resistance to disease were improved nutrition and environmental changes that made food safer and purer, especially for infants (Ornstein and Erlich, 1989). Other studies of the huge expansion of the availability of medical services found little or no effect on health " . . . in the five to ten percent range, results of much less consequence than such day to day factors as marital status, employment status, happiness in relationships, and the availability of care givers" (Ornstein and Erlich, 1989). Our state of health is largely determined by other factors than medical treatment. Over 80 percent of the factors which determine our state of health have to do with our environment, our relations with friends and enemies, the quality of our education, our status in the community and how we think about ourselves. It has only been during the last thirty years that medical practice could be said, on balance, to do more good than harm (Ornstein and Erlich, 1989).

Our state of health, then, is largely determined by how we live our everyday lives, our behaviors, emotions and, sometimes, our luck. Other than having the right genes, what is most important in determining health is our own personal habits and daily behaviors and our collective actions. If all forms of cancer were cured immediately, our life expectancies would go up an average of only two years, but if "good nutrition, exercise and good health habits (especially not smoking) were followed, average life expectancy would increase by seven years" (Ornstein and Erlich, 1989).

The Failure of Most Human Activities Done for the Sake of Health

If the way in which we lead our everyday lives and the condition of the environment in which we live have more to do with our state of health than does medical practice, it might be assumed that the individual act undertaken as a means to the end of improving health would be a critical determinant in one's state of health. Unfortunately, such acts usually fail. In terms of losing weight, for instance, 75 to 90 percent of those who undertake a diet have not lost weight one year later. Those who join organizations or seek treatment as a means of ending an addiction are generally no more likely to end the addiction than those who don't. Alcoholics who join Alcoholics Anonymous are no more likely to cease drinking than alcoholics who undergo no treatment (Peele, 1989). Joining an exercise class for "fitness" is highly unlikely to become a permanent part of one's style of life unless the activity becomes desired for its own sake. People who successfully change their dietary habits in order to eat foods which are healthful are unlikely to sustain these eating habits unless they come to prefer the taste and texture of more healthful foods. The activities which we undertake only as a means to an end, even the end of improved health, are not likely to succeed. Even when they do succeed temporarily, they are likely to cease once the perceived threat to health is minimized. There is, as psychologist B. F. Skinner would have identified it, a kind of aversive conditioning at work in such cases. That is, we do something only out of fear of punishment if we fail to do it. When this fear is removed, we return to our former way of behaving.

Rethinking Concepts of Health and Illness

Both "health" and "illness" are concepts which are in a remarkable state of change in our society. Although modern scientific concepts have sometimes thought of disease as an outside agent which invades the body or as a localized phenomenon within the body, many of our ideas are in a state of flux. Illness may be thought of as an imbalance and the imbalance may be thought of in terms not only of the physical, psychological and social aspects of the individual, but also as an imbalance between the individual, society and the ecosystem.

Illness, then, like life itself, may be thought of as a complex web of interrelationships throughout the universe or as something negative which happens to the body of an individual. This variation in thought extends to issues surrounding specific illnesses, such as cancer. Cancer expert Carl Simonton has argued that cancer must be understood as a disorder of the entire system . . . "a disease that has a localized appearance but has the ability to spread, and that really involves the entire organism—the mind as well as the body. The original tumor is merely the tip of the iceberg" (Simonton, 1988).

People, according to Simonton, may develop illness as a problem solver. That is, they may respond to stressful situations by getting ill when they find it impossible to solve their problems in a healthy way. Individuals who suffer from depression, in some cases may essentially shut down their systems as a means of escaping problems which are beyond their ability to handle. They may also do this by using a "social illness"—pathological behavior such as crime, violence or drug abuse.

New ways of thinking about health and illness have resulted in the increasingly widespread use of the concepts of "wellness," "well-being" and "optimal health."

> The concept of well-being or optimal health involves a delicate balance intellectual, and social health. Physical health may be thought of in terms of fitness, nutrition, control of substance abuse, medical self-help, and so on. Emotional health may refer to such areas as stress management and care for emotional crises. Examples of spiritual health are those themes dealing with love, charity, purpose and meditation. Intellectual health encompasses topics in the realms of education, achievement, career development, and others, while subjects concerned with social health may include relationships among friends, families and communities (Alberta Centre for Well-Being, 1989).

This emerging concept assumes that our health or well-being is the product of a number of interrelated aspects of not only our physical being but also of our mind, emotions and spirit as well as the environment in which we live.

Leisure's Relation to Health

If the definition of leisure by Godbey (1990) is compared to definitions of well-being, many commonalities are discovered. That definition is, to repeat:

> Leisure is living in relative freedom from the external compulsive forces of one's culture and physical environment so as to be able to act from internally compelling love in ways which are personally pleasing, intuitively worthwhile, and provide a basis for faith.

This definition considers relative freedom from negative aspects of our culture and environment as being prerequisite to leisure. Many of these freedoms are of our own making. The notion of "prevention" is useful here. That is, our relative freedom and our health can be strengthened by the extent to which we act in ways which avoid illness rather than attempt to cure it after it occurs.

If we live in relative freedom, leisure involves "acting." Thus, our actions both help determine our relative freedom and involve acting "from internally compelling love." To act from internally compelling love must surely be related to both leisure and health. Philosopher Josef Pieper (1952), as discussed in Chapter 13, thought some people could not experience leisure because they could not joyfully celebrate the world and their own life within that world. Our ability to love and what we love are related to the will to act. The human will, we are presently beginning to understand, is of critical importance in our susceptibility to disease and our response to it. To act involves both purpose and exercising the human will. So, too, does leisure.

Strangely enough, when we act in ways which are "intuitively worthwhile" such acts likely have greater health benefits than activities which are undertaken as a means to an end. If you learn to love the game of tennis, for example, you are no longer doing it merely for health purposes. Skills, appreciations and socialization into the activity may all be necessary before one loves it for its own sake.

In summary, it may be said that we, like other animals, are motivated to a great extent by pleasure, but, unlike other animals, we are capable of learning to derive pleasure from new experiences, to come to regard them as leisure. This being the case, the extent to which healthy behaviors can become part of our leisure lives, part of what we would voluntarily do for its own sake, may be a critical variable in determining the extent to which we lead healthy lives.

The Existential Act as Healthy Leisure

From the above, the relation of leisure to wellness is evident. So, too, is its relation to the existential act. That is, to be healthy requires using leisure in ways which involve individual decision and action, rather than the mere consumption of that which exists. As Kelly noted: "The realization of freedom, in leisure or any other mode of action, requires acting on a definition of self and environment that sees the possibilities beyond those presented by the social consensus" (Kelly, 1987, p. 56). The decision and act involved in leisure require individual uniqueness. "If the actor believes that freedom is simply following the norms and dictums of some external authority or guide, then leisure may be a prison as much as any other domain of life. In fact, an illusion of freedom would be the very heart of such leisure bad faith. A perception of freedom would serve to shield the actor from really decisive action" (Kelly, 1987, p. 56). The "healthy" use of leisure involves deciding and acting in ways in addition to those which are laid out in advance by society. To do this involves a consciousness which understands the necessity of doing so as well as sufficient will to do so. Perhaps this is what the ancient Athenians understood since they viewed the elite life of leisure as a difficult life to pursue; one devoted to self-understanding and perfection. Such understanding and perfection must be rooted in comprehending how one is different from the rest of society as well as how one is similar. Only such an understanding can ultimately contribute to the common good— and to one's health.

Controlling Technology

As discussed in Chapter 35, postindustrial nations pursue a style of leisure which cannot be either imitated by developing nations or, indeed, sustained by themselves. Such leisure is not only highly consumptive but is often guided by nothing more than technological advance. Thus, for instance, the creation of a variety of all-terrain vehicles has reshaped how deserts and forests are used for recreation. VCRs have led to millions of Americans spending millions of hours watching rented movies. This has created a situation in which leisure behavior springs less from the uniqueness of the individual or the consensus of the culture, than from a combination of technological innovation and advertising.

Since the beginnings of the Industrial Revolution, human behavior in all realms of life has been shaped by the products of technology. Technological advance has allowed us to consume more and more—" . . . since the beginning of the eighteenth century, while world population has grown by a factor of eight, production has increased one-hundred fold. In just the last forty years alone, industrial production has multiplied by seven and the consumption of mineral resources has tripled" (Attali, 1991, p. 79). Many futurists believe that we are entering a period of hyperindustrialization in which the creation of new products will increasingly shape all forms of behavior, including our use of leisure. The new products of technology increasingly shape or define the ways in which people will interact with them. Computers, for example, as Fraser (1987) observed, have not so much become "user friendly" as humans have had to become "computer friendly."

Such a situation, in some ways, is the essence of the basis of the existential protest. Life has been ordered to such a great extent that its unfolding produces only alienation and passive pleasure seeking. Americans during their leisure spend the bulk of time watching television, reading mass-produced newspapers and magazines, or shopping for mass-produced goods in shopping malls which have a striking similarity. These behaviors are shaped and reshaped by technology but allow little room for individual acts which are unique and authenticating.

Since leisure, according to Kelly (1987, p. 56) is " . . . the actualization of meaning-producing action that is not instrumentally determined by the social forces of a consensual or power-shaped system" much of the free time use of the products of high technology may not be considered leisure. Controlling the role of technology, especially during our free time, may therefore be critical to our transformation to a society in which leisure is more central. There may be numerous ways in which such change comes about. One example may be limiting our use of television. While today, much television viewing is exploratory and involves clicking from channel to channel, people may go on a television "diet," watching a limited number of hours and only those programs they have identified in advance as worthwhile. Some other forms of technology may simply be banned from certain recreation areas.

There are already precedents for this. "Boom boxes" have been banned from some sections of beaches, off-road vehicles have been banned from some public outdoor recreation areas, some cocktail lounges and bars have removed their television sets.

While such examples may have a slight impact on the extent to which technology shapes our leisure, the coming period of "hyperindustrialism" (Attali, 1991) in which technologically advanced products reshape every aspect of our lives may overwhelm these small changes. How to resist such technological advance may be the critical issue in terms of our use of leisure and the quality of our lives. Perhaps it may be said that the impulse for any such resistance will be spiritual. It may also require that people be educated for leisure in new ways.

Education for Leisure

Education for leisure, in the coming years, is likely to have two components: first, learning about and directly experiencing a variety of leisure activities and, second, the development of an understanding of why choice itself must be limited. Both these agendas, of course, are dependent upon the quality of all education.

Let us first deal with the traditional notion of education for leisure. For recreation educator Charles Brightbill, who popularized the term "education for leisure" during the 1950s, education for leisure involved exposing people in their homes, schools and communities to experiences which help them develop appreciations and skills to use in their increasingly available non work time (Brightbill, 1960).

Leisure education has also implied helping people learn more about leisure alternatives within their own community or elsewhere in the world. In leisure counseling, individuals may clarify values, expand their consciousness or make judgements about the appropriateness of various leisure alternatives.

While such ideas may be valuable, they do not begin to go as far as the ancient Athenian notion that education concerned itself first and foremost with learning that would enable the individual to live a life of leisure. Vocational training was of a distinctly lesser order. Education for leisure was education for the use of freedom and the assumption was that a free life could not be lived in ignorance. Such education was thus the basis of democracy, although democracy for a limited number. Today the issue of whether freedom can survive in the absence of education is a central one. Such education must provide a basis from which to make intelligent choices which benefit both the people and the environment in which they live. Further, in opposition to Greek philosophy, all men and women must be considered fully human and capable of exercising freedom.

Education for leisure must also show humans why their exercise of choice must be limited. "The great paradox of a global consumer democracy is that the right to pleasure and happiness, the right to choice in the present, may well be a toxic elixir we are forcing our children to drink. If man, the marginal parasite, turns the earth into a dead artifact, the dream of material pleasure will have murdered life itself. In order to survive the triumph of our secular ideals, we need a new idea of the sacred" (Attali, 1991, pp. 17-18). If our use of leisure is viewed only in terms of individual freedom, our culture cannot be sustained nor can life itself. Limits must be set on our use of leisure. The only alternative to individuals setting such limits is for the state to set them through the use of force. While the state will undoubtedly set more limits in attempts to protect our environment and hence our children's heritage, education for leisure must allow individuals to better understand that the goals of leisure transcend individual pleasure and relate to individual understanding and communal improvement. This was the assumption of the ancient Athenians and it must now be made universal in a divided world.

Leisure, in particular, must be understood as a life of discipline rather than of mere consumerism. Such discipline requires that freedom be viewed as a non absolute commodity which has the capacity to do great harm as well as great good. Leisure must also be understood as being a meaningless notion away from the expression of ideals. "Leisure always carries with it the responsibility for inventing an ideal" (Goodale and Godbey, 1988, p. xiii). If it does not matter to individuals what they do, then other people will shape their lives for them to an increasing extent. Leisure requires the invention of what is worthwhile at a personal level. Further, leisure in the modern world is much more concerned with the invention of meaning than with the search for pleasure. Finding things which are worth doing for their own sake, however, produces meaning—makes sense of the world at a spiritual level. Such a process produces pleasure as a byproduct.

It must also produce and reflect the spiritual impulse. The transition to a society of leisure, dreamed of by humans for centuries, is today not so much a matter of technical advance but of understanding the basis upon which the universe, all life within it, and even our very selves can be celebrated and are therefore sacred.

REFERENCES

Alberta Centre for Well-Being. (1989). Newsletter. Edmonton, Alberta, Canada: University of Alberta.

Attali, J. (1991). *Millennium—Winners and losers in the coming world order.* New York, NY: Random House.

Barrett, W. (1958). *Irrational man—A study of existential philosophy.* New York, NY: Doubleday and Co.

Brightbill, C. (1960). *The challenge of leisure.* Englewood Cliffs, NJ: Prentice-Hall.

Fraser, J. (1987). *Time—The familiar stranger.* Redmond, WA: Tempus Books.

Godbey, G. (1990). *Leisure in your life: An exploration,* (3rd ed.). State College, PA: Venture Publishing, Inc.

Goodale, T., and Godbey, G. (1988). *The evolution of leisure: Historical and philosophical perspectives.* State College, PA: Venture Publishing, Inc., p. xiii.

Heinemann, F. H. (1953). *Existentialism and the modern predicament.* New York, NY: Harper Torchbooks.

Kaufmann, Walter. (1956). *Existentialism from Dostoevsky to Sartre.* New York, NY: Meridian Books.

Kelly, J. (1987). *Freedom to be—A new sociology of leisure.* New York, NY: Macmillan.

McKinley, J., and McKinley, S. (1989). Quoted in R. Ornstein and P. Erlich, *New world—New mind.* New York, NY: Doubleday.

Ornstein, R., and Erlich, P. (1989). *New world—New mind.* New York, NY: Doubleday.

Peele, S. (1989). *The diseasing of America: Addiction treatment out of control.* New York, NY: Lexington Books.

Pieper, J. (1952). *Leisure: The basis of culture.* New York, NY: New American Library

Simonton, C. (1978). Getting Well Again. Los Angeles, CA: Tarcher. Cited in F. Capra (1988) *Conversations with remarkable people.* New York, NY: Simon and Schuster.

Skinner. B. F. (1978). *Reflections on behavioralism and society.* Englewood Cliffs, NJ: Prentice-Hall.

Author Index

A

B

T

V

W

Z

Subject Index

S

T

BOOKS FROM VENTURE PUBLISHING

Acquiring Parks and Recreation Facilities through Mandatory Dedication: A Comprehensive Guide
    by Ronald A. Kaiser and James D. Mertes

The Activity Gourmet
    by Peggy Powers

Adventure Education
    edited by John C. Miles and Simon Priest

Amenity Resource Valuation: Integrating Economics with Other Disciplines
    edited by George L. Peterson, B. L. Driver and Robin Gregory

Behavior Modification in Therapeutic Recreation: An Introductory Learning Manual
    by John Dattilo and William D. Murphy

Benefits of Leisure
    edited by B. L. Driver, Perry J. Brown and George L. Peterson

Beyond Bingo: Innovative Programs for the New Senior
    by Sal Arrigo, Jr., Ann Lewis and Hank Mattimore

Beyond the Bake Sale—A Fund Raising Handbook for Public Agencies
    by Bill Moskin

The Community Tourism Industry Imperative—The Necessity, The Opportunities, Its Potential
    by Uel Blank

Dimensions of Choice: A Qualitative Approach to Recreation, Parks, and Leisure Research
    by Karla A. Henderson

Doing More With Less in the Delivery of Recreation and Park Services: A Book of Case Studies
    by John Crompton

Evaluation of Therapeutic Recreation Through Quality Assurance
    edited by Bob Riley

The Evolution of Leisure: Historical and Philosophical Perspectives
    by Thomas Goodale and Geoffrey Godbey

The Future of Leisure Services: Thriving on Change
    by Geoffrey Godbey

The Game Finder—A Leader's Guide to Great Activities
    by Annette C. Moore

Gifts to Share—A Gifts Catalogue How-To Manual for Public Agencies
    by Lori Harder and Bill Moskin

Great Special Events and Activities
    by Annie Morton, Angie Prosser and Sue Spangler

Internships in Recreation and Leisure Services: A Practical Guide for Students
    by Edward E. Seagle, Jr., Ralph W. Smith and Lola M. Dalton

Leadership and Administration of Outdoor Pursuits
    by Phyllis Ford and James Blanchard

The Leisure Diagnostic Battery: Users Manual and Sample Forms
    by Peter A. Witt and Gary Ellis

Leisure Diagnostic Battery Computer Software
    by Gary Ellis and Peter A. Witt

Leisure Education: A Manual of Activities and Resources
    by Norma J. Stumbo and Steven R. Thompson

Leisure Education II: More Activities and Resources
    by Norma J. Stumbo

Leisure Education: Program Materials for Persons with Developmental Disabilities
    by Kenneth F. Joswiak

Leisure Education Program Planning: A Systematic Approach
    by John Dattilo and William D. Murphy

Leisure in Your Life: An Exploration, Third Edition
    by Geoffrey Godbey

A Leisure of One's Own: A Feminist Perspective on Women's Leisure
    by Karla Henderson, M. Deborah Bialeschki, Susan M. Shaw and Valeria J.
        Freysinger

Marketing for Parks, Recreation, and Leisure
    by Ellen L. O'Sullivan

Outdoor Recreation Management: Theory and Application, Revised and Enlarged
    by Alan Jubenville, Ben Twight and Robert H. Becker

Planning Parks for People,
    by John Hultsman, Richard L. Cottrell and Wendy Zales Hultsman

Private and Commercial Recreation
    edited by Arlin Epperson

The Process of Recreation Programming Theory and Technique, Third Edition
    by Patricia Farrell and Herberta M. Lundegren

Quality Management: Applications for Therapeutic Recreation
    edited by Bob Riley

Recreation and Leisure: Issues in an Era of Change, Third Edition
    edited by Thomas Goodale and Peter A. Witt

Recreation Economic Decisions: Comparing Benefits and Costs
    by Richard G. Walsh

Recreation Programming And Activities For Older Adults
    by Jerold E. Elliott and Judith A. Sorg-Elliott

Risk Management in Therapeutic Recreation: A Component of Quality Assurance
    by Judith Voelkl

A Social History of Leisure Since 1600
    by Gary Cross

A Study Guide for National Certification in Therapeutic Recreation
    by Gerald O'Morrow and Ron Reynolds

Therapeutic Recreation: Cases and Exercises
    by Barbara C. Wilhite and M. Jean Keller

Therapeutic Recreation Protocol for Treatment of Substance Addictions
    by Rozanne W. Faulkner

Understanding Leisure and Recreation: Mapping the Past, Charting the Future
    edited by Edgar L. Jackson and Thomas L. Burton

Venture Publishing, Inc
1999 Cato Avenue
State College, PA 16801
814-234-4561